A SPECIAL NOTE TO STUDENTS

Unlike other business courses that concentrate narrowly on a particular function or piece of the business—accounting, finance, marketing, production, human resources, or information systems—strategic management is a big picture course. It cuts across the whole spectrum of business and management. The center of attention is the *total enterprise*—the industry and competitive environment in which it operates, its long-term direction and strategy, its resources and competitive capabilities, and its prospects for success.

Throughout the course, the spotlight will be trained on the foremost issue in running a business enterprise: What must managers do, and do well, to make the company a winner in the game of business? The answer that emerges and the theme of the course is that good strategy making and good strategy execution are always the most reliable signs of good management. The task of this course is to explore why good strategic management leads to good business performance, to present the basic concepts and tools of strategic analysis, and to drill you in the methods of crafting a well-conceived strategy and executing it competently.

You'll be called on to probe, question, and evaluate all aspects of a company's external and internal situation. You'll grapple with sizing up a company's standing in the marketplace and its ability to go head-to-head with rivals, learn to tell the difference between winning strategies and mediocre strategies, and become more skilled in spotting ways to improve a company's strategy or its execution.

In the midst of all this, another purpose is accomplished: to help you synthesize what you have learned in prior business courses. Dealing with the grand sweep of how to manage all the pieces of a business makes strategic management an integrative, capstone course in which you reach back to use concepts and techniques covered in previous courses. For perhaps the first time you'll see how the various pieces of the business puzzle fit together and why the different parts of a business need to be managed in strategic harmony for the organization to operate in a winning fashion.

The journey ahead is exciting, fun, and immensely worthwhile. No matter what your major is, the content of this course has all the ingredients to be the best course you've taken—best in the sense of learning a great deal about business, holding your interest from beginning to end, and enhancing your powers of business judgment. As you tackle the subject matter, ponder Ralph Waldo Emerson's observation, "Commerce is a game of skill which many people play, but which few play well." What we've put between these covers is aimed squarely at helping you become a savvy player. Good luck!

Arthur A. Thompson
John E. Gamble
A. J. Strickland

STRATEGY

Core Concepts • Analytical Tools • Readings

Arthur A. Thompson, Jr.
University of Alabama

John E. Gamble
University of South Alabama

A. J. Strickland III
University of Alabama

 Irwin

Boston   Burr Ridge, IL   Dubuque, IA   Madison, WI   New York   San Francisco   St. Louis
Bangkok   Bogotá   Caracas   Kuala Lumpur   Lisbon   London   Madrid   Mexico City
Milan   Montreal   New Delhi   Santiago   Seoul   Singapore   Sydney   Taipei   Toronto

Irwin

STRATEGY: CORE CONCEPTS, ANALYTICAL TOOLS, READINGS

Published by McGraw-Hill/Irwin, a business unit of The McGraw-Hill Companies, Inc., 1221 Avenue of the Americas, New York, NY 10020. Copyright © 2004 by The McGraw-Hill Companies, Inc. All rights reserved. No part of this publication may be reproduced or distributed in any form or by any means, or stored in a database or retrieval system, without the prior written consent of The McGraw Hill Companies, Inc., including, but not limited to, in any network or other electronic storage or transmission, or broadcast for distance learning.
Some ancillaries, including electronic and print components, may not be available to customers outside the United States.

This book is printed on acid-free paper.

domestic   1 2 3 4 5 6 7 8 9 0 DOW/DOW 0 9 8 7 6 5 4 3
international 1 2 3 4 5 6 7 8 9 0 DOW/DOW 0 9 8 7 6 5 4 3

ISBN 0-07-291830-6

Editor in chief: *John E. Biernat*
Executive editor: *John Weimeister*
Managing developmental editor: *Laura Hurst Spell*
Executive marketing manager: *Ellen Cleary*
Producer, Media technology: *Mark Molsky*
Lead project manager: *Mary Conzachi*
Senior production supervisor: *Rose Hepburn*
Design team leader: *Mary L. Christianson*
Photo research coordinator: *Kathy Shive*
Supplement producer: *Joyce J. Chappetto*
Senior digital content specialist: *Brian Nacik*
Cover and interior design: *Jamie O'Neal*
Cover image: © *SuperStock*
Typeface: *10.5/12 Times*
Compositor: *GAC Indianapolis*
Printer: *R. R. Donnelley*

Library of Congress Cataloging-in-Publication Data
Thompson, Arthur A., 1940-
     Strategy : core concepts, analytical tools, readings / Arthur A. Thompson, Jr., John E.
  Gamble, A.J. Strickland III.
       p. cm.
     Includes index.
     ISBN 0-07-291830-6 (alk. paper) — ISBN 0-07-121801-7 (international : alk. paper)
     1. Strategic planning. 2. Management. 3. Strategic planning—Case studies. 4.
  Management—Case studies. I. Gamble, John (John E.) II. Strickland, A. J. (Alonzo J.) III.
  Title.
HD30.28.T537 2004
658.4'012—dc21

                                                                    2003044229

INTERNATIONAL EDITION ISBN 0-07-121802-5
Copyright © 2004 Exclusive rights by The McGraw-Hill Companies, Inc. for manufacture and export. This book cannot be re-exported from the country to which it is sold by McGraw-Hill. The International Edition is not available in North America.

www.mhhe.com

To our families and especially our wives:
Hasseline, Debra, and Kitty

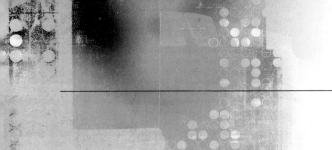

About the Authors

Arthur A. Thompson, Jr., earned his BS and PhD degrees in economics from the University of Tennessee in 1961 and 1965, respectively; spent three years on the economics faculty at Virginia Tech; and served on the faculty of the University of Alabama's College of Commerce and Business Administration for 24 years. In 1974 and again in 1982, Dr. Thompson spent semester-long sabbaticals as a visiting scholar at the Harvard Business School.

His areas of specialization are business strategy, competition and market analysis, and the economics of business enterprises. He has published over 30 articles in some 25 different professional and trade publications and has authored or co-authored five textbooks and four computer-based simulation exercises.

Dr. Thompson is a frequent speaker and consultant on the strategic issues confronting the electric utility industry, particularly as concerns the challenges posed by industry restructuring, re-regulation, competition, and customers' freedom of choice. He spends much of his off-campus time giving presentations to electric utility groups and conducting management development programs for electric utility executives all over the world.

Dr. Thompson and his wife of 42 years have two daughters, two grandchildren, and a Yorkshire terrier.

John E. Gamble is currently Chairman of the Department of Management and Associate Professor of Management in the Mitchell College of Business at The University of South Alabama. His teaching specialty at USA is strategic management and he also conducts a course in strategic management in Germany through a collaborative MBA program sponsored by the University of Applied Sciences in Ludwigshafen/Worms, the State of Rhineland Westphalia, and the University of South Alabama.

Dr. Gamble's research interests center on strategic issues in entrepreneurial, health care, and manufacturing settings. His work has been published in such scholarly journals as *Journal of Business Venturing*, *Journal of Labor Research*, *Health Care Management Review*, and *Labor Studies Journal*. He is the author or co-author of more than 20 case studies published in various strategic management and strategic marketing texts. He has done consulting on industry and market analysis and strategy formulation and implementation issues with clients in public utilities, technology, non-profit, and entrepreneurial businesses.

Professor Gamble received his Ph.D. in management from the University of Alabama in 1995. Dr. Gamble also has a Bachelor of Science degree and a Master of Arts degree from The University of Alabama.

Dr. A. J. (Lonnie) Strickland, a native of North Georgia, attended the University of Georgia, where he received a bachelor of science degree in math and physics in 1965. Afterward he entered the Georgia Institute of Technology, where he received a master of science in industrial management. He earned a PhD in business administration from Georgia State University in 1969. He currently holds the title of Professor of Strategic Management in the Graduate School of Business at the University of Alabama.

Dr. Strickland's experience in consulting and executive development is in the strategic management area, with a concentration in industry and competitive analysis. He has developed strategic planning systems for such firms as the Southern Company, BellSouth, South Central Bell, American Telephone and Telegraph, Gulf States Paper, Carraway Methodist Medical Center, Delco Remy, Mark IV Industries, Amoco Oil Company, USA Group, General Motors, and Kimberly Clark Corporation (Medical Products). He is a very popular speaker on the subject of implementing strategic change and serves on several corporate boards.

He has served as director of marketing for BellSouth, where he had responsibility for $1 billion in revenues and $300 million in profits.

In the international arena, Dr. Strickland has done extensive work in Europe, the Middle East, Central America, Malaysia, Australia, and Africa. In France he developed a management simulation of corporate decision making that enables management to test various strategic alternatives.

In the area of research, he is the author of 15 books and texts. His management simulations, Tempomatic IV and Micromatic, were pioneering innovations that enjoyed prominent market success for two decades.

Recent awards for Dr. Strickland include the Outstanding Professor Award for the Graduate School of Business and the Outstanding Commitment to Teaching Award for the University of Alabama, in which he takes particular pride. He is a member of various honor leadership societies: Mortar Board, Order of Omega, Beta Gamma Sigma, Omicron Delta Kappa, and Jasons. He is past national president of Pi Kappa Phi social fraternity.

Preface

The objective of this text is to effectively and interestingly cover what every senior-level or MBA student needs to know about crafting and executing business strategies. It features a *streamlined* and *substantive* 320-page presentation of core concepts and analytical techniques and a collection of 14 relatively short and quite current readings that amplify important topics in managing a company's strategy-making, strategy-executing process. This book is particularly suited for courses where the instructor wishes to provide students with a foundation in the core concepts and analytical tools of strategic management before having them tackle a customized set of cases and/or a simulation exercise.

In developing this book, we have attempted to put together a text that (1) is sufficiently comprehensive in its coverage of important concepts and analytical tools, (2) has a desirable degree of depth and substance, (3) is flush with convincing examples of strategy in action, (4) maintains a straightforward, integrated flow from one chapter to the next, and (5) makes the discipline of business strategy relevant and professionally interesting to students.

On-Target Content

To have adequately on-target content, a strategy text must:

- Explain core concepts and provide examples of their relevance and use by actual companies.
- Present understandable explanations of what the essential analytical tools are, how they are used, and where they fit into the managerial process of crafting and executing strategy.
- Be up-to-date and comprehensive, with solid coverage of the landmark changes in competitive markets and company strategies being driven by globalization and Internet technology.
- Focus squarely on what every student needs to know about crafting, implementing, and executing business strategies in today's market environments.

The 9 text chapters and the 14 supplemental readings (that can be assigned in whole or part) do all these things without posing a formidable number of pages for instructors to cover and students to absorb in one semester. Chapter discussions cut straight to the chase, but we have described core concepts and analytical tools at some length, the rationale being that overly brief or shallow explanations carry little punch and have almost no pedagogical value. We tried to use examples that students can easily relate to and have strived to incorporate all relevant state-of-the-art research that is pertinent in a first course in strategy.

Chapter Features and Organization

The content of the chapter presentations reflect a host of developments in the theory and practice of strategic management: the growing scope and strategic importance of collaborative alliances, the continuing march of industries and companies to wider globalization, the inclusion of the resource-based view of the firm as a standard part of strategic analysis, the spread of high-velocity change to more industries and company environments, and how implementation of Internet technology applications in companies all across the world is driving fundamental changes in both strategy and internal operations. The text chapters emphasize that a company's strategy must be matched *both* to its external market circumstances and to its internal resources and competitive capabilities. The resource-based view of the firm is prominently integrated into our coverage of crafting both single-business and multi-business strategies; two of the three chapters on executing strategy have a strong resource-based perspective, stressing the importance of intellectual capital, core competencies, and competitive capabilities.

The following rundown summarizes the noteworthy chapter features and topical emphasis of our nine-chapter presentation:

- Chapter 1 introduces and defines a host of core concepts—strategy, business model, strategic visions and business missions, strategic versus financial objectives, strategic intent, strategic plans, crafting strategy, and executing strategy. Clear distinction is made between a company's strategy and its business model. A section on strategic visions and mission statements hammers home the importance of clear direction setting and a motivating strategic vision; there's an accompanying discussion of how core values and ethics tie in to a company's vision and business purpose. Emphasis is placed on why companies have to rapidly adapt strategy to newly unfolding market conditions and why strategy life cycles are often short. Following Henry Mintzberg's pioneering research, we stress how and why a company's strategy emerges from (1) the deliberate and purposeful actions of management and (2) as-needed reactions to fresh developments and changing competitive pressures. There's a section on corporate intrapreneuring to help underscore that a company's strategic plan is a collection of strategies devised by different managers at different levels in the organizational hierarchy. We've taken pains to explain why *all managers are on a company's strategy-making, strategy-executing team*, why every manager is well advised to make the concepts and techniques of strategic management a basic part of his or her tool kit, and why the best companies want their personnel to be true students of the business. The chapter winds up with a section on corporate governance and a discussion of why strategy is important.

- Chapter 2 sets forth the now-familiar analytical tools and concepts of industry and competitive analysis and demonstrates the importance of tailoring strategy to fit the circumstances of a company's industry and competitive environment. The standout feature of this chapter is a dramatically enhanced presentation of Michael E. Porter's "five-forces model of competition"—we think it is the clearest, most straightforward five-forces model discussion of any text in the field. Globalization and Internet technology are treated as potent driving forces capable of reshaping industry competition—their roles as change agents have become factors that most companies in most industries must reckon with in forging winning strategies.

- Chapter 3 establishes the equal importance of doing solid company situation analysis as a basis for matching strategy to organizational resources, competencies, and competitive capabilities. The roles of core competencies and organizational re-sources and capabilities in creating customer value and helping build competitive advantage are *center stage* in the discussions of company resource strengths and weaknesses. SWOT analysis is cast as a simple, easy-to-use way to assess a company's resources and overall situation. There are sections describing the now-standard tools of value chain analysis, benchmarking, and competitive strength assessments—all of which, we believe, provide insight into a company's relative cost position and market standing vis-à-vis rivals. There's discussion of how company implementation of Internet technology is altering the value chain and the performance of particular value chain activities.

- Chapter 4 puts the spotlight on a company's quest for competitive advantage—the options for crafting a strategy that simultaneously hold good prospects for competitive advantage while also being well suited both to industry and competitive conditions and to its own resources and competitive circumstances. While the chapter is framed around the five generic competitive strategies—low-cost leadership, differentiation, best-cost provider, focused differentiation, and focused low-cost—it also contains important sections on what use to make of strategic alliances and collaborative partnerships; what use to make of mergers and acquisitions in strengthening the company's competitiveness; when to integrate backward or forward into more stages of the industry value chain; the merits of outsourcing certain value chain activities from outside specialists; whether and when to employ offensive and defensive moves; and the different ways a company can use the Internet as a distribution channel to position itself in the marketplace.

- Chapter 5 explores a company's strategy options for expanding beyond its domestic boundary and competing in the markets of either a few or a great many countries—options ranging from an export strategy to licensing and franchising to multicountry strategies to global strategies to heavy reliance on strategic alliances and joint ventures. Four strategic issues unique to competing multinationally are given special attention: (1) whether to customize the company's offerings in each different country market to match the tastes and preferences of local buyers or whether to offer a mostly standardized product worldwide, (2) whether to employ essentially the same basic competitive strategy in the markets of all countries where the company operates or whether to modify the company's competitive approach country by country as needed to fit specific market conditions and competitive circumstances, (3) how to locate production facilities, distribution centers, and customer service operations to maximum competitive advantage, and (4) how to use efficient cross-border transfer of a company's resource strengths and capabilities to build competitive advantage. There's also coverage of profit sanctuaries and cross-market subsidization; the special problems associated with entry into the markets of emerging countries; and strategies that local companies in such emerging countries as India, China, Brazil, and Mexico can use to defend against the invasion of opportunity-seeking, resource-rich global giants.

- The treatment of diversification strategies for multibusiness enterprises in Chapter 6 lays out the various paths for becoming diversified, explains how a company can use diversification to create or compound competitive advantage for its business units, and examines the strategic options an already-diversified company has to improve its overall performance. In the last part of the chapter, the analytical spotlight is on the techniques and procedures for assessing the strategic attractiveness of a diversified company's business portfolio—the relative attractiveness of the various businesses the company has diversified into, a multi-industry company's competitive strength in each of its lines of business, and the *strategic fits* and *resource fits* among a diversified company's different businesses.

▪ The three-chapter module on executing strategy (Chapters 7–9) is anchored around a solid, compelling conceptual framework: (1) building the resource strengths and organizational capabilities needed to execute the strategy in competent fashion; (2) allocating ample resources to strategy-critical activities; (3) ensuring that policies and procedures facilitate rather than impede strategy execution; (4) instituting best practices and pushing for continuous improvement in how value chain activities are performed; (5) installing information and operating systems that enable company personnel to better carry out their strategic roles proficiently; (6) tying rewards and incentives directly to the achievement of performance targets and good strategy execution; (7) shaping the work environment and corporate culture to fit the strategy; and (8) exerting the internal leadership needed to drive execution forward. The recurring theme of these three chapters is that implementing and executing strategy entails figuring out the specific actions, behaviors, and conditions that are needed for a smooth strategy-supportive operation and then following through to get things done and deliver results—the goal here is to ensure that students understand the strategy-implementing/strategy-executing phase is a managerial exercise in making things happen and making them happen right.

Our top priority has been to ensure that the nine chapters of text hit the bull's-eye with respect to content and represent the best thinking of both academics and practitioners. But at the same time we've gone the extra mile to stay on message with clear, crisp explanations laced with enough relevant examples to make the presentation convincing, pertinent, and worthwhile to students preparing for careers in management and business. We believe our enthusiasm for the subject matter will come across to readers. And the boxed Company Spotlights and Global Spotlights in each chapter relate stories aimed at both informing students and persuading them that the discipline of strategy merits their rapt attention.

The Collection of Readings

In selecting a set of readings to accompany the chapter presentations, we opted for readings that (1) were current (most appeared in 2002), (2) extended the chapter coverage and expanded on a topic of strategic importance, and (3) were quite readable and relatively short. At the same time, we endeavored to be highly selective, deciding that a small number of on-target readings was a better fit with the teaching/learning objectives of a first course in strategy than a more sweeping collection of readings. The 14 readings we chose come from such sources as *Business Strategy Review*, *MIT Sloan Management Review*, *Business Horizons*, *California Management Review*, *Business and Society Review*, *Journal of Business Strategy*, and *Strategic Change*.

Aside from providing an introductory look at the literature of strategic management literature, the readings offer nice variety. For instance, Constantos Markides article on "Strategy as Balance" deals with some passionately argued differences on the content and process of developing strategy. Kathleen Eisenhart's essay on "Has Strategy Changed?" describes how the powerful forces of globalization are fundamentally changing the nature and dimension of strategy. The article by Slater and Olson provides an augmented look at Porter's five forces model that takes into account the roles of "complementors", market turbulence, and the impact of market structure on risk, while also adding some new insights on rivalry, and both customer and supplier bargaining power. Clayton Christensen's article on "The Past and Future of Competitive Advantage" explains why company managers are obliged to continually seek new ways to build competitive advantage as changes in basic underlying factors act to dissipate existing advantages. The timely reading on "Sowing Growth in Your Own Backyard" provides useful perspectives on the difficulties of competing in stagnant markets and looks at the strategic options of growing a company's business in tough economic times. Yoffie and Kwan's intriguing article on "Judo Strategy: 10 Techniques for Beating a Stronger Opponent" offers a framework of strategic maneuvers that companies can employ to outcompete stronger rivals. There's a pertinent article on outsourcing that disavows the simplistic core or non-core approach and looks at how four companies successfully managed their outsourcing/insourcing decisions. To enhance the text treatment of strategy-ethics issues we included a reading dealing with ethical concerns in international businesses and a second reading on why ethics and compliance programs can fail.

The All-New Companion *GLO-BUS* Online Simulation Exercise

GLO-BUS: Developing Winning Competitive Strategies, a completely online simulation co-created by the senior author of this text with two others, is being marketed by the publisher as a companion supplement for use with this and other texts in the field. All three co-authors of this book are avid longtime simulation users. Our own experiences, together with numerous discussions with colleagues around the world, have convinced us that competition-based simulation games are *the single most effective, most stimulating exercise available* for giving students valuable practice in being active strategic thinkers and in reading the signs of industry change, reacting to the moves of competitors, evaluating strengths and weaknesses in their company's competitive position, and deciding what to do to improve a company's financial performance. The competitive circumstances of an industry simulation force participants to wrestle with charting a long-term direction for their company, setting strategic and financial objectives, and crafting strategies that produce good results and perhaps lead to competitive advantage. And by having to live with the decisions they make, players experience what it means to be accountable for their decisions and achieve satisfactory results. All this serves to drill students in responsible decision making and to improve their business acumen and managerial judgment. We think putting students through a simulation exercise helps make the strategy course a true capstone experience.

A Bird's-Eye View of *GLO-BUS*

This all-new, totally online simulation is modeled around the digital camera industry, a contemporary high-tech business students can readily identify with and understand. The market for digital cameras displays the characteristics of many globally competitive industries—fast growth, worldwide use of the product, competition among companies from several continents, production located in low-wage locations, and a marketplace where a variety of competitive approaches and business strategies can coexist. Companies design and assemble their lines of entry-level and multifeatured cameras in an Asian assembly facility and ship finished goods directly to camera retailers in North America, Asia-Pacific, Europe-Africa, and Latin America.

Competition is head-to-head—each team of students must match strategic wits against the other company teams. Depending on class size and the number of comanagers assigned to each company, an industry consists of 4, 8, or 12 competing companies. While at the beginning of the simulation each company starts off as the same overall size with the same financial condition and sells its cameras in all four geographic regions of the world market, competing companies do not begin the simulation with the same market shares in each geographic area—one-fourth of the competitors have their biggest market share in Europe-Africa, one-fourth have their biggest share in North America, and so on. As the simulation unfolds, companies can reposition themselves in the four geographic market segments and two product segments (entry-level and multifeatured cameras) however they see fit, pursuing additional sales and market share in some geographic areas and de-emphasizing or abandoning others. All companies have the flexibility to adjust their annual shipments of digital camera to mitigate the impact of fluctuating exchange rates.

Low-cost leadership, differentiation strategies, best-cost producer strategies, and focus strategies are all viable competitive options. Company managers can try to gain an edge over rivals with more advertising, longer and more frequent promotions, longer warranties, wider product selection, or better technical support. They can have a strategy aimed at being the clear market leader in either entry-level cameras, upscale multi-featured cameras, or both. They can focus on one or two geographic regions or strive for geographic balance. They can pursue essentially the same strategy worldwide or craft slightly or very different strategies for the Europe-Africa, Asia-Pacific, Latin America, and North America markets.

Company co-managers make 44 types of decisions each period, ranging from R&D, camera components, and camera performance (10 decisions) to production operations and work compensation (15 decisions) to pricing and marketing (15 decisions) to the financing of company operations (4 decisions). Cause–effect relationships are based on sound business and economic principles.

The *GLO-BUS* participant's guide (about 25 pages) is delivered online—students can read it on their monitors or print out a copy, as they prefer. There are built-in help screens and on-screen information that provide students with the relevant information and full instructions. Students make all *GLO-BUS* decisions online and access all the results online. While decisions are made annually, there is an option that instructors can turn on allowing students to review the results by quarter and to make changes for upcoming quarters in prices, special promotions, and production levels. Decisions are processed online automatically according to times and dates set by the instructor—nothing is required on the part of instructors beyond assigning students to teams, specifying the desired simulation schedule (done online), monitoring the results as they occur, counseling with students who may request advice about their company's performance, and deciding on a simulation grade (based on automatically calculated scores of company and individual performances using scoring weights specified by the instructor). Technical support is provided directly by the simulation co-authors and the staff at GLO-BUS.com. There is no software for students or instructors to download or install. The only requirement of players and instructors is that user PCs must be equipped with Microsoft Excel (versions 2000 or later), Internet Explorer and have access to an Internet connection.

For more information and details, please visit www.glo-bus.com.

Instructor Support Materials

Instructor's Manual

The accompanying IM contains a section on suggestions for organizing and structuring your course, sample syllabi and course outlines, and a test bank containing about 900 multiple-choice and essay questions.

Computest

A computerized version of the test bank allows you to generate tests quite conveniently and to add in your own questions.

PowerPoint Slides

To facilitate preparation of your lectures and to serve as detailed chapter outlines, you'll have access to approximately 500 colorful, professional-looking slides displaying core concepts, analytical procedures, key points, and all the figures in the text chapters. The slides are the creation of Professor Jana Kuzmicki of Troy State University.

Presentation CD-ROM

The instructor's manual and all of the PowerPoint slides have been installed on a CD for easy access in preparing a syllabus and daily course schedule, preparing customized lectures, and teaching the cases.

Website: www.mhhe.com/thompson1e

The instructor portion of the website contains a password-protected section that provides an assortment of instructor's manual and other support-related materials that can be downloaded directly.

The *GLO-BUS* Online Simulation

The optional companion simulation of the digital camera industry is a powerful and constructive way of emotionally connecting students to the subject matter of the course. We know of no more powerful way to stimulate the competitive energy of students and prepare them for the rigors of real-world business decision making than to have them match strategic wits with classmates in running a company in head-to-head competition for global market leadership.

Student Support Materials

Chapter-End Exercises

Each chapter contains a select number of exercises, most related to research on the Internet, that reinforce key concepts and topics covered in the chapters.

Website: www.mhhe.com/thompson1e

The student portion of the website features 20-question self-scoring chapter tests and a select number of PowerPoint slides for each chapter.

PowerWeb

With each new book, students gain access to the publisher's PowerWeb site offering current news, articles from 6,300 premium sources, a Web research guide, current readings from annual editions, and links to related sites.

Acknowledgments

A great number of colleagues and students at various universities, business acquaintances, and people at McGraw-Hill provided inspiration, encouragement, and counsel during the course of this project. From an intellectual perspective, we are indeed indebted to the many academics whose research and writing have blazed new trails and advanced the discipline of strategic management. We particularly acknowledge the work of the authors of the 14 readings we have included in this edition.

The following reviewers provided seasoned advice and suggestions that further guided our preparation of the text chapters:

Seyda Deligonul, *St. John Fisher College and Michigan State University*

David Flanagan, *Western Michigan University*

Esmeralda Garbi, *Florida Atlantic University*

Mohsin Habib, *University of Massachusetts–Boston*

Kim Hester, *Arkansas State University*

Jeffrey E. McGee, *The University of Texas at Arlington*

Diana J. Wong, *Eastern Michigan University*

As always, we value your recommendations and thoughts about the book. Your comments regarding coverage and contents will be taken to heart, and we always are grateful for the time you take to call our attention to printing errors, deficiencies, and other shortcomings. Please e-mail us at athompso@cba.ua.edu, jgamble@usouthal.edu, or astrickl@cba.ua.edu; fax us at (205) 348-6695; or write us at P.O. Box 870225, Department of Management and Marketing, The University of Alabama, Tuscaloosa, Alabama 35487-0225.

Arthur A. Thompson
John E. Gamble
A. J. Strickland

CHAPTER 1

What Is Strategy and Why Is It Important?

Unless we change our direction we are likely to end up where we are headed.
—Ancient Chinese proverb

If we can know where we are and something about how we got there, we might see where we are trending—and if the outcomes which lie naturally in our course are unacceptable, to make timely change.
—Abraham Lincoln

If you don't know where you are going, any road will take you there.
—The Koran

Without a strategy the organization is like a ship without a rudder.
—Joel Ross and Michael Kami

Each chapter begins with a series of pertinent quotes and an introductory preview of its contents.

In-depth examples—Company Spotlights and Global Spotlights—appear in boxes throughout each chapter to illustrate important chapter topics, connect the text presentation to real-world companies, and convincingly demonstrate strategy in action.

COMPANY SPOTLIGHT 1.1

A Strategy Example: Southwest Airlines

Southwest Airlines is the only major short-hop, low-fare, point-to-point carrier in the U.S. airline industry. It is one of the industry's great success stories and is the only airline that made a profit in each of the past 25 years. In 2003, Southwest operated 375 jets to 58 airports in 30 states. The company's no-frills strategy offers passengers a single class of service at the lowest possible fares.

Aside from its low fares, which make air travel affordable to a wide segment of the U.S. population, Southwest has made friendly service a core piece of its strategy and one of its trademarks. Company personnel work hard at creating a positive, enjoyable flying experience for passengers. Gate personnel are cheery and witty, sometimes entertaining those in the gate area with trivia questions or contests. Casually dressed flight attendants warmly greet passengers coming onto planes, directing them to open seats and helping them store their bags. Southwest's attendants, all screened carefully for fun-loving and outgoing personalities, joke and chat with passengers—some even sing the announcements on take-off and landing.

Southwest's market focus is flying between pairs of cities ranging anywhere from 150 to 700 miles apart where traffic potential is high enough for Southwest to offer several daily flights. Most recently, however, Southwest has begun offering longer range flights, using its low-cost advantage to horn in on the most profitable flights of such rivals as American, United, Northwest, Delta, and US Airways. Southwest grows its business by adding more flights on existing routes and by initiating service to new airports—its objective is steady growth year after year, not rapid growth for a few years that then becomes impossible to sustain.

Recognizing that low fares necessitate zealous pursuit of low operating costs, Southwest has perfected a number of operating strategies for keeping its costs below those of rival carriers:

» The company's aircraft fleet consists entirely of Boeing 737s, thus minimizing spare parts inventories, making it easier to train maintenance and repair personnel, improving the proficiency and speed of maintenance routines, and simplifying the task of scheduling planes for particular flights.

» As the launch customer for Boeing's 737-300, 737-500, and 737-700 models, Southwest acquires its new aircraft at favorable prices.

» Southwest encourages customers to make reservations and purchase tickets on the company's website. Selling a ticket on its website costs Southwest one-tenth as much as delivering a ticket through a travel agent and about

» with the practice of assigning each passenger a reserved seat. Instead, passengers are given boarding passes imprinted with A, B, or C at check-in and then board in groups of 30 according to their assigned letters, sitting in whatever seat is open when they get on the plane.

» Southwest flight attendants are responsible for cleaning up trash left by deplaning passengers

GLOBAL SPOTLIGHT 5.1

Microsoft, McDonald's, and Nestlé: Users of Multicountry Strategies

Microsoft's Multicountry Strategy in PC Software

In order to best serve the needs of users in foreign countries, Microsoft localizes many of its software products to reflect local languages. In France, for example, all user messages and documentation are in French and all monetary references are in euros. In the United Kingdom, monetary references are in British pounds and user messages and documentation reflect certain British conventions. Various Microsoft products have been localized into more than 30 languages.

McDonald's Multicountry Strategy in Fast Food

McDonald's has been highly successful in markets outside the United States, partly because it has been adept in altering its menu offerings to cater to local tastes. In Taiwan and Singapore, McDonald's outlets offer a bone-in fried chicken dish called Chicken Mc-Crispy. In Great Britain, there's the McChicken Tikka Naan to appeal to British cravings for Indian food. In India, McDonald's features the Maharajah Mac sandwich (an Indian version of the Big Mac); in Japan, there's the Chicken Tatsuta sandwich and a Teriyaki Burger sandwich; in Australia, there's a McOz Burger. However, the infrastructure and operating systems that are employed in the outlets are largely the same, enabling McDonald's to achieve low-cost leadership status once it builds volume up at its outlets (sometimes a 5-year process) and once it has enough outlets operating in a country to achieve full economies of scale (sometimes a 5- to 10-year process in the largest foreign markets).

Nestlé's Multicountry Strategy in Instant Coffee

Swiss-based Nestlé, the largest food company in the world, is also the largest producer of coffee. With a total workforce of 22,541 people operating in nearly 480 factories in 100 countries, Nestlé's presence is clearly multinational. Chief executive Peter Brabeck-Letmathe advocates understanding the distinctions between the cultures in which Nestlé markets its products. "[If] you are open to new languages, you are also open to new cultures," he explains. Thus, instant coffee names like Nescafé, Taster's Choice, Ricore, and Ricoffy line grocery shelves in various countries. If customers prefer roast or ground coffee, they can purchase Nespresso, Bonka, Zoegas, or Loumidis, depending on where they live.

Nestlé produces 200 types of instant coffee, from lighter blends for the U.S. market to dark espressos for Latin America. To keep its instant coffees matched to consumer tastes in different countries (and areas within some countries), Nestlé operates four coffee research labs that experiment with new blends in aroma, flavor, and color. The strategy is to match the blends marketed in each country to the tastes and preferences of coffee drinkers in that country, introducing new blends to develop new segments when opportunities appear and altering blends as needed to respond to changing tastes and buyer habits. In Britain, Nescafé was promoted extensively to build a wider base of instant-coffee drinkers. In Japan, where Nescafé was considered a luxury item, the company made its Japanese blends available in fancy containers suitable for gift-giving.

Sources: Nestlé website (www.nestle.com), accessed August 15, 2001; "Nestlé S.A.," Hoover's Online (www.hoovers.com), accessed August 15, 2001; Tom Mudd, "Nestlé Plays to Global Audience," Industry Week (www.industryweek.com), August 13, 2001; company annual reports; Shawn Tully, "Nestlé Shows How to Gobble Markets," Fortune, January 16, 1989, pp. 74–78; and "Nestlé: A Giant in a Hurry," Business Week, March 22, 1993, pp. 50–54.

and fresh market conditions (see Figure 1.2).[1] The biggest portion of a company's current strategy flows from previously initiated actions and business approaches that are working well enough to merit continuation and newly launched managerial initiatives to strengthen the company's overall position and performance. This part of management's game plan is deliberate and proactive, standing as the product of management's analysis and strategic thinking about the company's situation and its conclusions about how to position the company in the marketplace and tackle the task of competing for buyer patronage. But the uncertainty and unpredictability of future business conditions prevent company managers from plotting every needed strategic action in advance. A portion of a company's strategy is always developed on the fly, coming as a reasoned response to changing customer preferences, the latest strategic maneuvers of rival firms, new requirements and expectations on the part of customers, emerging technologies and market opportunities, a shifting political or economic climate, and other unforeseeable happenings. Crafting a strategy thus involves not only stitching together a comprehensive *intended strategy* but also modifying first one piece and then another as events unfold and circumstances surrounding the company's situation change (*adaptive/reactive strategy*). In short, a company's actual strategy is something managers shape and reshape as circumstances dictate and as managers learn from experience and seek out improvements.

As a rule, most multinational competitors endeavor to employ as global a strategy as customer needs permit. Philips N.V., the Netherlands-based electronics and consumer products company, operated successfully with a multicountry strategy for many years but has recently begun moving more toward a unified strategy within the European Union and within North America.[5] A global strategy can concentrate on building the resource strengths to secure a sustainable low-cost or differentiation-based competitive advantage over both domestic rivals and global rivals racing for world market leadership. Whenever country-to-country differences are small enough to be accommodated

6

172

Figures scattered throughout the chapters provide conceptual and analytical frameworks.

Margin notes define core concepts and call attention to important ideas and principles.

Figure 2.5   Factors Affecting the Threat of Entry

Entry threats are weaker when:
- The pool of entry candidates is small.
- Entry barriers are high.
- Existing competitors are struggling to earn good profits.
- The industry's outlook is risky or uncertain.
- Buyer demand is growing slowly or is stagnant.

Rivalry among Competing Sellers

How strong are the competitive pressures associated with the entry threat from new rivals?

Potential New Entrants

Entry threats are stronger when:
- The pool of entry candidates is large and some of the candidates have resources that would make them formidable market contenders.
- Entry barriers are low or can be readily hurdled by the likely candidates.
- When existing industry members are looking to expand their market reach by entering product segments or geographic areas where they currently do not have a presence.
- Newcomers can expect to earn attractive profits.
- Buyer demand is growing rapidly.
- Industry members are unable (or unwilling) to strongly contest the entry of newcomers.

However, even if a potential entrant has or can acquire the needed competencies and resources to attempt entry, it still faces the issue of how existing firms will react. Will incumbent firms offer only passive resistance, or will they aggressively defend their market positions using price cuts, increased advertising, product improvements, and whatever else they can think of to give a new entrant (as well as other rivals) a hard time? A potential entrant can have second thoughts when financially strong incumbent firms send clear signals that they will stoutly defend their market positions against newcomers. A potential entrant may also turn away when incumbent firms can leverage distributors and customers to retain their business.

The best test of whether potential entry is a strong or weak competitive force in the marketplace is to ask if the industry's growth and profit prospects are strongly attractive to potential entry candidates. When the answer is no, potential entry is a weak competitive force. When the answer is yes and there are entry candidates with

> The threat of entry is stronger when entry barriers are low, when there's a sizable pool of entry candidates, when industry growth is rapid and profit potentials are high, and when incumbent firms are unable or unwilling to vigorously contest a newcomer's entry.

When a company decides an industry is fundamentally attractive and presents good opportunities, a strong case can be made that it should invest aggressively to capture the opportunities it sees and to improve its long-term competitive position in the business. When a strong competitor concludes an industry is relatively unattractive and lacking in opportunity, it may elect to simply protect its present position, investing cautiously if at all and looking for opportunities in other industries. A competitively weak company in an unattractive industry may see its best option as finding a buyer, perhaps a rival, to acquire its business.

Key Points

Thinking strategically about a company's external situation involves probing for answers to the following seven questions:

1. *What are the industry's strategy-shaping economic features?* Industries differ significantly on such factors as market size and growth rate, the geographic scope of competitive rivalry, the number and relative sizes of both buyers and sellers, ease of entry and exit, the extent of vertical integration, how fast basic technology is changing, the extent of scale economies and learning-curve effects, the degree of product standardization or differentiation, and overall profitability. While setting the stage for the analysis to come, identifying an industry's economic features also promotes understanding of the kinds of strategic moves that industry members are likely to employ.

2. *What kinds of competitive forces are industry members facing, and how strong is each force?* The strength of competition is a composite of five forces: the rivalry among competing sellers, the presence of attractive substitutes, the potential for new entry, the competitive pressures stemming from supplier bargaining power and supplier–seller collaboration, and the competitive pressures stemming from buyer bargaining power and seller–buyer collaboration. These five forces have to be examined one by one to identify the specific competitive pressures they each comprise and to decide whether these pressures constitute a strong or weak competitive force. The next step in competition analysis is to evaluate the collective strength of the five forces and determine whether the state of competition is conducive to good profitability. Working through the five-forces model step by step not only aids strategy makers in assessing whether the intensity of competition allows good profitability but also promotes sound strategic thinking about how to better match company strategy to the specific competitive character of the marketplace. Effectively matching a company's strategy to the particular competitive pressures and competitive conditions that exist has two aspects: (1) pursuing avenues that shield the firm from as many of the prevailing competitive pressures as possible, and (2) initiating actions calculated to produce sustainable competitive advantage, thereby shifting competition in the company's favor, putting added competitive pressure on rivals, and perhaps even defining the business model for the industry.

3. *What forces are driving changes in the industry, and what impact will these changes have on competitive intensity and industry profitability?* Industry and competitive conditions change because forces are in motion that create incentives or pressures for change. The first phase is to identify the forces that are driving

Key Points sections at the end of each chapter provide a handy summary of essential ideas and things to remember.

Once all the higher-level strategic choices have been made, company managers can turn to the task of crafting functional and operating-level strategies to flesh out the details of the company's overall business and competitive strategy.

The timing of strategic moves also has relevance in the quest for competitive advantage. Because of the competitive importance that is sometimes associated with when a strategic move is made, company managers are obligated to carefully consider the advantages or disadvantages that attach to being a first-mover versus a fast-follower versus a wait-and-see late-mover. At the end of the day, though, the proper objective of a first-mover is that of being the first competitor to put together the precise combination of features, customer value, and sound revenue/cost/profit economics that puts it ahead of the pack in capturing an attractive market opportunity. Sometimes the company that first unlocks a profitable market opportunity is the first-mover and sometimes it is not—but the company that comes up with the key is surely the smart mover.

Exercises

1. Log on to www.business-ethics.com and review which companies are on the latest list of the 100 Best Corporate Citizens. Also review the criteria for earning a spot on this list. Are these criteria sound? Is there ample reason to believe that the 100 companies on this list pursue strategies that are ethical? Why or why not?

2. Go to www.google.com and do a search for "low-cost producer." See if you can identify five companies that are pursuing a low-cost strategy in their respective industries.

3. Using the advanced search engine function at www.google.com, enter "best-cost producer" in the exact phrase box and see if you can locate three companies that indicate they are employing a best-cost producer strategy.

Several short, mostly Internet research exercises at the end of each chapter provide a supplement to assigned cases and a further way to reinforce core concepts.

For Students: An Assortment of Support Materials

Website: www.mhhe.com/thompson1e

The student portion of the website features a "Guide to Case Analysis," with special sections on what a case is, why cases are a standard part of courses in strategy, preparing a case for class discussion, doing a written case analysis, doing an oral presentation, and using financial ratio analysis to assess a company's financial condition. In addition, there are self-scoring 20-question chapter tests and a select number of PowerPoint slides for each chapter.

The *GLO-BUS* Online Simulation

This course supplement emotionally connects students to the subject matter of the course by having teams assigned to manage companies in a head-to-head contest for global market leadership in the digital camera industry. The simulation puts students in a situation where they have to make decisions relating to product design, production, workforce compensation, pricing, advertising, warranties, sales promotions, and finance. It is students' job to craft and execute a strategy for their company that is powerful enough to deliver good bottom-line performance despite the efforts of rival companies to take away the company's sales and market share. Each company competes in North America, Latin America, Europe, and Asia.

PowerWeb

With each new book, students gain access to the publisher's PowerWeb site offering current news, articles from 6,300 premium sources, a Web research guide, current readings from annual editions, and links to related sites.

Contents
in Brief

Contents

Part III Crafting the Strategy

4 Crafting a Strategy: The Quest for Competitive Advantage 108

5 Competing in Foreign Markets 160

6 Diversification: Strategies for Managing a Group of Businesses 190

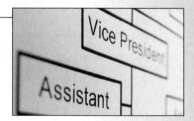

9 Corporate Culture and Leadership 294

STRATEGY

CHAPTER 1

What Is Strategy and Why Is It Important?

Unless we change our direction we are likely to end up where we are headed.
—Ancient Chinese proverb

If we can know where we are and something about how we got there, we might see where we are trending—and if the outcomes which lie naturally in our course are unacceptable, to make timely change.
—Abraham Lincoln

If you don't know where you are going, any road will take you there.
—The Koran

Without a strategy the organization is like a ship without a rudder.
—Joel Ross and Michael Kami

Management's job is not to see the company as it is . . . but as it can become.
—John W. Teets, former CEO Greyhound Corp.

Managers

at all companies face three basic, critical questions in thinking strategically about their company's present circumstances and prospects: Where are we now? Where do we want to go? How will we get there? A probing answer to *Where are we now?* must consider the company's market position and the competitive pressures it confronts, its resource strengths and capabilities, its competitive shortcomings, the appeal its products and services have to customers, and its current performance. *Where do we want to go?* deals with the direction in which management believes the company should be headed in light of the company's present situation and the winds of market change—new markets and customer groups that the company should be positioning itself to serve, new or different capabilities the company should be adding, the improvements in competitive market position the company is aiming for, and the geographic scope and product-line makeup of the company's business in the years to come. Finally, *How will we get there?* concerns the ins and outs of crafting and executing a strategy to get the company from where it is to where it wants to go.

What Is Strategy?

The tasks of crafting and executing company strategies are the heart and soul of managing a business enterprise and winning in the marketplace. A company's **strategy** is the game plan management is using to stake out a market position, attract and please customers, compete successfully, conduct operations, and achieve organizational objectives. In crafting a strategy, management is, in effect, saying: "Among all the paths we could have chosen, we have decided to focus on these markets and customer needs, compete in this fashion, allocate our resources and energies in these ways, and use these particular approaches to doing business." A company's strategy thus indicates the choices its managers have made among alternative markets, competitive approaches, and ways of operating. It is partly the result of trial-and-error organizational learning about what worked in the past and what didn't, and partly the product of managerial analysis and strategic thinking about all the circumstances surrounding the company's situation.

> ## Core Concept
>
> A company's **strategy** consists of the combination of competitive moves and business approaches that managers employ to please customers, compete successfully, conduct operations, and achieve organizational objectives.

Striving for Competitive Advantage

The central thrust of a company's strategy is undertaking moves to strengthen the company's long-term competitive position and financial performance. Typically, a company's strategy consists of both offensive and defensive elements—some actions mount direct challenges to competitors' market positions and seek to establish a competitive edge; others aim at defending against competitive pressures, the maneuvers of rivals, and other developments that threaten the company's well-being. *What separates a powerful strategy from an ordinary or weak one is management's ability to forge a series of moves, both in the marketplace and internally, that produce sustainable competitive advantage.* With competitive advantage, a company has good prospects for winning in the marketplace and realizing above-average profitability. Without competitive advantage, a company risks being outcompeted by rivals and/or locked into mediocre financial performance.

Four of the most frequently used strategic approaches to building competitive advantage are:

1. *Striving to be the industry's low-cost provider, thereby aiming for a cost-based competitive advantage over rivals.* Wal-Mart and Southwest Airlines have earned market-leading positions because of the low-cost advantages they have achieved over their rivals.

2. *Outcompeting rivals based on such differentiating features as high quality, wide product selection, reliable performance, excellent service, attractive styling, technological superiority, or unusually good value for the money.* Successful adopters of differentiation strategies include Johnson & Johnson (product reliability), Chanel and Rolex (prestige and distinctiveness), Mercedes-Benz and BMW (engineering design and performance), L. L. Bean (good value), and Amazon.com (wide selection and convenience).

3. *Focusing on a narrow market niche and winning a competitive edge by doing a better job than rivals of satisfying the special needs and tastes of buyers comprising the niche.* Prominent companies that enjoy competitive success in a specialized market niche include eBay in online auctions, Jiffy Lube International in quick oil changes, and Whole Foods Market in natural and organic foods.

4. *Developing expertise and resource strengths that give the company competitive capabilities rivals can't easily imitate or trump with capabilities of their own.* Federal Express has superior capabilities in next-day delivery of small packages; Walt Disney has hard-to-beat capabilities in theme park management and family entertainment, and IBM has wide-ranging capabilities in supporting the information systems and information technology needs of large enterprises.

Most companies recognize that winning a durable competitive edge over rivals hinges more on building competitively valuable expertise and capabilities than it does on having superior products. Rivals can nearly always copy the attributes of a popular or innovative product. But for rivals to match experience, know-how, and specialized competitive capabilities that a company has developed and perfected over a long period of time is substantially harder to duplicate and takes much longer—Kmart, Sears, and other discount retailers and supermarket chains have found it virtually impossible to match Wal-Mart's sophisticated distribution systems and its finely honed merchandising expertise despite years of trying. Company initiatives to build competencies and capabilities that rivals don't have and cannot readily match can relate to getting innovative new products to market faster than rivals (3M Corporation), better mastery of a complex technological process (Michelin in making radial tires), expertise in defect-free manufacturing (Toyota and Honda), specialized marketing and merchandising know-how (Coca-Cola), global sales and distribution capability (Black & Decker in power tools), superior e-commerce capabilities (Dell Computer), personalized customer service (Ritz-Carlton and Four Seasons hotels), or anything else that constitutes a competitively valuable strength in creating, producing, distributing, or marketing the company's product or service.

Identifying a Company's Strategy

Except for changes that remain under wraps and in the planning stage and some about-to-be launched moves, there's usually nothing secret or mysterious about what a company's present strategy is. Its competitive approaches and actions in the marketplace

Figure 1.1   Identifying a Company's Strategy:
What to Look For

are usually visible to studious observers and, in the case of publicly owned enterprises, often have been openly discussed by company managers or summarized in press releases or other widely available company documents. Hence the content of a company's strategy can normally be deduced from its actions in the marketplace and publicly available information. Some strategy features may remain hidden for competitively sensitive or legal reasons until the company's actions become public, but to maintain the confidence of investors and Wall Street, most public companies have to be fairly open about their strategies.

Figure 1.1 depicts what to look for in identifying the substance of a company's overall strategy. To get a better grip on the content of company strategies, read the description of Southwest Airlines' strategy in Company Spotlight 1.1.

Strategy Is Partly Proactive and Partly Reactive

A company's strategy is typically a blend of (1) proactive and purposeful actions on the part of company managers and (2) as-needed reactions to unanticipated developments

Southwest Airlines is the only major short-hop, low-fare, point-to-point carrier in the U.S. airline industry. It is one of the industry's great success stories and is the only airline that made a profit in each of the past 25 years. In 2003, Southwest operated 375 jets to 58 airports in 30 states. The company's no-frills strategy offers passengers a single class of service at the lowest possible fares.

Aside from its low fares, which make air travel affordable to a wide segment of the U.S. population, Southwest has made friendly service a core piece of its strategy and one of its trademarks. Company personnel work hard at creating a positive, enjoyable flying experience for passengers. Gate personnel are cheery and witty, sometimes entertaining those in the gate area with trivia questions or contests. Casually dressed flight attendants warmly greet passengers coming onto planes, directing them to open seats and helping them store their bags. Southwest's attendants, all screened carefully for fun-loving and outgoing personalities, joke and chat with passengers—some even sing the announcements on take-off and landing.

Southwest's market focus is flying between pairs of cities ranging anywhere from 150 to 700 miles apart where traffic potential is high enough for Southwest to offer several daily flights. Most recently, however, Southwest has begun offering longer range flights, using its low-cost advantage to horn in on the most profitable flights of such rivals as American, United, Northwest, Delta, and US Airways. Southwest grows its business by adding more flights on existing routes and by initiating service to new airports—its objective is steady growth year after year, not rapid growth for a few years that then becomes impossible to sustain.

Recognizing that low fares necessitate zealous pursuit of low operating costs, Southwest has perfected a number of operating strategies for keeping its costs below those of rival carriers:

■ The company's aircraft fleet consists entirely of Boeing 737s, thus minimizing spare parts inventories, making it easier to train maintenance and repair personnel, improving the proficiency and speed of maintenance routines, and simplifying the task of scheduling planes for particular flights.

and fresh market conditions (see Figure 1.2).[1] The biggest portion of a company's current strategy flows from previously initiated actions and business approaches that are working well enough to merit continuation and newly launched managerial initiatives to strengthen the company's overall position and performance. This part of management's game plan is deliberate and proactive, standing as the product of management's analysis and strategic thinking about the company's situation and its conclusions about how to position the company in the marketplace and tackle the task of competing for buyer patronage. But the uncertainty and unpredictability of future business conditions prevent company managers from plotting every needed strategic action in advance. A portion of a company's strategy is always developed on the fly, coming as a reasoned response to changing customer preferences, the latest strategic maneuvers of rival firms, new requirements and expectations on the part of customers, emerging technologies and market opportunities, a shifting political or economic climate, and other unforeseeable happenings. Crafting a strategy thus involves not only stitching together a comprehensive *intended strategy* but also modifying first one piece and then another as events unfold and circumstances surrounding the company's situation change (*adaptive/reactive strategy*). In short, a company's actual strategy is something managers shape and reshape as circumstances dictate and as managers learn from experience and seek out improvements.

- As the launch customer for Boeing's 737-300, 737-500, and 737-700 models, Southwest acquires its new aircraft at favorable prices.

- Southwest encourages customers to make reservations and purchase tickets at the company's website. Selling a ticket on its website costs Southwest one-tenth as much as delivering a ticket through a travel agent and about one-half as much as processing a paper ticket through its own internal reservation system.

- Southwest avoids flying into congested airports, stressing instead routes between medium-sized cities and small airports close to major metropolitan areas. This improves on-time performance and reduces the fuel costs associated with planes sitting in line on crowded taxiways or circling airports waiting for clearance to land. Moreover, the company pays lower landing fees and terminal gate costs than it would at high-traffic airports like Atlanta's Hartsfield International, Chicago's O'Hare, Denver International, and Dallas–Fort Worth.

- Southwest's point-to-point route system is highly efficient, reducing both the number of aircraft and the terminal gates needed to support flight operations compared to hub-and-spoke systems of rival carriers.

- To speed the reservation process and to economize on check-in time, Southwest dispensed with the practice of assigning each passenger a reserved seat. Instead, passengers are given boarding passes imprinted with A, B, or C at check-in and then board in groups of 30 according to their assigned letters, sitting in whatever seat is open when they get on the plane.

- Southwest flight attendants are responsible for cleaning up trash left by deplaning passengers and otherwise getting the plane presentable for passengers to board for the next flight (other carriers have cleaning crews come on board to perform this function). Attendants usually have planes ready for boarding within minutes of the last passenger's exit from the plane. On occasion, pilots pitch in to facilitate turnarounds.

- Southwest has no first-class section in any of its planes, has no fancy clubs for its frequent flyers to relax in at terminals, and serves no meals on its flights (passengers are offered beverages, peanuts, and pretzel mixes only). Reprovisioning planes is simpler, faster, and cheaper when meals are not a factor.

- Southwest planes' all-leather seats are more durable and easier to maintain than cloth seats, despite higher initial costs.

- Southwest does not provide passengers with baggage transfer services to other carriers.

Source: Company documents.

Figure 1.2 A Company's Actual Strategy Is Partly Proactive and Partly Reactive to Changing Circumstances

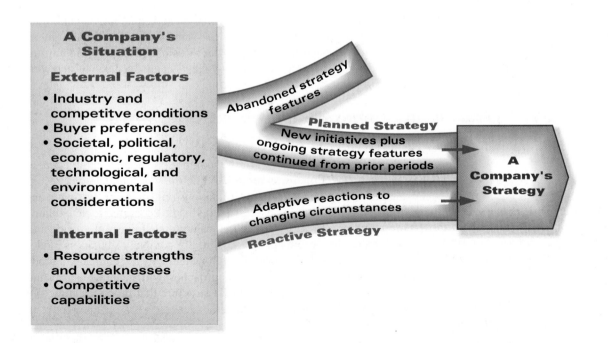

A Company's Situation

External Factors
- Industry and competitve conditions
- Buyer preferences
- Societal, political, economic, regulatory, technological, and environmental considerations

Internal Factors
- Resource strengths and weaknesses
- Competitive capabilities

Abandoned strategy features

Planned Strategy
New initiatives plus ongoing strategy features continued from prior periods

Adaptive reactions to changing circumstances

Reactive Strategy

A Company's Strategy

A Company's Strategy Evolves over Time   Because constantly developing external and internal events make it commonplace for managers to initiate fresh strategic moves and business approaches of one kind or another, *a company's strategy is a work in progress.* Most of the time a company's strategy evolves incrementally from management's ongoing efforts to fine-tune this or that piece of the strategy and to adjust certain strategy elements in response to unfolding events. Frequently making sweeping changes in strategy can be disruptive to the organization and confusing to customers—and such changes are usually unnecessary. In general, persistently tweaking a basically sound strategy to keep it freshly tuned to changing market circumstances offers greater rewards than does trying to change the basic strategy at every turn.

Nonetheless, on occasion—when a strategy is clearly failing, market conditions or buyer preferences are undergoing significant change, an opening is appearing for new strategy elements with powerful buyer appeal, competitors are doing something that demands a dramatic response, important technological breakthroughs are occurring, or the company is being hit with a major financial crisis—fine-tuning the existing strategy is not enough and major strategy shifts are called for. During periods of market turbulence (like the Internet gold rush and subsequent dot-com crash that occurred in 1997–2002), companies find it essential to revise demand forecasts, adjust key elements of their strategies, and update their financial projections at least quarterly and sometimes more frequently. At Ingram Micro, a contract manufacturer and distributor of PCs, market changes and strategic adjustments come so quickly that "rolling forecasts" of financial projections are devised for five quarters out and then updated every 60 days. Bluefly.com, a clothing e-tailer, revises its product offerings and operating budget weekly to react to daily sales patterns. Industry environments characterized by high-velocity change often require frequent shifts in strategy.[2]

> **Core Concept**
>
> Changing circumstances dictate that a company's strategy change and evolve over time—a condition that makes strategy making an ongoing process, not a one-time event.

Regardless of whether a company's strategy changes gradually or swiftly, the important point is that it is always temporary and on trial, awaiting new ideas for improvement on management's part, the appearance of new market and competitive conditions, and any other changes in the company's situation that managers believe warrant strategy adjustments. Since neither market and competitive conditions nor the company's situation stay the same for long, company managers are obligated to continually reevaluate their strategy, recrafting it as often and as extensively as they feel is needed to keep in step with changing times.

The Relationship Between a Company's Strategy and Its Business Model

> **Core Concept**
>
> A company's **business model** deals with whether the revenue/cost/profit economics of its strategy demonstrate the viability of the business enterprise as a whole.

Closely related to the concept of a company's strategy is the concept of a company's **business model.** While the word *model* conjures up images of empirical, ivory-tower relationships, such images do not apply here. A company's business model is the economic logic explaining how an enterprise can deliver value to customers at a price and cost that yields acceptable profitability.[3] A company's business model is thus management's storyline for how and why the company's product offerings and competitive approaches will generate a revenue stream and have an associated cost structure that produces attractive earnings and returns on investment.

The nitty-gritty issue surrounding a company's business model is whether the chosen strategy makes good business sense from a moneymaking perspective. The concept of a company's business model is, consequently, more narrowly focused than the concept of a company's business strategy. A company's strategy *relates broadly to its competitive initiatives and business approaches (regardless of the financial outcomes it produces), whereas its* business model *concerns whether the revenues and costs flowing from the strategy demonstrate business viability.* Companies that have been in business for a while and are making acceptable profits have a proven business model—there is clear evidence that their strategy is capable of profitability and that they have a viable enterprise. Companies that are in a start-up mode and established companies that are losing money have questionable business models: Their strategies are not producing good bottom-line results, putting their storyline about how they intend to make money and their viability as enterprises in doubt. Company Spotlight 1.2 discusses the contrasting business models of Microsoft and Red Hat Linux.

What Does the Strategy-Making, Strategy-Executing Process Entail?

The managerial process of crafting and executing a company's strategy consists of five interrelated and integrated phases:

1. *Forming a strategic vision of where the company needs to head,* a task that provides long-term direction, infuses the organization with a sense of purposeful action, and communicates to stakeholders what management's aspirations for the company are.
2. *Setting objectives* that convert the strategic vision into specific performance outcomes for the company to achieve.
3. *Crafting a strategy to achieve the objectives* and move the company toward where it wants to go.
4. *Implementing and executing the chosen strategy efficiently and effectively.*
5. *Evaluating performance and initiating corrective adjustments* in vision, long-term direction, objectives, strategy, or execution in light of actual experience, changing conditions, new ideas, and new opportunities.

Figure 1.3 displays this five-task process. Let's examine each task in enough detail to set the stage for the forthcoming chapters and give you a bird's-eye view of what this book is about.

Developing a Strategic Vision: Phase 1 of the Strategy-Making, Strategy-Executing Process

Very early in the strategy-making process, a company's senior managers need to decide what direction the company should be headed in and why such a direction makes good business sense. To draw carefully reasoned conclusions about the directional path

COMPANY SPOTLIGHT 1.2

Microsoft and Red Hat Linux: Contrasting Business Models

Different companies have different business models and strategies, sometimes strikingly so. Consider, for example, the business models for Microsoft and Red Hat Linux in operating system (OS) software for personal computers (PCs).

Microsoft is one of the world's most successful and profitable companies, partly because of its dominant market position in OS software for PCs—first DOS, then Windows 95, Windows NT, Windows 98, Windows 2000, and Windows XP. Microsoft's business model for making money from its OS products is based on the following business logic:

■ Employ a cadre of highly skilled programmers to develop proprietary Microsoft code; keep the source code hidden from users.

■ Sell the resulting OS and software package to PC makers and to PC users at relatively attractive prices, and achieve large unit sales.

■ Since most of Microsoft's costs are fixed (having been incurred on the front end in developing the code for the software), each copy of the software sold generates substantial margins over the variable costs of producing and packaging the CDs provided to users, which amount to only a couple of dollars per copy.

■ Provide technical support to users at no cost.

Red Hat Linux, a new company formed to market the Linux OS in competition against Microsoft's Windows OS, employs a sharply different business model:

■ Rely on the collaborative efforts of interested programmers from all over the world who volunteer their time and contribute bits and pieces of code to improve and polish the Linux system. Make the source code open and available to all users, allowing them to freely change the code to create a customized version of Linux. The global community of thousands of programmers who work on Linux in their spare time do what they do because they love it; because they are fervent believers that all software should be free (as in free speech); and, in some cases, because they are anti-Microsoft and want to have a part in undoing what they see as a Microsoft monopoly.

■ Add value to the free, downloadable version of Linux by offering users Red Hat Linux systems containing upgraded and tested features. Linux originator Linus Torvalds and a team of more than 300 Red Hat engineers and software developers collect enhancements and new applications submitted by the "open-source" community of volunteer programmers. Thus Red Hat, unlike Microsoft, essentially has very modest upfront product development costs—all stemming from evaluating new submissions, picking and choosing which to integrate and test for performance and compatibility, and deciding which to include in new releases of Red Hat Linux.

■ Charge a modest fee to those who prefer to subscribe to the Red Hat Linux version; the subscription fee includes a limited number of days of Red Hat's Web-based service and support.

■ Employ a cadre of technical support personnel who provide technical support to users for a fee. Because Linux can be a bit troublesome to install and use in some multiserver, multiprocessor applications, corporate users of Linux often require technical support during start-up.

■ Make as much or more money on providing technical support services, training, and consulting as on selling subscriptions to Red Hat Linux. Fees for technical support services, training, and consulting provide more than 50 percent of Red Hat's revenues.

Microsoft's business model—sell proprietary code software and give service away free—is a proven moneymaker that generates billions in profits annually. On the other hand, the jury is still out on Red Hat's business model of marketing open-source software developed mainly by volunteers and depending heavily on sales of technical support services, training, and consulting; in the early 2000s the company had less than $100 million in annual revenues and had operating losses.

Source: Company documents.

Figure 1.3   The Strategy-Making, Strategy-Executing Process

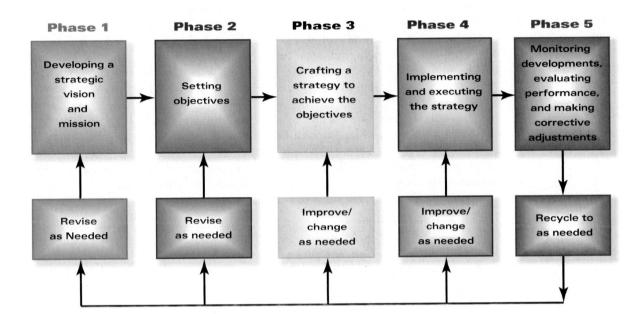

the company should take, managers must think strategically about the company's external and internal environment and answer the following direction-shaping questions:

Externally Focused Questions	Internally Focused Questions
■ How and at what pace is the company's market environment evolving?	■ What are our ambitions for the company? What industry standing do we want the company to have?
■ What factors are driving market change and what impact will they have?	■ What organizational strengths should we be trying to leverage and what weaknesses do we need to correct?
■ What are competitors up to? In what ways are competitive conditions growing stronger or weaker?	■ Will our present business generate adequate growth and profitability?
■ What does the changing market and competitive landscape mean for the company's business over the next five years and beyond?	■ What new products/services (or businesses) do we need to add?
■ What new markets and customer groups should we be moving in position to serve? What should we abandon?	■ What new capabilities do we need to be successful in the marketplace of the future?

Top management's views and conclusions about what the company's direction should be and the product-customer-market-technology focus it intends to pursue constitute a **strategic vision** for the company. A strategic vision thus delineates management's aspirations for the business, providing a panoramic view of "where are we going" and a convincing rationale for why this destination makes good business sense for the company. A strategic vision points an organization in a particular direction, charts a strategic path for it to follow, and molds organizational identity.

Well-stated visions are distinctive and specific to a particular organization; they avoid generic language like "we will become a global leader and the first choice of customers in every market we choose to serve," which could apply to scores of organizations.[4] Company Spotlight 1.3 provides examples of well-stated strategic visions developed by several prominent companies and nonprofit organizations.

According to one recent study of company vision statements:[5]

Most visions consist of easy options like "market leadership" or "leader in quality" or "the No. 1 choice of customers." They make people feel good, require little imaginative effort, and attract consensus.

Strong visions are different. They excite strong emotions. They are challenging, uncomfortable, nail biting . . . the critical mass of people who believe strongly in the vision will turn it into reality.

Strong visions only emerge from organizations with demanding and determined leaders.

Visions range from strong and clear to ill-conceived and bland. A surprising number of the vision statements found on company websites and in annual reports are dull, blurry, and uninspiring, coming across as written by a committee to satisfy a variety of organizational stakeholders and public relations expectations.[6] The one-sentence vision statement a company makes available to the public, of course, provides only a glimpse of what company executives are really thinking and where the company is headed and why. A vision statement is not a panacea but rather a useful management tool for giving an organization a sense of future direction. Like any tool, it can be used properly or improperly, either strongly conveying a company's future strategic course or not.

A Strategic Vision Is Different from a Mission Statement

Whereas a strategic vision is chiefly concerned with "where we are going and why," a company mission statement usually deals with the company's *present* business scope and purpose—"who we are, what we do, and why we are here." (Many companies prefer *business purpose* to *mission statement,* but the two terms are conceptually identical and are used interchangeably.) A typical example is the mission statement of Trader Joe's, a unique grocery store chain:

The mission of Trader Joe's is to give our customers the best food and beverage values that they can find anywhere and to provide them with the information required for informed buying decisions. We provide these with a dedication to the highest quality of customer satisfaction delivered with a sense of warmth, friendliness, fun, individual pride, and company spirit.

Verizon Communications

To be the customer's first choice for communications and information services in every market we serve, domestic and international.

Levi Strauss & Company

We will clothe the world by marketing the most appealing and widely worn casual clothing in the world.

Microsoft Corporation

Empower people through great software—any time, any place, and on any device.

Mayo Clinic

The best care to every patient every day.

Scotland Yard

To make London the safest city in the world.

Toyota

We want to set the tone for the era . . . green and affordable . . . that means establishing a new paradigm for harmonizing personal transport with the environment. It means revolutionary cost savings in products and production processes.

Greenpeace

To halt environmental abuse and promote environmental solutions.

Intel

Our vision: Getting to a billion connected computers worldwide, millions of servers, and trillions of dollars of e-commerce. Intel's core mission is being the building-block supplier to the Internet economy and spurring efforts to make the Internet more useful. Being connected is now at the center of people's computing experience. We are helping to expand the capabilities of the PC platform and the Internet.

As we look to the future, our strategies are based on the fundamental belief that we have seen only the early stages of deployment of digital technologies. The two areas that our business focuses on, computing and communications, are the backbone of the digital infrastructure, and our products are the building blocks that make up this infrastructure.

Goldman Sachs

To be the world's premier investment bank in every sector.

General Electric

We will become number one or number two in every market we serve, and revolutionize this company to have the speed and agility of a small enterprise.

Sources: Company documents and websites and Hugh Davidson, *The Committed Enterprise* (Oxford: Butterworth Heinemann, 2002), pp. 11, 65, 91, 92.

The mission statements that appear in company annual reports or on company websites almost always stress the company's present products and services and the types of customer it serves; sometimes they indicate the company's present market standing (whether it is a market leader or the industry's fastest growing company) as well as the company's technological and business capabilities. Rarely do they say much about where the company is headed, the coming changes in its business, or its future business aspirations. Hence the conceptual distinction between a strategic vision and a mission statement is fairly clear-cut: A strategic vision portrays a company's future business scope ("where we are going"), whereas a company's mission typically describes its present business scope and business purpose ("what we do, why we are here, and where we are now").

Sometimes companies word their mission statements around "making a profit." This is misguided: Profit is more correctly an *objective* and a *result* of what a company does. Making a profit is the obvious intent of every commercial enterprise, and mission statements structured around making a profit reveal nothing valuable about a company's business or the market arena in which it operates. The valuable part of a mission statement is in distinguishing the business purpose of one profit-seeking enterprise from the business purpose of another and, further, describing the company's business in language specific enough to give the company its own identity. To learn much of value from a company's mission statement, we must know management's answer to "Making a profit doing what and for whom?"

Communicating the Strategic Vision

Effectively communicating the strategic vision down the line to lower-level managers and employees is almost as important as ensuring the strategic soundness of the orga-nization's long-term direction and business model. Not only do people have a need to believe that the company's management knows where it's trying to take the company and what changes lie ahead both exter-nally and internally, but if frontline employees don't know what a company's vision is, they are unlikely to be emotionally committed to making the vision a reality. Generally, a strategic vision has to be put in writing so that it can be communicated organizationwide and then evaluated and debated by organization members.

> Strategic visions become real only when the vision statement is imprinted in the minds of organi-zation members and then translated into hard objectives and strategies.

Ideally, executives should present their vision for the company in language that reaches out and grabs people, that creates a vivid image, and that provokes emotion and enthusiasm. Expressing the strategic vision in engaging language has enormous motivational value—building a cathedral is more inspiring than laying stones. When a vision articulates a clear and compelling picture of what might be, organizational members begin to say "This is interesting. I would like to be involved and contribute to helping make it happen." In sum, a well-stated vision contains memorable language; clearly maps the company's future direction; and motivates organization members, ideally giving them the feeling their lives and their work are intertwined. If a vision doesn't move people, it is unlikely to have much beneficial organizational impact.[7]

Linking the Vision with Company Values

In the course of deciding who we are and where we are going, many companies also come up with a statement of values to guide the company's pursuit of its vision. By *values,* we mean the beliefs, business principles, and ways of doing things that are in-corporated into the company's operations and the behavior of organization members. Values, good and bad, exist in every organization. They relate to such things as fair-ness, integrity, ethics, innovativeness, teamwork, quality, customer service, social re-sponsibility, and community citizenship. Company values statements tend to contain between four and eight values, which, ideally, are tightly connected to and reinforce the company's vision, strategy, and operating practices. Home Depot embraces eight values (entrepreneurial spirit, excellent customer service, giving back to the commu-nity, respect for all people, doing the right thing, taking care of people, building strong relationships, and creating shareholder value) in its quest to become the world's largest home improvement retailer by operating warehouse stores filled with a wide assort-ment of products at the lowest prices with trained associates giving absolutely the best customer service in the industry. Du Pont stresses four values—safety, ethics, respect for people, and environmental stewardship; the first three have been in place since the company was founded 200 years ago by the Du Pont family. Loblaw, a major grocery chain in Canada, focuses on just two main values in operating its stores—competence and honesty; it expects employees to display both, and top management strives to promote only those employees who are smart and honest. At Johnson & Johnson, the two core values are teamwork and manufacturing the highest quality products.

Company managers connect values to the strategic vision in one of two ways. In companies with long-standing and deeply entrenched values, managers go to great lengths to explain how the vision matches the company's values, sometimes reinterpreting the meaning of existing values to indicate their relevance to the strategic vision. In new companies or companies having weak or incomplete sets of values, top management considers what values, beliefs, and operating principles will help drive the vision forward. Then new values that fit the vision are drafted and circulated among managers and employees for discussion and possible modification. A final values statement that connects to the vision and that reflects the beliefs and principles the company wants to uphold is then officially adopted. Some companies combine their vision and values into a single statement or document provided to all organization members and often posted on the company's website.

Of course, a wide gap sometimes opens between a company's stated values and business practices. Enron, for example, touted its four corporate values—respect, integrity, communication, and excellence—but as recent events demonstrated, some top officials did not behave in accordance with those values and the company imploded. Once one of the world's Big Five public accounting firms, Arthur Andersen was renowned for its commitment to the highest standards of audit integrity, but its high-profile audit failures at Enron, WorldCom, and other companies led to Andersen's demise.

Setting Objectives: Phase 2 of the Strategy-Making, Strategy-Executing Process

The managerial purpose of setting **objectives** is to convert the strategic vision into specific performance targets—results and outcomes the company's management wants to achieve—and then use these objectives as yardsticks for tracking the company's progress and performance. Well-stated objectives are *quantifiable,* or *measurable,* and contain a *deadline for achievement.* As Bill Hewlett, cofounder of Hewlett-Packard, shrewdly observed, "You cannot manage what you cannot measure . . . And what gets measured gets done."[8] The experiences of countless companies and managers teach that precisely spelling out *how much* of *what kind* of performance *by when* and then pressing forward with actions and incentives calculated to help achieve the targeted outcomes greatly improve a company's actual performance. It definitely beats setting vague targets like "maximize profits," "reduce costs," "become more efficient," or "increase sales" which specify neither how much nor when or else exhorting company personnel to try hard, do the best they can, and then living with whatever results they deliver.

> ### Core Concept
>
> **Objectives** are an organization's performance targets—the results and outcomes it wants to achieve. They function as yardsticks for tracking an organization's performance and progress.

Ideally, managers ought to use the objective-setting exercise as a tool for *stretching an organization to reach its full potential.* Challenging company personnel to go all out and deliver big gains in performance pushes an enterprise to be more inventive, to exhibit some urgency in improving both its financial performance and its business position, and to be more intentional and focused in its actions. Stretch objectives help

> **Core Concept**
>
> *Financial objectives* relate to the financial performance targets management has established for the organization to achieve. *Strategic objectives* relate to target outcomes that indicate a company is strengthening its market standing, competitive vitality, and future business prospects.

build a firewall against contentment with slow, incremental improvements in organizational performance. As Mitchell Leibovitz, CEO of the auto parts and service retailer Pep Boys, once said, "If you want to have ho-hum results, have ho-hum objectives."

What Kinds of Objectives to Set—The Need for a Balanced Scorecard

Two very distinct types of performance yardsticks are required: those relating to *financial performance* and those relating to *strategic performance*. Examples of commonly used financial and strategic objectives include the following:

Financial Objectives	Strategic Objectives
An *x* percent increase in annual revenues.	Winning additional market share (or reaching an *x* percent market share).
An *x* percent increase annually in after-tax profits.	Consistently getting new or improved products to market ahead of rivals.
An *x* percent increase annually in earnings per share.	Overtaking key competitors on product performance or quality or customer service.
Regular dividend increases.	
A larger gross profit margin.	Achieving lower overall costs than rivals.
A larger operating profit margin.	Deriving *x* percent of revenues from the sale of new products introduced within the past five years.
A larger net profit margin.	
An *x* percent return on capital employed (ROCE).	
An *x* percent return on assets (ROA).	Achieving national or global market coverage for the firm's products.
An *x* percent return on shareholder investment (ROE).	Being a recognized technological leader.
An upward-trending stock price that builds significant shareholder value over time.	Having broader or more attractive product selection than rivals.
Strong bond and credit ratings.	Deriving *x* percent of revenues from online sales.
Reduced levels of debt.	
Sufficient internal cash flows to fund new capital investment.	Having a better-known or more respected brand name than rivals.
Recognition as a blue-chip company.	Improving global sales and distribution capabilities.
A diversified revenue base.	
Stable earnings during periods of recession.	Having a larger network of wholesale distributors and/or retail dealers than rivals.

Achieving acceptable financial results is crucial. Without adequate profitability and financial strength, a company's pursuit of its strategic vision, as well as its long-term health and ultimate survival, is jeopardized. Neither shareowners nor lenders will continue to sink additional capital into an enterprise that can't deliver satisfactory financial

Unilever *(Strategic and financial objectives)*

"Grow revenues by 5–6 percent annually; increase operating profit margins from 11 percent to 16 percent within five years; trim the company's 1,200 food, household, and personal care products down to 400 core brands; focus sales and marketing efforts on those brands with potential to become respected, market-leading global brands; and streamline the company's supply chain."

Bank One Corporation *(Strategic objective)*

"To be one of the top three banking companies in terms of market share in all significant markets we serve."

Ford Motor Company *(Strategic objectives)*

"To satisfy our customers by providing quality cars and trucks, developing new products, reducing the time it takes to bring new vehicles to market, improving the efficiency of all our plants and processes, and building on our teamwork with employees, unions, dealers, and suppliers."

Alcan Aluminum *(Strategic and financial objectives)*

"To be the lowest-cost producer of aluminum and to outperform the average return on equity of the Standard & Poor's industrial stock index."

Bristol-Myers Squibb *(Strategic objective)*

"To focus globally on those businesses in health and personal care where we can be number one or number two through delivering superior value to the customer."

3M Corporation *(Financial and strategic objectives)*

"To achieve annual growth in earnings per share of 10 percent or better, on average; a return on stockholders' equity of 20–25 percent; a return on capital employed of 27 percent or better; and have at least 30 percent of sales come from products introduced in the past four years."

Source: Company documents.

---

results. Subpar earnings and a weak balance sheet alarm creditors and shareholders, impair a company's ability to fund needed initiatives, and perhaps even put its very survival at risk (not to mention the jobs of senior executives).

But company achievement of satisfactory financial performance, by itself, is not enough. Of equal or greater importance is a company's performance on the measures of its strategic well-being—its competitiveness and market position. Unless a company's performance in the marketplace reflects improving competitive strength and market penetration, its progress is less than inspiring and its ability to continue delivering good financial performance is suspect. A company's financial performance measures are really "lagging indicators" that reflect the results of past decisions and organizational activities. The "lead indicators" of a company's future financial performance and business prospects are its current achievement of strategic targets that reflect growing competitiveness and strength in the marketplace.

A balanced scorecard for measuring company performance thus requires setting both financial objectives and strategic objectives and tracking their achievement. Unless a company is in deep financial difficulty, such that its very survival is threatened, company managers are well advised to give the achievement of strategic objectives a higher priority than the achievement of financial objectives whenever a trade-off has to be made. *The surest path to sustained future profitability quarter after quarter and year after year is to relentlessly pursue strategic outcomes that strengthen a company's business position and yield sustainable competitive advantage.* Improving competitive vitality and market position enable a company to deliver steadily improving financial results. Company Spotlight 1.4 shows selected objectives of several prominent companies.

As a rule, a company's set of financial and strategic objectives ought to include both near-term and longer-term performance targets. Having quarterly or annual objectives focuses attention on delivering immediate performance improvements. Targets to be achieved within three to five years prompt considerations of what to do *now* to put the company in position to perform better later. If trade-offs have to be made between achieving long-run objectives and achieving short-run objectives, the long-run objectives should generally take precedence. A company rarely prospers from repeated management actions that put better short-term performance ahead of better long-run performance.

Company Spotlight 1.5 describes why a growing number of organizations are combining the use of financial and strategic objectives to create a "balanced scorecard" approach to measuring performance.

The Concept of Strategic Intent   A company's objectives sometimes play another role: Very ambitious or aggressive objectives often signal **strategic intent** to stake out a particular business position and be a winner in the marketplace, often against long odds.[9] Strategic intent can be thought of as a "big, hairy, audacious goal," or BHAG (pronounced *bee-hag*), that generally takes a long time to

> ### Core Concept
>
> A company exhibits **strategic intent** when it relentlessly pursues an ambitious strategic objective and concentrates its full resources and competitive actions on achieving that objective.

achieve (maybe as long as a decade or two). A company's strategic intent or BHAG can entail becoming the recognized industry leader, unseating the existing industry leader, delivering the best customer service of any company in the industry (or the world), or turning a new technology into products capable of changing the way people work and live. Ambitious companies almost invariably begin with strategic intents that are out of proportion to their immediate capabilities and market positions. But they set aggressive stretch objectives and pursue them relentlessly, sometimes even obsessively. Consider the following examples:

> Companies driving hard to achieve demanding performance targets make formidable competitors.

- In the 1960s, Komatsu, Japan's leading earth-moving equipment company, was less than one-third the size of its U.S. rival Caterpillar, had little market presence outside Japan, and depended on its small bulldozers for most of its revenue. But Komatsu's strategic intent was to eventually "encircle Caterpillar" with a broader product line and then compete globally against Caterpillar—its motivating battle cry among managers and employees was "Beat Caterpillar." By the late 1980s, Komatsu was the industry's second-ranking company, with a strong sales presence in North America, Europe, and Asia plus a product line that included industrial robots and semiconductors as well as a broad selection of earth-moving equipment.

- Nike's strategic intent during the 1960s was to overtake Adidas (which connected nicely with Nike's core purpose "to experience the emotion of competition, winning, and crushing competitors").

- Throughout the 1980s, Wal-Mart's strategic intent was to "overtake Sears" as the largest U.S. retailer (a feat accomplished in 1990).

- America Online's strategic intent is to build the strongest, most recognized brand name on the Internet.

- For some years, Toyota has been driving to overtake General Motors as the world's largest motor vehicle producer.

- When Yamaha overtook Honda in the motorcycle market, Honda responded with a warlike strategic intent: *Yamaha wo tsubusu* ("We will crush, squash, slaughter Yamaha").

Capably managed, up-and-coming enterprises with strategic intents exceeding their present reach and resources often prove to be more formidable competitors over time than larger, cash-rich rivals with modest market ambitions.

The Need for Objectives at All Organizational Levels   Objective setting should not stop with top management's establishing of companywide performance targets. Company objectives need to be broken down into performance targets for each of the organization's separate businesses, product lines, functional departments, and individual work units. Company performance can't reach full potential without each area of the organization doing its part and contributing directly to the desired companywide outcomes and results. This means setting performance targets for each organization unit that support—rather than conflict with or negate—the achievement of companywide strategic and financial objectives. The ideal situation is a team effort in which each organizational unit strives to produce results in its area of responsibility that contribute to the achievement of the company's performance targets and strategic vision. Such consistency of purpose signals that organizational units know their strategic role and are on board in helping the company move down the chosen strategic path and produce the desired results.

Crafting a Strategy: Phase 3 of the Strategy-Making, Strategy-Executing Process

Crafting strategy is partly an exercise in astute entrepreneurship—actively searching for opportunities to do new things or to do existing things in new ways. The faster a company's business environment is changing, the more critical the need for its managers to be good entrepreneurs in diagnosing the direction and force of the changes underway and in responding with timely strategic modifications.[10] Managers are always under the gun to pick up on happenings in the external environment and steer company activities in whatever new directions are dictated by shifting market conditions. This means studying market trends and the actions of competitors, listening to customers and anticipating their changing needs and expectations, scrutinizing the business possibilities that spring from new technological developments, building the firm's market position via acquisitions or new product introductions, and pursuing ways to strengthen the firm's competitive capabilities. Good strategy making is therefore inseparable from good business entrepreneurship. One cannot exist without the other.

The task of stitching a strategy together entails addressing a series of hows: *how* to grow the business, *how* to please customers, *how* to outcompete rivals, *how* to respond to changing market conditions, *how* to manage each functional piece of the business and develop needed organizational capabilities, *how* to achieve strategic and financial objectives. Companies usually have a wide degree of strategic freedom in addressing the hows of strategy. They can diversify broadly or narrowly, into related or unrelated industries, via acquisition, joint venture, strategic alliances, or internal start-up. Most industries are sufficiently diverse to offer competing companies enough strategy-making latitude to avoid carbon-copy strategies—some rivals have wide product lines, while others have narrow product lines; some target the high end of the market, while others go after the middle or low end; some strive for a competitive advantage based on lower costs than rivals, while others aim for a competitive edge based on product superiority or personalized customer service or added convenience. Some competitors position themselves in only one part of the industry's chain of production–distribution activities (preferring to be just in manufacturing or wholesale distribution or retailing), while others are integrated, with operations ranging from components production to manufacturing and assembly to wholesale distribution or company-owned retail stores. Some rivals deliberately confine their operations to local or regional markets; others opt to compete nationally, internationally (several countries), or globally (as many countries as possible). Opportunities abound for fashioning a strategy that tightly fits a company's own particular situation and that is discernibly different from the strategies of rivals.

The Ethical Component of Strategy Making

In choosing among strategic alternatives, corporate managers are well advised to embrace aboveboard actions that can pass the test of moral scrutiny. Crafting an ethical strategy means more than keeping a company's strategic actions within the bounds of what is legal. Ethical and moral standards go beyond the prohibitions of law and the language of "shall not" to the issues of *duty* and the language of "should and should not." A strategy is ethical only if all its pieces are consistent with the ethical duty management has to owners/shareholders, employees, customers, suppliers, and the community at large.

Recent headlines concerning Enron, WorldCom, Tyco, Adelphia, Dynegy, and other companies leave no room to doubt the damage that can result from ethical misconduct, corporate malfeasance, and even criminal behavior on the part of company personnel. Aside from just the embarrassment and black marks that accompany headline exposure of a company's unethical practices, the hard fact is that many customers and many suppliers are very wary of doing business with a company that engages in sleazy practices or that turns a blind eye to below-board behavior on the part of employees. They are turned off by unethical strategies or behavior and, rather than become victims or get burned themselves, wary customers will do their business elsewhere and wary suppliers will tread carefully in any business dealings they have with companies they view as unethical. Moreover, employees with character and integrity do not want to work for a company that has a shady strategy or whose executives are dishonest or unethical. There are few lasting upside benefits to unethical strategies and behavior, and the downside risks can be substantial—besides, such actions are plain wrong.

Admittedly, strategic behavior is not always easily categorized as definitely ethical or definitely unethical; many strategic actions fall in the gray zone, and whether they are ultimately deemed ethical or unethical often depends on how high one sets the bar. For example, is it ethical for a brewer of beer to advertise its products on TV at times when the ads are likely to be seen by underage viewers? Anheuser-Busch responded to concerns about the ethics of such advertising by announcing it would no longer run its beer commercials on MTV. Is it ethical for the manufacturers of firearms to encourage police departments and retired policemen to trade in or return automatic weapons whose manufacture has since been banned by Congress so they can gain access to a supply of weapons for resale? (A legal loophole allows them to traffic in weapons that were manufactured prior to the bans.) Similarly, is it ethical for firearms makers to change the designs of their automatic weapons just enough to escape the bans and prohibitions on automatic firearms instituted by Congress? Is it ethical for a meat packer to export meat products that do not meet safe standards in its home country to those countries where the safety standards are low and inspection is lax? Is it ethical for an apparel retailer attempting to keep prices attractively low to source clothing from low-cost foreign manufacturers who pay substandard wages or employ child labor?

Senior executives with strong character and ethical convictions are generally proactive in linking strategic action and ethics, forbidding the pursuit of ethically questionable business opportunities, and insisting that all aspects of company strategy reflect high ethical standards.[11] They make it clear that all company personnel are expected to act with integrity, and they put organizational systems and checks into place to monitor behavior, enforce ethical codes of conduct, and provide guidance to employees regarding any gray areas. They go beyond lip service to make a genuine commitment to conducting the company's business in an ethical manner.

Merging the Strategic Vision, Objectives, and Strategy into a Strategic Plan

Developing a strategic vision and mission, setting objectives, and crafting a strategy are basic direction-setting tasks. They map out where a company is headed, its short-range and long-range performance targets, and the competitive moves and internal action approaches to be used in achieving the targeted business results. Together, they constitute a **strategic plan** for coping with industry and competitive conditions, the expected actions of the industry's key

Core Concept

A company's **strategic plan** lays out its mission and future direction, performance targets, and strategy.

players, and the challenges and issues that stand as obstacles to the company's success.[12] In companies committed to regular strategy reviews and the development of explicit strategic plans, the strategic plan may take the form of a written document that is circulated to most managers and perhaps selected employees. In small, privately owned companies, strategic plans usually take the form of oral understandings and commitments among managers and key employees about where to head, what to accomplish, and how to proceed. Near-term performance targets are the part of the strategic plan most often spelled out explicitly and communicated to managers and employees. A number of companies summarize key elements of their strategic plans in the company's annual report to shareholders, in postings on their website, or in statements provided to the business media, whereas others, perhaps for reasons of competitive sensitivity, make only vague, general statements about their strategic plans that could apply to most any company.

Who Participates in Crafting a Company's Strategy?

A company's senior executives obviously have important strategy-making roles. The chief executive officer (CEO), as captain of the ship, carries the mantles of chief direction setter, chief objective setter, chief strategy maker, and chief strategy implementer for the total enterprise. Ultimate responsibility for *leading* the strategy-making, strategy-executing process rests with the CEO. In some enterprises the CEO or owner functions as strategic visionary and chief architect of strategy, personally deciding which of several strategic options to pursue, although others may well assist with data gathering and analysis and the CEO may seek the advice of other senior managers and key employees on which way to go. Such an approach to strategy development is characteristic of small owner-managed companies and sometimes large corporations that have been founded by the present CEO—Michael Dell at Dell Computer, Bill Gates at Microsoft, and Howard Schultz at Starbucks are prominent examples of corporate CEOs who maintain a heavy hand in shaping their company's strategy.

In most companies, however, the heads of business divisions and major product lines, the chief financial officer, and vice presidents for production, marketing, human resources, and other functional departments have influential strategy-making roles. Normally, a company's chief financial officer is in charge of devising and implementing an appropriate financial strategy; the production vice president takes the lead in developing and executing the company's production strategy; the marketing vice president orchestrates sales and marketing strategy; a brand manager is in charge of the strategy for a particular brand in the company's product lineup, and so on.

But it is a mistake to view strategy making as exclusively a top management function, the province of owner-entrepreneurs, CEOs, and other senior executives. The more wide-ranging a company's operations, the more that strategy making is a collaborative team effort involving managers (and sometimes key employees) down through the whole organization hierarchy. Consider Toshiba, a $43 billion corporation with 300 subsidiaries, thousands of products, and operations extending across the world. Any notion that a few senior executives in Toshiba headquarters have either the expertise or a sufficiently detailed understanding of all the relevant factors to wisely craft all the strategic initiatives taken in Toshiba's numerous and diverse organizational units is farfetched and erroneous. Rather, it takes involvement on the part of Toshiba's entire management team to

Core Concept

Every company manager has a strategy-making, strategy-executing role; viewing the tasks of managing strategy as something only high-level managers do is flawed thinking.

craft and execute the thousands of strategic initiatives that constitute the whole of Toshiba's strategy.

Major organizational units in a company—business divisions, product groups, functional departments, plants, geographic offices, distribution centers—normally have a leading or supporting role in the company's strategic game plan. Because senior executives in the corporate office seldom know enough about the situation in every geographic area and operating unit to direct every strategic move made in the field, it is common practice for top-level managers to delegate strategy-making authority to middle- and lower-echelon managers who head the organizational subunits where specific strategic results must be achieved. The more that a company's operations cut across different products, industries, and geographical areas, the more that headquarters executives are prone to delegate considerable strategy-making authority to on-the-scene personnel who have firsthand knowledge of customer requirements, can accurately evaluate market opportunities, and know how to keep the strategy responsive to changing market and competitive conditions. While managers further down in the managerial hierarchy obviously have a narrower, more specific strategy-making, strategy-executing role than managers closer to the top, the important point here is that in most of today's companies *every company manager typically has a strategy-making, strategy-executing role—ranging from major to minor—for the area he or she heads.*

Hence any notion that an organization's strategists are at the top of the management hierarchy and that midlevel and frontline managers and employees merely carry out the strategic directives of senior managers needs to be cast aside. With decentralized decision making becoming common at companies of all stripes, key pieces of a company's strategy now typically originate in a company's middle and lower ranks.[13] For example, Electronic Data Systems conducted a year-long strategy review that involved 2,500 of its 55,000 employees and was coordinated by a core of 150 managers and staffers from all over the world.[14] J. M. Smucker, well known for its jams and jellies, formed a team of 140 employees (7 percent of its 2,000-person workforce) who spent 25 percent of their time over a six-month period looking for ways to rejuvenate the company's growth; the team, which solicited input from all employees, came up with 12 initiatives to double the company's revenues over the next five years.

Involving teams of people to dissect complex situations and find market-driven, customer-driven solutions is becoming increasingly necessary in many businesses. Many strategic issues are not only too far-reaching or complex for a single manager to handle but also cross-functional and cross-departmental, thus requiring the contributions of many disciplinary experts and the collaboration of managers from different parts of the organization. A valuable strength of collaborative strategy making is that the group of people charged with crafting the strategy can easily include the very people who will also be charged with implementing it. Giving people an influential stake in crafting the strategy they must later help implement and execute builds motivation and commitment; furthermore, it allows the company to hold these people accountable for putting the strategy into place and making it work—the tired excuse of "It wasn't my idea to do this" won't fly.

In some companies, top management makes a regular practice of encouraging individuals and teams to develop and champion proposals for new product lines and new business ventures. The idea is to unleash the talents and energies of promising "corporate intrapreneurs," letting them try out untested business ideas and giving them the room to pursue new strategic initiatives. Executives judge which proposals merit support, give the chosen intrapreneurs the organizational and budgetary support they need, and let them run with the ball. Thus important pieces of company strategy originate with those intrapreneurial individuals and teams who succeed in championing a proposal through the approval stage and then end up being charged with the lead role in launching new products, overseeing the company's entry into new geographic markets, or heading up new business ventures. W. L. Gore and Associates, a privately owned company famous for its Gore-Tex waterproofing film, is an avid and highly successful practitioner of the corporate intrapreneur approach to strategy making. Gore expects all employees to initiate improvements and to display innovativeness. Each employee's intrapreneurial contributions are prime considerations in determining raises, stock option bonuses, and promotions. W. L. Gore's commitment to intrapreneurship has produced a stream of product innovations and new strategic initiatives that has kept the company vibrant and growing for nearly two decades.

A Company's Strategy-Making Hierarchy

It thus follows that *a company's overall strategy is a collection of strategic initiatives and actions* devised by managers and key employees up and down the whole organizational hierarchy. The larger and more diverse the operations of an enterprise, the more points of strategic initiative it has and the more managers and employees at more levels of management that have a relevant strategy-making role. Figure 1.4 shows who is generally responsible for devising what pieces of a company's overall strategy.

In diversified, multibusiness companies where the strategies of several different businesses have to be managed, the strategy-making task involves four distinct types or levels of strategy, each of which involves different facets of the company's overall strategy:

- *Corporate strategy* consists of the kinds of initiatives the company uses to establish business positions in different industries, the approaches corporate executives pursue to boost the combined performance of the set of businesses the company has diversified into, and the means of capturing cross-business synergies and turning them into competitive advantage. Senior corporate executives normally have lead responsibility for devising corporate strategy and for choosing among whatever recommended actions bubble up from the organization below. Key business-unit heads may also be influential, especially in strategic decisions affecting the businesses they head. Major strategic decisions are usually reviewed and approved by the company's board of directors. We will look deeper into the strategy-making process at diversified companies when we get to Chapter 6.

- *Business strategy* concerns the actions and the approaches crafted to produce successful performance in one specific line of business. The key focus is crafting responses to changing market circumstances and initiating actions to strengthen market position, build competitive advantage, and develop strong competitive capabilities. Orchestrating the development of business-level strategy is the responsibility of the manager in charge of the business. The business head has at least two other strategy-related roles: (1) seeing that lower-level strategies are well conceived, consistent, and adequately matched to the overall business strategy, and (2) getting major business-level strategic moves approved by corporate-level officers (and sometimes the board of directors) and keeping them informed of emerging strategic issues. In diversified companies, business-unit heads may have the additional obligation of making sure business-level objectives and strategy conform to corporate-level objectives and strategy themes.

Figure 1.4   A Company's Strategy-Making Hierarchy

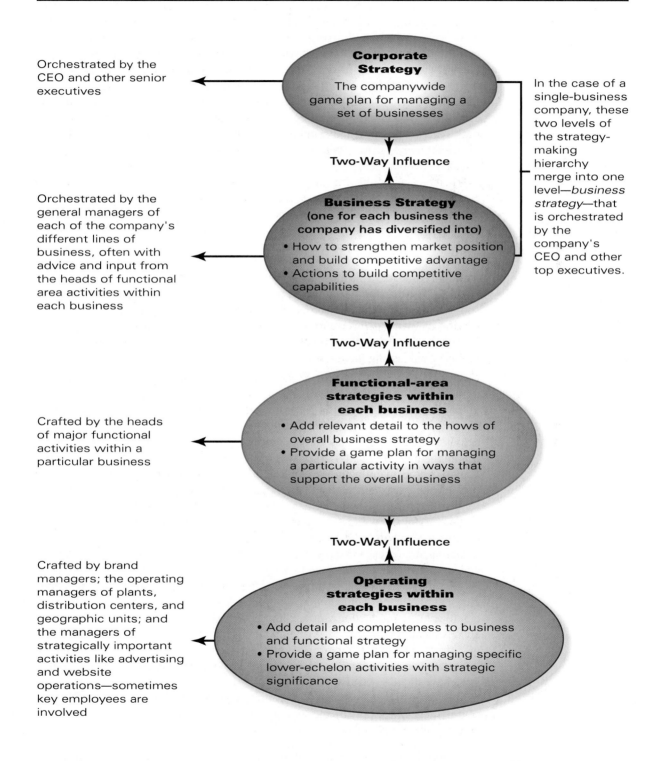

Orchestrated by the CEO and other senior executives

Orchestrated by the general managers of each of the company's different lines of business, often with advice and input from the heads of functional area activities within each business

Crafted by the heads of major functional activities within a particular business

Crafted by brand managers; the operating managers of plants, distribution centers, and geographic units; and the managers of strategically important activities like advertising and website operations—sometimes key employees are involved

Corporate Strategy
The companywide game plan for managing a set of businesses

In the case of a single-business company, these two levels of the strategy-making hierarchy merge into one level—*business strategy*—that is orchestrated by the company's CEO and other top executives.

Two-Way Influence

Business Strategy (one for each business the company has diversified into)
• How to strengthen market position and build competitive advantage
• Actions to build competitive capabilities

Two-Way Influence

Functional-area strategies within each business
• Add relevant detail to the hows of overall business strategy
• Provide a game plan for managing a particular activity in ways that support the overall business

Two-Way Influence

Operating strategies within each business
• Add detail and completeness to business and functional strategy
• Provide a game plan for managing specific lower-echelon activities with strategic significance

▪ *Functional-area strategies* concern the actions, approaches, and practices to be employed in managing particular functions or business processes or key activities within a business. A company's marketing strategy, for example, represents the managerial game plan for running the sales and marketing part of the business. A company's product development strategy represents the managerial game plan for keeping the company's product lineup fresh and in tune with what buyers are looking for. Functional strategies add specifics to the hows of business-level strategy. Plus, they aim at establishing or strengthening a business unit's competencies and capabilities in performing strategy-critical activities so as to enhance the business's market position and standing with customers. The primary role of a functional strategy is to *support* the company's overall business strategy and competitive approach.

Lead responsibility for functional strategies within a business is normally delegated to the heads of the respective functions, with the general manager of the business having final approval and perhaps even exerting a strong influence over the content of particular pieces of the strategies. To some extent, functional managers have to collaborate and coordinate their strategy-making efforts to avoid uncoordinated or conflicting strategies. For the overall business strategy to have maximum impact, a business's marketing strategy, production strategy, finance strategy, customer service strategy, product development strategy, and human resources strategy should be compatible and mutually reinforcing rather than each serving its own narrower purposes. If inconsistent functional-area strategies are sent up the line for final approval, the business head is responsible for spotting the conflicts and getting them resolved.

▪ *Operating strategies* concern the relatively narrow strategic initiatives and approaches for managing key operating units (plants, distribution centers, geographic units) and specific operating activities with strategic significance (advertising campaigns, the management of specific brands, supply chain–related activities, and website sales and operations). A plant manager needs a strategy for accomplishing the plant's objectives, carrying out the plant's part of the company's overall manufacturing game plan, and dealing with any strategy-related problems that exist at the plant. A company's advertising manager needs a strategy for getting maximum audience exposure and sales impact from the ad budget. Operating strategies, while of limited scope, add further detail and completeness to functional strategies and to the overall business strategy. Lead responsibility for operating strategies is usually delegated to frontline managers, subject to review and approval by higher-ranking managers.

Even though operating strategy is at the bottom of the strategy-making hierarchy, its importance should not be downplayed. A major plant that fails in its strategy to achieve production volume, unit cost, and quality targets can undercut the achievement of company sales and profit objectives and wreak havoc with strategic efforts to build a quality image with customers. Frontline managers are thus an important part of an organization's strategy-making team because many operating units have strategy-critical performance targets and need to have strategic action plans in place to achieve them. One cannot reliably judge the strategic importance of a given action simply by the strategy level or location within the managerial hierarchy where it is initiated.

In single-business enterprises, the corporate and business levels of strategy-making merge into one level—business strategy—because the strategy for the whole company involves only one distinct line of business. Thus a single-business enterprise has three levels of strategy: business strategy for the company as a whole, functional-area strategies for each main area within the business, and operating strategies undertaken by lower-echelon managers to flesh out strategically significant aspects for the company's business and functional-area strategies. Proprietorships, partnerships, and owner-managed enterprises may have only one or two strategy-making levels since their strategy-making, strategy-executing process can be handled by just a few key people.

Uniting the Strategy-Making Effort   Ideally, the pieces of a company's strategy should fit together like a jigsaw puzzle. To achieve such unity, the strategizing process must generally proceed from the corporate level to the business level and then from the business level to the functional and operating levels. *Midlevel and frontline managers cannot do good strategy making without understanding the company's long-term direction and higher-level strategies.* The strategic disarray that occurs in an organization when senior managers don't exercise strong top-down direction setting and set forth a clearly articulated companywide strategy is akin to what would happen to a football team's offensive performance if the quarterback decided not to call a play for the team but instead let each

> **Core Concept**
>
> A company's strategy is at full power only when its many pieces are united.

player pick whatever play he thought would work best at his respective position. In business, as in sports, all the strategy makers in a company are on the same team and the many different pieces of the overall strategy crafted at various organizational levels need to be in sync and united. Anything less than a unified collection of strategies weakens company performance.

Achieving unity is partly a function of communicating the company's basic strategy themes effectively across the organization and establishing clear strategic principles and guidelines for lower-level strategy making. Cohesive strategy making becomes easier to achieve when company strategy is distilled into pithy, easy-to-grasp terminology that can be used to drive consistent strategic action down through the hierarchy.[15] The greater the numbers of company personnel who know, understand, and buy into the company's basic direction and strategy, the smaller the risk that people and organization units will go off in conflicting strategic directions when decision making is pushed down to frontline levels and many people are given a strategy-making role. Good communication of strategic themes and guiding principles thus serves a valuable strategy-unifying purpose.

What Makes a Strategy a Winner?

Being able to tell a winning strategy from a losing or mediocre strategy is a valuable skill. There are three tests for evaluating the merits of one strategy over another and gauging how good a company's strategy is:

The Goodness of Fit Test—To qualify as a winner, a strategy has to be well matched to industry and competitive conditions, market opportunities and threats, and other aspects of the enterprise's external environment. At the same time, it has to be tailored to company's resource strengths and weaknesses, competencies, and competitive capabilities. Unless a strategy tightly fits both the external and internal aspects of a company's overall situation, it is suspect and likely to produce less than the best possible business results.

The Competitive Advantage Test—Good strategies enable a company to build sustainable competitive advantage and then defend or protect it. The bigger the competitive edge it helps build, the more powerful and appealing the strategy is.

The Performance Test—A good strategy boosts company performance. Two kinds of performance improvement tell the most about the caliber of a company's strategy: gains in profitability and gains in the company's competitive strength and market standing.

> ### Core Concept
>
> A winning strategy must fit the enterprise's external and internal situation, build sustainable competitive advantage, and improve company performance.

Once a company commits to a particular strategy and enough time elapses to assess how well that strategy fits the situation and whether it is actually delivering competitive advantage and better performance, these tests can be used to determine what grade to assign the strategy. Strategies that come up short on one or more of these tests are plainly less appealing than strategies that pass all three with flying colors.

Managers can also apply the tests in picking and choosing among alternative strategic actions. A company debating which of several strategic options to employ can evaluate each for goodness of fit, competitive advantage, and performance. The strategic option with the highest prospective passing scores on all three tests can be regarded as the most attractive strategic alternative.

Other relevant criteria for judging the merits of a particular strategy include how consistent all its pieces are, what degree of risk it poses compared to alternative strategies, how adaptable it is to changing circumstances, and whether it represents a viable business model. These criteria merit consideration, but they seldom override the importance of the three tests listed above.

Implementing and Executing the Strategy: Phase 4 of the Strategy-Making, Strategy-Executing Process

Managing the implementation and execution of strategy is an operations-oriented, make-things-happen activity aimed at shaping the performance of core business activities in a strategy-supportive manner. It is easily the most demanding and time-consuming part of the strategy management process. Converting strategic plans into actions and results tests a manager's ability to direct organizational change, motivate people, build and strengthen company competencies and competitive capabilities, create a strategy-supportive work climate, and meet or beat performance targets. Initiatives have to be launched and managed on many organizational fronts.

Management's action agenda for implementing and executing the chosen strategy emerges from assessing what the company will have to do differently or better, given its particular operating practices and organizational circumstances, to execute the strategy proficiently and achieve the targeted performance. Each company manager has to think through the answer to "What has to be done in my area to execute my piece of the strategic plan, and what actions should I take to get the process under way?" How much internal change is needed depends on how much of the strategy is new, how far internal practices and competencies deviate from what the strategy requires, and how well the present work climate/culture supports good strategy execution. Depending on the amount of internal change involved, full implementation and proficient execution of company strategy (or important new pieces thereof) can take several months to several years.

In most situations, managing the strategy execution process includes the following principal aspects:

- Staffing the organization with the needed skills and expertise, consciously building and strengthening strategy-supportive competencies and competitive capabilities, and organizing the work effort.

- Developing budgets that steer ample resources into those activities critical to strategic success.

- Ensuring that policies and operating procedures facilitate rather than impede effective execution.

- Using the best-known practices to perform core business activities and pushing for continuous improvement. Organizational units have to periodically reassess how things are being done and diligently pursue useful changes and improvements.

- Installing information and operating systems that enable company personnel to better carry out their strategic roles day in and day out.

- Motivating people to pursue the target objectives energetically and, if need be, modifying their duties and job behavior to better fit the requirements of successful strategy execution.

- Tying rewards and incentives directly to the achievement of performance objectives and good strategy execution.

- Creating a company culture and work climate conducive to successful strategy implementation and execution.

- Exerting the internal leadership needed to drive implementation forward and keep improving on how the strategy is being executed. When stumbling blocks or weaknesses are encountered, management has to see that they are addressed and rectified on a timely basis.

Good strategy execution requires creating strong fits between strategy and organizational capabilities, between strategy and the reward structure, between strategy and internal operating systems, and between strategy and the organization's work climate and culture. The stronger these fits—that is, the more that the company's capabilities, reward structure, internal operating systems, and culture facilitate and promote proficient strategy execution—the better the execution and the higher the company's odds of achieving its performance targets. Furthermore, deliberately shaping the performance of core business activities around the strategy helps unite the organization.

Evaluating Performance and Initiating Corrective Adjustments: Phase 5 of the Strategy-Making, Strategy-Executing Process

The fifth phase of the strategy management process—evaluating the company's progress, assessing the impact of new external developments, and making corrective adjustments—is the trigger point for deciding whether to continue or change the company's vision, objectives, strategy, and/or strategy execution methods. So long as the company's direction and strategy seem well matched to industry and competitive conditions and performance targets are being met, company executives may well decide to stay the course. Simply fine-tuning the strategic plan and continuing with efforts to improve strategy execution are sufficient.

> **Core Concept**
>
> A company's vision, objectives, strategy, and approach to strategy execution are never final; managing strategy is an ongoing process, not a start–stop event.

But whenever a company encounters disruptive changes in its environment, questions need to be raised about the appropriateness of its direction and strategy. If a company experiences a downturn in its market position or shortfalls in performance, then company managers are obligated to ferret out the causes—do they relate to poor strategy, poor strategy execution, or both?—and take timely corrective action. A company's direction, objectives, and strategy have to be revisited anytime external or internal conditions warrant. It is to be expected that a company will modify its strategic vision, direction, objectives, and strategy over time.

Likewise, it is not unusual for a company to find that one or more aspects of its strategy implementation and execution are not going as well as intended. Proficient strategy execution is always the product of much organizational learning. It is achieved unevenly—coming quickly in some areas and proving nettlesome in others. It is both normal and desirable to periodically assess strategy execution to determine which aspects are working well and which need improving. Successful strategy execution entails vigilantly searching for ways to improve and then making corrective adjustments whenever and wherever it is useful to do so.

What Is the Role of the Board of Directors in the Strategy-Making, Strategy-Executing Process?

Since *lead responsibility* for crafting and executing strategy falls to top executives, the chief strategic role of an organization's board of directors is to exercise oversight and see that all five phases of managing the strategy-making, strategy-executing process are carried out in a manner that benefits shareholders (in the case of investor-owned enterprises) or stakeholders (in the case of not-for-profit organizations). The specter of stockholder lawsuits and the escalating costs of liability insurance for directors underscore the responsibility that corporate board members have for overseeing a company's strategic actions. Moreover, holders of large blocks of shares (mutual funds and pension funds), regulatory authorities, and the financial press consistently urge that board members, especially outside directors, be active in their oversight of company strategy and the actions and capabilities of executives.

It is standard procedure for executives to brief board members on important strategic moves and to submit the company's strategic plans to the board for official approval. But directors rarely can or should play a direct, hands-on role in crafting or executing strategy. Many outside directors, especially if they are relatively new, have limited industry-specific and company-specific knowledge. Boards of directors typically meet no more than once a month for six to eight hours. Outside board members can scarcely be expected to have detailed command of all the strategic issues or know the ins and outs of the various strategic options. They can hardly be expected to come up with compelling strategy proposals of their own to debate against those put forward by senior management. But such a hands-on role is unnecessary for good oversight. The chief task of directors is to be *inquiring critics* and *overseers,* asking probing questions and drawing on their experience and knowledge to make independent judgments about whether proposals have been adequately analyzed and whether proposed strategic actions appear to have greater promise than alternatives.[16] If executive management is bringing well-supported and reasoned strategy proposals to the board, there's little reason for board members to aggressively challenge and try to pick apart everything put before them. Asking probing questions and following up on superficial or unpersuasive answers is usually sufficient to test whether the case for the proposals is compelling and to exercise vigilant oversight. However, if the company is experiencing gradual erosion of profits and market share, and certainly when there is a precipitous collapse in profitability, board members have a duty to forcefully express their concerns about the validity of the strategy, initiate debate about the company's strategic path, hold one-on-one discussions with key executives and other board members, and perhaps directly intervene as a group to alter both the strategy and the company's executive leadership.

> **Core Concept**
>
> The central roles of a company's board of directors are (1) to critically appraise and ultimately approve strategic action plans, and (2) to evaluate the strategic leadership skills of the CEO and others in line to succeed the incumbent CEO.

Insofar as strategy is concerned, the primary hands-on role of directors is to evaluate the caliber of senior executives' strategy-making and strategy-implementing skills. The board is always responsible for determining whether the current CEO is doing a good job of strategic management (as a basis for awarding salary increases and bonuses and deciding on retention or removal). Boards must also exercise due diligence in evaluating the strategic leadership skills of other senior executives in line to succeed the CEO. When the incumbent CEO retires, the board must elect a successor, either going with an insider (frequently nominated by the retiring CEO) or deciding that an outsider is needed to perhaps radically change the company's strategic course. Board oversight and vigilance are therefore very much in play in the strategy arena, but the board's tasks seldom extend to relieving top executives of their strategy-making, strategy-implementing responsibilities and taking over these functions themselves.

Why Is Strategy Important?

Crafting and executing strategy are top-priority managerial tasks for two very big reasons. First, there is a compelling need for managers to *proactively shape* how the company's business will be conducted. A clear and reasoned strategy is management's prescription for doing business, its road map to competitive advantage, its game plan for pleasing customers and achieving performance targets. Winning in the marketplace requires a well-conceived opportunistic strategy, usually one characterized by strategic offensives to outinnovate and outmaneuver rivals and secure sustainable competitive advantage, then using this market edge to achieve superior financial performance. A powerful strategy that delivers a home run in the marketplace can propel a firm from a trailing position into one of leadership such that the firm's products/services become the industry standard. High-achieving enterprises are nearly always the product of shrewd strategy making—companies don't get to the top of the industry rankings or stay there with strategies built around timid efforts to do better. And only a handful of companies can boast of strategies that hit home runs in the marketplace due to lucky breaks or the good fortune of having stumbled into the right market at the right time with the right product. So there can be little argument that the caliber of a company's strategy matters—and matters a lot.

Second, a strategy-focused organization is more likely to be a strong bottom-line performer than an organization that views strategy as secondary and puts its priorities elsewhere. The quality of managerial strategy making and strategy execution has a highly positive impact on earnings, cash flow, and return on investment. A company that lacks clear-cut direction, has vague or undemanding objectives, has a muddled or flawed strategy, or can't seem to execute its strategy competently is a company whose financial performance is probably suffering, whose business is at long-term risk, and whose management is sorely lacking. On the other hand, when the five phases of the strategy-making, strategy-executing process drive management's whole approach to managing the company, the odds are much greater that the initiatives and activities of different divisions, departments, managers, and work groups will be unified into a *coordinated, cohesive effort*. Mobilizing the full complement of company resources in a total team effort behind good execution of the chosen strategy and achievement of the targeted performance allows a company to operate at full power. The chief executive officer of one successful company put it well when he said:

> In the main, our competitors are acquainted with the same fundamental concepts and techniques and approaches that we follow, and they are as free to pursue them as we are. More often than not, the difference between their level of success and ours lies in the relative thoroughness and self-discipline with which we and they develop and execute our strategies for the future.

Good Strategy + Good Strategy Execution = Good Management

Crafting and executing strategy are thus core management functions. Among all the things managers do, nothing affects a company's ultimate success or failure more fundamentally than how well its management team charts the company's direction, develops competitively effective strategic moves and business approaches, and pursues what needs to be done internally to produce good day-in, day-out strategy execution. Indeed, *good strategy and good strategy execution are the most trustworthy signs of good management.* Managers don't deserve a gold star for designing a potentially brilliant strategy but failing to put the organizational means in place to carry it out in high-caliber fashion; weak implementation and execution undermine the strategy's potential and pave the way for shortfalls in customer satisfaction and company performance. Competent execution of a mediocre strategy scarcely merits enthusiastic applause for management's efforts either. The rationale for using the twin standards of good strategy making and good strategy execution to determine whether a company is well managed is therefore compelling: The better conceived a company's strategy and the more competently it is executed, the more likely the company will be a standout performer in the marketplace.

Throughout the text chapters to come and the accompanying case collection, the spotlight is trained on the foremost question in running a business enterprise: What must managers do, and do well, to make a company a winner in the marketplace? The answer that emerges, and that becomes the message of this book, is that doing a good job of managing inherently requires good strategic thinking and good management

Core Concept

Excellent execution of an excellent strategy is the best test of managerial excellence—and the most reliable recipe for winning in the marketplace.

of the strategy-making, strategy-executing process. The mission of this book is to explore what "good strategic thinking" entails, to present the core concepts and tools of strategic analysis, to describe the ins and outs of crafting and executing strategy, and, through the cases that are included, to help you build your skills both in diagnosing how well the five aspects of managing strategy are being performed in actual companies and in making analysis-based recommendations for improvement. As you tackle the following pages, ponder an observation once made by Ralph Waldo Emerson: "Commerce is a game of skill which many people play, but which few play well." The overriding objective of this book is to help you become a more savvy player and equip you to succeed in business—capabilities in crafting and executing strategy are basic to managing successfully and a standard component of the managerial toolkit.

Key Points

The tasks of crafting and executing company strategies are the heart and soul of managing a business enterprise and winning in the marketplace. A company's strategy is the game plan management is using to stake out a market position, conduct its operations, attract and please customers, compete successfully, and achieve organizational objectives. The central thrust of a company's strategy is undertaking moves to build and strengthen the company's long-term competitive position and financial performance and, ideally, gain a competitive advantage over rivals that then becomes a company's ticket to above-average profitability. A company's strategy typically evolves and re-forms over time, emerging from a blend of (1) proactive and purposeful actions on the part of company managers, and (2) as-needed reactions to unanticipated developments and fresh market conditions.

Closely related to the concept of strategy is the concept of a company's business model. A company's business model is management's storyline for how and why the company's product offerings and competitive approaches will generate a revenue stream and have an associated cost structure that produces attractive earnings and return on investment; in effect a company's business model sets forth the economic logic for answering the question "How do we intend to make money in this business, given our current strategy?"

The managerial process of crafting and executing a company's strategy consists of five interrelated and integrated phases:

1. *Developing a strategic vision* of where the company needs to head and what market position it is trying to stake out. This managerial step provides long-term direction, infuses the organization with a sense of purposeful action, and communicates to stakeholders what management's aspirations for the company are.

2. *Setting objectives*—managerial actions that convert the strategic vision into specific performance outcomes for the company to achieve. Objectives need to spell out *how much* of *what kind* of performance *by when* and they need to require a significant amount of organizational stretch. A balanced scorecard approach for measuring company performance entails setting both *financial objectives* and *strategic objectives.* Judging how well a company is doing by its financial performance is not enough, because financial outcomes are "lag indicators" that reflect the impacts of past decisions and organizational activities. But the "lead indicators" of a company's future financial performance are its current achievement of strategic

targets that indicate a company is strengthening its marketing standing, competitive vitality, and future business prospects.

3. *Crafting a strategy to achieve the objectives and move the company toward where it wants to go.* Crafting strategy is concerned principally with forming responses to changes under way in the external environment, devising competitive moves and market approaches aimed at producing sustainable competitive advantage, building competitively valuable competencies and capabilities, and uniting the strategic actions initiated in various parts of the company. The more wide-ranging a company's operations, the more that strategy making is a collaborative team effort involving managers (and sometimes key employees) down through the whole organization hierarchy; the overall strategy that emerges in such companies is really a collection of strategic actions and business approaches initiated partly by senior company executives, partly by the heads of major business divisions, partly by functional area managers, and partly by operating managers on the frontlines. The tests of a winning strategy are how well matched it is to the company's external and internal situation, whether it is producing sustainable competitive advantage, and whether it is boosting company performance.

4. *Implementing and executing the chosen strategy efficiently and effectively.* Managing the implementation and execution of strategy is an operations-oriented, make-things-happen activity aimed at shaping the performance of core business activities in a strategy-supportive manner. Converting a company's strategy into actions and results tests a manager's ability to direct organizational change, motivate people with a reward and incentive compensation system tied to good strategy execution and the achievement of target outcomes, build and strengthen company competencies and competitive capabilities, create a strategy-supportive work climate, and deliver the desired results. The quality of a company's operational excellence in executing the chosen strategy is a major driver of how well the company ultimately performs.

5. *Evaluating performance and initiating corrective adjustments in vision, long-term direction, objectives, strategy, or execution in* light of actual experience, changing conditions, new ideas, and new opportunities. This phase of the strategy management process is the trigger point for deciding whether to continue or change the company's vision, objectives, strategy, and/or strategy execution methods. Sometimes simply fine-tuning the strategic plan and continuing with efforts to improve strategy execution suffices. At other times, major overhauls are required.

Developing a strategic vision and mission, setting objectives, and crafting a strategy are the basic direction-setting tasks that together constitute a *strategic plan* for coping with industry and competitive conditions, the actions of rivals, and the challenges and issues that stand as obstacles to the company's success.

Crafting and executing strategy are core management functions. Whether a company wins or loses in the marketplace is directly attributable to the caliber with which it performs the five tasks that comprise the strategy-making, strategy-executing process.

Exercises

1. Go to www.redhat.com and check whether the company's business model is working. That is, is the company profitable? Is its revenue stream from selling technical support services growing or declining as a percentage of total revenues? Does your review of the company's recent financial performance suggest that its business model and strategy are changing? Explain.

2. Go to www.levistrauss.com/about/vision and read what Levi Strauss & Company says about how its corporate values of originality, empathy, integrity, and courage are connected to its vision of clothing the world by marketing the most appealing and widely worn casual clothing in the world. Do you buy what the company says, or are its statements just a bunch of nice pontifications that represent the personal values of the CEO (and make for good public relations)? Explain.

CHAPTER 2

Analyzing a Company's External Environment

Analysis is the critical starting point of strategic thinking.
—Kenichi Ohmae, consultant and author

Things are always different—the art is figuring out which differences matter.
—Laszlo Birinyi, investments manager

Competitive battles should be seen not as one-shot skirmishes but as a dynamic multiround game of moves and countermoves.
—Anil K. Gupta, Professor

Managers

are not prepared to act wisely in steering a company in a different direction or altering its strategy until they have a deep understanding of the pertinent factors surrounding the company's situation. Probing, analysis-based answers to "Where are we now and what's the situation we face?" require thinking strategically about two facets of the company's situation. One is the industry and competitive environment in which the company operates and the forces acting to reshape this environment. The other is the company's own market position and competitiveness: its resources and capabilities, its strengths and weaknesses vis-à-vis rivals, and its windows of opportunity.

A perceptive diagnosis of a company's external and internal environment is a prerequisite for managers to succeed in crafting a strategy that is an especially good fit with the company's situation, is capable of building competitive advantage, and holds good prospect for boosting company performance—the three criteria of a winning strategy. The proper sequence for managers to observe in developing company strategy begins with a strategic appraisal of the company's external and internal situation (to form a strategic vision of where the company needs to head) and moves toward an evaluation of the most promising alternative strategies and business models, and finally to a choice of strategy (see Figure 2.1).

This chapter presents the concepts and analytical tools for assessing a single-business company's external environment. Attention centers on the competitive arena in which a company operates, together with whatever other pertinent technological, societal, regulatory, or demographic influences in the larger macroenvironment are acting to reshape the company's future market arena. In Chapter 3 we explore the methods of evaluating a company's internal circumstances and competitiveness.

Figure 2.1   From Thinking Strategically to Choosing a Strategy

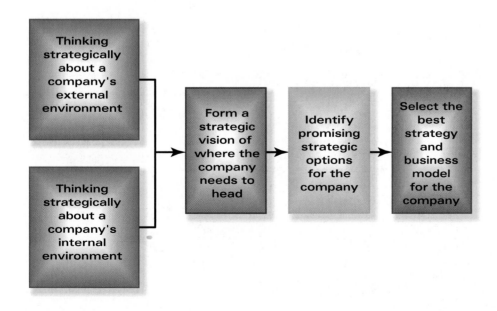

The Strategically Relevant Components of a Company's External Environment

All companies operate in a "macroenvironment" shaped by influences emanating from the economy at large; population demographics; societal values and lifestyles; governmental legislation and regulation; technological factors; and, closer to home, the industry and competitive arena in which the company operates (see Figure 2.2). Strictly speaking, a company's macroenvironment includes *all relevant factors and influences* outside the company's boundaries; by *relevant,* we mean important enough to have a bearing on the decisions the company ultimately makes about its direction, objectives,

Figure 2.2   The Components of a Company's Macroenvironment

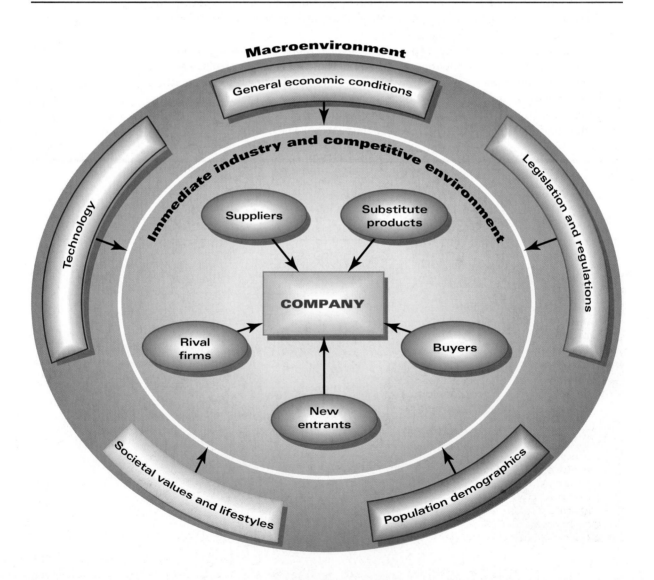

strategy, and business model. For the most part, influences coming from the outer ring of the macroenvironment have a low impact on a company's business situation and shape only the edges of the company's direction and strategy. (There are notable exceptions, though. The strategic opportunities of cigarette producers to grow their business are greatly reduced by antismoking ordinances and the growing cultural stigma attached to smoking; the market growth potential for health care and prescription drug companies is quite favorably affected by the demographics of an aging population and longer life expectancies; and companies in most all industries, seeking to capitalize on the benefits of Internet technology applications, are rushing to incorporate e-commerce elements into their strategies.) But while the strategy-shaping impact of outer-ring influences is normally low, there are enough strategically relevant trends and developments in the outer ring of the macroenvironment to justify a watchful eye. As company managers scan the external environment, they must be alert for potentially important outer-ring forces, assess their impact and influence, and adapt the company's direction and strategy as needed.

However, the factors and forces in a company's macroenvironment having the biggest strategy-shaping impact almost always pertain to the company's immediate industry and competitive environment. Consequently, it is on these factors that we concentrate our attention in this chapter.

Thinking Strategically about a Company's Industry and Competitive Environment

To gain a deep understanding of a company's industry and competitive environment, managers do not need to gather all the information they can find and spend lots of time digesting it. Rather, the task is much more focused. Thinking strategically about a company's industry and competitive environment entails using some well-defined concepts and analytical tools to get clear answers to seven questions:

1. What are the industry's strategy-shaping economic features?
2. What kinds of competitive forces are industry members facing, and how strong is each force?
3. What forces are driving changes in the industry, and what impact will these changes have on competitive intensity and industry profitability?
4. What market positions do industry rivals occupy—who is strongly positioned and who is not?
5. What strategic moves are rivals likely to make next?
6. What are the key factors for future competitive success?
7. Does the outlook for the industry present the company with sufficiently attractive prospects for profitability?

Analysis-based answers to these questions provide managers with a solid diagnosis of the industry and competitive environment. The remainder of this chapter is devoted to describing the methods of analyzing a company's industry and competitive environment.

Identifying Strategically Relevant Industry Features

Because industries differ so significantly in their basic character and structure, analyzing a company's industry and competitive environment begins with an overview of the industry's dominant economic features. The following economic features and corresponding questions need to be considered.

Economic Feature	Strategically Relevant Questions
▦ Market size and growth rate	▦ Is the industry big enough or growing fast enough to attract the attention of opportunity-seeking new entrants?
	▦ Is slowly growing buyer demand spurring increased rivalry and the acquisition or exit of weak competitors?
▦ Position in the life cycle	▦ What does the industry's position in the growth cycle (early development, rapid growth and takeoff, early maturity, maturity, saturation and stagnation, decline) indicate about the industry's growth prospects?
▦ Number of rivals	▦ Is the industry fragmented into many small companies or concentrated and dominated by a few large companies?
	▦ Is the industry going through a period of consolidation to a smaller number of competitors?
▦ Buyer needs and requirements	▦ Are buyer needs or requirements changing and, if so, what is driving the changes?
	▦ What are buyers looking for? What attributes prompt buyers to choose one brand over another?
▦ Production capacity	▦ Is a surplus of capacity pushing prices and profit margins down?
	▦ Is the industry overcrowded?
▦ Pace of technological change	▦ What role does advancing technology play in this industry?
	▦ Are ongoing upgrades of facilities/equipment essential because of rapidly advancing production process technologies?
	▦ Do most industry members have or need strong technological capabilities? Why?
▦ Vertical integration	▦ Are there important cost differences among fully integrated versus partially integrated versus nonintegrated firms?
	▦ Do fully or partially integrated firms have any competitive advantage over nonintegrated firms?

- Product innovation

  - Are there opportunities to overtake key rivals by being first to market with next-generation products?
  - Is the industry characterized by rapid product innovation and short product life cycles?
  - How important is R&D and product innovation?

- Degree of product differentiation

  - Are the products of rivals becoming more differentiated or less differentiated?
  - Are increasingly look-alike products of rivals causing heightened price competition?

- Scope of competitive rivalry

  - Is the geographic area over which most companies compete local, regional, national, multinational, or global?
  - Is having a presence in foreign-country markets becoming more important to a company's long-term competitive success?

- Economies of scale

  - Is the industry characterized by economies of scale in purchasing, manufacturing, advertising, shipping, or other activities?
  - Do companies with large-scale operations have an important cost advantage over small-scale firms?

- Experience and learning-curve effects

  - Are certain industry activities characterized by strong learning-curve and experience ("learning by doing") effects such that unit costs decline as a company's experience in performing the activity builds?[1]
  - Do any companies have significant cost advantages because of their learning/experience in performing particular activities?

Identifying an industry's economic features not only sets the stage for the analysis to come but also promotes understanding of the kinds of strategic moves that industry members are likely to employ. For example, in an industry characterized by important scale economies and/or learning-experience curve effects, industry members are strongly motivated to go after increased sales volumes and capture the cost-saving economies of larger-scale operations; small-scale firms are under considerable pressure to grow sales in order to become more cost-competitive with large-volume rivals. In industries characterized by one product advance after another, companies must invest in R&D and develop strong product innovation capabilities; a strategy of continuous product innovation becomes a condition of survival. An industry that has recently passed through the rapid-growth stage and is looking at single-digit percentage increases in buyer demand is likely to be experiencing a competitive shake-out and much stronger strategic emphasis on cost reduction and improved customer service.

Analyzing the Nature and Strength of Competitive Forces

The character, mix, and subtleties of the competitive forces operating in a company's industry are never the same from one industry to another. Far and away the most powerful and widely used tool for systematically diagnosing the principal competitive pressures in a market and assessing the strength and importance of each is the *five-forces model of competition*.[2] This model, depicted in Figure 2.3, holds that the state of competition in an industry is a composite of competitive pressures operating in five areas of the overall market:

1. Competitive pressures associated with the market maneuvering and jockeying for buyer patronage that goes on among *rival sellers* in the industry.

2. Competitive pressures associated with the threat of *new entrants* into the market.

3. Competitive pressures coming from the attempts of companies in other industries to win buyers over to their own *substitute products*.

4. Competitive pressures stemming from *supplier* bargaining power and supplier–seller collaboration.

5. Competitive pressures stemming from *buyer* bargaining power and seller–buyer collaboration.

The way one uses the five-forces model to determine what competition is like in a given industry is to build the picture of competition in three steps or stages. Step 1 is to identify the specific competitive pressures associated with each of the five forces. Step 2 is to evaluate how strong the pressures comprising each of the five forces are (fierce, strong, moderate to normal, or weak). Step 3 is to consider the overall pattern of competition and the collective impact of all five forces. The analytical process is straightforward and logical.

The Rivalry among Competing Sellers

The strongest of the five competitive forces is nearly always the market maneuvering and jockeying for buyer patronage that goes on among rival sellers of a product or service. In effect, *a market is a competitive battlefield* where it is customary for rival sellers to employ whatever weapons they have in their competitive arsenal to improve their market positions and business performance. Managers have a duty to craft a competitive strategy that, at the very least, allows their company to hold its own against rivals and that, ideally, strengthens the company's standing with buyers, delivers good profitability, and *produces a competitive edge over rivals*. But when one firm makes a strategic move that produces good results, its rivals often react and respond with offensive or defensive countermoves. This pattern of action and reaction, move and countermove, is what makes competitive rivalry a combative contest. Market battles for buyer patronage are dynamic, with the competitive landscape continually changing as industry rivals initiate new rounds of market maneuvers (with some gaining and some losing momentum in the marketplace) and as their emphasis swings from one combination of product attributes, marketing tactics, and competitive capabilities to another.

Core Concept

Competitive jockeying among industry rivals is ever-changing, as fresh offensive and defensive moves are initiated and rivals emphasize first one mix of competitive weapons and tactics, then another.

Figure 2.3   The Five-Forces Model of Competition: A Key Analytical Tool

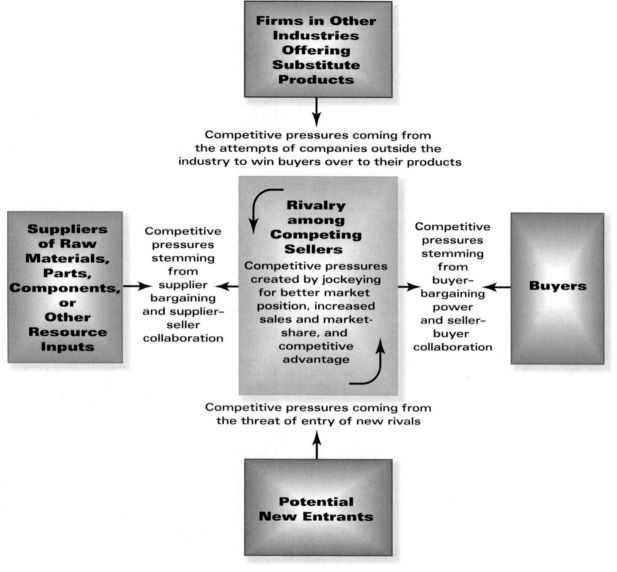

Source: Adapted from Michael E. Porter, "How Competitive Forces Shape Strategy," *Harvard Business Review* 57, no. 2 (March–April 1979), pp. 137–45.

Figure 2.4 shows a sampling of competitive weapons that firms can deploy in battling rivals and indicates the factors that influence the intensity of their rivalry. A brief discussion of some of the factors that influence the tempo of rivalry among industry competitors is in order:[3]

▪ *Rivalry among competing sellers intensifies the more frequently and more aggressively that industry members undertake fresh actions to boost their market standing and performance—perhaps at the expense of rivals.* Rivalry tends to be fairly

Figure 2.4   Weapons for Competing and Factors Affecting the Strength of Rivalry

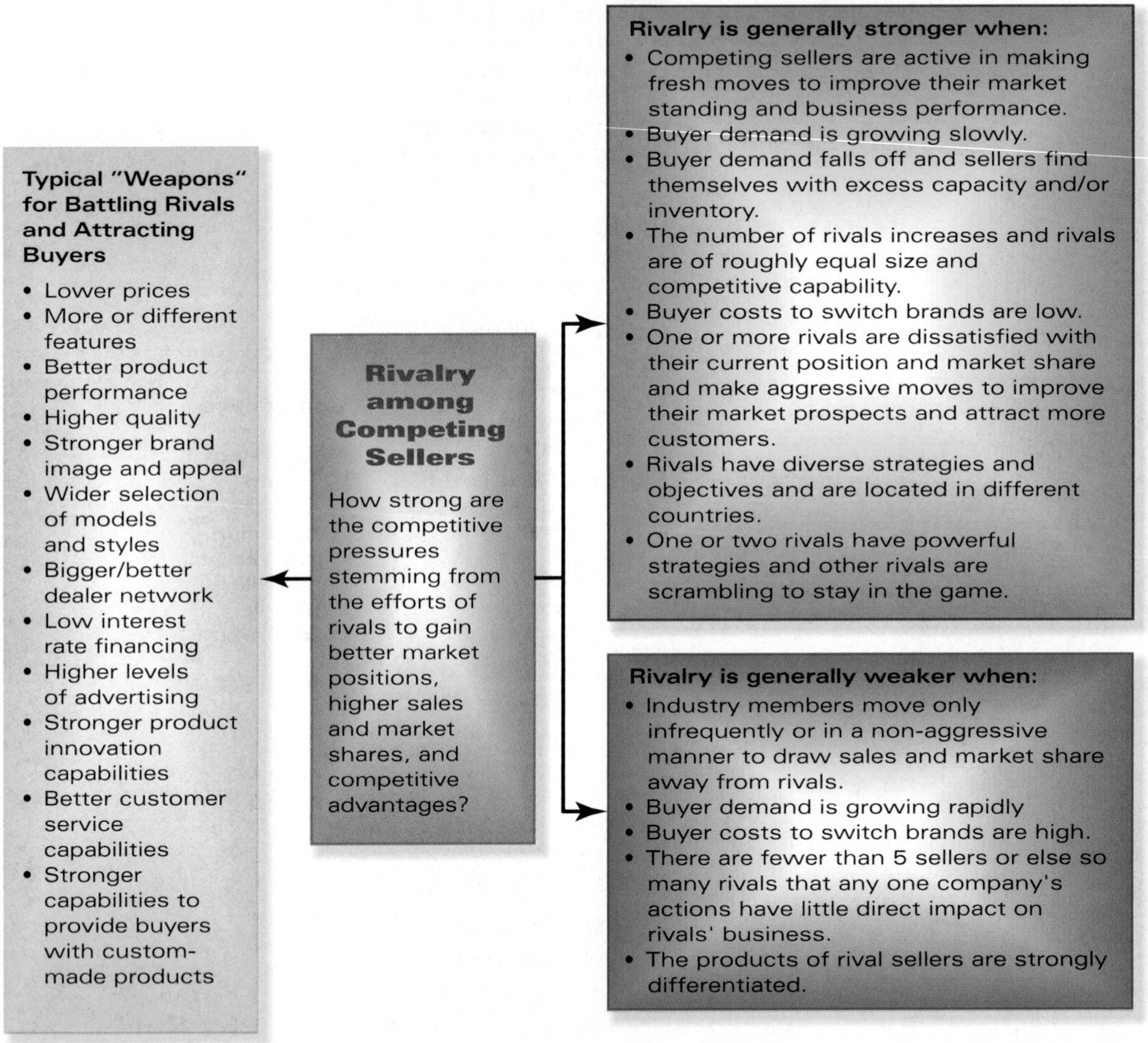

Typical "Weapons" for Battling Rivals and Attracting Buyers

- Lower prices
- More or different features
- Better product performance
- Higher quality
- Stronger brand image and appeal
- Wider selection of models and styles
- Bigger/better dealer network
- Low interest rate financing
- Higher levels of advertising
- Stronger product innovation capabilities
- Better customer service capabilities
- Stronger capabilities to provide buyers with custom-made products

Rivalry among Competing Sellers

How strong are the competitive pressures stemming from the efforts of rivals to gain better market positions, higher sales and market shares, and competitive advantages?

Rivalry is generally stronger when:

- Competing sellers are active in making fresh moves to improve their market standing and business performance.
- Buyer demand is growing slowly.
- Buyer demand falls off and sellers find themselves with excess capacity and/or inventory.
- The number of rivals increases and rivals are of roughly equal size and competitive capability.
- Buyer costs to switch brands are low.
- One or more rivals are dissatisfied with their current position and market share and make aggressive moves to improve their market prospects and attract more customers.
- Rivals have diverse strategies and objectives and are located in different countries.
- One or two rivals have powerful strategies and other rivals are scrambling to stay in the game.

Rivalry is generally weaker when:

- Industry members move only infrequently or in a non-aggressive manner to draw sales and market share away from rivals.
- Buyer demand is growing rapidly
- Buyer costs to switch brands are high.
- There are fewer than 5 sellers or else so many rivals that any one company's actions have little direct impact on rivals' business.
- The products of rival sellers are strongly differentiated.

intense whenever sellers actively engage in vigorous price competition—lively price competition pressures rival companies to aggressively pursue ways to drive costs out of the business; high-cost companies are hard-pressed to survive. Other indicators of the intensity of rivalry among industry members include:

- Whether industry members are racing to offer better performance features or higher quality or improved customer service or a wider product selection.

- How frequently rivals resort to such marketing tactics as special sales promotions, heavy advertising, rebates, or low-interest-rate financing to drum up additional sales.

- How actively industry members are pursuing efforts to build stronger dealer networks or establish positions in foreign markets or otherwise expand their distribution capabilities and market presence.
- The frequency with which rivals introduce new and improved products (and thus are competing on the basis of their product innovation capabilities).
- How hard companies are striving to gain a market edge over rivals by developing valuable expertise and capabilities.

Normally, industry members are proactive in drawing on their arsenal of competitive weapons and deploying their organizational resources in a manner calculated to strengthen their market positions and performance.

- *Rivalry intensifies as the number of competitors increases and as competitors become more equal in size and capability.* Competition is not as strong in PC operating systems, where Linux is one of the few challengers to Microsoft, as it is in fast-food restaurants, where buyers have many choices. Up to a point, the greater the number of competitors, the greater the probability of fresh, creative strategic initiatives. In addition, when rivals are nearly equal in size and capability, they can usually compete on a fairly even footing, making it harder for one or two firms to win the competitive battle and dominate the market.

- *Rivalry is usually weaker when there are fewer than five competitors or else so many rivals that the impact of any one company's actions is spread thinly across all industry members.* When an industry contains only a few rival sellers, each company tends to recognize that its actions can have immediate and significant impact on the others and, if aggressive, may provoke direct retaliation. Although occasional warfare can break out, competition among the few tends to produce a live-and-let-live approach to competing and thus a restrained use of competitive weaponry. Rivalry also tends to be weak when an industry is fragmented with so many competitors that successful moves by one have little discernible adverse impact on the others and thus may provoke no immediate response or countermove on the part of its rivals.

- *Rivalry is usually stronger in slow-growing markets and weaker in fast-growing markets.* Rapidly expanding buyer demand produces enough new business for all industry members to grow. Indeed, in a fast-growing market, a company may find itself stretched just to keep abreast of incoming orders, let alone devote resources to stealing customers away from rivals. But in markets where growth is sluggish or where buyer demand drops off unexpectedly, expansion-minded firms and/or firms with excess capacity often are quick to cut prices and initiate other sales-increasing tactics, thereby igniting a battle for market share that can result in a shake-out of weak, inefficient firms.

- *Rivalry increases as the products of rival sellers become more standardized and/or when buyer costs to switch from one brand to another are low.* When the offerings of rivals are identified it is usually easy and inexpensive for buyers to switch their purchases from one seller to another. Strongly differentiated products raise the probability that buyers will find it costly to switch brands.

- *Rivalry is more intense when industry conditions tempt competitors to use price cuts or other competitive weapons to boost unit volume.* When a product is perishable, seasonal, or costly to hold in inventory, or when demand slacks off, competitive pressures build quickly anytime one or more firms decide to cut prices and dump excess supplies on the market. Likewise, whenever fixed costs account for a large fraction of total cost so that unit costs tend to be lowest at or near full capacity, then firms come under significant pressure to cut prices or otherwise try to boost sales. Unused capacity imposes a significant cost-increasing penalty because there are fewer units over which to spread fixed costs. The pressure of high fixed costs can push rival firms into price concessions, special discounts, rebates, low-interest-rate financing, and other volume-boosting tactics.

- *Rivalry increases when one or more competitors become dissatisfied with their market position and launch moves to bolster their standing at the expense of rivals.* Firms that are losing ground or in financial trouble often react aggressively by acquiring smaller rivals, introducing new products, boosting advertising, discounting prices, and so on. Such actions heighten rivalry and can trigger a hotly contested battle for market share. The market maneuvering among rivals usually heats up when a competitor makes new offensive moves—because it sees an opportunity to better please customers or is under pressure to improve its market share or profitability.

- *Rivalry increases in proportion to the size of the payoff from a successful strategic move.* The greater the benefits of going after a new opportunity, the more likely it is that one or more rivals will initiate moves to capture it. Competitive pressures nearly always intensify when several rivals start pursuing the same opportunity. For example, competition in online music sales heated up with the entries of Amazon.com, Barnesandnoble.com, and Buy.com. Furthermore, the size of the strategic payoff can vary with the speed of retaliation. When competitors respond slowly (or not at all), the initiator of a fresh competitive strategy can reap benefits in the intervening period and perhaps gain a first-mover advantage that is not easily surmounted. The greater the benefits of moving first, the more likely some competitor will accept the risk and try it.

- *Rivalry becomes more volatile and unpredictable as the diversity of competitors increases in terms of visions, strategic intents, objectives, strategies, resources, and countries of origin.* A diverse group of sellers often contains one or more mavericks willing to try novel or high-risk or rule-breaking market approaches, thus generating a livelier and less predictable competitive environment. Globally competitive markets often contain rivals with different views about where the industry is headed and a willingness to employ perhaps radically different competitive approaches. Attempts by cross-border rivals to gain stronger footholds in each other's domestic markets usually boost the intensity of rivalry, especially when the aggressors have lower costs or products with more attractive features.

- *Rivalry increases when strong companies outside the industry acquire weak firms in the industry and launch aggressive, well-funded moves to transform their newly acquired competitors into major market contenders.* A concerted effort to turn a weak rival into a market leader nearly always entails launching well-financed strategic initiatives to dramatically improve the competitor's product offering, excite buyer interest, and win a much bigger market share—actions that, if successful, put added pressure on rivals to counter with fresh strategic moves of their own.

- *A powerful, successful competitive strategy employed by one company greatly intensifies the competitive pressures on its rivals to develop effective strategic responses or be relegated to also-ran status.*

Rivalry can be characterized as *cutthroat* or *brutal* when competitors engage in protracted price wars or habitually employ other aggressive tactics that are mutually destructive to profitability. Rivalry can be considered *fierce* to *strong* when the battle for market share is so vigorous that the profit margins of most industry members are squeezed to bare-bones levels. Rivalry can be characterized as *moderate* or *normal* when the maneuvering among industry members, while lively and healthy, still allows most industry members to earn acceptable profits. Rivalry is *weak* when most companies in the industry are relatively well satisfied with their sales growth and market shares, rarely undertake offensives to steal customers away from one another, and have comparatively attractive earnings and returns on investment.

The Potential Entry of New Competitors

Several factors affect the strength of the competitive threat of potential entry in a particular industry (see Figure 2.5). One factor relates to the size of the pool of likely entry candidates and the resources at their command. As a rule, competitive pressures intensify the bigger the pool of entry candidates. This is especially true when some of the likely entry candidates have ample resources and the potential to become formidable contenders for market leadership. Frequently, the strongest competitive pressures associated with potential entry come not from outsiders but from current industry participants looking for growth opportunities. *Existing industry members are often strong candidates to enter market segments or geographic areas where they currently do not have a market presence.* Companies already well established in certain product categories or geographic areas often possess the resources, competencies, and competitive capabilities to hurdle the barriers of entering a different market segment or new geographic area.

A second factor concerns whether the likely entry candidates face high or low entry barriers. The most widely encountered barriers that entry candidates must hurdle include:[4]

- *The presence of sizable economies of scale in production or other areas of operation*—When incumbent companies enjoy cost advantages associated with large-scale operation, outsiders must either enter on a large scale (a costly and perhaps risky move) or accept a cost disadvantage and consequently lower profitability. Trying to overcome the disadvantages of small size by entering on a large scale at the outset can result in long-term overcapacity problems for the new entrant (until sales volume builds up), and it can so threaten the market shares of existing firms that they launch strong defensive maneuvers (price cuts, increased advertising and sales promotion, and similar blocking actions) to maintain their positions and make things hard on a newcomer.

- *Cost and resource disadvantages not related to size*—Existing firms may have low unit costs as a result of experience or learning-curve effects, key patents, partnerships with the best and cheapest suppliers of raw materials and components, proprietary technology know-how not readily available to newcomers, favorable locations, and low fixed costs (because they have older plants that have been mostly depreciated).

- *Brand preferences and customer loyalty*—In some industries, buyers are strongly attached to established brands. Japanese consumers, for example, are fiercely loyal to Japanese brands of motor vehicles, electronics products, cameras, and film. European consumers have traditionally been loyal to European brands of major household appliances. High brand loyalty means that a potential entrant must commit to spending enough money on advertising and sales promotion to overcome customer loyalties and build its own clientele. Establishing brand recognition and building customer loyalty can be a slow and costly process. In addition, if it is difficult or costly for a customer to switch to a new brand, a new entrant must persuade buyers that its brand is worth the switching costs. To overcome switching-cost barriers, new entrants may have to offer buyers a discounted price or an extra margin of quality or service. All this can mean lower expected profit margins for new entrants, which increases the risk to start-up companies dependent on sizable early profits to support their new investments.

▪ *Capital requirements*—The larger the total dollar investment needed to enter the market successfully, the more limited the pool of potential entrants. The most obvious capital requirements for new entrants are those associated with investing in the necessary manufacturing facilities and equipment, being able to finance the introductory advertising and sales promotion campaigns to build brand awareness and establish a clientele, securing the working capital to finance inventories and customer credit, and having sufficient cash reserves to cover start-up losses.

▪ *Access to distribution channels*—In consumer goods industries, a potential entrant may face the barrier of gaining adequate access to consumers. Wholesale distributors may be reluctant to take on a product that lacks buyer recognition. A network of retail dealers may have to be set up from scratch. Retailers have to be convinced to give a new brand ample display space and an adequate trial period. Entry is tough when existing producers have strong, well-functioning distributor–dealer networks and a newcomer must struggle to squeeze its way into existing distribution channels. To overcome the barrier of gaining adequate access to consumers, potential entrants may have to "buy" their way into wholesale or retail channels by cutting their prices to provide dealers and distributors with higher markups and profit margins or by giving them big advertising and promotional allowances. As a consequence, a potential entrant's own profits may be squeezed unless and until its product gains enough consumer acceptance that distributors and retailers want to carry it.

▪ *Regulatory policies*—Government agencies can limit or even bar entry by requiring licenses and permits. Regulated industries like cable TV, telecommunications, electric and gas utilities, radio and television broadcasting, liquor retailing, and railroads entail government-controlled entry. In international markets, host governments commonly limit foreign entry and must approve all foreign investment applications. Stringent government-mandated safety regulations and environmental pollution standards are entry barriers because they raise entry costs.

▪ *Tariffs and international trade restrictions*—National governments commonly use tariffs and trade restrictions (antidumping rules, local content requirements, quotas, etc.) to raise entry barriers for foreign firms and protect domestic producers from outside competition.

Whether an industry's entry barriers ought to be considered high or low and how hard it is for new entrants to compete on a level playing field depend on the resources and competencies possessed by the pool of potential entrants. Entry barriers can be formidable for newly formed enterprises that have to find some way to gain a market foothold and then over time make inroads against well-established companies. But opportunity-seeking companies in other industries, if they have suitable resources, competencies, and brand-name recognition, may be able to hurdle an industry's entry barriers rather easily. In evaluating the potential threat of entry, company managers must look at (1) how formidable the entry barriers are for each type of potential entrant—start-up enterprises, specific candidate companies in other industries, and current industry participants looking to expand their market reach—and (2) how attractive the growth and profit prospects are for new entrants. *Rapidly growing market demand and high potential profits act as magnets, motivating potential entrants to commit the resources needed to hurdle entry barriers.*[5]

Figure 2.5   Factors Affecting the Threat of Entry

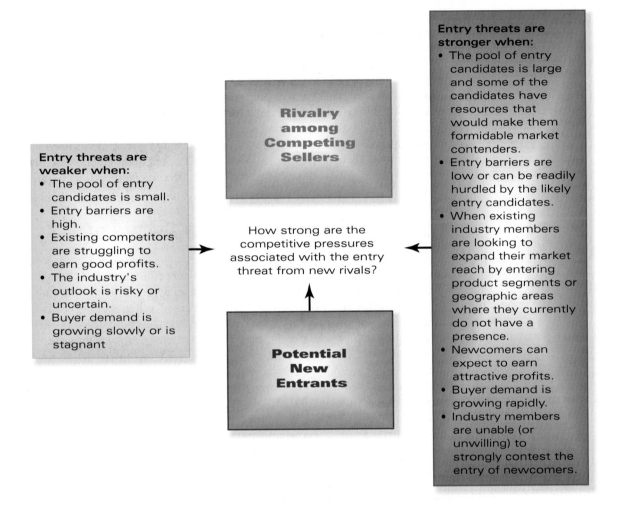

Entry threats are weaker when:
- The pool of entry candidates is small.
- Entry barriers are high.
- Existing competitors are struggling to earn good profits.
- The industry's outlook is risky or uncertain.
- Buyer demand is growing slowly or is stagnant

Rivalry among Competing Sellers

How strong are the competitive pressures associated with the entry threat from new rivals?

Potential New Entrants

Entry threats are stronger when:
- The pool of entry candidates is large and some of the candidates have resources that would make them formidable market contenders.
- Entry barriers are low or can be readily hurdled by the likely entry candidates.
- When existing industry members are looking to expand their market reach by entering product segments or geographic areas where they currently do not have a presence.
- Newcomers can expect to earn attractive profits.
- Buyer demand is growing rapidly.
- Industry members are unable (or unwilling) to strongly contest the entry of newcomers.

However, even if a potential entrant has or can acquire the needed competencies and resources to attempt entry, it still faces the issue of how existing firms will react.[6] Will incumbent firms offer only passive resistance, or will they aggressively defend their market positions using price cuts, increased advertising, product improvements, and whatever else they can think of to give a new entrant (as well as other rivals) a hard time? A potential entrant can have second thoughts when financially strong incumbent firms send clear signals that they will stoutly defend their market positions against newcomers. A potential entrant may also turn away when incumbent firms can leverage distributors and customers to retain their business.

The best test of whether potential entry is a strong or weak competitive force in the marketplace is to ask if the industry's growth and profit prospects are strongly attractive to potential entry candidates. When the answer is no, potential entry is a weak competitive force. When the answer is yes and there are entry candidates with

> The threat of entry is stronger when entry barriers are low, when there's a sizable pool of entry candidates, when industry growth is rapid and profit potentials are high, and when incumbent firms are unable or unwilling to vigorously contest a newcomer's entry.

sufficient expertise and resources, then potential entry adds significantly to competitive pressures in the marketplace. The stronger the threat of entry, the more that incumbent firms are driven to seek ways to fortify their positions against newcomers, pursuing strategic moves not only to protect their market shares but also to make entry more costly or difficult.

One additional point: *The threat of entry changes as the industry's prospects grow brighter or dimmer and as entry barriers rise or fall.* For example, in the pharmaceutical industry the expiration of a key patent on a widely prescribed drug virtually guarantees that one or more drug makers will enter with generic offerings of their own. Use of the Internet for shopping is making it much easier for e-tailers to enter into competition against some of the best-known retail chains. In international markets, entry barriers for foreign-based firms fall as tariffs are lowered, as host governments open up their domestic markets to outsiders, as domestic wholesalers and dealers seek out lower-cost foreign-made goods, and as domestic buyers become more willing to purchase foreign brands.

Competitive Pressures from the Sellers of Substitute Products

Companies in one industry come under competitive pressure from the actions of companies in a closely adjoining industry whenever buyers view the products of the two industries as good substitutes. For instance, the producers of sugar experience competitive pressures from the sales and marketing efforts of the makers of artificial sweeteners. Similarly, the producers of eyeglasses and contact lenses are currently facing mounting competitive pressures from growing consumer interest in corrective laser surgery. Newspapers are feeling the competitive force of the general public turning to cable news channels for late-breaking news and using Internet sources to get information about sports results, stock quotes, and job opportunities.

Just how strong the competitive pressures are from the sellers of substitute products depends on three factors: (1) whether substitutes are readily available and attractively priced; (2) whether buyers view the substitutes as being comparable or better in terms of quality, performance, and other relevant attributes; and (3) how much it costs end users to switch to substitutes. Figure 2.6 lists factors affecting the strength of competitive pressures from substitute products and signs that indicate substitutes are a strong competitive force.

The presence of readily available and attractively priced substitutes creates competitive pressure by placing a ceiling on the prices industry members can charge without giving customers an incentive to switch to substitutes and risking sales erosion.[7] This price ceiling, at the same time, puts a lid on the profits that industry members can earn unless they find ways to cut costs. When substitutes are cheaper than an industry's product, industry members come under heavy competitive pressure to reduce their prices and find ways to absorb the price cuts with cost reductions.

The availability of substitutes inevitably invites customers to compare performance, features, ease of use, and other attributes as well as price. For example, ski boat manufacturers are experiencing strong competition from personal water-ski craft because water sports enthusiasts are finding that personal water skis are fun to ride and less expensive. The users of paper cartons constantly weigh the performance trade-offs with plastic containers and metal cans. Competition from good-performing substitute products pushes industry participants to incorporate new performance features and

Figure 2.6   Factors Affecting Competition from Substitute Products

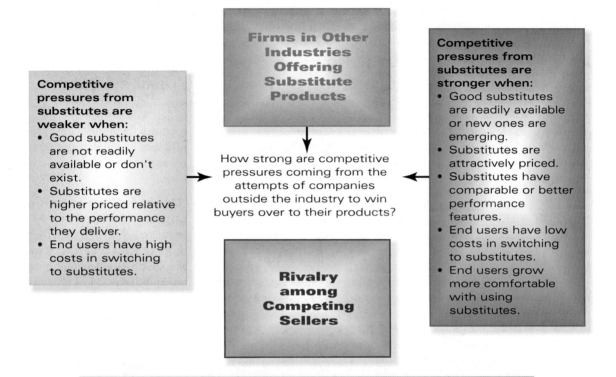

Competitive pressures from substitutes are weaker when:
- Good substitutes are not readily available or don't exist.
- Substitutes are higher priced relative to the performance they deliver.
- End users have high costs in switching to substitutes.

Firms in Other Industries Offering Substitute Products

How strong are competitive pressures coming from the attempts of companies outside the industry to win buyers over to their products?

Rivalry among Competing Sellers

Competitive pressures from substitutes are stronger when:
- Good substitutes are readily available or new ones are emerging.
- Substitutes are attractively priced.
- Substitutes have comparable or better performance features.
- End users have low costs in switching to substitutes.
- End users grow more comfortable with using substitutes.

Signs That Competition from Substitutes Is Strong
- Sales of substitutes are growing faster than sales of the industry being analyzed.
- Producers of substitutes are moving to add new capacity.
- Profits of the producers of substitutes are on the rise.

heighten efforts to convince customers their product has attributes that are superior to those of substitutes.

The strength of competition from substitutes is significantly influenced by how difficult or costly it is for the industry's customers to switch to a substitute.[8] Typical switching costs include the time and inconvenience that may be involved, the costs of additional equipment, the time and cost in testing the quality and reliability of the substitute, the psychological costs of severing old supplier relationships and establishing new ones, payments for technical help in making the changeover, and employee retraining costs. When buyers incur high costs in switching to substitutes, the competitive pressures that industry members experience from substitutes are usually lessened unless the sellers of substitutes begin offering price discounts or major performance benefits that entice the industry's customers away. When switching costs are low, it's much easier for sellers of substitutes to convince buyers to change to their products.

As a rule, then, the lower the price of substitutes, the higher their quality and performance, and the lower the user's switching costs, the more intense the competitive pressures posed by substitute products. Good indicators of the competitive strength of substitute products are the rate at which their sales and profits are growing, the market inroads they are making, and their plans for expanding production capacity.

Competitive Pressures Stemming from Supplier Bargaining Power and Supplier–Seller Collaboration

Whether supplier–seller relationships represent a weak or strong competitive force depends on (1) whether the major suppliers can exercise sufficient bargaining power to influence the terms and conditions of supply in their favor, and (2) the nature and extent of supplier–seller collaboration in the industry.

How Supplier Bargaining Power Can Create Competitive Pressures
Whenever the major suppliers to an industry have considerable leverage in determining the terms and conditions of the item they are supplying, then they are in a position to exert competitive pressure on one or more rival sellers. For instance, Microsoft and Intel, both of whom supply PC makers with products that most PC users consider essential, are known for using their dominant market status not only to charge PC makers premium prices but also to leverage PC makers in other ways. Microsoft pressures PC makers to load only Microsoft products on the PCs they ship and to position the icons for Microsoft software prominently on the screens of new computers that come with factory-loaded software. Intel pushes greater use of Intel microprocessors in PCs by granting PC makers sizable advertising allowances on PC models equipped with "Intel Inside" stickers; it also tends to give PC makers who use the biggest percentages of Intel chips in their PC models top priority in filling orders for newly introduced Intel chips. Being on Intel's list of preferred customers helps a PC maker get an allocation of the first production runs of Intel's latest and greatest chips and thus get new PC models equipped with these chips to market ahead of rivals who are heavier users of chips made by Intel's rivals. The ability of Microsoft and Intel to pressure PC makers for preferential treatment of one kind or another in turn affects competition among rival PC makers.

Several other instances of supplier bargaining power are worth citing. Small-scale retailers must often contend with the power of manufacturers whose products enjoy prestigious and well-respected brand names; when a manufacturer knows that a retailer needs to stock the manufacturer's product because consumers expect to find the product on the shelves of retail stores where they shop, the manufacturer usually has some degree of pricing power and can also push hard for favorable shelf displays. Motor vehicle manufacturers typically exert considerable power over the terms and conditions with which they supply new vehicles to their independent automobile dealerships. The operators of franchised units of such chains as Krispy Kreme Doughnuts, Burger King, Pizza Hut, and Hampton Inns must frequently agree not only to source some of their supplies from the franchisor at prices and terms favorable to that franchisor but also to operate their facilities in a manner largely dictated by the franchisor. Strong supplier bargaining power is a competitive factor in industries where unions have been able to organize the workforces of some industry members but not others; those industry members that must negotiate wages, fringe benefits, and working conditions with powerful unions (which control the supply of labor) often find themselves with higher labor costs than their competitors with nonunion labor forces. The bigger the gap between union and nonunion labor costs in an industry, the more that unionized industry members must scramble to find ways to relieve the competitive pressure associated with their disadvantage on labor costs.

The factors that determine whether any of the suppliers to an industry are in a position to exert substantial bargaining power or leverage are fairly clear-cut:[9]

- *Whether the item being supplied is a commodity that is readily available from many suppliers at the going market price.* Suppliers have little or no bargaining power or leverage whenever industry members have the ability to source their requirements at competitive prices from any of several alternative and eager suppliers, perhaps dividing their purchases among two or more suppliers to promote lively competition for orders. The suppliers of commoditylike items have market power only when supplies become quite tight and industry members are so eager to secure what they need that they agree to terms more favorable to suppliers.

- *Whether a few large suppliers are the primary sources of a particular item.* The leading suppliers may well have pricing leverage unless they are plagued with excess capacity and are scrambling to secure additional orders for their products. Major suppliers with good reputations and strong demand for the items they supply are harder to wring concessions from than struggling suppliers striving to broaden their customer base or more fully utilize their production capacity.

- *Whether it is difficult or costly for industry members to switch their purchases from one supplier to another or to switch to attractive substitute inputs.* High switching costs signal strong bargaining power on the part of suppliers, whereas low switching costs and ready availability of good substitute inputs signal weak bargaining power. Soft-drink bottlers, for example, can counter the bargaining power of aluminum can suppliers by shifting or threatening to shift to greater use of plastic containers and introducing more attractive plastic container designs.

- *Whether certain needed inputs are in short supply.* Suppliers of items in short supply have some degree of pricing power, whereas a surge in the availability of particular items greatly weakens supplier pricing power and bargaining leverage.

- *Whether certain suppliers provide a differentiated input that enhances the performance or quality of the industry's product.* The more valuable that a particular input is in terms of enhancing the performance or quality of the products of industry members or of improving the efficiency of their production processes, the more bargaining leverage its suppliers are likely to possess.

- *Whether certain suppliers provide equipment or services that deliver valuable cost-saving efficiencies to industry members in operating their production processes.* Suppliers who provide cost-saving equipment or other valuable or necessary production-related services are likely to possess bargaining leverage. Industry members that do not source from such suppliers may find themselves at a cost disadvantage and thus under competitive pressure to do so (on terms that are favorable to the suppliers).

- *Whether suppliers provide an item that accounts for a sizable fraction of the costs of the industry's product.* The bigger the cost of a particular part or component, the more opportunity for the pattern of competition in the marketplace to be affected by the actions of suppliers to raise or lower their prices.

- *Whether industry members are major customers of suppliers.* As a rule, suppliers have less bargaining leverage when their sales to members of this one industry constitute a big percentage of their total sales. In such cases, the well-being of suppliers is closely tied to the well-being of their major customers. Suppliers then have a big incentive to protect and enhance their customers' competitiveness via reasonable prices, exceptional quality, and ongoing advances in the technology of the items supplied.

■ *Whether it makes good economic sense for industry members to integrate backward and self-manufacture items they have been buying from suppliers.* The make-or-buy issue generally boils down to whether suppliers who specialize in the production of a particular part or component and make them in volume for many different customers have the expertise and scale economies to supply as good or better component at a lower cost than industry members could achieve via self-manufacture. Frequently, it is difficult for industry members to self-manufacture parts and components more economically than they can obtain them from suppliers who specialize in making such items. For instance, most producers of outdoor power equipment (lawn mowers, rotary tillers, leaf blowers, etc.) find it cheaper to source the small engines they need from outside manufacturers who specialize in small engine manufacture rather than make their own engines because the quantity of engines they need is too small to justify the investment in manufacturing facilities, master the production process, and capture scale economies. Specialists in small-engine manufacture, by supplying many kinds of engines to the whole power equipment industry, can obtain a big enough sales volume to fully realize scale economies, become proficient in all the manufacturing techniques, and keep costs low. As a rule, suppliers are safe from the threat of self-manufacture by their customers *until* the volume of parts a customer needs becomes large enough for the customer to justify backward integration into self-manufacture of the component. Suppliers also gain bargaining power when they have the resources and profit incentive to integrate forward into the business of the customers they are supplying and thus become a strong rival.

Figure 2.7 summarizes the conditions that tend to make supplier bargaining power strong or weak.

How Seller–Supplier Partnerships Can Create Competitive Pressures In more and more industries, sellers are forging strategic partnerships with select suppliers in efforts to (1) reduce inventory and logistics costs (e.g., through just-in-time deliveries), (2) speed the availability of next-generation components, (3) enhance the quality of the parts and components being supplied and reduce defect rates, and (4) squeeze out important cost savings for both themselves and their suppliers. Numerous Internet technology applications are now available that permit real-time data sharing, eliminate paperwork, and produce cost savings all along the supply chain. The many benefits of effective seller–supplier collaboration can translate into competitive advantage for industry members who do the best job of managing supply chain relationships.

Dell Computer has used strategic partnering with key suppliers as a major element in its strategy to be the world's lowest-cost supplier of branded PCs, servers, and workstations. Because Dell has managed its supply chain relationships in ways that contribute to a low-cost, high-quality competitive edge in components supply, it has put enormous pressure on its PC rivals to try to imitate its supply chain management

Figure 2.7   Factors Affecting the Bargaining Power of Suppliers

Supplier bargaining power is stronger when:
- Industry members incurs high costs in switching their purchases to alternative suppliers.
- Needed inputs are in short supply (which gives suppliers more leverage in setting prices).
- A supplier has a differentiated input that enhances the quality or performance of sellers' products or is a valuable or critical part of sellers' production process.
- There are only a few suppliers of a particular input.
- Some suppliers threaten to integrate forward into the business of industry members and perhaps become a powerful rival.

Supplier bargaining power is weaker when:
- The item being supplied is a commodity that is readily available from many suppliers at the going market price.
- Seller switching costs to alternative suppliers are low.
- Good substitute inputs exist or new ones emerge.
- There is a surge in the availability of supplies (thus greatly weakening supplier pricing power).
- Industry members account for a big fraction of suppliers' total sales and continued high volume purchases are important to the well-being of suppliers.
- Industry members are a threat to integrate backward into the business of suppliers and to self-manufacture their own requirements.
- Seller collaboration or partnering with selected suppliers provides attractive win–win opportunities.

practices. Effective partnerships with suppliers on the part of one or more industry members can thus become a major source of competitive pressure for rival firms.

The more opportunities that exist for win–win efforts between a company and its suppliers, the less their relationship is characterized by who has the upper hand in bargaining with the other. So long as the relationship is producing valuable benefits for both parties, it will last; only if a supply partner is falling behind alternative suppliers is a company likely to switch suppliers and incur the costs and trouble of building close working ties with a different supplier.

Competitive Pressures Stemming from Buyer Bargaining Power and Seller–Buyer Collaboration

Whether seller–buyer relationships represent a weak or strong competitive force depends on (1) whether some or many buyers have sufficient bargaining leverage to obtain price concessions and other favorable terms and conditions of sale, and (2) the extent and competitive importance of seller–buyer strategic partnerships in the industry.

How Buyer Bargaining Power Can Create Competitive Pressures   As with suppliers, the leverage that certain types of buyers have in negotiating favorable terms can range from weak to strong. Individual consumers, for example, rarely have much bargaining power in negotiating price concessions or other favorable terms with sellers; the primary exceptions involve situations in which price haggling is customary, such as the purchase of new and used motor vehicles, homes, and certain big-ticket items like luxury watches, jewelry, and pleasure boats. For most consumer goods and services, individual buyers have no bargaining leverage—their option is to pay the seller's posted price or take their business elsewhere.

In contrast, large retail chains like Wal-Mart, Circuit City, Target, and Home Depot typically have considerable negotiating leverage in purchasing products from manufacturers because of manufacturers' need for broad retail exposure and the most appealing shelf locations. Retailers may stock two or three competing brands of a product but rarely all competing brands, so competition among rival manufacturers for visibility on the shelves of popular multistore retailers gives such retailers significant bargaining strength. Major supermarket chains like Kroger, Safeway, and Royal Ahold, which provide access to millions of grocery shoppers, have sufficient bargaining power to demand promotional allowances and lump-sum payments (called slotting fees) from food products manufacturers in return for stocking certain brands or putting them in the best shelf locations. Motor vehicle manufacturers have strong bargaining power in negotiating to buy original equipment tires from Goodyear, Michelin, Bridgestone/Firestone, Continental, and Pirelli not only because they buy in large quantities but also because tire makers believe they gain an advantage in supplying replacement tires to vehicle owners if their tire brand is original equipment on the vehicle. "Prestige" buyers have a degree of clout in negotiating with sellers because a seller's reputation is enhanced by having prestige buyers on its customer list.

Even if buyers do not purchase in large quantities or offer a seller important market exposure or prestige, they gain a degree of bargaining leverage in the following circumstances:[10]

- *If buyers' costs of switching to competing brands or substitutes are relatively low*—Buyers who can readily switch brands or source from several sellers have more negotiating leverage than buyers who have high switching costs. When the products of rival sellers are virtually identical, it is relatively easy for buyers to switch from seller to seller at little or no cost and anxious sellers may be willing to make concessions to win or retain a buyer's business.

- *If the number of buyers is small or if a customer is particularly important to a seller*—The smaller the number of buyers, the less easy it is for sellers to find alternative buyers when a customer is lost to a competitor. The prospect of losing a customer not easily replaced often makes a seller more willing to grant concessions of one kind or another.

▪ *If buyer demand is weak and sellers are scrambling to secure additional sales of their products*—Weak or declining demand creates a "buyers' market"; conversely, strong or rapidly growing demand creates a "sellers' market" and shifts bargaining power to sellers.

▪ *If buyers are well-informed about sellers' products, prices, and costs*—The more information buyers have, the better bargaining position they are in. The mushrooming availability of product information on the Internet is giving added bargaining power to individuals. Buyers can easily use the Internet to compare prices and features of vacation packages, shop for the best interest rates on mortgages and loans, and find the best prices on big-ticket items such as digital cameras. Bargain-hunting individuals can shop around for the best deal on the Internet and use that information to negotiate a better deal from local retailers; this method is becoming commonplace in buying new and used motor vehicles. Further, the Internet has created opportunities for manufacturers, wholesalers, retailers, and sometimes individuals to join online buying groups to pool their purchasing power and approach vendors for better terms than could be gotten individually. A multinational manufacturer's geographically scattered purchasing groups can use Internet technology to pool their orders with parts and components suppliers and bargain for volume discounts. Purchasing agents at some companies are banding together at third-party websites to pool corporate purchases to get better deals or special treatment.

▪ *If buyers pose a credible threat of integrating backward into the business of sellers*—Companies like Anheuser-Busch, Coors, and Heinz have integrated backward into metal can manufacturing to gain bargaining power in obtaining the balance of their can requirements from otherwise powerful metal can manufacturers. Retailers gain bargaining power by stocking and promoting their own private-label brands alongside manufacturers' name brands. Wal-Mart, for example, has elected to compete against Procter & Gamble, its biggest supplier, with its own brand of laundry detergent, called Sam's American Choice, which is priced 25 to 30 percent lower than P&G's Tide.

▪ *If buyers have discretion in whether and when they purchase the product*—Many consumers, if they are unhappy with the present deals offered on major appliances or hot tubs or home entertainment centers, may be in a position to delay purchase until prices and financing terms improve. If business customers are not happy with the prices or security features of bill-payment software systems, they can either delay purchase until next-generation products become available or attempt to develop their own software in-house. If college students believe that the prices of new textbooks are too high, they can purchase used copies.

Figure 2.8 summarizes the circumstances that make for strong or weak bargaining power on the part of buyers.

A final point to keep in mind is that *not all buyers of an industry's product have equal degrees of bargaining power with sellers*, and some may be less sensitive than others to price, quality, or service differences. For example, independent tire retailers have less bargaining power in purchasing tires than do Honda, Ford, and Daimler-Chrysler (which buy in much larger quantities), and they are also less sensitive to quality. Motor vehicle manufacturers are very particular about tire quality and tire performance because of the effects on vehicle performance, and they drive a hard bargain with tire manufacturers on both price and quality. Apparel manufacturers confront

Figure 2.8   Factors Affecting the Bargaining Power of Buyers

Buyer bargaining power is stronger when:
- Buyer switching costs to competing brands or substitute products are low.
- Buyers are large and can demand concessions when purchasing large quantities.
- Large-volume purchases by buyers are important to sellers.
- Buyer demand is weak or declining.
- There are only a few buyers—so that each one's business is important to sellers.
- Identity of buyer adds prestige to the seller's list of customers.
- Quantity and quality of information available to buyers improves.
- Buyers have the ability to postpone purchases until later if they do not like the present deals being offered by sellers.
- Some buyers are a threat to integrate backward into the business of sellers and become an important competitor.

Buyer bargaining power is weaker when:
- Buyers purchase the item infrequently or in small quantities.
- Buyer switching costs to competing brands are high.
- There is a surge in buyer demand that creates a "sellers' market."
- A seller's brand reputation is important to a buyer.
- A particular seller's product delivers quality or performance that is very important to buyer and that is not matched in other brands.
- Buyer collaboration or partnering with selected sellers provides attractive win–win opportunities.

significant bargaining power when selling to retail chains like JCPenney, Sears, or Macy's, but they can command much better prices selling to small owner-managed apparel boutiques.

How Seller–Buyer Partnerships Can Create Competitive Pressures   Partnerships between sellers and buyers are an increasingly important element of the competitive picture in *business-to-business relationships* (as opposed to business-to-consumer relationships). Many sellers that provide items to business customers have found it in their mutual interest to collaborate closely on such matters as just-in-time deliveries, order processing, electronic invoice payments, and data sharing. Wal-Mart, for example, provides the manufacturers with whom it does business (like Procter & Gamble) with daily sales at each of its stores so that the manufacturers can maintain sufficient inventories at Wal-Mart's distribution centers to keep the shelves at each Wal-Mart store amply stocked. Dell Computer has partnered with its largest customers to create online systems for over 50,000 corporate customers, providing their employees with information on approved product configurations, global pricing, paperless purchase orders, real-time order tracking, invoicing, purchasing history, and other efficiency tools. Dell also loads a customer's software at the factory and installs asset tags so that customer setup time is minimal; it also helps customers upgrade their PC systems to next-generation hardware and software. Dell's partnerships with its corporate customers have put significant competitive pressure on other PC makers.

Determining Whether the Collective Strength of the Five Competitive Forces Is Conducive to Good Profitability

Scrutinizing each of the five competitive forces one by one provides a powerful diagnosis of what competition is like in a given market. Once the strategist has gained an understanding of the specific competitive pressures comprising each force and determined whether these pressures constitute a strong or weak competitive force, the next step is to evaluate the collective strength of the five forces and determine whether the state of competition is conducive to good profitability. Is the collective impact of the five competitive forces stronger than "normal"? Are some of the competitive forces sufficiently strong to undermine industry profitability? Can companies in this industry reasonably expect to earn decent profits in light of the prevailing competitive forces?

Is the State of Competition Conducive to Good Profitability?

As a rule, the stronger the collective impact of the five competitive forces, the lower the combined profitability of industry participants. The most extreme case of a "competitively unattractive" industry is when all five forces are producing strong competitive pressures: rivalry among sellers is vigorous, low entry barriers allow new rivals to gain a market foothold, competition from substitutes is intense, and both suppliers and customers are able to exercise considerable bargaining leverage. Fierce to strong competitive pressures coming from all five directions nearly always drive industry profitability to unacceptably low levels, frequently producing losses for many industry members and forcing some out of business. But an industry can be competitively unattractive without all five competitive forces being strong. Intense competitive pressures from just two or three of the five forces may suffice to destroy the conditions for good profitability and prompt some companies to exit the business. The manufacture of disk drives, for example, is brutally competitive; IBM recently announced the sale of its disk drive business to Hitachi, taking a loss of over $2 billion on its exit from the business. Especially intense competitive conditions seem to be the norm in tire manufacturing and apparel, two industries where profit margins have historically been thin.

> The stronger the forces of competition, the harder it becomes for industry members to earn attractive profits.

In contrast, when the collective impact of the five competitive forces is moderate to weak, an industry is competitively attractive in the sense that industry members can reasonably expect to earn good profits and a nice return on investment. The ideal competitive environment for earning superior profits is one in which both suppliers and customers are in weak bargaining positions, there are no good substitutes, high barriers block further entry, and rivalry among present sellers generates only moderate competitive pressures. Weak competition is the best of all possible worlds for also-ran companies because even they can usually eke out a decent profit—if a company can't make a decent profit when competition is weak, then its business outlook is indeed grim.

In most industries, the collective strength of the five competitive forces is somewhere near the middle of the two extremes of very intense and very weak, typically ranging from slightly stronger than normal to slightly weaker than normal and typically allowing well-managed companies with sound strategies to earn attractive profits.

Striving to Match Company Strategy to Competitive Conditions   Working through the five-forces model step by step not only aids strategy makers in assessing whether the intensity of competition allows good profitability but also promotes sound strategic thinking about how to better match company strategy to the specific competitive character of the marketplace. Effectively matching a company's strategy to the particular competitive pressures and competitive conditions that exist has two aspects:

1. Pursuing avenues that shield the firm from as many of the prevailing competitive pressures as possible.

2. Initiating actions calculated to produce sustainable competitive advantage, thereby shifting competition in the company's favor, putting added competitive pressure on rivals, and perhaps even defining the business model for the industry.

> A company's strategy is increasingly effective the more it provides some insulation from competitive pressures and shifts the competitive battle in the company's favor.

But making headway on these two fronts first requires identifying competitive pressures, gauging the relative strength of each, and gaining a deep enough understanding of the state of competition in the industry to know which strategy buttons to push.

The Drivers of Change: What Impacts Will They Have?

An industry's present conditions don't necessarily reveal much about the strategically relevant ways in which the industry environment is changing. All industries are characterized by trends and new developments that gradually or speedily produce changes important enough to require a strategic response from participating firms. The popular hypothesis that industries go through a life cycle of takeoff, rapid growth, early maturity, market saturation, and stagnation or decline helps explain industry change—but it is far from complete.[11] There are more causes of industry change than an industry's normal progression through the life cycle.

> **Core Concept**
>
> Industry conditions change because important forces are *driving* industry participants (competitors, customers, or suppliers) to alter their actions; the **driving forces** in an industry are the *major underlying causes* of changing industry and competitive conditions—some driving forces originate in the macroenvironment and some originate from within a company's immediate industry and competitive environment.

The Concept of Driving Forces

Although it is important to judge what growth stage an industry is in, there's more analytical value in identifying the specific factors causing fundamental industry and competitive adjustments. Industry and competitive conditions change because certain forces are enticing or pressuring industry participants to alter their actions.[12] **Driving forces** are those that have the biggest influence on what kinds of changes will take place in the industry's structure and competitive environment. Some driving forces originate in the company's macroenvironment;

some originate from within the company's more immediate industry and competitive environment. Driving-forces analysis has two steps: (1) identifying what the driving forces are, and (2) assessing the impact they will have on the industry.

Identifying an Industry's Driving Forces

Many events can affect an industry powerfully enough to qualify as driving forces. Some are unique and specific to a particular industry situation, but most drivers of change fall into one of the following categories:[13]

▨ *Growing use of the Internet and emerging new Internet technology applications*— The Internet and the adoption of Internet technology applications represent a driving force of historical and revolutionary proportions. The Internet is proving to be an important new distribution channel, allowing manufacturers to access customers directly rather than distribute exclusively through traditional wholesale and retail channels, and also making it easy for companies of all types to extend their geographic reach and vie for sales in areas where they formerly did not have a presence. Being able to reach consumers via the Internet can increase the number of rivals a company faces and escalate rivalry among sellers, sometimes pitting pure online sellers against combination brick-and-click sellers against pure brick-and-mortar sellers. The websites of rival sellers are only a few clicks apart and are "open for business" 24 hours a day every day of the year, giving buyers unprecedented ability to research the product offerings of competitors and shop the market for the best value. Companies can use the Internet to reach beyond their borders to find the best suppliers and, further, to collaborate closely with them to achieve efficiency gains and cost savings. Moreover, companies across the world are using a host of Internet technology applications to revamp internal operations and squeeze out cost savings. Internet technology has so many business applications that companies across the world are pursuing the operational benefits of Internet technology and making online systems a normal part of everyday operations. But the impacts vary from industry to industry and company to company, and the industry and competitive implications are continuously evolving. The challenges here are to assess precisely how the Internet and Internet technology applications are altering a particular industry's landscape and to factor these impacts into the strategy-making equation.

▨ *Increasing globalization of the industry*—Competition begins to shift from primarily a regional or national focus to an international or global focus when industry members begin seeking out customers in foreign markets or when production activities begin to migrate to countries where costs are lowest. Globalization of competition really starts to take hold when one or more ambitious companies precipitate a race for worldwide market leadership by launching initiatives to expand into more and more country markets. Globalization can also be precipitated by the blossoming of consumer demand in more and more countries and by the actions of government officials in many countries to reduce trade barriers or open up once-closed markets to foreign competitors, as is occurring in many parts of Europe, Latin America, and Asia. Significant differences in labor costs among countries give manufacturers a strong incentive to locate plants for labor-intensive products in low-wage countries and use these plants to supply market demand across the whole world. Wages in China, India, Singapore, Mexico, and Brazil, for example, are about one-fourth those in the United States, Germany, and Japan. The forces of globalization are sometimes such a strong driver that companies find it highly advantageous, if not necessary, to spread their operating reach into more and more country markets. Globalization is very much a driver of industry change in such industries as credit cards, mobile phones, motor vehicles, steel, refined petroleum products, public accounting, and textbook publishing.

■ *Changes in the long-term industry growth rate*—Shifts in industry growth up or down are a driving force for industry change, affecting the balance between industry supply and buyer demand, entry and exit, and the character and strength of competition. An upsurge in buyer demand triggers a race among established firms and newcomers to capture the new sales opportunities; ambitious companies with trailing market shares may see the upturn in demand as a golden opportunity to broaden their customer base and move up several notches in the industry standings to secure a place among the market leaders. A slowdown in the rate at which demand is growing nearly always portends mounting rivalry and increased efforts by some firms to maintain their high rates of growth by taking sales and market share away from rivals. If industry sales suddenly turn flat or begin to shrink after years of rising steadily, competition is certain to intensify as industry members scramble for the available business and as mergers and acquisitions result in industry consolidation to a smaller number of competitively stronger participants. Dimming sales prospects usually prompt both competitively weak and growth-oriented companies to sell their business operations to those industry members who elect to stick it out; as demand for the industry's product continues to shrink, the remaining industry members may be forced to close inefficient plants and retrench to a smaller production base—all of which results in a much-changed competitive landscape.

■ *Changes in who buys the product and how they use it*—Shifts in buyer demographics and new ways of using the product can alter the state of competition by opening the way to market an industry's product through a different mix of dealers and retail outlets; prompting producers to broaden or narrow their product lines; bringing different sales and promotion approaches into play; and forcing adjustments in customer service offerings (credit, technical assistance, maintenance and repair). The mushrooming popularity of downloading music from the Internet, storing music files on PC hard drives, and burning custom CDs has forced recording companies to reexamine their distribution strategies and raised questions about the future of traditional retail music stores; at the same time, it has stimulated sales of CD burners and blank CDs. Longer life expectancies and growing percentages of relatively well-to-do retirees are driving changes in such industries as health care, prescription drugs, recreational living, and vacation travel. The growing percentage of households with PCs and Internet access is opening opportunities for banks to expand their electronic bill-payment services and for retailers to move more of their customer services online.

■ *Product innovation*—Competition in an industry is always affected by rivals racing to be first to introduce one new product or product enhancement after another. An ongoing stream of product innovations tends to alter the pattern of competition in an industry by attracting more first-time buyers, rejuvenating industry growth, and/or creating wider or narrower product differentiation among rival sellers. Successful new product introductions strengthen the market positions of the innovating companies, usually at the expense of companies that stick with their old products or are slow to follow with their own versions of the new product. Product innovation has been a key driving force in such industries as digital cameras, golf clubs, video games, toys, and prescription drugs.

■ *Technological change*—Advances in technology can dramatically alter an industry's landscape, making it possible to produce new and better products at lower cost and opening up whole new industry frontiers. Technological developments can also produce competitively significant changes in capital requirements, minimum efficient plant sizes, distribution channels and logistics, and experience or learning-curve effects. In the steel industry, ongoing advances in minimill technology (which involve recycling scrap steel to make new products) have allowed steelmakers with state-of-the-art minimills to gradually expand into the production of more and more steel products, steadily taking sales and market share from higher-cost integrated producers (which make steel from scratch using iron ore, coke, and traditional blast furnace technology). Nucor, the leader of the minimill technology revolution in the United States, came from nowhere in 1970 to emerge as the nation's biggest and the lowest-cost steel producer as of 2002, having overtaken U.S. Steel and Bethlehem Steel, both integrated producers and the longtime market leaders. In a space of 30 years, advances in minimill technology have changed the face of the steel industry worldwide.

■ *Marketing innovation*—When firms are successful in introducing new ways to market their products, they can spark a burst of buyer interest, widen industry demand, increase product differentiation, and lower unit costs—any or all of which can alter the competitive positions of rival firms and force strategy revisions. In today's world, Internet marketing is shaking up competition in such industries as electronics retailing, stock brokerage (where online brokers have taken significant business away from traditional brokers), and office supplies (where Office Depot, Staples, and Office Max are using their websites to market office supplies to corporations, small businesses, schools and universities, and government agencies).

■ *Entry or exit of major firms*—The entry of one or more foreign companies into a geographic market once dominated by domestic firms nearly always shakes up competitive conditions. Likewise, when an established domestic firm from another industry attempts entry either by acquisition or by launching its own start-up venture, it usually applies its skills and resources in some innovative fashion that pushes competition in new directions. Entry by a major firm often produces a new ballgame, not only with new key players but also with new rules for competing. Similarly, exit of a major firm changes the competitive structure by reducing the number of market leaders (perhaps increasing the dominance of the leaders who remain) and causing a rush to capture the exiting firm's customers.

■ *Diffusion of technical know-how across more companies and more countries*—As knowledge about how to perform a particular activity or execute a particular manufacturing technology spreads, the competitive advantage held by firms originally possessing this know-how erodes. Knowledge diffusion can occur through scientific journals, trade publications, on-site plant tours, word of mouth among suppliers and customers, employee migration, and Internet sources. It can also occur when those possessing technological know-how license others to use it for a royalty fee or team up with a company interested in turning the technology into a new business venture. Quite often, technological know-how can be acquired by simply buying a company that has the wanted skills, patents, or manufacturing capabilities. In recent years, rapid technology transfer across national boundaries has been a prime factor in causing industries to become more globally competitive. As companies worldwide gain access to valuable technical know-how, they upgrade their manufacturing capabilities in a long-term effort to compete head-on against established companies. Cross-border technology transfer has made the once domestic industries of automobiles, tires, consumer electronics, telecommunications, computers, and others, increasingly global.

■ *Changes in cost and efficiency*—Widening or shrinking differences in the costs among key competitors tend to dramatically alter the state of competition. The low cost of e-mail and fax transmission has put mounting competitive pressure on the relatively inefficient and high-cost operations of the U.S. Postal Service—sending a one-page fax is cheaper and far quicker than sending a first-class letter; sending e-mail is faster and cheaper still. In the electric power industry, sharply lower costs to generate electricity at newly constructed combined-cycle generating plants during 1998–2001 forced older coal-fired and gas-fired plants to lower their production costs to remain competitive. Shrinking cost differences in producing multifeatured mobile phones is turning the mobile phone market into a commodity business and causing more buyers to base their purchase decisions on price.

■ *Growing buyer preferences for differentiated products instead of a commodity product (or for a more standardized product instead of strongly differentiated products)*—When buyer tastes and preferences start to diverge, sellers can win a loyal following with product offerings that stand apart from those of rival sellers. In recent years, beer drinkers have grown less loyal to a single brand and have begun to drink a variety of domestic and foreign beers; as a consequence, beer manufacturers have introduced a host of new brands and malt beverages with different tastes and flavors. Buyer preferences for motor vehicles are becoming increasingly diverse, with few models generating sales of more than 250,000 units annually. When a shift from standardized to differentiated products occurs, the driver of change is the contest among rivals to cleverly outdifferentiate one another.

On the other hand, buyers sometimes decide that a standardized, budget-priced product suits their requirements as well as or better than a premium-priced product with lots of snappy features and personalized services. Online brokers, for example, have used the lure of cheap commissions to attract many investors willing to place their own buy–sell orders via the Internet; growing acceptance of online trading has put significant competitive pressures on full-service brokers whose business model has always revolved around convincing clients of the value of asking for personalized advice from professional brokers and paying their high commission fees to make trades. Pronounced shifts toward greater product standardization usually spawn lively price competition and force rival sellers to drive down their costs to maintain profitability. The lesson here is that competition is driven partly by whether the market forces in motion are acting to increase or decrease product differentiation.

■ *Reductions in uncertainty and business risk*—An emerging industry is typically characterized by much uncertainty over potential market size, how much time and money will be needed to surmount technological problems, and what distribution channels and buyer segments to emphasize. Emerging industries tend to attract only risk-taking entrepreneurial companies. Over time, however, if the business model of industry pioneers proves profitable and market demand for the product appears durable, more conservative firms are usually enticed to enter the market. Often, these later entrants are large, financially strong firms looking to invest in attractive growth industries.

Lower business risks and less industry uncertainty also affect competition in international markets. In the early stages of a company's entry into foreign markets, conservatism prevails and firms limit their downside exposure by using less risky strategies like exporting, licensing, joint marketing agreements, or joint ventures with local companies to accomplish entry. Then, as experience accumulates and perceived risk levels decline, companies move more boldly and more independently, making acquisitions, constructing their own plants, putting in their own sales and marketing capabilities to build strong competitive positions in each country market, and beginning to link the strategies in each country to create a more globalized strategy.

- *Regulatory influences and government policy changes*—Government regulatory actions can often force significant changes in industry practices and strategic approaches. Deregulation has proved to be a potent procompetitive force in the airline, banking, natural gas, telecommunications, and electric utility industries. Government efforts to reform Medicare and health insurance have become potent driving forces in the health care industry. In international markets, host governments can drive competitive changes by opening their domestic markets to foreign participation or closing them to protect domestic companies. Note that this driving force is spawned by forces in a company's macroenvironment.

- *Changing societal concerns, attitudes, and lifestyles*—Emerging social issues and changing attitudes and lifestyles can be powerful instigators of industry change. Growing antismoking sentiment has emerged as a major driver of change in the tobacco industry; concerns about terrorism are having a big impact on the travel industry. Consumer concerns about salt, sugar, chemical additives, saturated fat, cholesterol, and nutritional value have forced food producers to revamp food-processing techniques, redirect R&D efforts into the use of healthier ingredients, and compete in developing nutritious, good-tasting products. Safety concerns have transformed the automobile, toy, and outdoor power equipment industries, to mention a few. Increased interest in physical fitness has spawned new industries in exercise equipment, mountain biking, outdoor apparel, sports gyms and recreation centers, vitamin and nutrition supplements, and medically supervised diet programs. Social concerns about air and water pollution have forced industries to incorporate expenditures for controlling pollution into their cost structures. Shifting societal concerns, attitudes, and lifestyles alter the pattern of competition, usually favoring those players that respond quickly and creatively with products targeted to the new trends and conditions. As with the preceding driving force, this driving force springs from factors at work in a company's macroenvironment.

That there are so many different *potential driving forces* explains why it is too simplistic to view industry change only in terms of the life-cycle model and why a full understanding of the *causes* underlying the emergence of new competitive conditions is a fundamental part of industry analysis. However, while many forces of change may be at work in a given industry, no more than three or four are likely to be true driving forces powerful enough to qualify as the *major determinants* of why and how the industry is changing. Thus company strategists must resist the temptation to label every change they see as a driving force; the analytical task is to evaluate the forces of industry and competitive change carefully enough to separate major factors from minor ones.

Assessing the Impact of the Driving Forces

The second phase of driving forces analysis is to determine whether the driving forces are, on the whole, acting to make the industry environment more or less attractive. Answers to three questions are needed here:

1. Are the driving forces causing demand for the industry's product to increase or decrease?

2. Are the driving forces acting to make competition more or less intense?

3. Will the driving forces lead to higher or lower industry profitability?

Getting a handle on the collective impact of the driving forces usually requires looking at the likely effects of each force separately, since the driving forces may not all be pushing change in the same direction. For example, two driving forces may be acting to spur demand for the industry's product while one driving force may be working to curtail demand. Whether the net effect on industry demand is up or down hinges on which driving forces are the more powerful. The analyst's objective here is to get a good grip on what external factors are shaping industry change and what difference these factors will make.

The Link between Driving Forces and Strategy

Sound analysis of an industry's driving forces is a prerequisite to sound strategy making. Without understanding the forces driving industry change and the impacts these forces will have on the character of the industry environment and on the company's business over the next one to three years, managers are ill-prepared to craft a strategy tightly matched to emerging conditions. Similarly, if managers are uncertain about the implications of each driving force, or if their views are incomplete or off-base, it's difficult for them to craft a strategy that is responsive to the driving forces and their consequences for the industry. So driving-forces analysis is not something to take lightly; it has practical value and is basic to the task of thinking strategically about where the industry is headed and how to prepare for the changes.

Diagnosing the Market Positions of Industry Rivals: Who is Strongly Positioned and Who Is Not?

Core Concept

Strategic group mapping is a technique for displaying the different market or competitive positions that rival firms occupy in the industry.

Since competing companies commonly sell in different price/quality ranges, emphasize different distribution channels, incorporate product features that appeal to different types of buyers, have different geographic coverage, and so on, it stands to reason that some companies enjoy stronger or more attractive market positions than other companies. Understanding which companies are strongly positioned and which are weakly positioned is an integral part of analyzing an industry's competitive structure. The best technique for revealing the market positions of industry competitors is **strategic group mapping**.[14] This analytical tool is useful for comparing the market positions of each firm separately or for grouping them into like positions when an industry has so many competitors that it is not practical to examine each one in depth.

Using Strategic Group Maps to Assess the Market Positions of Key Competitors

A **strategic group** consists of those industry members with similar competitive approaches and positions in the market.[15] Companies in the same strategic group can

resemble one another in any of several ways: they may have comparable product-line breadth, sell in the same price/quality range, emphasize the same distribution channels, use essentially the same product
attributes to appeal to similar types of buyers, depend on identical
technological approaches, or offer buyers similar services and technical assistance.[16] An industry contains only one strategic group when
all sellers pursue essentially identical strategies and have comparable
market positions. At the other extreme, an industry may contain as many strategic
groups as there are competitors when each rival pursues a distinctively different competitive approach and occupies a substantially different market position.

> **Core Concept**
>
> A **strategic group** is a cluster of firms in an industry with similar competitive approaches and market positions.

The procedure for constructing a *strategic group map* is straightforward:

- Identify the competitive characteristics that differentiate firms in the industry; typical variables are price/quality range (high, medium, low), geographic coverage
(local, regional, national, global), degree of vertical integration (none, partial,
full), product-line breadth (wide, narrow), use of distribution channels (one, some,
all), and degree of service offered (no-frills, limited, full).

- Plot the firms on a two-variable map using pairs of these differentiating characteristics.

- Assign firms that fall in about the same strategy space to the same strategic group.

- Draw circles around each strategic group, making the circles proportional to the
size of the group's share of total industry sales revenues.

This produces a two-dimensional diagram like the one for the retailing industry in
Company Spotlight 2.1.

Several guidelines need to be observed in mapping the positions of strategic
groups in the industry's overall strategy space.[17] First, the two variables selected as
axes for the map should *not* be highly correlated; if they are, the circles on the map will
fall along a diagonal and strategy makers will learn nothing more about the relative positions of competitors than they would by considering just one of the variables. For instance, if companies with broad product lines use multiple distribution channels while
companies with narrow lines use a single distribution channel, then looking at broad
versus narrow product lines reveals just as much about who is positioned where as
looking at single versus multiple distribution channels; that is, one of the variables is
redundant. Second, the variables chosen as axes for the map should expose big differences in how rivals position themselves to compete in the marketplace. This, of course,
means analysts must identify the characteristics that differentiate rival firms and use
these differences as variables for the axes and as the basis for deciding which firm belongs in which strategic group. Third, the variables used as axes don't have to be either
quantitative or continuous; rather, they can be discrete variables or defined in terms of
distinct classes and combinations. Fourth, drawing the sizes of the circles on the map
proportional to the combined sales of the firms in each strategic group allows the map
to reflect the relative sizes of each strategic group. Fifth, if more than two good competitive variables can be used as axes for the map, several maps can be drawn to give
different exposures to the competitive positioning relationships present in the industry's structure. Because there is not necessarily one best map for portraying how competing firms are positioned in the market, it is advisable to experiment with different
pairs of competitive variables.

Comparative Market Positions of Selected Retail Chains: A Strategic Group Map Application

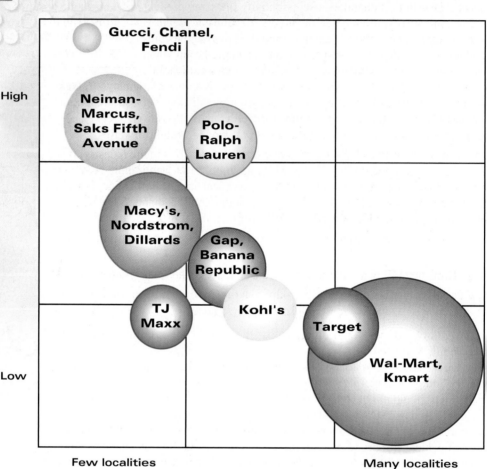

Note: Circles are drawn roughly proportional to the sizes of the chains, according to revenues.

What Can Be Learned from Strategic Group Maps

Driving forces and competitive pressures do not affect all strategic groups evenly. Profit prospects vary from group to group based on the relative attractiveness of their market positions.

One thing to look for is to what extent *industry driving forces and competitive pressures favor some strategic groups and hurt others.*[18] Firms in adversely affected strategic groups may try to shift to a more favorably situated group; how hard such a move proves to be depends on whether entry barriers for the target strategic group are high or low. Attempts by rival firms to enter a new strategic group nearly always increase competitive pressures. If certain firms are known to be trying to change their competitive positions on the map, then attaching arrows to the circles showing the targeted direction helps clarify the picture of competitive maneuvering among rivals.

Another consideration is to what extent *the profit potential of different strategic groups varies due to the strengths and weaknesses in each group's market position.* Differences in profitability can occur because of differing degrees of bargaining leverage or collaboration with suppliers and/or customers, differing degrees of exposure to competition from substitute products outside the industry, differing degrees of competitive rivalry within strategic groups, and differing growth rates for the principal buyer segments served by each group.

Generally speaking, *the closer strategic groups are to each other on the map, the stronger the cross-group competitive rivalry tends to be.* Although firms in the same strategic group are the closest rivals, the next closest rivals are in the immediately adjacent groups.[19] Often, firms in strategic groups that are far apart on the map hardly compete at all. For instance, Tiffany & Co. and Wal-Mart both sell gold and silver jewelry, but their clientele and the prices and quality of their products are much too different to justify calling them competitors. For the same reason, Timex is not a meaningful competitive rival of Rolex, and Subaru is not a close competitor of Lincoln or Mercedes-Benz.

Predicting the Next Strategic Moves Rivals are Likely to Make

Unless a company pays attention to what competitors are doing and knows their strengths and weaknesses, it ends up flying blind into competitive battle. As in sports, scouting the opposition is essential. **Competitive intelligence** about rivals' strategies, their latest actions and announcements, their resource strengths and weaknesses, the efforts being made to improve their situation, and the thinking and leadership styles of their executives is valuable for predicting or anticipating the strategic moves competitors are likely to make next in the marketplace. Having good information to predict the strategic direction and likely moves of key competitors allows a company to prepare defensive countermoves, to craft its own strategic moves with some confidence about what market maneuvers to expect from rivals, and to exploit any openings that arise from competitors' missteps or strategy flaws.

> Good scouting reports on rivals provide a valuable assist in anticipating what moves rivals are likely to make next and outmaneuvering them in the marketplace.

Identifying Competitors' Strategies and Resource Strengths and Weaknesses

Keeping close tabs on a competitor's strategy entails monitoring what the rival is doing in the marketplace, what its management is saying in company press releases, information posted on the company's website (especially press releases and the presentations management has recently made to securities analysts), and such public documents as annual reports and 10-K filings, articles in the business media, and the reports of securities analysts. (Figure 1.1 in Chapter 1 indicates what to look for in identifying a company's strategy.) Company personnel may be able to pick up useful information from a rival's exhibits at trade shows and from conversations with a rival's customers, suppliers, and former employees.[20] Many companies have a competitive intelligence unit that sifts through the available information to construct up-to-date strategic profiles of rivals—their current strategies, their resource strengths and competitive capabilities, their competitive shortcomings, and the latest pronouncements and leadership styles of their executives. Such profiles are typically updated regularly and made available to managers and other key personnel.

Those who gather competitive intelligence on rivals, however, can sometimes cross the fine line between honest inquiry and unethical or even illegal behavior. For example, calling rivals to get information about prices, the dates of new product introductions, or wage and salary levels is legal, but misrepresenting one's company affiliation during such calls is unethical. Pumping rivals' representatives at trade shows is ethical only if one wears a name tag with accurate company affiliation indicated. Avon Products at one point secured information about its biggest rival, Mary Kay Cosmetics (MKC), by having its personnel search through the garbage bins outside MKC's headquarters.[21] When MKC officials learned of the action and sued, Avon claimed it did nothing illegal, since a 1988 Supreme Court case had ruled that trash left on public property (in this case, a sidewalk) was anyone's for the taking. Avon even produced a videotape of its removal of the trash at the MKC site. Avon won the lawsuit—but Avon's action, while legal, scarcely qualifies as ethical.

In sizing up the strategies and the competitive strengths and weaknesses of competitors, it makes sense for company strategists to make three assessments:

1. Which competitor has the best strategy? Which competitors appear to have flawed or weak strategies?

2. Which competitors are poised to gain market share, and which ones seem destined to lose ground?

3. Which competitors are likely to rank among the industry leaders five years from now? Do one or more up-and-coming competitors have powerful strategies and sufficient resource capabilities to overtake the current industry leader?

The industry's *current* major players are generally easy to identify, but some of the leaders may be plagued with weaknesses that are causing them to lose ground; others may lack the resources and capabilities to remain strong contenders given the superior strategies and capabilities of up-and-coming companies. In evaluating which competitors are favorably or unfavorably positioned to gain market ground, company strategists need to focus on why there is potential for some rivals to do better or worse than other rivals. Usually, a competitor's prospects are a function of its vulnerability to driving forces and competitive pressures, whether its strategy has resulted in competitive advantage or disadvantage, and whether its resources and capabilities are well suited for competing on the road ahead.

> Today's market leaders don't automatically become tomorrow's.

Predicting Competitors' Next Moves

Predicting the next strategic moves of competitors is the hardest yet most useful part of competitor analysis. Good clues about what actions a specific company is likely to undertake can often be gleaned from how well it is faring in the marketplace, the problems or weaknesses it needs to address, and how much pressure it is under to improve its financial performance. Content rivals are likely to continue their present strategy with only minor fine-tuning. Ailing rivals can be performing so poorly that fresh strategic moves are virtually certain. Ambitious rivals looking to move up in the industry ranks are strong candidates for launching new strategic offensives to pursue emerging market opportunities and exploit the vulnerabilities of weaker rivals.

Since the moves a competitor is likely to make are generally predicated on the views their executives have about the industry's future and their beliefs about their firm's situation, it makes sense to closely scrutinize the public pronouncements of rival company executives about where the industry is headed and what it will take to be successful, what they are saying about their firm's situation, information from the grapevine about what they are doing, and their past actions and leadership styles. Other considerations in trying to predict what strategic moves rivals are likely to make next include the following:

- Which rivals badly need to increase their unit sales and market share? What strategic options are they most likely to pursue: lowering prices, adding new models and styles, expanding their dealer networks, entering additional geographic markets, boosting advertising to build better brand-name awareness, acquiring a weaker competitor, or placing more emphasis on direct sales via their website?

- Which rivals have a strong incentive, along with the resources, to make major strategic changes, perhaps moving to a different position on the strategic group map? Which rivals are probably locked in to pursuing the same basic strategy with only minor adjustments?

- Which rivals are good candidates to be acquired? Which rivals may be looking to make an acquisition and are financially able to do so?

- Which rivals are likely to enter new geographic markets?

- Which rivals are strong candidates to expand their product offerings and enter new product segments where they do not currently have a presence?

To succeed in predicting a competitor's next moves, company strategists need to have a good feel for each rival's situation, how its managers think, and what its best options are. Doing the necessary detective work can be tedious and time-consuming, but scouting competitors well enough to anticipate their next moves allows managers to prepare effective countermoves (perhaps even beat a rival to the punch) and to take rivals' probable actions into account in crafting their own best course of action.

> Managers who fail to study competitors closely risk being caught napping by the new strategic moves of rivals.

Pinpointing the Key Factors for Future Competitive Success

An industry's **key success factors (KSFs)** are those competitive factors that most affect industry members' ability to prosper in the marketplace—the particular strategy elements, product attributes, resources, competencies, competitive capabilities, and market achievements that spell the difference between being a strong competitor and a weak competitor—and sometimes between profit and loss. KSFs by their very nature are so important to future competitive success that *all firms* in the industry must pay close attention to them or risk becoming an industry also-ran. To indicate the significance of KSFs another way, how well a company's product offering, resources, and capabilities measure up against an industry's KSFs determines just how financially and competitively successful that company will be. Identifying KSFs, in light of the prevailing and anticipated industry and competitive conditions, is therefore always a

> **Core Concept**
>
> **Key success factors** are the product attributes, competencies, competitive capabilities, and market achievements with the greatest impact on future competitive success in the marketplace.

top priority analytical and strategy-making consideration. Company strategists need to understand the industry landscape well enough to separate the factors most important to competitive success from those that are less important.

In the beer industry, the KSFs are full utilization of brewing capacity (to keep manufacturing costs low), a strong network of wholesale distributors (to get the company's brand stocked and favorably displayed in retail outlets where beer is sold), and clever advertising (to induce beer drinkers to buy the company's brand and thereby pull beer sales through the established wholesale/retail channels). In apparel manufacturing, the KSFs are appealing designs and color combinations (to create buyer interest) and low-cost manufacturing efficiency (to permit attractive retail pricing and ample profit margins). In tin and aluminum cans, because the cost of shipping empty cans is substantial, one of the keys is having can-manufacturing facilities located close to end-use customers. Key success factors thus vary from industry to industry, and even from time to time within the same industry, as driving forces and competitive conditions change. Table 2.1 lists the most common types of key success factors.

An industry's key success factors can usually be deduced from what was learned from the previously described analysis of the industry and competitive environment. Which factors are most important to future competitive success flow directly from the industry's dominant characteristics, what competition is like, the impacts of the driving forces, the comparative market positions of industry members, and the likely next moves of key rivals. In addition, the answers to three questions help identify an industry's key success factors:

1. On what basis do buyers of the industry's product choose between the competing brands of sellers? That is, what product attributes are crucial?

2. Given the nature of competitive rivalry and the competitive forces prevailing in the marketplace, what resources and competitive capabilities does a company need to have to be competitively successful?

3. What shortcomings are almost certain to put a company at a significant competitive disadvantage?

Only rarely are there more than five or six key factors for future competitive success. And even among these, two or three usually outrank the others in importance. Managers should therefore bear in mind the purpose of identifying key success factors—to determine which factors are most important to future competitive success—and resist the temptation to label a factor that has only minor importance a KSF. To compile a list of every factor that matters even a little bit defeats the purpose of concentrating management attention on the factors truly critical to long-term competitive success.

Correctly diagnosing an industry's KSFs raises a company's chances of crafting a sound strategy. The goal of company strategists should be to design a strategy aimed at stacking up well on all of the industry's future KSFs and trying to be *distinctively better* than rivals on one (or possibly two) of the KSFs. Indeed, companies that stand out or excel on a particular KSF are likely to enjoy a stronger market position—*being distinctively better than rivals on one or two key success factors tends to translate into competitive advantage*. Hence, using the industry's KSFs as *cornerstones* for the company's strategy and trying to gain sustainable competitive advantage by excelling at one particular KSF is a fruitful competitive strategy approach.[22]

Core Concept

Industry key success factors need to be the cornerstones of a company's strategy.

Table 2.1   COMMON TYPES OF INDUSTRY KEY SUCCESS FACTORS

Technology-related KSFs	■ Expertise in a particular technology or in scientific research (important in pharmaceuticals, Internet applications, mobile communications, and most high-tech industries)
	■ Proven ability to improve production processes (important in industries where advancing technology opens the way for higher manufacturing efficiency and lower production costs)
Manufacturing-related KSFs	■ Ability to achieve scale economies and/or capture learning-curve effects (important to achieving low production costs)
	■ Quality control know-how (important in industries where customers insist on product reliability)
	■ High utilization of fixed assets (important in capital-intensive/high-fixed-cost industries)
	■ Access to adequate supplies of skilled labor
	■ High labor productivity (important for items with high labor content)
	■ Low-cost product design and engineering (reduces manufacturing costs)
	■ Ability to manufacture or assemble products that are customized to buyer specifications
Distribution-related KSFs	■ A strong network of wholesale distributors/dealers
	■ Strong direct sales capabilities via the Internet and/or having company-owned retail outlets
	■ Ability to secure favorable display space on retailer shelves
Marketing-related KSFs	■ Breadth of product line and product selection
	■ A well-known and well-respected brand name
	■ Fast, accurate technical assistance
	■ Courteous, personalized customer service
	■ Accurate filling of buyer orders (few back orders or mistakes)
	■ Customer guarantees and warranties (important in mail-order and online retailing, big-ticket purchases, new product introductions)
	■ Clever advertising
Skills- and capability-related KSFs	■ A talented workforce (important in professional services like accounting and investment banking)
	■ National or global distribution capabilities
	■ Product innovation capabilities (important in industries where rivals are racing to be first to market with new product attributes or performance features)
	■ Design expertise (important in fashion and apparel industries)
	■ Short delivery time capability
	■ Supply chain management capabilities
	■ Strong e-commerce capabilities—a user-friendly website and/or skills in using Internet technology applications to streamline internal operations
Other types of KSFs	■ Overall low costs (not just in manufacturing) so as to be able to profitably meet low price expectations of customers
	■ Convenient locations (important in many retailing businesses)
	■ Ability to provide fast, convenient after-the-sale repairs and service
	■ A strong balance sheet and access to financial capital (important in newly emerging industries with high degrees of business risk and in capital-intensive industries)
	■ Patent protection

Deciding Whether the Industry Presents an Attractive Opportunity

The final step in evaluating the industry and competitive environment is to use the preceding analysis to decide whether the outlook for the industry presents the company with a sufficiently attractive business opportunity. The important factors on which to base such a conclusion include:

- The industry's growth potential.

- Whether powerful competitive forces are squeezing industry profitability to subpar levels and whether competition appears destined to grow stronger or weaker.

- Whether industry profitability will be favorably or unfavorably affected by the prevailing driving forces.

- The degrees of risk and uncertainty in the industry's future.

- Whether the industry as a whole confronts severe problems—regulatory or environmental issues, stagnating buyer demand, industry overcapacity, mounting competition, and so on.

- The company's competitive position in the industry vis-à-vis rivals. (Being a well-entrenched leader or strongly positioned contender in a lackluster industry may present adequate opportunity for good profitability; however, having to fight a steep uphill battle against much stronger rivals may hold little promise of eventual market success or good return on shareholder investment, even though the industry environment is attractive.)

- The company's potential to capitalize on the vulnerabilities of weaker rivals (perhaps converting a relatively unattractive *industry* situation into a potentially rewarding *company* opportunity).

- Whether the company has sufficient competitive strength to defend against or counteract the factors that make the industry unattractive.

- Whether continued participation in this industry adds importantly to the firm's ability to be successful in other industries in which it may have business interests.

As a general proposition, *if an industry's overall profit prospects are above average, the industry environment is basically attractive; if industry profit prospects are below average, conditions are unattractive.* However, it is a mistake to think of a particular industry as being equally attractive or unattractive to all industry participants and all potential entrants. Attractiveness is relative, not absolute, and conclusions one way or the other have to be drawn from the perspective of a particular company. Industries attractive to insiders may be unattractive to outsiders. Companies on the outside may look at an industry's environment and conclude that it is an unattractive business for them to get into, given the prevailing entry barriers, the difficulty of challenging current market leaders with their particular resources and competencies, and the opportunities they have elsewhere. Industry environments unattractive to weak competitors may be attractive to strong competitors. A favorably positioned company may survey a business environment and see a host of opportunities that weak competitors cannot capture.

> **Core Concept**
>
> The degree to which an industry is attractive or unattractive is not the same for all industry participants and all potential entrants; the opportunities an industry presents depends partly on a company's ability to capture them.

When a company decides an industry is fundamentally attractive and presents good opportunities, a strong case can be made that it should invest aggressively to capture the opportunities it sees and to improve its long-term competitive position in the business. When a strong competitor concludes an industry is relatively unattractive and lacking in opportunity, it may elect to simply protect its present position, investing cautiously if at all and looking for opportunities in other industries. A competitively weak company in an unattractive industry may see its best option as finding a buyer, perhaps a rival, to acquire its business.

Key Points

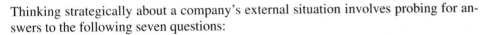

Thinking strategically about a company's external situation involves probing for answers to the following seven questions:

1. *What are the industry's strategy-shaping economic features?* Industries differ significantly on such factors as market size and growth rate, the geographic scope of competitive rivalry, the number and relative sizes of both buyers and sellers, ease of entry and exit, the extent of vertical integration, how fast basic technology is changing, the extent of scale economies and learning-curve effects, the degree of product standardization or differentiation, and overall profitability. While setting the stage for the analysis to come, identifying an industry's economic features also promotes understanding of the kinds of strategic moves that industry members are likely to employ.

2. *What kinds of competitive forces are industry members facing, and how strong is each force?* The strength of competition is a composite of five forces: the rivalry among competing sellers, the presence of attractive substitutes, the potential for new entry, the competitive pressures stemming from supplier bargaining power and supplier–seller collaboration, and the competitive pressures stemming from buyer bargaining power and seller–buyer collaboration. These five forces have to be examined one by one to identify the specific competitive pressures they each comprise and to decide whether these pressures constitute a strong or weak competitive force. The next step in competition analysis is to evaluate the collective strength of the five forces and determine whether the state of competition is conducive to good profitability. Working through the five-forces model step by step not only aids strategy makers in assessing whether the intensity of competition allows good profitability but also promotes sound strategic thinking about how to better match company strategy to the specific competitive character of the marketplace. Effectively matching a company's strategy to the particular competitive pressures and competitive conditions that exist has two aspects: (1) pursuing avenues that shield the firm from as many of the prevailing competitive pressures as possible, and (2) initiating actions calculated to produce sustainable competitive advantage, thereby shifting competition in the company's favor, putting added competitive pressure on rivals, and perhaps even defining the business model for the industry.

3. *What forces are driving changes in the industry, and what impact will these changes have on competitive intensity and industry profitability?* Industry and competitive conditions change because forces are in motion that create incentives or pressures for change. The first phase is to identify the forces that are driving

change in the industry; the most common driving forces include the Internet and Internet technology applications, globalization of competition in the industry, changes in the long-term industry growth rate, changes in buyer composition, product innovation, entry or exit of major firms, changes in cost and efficiency, changing buyer preferences for standardized versus differentiated products or services, regulatory influences and government policy changes, changing societal and lifestyle factors, and reductions in uncertainty and business risk. The second phase of driving-forces analysis is to determine whether the driving forces, taken together, are acting to make the industry environment more or less attractive. Are the driving forces causing demand for the industry's product to increase or decrease? Are the driving forces acting to make competition more or less intense? Will the driving forces lead to higher or lower industry profitability?

4. *What market positions do industry rivals occupy—who is strongly positioned and who is not?* Strategic group mapping is a valuable tool for understanding the similarities, differences, strengths, and weaknesses inherent in the market positions of rival companies. Rivals in the same or nearby strategic groups are close competitors, whereas companies in distant strategic groups usually pose little or no immediate threat. The lesson of strategic group mapping is that some positions on the map are more favorable than others. The profit potential of different strategic groups varies due to strengths and weaknesses in each group's market position. Often, industry driving forces and competitive pressures favor some strategic groups and hurt others.

5. *What strategic moves are rivals likely to make next?* This analytical step involves identifying competitors' strategies, deciding which rivals are likely to be strong contenders and which are likely to be weak, evaluating rivals' competitive options, and predicting their next moves. Scouting competitors well enough to anticipate their actions can help a company prepare effective countermoves (perhaps even beating a rival to the punch) and allows managers to take rivals' probable actions into account in designing their own company's best course of action. Managers who fail to study competitors risk being caught unprepared by the strategic moves of rivals.

6. *What are the key factors for competitive success?* An industry's key success factors (KSFs) are the particular strategy elements, product attributes, competitive capabilities, and business outcomes that spell the difference between being a strong competitor and a weak competitor—and sometimes between profit and loss. KSFs by their very nature are so important to competitive success that *all firms* in the industry must pay close attention to them or risk becoming an industry also-ran. Correctly diagnosing an industry's KSFs raises a company's chances of crafting a sound strategy. The goal of company strategists should be to design a strategy aimed at stacking up well on all of the industry KSFs and trying to be *distinctively better* than rivals on one (or possibly two) of the KSFs. Indeed, using the industry's KSFs as *cornerstones* for the company's strategy and trying to gain sustainable competitive advantage by excelling at one particular KSF is a fruitful competitive strategy approach.

7. *Does the outlook for the industry present the company with sufficiently attractive prospects for profitability?* The answer to this question is a major driver of company strategy. An assessment that the industry and competitive environment is fundamentally attractive typically suggests employing a strategy calculated to

build a stronger competitive position in the business, expanding sales efforts, and investing in additional facilities and equipment as needed. If the industry is relatively unattractive, outsiders considering entry may decide against it and look elsewhere for opportunities, weak companies in the industry may merge with or be acquired by a rival, and strong companies may restrict further investments and employ cost-reduction strategies or product innovation strategies to boost long-term competitiveness and protect their profitability. On occasion, an industry that is unattractive overall is still very attractive to a favorably situated company with the skills and resources to take business away from weaker rivals.

A competently conducted industry and competitive analysis generally tells a clear, easily understood story about the company's external environment. Different analysts can have different judgments about competitive intensity, the impacts of driving forces, how industry conditions will evolve, how good the outlook is for industry profitability, and the degree to which the industry environment offers the company an attractive business opportunity. However, while no method can guarantee a single conclusive diagnosis about the state of industry and competitive conditions and an industry's future outlook, this doesn't justify shortcutting hardnosed strategic analysis and relying instead on opinion and casual observation. Managers become better strategists when they know what questions to pose and what tools to use. This is why this chapter has concentrated on suggesting the right questions to ask, explaining concepts and analytical approaches, and indicating the kinds of things to look for. There's no substitute for staying on the cutting edge of what's happening in the industry—anything less weakens managers' ability to craft strategies that are well matched to the industry and competitive situation.

Exercises

1. As the owner of a new fast-food enterprise seeking a loan from a bank to finance the construction and operation of three new store locations, you have been asked to provide the loan officer with a brief analysis of the competitive environment in fast food. Draw a five-forces diagram for the fast-food industry, and briefly discuss the nature and strength of each of the five competitive forces in fast food.

2. Based on the strategic group map in Company Spotlight 2.1: Who are Wal-Mart's two closest competitors? Between which two strategic groups is competition the weakest? Which strategic group faces the weakest competition from the members of other strategic groups?

3. Based on your knowledge of the ice cream industry, which of the following factors might qualify as possible driving forces capable of causing fundamental change in the industry's structure and competitive environment?
   a) Increasing sales of frozen yogurt and frozen sorbets.
   b) The potential for additional makers of ice cream to enter the market.
   c) Growing consumer interest in low-calorie/low-fat dessert alternatives.
   d) A slowdown in the rate of consumer demand for ice cream products.
   e) An increase in the prices of milk and sugar.
   f) A decision by Häagen-Dazs to increase its prices by 10 percent.
   g) A decision by Ben & Jerry's to add five new flavors to its product line.
   h) A trend in ice cream manufacturers to promoting their brands on the Internet.

CHAPTER 3

Analyzing a Company's Resources and Competitive Position

Before executives can chart a new strategy, they must reach common understanding of the company's current position.

—W. Chan Kim and Renée Mauborgne

The real question isn't how well you're doing today against your own history, but how you're doing against your competitors.

—Donald Kress

Organizations succeed in a competitive marketplace over the long run because they can do certain things their customers value better than can their competitors.

—Robert Hayes, Gary Pisano, and David Upton

Only firms who are able to continually build new strategic assets faster and cheaper than their competitors will earn superior returns over the long term.

—C. C. Markides and P. J. Williamson

In Chapter 2 we described how to use the tools of industry and competitive analysis to assess a company's external environment and lay the groundwork for matching a company's strategy to its external situation. In this chapter we discuss the techniques of evaluating a company's resource capabilities, relative cost position, and competitive strength versus rivals. The analytical spotlight will be trained on five questions:

1. How well is the company's present strategy working?
2. What are the company's resource strengths and weaknesses, and its external opportunities and threats?
3. Are the company's prices and costs competitive?
4. Is the company competitively stronger or weaker than key rivals?
5. What strategic issues and problems merit front-burner managerial attention?

In probing for answers to these questions, four analytical tools—SWOT analysis, value chain analysis, benchmarking, and competitive strength assessment—will be used. All four are valuable techniques for revealing a company's competitiveness and for helping company managers match their strategy to the company's own particular circumstances.

Evaluating How Well a Company's Present Strategy Is Working

In evaluating how well a company's present strategy is working, a manager has to start with what the strategy is. Figure 3.1 shows the key components of a single-business company's strategy. The first thing to pin down is the company's competitive approach. Is the company striving to be a low-cost leader *or* stressing ways to differentiate its product offering from rivals? Is it concentrating its efforts on serving a broad spectrum of customers *or* a narrow market niche? Another strategy-defining consideration is the firm's competitive scope within the industry—what its geographic market coverage is and whether it operates in just a single stage of the industry's production/distribution chain or is vertically integrated across several stages. Another good indication of the company's strategy is whether the company has made moves recently to improve its competitive position and performance—for instance, by cutting prices, improving design, stepping up advertising, entering a new geographic market (domestic or foreign), or merging with a competitor. The company's functional strategies in R&D, production, marketing, finance, human resources, information technology, and so on further characterize company strategy.

While there's merit in evaluating the strategy from a *qualitative* standpoint (its completeness, internal consistency, rationale, and relevance), the best *quantitative* evidence of how well a company's strategy is working comes from its results. The two best empirical indicators are (1) whether the company is achieving its stated financial and strategic objectives, and (2) whether the company is an above-average industry performer. Persistent shortfalls in meeting company performance targets and weak performance relative to rivals are reliable warning signs that the company suffers from

Figure 3.1   Identifying the Components of a Single-Business Company's Strategy

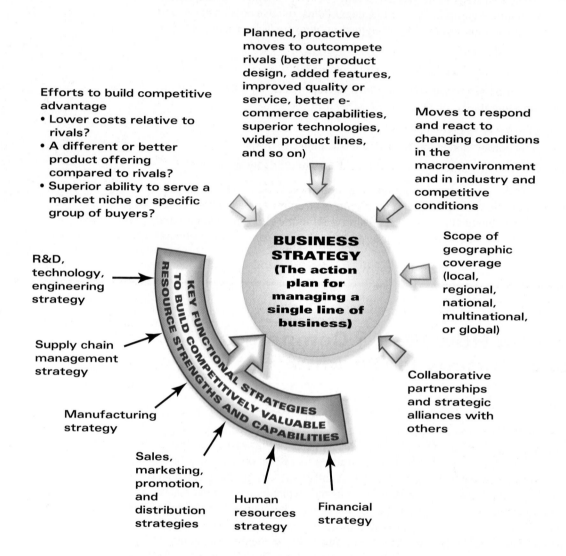

Planned, proactive moves to outcompete rivals (better product design, added features, improved quality or service, better e-commerce capabilities, superior technologies, wider product lines, and so on)

Efforts to build competitive advantage
- Lower costs relative to rivals?
- A different or better product offering compared to rivals?
- Superior ability to serve a market niche or specific group of buyers?

Moves to respond and react to changing conditions in the macroenvironment and in industry and competitive conditions

R&D, technology, engineering strategy

Supply chain management strategy

Manufacturing strategy

Sales, marketing, promotion, and distribution strategies

Human resources strategy

Financial strategy

BUSINESS STRATEGY (The action plan for managing a single line of business)

KEY FUNCTIONAL STRATEGIES TO BUILD COMPETITIVELY VALUABLE RESOURCE STRENGTHS AND CAPABILITIES

Scope of geographic coverage (local, regional, national, multinational, or global)

Collaborative partnerships and strategic alliances with others

poor strategy making, less-than-competent strategy execution, or both. Other indicators of how well a company's strategy is working include:

- Whether the firm's sales are growing faster, slower, or about the same pace as the market as a whole, thus resulting in a rising, eroding, or stable market share.

- Whether the company is acquiring new customers at an attractive rate as well as retaining existing customers.

- Whether the firm's profit margins are increasing or decreasing and how well its margins compare to rival firms' margins.

- Trends in the firm's net profits and return on investment and how these compare to the same trends for other companies in the industry.

- Whether the company's overall financial strength and credit rating are improving or on the decline.

- Whether the company can demonstrate continuous improvement in such internal performance measures as days of inventory, employee productivity, unit cost, defect rate, scrap rate, misfilled orders, delivery times, warranty costs, and so on.

- How shareholders view the company based on trends in the company's stock price and shareholder value (relative to the stock price trends at other companies in the industry).

- The firm's image and reputation with its customers.

- How well the company stacks up against rivals on technology, product innovation, customer service, product quality, delivery time, price, getting newly developed products to market quickly, and other relevant factors on which buyers base their choice of brands.

The stronger a company's current overall performance, the less likely the need for radical changes in strategy. The weaker a company's financial performance and market standing, the more its current strategy must be questioned. Weak performance is almost always a sign of weak strategy, weak execution, or both.

> The stronger a company's financial performance and market position, the more likely it has a well-conceived, well-executed strategy.

Sizing Up a Company's Resource Strengths and Weaknesses and Its External Opportunities and Threats

Appraising a company's resource **s**trengths and **w**eaknesses and its external **o**pportunities and **t**hreats, commonly known as **SWOT analysis,** provides a good overview of whether its overall situation is fundamentally healthy or unhealthy. Just as important, a first-rate SWOT analysis provides the basis for crafting a strategy that capitalizes on the company's resources, aims squarely at capturing the company's best opportunities, and defends against the threats to its well-being.

> **SWOT analysis** is a simple but powerful tool for sizing up a company's resource capabilities and deficiencies, its market opportunities, and the external threats to its future well-being.

Identifying Company Resource Strengths and Competitive Capabilities

A *strength* is something a company is good at doing or an attribute that enhances its competitiveness. A strength can take any of several forms:

- *A skill or important expertise*—low-cost manufacturing capabilities, strong e-commerce expertise, technological know-how, skills in improving production processes, a proven track record in defect-free manufacture, expertise in providing consistently good customer service, excellent mass merchandising skills, or unique advertising and promotional talents.

- *Valuable physical assets*—state-of-the-art plants and equipment, attractive real estate locations, worldwide distribution facilities, or ownership of valuable natural resource deposits.

- *Valuable human assets*—an experienced and capable workforce, talented employees in key areas, cutting-edge knowledge and intellectual capital, collective learning embedded in the organization and built up over time, or proven managerial know-how.[1]

- *Valuable organizational assets*—proven quality control systems, proprietary technology, key patents, mineral rights, a cadre of highly trained customer service representatives, sizable amounts of cash and marketable securities, a strong balance sheet and credit rating (thus giving the company access to additional financial capital), or a comprehensive list of customers' e-mail addresses.

- *Valuable intangible assets*—a powerful or well-known brand name, a reputation for technological leadership, or strong buyer loyalty and goodwill.

- *Competitive capabilities*—product innovation capabilities, short development times in bringing new products to market, a strong dealer network, cutting-edge supply chain management capabilities, quickness in responding to shifting market conditions and emerging opportunities, or state-of-the-art systems for doing business via the Internet.

- *An achievement or attribute that puts the company in a position of market advantage*—low overall costs relative to competitors, market share leadership, a superior product, a wider product line than rivals, wide geographic coverage, a well-known brand name, superior e-commerce capabilities, or exceptional customer service.

- *Competitively valuable alliances or cooperative ventures*—fruitful partnerships with suppliers that reduce costs and/or enhance product quality and performance; alliances or joint ventures that provide access to valuable technologies, competencies, or geographic markets.

Taken together, a company's strengths determine the complement of competitively valuable *resources* with which it competes—a company's resource strengths represent *competitive assets*. The caliber of a firm's resource strengths and competitive capabilities, along with its ability to mobilize them in the pursuit of competitive advantage, are big determinants of how well a company will perform in the marketplace.[2]

> **Core Concept**
> A company is better positioned to succeed if it has a competitively valuable complement of resources at its command.

Company Competencies and Competitive Capabilities   Sometimes a company's resource strengths relate to fairly specific skills and expertise (like just-in-time inventory control) and sometimes they flow from pooling the knowledge and expertise of different organizational groups to create a company competence or competitive capability. Competence or capability in continuous product innovation, for example, comes from teaming the efforts of people and groups with expertise in market research, new product R&D, design and engineering, cost-effective manufacturing, and market testing.[3] Company competencies can range from merely a competence in performing an activity to a core competence to a distinctive competence:

1. A **competence** is something an organization is good at doing. It is nearly always the product of experience, representing an accumulation of learning and the buildup of proficiency in performing an internal activity. Usually a company competence originates with deliberate efforts to develop the organizational ability to do something, however imperfectly or inefficiently. Such efforts involve selecting people with the requisite knowledge and skills, upgrading or expanding individual abilities as needed, and then molding the efforts and work products of individuals

into a cooperative group effort to create organizational ability. Then, as experience builds, such that the company gains proficiency in performing the activity consistently well and at an acceptable cost, the ability evolves into a true competence and company capability. Examples of competencies include proficiency in merchandising and product display, the capability to create attractive and easy-to-use websites, expertise in a specific technology, proven capabilities in selecting good locations for retail outlets, and a proficiency in working with customers on new applications and uses of the product.

2. A **core competence** is a proficiently performed internal activity that is *central* to a company's strategy and competitiveness. A core competence is a more valuable resource strength than a competence because of the well-performed activity's core role in the company's strategy and the contribution it makes to the company's success in the marketplace. A core competence can relate to any of several aspects of a company's business: expertise in integrating multiple technologies to create families of new products, know-how in creating and operating systems for cost-efficient supply chain management, the capability to speed new or next-generation products to market, good after-sale service capabilities, skills in manufacturing a high-quality product at a low cost, or the capability to fill customer orders accurately and swiftly. A company may have more than one core competence in its resource portfolio, but rare is the company that can legitimately claim more than two or three core competencies. Most often, *a core competence is knowledge-based, residing in people and in a company's intellectual capital and not in its assets on the balance sheet.* Moreover, a core competence is more likely to be grounded in cross-department combinations of knowledge and expertise rather than being the product of a single department or work group.

> ### Core Concept
>
> A **core competence** is a competitively important activity that a company performs better than other internal activities; a **distinctive competence** is something that a company does better than its rivals.

3. A **distinctive competence** is a competitively valuable activity that a company *performs better than its rivals.* A distinctive competence thus represents a *competitively superior resource strength.* A company may well perform one competitively important activity well enough to claim that activity as a core competence. But what a company does best internally doesn't translate into a distinctive competence unless the company enjoys *competitive superiority in performing that activity.* For instance, most retailers believe they have core competencies in product selection and in-store merchandising, but many retailers run into trouble in the marketplace because they encounter rivals whose core competencies in product selection and in-store merchandising are better than theirs. Consequently, *a core competence becomes a basis for competitive advantage only when it rises to the level of a distinctive competence.* Sharp Corporation's distinctive competence in flat-panel display technology has enabled it to dominate the worldwide market for liquid crystal displays (LCDs). The distinctive competencies of Toyota and Honda in low-cost, high-quality manufacturing and in short design-to-market cycles for new models have proved to be considerable competitive advantages in the global market for motor vehicles. Intel's distinctive competence in rapidly developing new generations of ever more powerful semiconductor chips for PCs and network servers has helped give the company a dominating presence in the semiconductor industry. Starbucks' distinctive competence in store ambience and innovative coffee drinks has propelled it to the forefront among coffee retailers.

The conceptual differences between a competence, a core competence, and a distinctive competence draw attention to the fact that competitive capabilities are not all equal. Some competencies and competitive capabilities merely enable market survival because most rivals have them—indeed, not having a competence or capability that rivals have can result in competitive disadvantage. Core competencies are *competitively* more important than competencies because they add power to the company's strategy and have a bigger positive impact on its market position and profitability. On occasion, a company may have a uniquely strong competitive capability that holds the potential for creating competitive advantage if it meets the criterion for a distinctive competence and delivers value to buyers.[4] *The importance of a distinctive competence to strategy-making rests with (1) the competitively valuable capability it gives a company, (2) its potential for being the cornerstone of strategy, and (3) the competitive edge it can produce in the marketplace.* It is always easier to build competitive advantage when a firm has a distinctive competence in performing an activity important to market success, when rival companies do not have offsetting competencies, and when it is costly and time-consuming for rivals to imitate the competence. A distinctive competence is thus potentially the mainspring of a company's success—unless it is trumped by more powerful resources of rivals.

What Is the Competitive Power of a Resource Strength?   It is not enough to simply compile a list of a company's resource strengths and competitive capabilities. What is most telling about a company's strengths, individually and collectively, is how powerful they are in the marketplace. The competitive power of a company strength is measured by how many of the following four tests it can pass:[5]

1. *Is the resource strength hard to copy?* The more difficult and more expensive it is to imitate a company's resource strength, the greater its potential competitive value. Resources tend to be difficult to copy when they are unique (a fantastic real estate location, patent protection), when they must be built over time in ways that are difficult to imitate (a brand name, mastery of a technology), and when they carry big capital requirements (a cost-effective plant to manufacture cutting-edge microprocessors). Wal-Mart's competitors have failed miserably in their attempts over the past two decades to match Wal-Mart's superefficient state-of-the-art distribution capabilities. Hard-to-copy strengths and capabilities are valuable competitive assets, adding to a company's market strength and contributing to sustained profitability.

2. *Is the resource strength durable—does it have staying power?* The longer the competitive value of a resource lasts, the greater its value. Some resources lose their clout in the marketplace quickly because of the rapid speeds at which technologies or industry conditions are moving. The value of Eastman Kodak's resources in film and film processing is rapidly being undercut by the growing popularity of digital cameras. The investments that commercial banks have made in branch offices is a rapidly depreciating asset because of growing use of direct deposits, automated teller machines, and telephone and Internet banking options.

3. *Is the resource really competitively superior?* Companies have to guard against pridefully believing that their core competences are distinctive competences or that their brand name is more powerful than the brand names of rivals. Who can really say whether Coca-Cola's consumer marketing prowess is better than Pepsi-Cola's or whether the Mercedes-Benz brand name is more powerful than that of BMW or Lexus?

4. *Can the resource strength be trumped by the different resource strengths and competitive capabilities of rivals?* Many commercial airlines (American Airlines, Delta Airlines, Continental Airlines, Singapore Airlines) have attracted large numbers of passengers because of their resources and capabilities in offering safe, convenient, reliable air transportation services and in providing an array of amenities to passengers. However, Southwest Airlines has consistently been a more profitable air carrier because it provides safe, reliable, basic services at radically lower fares. The prestigious brand names of Cadillac and Lincoln have faded in the market for luxury cars because Mercedes, BMW, Audi, and Lexus have introduced the most appealing luxury vehicles in recent years. Amazon.com is putting a big dent in the business prospects of brick-and-mortar bookstores; likewise, Wal-Mart (with its lower prices) is putting major competitive pressure on Toys "R" Us, at one time the leading toy retailer in the United States.

The vast majority of companies are not well endowed with competitively valuable resources, much less with competitively superior resources capable of passing all four tests with high marks. Most firms have a mixed bag of resources—one or two quite valuable, some good, many satisfactory to mediocre. Only a few companies, usually the strongest industry leaders or up-and-coming challengers, possess a distinctive competence or competitively superior resource.

But even if a company doesn't possess a competitively superior resource, it can still marshal potential for winning in the marketplace. Sometimes a company derives significant competitive vitality, maybe even competitive advantage, from a collection of good-to-adequate resources that collectively have competitive power in the marketplace. Toshiba's laptop computers were the market share leader throughout most of the 1990s—an indicator that Toshiba had competitively valuable resource strengths. Yet Toshiba's laptops were not demonstrably faster than rivals' laptops; nor did they have bigger screens, more memory, longer battery power, a better pointing device, or other superior performance features; nor did Toshiba provide clearly superior technical support services to buyers of its laptops. Further, Toshiba laptops were definitely not cheaper, model for model, than the comparable models of its rivals, and they seldom ranked first in the overall performance ratings done by various organizations. Rather, Toshiba's market share leadership stemmed from a *combination* of *good* resource strengths and capabilities—its strategic partnerships with suppliers of laptop components, efficient assembly capability, design expertise, skills in choosing quality components, a wide selection of models, the attractive mix of built-in performance features found in each model when balanced against price, the better-than-average reliability of its models (based on buyer ratings), and very good technical support services (based on buyer ratings). The verdict from the marketplace was that PC buyers considered Toshiba laptops as better, all things considered, than competing brands. (More recently, however, Toshiba has been overtaken by Dell Computer, the present market leader in laptop PCs.)

> Winning in the marketplace becomes more certain when a company has appropriate and ample resources with which to compete, and especially when it has strengths and capabilities with competitive advantage potential.

Identifying Company Resource Weaknesses and Competitive Deficiencies

A *weakness,* or *competitive deficiency,* is something a company lacks or does poorly (in comparison to others) or a condition that puts it at a disadvantage in the marketplace. A company's weaknesses can relate to (1) inferior or unproven skills, expertise,

Table 3.1   WHAT TO LOOK FOR IN IDENTIFYING A COMPANY'S STRENGTHS, WEAKNESSES, OPPORTUNITIES, AND THREATS

Potential Resource Strengths and Competitive Capabilities	Potential Resource Weaknesses and Competitive Deficiencies
■ A powerful strategy	■ No clear strategic direction
■ Core competencies in . . .	■ Resources that are not well matched to industry key success factors
■ A distinctive competence in . . .	■ No well-developed or proven core competencies
■ A product that is strongly differentiated from that of rivals	■ A weak balance sheet; too much debt
■ Competencies and capabilities that are well matched to industry key success factors	■ Higher overall unit costs relative to key competitors
■ A strong financial condition; ample financial resources to grow the business	■ Weak or unproven innovation capabilities
■ Strong brand-name image/company reputation	■ A product/service with ho-hum attributes or features inferior to those of rivals
■ An attractive customer base	■ Too narrow a product line relative to rivals
■ Ability to take advantage of economies of scale and/or experience and learning-curve effects	■ Weak brand image or reputation
■ Proprietary technology, superior technological skills, important patents	■ Weaker dealer network than key rivals and/or lack of adequate global distribution capability
■ Superior intellectual capital relative to key rivals	■ Behind on product quality, R&D, and/or technological know-how
■ Cost advantages	■ In the wrong strategic group
■ Strong advertising and promotion	■ Losing market share because . . .
■ Product innovation capabilities	■ Lack of management depth
■ Proven capabilities in improving production processes	■ Inferior intellectual capital relative to leading rivals
■ Good supply chain management capabilities	■ Subpar profitability because . . .
■ Good customer service capabilities	■ Plagued with internal operating problems or obsolete facilities
■ Better product quality relative to rivals	■ Behind rivals in e-commerce capabilities
■ Wide geographic coverage and/or strong global distribution capability	■ Short on financial resources to grow the business and pursue promising initiatives
■ Alliances/joint ventures with other firms that provide access to valuable technology, competencies, and/or attractive geographic markets	■ Too much underutilized plant capacity

or intellectual capital in competitively important areas of the business; (2) deficiencies in competitively important physical, organizational, or intangible assets; or (3) missing or competitively inferior capabilities in key areas. *Internal weaknesses are thus shortcomings in a company's complement of resources and represent competitive liabilities.* Nearly all companies have competitive liabilities of one kind or another. Whether a company's resource weaknesses make it competitively vulnerable depends on how much they matter in the marketplace and whether they are offset by the company's resource strengths.

Table 3.1 lists the kinds of factors to consider in compiling a company's resource strengths and weaknesses. Sizing up a company's complement of resource capabilities and deficiencies is akin to constructing a *strategic balance sheet,* on which resource strengths represent *competitive assets* and resource weaknesses represent *competitive liabilities.* Obviously, the ideal condition is for the company's competitive assets to outweigh its competitive liabilities by an ample margin—a 50–50 balance is definitely not the desired condition!

Core Concept

A company's resource strengths represent competitive assets; its resource weaknesses represent competitive liabilities.

Potential Market Opportunities	**Potential External Threats to a Company's Well-Being**
■ Openings to take market share away from rivals ■ Ability to grow rapidly because of sharply rising buyer demand for the industry's product ■ Serving additional customer groups or market segments ■ Expanding into new geographic markets or product segments ■ Expanding the company's product line to meet a broader range of customer needs ■ Utilizing existing company skills or technological know-how to enter new product lines or new businesses ■ Online sales via the Internet ■ Integrating forward or backward ■ Falling trade barriers in attractive foreign markets ■ Acquiring rival firms or companies with attractive technological expertise ■ Entering into alliances or joint ventures to expand the firm's market coverage or boost its competitive capability ■ Openings to exploit emerging new technologies	■ Increasing intensity of competition among industry rivals—may squeeze profit margins ■ Slowdowns in market growth ■ Likely entry of potent new competitors ■ Loss of sales to substitute products ■ Growing bargaining power of customers or suppliers ■ A shift in buyer needs and tastes away from the industry's product ■ Adverse demographic changes that threaten to curtail demand for the industry's product ■ Vulnerability to industry driving forces ■ Restrictive trade policies on the part of foreign governments that block access to attractive foreign markets ■ Costly new regulatory requirements

Identifying a Company's Market Opportunities

Market opportunity is a big factor in shaping a company's strategy. Indeed, managers can't properly tailor strategy to the company's situation without first identifying its opportunities and appraising the growth and profit potential each one holds. Depending on the prevailing circumstances, a company's opportunities can be plentiful or scarce and can range from wildly attractive (an absolute "must" to pursue) to marginally interesting (because the growth and profit potential are questionable) to unsuitable (because there's not a good match with the company's strengths and capabilities). A checklist of potential market opportunities is included in Table 3.1.

In evaluating a company's market opportunities and ranking their attractiveness, managers have to guard against viewing every *industry* opportunity as a *company* opportunity. Not every company is equipped with the resources to successfully pursue each opportunity that exists in its industry. Some companies are more capable of going after particular opportunities than others, and a few companies may be

> A company is well advised to pass on a particular market opportunity unless it has or can acquire the resources to capture it.

hopelessly outclassed. Deliberately adapting a company's resource base to put it in position to contend for attractive growth opportunities is something strategists must pay keen attention to. *The market opportunities most relevant to a company are those that match up well with the company's financial and organizational resource capabilities, offer the best growth and profitability, and present the most potential for competitive advantage.*

Identifying the Threats to a Company's Future Profitability

Often, certain factors in a company's external environment pose *threats* to its profitability and competitive well-being. Threats can stem from the emergence of cheaper or better technologies, rivals' introduction of new or improved products, the entry of lower-cost foreign competitors into a company's market stronghold, new regulations that are more burdensome to a company than to its competitors, vulnerability to a rise in interest rates, the potential of a hostile takeover, unfavorable demographic shifts, adverse changes in foreign exchange rates, political upheaval in a foreign country where the company has facilities, and the like. External threats may pose no more than a moderate degree of adversity (all companies confront some threatening elements in the course of doing business), or they may be so imposing as to make a company's situation and outlook quite tenuous. It is management's job to identify the threats to the company's future well-being and to evaluate what strategic actions can be taken to neutralize or lessen their impact.

A list of potential threats to a company's future profitability and market position is included in Table 3.1.

What Do the SWOT Listings Reveal?

> Simply making lists of a company's strengths, weaknesses, opportunities, and threats is not enough; the payoff from SWOT analysis comes from the conclusions about a company's situation and the implications for strategy improvement that flow from the four lists.

SWOT analysis involves more than making four lists. The two most important parts of SWOT analysis are *drawing conclusions* from the SWOT listings about the company's overall situation, and *acting on those conclusions* to better match the company's strategy to its resource strengths and market opportunities, to correct the important weaknesses, and to defend against external threats. Figure 3.2 shows the three steps of SWOT analysis.

Just what story the SWOT listings tell about the company's overall situation is often revealed in the answers to the following sets of questions:

■ Does the company have an attractive set of resource strengths? Does it have any strong core competencies or a distinctive competence? Are the company's strengths and capabilities well matched to the industry key success factors? Do they add adequate power to the company's strategy, or are more or different strengths needed? Will the company's current strengths and capabilities matter in the future?

■ How serious are the company's weaknesses and competitive deficiencies? Are they mostly inconsequential and readily correctable, or could one or more prove fatal if not remedied soon? Are some of the company's weaknesses in areas that relate to the industry's key success factors? Are there any weaknesses that if uncorrected, would keep the company from pursuing an otherwise attractive opportunity? Does the company have important resource gaps that need to be filled for it to move up in the industry rankings and/or boost its profitability?

Figure 3.2   The Three Steps of SWOT Analysis: Identify, Draw Conclusions, Translate into Strategic Action

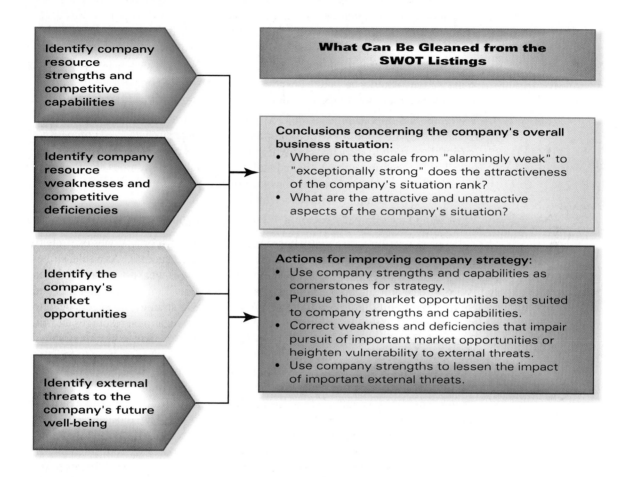

- Do the company's resource strengths and competitive capabilities (its competitive assets) outweigh its resource weaknesses and competitive deficiencies (its competitive liabilities) by an attractive margin?

- Does the company have attractive market opportunities that are well suited to its resource strengths and competitive capabilities? Does the company lack the resources and capabilities to pursue any of the most attractive opportunities?

- Are the threats alarming, or are they something the company appears able to deal with and defend against?

- All things considered, how strong is the company's overall situation? Where on a scale of 1 to 10 (where 1 is alarmingly weak and 10 is exceptionally strong) should the firm's position and overall situation be ranked? What aspects of the company's situation are particularly attractive? What aspects are of the most concern?

The final piece of SWOT analysis is to translate the diagnosis of the company's situation into actions for improving the company's strategy and business prospects. The following questions point to implications the SWOT listings have for strategic action:

▦   Which competitive capabilities need to be strengthened immediately (so as to add greater power to the company's strategy and boost sales and profitability)? Do new types of competitive capabilities need to be put in place to help the company better respond to emerging industry and competitive conditions? Which resources and capabilities need to be given greater emphasis, and which merit less emphasis? Should the company emphasize leveraging its existing resource strengths and capabilities, or does it need to create new resource strengths and capabilities?

▦   What actions should be taken to reduce the company's competitive liabilities? Which weaknesses or competitive deficiencies are in urgent need of correction?

▦   Which market opportunities should be top priority in future strategic initiatives (because they are good fits with the company's resource strengths and competitive capabilities, present attractive growth and profit prospects, and/or offer the best potential for securing competitive advantage)? Which opportunities should be ignored, at least for the time being (because they offer less growth potential or are not suited to the company's resources and capabilities)?

▦   What should the company be doing to guard against the threats to its well-being?

A company's resource strengths should generally form the cornerstones of strategy because they represent the company's best chance for market success.[6] As a rule, strategies that place heavy demands on areas where the company is weakest or has unproven ability are suspect and should be avoided. If a company doesn't have the resources and competitive capabilities around which to craft an attractive strategy, managers need to take decisive remedial action either to upgrade existing organizational resources and capabilities and add others as needed or to acquire them through partnerships or strategic alliances with firms possessing the needed expertise. Plainly, managers have to look toward correcting competitive weaknesses that make the company vulnerable, hold down profitability, or disqualify it from pursuing an attractive opportunity.

At the same time, sound strategy making requires sifting through the available market opportunities and aiming strategy at capturing those that are most attractive and suited to the company's circumstances. Rarely does a company have the resource depth to pursue all available market opportunities simultaneously without spreading itself too thin. How much attention to devote to defending against external threats to the company's market position and future performance hinges on how vulnerable the company is, whether there are attractive defensive moves that can be taken to lessen their impact, and whether the costs of undertaking such moves represent the best use of company resources.

Analyzing Whether a Company's Prices and Costs Are Competitive

Company managers are often stunned when a competitor cuts its price to "unbelievably low" levels or when a new market entrant comes on strong with a very low price. The competitor may not, however, be "dumping" (an economic term for selling large amounts of goods below market price), buying market share, or waging a desperate move to gain sales; it may simply have substantially lower costs. One of the most telling signs of whether a company's business position is strong or precarious is whether its prices and costs are competitive with industry rivals. Price–cost comparisons are especially critical in a commodity-product industry where the value provided to buyers is the same from seller to seller, price competition is typically the ruling market force, and lower-cost companies have the upper hand. But even in industries where products are differentiated and competition centers on the different attributes of competing brands as much as on price, rival companies have to keep their costs *in line* and make sure that any added costs they incur, and any price premiums they charge, create ample buyer value.

For a company to compete successfully, its costs must be *in line* with those of close rivals. While some cost disparity is justified so long as the products or services of closely competing companies are sufficiently differentiated, a high-cost firm's market position becomes increasingly vulnerable the more its costs exceed those of close rivals.

> The higher a company's costs are above those of close rivals, the more competitively vulnerable it becomes.

Two analytical tools are particularly useful in determining whether a company's prices and costs are competitive and thus conducive to winning in the marketplace: value chain analysis and benchmarking.

The Concept of a Company Value Chain

Every company's business consists of a collection of activities undertaken in the course of designing, producing, marketing, delivering, and supporting its product or service. A company's **value chain** consists of the linked set of value-creating activities the company performs internally. As shown in Figure 3.3, the value chain consists of two broad categories of activities: the *primary activities* that are foremost in creating value for customers and the requisite *support activities* that facilitate and enhance the performance of the primary activities.[7] The value chain includes a profit margin because a markup over the cost of performing the firm's value-creating activities is customarily part of the price (or total cost) borne by buyers—a fundamental objective of every enterprise is to create and deliver a value to buyers whose margin over cost yields an attractive profit.

> **Core Concept**
> A company's **value chain** identifies the primary activities that create customer value and the related support activities.

Disaggregating a company's operations into primary and secondary activities exposes the major elements of the company's cost structure. Each activity in the value chain gives rise to costs and ties up assets; assigning the company's operating costs and assets to each individual activity in the chain provides cost estimates and capital requirements. Quite often, there are links between activities such that the manner in which one activity is done can affect the costs of performing other activities. For instance, Japanese producers of videocassette recorders (VCRs) were able to reduce prices from around $1,300 in 1977 to under $300 in 1984 by spotting the impact of an early step in the value chain (product design) on a later step (production) and deciding to change the product design to drastically reduce the number of parts in each VCR.[8]

The combined costs of all the various activities in a company's value chain define the company's internal cost structure. Further, the cost of each activity contributes to whether the company's overall cost position relative to rivals is favorable or unfavorable. The tasks of value chain analysis and benchmarking are to develop the data for comparing a company's costs activity by activity against the costs of key rivals and to learn which internal activities are a source of cost advantage or disadvantage. A company's relative cost position is a function of how the overall costs of the activities it performs in conducting business compare to the overall costs of the activities performed by rivals.

Figure 3.3   Representative Company Value Chain

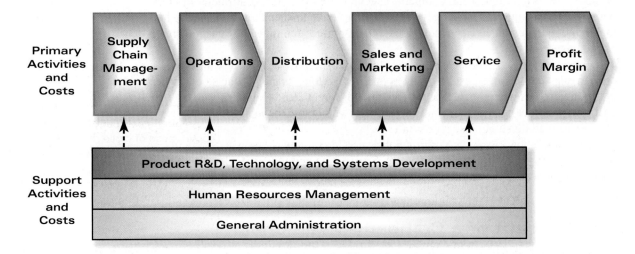

PRIMARY ACTIVITIES

- **Supply Chain Management**—Activities, costs, and assets associated with purchasing fuel, energy, raw materials, parts and components, merchandise, and consumable items from vendors; receiving, storing, and disseminating inputs from suppliers; inspection; and inventory management.

- **Operations**—Activities, costs, and assets associated with converting inputs into final product form (production, assembly, packaging, equipment maintenance, facilities, operations, quality assurance, environmental protection).

- **Distribution**—Activities, costs, and assets dealing with physically distributing the product to buyers (finished goods warehousing, order processing, order picking and packing, shipping, delivery vehicle operations, establishing and maintaining a network of dealers and distributors).

- **Sales and Marketing**—Activities, costs, and assets related to sales force efforts, advertising and promotion, market research and planning, and dealer/distributor support.

- **Service**—Activities, costs, and assets associated with providing assistance to buyers, such as installation, spare parts delivery, maintenance and repair, technical assistance, buyer inquiries, and complaints.

SUPPORT ACTIVITIES

- **Product R&D, Technology, and Systems Development**—Activities, costs, and assets relating to product R&D, process R&D, process design improvement, equipment design, computer software development, telecommunications systems, computer-assisted design and engineering, database capabilities, and development of computerized support systems.

- **Human Resources Management**—Activities, costs, and assets associated with the recruitment, hiring, training, development, and compensation of all types of personnel; labor relations activities; and development of knowledge-based skills and core competencies.

- **General Administration**—Activities, costs, and assets relating to general management, accounting and finance, legal and regulatory affairs, safety and security, management information systems, forming strategic alliances and collaborating with strategic partners, and other "overhead" functions.

Source: Adapted from Michael E. Porter, *Competitive Advantage* (New York: Free Press, 1985), pp. 37–43.

Why the Value Chains of Rival Companies Often Differ

A company's value chain and the manner in which it performs each activity reflect the evolution of its own particular business and internal operations, its strategy, the approaches it is using to execute its strategy, and the underlying economics of the activities themselves.[9] Because these factors differ from company to company, the value chains of rival companies sometimes differ substantially—a condition that complicates the task of assessing rivals' relative cost positions. For instance, competing companies may differ in their degrees of vertical integration. Comparing the value chains of a fully integrated rival and a partially integrated rival requires adjusting for differences in the scope of activities performed. Clearly the internal costs for a manufacturer that *makes* all of its own parts and components will be greater than the internal costs of a producer that *buys* the needed parts and components from outside suppliers and only performs assembly operations.

Likewise, there is legitimate reason to expect value chain and cost differences between a company that is pursuing a low-cost/low-price strategy and a rival that is positioned on the high end of the market. The costs of certain activities along the low-cost company's value chain should indeed be relatively low, whereas the high-end firm may understandably be spending relatively more to perform those activities that create the added quality and extra features of its products.

Moreover, cost and price differences among rival companies can have their origins in activities performed by suppliers or by distribution channel allies involved in getting the product to end users. Suppliers or wholesale/retail dealers may have excessively high cost structures or profit margins that jeopardize a company's cost-competitiveness even though its costs for internally performed activities are competitive. For example, when determining Michelin's cost-competitiveness vis-à-vis Goodyear and Bridgestone in supplying replacement tires to vehicle owners, we have to look at more than whether Michelin's tire manufacturing costs are above or below Goodyear's and Bridgestone's. Let's say that a buyer has to pay $400 for a set of Michelin tires and only $350 for a comparable set of Goodyear or Bridgestone tires; Michelin's $50 price disadvantage can stem not only from higher manufacturing costs (reflecting, perhaps, the added costs of Michelin's strategic efforts to build a better-quality tire with more performance features) but also from (1) differences in what the three tire makers pay their suppliers for materials and tire-making components, and (2) differences in the operating efficiencies, costs, and markups of Michelin's wholesale–retail dealer outlets versus those of Goodyear and Bridgestone. Thus, determining whether a company's prices and costs are competitive from an end user's standpoint requires looking at the activities and costs of competitively relevant suppliers and forward allies, as well as the costs of internally performed activities.

The Value Chain System for an Entire Industry

As the tire industry example makes clear, a company's value chain is embedded in a larger system of activities that includes the value chains of its suppliers and its distribution channel allies engaged in getting its product or service to end users.[10] *Accurately assessing a company's competitiveness in end-use markets requires that company managers understand the entire value chain system for delivering a product or service to end users, not just the company's own value chain.* At the very least, this means considering the value chains of suppliers and forward channel allies (if any), as shown in Figure 3.4.

Suppliers' value chains are relevant because suppliers perform activities and incur costs in creating and delivering the purchased inputs used in a company's own value chain. The costs, performance features, and quality of these inputs influence a company's own costs and product differentiation capabilities. Anything a company can do to help its suppliers' take costs out of their value chain activities or improve the quality

Figure 3.4   Representative Value Chain for an Entire Industry

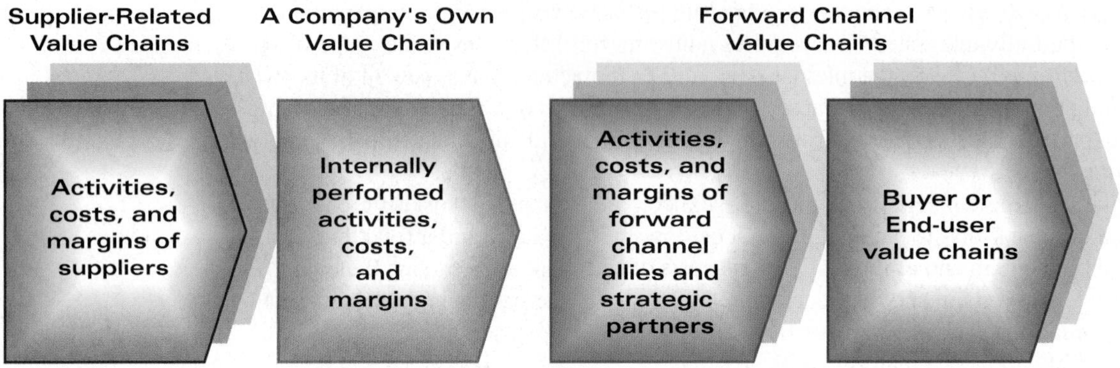

Supplier-Related Value Chains	A Company's Own Value Chain	Forward Channel Value Chains	
Activities, costs, and margins of suppliers	Internally performed activities, costs, and margins	Activities, costs, and margins of forward channel allies and strategic partners	Buyer or End-user value chains

Source: Adapted from Michael E. Porter, *Competitive Advantage* (New York: Free Press, 1985), p. 35.

and performance of the items being supplied can enhance its own competitiveness—a powerful reason for working collaboratively with suppliers in managing supply chain activities.

Forward channel and customer value chains are relevant because (1) the costs and margins of a company's distribution allies are part of the price the end user pays, and (2) the activities that distribution allies perform affect the end user's satisfaction. For these reasons, companies normally work closely with their forward channel allies (who are their direct customers) to perform value chain activities in mutually beneficial ways. For instance, some aluminum can producers have constructed plants next to beer breweries and deliver cans on overhead conveyors directly to the breweries' can-filling lines; this has resulted in significant savings in production scheduling, shipping, and inventory costs for both container producers and breweries.[11] Many automotive parts suppliers have built plants near the auto assembly plants they supply to facilitate just-in-time deliveries, reduce warehousing and shipping costs, and promote close collaboration on parts design and production scheduling. Irrigation equipment companies, suppliers of grape-harvesting and winemaking equipment, and firms making barrels, wine bottles, caps, corks, and labels all have facilities in the California wine country to be close to the nearly 700 winemakers they supply.[12] The lesson here is that a company's value chain activities are often closely linked to the value chains of their suppliers and the forward allies or customers to whom they sell.

> A company's cost-competitiveness depends not only on the costs of internally performed activities (its own value chain) but also on costs in the value chain of its suppliers and forward channel allies.

Although the value chains in Figures 3-3 and 3-4 are representative, actual value chains vary by industry and by company. The primary value chain activities in the pulp and paper industry (timber farming, logging, pulp mills, and papermaking) differ from the primary value chain activities in the home appliance industry (parts and components manufacture, assembly, wholesale distribution, retail sales). The value chain for the soft-drink industry (processing of basic ingredients and syrup manufacture, bottling and can filling, wholesale distribution, advertising, and retail merchandising) differs from that for the computer software industry (programming, disk loading, marketing, distribution). A producer of bathroom and kitchen faucets depends heavily on the activities of wholesale distributors and building supply retailers in winning sales to

Table 3.2   THE DIFFERENCE BETWEEN TRADITIONAL COST ACCOUNTING AND ACTIVITY-BASED COST ACCOUNTING: A PURCHASING DEPARTMENT EXAMPLE

Traditional Cost Accounting Categories in Purchasing Department Budget		Cost of Performing Specific Purchasing Department Activities Using Activity-Based Cost Accounting	
Wages and salaries	$340,000	Evaluate supplier capabilities	$100,300
Employee benefits	95,000	Process purchase orders	82,100
Supplies	21,500	Collaborate with suppliers on just-in-time deliveries	140,200
Travel	12,400	Share data with suppliers	59,550
Depreciation	19,000	Check quality of items purchased	94,100
Other fixed charges (office space, utilities)	112,000	Check incoming deliveries against purchase orders	48,450
Miscellaneous operating expenses	40,250	Resolve disputes	15,250
		Conduct internal administration	100,200
	$640,150		$640,150

Source: Adapted from information in Terence P. Paré, "A New Tool for Managing Costs," *Fortune,* June 14, 1993, pp. 124–29.

homebuilders and do-it-yourselfers; a producer of small gasoline engines internalizes its distribution activities by selling directly to the makers of lawn and garden equipment. A wholesaler's most important activities and costs deal with purchased goods, inbound logistics, and outbound logistics. A hotel's most important activities and costs are in operations—check-in and check-out, maintenance and housekeeping, dining and room service, conventions and meetings, and accounting. Outbound logistics is a crucial activity at Domino's Pizza but comparatively insignificant at Blockbuster. Advertising and promotion are dominant activities at Anheuser-Busch but only minor activities at interstate gas pipeline companies. Consequently, generic value chains like those in Figures 3.3 and 3.4 are illustrative, not absolute, and have to be drawn to fit the activities of a particular company or industry.

Developing the Data to Measure a Company's Cost Competitiveness

Once the major value chain activities are identified, the next step in evaluating a company's cost-competitiveness involves breaking down departmental cost accounting data into the costs of performing specific activities.[13] The appropriate degree of disaggregation depends on the economics of the activities and how valuable it is to develop cross-company cost comparisons for narrowly defined activities as opposed to broadly defined activities. A good guideline is to develop separate cost estimates for activities having different economics and for activities representing a significant or growing proportion of cost.[14]

Traditional accounting identifies costs according to broad categories of expenses—wages and salaries, employee benefits, supplies, maintenance, utilities, travel, depreciation, R&D, interest, general administration, and so on. A newer method, *activity-based costing,* entails defining expense categories according to the specific activities being performed and then assigning costs to the activity responsible for creating the cost. An illustrative example is shown in Table 3.2.[15] Perhaps 25 percent of the companies that have explored the feasibility of activity-based costing have adopted

Value Chain Costs for Companies in the Business of Recording and Distributing Music CDs

The table below presents the representative costs and markups associated with producing and distributing a music CD retailing for $15.

1. Record company direct production costs		$2.40
Artists and repertoire	$0.75	
Pressing of CD and packaging	1.65	
2. Royalties		.99
3. Record company marketing expenses		1.50
4. Record company overhead		1.50
5. Total record company costs		6.39
6. Record company's operating profit		1.86
7. Record company's selling price to distributor/wholesaler		8.25
8. Average wholesale distributor markup to cover distribution activities and profit margins		1.50
9. Average wholesale price charged to retailer		9.75
10. Average retail markup over wholesale cost		5.25
11. Average price to consumer at retail		$15.00

Source: Developed from information in "Fight the Power," a case study prepared by Adrian Aleyne, Babson College, 1999.

---

this accounting approach. To fully understand the costs of activities all along the industry value chain, cost estimates for activities performed in the competitively relevant portions of suppliers' and customers' value chains also have to be developed—an advanced art in competitive intelligence. But despite the tediousness of developing cost estimates activity by activity and the imprecision of some of the estimates, the payoff in exposing the costs of particular activities makes activity-based costing a valuable analytical tool.[16] Company Spotlight 3.1 shows representative costs for various activities performed by the producers and marketers of music CDs.

The most important application of value chain analysis is to expose how a particular firm's cost position compares with the cost positions of its rivals. What is needed are competitor-versus-competitor cost estimates for supplying a product or service to a well-defined customer group or market segment. The size of a company's cost advantage or disadvantage can vary from item to item in the product line, from customer group to customer group (if different distribution channels are used), and from geographic market to geographic market (if cost factors vary across geographic regions).

Core Concept

Benchmarking has proved to be a potent tool for learning which companies are best at performing particular activities and then using their techniques (or "best practices") to improve the cost and effectiveness of a company's own internal activities.

Benchmarking the Costs of Key Value Chain Activities

Many companies today are **benchmarking** their costs of performing a given activity against competitors' costs (and/or against the costs of a noncompetitor in another industry that efficiently and effectively performs much the same activity). Benchmarking is a tool that allows a company to determine whether the manner in which it performs particular functions and activities represents industry "best practices" when both cost and effectiveness are taken into account.

Benchmarking entails comparing how different companies perform various value chain activities—how materials are purchased, how suppliers are paid, how inventories are managed, how products are assembled, how fast the company can get new products to market, how the quality control function is performed, how customer orders are filled and shipped, how employees are trained, how payrolls are processed, and how maintenance is performed—and then making cross-company comparisons of the costs of these activities.[17] The objectives of benchmarking are to identify the best practices in performing an activity, to learn how other companies have actually achieved lower costs or better results in performing benchmarked activities, and to take action to improve a company's competitiveness whenever benchmarking reveals that its costs and results of performing an activity do not match those of other companies (either competitors or noncompetitors).

In 1979, Xerox became an early pioneer in the use of benchmarking when Japanese manufacturers began selling midsize copiers in the United States for $9,600 each— less than Xerox's production costs.[18] Although Xerox management suspected its Japanese competitors were dumping, it sent a team of line managers to Japan, including the head of manufacturing, to study competitors' business processes and costs. Fortunately, Xerox's joint venture partner in Japan, Fuji-Xerox, knew the competitors well. The team found that Xerox's costs were excessive due to gross inefficiencies in the company's manufacturing processes and business practices; the study proved instrumental in Xerox's efforts to become cost-competitive and prompted Xerox to embark on a long-term program to benchmark 67 of its key work processes against companies identified as having the best practices in performing these processes. Xerox quickly decided not to restrict its benchmarking efforts to its office equipment rivals but to extend them to any company regarded as "world class" in performing *any activity* relevant to Xerox's business.

Thus, benchmarking has quickly come to be a tool for comparing a company against rivals not only on cost but on most any relevant activity or competitively important measure. Toyota managers got their idea for just-in-time inventory deliveries by studying how U.S. supermarkets replenished their shelves. Southwest Airlines reduced the turnaround time of its aircraft at each scheduled stop by studying pit crews on the auto racing circuit. Over 80 percent of Fortune 500 companies reportedly engage in some form of benchmarking.

The tough part of benchmarking is not whether to do it but rather how to gain access to information about other companies' practices and costs. Sometimes benchmarking can be accomplished by collecting information from published reports, trade groups, and industry research firms and by talking to knowledgeable industry analysts, customers, and suppliers. On occasion, customers, suppliers, and joint-venture partners often make willing benchmarking allies. Usually, though, benchmarking requires field trips to the facilities of competing or noncompeting companies to observe how things are done, ask questions, compare practices and processes, and perhaps exchange data on productivity, staffing levels, time requirements, and

> Benchmarking the costs of company activities against rivals provides hard evidence of a company's cost-competitiveness.

other cost components. The problem is that, because benchmarking involves competitively sensitive cost information, close rivals can't be expected to be completely open, even if they agree to host facilities tours and answer questions. Making reliable cost comparisons is complicated by the fact that participants often use different cost accounting systems.

However, the explosive interest of companies in benchmarking costs and identifying best practices has prompted consulting organizations (e.g., Accenture, A. T. Kearney, Best Practices Benchmarking & Consulting, Towers Perrin) and several newly formed councils and associations (the International Benchmarking Clearinghouse, the Strategic Planning Institute's Council on Benchmarking) to gather benchmarking data, do benchmarking studies, and distribute information about best practices without identifying the sources. Having an independent group gather the information and report it in a manner that disguises the names of individual companies permits companies to avoid having to disclose competitively sensitive data to rivals and reduces the risk of ethical problems.

Strategic Options for Remedying a Cost Disadvantage

Value chain analysis and benchmarking can reveal a great deal about a firm's cost competitiveness. Examining the costs of a company's own value chain activities and comparing them to rivals' indicates who has how much of a cost advantage or disadvantage and which cost components are responsible. Such information is vital in strategic actions to eliminate a cost disadvantage or create a cost advantage. One of the fundamental insights of value chain analysis and benchmarking is that a company's competitiveness on cost depends on how efficiently it manages its value chain activities relative to how well competitors manage theirs.[19] There are three main areas in a company's overall value chain where important differences in the costs of competing firms can occur: a company's own activity segments, suppliers' part of the industry value chain, and the forward channel portion of the industry chain.

When the source of a firm's cost disadvantage is internal, managers can use any of the following eight strategic approaches to restore cost parity:[20]

1. Implement the use of best practices throughout the company, particularly for high-cost activities.
2. Try to eliminate some cost-producing activities altogether by revamping the value chain. Examples include cutting out low-value-added activities or bypassing the value chains and associated costs of distribution allies and marketing directly to end users (the approach used by Gateway and Dell in PCs).
3. Relocate high-cost activities (such as R&D or manufacturing) to geographic areas where they can be performed more cheaply.
4. Search out activities that can be outsourced from vendors or performed by contractors more cheaply than they can be done internally.
5. Invest in productivity-enhancing, cost-saving technological improvements (robotics, flexible manufacturing techniques, state-of-the-art electronic networking).
6. Innovate around the troublesome cost components—computer chip makers regularly design around the patents held by others to avoid paying royalties; automakers have substituted lower-cost plastic and rubber for metal at many exterior body locations.
7. Simplify the product design so that it can be manufactured or assembled quickly and more economically.

Table 3.3   OPTIONS FOR ATTACKING COST DISADVANTAGES ASSOCIATED WITH SUPPLY CHAIN ACTIVITIES OR FORWARD CHANNEL ALLIES

Options for Attacking the High Costs of Items Purchased from Suppliers	Options for Attacking the High Costs of Forward Channel Allies
■ Negotiate more favorable prices with suppliers. ■ Work with suppliers on the design and specifications for what is being supplied to identify cost savings that will allow them to lower their prices. ■ Switch to lower-priced substitute inputs. ■ Collaborate closely with suppliers to identify mutual cost-saving opportunities. For example, just-in-time deliveries from suppliers can lower a company's inventory and internal logistics costs and may also allow its suppliers to economize on their warehousing, shipping, and production scheduling costs—a win–win outcome for both. ■ Integrate backward into the business of high-cost suppliers to gain control over the costs of purchased items—seldom an attractive option. ■ Try to make up the difference by cutting costs elsewhere in the chain—usually a last resort.	■ Push distributors and other forward channel allies to reduce their markups. ■ Work closely with forward channel allies to identify win–win opportunities to reduce costs. A chocolate manufacturer learned that by shipping its bulk chocolate in liquid form in tank cars instead of 10-pound molded bars, it could not only save its candy-bar manufacturing customers the costs associated with unpacking and melting but also eliminate its own costs of molding bars and packing them. ■ Change to a more economical distribution strategy, including switching to cheaper distribution channels (perhaps direct sales via the Internet) or perhaps integrating forward into company-owned retail outlets. ■ Try to make up the difference by cutting costs earlier in the cost chain—usually a last resort.

Source: Based in part on Michael E. Porter, *Competitive Advantage* (New York: Free Press, 1985), Chapter 3

8. Try to make up the internal cost disadvantage by achieving savings in other two parts of the value chain system—usually a last resort.

If a firm finds that it has a cost disadvantage stemming from costs in the supplier or forward channel portions of the industry value chain, then the task of reducing its costs to levels more in line with competitors usually has to extend beyond the firm's own in-house operations. Table 3.3 presents the strategy options for attacking high costs associated with supply chain activities or forward channel allies.

Translating Proficient Performance of Value Chain Activities into Competitive Advantage

A company that does a first rate job of managing its value chain activities relative to competitors stands a good chance of leveraging its competitively valuable competencies and capabilities into sustainable competitive advantage. With rare exceptions, company attempts to achieve competitive advantage with unique attributes and performance features seldom result in a durable competitive advantage. It is too easy for resourceful competitors to clone, improve on, or find an effective substitute for any unique features of a product or service.[21] A more fruitful approach to achieving and sustaining a competitive edge over rivals is for a company to develop competencies and capabilities that please buyers and that rivals don't have or can't quite match.

The process of translating proficient company performance of value chain activities into competitive advantage is shown in Figure 3.5. The road to competitive advantage begins with management efforts to build more organizational expertise in performing certain competitively important value chain activities, deliberately striving to develop competencies and capabilities that add power to its strategy

> Performing value chain activities in ways that give a company the capabilities to outmatch rivals is a source of competitive advantage.

Figure 3.5   Translating Company Performance of Value Chain Activities into Competitive Advantage

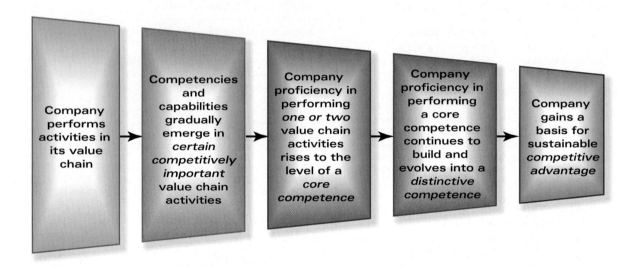

and competitiveness. If management begins to make one or two of these competencies and capabilities cornerstones of its strategy and continues to invest resources in building greater and greater proficiency in performing them, then over time one (or maybe both) of the targeted competencies/capabilities may rise to the level of a core competence. Later, following additional organizational learning and investments in gaining still greater proficiency, the core competence could evolve into a distinctive competence, giving the company superiority over rivals. Such superiority, if it gives the company significant competitive clout in the marketplace, could produce an attractive competitive edge over rivals and, more important, prove difficult for rivals to match or offset with competencies and capabilities of their own making. As a general rule, it is substantially harder for rivals to achieve "best in industry" proficiency in performing a key value chain activity than it is for them to clone the features and attributes of a hot-selling product or service. This is especially true when a company with a distinctive competence avoids becoming complacent and works diligently to maintain its industry-leading expertise and capability.

There are numerous examples of companies that have gained a competitive edge by building competencies and capabilities that outmatch those of rivals. Merck and Glaxo, two of the world's most competitively capable pharmaceutical companies, built their business positions around expert performance of a few competitively crucial activities: extensive R&D to achieve first discovery of new drugs, a carefully constructed approach to patenting, skill in gaining rapid and thorough clinical clearance through regulatory bodies, and unusually strong distribution and sales force capabilities.[22] Federal Express has linked and integrated the performance of its aircraft fleet, truck fleet, support systems, and personnel so tightly and smoothly across the company's different value chain activities that it has created the capability to provide customers with guaranteed overnight delivery services. McDonald's can turn out identical-quality fast-food items at some 25,000-plus outlets around the world—an impressive demonstration of its capability to replicate its operating systems at many locations via an omnibus manual of detailed rules and procedures for each activity and intensive training of franchise operators and outlet managers.

Assessing a Company's Competitive Strength

Using value chain analysis and benchmarking to determine a company's competitiveness on price and cost is necessary but not sufficient. A more comprehensive assessment needs to be made of the company's overall competitive strength. The answers to two questions are of particular interest: First, how does the company rank relative to competitors on each of the important factors that determine market success? Second, all things considered, does the company have a net competitive advantage or disadvantage vis-à-vis major competitors?

An easy-to-use method for answering the two questions posed above involves developing quantitative strength ratings for the company and its key competitors on each industry key success factor and each competitively decisive resource capability. Much of the information needed for doing a competitive strength assessment comes from previous analyses. Industry and competitive analysis reveals the key success factors and competitive capabilities that separate industry winners from losers. Benchmarking data and scouting key competitors provide a basis for judging the competitive strength of rivals on such factors as cost, key product attributes, customer service, image and reputation, financial strength, technological skills, distribution capability, and other competitively important resources and capabilities. SWOT analysis reveals how the company in question stacks up on these same strength measures.

Step 1 in doing a competitive strength assessment is to make a list of the industry's key success factors and most telling measures of competitive strength or weakness (6 to 10 measures usually suffice). Step 2 is to rate the firm and its rivals on each factor. Numerical rating scales (e.g., from 1 to 10) are best to use, although ratings of stronger (+), weaker (−), and about equal (=) may be appropriate when information is scanty and assigning numerical scores conveys false precision. Step 3 is to sum the strength ratings on each factor to get an overall measure of competitive strength for each company being rated. Step 4 is to use the overall strength ratings to draw conclusions about the size and extent of the company's net competitive advantage or disadvantage and to take specific note of areas of strength and weakness.

Table 3.4 provides two examples of competitive strength assessment, using the hypothetical ABC Company against four rivals. The first example employs an *unweighted rating system*. With unweighted ratings, each key success factor/competitive strength measure is assumed to be equally important (a rather dubious assumption). Whichever company has the highest strength rating on a given measure has an implied competitive edge on that factor; the size of its edge is mirrored in the margin of difference between its rating and the ratings assigned to rivals—a rating of 9 for one company versus ratings of 5, 4, and 3, respectively, for three other companies indicates a bigger advantage than a rating of 9 versus ratings of 8, 7, and 6. Summing a company's ratings on all the measures produces an overall strength rating. The higher a company's overall strength rating, the stronger its overall competitiveness versus rivals. The bigger the difference between a company's overall rating and the scores of *lower-rated* rivals, the greater its implied *net competitive advantage*.

> High competitive strength ratings signal a strong competitive position and possession of competitive advantage; low ratings signal a weak position and competitive disadvantage.

Table 3.4 ILLUSTRATIONS OF UNWEIGHTED AND WEIGHTED COMPETITIVE STRENGTH ASSESSMENTS

A. Sample of an Unweighted Competitive Strength Assessment

Rating scale: 1 = Very weak; 10 = Very strong

Key Success Factor/ Strength Measure	ABC Co.	Rival 1	Rival 2	Rival 3	Rival 4
Quality/product performance	8	5	10	1	6
Reputation/image	8	7	10	1	6
Manufacturing capability	2	10	4	5	1
Technological skills	10	1	7	3	8
Dealer network/distribution capability	9	4	10	5	1
New product innovation capability	9	4	10	5	1
Financial resources	5	10	7	3	1
Relative cost position	5	10	3	1	4
Customer service capabilities	5	7	10	1	4
Unweighted overall strength rating	61	58	71	25	32

B. Sample of a Weighted Competitive Strength Assessment

Rating scale: 1 = Very weak; 10 = Very strong

Key Success Factor/ Strength Measure	Importance Weight	Ratings/Scores				
		ABC Co.	Rival 1	Rival 2	Rival 3	Rival 4
Quality/product performance	0.10	8/0.80	5/0.50	10/1.00	1/0.10	6/0.60
Reputation/image	0.10	8/0.80	7/0.70	10/1.00	1/0.10	6/0.60
Manufacturing capability	0.10	2/0.20	10/1.00	4/0.40	5/0.50	1/0.10
Technological skills	0.05	10/0.50	1/0.05	7/0.35	3/0.15	8/0.40
Dealer network/distribution capability	0.05	9/0.45	4/0.20	10/0.50	5/0.25	1/0.05
New product innovation capability	0.05	9/0.45	4/0.20	10/0.50	5/0.25	1/0.05
Financial resources	0.10	5/0.50	10/1.00	7/0.70	3/0.30	1/0.10
Relative cost position	0.30	5/1.50	10/3.00	3/0.95	1/0.30	4/1.20
Customer service capabilities	0.15	5/0.75	7/1.05	10/1.50	1/0.15	4/0.60
Sum of importance weights	1.00					
Weighted overall strength rating		5.95	7.70	6.85	2.10	3.70

Conversely, the bigger the difference between a company's overall rating and the scores of *higher-rated* rivals, the greater its implied *net competitive disadvantage*. Thus, ABC's total score of 61 (see the top half of Table 3.4) signals a much greater net competitive advantage over Rival 4 (with a score of 32) than over Rival 1 (with a score of 58) but indicates a moderate net competitive disadvantage against Rival 2 (with an overall score of 71).

However, a better method is a *weighted rating system* (shown in the bottom half of Table 3.4) because the different measures of competitive strength are unlikely to be equally important. In an industry where the products/services of rivals are virtually identical, for instance, having low unit costs relative to rivals is nearly always the most important determinant of competitive strength. In an industry with strong product differentiation, the most significant measures of competitive strength may be brand awareness, amount of advertising, product attractiveness, and distribution capability. In a weighted rating system each measure of competitive strength is assigned a weight based on its perceived importance in shaping competitive success. A weight could be as high as 0.75 (maybe even higher) in situations where one particular competitive variable is overwhelmingly decisive, or a weight could be as low as 0.20 when two or three strength measures are more important than the rest. Lesser competitive strength indicators can carry weights of 0.05 or 0.10. No matter whether the differences between the importance weights are big or little, *the sum of the weights must add up to 1.0.*

Weighted strength ratings are calculated by rating each competitor on each strength measure (using the 1 to 10 rating scale) and multiplying the assigned rating by the assigned weight (a rating of 4 times a weight of 0.20 gives a weighted rating, or score, of 0.80). Again, the company with the highest rating on a given measure has an implied competitive edge on that measure, with the size of its edge reflected in the difference between its rating and rivals' ratings. The weight attached to the measure indicates how important the edge is. Summing a company's weighted strength ratings for all the measures yields an overall strength rating. Comparisons of the weighted overall strength scores indicate which competitors are in the strongest and weakest competitive positions and who has how big a net competitive advantage over whom.

> A weighted competitive strength analysis is conceptually stronger than an unweighted analysis because of the inherent weakness in assuming that all the strength measures are equally important.

Note in Table 3.4 that the unweighted and weighted rating schemes produce different orderings of the companies. In the weighted system, ABC Company drops from second to third in strength, and Rival 1 jumps from third into first because of its high strength ratings on the two most important factors. Weighting the importance of the strength measures can thus make a significant difference in the outcome of the assessment.

Competitive strength assessments provide useful conclusions about a company's competitive situation. The ratings show how a company compares against rivals, factor by factor or capability by capability, thus revealing where it is strongest and weakest, and against whom. Moreover, the overall competitive strength scores indicate how all the different factors add up—whether the company is at a net competitive advantage or disadvantage against each rival. The firm with the largest overall competitive strength rating enjoys the strongest competitive position, with the size of its net competitive advantage reflected by how much its score exceeds the scores of rivals.

Knowing where a company is competitively strong and where it is weak in comparison to specific rivals is valuable in deciding on specific actions to strengthen its ability to compete. As a general rule, a company should try to leverage its competitive strengths (areas where it scores higher than rivals) into sustainable competitive advantage. Furthermore, it makes sense for the company to initiate actions to remedy its important competitive weaknesses (areas where its scores are below those of rivals); at the very least, it should try to narrow the gap against companies with higher strength ratings—when the leader is at 10, improving from a rating of 3 to a rating of 7 can be significant.

In addition, the competitive strength ratings point to which rival companies may be vulnerable to competitive attack and the areas where they are weakest. When a company has important competitive strengths in areas where one or more rivals are weak, it makes sense to consider offensive moves to exploit rivals' competitive weaknesses.

> High competitive strength ratings vis-à-vis competitors signal opportunity for a company to improve its long-term market position.

Identifying the Strategic Issues That Merit Managerial Attention

The final and most important analytical step is to zero in on exactly what strategic issues that company managers need to address—and resolve—for the company to be

> Zeroing in on the strategic issues a company faces and compiling a "worry list" of problems and roadblocks creates a strategic agenda of problems that merit prompt managerial attention.

more financially and competitively successful in the years ahead. This step involves drawing on the results of both industry and competitive analysis and the evaluations of the company's own competitiveness. The task here is to get a clear fix on exactly what strategic and competitive challenges confront the company, which of the company's competitive shortcomings need fixing, what obstacles stand in the way of improving the company's competitive position in the marketplace, and what specific problems merit front-burner attention by company

managers. *Pinpointing the precise things that management needs to worry about sets the agenda for deciding what actions to take next to improve the company's performance and business outlook.*

The "worry list" of issues and problems that have to be wrestled with can include such things as *how* to stave off market challenges from new foreign competitors, *how* to combat the price discounting of rivals, *how* to reduce the company's high costs and pave the way for price reductions, *how* to sustain the company's present rate of growth in light of slowing buyer demand, *whether* to expand the company's product line, *whether* to correct the company's competitive deficiencies by acquiring a rival company with the missing strengths, *whether* to expand into foreign markets rapidly or cautiously, *whether* to reposition the company and move to a different strategic group, *what to do* about growing buyer interest in substitute products, and *what to do* about the aging demographics of the company's customer base.

What turns up on the list of concerns about "how to . . . ,"

> A good strategy must contain ways to deal with all the strategic issues and obstacles that stand in the way of the company's financial and competitive success in the years ahead.

"whether to . . . ," and "what to do about . . . " signals whether the company will be able to continue the same basic strategy with minor adjustments or whether major overhaul is called for. If the worry list is relatively minor, thus suggesting the company's strategy is mostly on track and reasonably well matched to the company's overall situation, company managers seldom need to go much beyond fine-tuning of the present strategy. If, however, the issues and problems confronting the

company are serious and indicate the present strategy is not well suited for the road ahead, the task of crafting a better strategy has got to go to the top of management's action agenda.

Key Points

There are five key questions to consider in analyzing a company's own particular competitive circumstances and its competitive position vis-à-vis key rivals:

1. *How well is the present strategy working?* This involves evaluating the strategy from a qualitative standpoint (completeness, internal consistency, rationale, and suitability to the situation) and also from a quantitative standpoint (the strategic and financial results the strategy is producing). The stronger a company's current

overall performance, the less likely the need for radical strategy changes. The weaker a company's performance and/or the faster the changes in its external situation (which can be gleaned from industry and competitive analysis), the more its current strategy must be questioned.

2. *What are the company's resource strengths and weaknesses, and its external opportunities and threats?* A SWOT analysis provides an overview of a firm's situation and is an essential component of crafting a strategy tightly matched to the company's situation. The two most important parts of SWOT analysis are (1) drawing conclusions about what story the compilation of strengths, weaknesses, opportunities, and threats tells about the company's overall situation, and (2) acting on those conclusions to better match the company's strategy, to its resource strengths and market opportunities, to correct the important weaknesses, and to defend against external threats. A company's resource strengths, competencies, and competitive capabilities are strategically relevant because they are the most logical and appealing building blocks for strategy; resource weaknesses are important because they may represent vulnerabilities that need correction. External opportunities and threats come into play because a good strategy necessarily aims at capturing a company's most attractive opportunities and at defending against threats to its well-being.

3. *Are the company's prices and costs competitive?* One telling sign of whether a company's situation is strong or precarious is whether its prices and costs are competitive with those of industry rivals. Value chain analysis and benchmarking are essential tools in determining whether the company is performing particular functions and activities cost-effectively, learning whether its costs are in line with competitors, and deciding which internal activities and business processes need to be scrutinized for improvement. Value chain analysis teaches that how competently a company manages its value chain activities relative to rivals is a key to building valuable competencies and competitive capabilities and then leveraging them into sustainable competitive advantage.

4. *Is the company competitively stronger or weaker than key rivals?* The key appraisals here involve how the company matches up against key rivals on industry key success factors and other chief determinants of competitive success and whether and why the company has a competitive advantage or disadvantage. Quantitative competitive strength assessments, using the method presented in Table 3.4, indicate where a company is competitively strong and weak, and provide insight into the company's ability to defend or enhance its market position. As a rule a company's competitive strategy should be built around its competitive strengths and should aim at shoring up areas where it is competitively vulnerable. Also, the areas where company strengths match up against competitor weaknesses represent the best potential for new offensive initiatives.

5. *What strategic issues and problems merit front-burner managerial attention?* This analytical step zeros in on the strategic issues and problems that stand in the way of the company's success. It involves using the results of both industry and competitive analysis and company situation analysis to identify a "worry list" of issues to be resolved for the company to be financially and competitively successful in the years ahead.

Good company situation analysis, like good industry and competitive analysis, is a valuable precondition for good strategy-making. A competently done evaluation of a company's resource capabilities and competitive strengths exposes strong and weak points in the present strategy and how attractive or unattractive the company's competitive position is and why. Managers need such understanding to craft a strategy that is well suited to the company's competitive circumstances.

Exercise
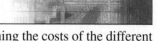

Review the information in Company Spotlight 3.1 concerning the costs of the different value chain activities associated with recording and distributing music CDs through traditional brick-and-mortar retail outlets. Then answer the following questions:

1. Does the growing popularity of downloading music from the Internet give rise to a new music industry value chain that differs considerably from the traditional value chain? Explain why or why not.

2. What costs are being cut out of the traditional value chain or bypassed as recording studios begin to sell downloadable files of artists' recordings and buyers make their own custom CDs (or play music directly from their PCs)?

3. How much more cost-effective is the value chain for selling downloadable files direct to consumers than the traditional industry value chain?

4. What do you think the growing popularity of downloading music from the Internet is doing to the competitiveness and future business prospects of brick-and-mortar retail music chains?

CHAPTER 4

Crafting a Strategy
The Quest for Competitive Advantage

Successful business strategy is about actively shaping the game you play, not just playing the game you find.
—Adam M. Brandenburger and Barry J. Nalebuff

The essence of strategy lies in creating tomorrow's competitive advantages faster than competitors mimic the ones you possess today.
—Gary Hamel and C. K. Prahalad

Competitive strategy is about being different. It means deliberately choosing to perform activities differently or to perform different activities than rivals to deliver a unique mix of value.
—Michael E. Porter

Strategies for taking the hill won't necessarily hold it.
—Amar Bhide

This chapter focuses on a company's quest for competitive advantage—the strategy options for competing successfully in a particular industry and securing an attractive market position. This chapter surveys the menu of options a company has for crafting a strategy that is well suited both to industry and competitive conditions and to its own resources and competitive circumstances and that holds good prospects for competitive advantage. We begin by describing the five *basic competitive strategy options*—which of the five to employ is a company's first and foremost choice in crafting an overall strategy. Next on a company's menu of strategic choices are the various *strategic actions* it can take to complement its choice of a basic competitive strategy:

■ What use to make of strategic alliances and collaborative partnerships.

■ What use to make of mergers and acquisitions.

■ Whether to integrate backward or forward into more stages of the industry value chain.

■ Whether to outsource certain value chain activities or perform them in-house.

■ Whether and when to employ offensive and defensive moves.

■ Which of several ways to use the Internet as a distribution channel in positioning the company in the marketplace.

This chapter contains sections discussing the pros and cons of each of the above complementary strategic options. The next-to-last section in the chapter discusses the need for strategic choices in each functional area of a company's business (R&D, production, sales and marketing, finance, and so on) to support its basic competitive approach and complementary strategic moves. The chapter concludes with a brief look at the competitive importance of timing strategic moves—when it is advantageous to be a first-mover and when it is better to be a fast-follower or late-mover.

Figure 4.1 shows the menu of options a company has in crafting a strategy and the order in which the choices should generally be made. It also illustrates the structure of the chapter and the topics that will be covered.

The Five Generic Competitive Strategies

A company's **competitive strategy** deals exclusively with its plans for competing successfully—its specific efforts to please customers, its offensive and defensive moves to counter the maneuvers of rivals, its responses to whatever market conditions prevail at the moment, and its initiatives to strengthen its market position. Companies the world over are imaginative in conceiving competitive strategies to win customer favor. At most companies the aim, quite simply, is to do a significantly better job than rivals of providing what buyers are looking for and thereby secure a market edge over rivals. Winning in the marketplace is nearly always a result of actions to seek and secure a sustainable competitive advantage. A company has *competitive advantage* whenever it has an edge over rivals in attracting buyers and coping with competitive forces. There are many routes to competitive advantage, but they all involve giving buyers what they

> **Core Concept**
>
> The objective of **competitive strategy** is to knock the socks off rival companies by doing a better job of providing what buyers are looking for.

Figure 4.1   A Company's Menu of Strategy Options for Winning in the Marketplace

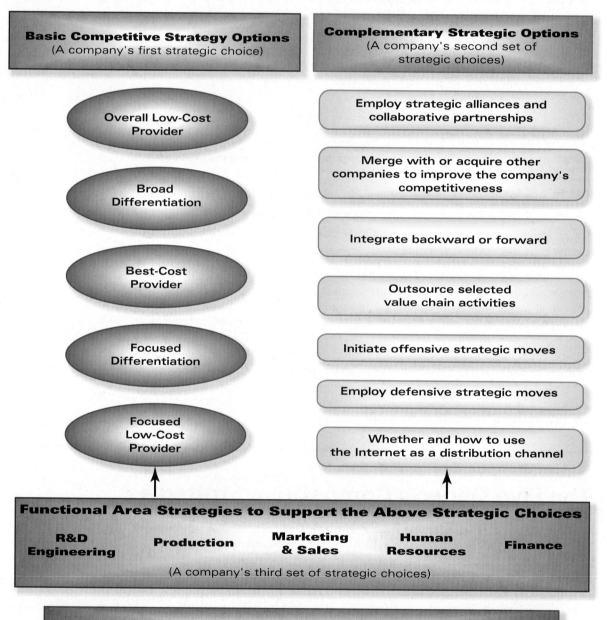

perceive as superior value—a good product at a low price; a superior product that is worth paying more for; or a best-value offering that represents an attractive combination of price, features, quality, service, and other appealing attributes. Delivering superior value—whatever form it takes—nearly always requires performing value chain activities differently than rivals and building competencies and resource capabilities that are not readily matched.

Because each company's strategic approach consists partly of custom-designed actions to fit its own circumstances and industry environment, there are countless variations in the competitive strategies that companies employ. Strictly speaking, there are as many competitive strategies as there are companies; the chances are indeed remote that any two companies—even companies in the same industry—will employ strategies that are exactly alike in every detail. However, when one strips away the details to get at the real substance, the biggest and most important differences among competitive strategies boil down to (1) whether a company's market target is broad or narrow, and (2) whether the company is pursuing a competitive advantage linked to low costs or product differentiation. Five distinct competitive strategy approaches stand out:[1]

1. *A low-cost provider strategy*—appealing to a broad spectrum of customers by being the overall low-cost provider of a product or service.

2. *A broad differentiation strategy*—seeking to differentiate the company's product/service offering from rivals' in ways that will appeal to a broad spectrum of buyers.

3. *A best-cost provider strategy*—giving customers more value for the money by incorporating good-to-excellent product attributes at a lower cost than rivals; the target is to have the lowest (best) costs and prices compared to rivals offering products with comparable attributes.

4. *A focused (or market niche) strategy based on lower cost*—concentrating on a narrow buyer segment and outcompeting rivals by serving niche members at a lower cost than rivals.

5. *A focused (or market niche) strategy based on differentiation*—concentrating on a narrow buyer segment and outcompeting rivals by offering niche members customized attributes that meet their tastes and requirements better than rivals' products.

Each of these five generic competitive approaches stakes out a different market position, as shown in Figure 4.2. Each involves distinctively different approaches to competing and operating the business. The listing in Table 4.1 highlights the contrasting features of these five competitive strategies; for simplicity, the two strains of focused strategies are combined under one heading since they differ fundamentally on only one feature—the basis of competitive advantage.

Low-Cost Provider Strategies

Striving to be the industry's overall low-cost provider is a powerful competitive approach in markets with many price-sensitive buyers. A company achieves low-cost leadership when it becomes the industry's lowest-cost provider rather than just being one of perhaps several competitors with comparatively low costs A low-cost provider's strategic target is meaningfully lower costs than rivals—but not the absolutely lowest possible cost. In striving for a cost advantage over rivals, managers must take care to include features and services that

> **Core Concept**
>
> A low-cost leader's basis for competitive advantage is lower overall costs than competitors. Successful low-cost leaders are exceptionally good at finding ways to drive costs out of their businesses.

Figure 4.2   The Five Generic Competitive Strategies:
Each Represents a Different Market Position

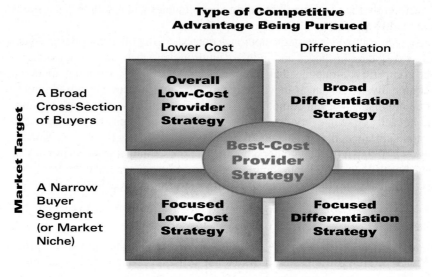

Source: Adapted from Michael E. Porter, *Competitive Strategy* (New York: Free Press, 1980), pp. 35–40.

buyers consider essential—*a product offering that is too frills-free sabotages the attractiveness of the company's product and can turn buyers off even if it is cheaper priced.* For maximum effectiveness, companies employing a low-cost provider strategy need to achieve their cost advantage in ways difficult for rivals to copy or match. If rivals find it relatively easy or inexpensive to imitate the leader's low-cost methods, then the leader's advantage will be too short-lived to yield a valuable edge in the marketplace.

A company has two options for translating a low-cost advantage over rivals into attractive profit performance. Option 1 is to use the lower-cost edge to underprice competitors and attract price-sensitive buyers in great enough numbers to increase total profits. The trick to profitably underpricing rivals is either to keep the size of the price cut smaller than the size of the firm's cost advantage (thus reaping the benefits of both a bigger profit margin per unit sold and the added profits on incremental sales) or to generate enough added volume to increase total profits despite thinner profit margins (larger volume can make up for smaller margins provided the underpricing of rivals brings in enough extra sales). Option 2 is to maintain the present price, be content with the present market share, and use the lower-cost edge to earn a higher profit margin on each unit sold, thereby raising the firm's total profits and overall return on investment.

Company Spotlight 4.1 describes Nucor Corporation's strategy for gaining low-cost leadership in manufacturing a variety of steel products.

The Two Major Avenues for Achieving a Cost Advantage   To achieve a cost advantage, a firm's cumulative costs across its overall value chain must be lower than competitors' cumulative costs. There are two ways to accomplish this:[2]

Table 4.1   DISTINGUISHING FEATURES OF THE FIVE GENERIC COMPETITIVE STRATEGIES

	Low-Cost Provider	Broad Differentiation	Best-Cost Provider	Focused Low-Cost Provider	Focused Differentiation
Strategic target	■ A broad cross-section of the market	■ A broad cross-section of the market	■ Value-conscious buyers	■ A narrow market niche where buyer needs and preferences are distinctively different	■ A narrow market niche where buyer needs and preferences are distinctively different
Basis of competitive advantage	■ Lower overall costs than competitors	■ Ability to offer buyers something attractively different from competitors	■ Ability to give customers more value for the money	■ Lower overall cost than rivals in serving niche members	■ Attributes that appeal specifically to niche members
Product line	■ A good basic product with few frills (acceptable quality and limited selection)	■ Many product variations; wide selection; emphasis on differentiating features	■ Items with appealing attributes; assorted upscale features	■ Features and attributes tailored to the tastes and requirements of niche members	■ Features and attributes tailored to the tastes and requirements of niche members
Production emphasis	■ A continuous search for cost reduction without sacrificing acceptable quality and essential features	■ Differentiating features buyers are willing to pay for; product superiority	■ Upscale features and appealing attributes at lower cost than rivals	■ A continuous search for cost reduction while incorporating features and attributes matched to niche member preferences	■ Custom-made products that match the tastes and requirements of niche members
Marketing emphasis	■ Try to make a virtue out of product features that lead to low cost	■ Tout differentiating features ■ Charge a premium price to cover the extra costs of differentiating features	■ Tout delivery of best value ■ Either deliver comparable features at a lower price than rivals or else match rivals on prices and provide better features	■ Communicate attractive features of a budget-priced product offering that fits niche buyers' expectations	■ Communicate how product offering does the best job of meeting niche buyers' expectations
Keys to sustaining the strategy	■ Economical prices/good value ■ Low costs, year after year, in every area of the business	■ Constant innovation to stay ahead of imitative competitors ■ A few key differentiating features	■ Unique expertise in simultaneously managing costs down while incorporating upscale features and attributes	■ Commitment to serving the niche at lowest overall cost; don't blur the firm's image by entering other market segments or adding other products to widen market appeal	■ Commitment to serving the niche better than rivals; don't blur the firm's image by entering other market segments or adding other products to widen market appeal

1. Outmanage rivals in the efficiency with which value chain activities are performed and in controlling the factors that drive the costs of value chain activities.
2. Revamp the firm's overall value chain to eliminate or bypass some cost-producing activities.

Let's look at each of the two approaches to securing a cost advantage.

COMPANY SPOTLIGHT 4.1
Nucor Corporation's Low-Cost Provider Strategy

Nucor Corporation is the leading minimill producer of such steel products as rolled steel, finished steel, steel joists, joist girders, steel decks, and grinding balls. It has over $4 billion in sales and produces over 10 million tons of steel annually. The company has pursued a strategy that has made it among the lowest-cost producers of steel in the world and has allowed the company to consistently outperform its rivals in terms of financial and market performance.

Nucor's low-cost strategy aims to give it a cost and pricing advantage in the commoditylike steel industry and leaves no part of the company's value chain neglected. The key elements of the strategy include the following:

- Using electric arc furnaces where scrap steel and directly reduced iron ore are melted and then sent to a continuous caster and rolling mill to be shaped into steel products, thereby eliminating an assortment of production processes from the value chain used by traditional integrated steel mills. Nucor's minimill value chain makes the use of coal, coke, and iron ore unnecessary; cuts investment in facilities and equipment (eliminating coke ovens, blast furnaces, basic oxygen furnaces, and ingot casters); and requires fewer employees than integrated mills.

- Striving hard for continuous improvement in the efficiency of its plants and frequently investing in state-of-the-art equipment to reduce unit costs. Nucor is known for its technological leadership and its aggressive pursuit of innovation.

- Carefully selecting plant sites to minimize inbound and outbound shipping costs and to take advantage of low rates for electricity (electric arc furnaces are heavy users of electricity). Nucor also avoids geographic areas where labor unions are a strong influence.

- Hiring a nonunion workforce that uses team-based incentive compensation systems (often opposed by unions). Operating and maintenance employees and supervisors are paid weekly bonuses based on the productivity of

Controlling the Cost Drivers There are nine major cost drivers that come into play in determining a company's costs in each activity segment of the value chain:[3]

1. *Economies or diseconomies of scale*—The costs of a particular value chain activity are often subject to economies or diseconomies of scale. Economies of scale arise whenever activities can be performed more cheaply at larger volumes than smaller volumes and from the ability to spread out certain costs like R&D and advertising over a greater sales volume. Astute management of activities subject to scale economies or diseconomies can be a major source of cost savings. For example, manufacturing economies can usually be achieved by simplifying the product line, scheduling longer production runs for fewer models, and using common parts and components in different models. In global industries, making separate products for each country market instead of selling a mostly standard product worldwide tends to boost unit costs because of lost time in model changeover, shorter production runs, and inability to reach the most economic scale of production for each country model.

2. *Experience and learning-curve effects*—The cost of performing an activity can decline over time as the learning and experience of company personnel builds. Learning/experience economies can stem from debugging and mastering newly introduced technologies, finding ways to improve plant layout and work flows, making product design modifications that streamline the assembly process, and the

their work group. The size of the bonus is based on the capabilities of the equipment employed and ranges from 80 percent to 150 percent of an employee's base pay; no bonus is paid if the equipment is not operating. Nucor's compensation program has boosted the company's labor productivity to levels nearly double the industry average while rewarding productive employees with annual compensation packages that exceed what their union counterparts earn by as much as 20 percent. Nucor has been able to attract and retain highly talented, productive, and dedicated employees. In addition, the company's healthy culture and results-oriented self-managed work teams allow the company to employ fewer supervisors than what would be needed with an hourly union workforce. Nucor is proud of the more than 7,000 employees that make up the total Nucor team.

- Heavily emphasizing consistent product quality and has rigorous quality systems.

- Minimizing general and administrative expenses by maintaining a lean staff at corporate headquarters (fewer than 125 employees) and allowing only four levels of management between the CEO and production workers. Headquarters offices are modestly furnished and located in an inexpensive building. The company minimizes reports, paperwork, and meetings to keep managers focused on value-adding activities. Nucor is noted not only for its streamlined organizational structure but also its frugality in travel and entertainment expenses—the company's top managers set the example by flying coach class, avoiding pricey hotels, and refraining from taking customers out for expensive dinners.

In 2001–2002, when many U.S. producers of steel products were in dire economic straits because of weak demand for steel and deep price discounting by foreign rivals, Nucor began acquiring state-of-the-art steel making facilities from bankrupt or nearly bankrupt rivals at bargain-basement prices, often at 20 percent to 25 percent of what it cost to construct the facilities. This gave Nucor much lower depreciation costs than rivals having comparable plants.

Nucor management's outstanding execution of its low-cost strategy and its commitment to drive out non-value-adding costs throughout its value chain has allowed it to grow at a considerably faster rate than its integrated steel mill rivals and maintain high industry-relative profit margins while aggressively competing on price. In 2002, Nucor became the largest U.S. producer of steel products, overtaking U.S. Steel, the industry leader for over 70 years.

Source: Company annual reports, news releases, and website.

---

added speed and knowledge that accrues from repeatedly siting and building new plants, retail outlets, or distribution centers. Aggressively managed low-cost providers pay diligent attention to capturing the benefits of learning and experience and to keeping the benefits proprietary to whatever extent possible.

3. *The cost of key resource inputs*—The cost of performing value chain activities depends in part on what a firm has to pay for key resource inputs. Competitors do not all incur the same costs for items purchased from suppliers or for other resources. How well a company manages the costs of acquiring key resource inputs is often a big driver of costs. Input costs are a function of four factors:

   a) *Union versus nonunion labor*—Avoiding the use of union labor is often a key to keeping labor input costs low, not just because unions demand high wages but also because union work rules can stifle productivity. Such highly regarded low-cost manufacturers as Nucor and Cooper Tire are noted for their incentive compensation systems that promote very high levels of labor productivity—at both companies, nonunion workers earn more than their unionized counterparts at rival companies but their high productivity results in lower labor costs per unit produced.

   b) *Bargaining power vis-à-vis suppliers*—Many large enterprises (e.g., Wal-Mart, Home Depot, the world's major motor vehicle producers) have used their bargaining clout in purchasing large volumes to wrangle good prices on their purchases from suppliers. Having greater buying power than rivals can be an important source of cost advantage.

    c) *Locational variables*—Locations differ in their prevailing wage levels, tax rates, energy costs, inbound and outbound shipping and freight costs, and so on. Opportunities may exist for reducing costs by relocating plants, field offices, warehousing, or headquarters operations.

    d) *Supply chain management expertise*—Some companies have more efficient supply chain expertise than others and are able to squeeze out cost savings via partnerships with suppliers that lower the costs of purchased materials and components, e-procurement systems, and inbound logistics.

4. *Links with other activities in the company or industry value chain*—When the cost of one activity is affected by how other activities are performed, costs can be managed downward by making sure that linked activities are performed in cooperative and coordinated fashion. For example, when a company's materials inventory costs or warranty costs are linked to the activities of suppliers, cost savings can be achieved by working cooperatively with key suppliers on the design of parts and components, quality-assurance procedures, just-in-time delivery, and integrated materials supply. The costs of new product development can often be managed downward by having cross-functional task forces (perhaps including representatives of suppliers and key customers) jointly work on R&D, product design, manufacturing plans, and market launch. Links with forward channels tend to center on location of warehouses, materials handling, outbound shipping, and packaging. Nail manufacturers, for example, learned that delivering nails in prepackaged 1-pound, 5-pound, and 10-pound assortments instead of 100-pound bulk cartons could reduce a hardware dealer's labor costs in filling individual customer orders. The lesson here is that effective coordination of linked activities anywhere in the value chain holds potential for cost reduction.

5. *Sharing opportunities with other organizational or business units within the enterprise*—Different product lines or business units within an enterprise can often share the same order processing and customer billing systems, utilize a common sales force to call on customers, share the same warehouse and distribution facilities, or rely on a common customer service and technical support team. Such combining of like activities and sharing of resources across sister units can create significant cost savings. Furthermore, there are times when the know-how gained in one division or geographic unit can be used to help lower costs in another; sharing know-how across organizational lines has significant cost-saving potential when cross-unit value chain activities are similar and know-how is readily transferred from one unit to another.

6. *The benefits of vertical integration versus outsourcing*—Partially or fully integrating into the activities of either suppliers or distribution channel allies can allow an enterprise to detour suppliers or buyers with considerable bargaining power. Vertical integration forward or backward also has potential if there are significant cost-savings from having a single firm perform adjacent activities in the industry value chain. But more often it is cheaper to outsource certain functions and activities to outside specialists, who by virtue of their expertise and volume can perform the activity/function more cheaply.

7. *Timing considerations associated with first-mover advantages and disadvantages*—Sometimes the first major brand in the market is able to establish and maintain its brand name at a lower cost than later brand arrivals. Competitors looking to go head-to-head against such first-movers as eBay, Yahoo!, and Amazon.com have to spend heavily to come close to achieving the same brand awareness and name recognition.

On other occasions, such as when technology is developing fast, late-purchasers can benefit from waiting to install second- or third-generation equipment that is both cheaper and more efficient; first-generation users often incur added costs associated with debugging and learning how to use an immature and unperfected technology. Likewise, companies that follow rather than lead new product development efforts sometimes avoid many of the costs that pioneers incur in performing pathbreaking R&D and opening up new markets.

8. *The percentage of capacity utilization*—Capacity utilization is a big cost driver for those value chain activities associated with substantial fixed costs. Higher rates of capacity utilization allow depreciation and other fixed costs to be spread over a larger unit volume, thereby lowering fixed costs per unit. The more capital-intensive the business, or the higher the percentage of fixed costs as a percentage of total costs, the more important this cost driver becomes because there's such a stiff unit-cost penalty for underutilizing existing capacity. In such cases, finding ways to operate close to full capacity year-round can be an important source of cost advantage.

9. *Strategic choices and operating decisions*—A company's costs can be driven up or down by a fairly wide assortment of managerial decisions:

   a) Adding/cutting the services provided to buyers.

   b) Incorporating more/fewer performance and quality features into the product.

   c) Increasing/decreasing the number of different channels utilized in distributing the firm's product.

   d) Lengthening/shortening delivery times to customers.

   e) Putting more/less emphasis than rivals on the use of incentive compensation, wage increases, and fringe benefits to motivate employees and boost worker productivity.

   f) Raising/lowering the specifications for purchased materials.

For a company to outmanage rivals in performing value chain activities cost-effectively, its managers must possess a sophisticated understanding of the factors that drive the costs of each activity. And then they must not only use their knowledge about the cost drivers to squeeze out cost savings all along the value chain but also be so much more ingenious and committed than rivals in achieving cost-saving efficiencies that the company ends up with a sustainable cost advantage.

> Outperforming rivals in controlling the factors that drive costs is a very demanding managerial exercise.

Revamping the Value Chain Dramatic cost advantages can emerge from finding innovative ways to eliminate or bypass cost-producing value chain activities. The primary ways companies can achieve a cost advantage by reconfiguring their value chains include:

▪ *Making greater use of Internet technology applications*—In recent years the Internet and Internet technology applications have become powerful and pervasive tools for reengineering company and industry value chains. For instance, Internet technology has revolutionized supply chain management. Using software packages from any of several vendors, company procurement personnel can—with only a few mouse clicks within one seamless system—check materials inventories against incoming customer orders, check suppliers' stocks, check the latest prices for parts and components at auction and e-sourcing websites, and check Federal Express delivery schedules. Electronic data interchange software permits the relevant details of incoming customer orders to be instantly shared with the suppliers of needed parts and components. All this lays the foundation for just-in-time deliveries of parts and components, and for the production of parts and components, to be matched closely to assembly plant requirements and production schedules—and such coordination produces savings for both suppliers and manufacturers. Via the Internet, manufacturers can collaborate closely with parts and components suppliers in designing new products and reducing the time it takes to get them into production. Warranty claims and product performance problems involving supplier components can be made available instantly to the relevant suppliers so that corrections can be expedited. Various e-procurement software packages streamline the purchasing process by eliminating much of the manual handling of data and by substituting electronic communication for paper documents such as requests for quotations, purchase orders, order acceptances, and shipping notices.

Manufacturers are using Internet applications to link customer orders to production at their plants and to deliveries of components from suppliers. Real-time sharing of customer orders with suppliers facilitates just-in-time deliveries of parts and slices parts inventory costs. It also allows both manufacturers and their suppliers to gear production to match demand for both components and finished goods. Online systems that monitor actual sales permit more accurate demand forecasting, thereby helping both manufacturers and their suppliers adjust their production schedules as swings in buyer demand are detected. Data sharing, starting with customer orders and going all the way back to components production, coupled with the use of enterprise resource planning (ERP) and manufacturing execution system (MES) software, can make custom manufacturing just as cheap as mass production—and sometimes cheaper. It can also greatly reduce production times and labor costs. J. D. Edwards, a specialist in ERP software, teamed with Camstar Systems, a specialist in MES software, to cut Lexmark's production time for inkjet printers from four hours to 24 minutes.

The instant communications features of the Internet, combined with all the real-time data sharing and information availability, have the further effect of breaking down corporate bureaucracies and reducing overhead costs. The whole "back-office" data management process (order processing, invoicing, customer accounting, and other kinds of transaction costs) can be handled fast, accurately, and with less paperwork and fewer personnel. The time savings and transaction cost reductions associated with doing business online can be quite significant across both company and industry value chains.

Company Spotlight 4.2 describes how one company is using Internet technology to improve both the effectiveness and the efficiency of the activities comprising its potato chip business.

▪ *Using direct-to-end-user sales and marketing approaches*—Costs in the wholesale/retail portions of the value chain frequently represent 35–50 percent of the price final consumers pay. Software developers are increasingly using the Internet to market and deliver their products directly to buyers; allowing customers to download software directly from the Internet eliminates the costs of producing and packaging CDs and cuts out the host of activities, costs, and markups associated with shipping and distributing software through wholesale and retail channels. By cutting all these costs and activities out of the value chain, software developers have the pricing room to boost their profit margins and still sell their products below levels that retailers would have to charge. The major airlines have stopped

Utz Quality Foods' Use of Internet Technology to Reengineer Value Chain Activities

Utz Quality Foods, the number three maker of salty snacks in the United States, with sales of over $200 million, recently implemented an Internet-based sales-tracking system called UtzFocus that monitors sales of the company's chips and pretzel products at each supermarket and convenience store that carries the brand. The 500 drivers/salespeople who deliver Utz snacks directly to retail stores scattered from Massachusetts to North Carolina use handheld computers to upload daily sales data (product by product and store by store) to headquarters. Managers carefully monitor the results to spot missed deliveries, pinpoint stores with lagging sales, and measure the effectiveness of special promotions.

The UtzFocus system also keeps delivery personnel up-to-date on which stores are running specials on Utz products so that drivers can make sure they have ample supplies of the right products on their trucks—and since drivers get a 10 percent commission on sales, they have a stake in making UtzFocus work. The company has also installed machines with monitoring capabilities in all of its plants, and efforts are under way to hook them up to the company's intranet to generate real-time data on the usage of ingredients, measure how close chip-slicing machines are coming to the ideal thickness of 0.057 of an inch, track how many bags of chips the main factory's seven lines are turning out, and keep inventories of ingredients and plastic bags matched to production and sales requirements. This reengineering of the value chain has produced cost-saving efficiencies, improved the effectiveness of Utz's operations, and helped boost sales.

paying commissions to travel agents on ticket sales, thereby saving hundreds of millions of dollars in commissions. Airlines now sell most of their tickets directly to passengers via their websites, ticket counter agents, and telephone reservation systems.

- *Simplifying product design*—Using computer-assisted design techniques, reducing the number of parts, standardizing parts and components across models and styles, and shifting to an easy-to-manufacture product design can all simplify the value chain.

- *Stripping away the extras*—Offering only basic products or services can help a company cut costs associated with multiple features and options. Stripping extras is a favorite technique of the no-frills airlines like Southwest Airlines.

- *Shifting to a simpler, less capital-intensive, or more streamlined or flexible technological process*—Computer-assisted design and manufacture, or other flexible manufacturing systems, can accommodate both low-cost efficiency and product customization.

- *Bypassing the use of high-cost raw materials or component parts*—High-cost raw materials and parts can be designed out of the product.

- *Relocating facilities*—Moving plants closer to suppliers, customers, or both can help curtail inbound and outbound logistics costs.

- *Dropping the "something for everyone" approach*—Pruning slow-selling items from the product lineup and being content to meet the needs of most buyers rather than all buyers can eliminate activities and costs associated with numerous product versions.

An example of accruing significant cost advantages from creating altogether new value chain systems can be found in the beef-packing industry. The traditional cost chain involved raising cattle on scattered farms and ranches, shipping them live to labor-intensive, unionized slaughtering plants, and then transporting whole sides of beef to grocery retailers whose butcher departments cut them into smaller pieces and packaged them for sale to grocery shoppers. Iowa Beef Packers revamped the traditional chain with a radically different strategy—large automated plants employing nonunion workers were built near economically transportable supplies of cattle, and the meat was partially butchered at the processing plant into small, high-yield cuts (sometimes sealed in plastic casing ready for purchase) before being boxed and shipped to retailers. Iowa Beef's inbound cattle transportation expenses, traditionally a major cost item, were cut significantly by avoiding the weight losses that occurred when live animals were shipped long distances; major outbound shipping cost savings were achieved by not having to ship whole sides of beef with their high waste factor. The company's strategy was so successful that Iowa Beef became the largest U.S. meatpacker, surpassing the former industry leaders, Swift, Wilson, and Armour.[4]

Southwest Airlines has reconfigured the traditional value chain of commercial airlines to lower costs and thereby offer dramatically lower fares to passengers. It has mastered fast turnarounds at the gates (about 25 minutes versus 45 minutes for rivals); because the short turnarounds allow the planes to fly more hours per day, Southwest can schedule more flights per day with fewer aircraft. Southwest does not offer inflight meals, assigned seating, baggage transfer to connecting airlines, or first-class seating and service, thereby eliminating all the cost-producing activities associated with these features. The company's online reservation system and e-ticketing capability encourage customers to bypass travel agents and also reduce staffing requirements at telephone reservation centers and at check-in counters.

Dell Computer has proved a pioneer in redesigning its value chain architecture in assembling and marketing PCs. Whereas Dell's major rivals (Compaq, Hewlett-Packard, Sony, and Toshiba) produce their models in volume and sell them through independent resellers and retailers, Dell has elected to market directly to customers, building its PCs as customers order them and shipping them to customers within a few days of receiving the order. Dell's value chain approach has proved cost-effective in coping with the PC industry's blink-of-an-eye product life cycle. The build-to-order strategy enables the company to avoid misjudging buyer demand for its various models and being saddled with quickly obsolete excess components and finished-goods inventories. Also, Dell's sell-direct strategy slices reseller/retailer costs and margins out of the value chain (although some of these savings are offset by the cost of Dell's direct marketing and customer support activities—functions that would otherwise be performed by resellers and retailers). Partnerships with suppliers that facilitate just-in-time deliveries of components and minimize Dell's inventory costs, coupled with Dell's extensive use of e-commerce technologies further reduce Dell's costs. Dell's value chain approach is widely considered to have made it the global low-cost leader in the PC industry.

The Keys to Success in Achieving Low-Cost Leadership

> Success in achieving a low-cost edge over rivals comes from exploring all the avenues for cost reduction and pressing for continuous cost reductions across all aspects of the company's value chain year after year.

To succeed with a low-cost-provider strategy, company managers have to scrutinize each cost-creating activity and determine what drives its cost. Then they have to use this knowledge about the cost drivers to manage the costs of each activity downward, exhaustively pursuing cost savings throughout the value chain. They have to be proactive in restructuring the value chain to eliminate nonessential work steps and low-value activities. Normally, low-cost producers work diligently to create cost-conscious corporate cultures that feature broad employee participation in continuous cost improvement efforts and limited perks and frills for executives. They strive to operate with exceptionally small corporate staffs to keep administrative costs to a minimum. Many successful low-cost leaders also benchmark costs against best-in-class performers of an activity to keep close tabs on how well they are doing at cost control.

But while low-cost providers are champions of frugality, they are usually aggressive in investing in resources and capabilities that promise to drive costs out of the business. Wal-Mart, one of the foremost practitioners of low-cost leadership, employs state-of-the-art technology throughout its operations—its distribution facilities are an automated showcase, it uses online systems to order goods from suppliers and manage inventories, it equips its stores with cutting-edge sales-tracking and check-out systems, and it operates a private satellite communications system that daily sends point-of-sale data to 4,000 vendors. Wal-Mart's information and communications systems and capabilities are more sophisticated than those of virtually any other retail chain in the world.

Other companies noted for their successful use of low-cost provider strategies include Lincoln Electric in arc welding equipment, Briggs & Stratton in small gasoline engines, Bic in ballpoint pens, Black & Decker in power tools, Stride Rite in footwear, Beaird-Poulan in chain saws, and General Electric and Whirlpool in major home appliances.

When a Low-Cost Provider Strategy Works Best A competitive strategy predicated on low-cost leadership is particularly powerful when:

- *Price competition among rival sellers is especially vigorous*—Low-cost providers are in the best position to compete offensively on the basis of price, to use the appeal of lower price to grab sales (and market share) from rivals, to remain profitable in the face of strong price competition, and to survive price wars.

- *The products of rival sellers are essentially identical and supplies are readily available from any of several eager sellers*—Commoditylike products and/or ample supplies set the stage for lively price competition; in such markets, it is less efficient, higher-cost companies whose profits get squeezed the most.

- *There are few ways to achieve product differentiation that have value to buyers*— When the differences between brands do not matter much to buyers, buyers are nearly always very sensitive to price differences and shop the market for the best price.

- *Most buyers use the product in the same ways*—With common user requirements, a standardized product can satisfy the needs of buyers, in which case low selling price, not features or quality, becomes the dominant factor in causing buyers to choose one seller's product over another's.

- *Buyers incur low costs in switching their purchases from one seller to another*— Low switching costs give buyers the flexibility to shift purchases to lower-priced sellers having equally good products or to attractively priced substitute products. A low-cost leader is well positioned to use low price to induce its customers not to switch to rival brands or substitutes.

- *Buyers are large and have significant power to bargain down prices*—Low-cost providers have partial profit-margin protection in bargaining with high-volume buyers, since powerful buyers are rarely able to bargain price down past the survival level of the next most cost-efficient seller.

■ *Industry newcomers use introductory low prices to attract buyers and build a customer base*—The low-cost leader can use price cuts of its own to make it harder for a new rival to win customers; the pricing power of the low-cost provider acts as a barrier for new entrants.

> A low-cost provider is in the best position to win the business of price-sensitive buyers, set the floor on market price, and still earn a profit.

As a rule, the more price-sensitive buyers are, the more appealing a low-cost strategy becomes. A low-cost company's ability to set the industry's price floor and still earn a profit erects protective barriers around its market position.

The Pitfalls of a Low-Cost Provider Strategy   Perhaps the biggest pitfall of a low-cost provider strategy is getting carried away with overly aggressive price cutting and ending up with lower, rather than higher, profitability. A low-cost/low-price advantage results in superior profitability only if (1) prices are cut by less than the size of the cost advantage or (2) the added gains in unit sales are large enough to bring in a bigger total profit despite lower margins per unit sold. A company with a 5 percent cost advantage cannot cut prices 20 percent, end up with a volume gain of only 10 percent, and still expect to earn higher profits!

A second big pitfall is not emphasizing avenues of cost advantage that can be kept proprietary or that relegate rivals to playing catch-up. The value of a cost advantage depends on its sustainability. Sustainability, in turn, hinges on whether the company achieves its cost advantage in ways difficult for rivals to copy or match.

> A low-cost provider's product offering must always contain enough attributes to be attractive to prospective buyers—low price, by itself, is not always appealing to buyers.

A third pitfall is becoming too fixated on cost reduction. Low cost cannot be pursued so zealously that a firm's offering ends up being too features-poor to generate buyer appeal. Furthermore, a company driving hard to push its costs down has to guard against misreading or ignoring increased buyer interest in added features or service, declining buyer sensitivity to price, or new developments that start to alter how buyers use the product. A low-cost zealot risks losing market ground if buyers start opting for more upscale or features-rich products.

Even if these mistakes are avoided, a low-cost competitive approach still carries risk. Cost-saving technological breakthroughs or the emergence of still-lower-cost value chain models can nullify a low-cost leader's hard-won position. The current leader may have difficulty in shifting quickly to the new technologies or value chain approaches because heavy investments lock it in (at least temporarily) to its present value chain approach.

Differentiation Strategies

> **Core Concept**
>
> The essence of a broad differentiation strategy is to be unique in ways that are valuable to a wide range of customers.

Differentiation strategies are attractive whenever buyers' needs and preferences are too diverse to be fully satisfied by a standardized product or by sellers with identical capabilities. A company attempting to succeed through differentiation must study buyers' needs and behavior carefully to learn what buyers consider important, what they think has value, and what they are willing to pay for. Then the company has to incorporate buyer-desired attributes into its product or service offering that will clearly set it apart from rivals. Competitive advantage results once a sufficient number of buyers become strongly attached to the differentiated attributes.

Successful differentiation allows a firm to:

- Command a premium price for its product, and/or

- Increase unit sales (because additional buyers are won over by the differentiating features), and/or

- Gain buyer loyalty to its brand (because some buyers are strongly attracted to the differentiating features and bond with the company and its products).

Differentiation enhances profitability whenever the extra price the product commands outweighs the added costs of achieving the differentiation. Company differentiation strategies fail when buyers don't value the brand's uniqueness and/or when a company's approach to differentiation is easily copied or matched by its rivals.

Types of Differentiation Themes Companies can pursue differentiation from many angles: a unique taste (Dr Pepper, Listerine); multiple features (Microsoft Windows, Microsoft Office); wide selection and one-stop shopping (Home Depot, Amazon.com); superior service (Federal Express); spare parts availability (Caterpillar guarantees 48-hour spare parts delivery to any customer anywhere in the world or else the part is furnished free); engineering design and performance (Mercedes, BMW); prestige and distinctiveness (Rolex); product reliability (Johnson & Johnson in baby products); quality manufacture (Karastan in carpets, Michelin in tires, Honda in automobiles); technological leadership (3M Corporation in bonding and coating products); a full range of services (Charles Schwab in stock brokerage); a complete line of products (Campbell's soups); and top-of-the-line image and reputation (Ralph Lauren and Starbucks).

The most appealing approaches to differentiation are those that are hard or expensive for rivals to duplicate. Indeed, resourceful competitors can, in time, clone almost any product or feature or attribute. If Coca-Cola introduces a vanilla-flavored soft drink, so can Pepsi; if Ford offers a 50,000-mile bumper-to-bumper warranty on its new vehicles, so can Volkswagen and Nissan. This is why *sustainable* differentiation usually has to be linked to core competencies, unique competitive capabilities, and superior management of value chain activities that competitors cannot readily match. As a rule, differentiation yields a longer-lasting and more profitable competitive edge when it is based on product innovation, technical superiority, product quality and reliability, comprehensive customer service, and unique competitive capabilities. Such differentiating attributes tend to be tough for rivals to copy or offset profitably, and buyers widely perceive them as having value.

> Easy-to-copy differentiating features cannot produce sustainable competitive advantage.

Where along the Value Chain to Create the Differentiating Attributes Differentiation is not something hatched in marketing and advertising departments, nor is it limited to the catchalls of quality and service. Differentiation opportunities can exist in activities all along an industry's value chain; possibilities include the following:

- *Supply chain activities* that ultimately spill over to affect the performance or quality of the company's end product. Starbucks gets high ratings on its coffees partly because it has very strict specifications on the coffee beans purchased from suppliers.

- *Product R&D activities* that aim at improved product designs and performance features, expanded end uses and applications, more frequent first-on-the-market victories, wider product variety and selection, added user safety, greater recycling capability, or enhanced environmental protection.

- *Production R&D and technology-related activities* that permit custom-order manufacture at an efficient cost; make production methods safer for the environment; or improve product quality, reliability, and appearance. Many manufacturers have developed flexible manufacturing systems that allow different models to be made or different options to be added on the same assembly line. Being able to provide buyers with made-to-order products can be a potent differentiating capability.

- *Manufacturing activities* that reduce product defects, prevent premature product failure, extend product life, allow better warranty coverages, improve economy of use, result in more end-user convenience, or enhance product appearance. The quality edge enjoyed by Japanese automakers stems partly from their distinctive competence in performing assembly-line activities.

- *Outbound logistics and distribution activities* that allow for faster delivery, more accurate order filling, lower shipping costs, and fewer warehouse and on-the-shelf stockouts.

- *Marketing, sales, and customer service activities* that result in superior technical assistance to buyers, faster maintenance and repair services, more and better product information provided to customers, more and better training materials for end users, better credit terms, quicker order processing, or greater customer convenience.

Managers need keen understanding of the sources of differentiation and the activities that drive uniqueness to devise a sound differentiation strategy and evaluate various differentiation approaches.

Achieving a Differentiation-Based Competitive Advantage

While it is easy enough to grasp that a successful differentiation strategy must entail creating buyer value in ways unmatched by rivals, the big question is which of four basic differentiating approaches to take in delivering unique buyer value. One approach is to *incorporate product attributes and user features that lower the buyer's overall costs of using the company's product.* Making a company's product more economical for a buyer to use can be done by reducing the buyer's raw materials waste (providing cut-to-size components), reducing a buyer's inventory requirements (providing just-in-time deliveries), increasing maintenance intervals and product reliability so as to lower a buyer's repair and maintenance costs, using online systems to reduce a buyer's procurement and order processing costs, and providing free technical support.

A second approach is to *incorporate features that raise product performance.*[5] This can be accomplished with attributes that provide buyers greater reliability, durability, convenience, or ease of use. Other performance-enhancing options include making the company's product or service cleaner, safer, quieter, or more maintenance-free than rival brands. A third approach is to *incorporate features that enhance buyer satisfaction in noneconomic or intangible ways.* Goodyear's Aquatread tire design appeals to safety-conscious motorists wary of slick roads. BMW, Ralph Lauren, and Rolex have differentiation-based competitive advantages linked to buyer desires for status, image, prestige, upscale fashion, superior craftsmanship, and the finer things in life. L. L. Bean makes its mail-order customers feel secure in their purchases by providing an unconditional guarantee with no time limit: "All of our products are guaranteed to give 100 percent satisfaction in every way. Return anything purchased from us at any time if it proves otherwise. We will replace it, refund your purchase price, or credit your credit card, as you wish."

Core Concept

A differentiator's basis for competitive advantage is either a product/service offering whose attributes differ significantly from the offerings of rivals or a set of capabilities for delivering customer value that rivals don't have.

A fourth approach is to differentiate on the basis of capabilities—*to deliver value to customers via competitive capabilities that rivals don't have or can't afford to match.*[6] Japanese automakers can bring new models to market faster than American and European automakers, thereby allowing the Japanese companies to satisfy changing consumer preferences for one vehicle style versus another. CNN has the capability to cover breaking news stories faster and more completely than the major networks. Microsoft has stronger capabilities to design, create, distribute, and advertise an array of software products for PC applications than any of its rivals.

Keeping the Cost of Differentiation in Line   Company efforts to achieve differentiation usually raise costs. The trick to profitable differentiation is either to keep the costs of achieving differentiation below the price premium the differentiating attributes can command in the marketplace (thus increasing the profit margin per unit sold) or to offset thinner profit margins with enough added volume to increase total profits. It usually makes sense to incorporate differentiating features that are not costly but that add to buyer satisfaction. Federal Express (FedEx) installed systems that allowed customers to track packages in transit by connecting to FedEx's website and entering the airbill number; some hotels and motels provide free continental breakfasts, exercise facilities, and in-room coffeemaking amenities; publishers are using their websites to deliver complementary educational materials to the buyers of their textbooks.

When a Differentiation Strategy Works Best   Differentiation strategies tend to work best in market circumstances where:

- *There are many ways to differentiate the product or service and many buyers perceive these differences as having value*—Unless buyers have strong preferences about certain features, profitable differentiation opportunities are very restricted.

- *Buyer needs and uses are diverse*—The more diverse buyer preferences are, the more room firms have to pursue different approaches to differentiation.

- *Few rival firms are following a similar differentiation approach*—There is less head-to-head rivalry when differentiating rivals go separate ways in pursuing uniqueness and try to appeal to buyers on different combinations of attributes.

- *Technological change is fast-paced and competition revolves around rapidly evolving product features*—Rapid product innovation and frequent introductions of next-version products help maintain buyer interest and provide space for companies to pursue separate differentiating paths.

The Pitfalls of a Differentiation Strategy   There are, of course, no guarantees that differentiation will produce a meaningful competitive advantage. If buyers see little value in the unique attributes or capabilities of a product, then the company's differentiation strategy will get a ho-hum market reception. In addition, attempts at differentiation are doomed to fail if competitors can quickly copy most or all of the appealing product attributes a company comes up with. Rapid imitation means that no rival achieves differentiation, since whenever one firm introduces some aspect of uniqueness that strikes the fancy of buyers, fast-following copycats quickly reestablish similarity. Thus, to build competitive advantage through differentiation a firm must search out sources of uniqueness that are time-consuming or burdensome for rivals to match. Other common pitfalls and mistakes in pursuing differentiation include:[7]

> **Core Concept**
>
> Any differentiating feature that works well tends to draw imitators.

- Trying to differentiate on the basis of something that does not lower a buyer's cost or enhance a buyer's well-being, as perceived by the buyer.
- Overdifferentiating so that the product quality or service level exceeds buyers' needs.
- Trying to charge too high a price premium. (The bigger the price differential, the harder it is to keep buyers from switching to lower-priced competitors.)

A low-cost provider strategy can defeat a differentiation strategy when buyers are satisfied with a basic product and don't think "extra" attributes are worth a higher price.

Best-Cost Provider Strategies

Best-cost provider strategies aim at giving customers *more value for the money*. The objective is to deliver superior value to buyers by satisfying their expectations on key quality/service/features/performance attributes and beating their expectations on price (given what rivals are charging for much the same attributes). A company achieves best-cost status from an ability to incorporate attractive attributes at a lower cost than rivals. To become a best-cost provider, a company must have the resources and capabilities to achieve good-to-excellent quality, incorporate appealing features, match product performance, and provide good-to-excellent customer service—all at a lower cost than rivals.

As Figure 4.1 indicates, best-cost provider strategies stake out a middle ground between pursuing a low-cost advantage and a differentiation advantage and between appealing to the broad market as a whole and a narrow market niche. From a competitive positioning standpoint, best-cost strategies are a *hybrid,* balancing a strategic emphasis on low cost against a strategic emphasis on differentiation (superior value). *The target market is value-conscious buyers,* perhaps a very sizable part of the overall market. *The competitive advantage of a best-cost provider is lower costs than rivals* in incorporating good-to-excellent attributes, putting the company in a position to underprice rivals whose products have similar appealing attributes.

A best-cost provider strategy is very appealing in markets where buyer diversity makes product differentiation the norm *and* where many buyers are also sensitive to price and value. This is because a best-cost provider can position itself near the middle of the market with either a medium-quality product at a below-average price or a high-quality product at an average price. Often, substantial numbers of buyers prefer midrange products rather than the cheap, basic products of low-cost producers or the expensive products of top-of-the-line differentiators. But unless a company has the resources, know-how, and capabilities to incorporate upscale product or service attributes at a lower cost than rivals, this strategy is ill-advised.

Company Spotlight 4.3 describes how Toyota has used a best-cost approach with its Lexus models.

The Big Risk of a Best-Cost Provider Strategy   The danger of a best-cost provider strategy is that a company using it will get squeezed between the strategies of firms using low-cost and differentiation strategies. Low-cost leaders may be able to siphon customers away with the appeal of a lower price. High-end differentiators may be able to steal customers away with the appeal of better product attributes. Thus, to be successful, a best-cost provider must offer buyers *significantly* better product attributes in order to justify a price above what low-cost leaders are charging. Likewise, it has to achieve significantly lower costs in providing upscale features so that it can outcompete high-end differentiators on the basis of an attractively lower price.

Toyota's Best-Cost Producer Strategy for Its Lexus Line

Toyota Motor Company is widely regarded as a low-cost producer among the world's motor vehicle manufacturers. Despite its emphasis on product quality, Toyota has achieved low-cost leadership because it has developed considerable skills in efficient supply chain management and low-cost assembly capabilities, and because its models are positioned in the low-to-medium end of the price spectrum, where high production volumes are conducive to low unit costs. But when Toyota decided to introduce its new Lexus models to compete in the luxury-car market, it employed a classic best-cost provider strategy. Toyota took the following four steps in crafting and implementing its Lexus strategy:

1. *Designing an array of high performance characteristics and upscale features into the Lexus models* so as to make them comparable in performance and luxury to other high-end models and attractive to Mercedes, BMW, Audi, Jaguar, Cadillac, and Lincoln buyers.

2. *Transferring its capabilities in making high-quality Toyota models at low cost to making premium-quality Lexus models at costs below other luxury-car makers.* Toyota's supply chain capabilities and low-cost assembly know-how allowed it to incorporate high-tech performance features and upscale quality into Lexus models at substantially less cost than Mercedes and BMW.

3. *Using its relatively lower manufacturing costs to underprice comparable Mercedes and BMW models.* Toyota believed that with its cost advantage it could price attractively equipped Lexus cars low enough to draw price-conscious buyers away from Mercedes and BMW and perhaps induce dissatisfied Lincoln and Cadillac owners to move up to a Lexus.

4. *Establishing a new network of Lexus dealers, separate from Toyota dealers, dedicated to providing a level of personalized, attentive customer service unmatched in the industry.*

Lexus models have consistently ranked among the top 10 models in the widely watched J. D. Power & Associates quality survey, and the prices of Lexus models are typically several thousand dollars below those of comparable Mercedes and BMW models—clear signals that Toyota has succeeded in becoming a best-cost producer with its Lexus brand.

Focused (or Market Niche) Strategies

What sets focused strategies apart from low-cost leadership or broad differentiation strategies is concentrated attention on a narrow piece of the total market. The target segment, or niche, can be defined by geographic uniqueness, by specialized requirements in using the product, or by special product attributes that appeal only to niche members. Examples of firms that concentrate on a well-defined market niche include eBay (in online auctions); Porsche (in sports cars); Cannondale (in top-of-the-line mountain bikes); Jiffy Lube International (a specialist in quick oil changes and simple maintenance for motor vehicles); Enterprise Rent-a-Car (specializing in providing rental cars to repair garage customers); Pottery Barn Kids (a retail chain featuring children's furniture and accessories); and Bandag (a specialist in truck tire recapping that promotes its recaps aggressively at over 1,000 truck stops). Microbreweries, local bakeries, bed-and-breakfast inns, and local owner-managed retail boutiques are all good examples of enterprises that have scaled their operations to serve narrow or local customer segments.

> Even though a focuser may be small, it still may have substantial competitive strength because of the attractiveness of its product offering and its strong expertise and capabilities in meeting the needs and expectations of niche members.

A Focused Low-Cost Strategy   A focused strategy based on low cost aims at securing a competitive advantage by serving buyers in the target market niche

Motel 6's Focused Low-Cost Strategy

Motel 6 caters to price-conscious travelers who want a clean, no-frills place to spend the night. To be a low-cost provider of overnight lodging, Motel 6 (1) selects relatively inexpensive sites on which to construct its units (usually near interstate exits and high traffic locations but far enough away to avoid paying prime site prices); (2) builds only basic facilities (no restaurant or bar and only rarely a swimming pool); (3) relies on standard architectural designs that incorporate inexpensive materials and low-cost construction techniques; and (4) provides simple room furnishings and decorations. These approaches lower both investment costs and operating costs. Without restaurants, bars, and all kinds of guest services, a Motel 6 unit can be operated with just front-desk personnel, room cleanup crews, and skeleton building-and-grounds maintenance.

To promote the Motel 6 concept with travelers who have simple overnight requirements, the chain uses unique, recognizable radio ads done by nationally syndicated radio personality Tom Bodett; the ads describe Motel 6's clean rooms, no-frills facilities, friendly atmosphere, and dependably low rates (usually under $40 a night).

Motel 6's basis for competitive advantage is lower costs than competitors in providing basic, economical overnight accommodations to price-constrained travelers.

at a lower cost and lower price than rival competitors. This strategy has considerable attraction when a firm can lower costs significantly by limiting its customer base to a well-defined buyer segment. The avenues to achieving a cost advantage over rivals also serving the target market niche are the same as for low-cost leadership—outmanage rivals in controlling the factors that drive costs and reconfigure the firm's value chain in ways that yield a cost edge over rivals.

Focused low-cost strategies are fairly common. Producers of private-label goods are able to achieve low costs in product development, marketing, distribution, and advertising by concentrating on making generic items imitative of name-brand merchandise and selling directly to retail chains wanting a basic house brand to sell to price-sensitive shoppers. Several small printer-supply manufacturers have begun making low-cost clones of the premium-priced replacement ink and toner cartridges sold by Hewlett-Packard, Lexmark, Canon, and Epson; the clone manufacturers dissect the cartridges of the name-brand companies and then reengineer a similar version that won't violate patents. The components for remanufactured replacement cartridges are acquired from various outside sources, and the clones are then marketed at prices as much as 50 percent below the name-brand cartridges. Cartridge remanufacturers have been lured to focus on this market because replacement cartridges constitute a multibillion-dollar business with considerable profit potential given their low costs and the premium pricing of the name brand companies. Company Spotlight 4.4 describes how Motel 6 has kept its costs low in catering to budget-conscious travelers.

A Focused Differentiation Strategy A focused strategy based on differentiation aims at securing a competitive advantage by offering niche members a product they perceive as well suited to their own unique tastes and preferences. Successful use of a focused differentiation strategy depends on the existence of a buyer segment that is looking for special product attributes or seller capabilities and on a firm's ability to stand apart from rivals competing in the same target market niche.

Companies like Godiva Chocolates, Chanel, Rolls-Royce, Häagen-Dazs, and W. L. Gore (the maker of Gore-Tex) employ successful differentiation-based focused strategies targeted at upscale buyers wanting products and services with world-class

Ritz-Carlton's Focused Differentiation Strategy

Ritz-Carlton caters to discriminating travelers and vacationers willing and able to pay for top-of-the-line accommodations and world-class personal service. Ritz-Carlton hotels feature (1) prime locations and scenic views from many rooms; (2) custom architectural designs; (3) fine restaurants with gourmet menus prepared by accomplished chefs; (4) elegantly appointed lobbies and bar lounges; (5) swimming pools, exercise facilities, and leisure-time options; (6) upscale room accommodations; (7) an array of guest services and recreation opportunities appropriate to the location; and (8) large, well-trained professional staffs who do their utmost to make each guest's stay an enjoyable experience.

Ritz-Carlton strives to differentiate itself from other high-end lodging rivals like Four Seasons and Hyatt based on its capability to provide superior accommodations and unmatched personal service for a well-to-do clientele. Despite polar–opposite strategies, both Motel 6 and Ritz-Carlton have been able to succeed because the market for lodging consists of diverse buyer segments with diverse preferences and abilities to pay.

attributes. Indeed, most markets contain a buyer segment willing to pay a big price premium for the very finest items available, thus opening the strategic window for some competitors to pursue differentiation-based focused strategies aimed at the very top of the market pyramid. Another successful focused differentiator is a "fashion food retailer" called Trader Joe's, a 150-store East and West Coast chain that is a combination gourmet deli and food warehouse.[8] Customers shop Trader Joe's as much for entertainment as for conventional grocery items—the store stocks out-of-the-ordinary culinary treats like raspberry salsa, salmon burgers, and jasmine fried rice, as well as the standard goods normally found in supermarkets. What sets Trader Joe's apart is not just its unique combination of food novelties and competitively priced grocery items but also its capability to turn an otherwise mundane grocery excursion into a whimsical treasure hunt that is just plain fun. Company Spotlight 4.5 describes Ritz-Carlton's focused differentiation strategy.

When Focusing Is Attractive   A focused strategy aimed at securing a competitive edge based either on low cost or differentiation becomes increasingly attractive as more of the following conditions are met:

- The target market niche is big enough to be profitable and offers good growth potential.

- Industry leaders do not see that having a presence in the niche is crucial to their own success—in which case focusers can often escape battling head-to-head against some of the industry's biggest and strongest competitors.

- It is costly or difficult for multisegment competitors to put capabilities in place to meet the specialized needs of the target market niche and at the same time satisfy the expectations of their mainstream customers.

- The industry has many different niches and segments, thereby allowing a focuser to pick a competitively attractive niche suited to its resource strengths and capabilities. Also, with more niches there is more room for focusers to avoid each other in competing for the same customers.

- Few, if any, other rivals are attempting to specialize in the same target segment— a condition that reduces the risk of segment overcrowding.

■   The focuser can compete effectively against challengers based on the capabilities and resources it has to serve the targeted niche and the customer goodwill it may have built up.

The Risks of a Focused Strategy   Focusing carries several risks. One is the chance that competitors will find effective ways to match the focused firm's capabilities in serving the target niche—perhaps by coming up with more appealing product offerings or by developing expertise and capabilities that offset the focuser's strengths. A second is the potential for the preferences and needs of niche members to shift over time toward the product attributes desired by the majority of buyers. An erosion of the differences across buyer segments lowers entry barriers into a focuser's market niche and provides an open invitation for rivals in adjacent segments to begin competing for the focuser's customers. A third risk is that the segment may become so attractive it is soon inundated with competitors, intensifying rivalry and splintering segment profits.

Strategic Alliances and Partnerships

During the past decade, companies in all types of industries and in all parts of the world have elected to form strategic alliances and partnerships to complement their own strategic initiatives and strengthen their competitiveness in domestic and international markets. This is an about-face from times past, when the vast majority of companies were content to go it alone, confident that they already had or could independently develop whatever resources and know-how were needed to be successful in their markets. But globalization of the world economy; revolutionary advances in technology across a broad front; and untapped opportunities in national markets in Asia, Latin America, and Europe that are opening up, deregulating, and/or undergoing privatization have made strategic partnerships of one kind or another integral to competing on a broad geographic scale.

Many companies now find themselves thrust into two very demanding competitive races: (1) *the global race to build a market presence in many different national markets* and join the ranks of companies recognized as global market leaders, and (2) *the race to seize opportunities on the frontiers of advancing technology* and build the resource strengths and business capabilities to compete successfully in the industries and product markets of the future.[9] Even the largest and most financially sound companies have concluded that simultaneously running the races for global market leadership and for a stake in the industries of the future requires more diverse and expansive skills, resources, technological expertise, and competitive capabilities than they can assemble and manage alone.

> Alliances and partnerships can be valuable competitive assets in racing against rivals to build a strong global presence and/or to stake out a position on new technological frontiers.

Indeed, the gaps in resources and competitive capabilities between industry rivals have become painfully apparent to disadvantaged enterprises. Allowing such gaps to go unaddressed can put a company in a precarious competitive position or even prove fatal. When rivals can develop new products faster or achieve better quality at lower cost or have more resources and know-how to exploit opportunities in attractive new market arenas, a company has little option but to try to close the resource and competency gaps quickly. Often, the fastest way to do this is to form an alliance that provides immediate access to needed capabilities and competitive strengths. In today's rapidly changing world, a company that cannot position itself quickly misses important opportunities. As a consequence, more and more enterprises, especially in fast-changing industries, are making strategic alliances a core part of their overall strategy. Alliances are so central to Corning's strategy that the company describes itself as a "network of organizations." Toyota has forged a network of long-term strategic partnerships with its suppliers of automotive parts and components. Microsoft collaborates very closely with independent software developers that create new programs to run on the next-generation versions of Windows. A recent study indicates that the average large corporation is involved in around 30 alliances today, versus fewer than 3 in the early 1990s.

Why and How Strategic Alliances Are Advantageous

Strategic alliances are cooperative agreements between firms that go beyond normal company-to-company dealings but fall short of merger or full joint venture partnership with formal ownership ties. (Some strategic alliances, however, do involve arrangements whereby one or more allies have minority ownership in certain of the other alliance members.) The value of an alliance stems not from the agreement or deal itself but rather from the capacity of the partners to defuse organizational frictions, collaborate effectively over time, and work their way through the maze of changes that lie in front of them—technological and competitive surprises, new market developments (which may come at a rapid-fire pace), and changes in their own priorities and competitive circumstances. Collaborative alliances nearly always entail an *evolving* relationship whose benefits and competitive value ultimately depend on mutual learning, cooperation, and adaptation to changing industry conditions. Competitive advantage can emerge if the combined resources and capabilities of a company and its allies give it an edge over rivals.

> **Core Concept**
> **Strategic alliances** are collaborative partnerships where two or more companies join forces to achieve mutually beneficial strategic outcomes.

The most common reasons why companies enter into strategic alliances are to collaborate on technology or the development of promising new products, to overcome deficits in their technical and manufacturing expertise, to acquire altogether new competencies, to improve supply chain efficiency, to gain economies of scale in production and/or marketing, and to acquire or improve market access through joint marketing agreements.[10]

> The best alliances are highly selective, focusing on particular value chain activities and on obtaining a particular competitive benefit. They tend to enable a firm to build on its strengths and to learn.

A company that is racing for *global market leadership* needs alliances to:

- Get into critical country markets quickly and accelerate the process of building a potent global market presence.

- Gain inside knowledge about unfamiliar markets and cultures through alliances with local partners. For example, U.S., European, and Japanese companies wanting to build market footholds in the fast-growing Chinese market have pursued partnership arrangements with Chinese companies to help in dealing with government regulations, to supply knowledge of local markets, to provide guidance on adapting their products to better match the buying preferences of Chinese consumers, to set up local manufacturing capabilities, and to assist in distribution, marketing, and promotional activities. The policy of the Chinese government has long been to limit foreign companies to a 50 percent ownership in local companies, making alliances with local Chinese companies a virtual necessity to gain market access.

- Access valuable skills and competencies that are concentrated in particular geographic locations (such as software design competencies in the United States, fashion design skills in Italy, and efficient manufacturing skills in Japan).

A company that is racing to *stake out a strong position in an industry of the future* needs alliances to:

- Establish a stronger beachhead for participating in the target industry.
- Master new technologies and build new expertise and competencies faster than would be possible through internal efforts.
- Open up broader opportunities in the target industry by melding the firm's own capabilities with the expertise and resources of partners.

Allies can learn much from one another in performing joint research, sharing technological know-how, and collaborating on complementary new technologies and products—sometimes enough to enable them to pursue other new opportunities on their own. Manufacturers typically pursue alliances with parts and components suppliers to gain the efficiencies of better supply chain management and to speed new products to market. By joining forces in components production and/or final assembly, companies may be able to realize cost savings not achievable with their own small volumes—Volvo, Renault, and Peugeot formed an alliance to make engines together for their large car models precisely because none of the three needed enough such engines to operate its own engine plant economically. Manufacturing allies can also learn much about how to improve their quality control and production procedures by studying one another's manufacturing methods. Often alliances are formed to utilize common dealer networks or to promote complementary products jointly, thereby mutually strengthening their access to buyers and economizing on forward channel distribution costs. United Airlines, American Airlines, Continental, Delta, and Northwest created an alliance to form Orbitz, an Internet travel site designed to compete with Expedia and Travelocity to provide consumers with low-cost airfares, rental cars, lodging, cruises, and vacation packages.

> The competitive attraction of alliances is in allowing companies to bundle competences and resources that are more valuable in a joint effort than when kept separate.

Strategic cooperation is a much-favored, indeed necessary, approach in industries where new technological developments are occurring at a furious pace along many different paths and where advances in one technology spill over to affect others (often blurring industry boundaries). Whenever industries are experiencing high-velocity technological change in many areas simultaneously, firms find it virtually essential to have cooperative relationships with other enterprises to stay on the leading edge of technology and product performance even in their own area of specialization.

Why Many Alliances Are Unstable or Break Apart   The stability of an alliance depends on how well the partners work together, their success in responding and adapting to changing internal and external conditions, and their willingness to renegotiate the bargain if circumstances so warrant. A successful alliance requires real in-the-trenches collaboration, not merely an arm's-length exchange of ideas. Unless partners place a high value on the skills, resources, and contributions each brings to the alliance and the cooperative arrangement results in valuable win–win outcomes, it is doomed. A surprisingly large number of alliances never live up to expectations. A study by Accenture, a global business consulting organization, revealed that 61 percent of alliances were either outright failures or "limping along."[11] Many alliances are dissolved after a few years. The high "divorce rate" among strategic allies has several causes—diverging objectives and priorities, an inability to work well together, changing conditions that render the purpose of the alliance obsolete, the emergence of more attractive technological paths, and marketplace rivalry between one or more allies.[12] Experience indicates that alliances stand a reasonable chance of helping a company reduce competitive disadvantage but very rarely have they proved a durable device for achieving a competitive edge over rivals.

The Strategic Dangers of Relying Heavily on Alliances and Cooperative Partnerships   The Achilles heel of alliances and cooperative strategies is the danger of becoming dependent on other companies for *essential* expertise and capabilities over the long term. To be a market leader (and perhaps even a serious market contender), a company must ultimately develop its own capabilities in areas where internal strategic control is pivotal to protecting its competitiveness and building competitive advantage. Moreover, some alliances hold only limited potential because the partner guards its most valuable skills and expertise; in such instances, acquiring or merging with a company possessing the desired resources is a better solution.

Merger and Acquisition Strategies

Mergers and acquisitions are much-used strategic options. They are especially suited for situations in which alliances and partnerships do not go far enough in providing a company with access to the needed resources and capabilities. Ownership ties are more permanent than partnership ties, allowing the operations of the merger/acquisition participants to be tightly integrated and creating more in-house control and autonomy. A *merger* is a pooling of equals, with the newly created company often taking on a new name. An *acquisition* is a combination in which one company, the acquirer, purchases and absorbs the operations of another, the acquired. The difference between a merger and an acquisition relates more to the details of ownership, management control, and financial arrangements than to strategy and competitive advantage. The resources, competencies, and competitive capabilities of the newly created enterprise end up much the same whether the combination is the result of acquisition or merger.

> No company can afford to ignore the strategic and competitive benefits of acquiring or merging with another company to strengthen its market position and open up avenues of new opportunity.

Many mergers and acquisitions are driven by strategies to achieve one of five strategic objectives:[13]

1. *To pave the way for the acquiring company to gain more market share and, further, create a more efficient operation out of the combined companies by closing high-cost plants and eliminating surplus capacity industrywide*—The merger that formed DaimlerChrysler was motivated in large part by the fact that the motor vehicle industry had far more production capacity worldwide than was needed; management at both Daimler Benz and Chrysler believed that the efficiency of the two companies could be significantly improved by shutting some plants and laying off workers; realigning which models were produced at which plants; and squeezing out efficiencies by combining supply chain activities, product design, and administration. Quite a number of acquisitions are undertaken with the objective of transforming two or more otherwise high-cost companies into one lean competitor with average or below-average costs.

2. *To expand a company's geographic coverage*—Many industries exist for a long time in a fragmented state, with local companies dominating local markets and no company having a significantly visible regional or national presence. Eventually,

though, expansion-minded companies will launch strategies to acquire local companies in adjacent territories. Over time, companies with successful growth via acquisition strategies emerge as regional market leaders and later perhaps as a company with national coverage. Often the acquiring company follows up on its acquisitions with efforts to lower the operating costs and improve the customer service capabilities of the local businesses it acquires.

3. *To extend the company's business into new product categories or international markets*—PepsiCo acquired Quaker Oats chiefly to bring Gatorade into the Pepsi family of beverages, and PepsiCo's Frito-Lay division has made a series of acquisitions of foreign-based snack foods companies to begin to establish a stronger presence in international markets. Companies like Nestlé, Kraft, Unilever, and Procter & Gamble—all racing for global market leadership—have made acquisitions an integral part of their strategies to widen their geographic reach and broaden the number of product categories in which they compete.

4. *To gain quick access to new technologies and avoid the need for a time-consuming R&D effort* (which might not succeed)—This type of acquisition strategy is a favorite of companies racing to establish attractive positions in emerging markets. Such companies need to fill in technological gaps, extend their technological capabilities along some promising new paths, and position themselves to launch next-wave products and services. Cisco Systems purchased over 75 technology companies to give it more technological reach and product breadth, thereby buttressing its standing as the world's biggest supplier of systems for building the infrastructure of the Internet. Intel has made over 300 acquisitions in the past five or so years to broaden its technological base, put it in a stronger position to be a major supplier of Internet technology, and make it less dependent on supplying microprocessors for PCs. This type of acquisition strategy enables a company to build a market position in attractive technologies quickly and serves as a substitute for extensive in-house R&D programs.

5. *To try to invent a new industry and lead the convergence of industries whose boundaries are being blurred by changing technologies and new market opportunities*—Such acquisitions are the result of a company's management betting that a new industry is on the verge of being born and deciding to establish an early position in this industry by bringing together the resources and products of several different companies. Examples include the merger of AOL and media giant Time Warner and Viacom's purchase of Paramount Pictures, CBS, and Blockbuster—both of which reflected bold strategic moves predicated on beliefs that all entertainment content will ultimately converge into a single industry and be distributed over the Internet.

In addition to the above objectives, there are instances when acquisitions are motivated by a company's desire to fill resource gaps, thus allowing the new company to do things it could not do before. Company Spotlight 4.6 describes how Clear Channel Worldwide has used mergers and acquisitions to build a leading global position in outdoor advertising and radio and TV broadcasting.

However, mergers and acquisitions do not always produce the hoped-for outcomes. Combining the operations of two companies, especially large and complex ones, often entails formidable resistance from rank-and-file organization members, hard-to-resolve conflicts in management styles and corporate cultures, and tough problems of integration. Cost savings, expertise sharing, and enhanced competitive capabilities may take substantially longer than expected to realize or, worse, may never materialize at all.

COMPANY SPOTLIGHT 4.6

How Clear Channel Has Used Mergers and Acquisitions to Become a Global Market Leader

In 2002, Clear Channel Communications was the fourth largest media company in the world behind Disney, AOL Time Warner, and Viacom/CBS. The company, founded in 1972 by Lowry Mays and Billy Joe McCombs, got its start by acquiring an unprofitable country-music radio station in San Antonio, Texas. Over the next 10 years, Mays learned the radio business and slowly bought other radio stations in a variety of states. Going public in 1984 helped the company raise the equity capital needed to fuel its strategy of expanding by acquiring radio stations in additional geographic markets.

In the late 1980s, following the decision of the Federal Communications Commission to loosen the rules regarding the ability of one company to own both radio and TV stations, Clear Channel broadened its strategy and began acquiring small, struggling TV stations. Soon thereafter, Clear Channel became affiliated with the Fox network, which was starting to build a national presence and challenge ABC, CBS, and NBC. Meanwhile, the company began selling programming services to other stations, and in some markets where it already had stations it took on the function of selling advertising for cross-town stations it did not own.

By 1998, Clear Channel had used acquisitions to build a leading position in radio and television stations. Domestically, it owned, programmed, or sold airtime for 69 AM radio stations, 135 FM stations, and 18 TV stations in 48 local markets in 24 states. The TV stations included affiliates of FOX, UPN, ABC, NBC, and CBS. Clear Channel was beginning to expand internationally. It purchased an ownership interest in a domestic Spanish-language radio broadcaster; owned two radio stations and a cable audio channel in Denmark; and acquired ownership interests in radio stations in Australia, Mexico, New Zealand, and the Czech Republic.

In 1997, Clear Channel acquired Phoenix-based Eller Media Company, an outdoor advertising company with over 100,000 billboard facings. This was quickly followed by additional acquisitions of outdoor advertising companies, the most important of which were ABC Outdoor in Milwaukee, Wisconsin; Paxton Communications (with operations in Tampa and Orlando, Florida); Universal Outdoor; and the More Group, with outdoor operations and 90,000 displays in 24 countries.

Then in October 1999, Clear Channel merged with AM-FM, Inc. After divesting some 125 properties needed to gain regulatory approval, Clear Channel Communications (the name adopted by the merged companies) operated in 32 countries and included 830 radio stations, 19 TV stations, and more than 425,000 outdoor displays.

Clear Channel's strategy was to buy radio, TV, and outdoor advertising properties with operations in many of the same local markets, share facilities and staffs to cut costs, improve programming, and sell advertising to customers in packages for all three media simultaneously. Packaging ads for two or three media allowed the company to combine its sales activities and have a common sales force for all three media, achieving significant cost savings and boosting profit margins.

Over the next four years, Clear Channel continued its strategy of growth via acquisitions. By 2002, Clear Channel Worldwide (the company's latest name) owned radio and television stations, outdoor displays, and entertainment venues in 66 countries around the world. Clear Channel operated approximately 1,225 radio and 37 television stations in the United States and had equity interests in over 240 radio stations internationally. In addition, the company operated approximately 776,000 outdoor advertising displays, including billboards, street furniture, and transit panels around the world. The company's Clear Channel Entertainment division was a leading promoter, producer, and marketer of live entertainment events and also owned leading athlete management and marketing companies.

Sources: Company documents and *Business Week,* October 19, 1999, p. 56.

Integrating the operations of two fairly large or culturally diverse companies is hard to pull off—only a few companies that use merger and acquisition strategies have proved they can consistently make good decisions about what to leave alone and what to meld into their own operations and systems. In the case of mergers between companies of roughly equal size, the management groups of the two companies frequently battle over which one is going to end up in control. A number of previously applauded mergers/acquisitions have yet to live up to expectations—the merger of AOL and Time Warner, the merger of Daimler Benz and Chrysler, the merger of J. P. Morgan and Chase Manhattan Bank, and Ford's acquisition of Jaguar. Ford paid a handsome price to acquire Jaguar but has yet to make the Jaguar brand a major factor in the luxury-car segment in competition against Mercedes, BMW, and Lexus. Novell acquired WordPerfect for $1.7 billion in stock in 1994, but the combination never generated enough punch to compete against Microsoft Word and Microsoft Office—Novell sold WordPerfect to Corel for $124 million in cash and stock less than two years later. The jury is out on whether Hewlett-Packard's acquisition of Compaq Computer will be a success.

Vertical Integration Strategies: Operating across More Stages of the Industry Value Chain

Vertical integration extends a firm's competitive and operating scope within the same industry. It involves expanding the firm's range of activities backward into sources of supply and/or forward toward end users. Thus, if a manufacturer invests in facilities to produce certain component parts that it formerly purchased from outside suppliers, it remains in essentially the same industry as before. The only change is that it has operations in two stages of the industry value chain. Similarly, if a paint manufacturer, Sherwin-Williams for example, elects to integrate forward by opening 100 retail stores to market its paint products directly to consumers, it remains in the paint business even though its competitive scope extends from manufacturing to retailing.

Vertical integration strategies can aim at *full integration* (participating in all stages of the industry value chain) or *partial integration* (building positions in selected stages of the industry's total value chain). A firm can pursue vertical integration by starting its own operations in other stages in the industry's activity chain or by acquiring a company already performing the activities it wants to bring in-house.

The Strategic Advantages of Vertical Integration

> **Core Concept**
>
> A vertical integration strategy has appeal *only* if it significantly strengthens a firm's competitive position.

The only good reason for investing company resources in vertical integration is to strengthen the firm's competitive position.[14] Vertical integration has no real payoff profitwise or strategywise unless it produces sufficient cost savings to justify the extra investment, adds materially to a company's technological and competitive strengths, or truly helps differentiate the company's product offering.

Integrating Backward to Achieve Greater Competitiveness   Integrating backward generates cost savings only when the volume needed is big enough to capture the same scale economies suppliers have and when suppliers' production efficiency can be matched or exceeded with no dropoff in quality. The best potential for being able to reduce costs via backward integration exists in situations where suppliers have sizable profit margins, where the item being supplied is a major cost component, and where the needed technological skills are easily mastered or can be gained by acquiring a supplier with the desired technological know-how. Integrating backward can sometimes significantly enhance a company's technological capabilities and give it expertise needed to stake out positions in the industries and products of the future. Intel, Cisco, and many other Silicon Valley companies have been active in acquiring companies that will help them speed the advance of Internet technology and pave the way for next-generation families of products and services.

Backward vertical integration can produce a differentiation-based competitive advantage when a company, by performing in-house activities that were previously outsourced, ends up with a better-quality product/service offering, improves the caliber of its customer service, or in other ways enhances the performance of its final product. On occasion, integrating into more stages along the industry value chain can add to a company's differentiation capabilities by allowing it to build or strengthen its core competencies, better master key skills or strategy-critical technologies, or add features that deliver greater customer value.

Other potential advantages of backward integration include sparing a company the uncertainty of being dependent on suppliers for crucial components or support services and lessening a company's vulnerability to powerful suppliers inclined to raise prices at every opportunity. Stockpiling, contracting for fixed prices, multiple sourcing, forming long-term cooperative partnerships, and using substitute inputs are not always attractive ways for dealing with uncertain supply conditions or with economically powerful suppliers. Companies that are low on a key supplier's customer priority list can find themselves waiting on shipments every time supplies get tight. If this occurs often and wreaks havoc in a company's own production and customer relations activities, backward integration can be an advantageous strategic solution.

Integrating Forward to Enhance Competitiveness The strategic impetus for forward integration is to gain better access to end users and better market visibility. In many industries, independent sales agents, wholesalers, and retailers handle competing brands of the same product; having no allegiance to any one company's brand, they tend to push whatever sells and earns them the biggest profits. Halfhearted commitments by distributors and retailers can frustrate a company's attempt to boost sales and market share; give rise to costly inventory pileups and frequent underutilization of capacity; and disrupt the economies of steady, near-capacity production. In such cases, it can be advantageous for a manufacturer to integrate forward into wholesaling or retailing via company-owned distributorships or a chain of retail stores. But often a company's product line is not broad enough to justify stand-alone distributorships or retail outlets. This leaves the option of integrating forward into the activity of selling directly to end users—perhaps via the Internet. Bypassing regular wholesale/retail channels in favor of direct sales and Internet retailing may lower distribution costs, produce a relative cost advantage over certain rivals, and result in lower selling prices to end users.

The Strategic Disadvantages of Vertical Integration

Vertical integration has some substantial drawbacks, however. It boosts a firm's capital investment in the industry, increasing business risk (what if industry growth and profitability go sour?) and perhaps denying financial resources to more worthwhile pursuits. A vertically integrated firm has vested interests in protecting its technology and production facilities. Because of the high costs of abandoning such investments before they are worn out, fully integrated firms tend to adopt new technologies slower than partially integrated or nonintegrated firms. Second, integrating forward or backward locks a firm into relying on its own in-house activities and sources of supply (which later may prove more costly than outsourcing) and potentially results in less flexibility in accommodating buyer demand for greater product variety. In today's world of close working relationships with suppliers and efficient supply chain management systems, very few businesses can make a case for integrating backward into the business of suppliers to ensure a reliable supply of materials and components or to reduce production costs.

Third, vertical integration poses all kinds of capacity-matching problems. In motor vehicle manufacturing, for example, the most efficient scale of operation for making axles is different from the most economic volume for radiators, and different yet again for both engines and transmissions. Building the capacity to produce just the right number of axles, radiators, engines, and transmissions in-house—and doing so at the lowest unit costs for each—is much easier said than done. If internal capacity for making transmissions is deficient, the difference has to be bought externally. Where internal capacity for radiators proves excessive, customers need to be found for the surplus. And if by-products are generated—as occurs in the processing of many chemical products—they require arrangements for disposal.

Fourth, integration forward or backward often calls for radical changes in skills and business capabilities. Parts and components manufacturing, assembly operations, wholesale distribution and retailing, and direct sales via the Internet are different businesses with different key success factors. Managers of a manufacturing company should consider carefully whether it makes good business sense to invest time and money in developing the expertise and merchandising skills to integrate forward into wholesaling and retailing. Many manufacturers learn the hard way that company-owned wholesale/retail networks present many headaches, fit poorly with what they do best, and don't always add the kind of value to their core business they thought they would. Selling to customers via the Internet poses still another set of problems—it is usually easier to use the Internet to sell to business customers than to consumers.

Integrating backward into parts and components manufacture isn't as simple or profitable as it sounds, either. Producing some or all of the parts and components needed for final assembly can reduce a company's flexibility to make desirable changes in using certain parts and components—it is one thing to design out a component made by a supplier and another to design out a component being made in-house. Companies that alter designs and models frequently in response to shifting buyer preferences often find outsourcing the needed parts and components cheaper and less complicated than making them in-house. Most of the world's automakers, despite their expertise in automotive technology and manufacturing, have concluded that purchasing many of their key parts and components from manufacturing specialists results in higher quality, lower costs, and greater design flexibility than does the vertical integration option.

Weighing the Pros and Cons of Vertical Integration   All in all, therefore, a strategy of vertical integration can have both important strengths and weaknesses. The tip of the scales depends on (1) whether vertical integration can enhance the performance of strategy-critical activities in ways that lower cost, build expertise, or increase differentiation; (2) the impact of vertical integration on investment costs, flexibility and response times, and the administrative costs of coordinating operations across more value chain activities; and (3) whether the integration substantially enhances a company's competitiveness. Vertical integration strategies have merit according to which capabilities and value-chain activities truly need to be performed in-house and which can be performed better or cheaper by outsiders. Absent solid benefits, integrating forward or backward is not likely to be an attractive competitive strategy option. In a growing number of instances, companies are proving that deintegrating (i.e., focusing on a narrower portion of the industry value chain) is a cheaper and more flexible competitive strategy.

Outsourcing Strategies: Narrowing the Boundaries of the Business

Outsourcing involves withdrawing from certain activities in the value chain and relying on outside vendors to supply the needed products, support services, or functional activities. Over the past decade, outsourcing has become increasingly popular. Some companies have found vertical integration to be so competitively burdensome that they have deintegrated and withdrawn from some stages of the industry value chain. Moreover, a number of single-business enterprises have begun outsourcing activities and concentrating their energies on a narrower portion of the value chain.

> **Core Concept**
>
> **Outsourcing** involves shifting the performance of value chain activities to outside specialists rather than performing them in-house.

Advantages of Outsourcing

Outsourcing pieces of the value chain to narrow the boundaries of a firm's business makes strategic sense whenever:

- An activity can be performed better or more cheaply by outside specialists. Many PC makers, for example, have shifted from assembling units in-house to using contract assemblers because of the sizable scale economies associated with purchasing PC components in large volumes and assembling PCs. Cisco outsources most all production and assembly of its routers and switching equipment to contract manufacturers that together operate 37 factories, all linked via the Internet.

- The activity is not crucial to the firm's ability to achieve sustainable competitive advantage and won't hollow out its core competencies, capabilities, or technical know-how. Outsourcing of maintenance services, data processing, accounting, and other administrative support activities to specialists has become commonplace. American Express, for instance, recently entered into a seven-year, $4 billion deal whereby IBM's Services division will host American Express's website, network servers, data storage, and help-desk support; American Express indicated that it would save several hundred million dollars by paying only for the services it needed when it needed them (as opposed to funding its own full-time staff).

- It reduces the company's risk exposure to changing technology and/or changing buyer preferences.

- It streamlines company operations in ways that improve organizational flexibility, cut cycle time, speed decision making, and reduce coordination costs.

- It allows a company to concentrate on its core business and do what it does best.

Often, many of the advantages of performing value chain activities in-house can be captured and many of the disadvantages avoided by forging close, long-term cooperative partnerships with key suppliers and tapping into the important competitive capabilities that able suppliers have painstakingly developed. In years past, many companies maintained arm's-length relationships with suppliers, insisting on items being made to precise specifications and negotiating long and hard over price.[15] Although a company might place orders with the same supplier repeatedly, there was no expectation that this would be the case; price usually determined which supplier was awarded an order, and companies maneuvered for leverage over suppliers to get the lowest possible prices. The threat of switching suppliers was the company's primary weapon. To make this threat credible, sourcing from several suppliers was preferred to dealing with only a single supplier.

Today, most companies are abandoning such approaches in favor of alliances and strategic partnerships with a small number of highly capable suppliers. Cooperative relationships are replacing contractual, purely price-oriented relationships. Relying on outside specialists to perform certain value chain activities offers a number of strategic advantages:[16]

■ Obtaining higher quality and/or cheaper components or services than internal sources can provide.

> **Core Concept**
>
> A company should generally *not* perform any value chain activity internally that can be performed more efficiently or effectively by its outside business partners—the chief exception is when a particular activity is strategically crucial and internal control over that activity is deemed essential.

■ Improving the company's ability to innovate by allying with "best-in-world" suppliers who have considerable intellectual capital and innovative capabilities of their own.

■ Enhancing the firm's strategic flexibility should customer needs and market conditions suddenly shift—seeking out new suppliers with the needed capabilities already in place is frequently quicker, easier, less risky, and cheaper than hurriedly retooling internal operations to disband obsolete capabilities and put new ones in place.

■ Increasing the firm's ability to assemble diverse kinds of expertise speedily and efficiently.

■ Allowing the firm to concentrate its resources on performing those activities internally that it can perform better than outsiders and/or that it needs to have under its direct control.

Dell Computer's partnerships with the suppliers of PC components have allowed it to operate with fewer than four days of inventory, to realize substantial savings in inventory costs, and to get PCs equipped with next-generation components into the marketplace in less than a week after the newly upgraded components start shipping. Cisco's contract suppliers work so closely with Cisco that they can ship Cisco products to Cisco customers without a Cisco employee ever touching the gear. This system of alliances saves $500 million to $800 million annually.[17] Hewlett-Packard, IBM, Silicon Graphics (now SGI), and others have sold plants to suppliers and then contracted to purchase the output. Starbucks finds purchasing coffee beans from independent growers far more advantageous than trying to integrate backward into the coffee-growing business.

The Pitfalls of Outsourcing

The biggest danger of outsourcing is that a company will farm out too many or the wrong types of activities and thereby hollow out its own capabilities. In such cases, a company loses touch with the very activities and expertise that over the long run determine its success. Cisco guards against loss of control and protects its manufacturing expertise by designing the production methods that its contract manufacturers must use. Cisco keeps the source code for its design proprietary and is thus the source of all improvements and innovations. Further, Cisco uses the Internet to monitor the factory operations of contract manufacturers around the clock, and can therefore know immediately when problems arise and whether to get involved.

Offensive and Defensive Strategies

Competitive advantage is nearly always achieved by successful *offensive* strategic moves—initiatives calculated to yield a cost advantage, a differentiation advantage, or a resource advantage. *Defensive* strategies, in contrast, can protect competitive advantage but rarely are the basis for creating the advantage. How long it takes for a successful offensive to create an edge varies with the competitive circumstances.[18] It can be short if the requisite resources and capabilities are already in place awaiting deployment or if buyers respond immediately (as can occur with a dramatic price cut, an imaginative ad campaign, or an especially appealing new product). Securing a competitive edge can take much longer if winning consumer acceptance of an innovative product will take some time or if the firm may need several years to debug a new technology or put new network systems or production capacity in place. Ideally, an offensive move builds competitive advantage quickly; the longer it takes, the more likely it is that rivals will spot the move, see its potential, and begin a counterresponse. The size of the advantage can be large (as in pharmaceuticals, where patents on an important new drug produce a substantial advantage) or small (as in apparel, where popular new designs can be imitated quickly).

> **Core Concept**
>
> Competent, resourceful rivals will exert strong efforts to overcome any competitive disadvantage they face—they won't be outcompeted without a fight.

However, competent, resourceful competitors can be counted on to counterattack with initiatives to overcome any market disadvantage they face—they are not going to be outcompeted without a fight.[19] Thus, to sustain an initially won competitive advantage, a firm must come up with follow-on offensive and defensive moves. Unless the firm initiates one series of offensive and defensive moves after another to protect its market position and retain customer favor, its market advantage will erode.

Basic Types of Offensive Strategies

Most every company must at times go on the offensive to improve its market position. While offensive attacks may or may not be aimed at particular rivals, they usually are motivated by a desire to win sales and market share at the expense of other companies in the industry. Several types of strategic offensives merit consideration.[20]

Initiatives to Match or Exceed Competitor Strengths   Offensive strategies are important when a company has no choice but to try to whittle away at a strong rival's competitive advantage and when it is possible to gain profitable market share at the expense of rivals despite whatever resource strengths and capabilities they have. The classic avenue for attacking a strong rival is to offer an equally good product at a lower price.[21] This can produce market share gains if the targeted competitor has sound reasons for not resorting to price cuts of its own and if the challenger convinces buyers that its product is just as good. However, such a strategy increases total profits only if the gains in additional unit sales are enough to offset the impact of lower prices and thinner margins per unit sold. A more potent and sustainable basis for mounting a price-aggressive challenge is to *first achieve a cost advantage* and then hit competitors with a lower price.[22] Other strategic options for attacking a competitor's strengths include leapfrogging into next-generation technologies to make the rival's products obsolete, adding new features that appeal to the rival's customers, running comparison ads, constructing major new plant capacity in the rival's backyard, expanding the product line to match the rival model for model, and developing customer service capabilities that the targeted rival doesn't have. As a rule, challenging a rival on competitive grounds where it is strong is an uphill struggle.

Initiatives to Capitalize on Competitor Weaknesses   Initiatives that exploit competitor weaknesses stand a better chance of succeeding than do those that challenge competitor strengths, especially if the weaknesses represent important vulnerabilities and the rival is caught by surprise with no ready defense.[23] Options for attacking the competitive weaknesses of rivals include going after the customers of those rivals whose products lag on quality, features, or product performance; making special sales pitches to the customers of those rivals who provide subpar customer service; trying to win customers away from rivals with weak brand recognition (an attractive option if the aggressor has strong marketing skills and a recognized brand name); emphasizing sales to buyers in geographic regions where a rival has a weak market share or is exerting less competitive effort; and paying special attention to buyer segments that a rival is neglecting or is weakly equipped to serve.

Simultaneous Initiatives on Many Fronts   On occasion a company may see merit in launching a grand competitive offensive involving multiple initiatives (price cuts, increased advertising, new product introductions, free samples, coupons, in-store promotions, rebates) across a wide geographic front. Such all-out campaigns can force a rival to try to protect many pieces of its customer base simultaneously and thus divide its attention. Multifaceted offensives have their best chance of success when a challenger not only comes up with an especially attractive product or service but also has a brand name and reputation to secure broad distribution and retail exposure. Then it can blitz the market with innovative new products and advertising, perhaps enticing large numbers of buyers to switch their brand allegiance.

End-Run Offensives   The idea of an end-run offensive is to maneuver *around* competitors, capture unoccupied or less contested market territory, and change the rules of the competitive game in the aggressor's favor.[24] Examples include launching initiatives to build strong positions in geographic areas where close rivals have little or no market presence and trying to create new segments by introducing products with different attributes and performance features to better meet the needs of selected buyers.

Guerrilla Offensives   Guerrilla offensives use the hit-and-run principle—an underdog tries to grab sales and market share wherever and whenever it catches rivals napping or spots an opening through which to lure customers away. Guerrilla offensives can involve making scattered, random raids on the leaders' customers with such tactics as occasional lowballing on price (to win a big order or steal a key account); surprising key rivals with sporadic but intense bursts of promotional activity (offering a 20 percent discount for one week to draw customers away from rival brands); or undertaking special campaigns to attract buyers away from rivals plagued with a strike or problems in meeting delivery schedules.[25] Guerrilla offensives are particularly well suited to small challengers who have neither the resources nor the market visibility to mount a full-fledged attack on industry leaders.[26]

Preemptive Strikes   Preemptive strategies involve moving first to secure an advantageous position that rivals are prevented or discouraged from duplicating. What makes a move preemptive is its one-of-a-kind nature—whoever strikes first stands to acquire competitive assets that rivals can't readily match. There are several ways a firm can bolster its competitive capabilities with preemptive moves: (1) securing exclusive or dominant access to the best distributors in a particular geographic region or country; (2) moving to obtain the most favorable site along a heavily traveled thoroughfare, at a new interchange or intersection, in a new shopping mall, in a natural beauty spot, close to cheap transportation or raw material supplies or market outlets, and so on; and (3) tying up the most reliable, high-quality suppliers via exclusive partnership, long-term contracts, or acquisition.[27] To be successful, a preemptive move doesn't have to totally block rivals from following or copying; it merely needs to give a firm a prime position that is not easily circumvented.

Choosing Which Rivals to Attack   Offensive-minded firms need to analyze which of their rivals to challenge as well as how to mount that challenge. The following are the best targets for offensive attacks:[28]

■ *Market leaders that are vulnerable*—Offensive attacks make good sense when a company that leads in terms of size and market share is not a true leader in terms of serving the market well. Signs of leader vulnerability include unhappy buyers, an inferior product line, a weak competitive strategy with regard to low-cost leadership or differentiation, strong emotional commitment to an aging technology the leader has pioneered, outdated plants and equipment, a preoccupation with diversification into other industries, and mediocre or declining profitability. Offensives to erode the positions of market leaders have real promise when the challenger is able to revamp its value chain or innovate to gain a fresh cost-based or differentiation-based competitive advantage.[29] To be judged successful, attacks on leaders don't have to result in making the aggressor the new leader; a challenger may "win" by simply becoming a stronger runner-up. Caution is well advised in challenging strong market leaders—there's a significant risk of squandering valuable resources in a futile effort or precipitating a fierce and profitless industrywide battle for market share.

■ *Runner-up firms with weaknesses where the challenger is strong*—Runner-up firms are an especially attractive target when a challenger's resource strengths and competitive capabilities are well suited to exploiting their weaknesses.

■ *Struggling enterprises that are on the verge of going under*—Challenging a hard-pressed rival in ways that further sap its financial strength and competitive position can weaken its resolve and hasten its exit from the market.

■ *Small local and regional firms with limited capabilities*—Because small firms typically have limited expertise and resources, a challenger with broader capabilities is well positioned to raid their biggest and best customers—particularly those who are growing rapidly, have increasingly sophisticated requirements, and may already be thinking about switching to a supplier with more full-service capability.

Choosing the Basis for Attack   A firm's strategic offensive should, at a minimum, be tied to what it does best—its core competencies, resource strengths, and competitive capabilities. Otherwise the prospects for success are indeed dim. The centerpiece of the offensive can be an important core competence, a unique competitive capability, much-improved performance features, an innovative new product, technological superiority, a cost advantage in manufacturing or distribution, or some kind of differentiation advantage. If the challenger's resources and competitive strengths amount to a competitive advantage over the targeted rivals, so much the better.

Defensive Strategy Options

> It is just as important to discern when to fortify a company's present market position with defensive actions as it is to seize the initiative and launch strategic offensives.

In a competitive market, all firms are subject to offensive challenges from rivals. The purposes of defensive strategies are to lower the risk of being attacked, weaken the impact of any attack that occurs, and influence challengers to aim their efforts at other rivals. While defensive strategies usually don't enhance a firm's competitive advantage, they can definitely help fortify its competitive position, protect its most valuable resources and capabilities from imitation, and defend whatever competitive advantage it might have. Defensive strategies can take either of two forms: actions to block challengers and signaling the likelihood of strong retaliation.

Blocking the Avenues Open to Challengers   The most frequently employed approach to defending a company's present position involves actions that restrict a challenger's options for initiating competitive attack. There are any number of

> There are many ways to throw obstacles in the path of challengers.

obstacles that can be put in the path of would-be challengers.[30] A defender can participate in alternative technologies to reduce the threat that rivals will attack with a better technology. A defender can introduce new features, add new models, or broaden its product line to close off gaps and vacant niches to would-be challengers. It can thwart the efforts of rivals to attack with a lower price by maintaining economy-priced options of its own. It can try to discourage buyers from trying competitors' brands by lengthening warranty coverages, offering free training and support services, developing the capability to deliver spare parts to users faster than rivals can, providing coupons and sample giveaways to buyers most prone to experiment, and making early announcements about impending new products or price changes to induce potential buyers to postpone switching, It can challenge the quality or safety of rivals' products. Finally, a defender can grant dealers and distributors volume discounts or better financing terms to discourage them from experimenting with other suppliers, or it can convince them to handle its product line *exclusively* and force competitors to use other distribution outlets.

Signaling Challengers That Retaliation Is Likely   The goal of signaling challengers that strong retaliation is likely in the event of an attack is either to dissuade challengers from attacking at all or to divert them to less threatening options. Either goal can be achieved by letting challengers know the battle will cost more than it is worth. Would-be challengers can be signaled by:[31]

- Publicly announcing management's commitment to maintain the firm's present market share.
- Publicly committing the company to a policy of matching competitors' terms or prices.
- Maintaining a war chest of cash and marketable securities.
- Making an occasional strong counterresponse to the moves of weak competitors to enhance the firm's image as a tough defender.

Strategies for Using the Internet as a Distribution Channel

As the Internet continues to weave its way into the fabric of everyday business and personal life, and as the second wave of Internet entrepreneurship takes root, companies of all types are addressing how best to make the Internet a fundamental part of their business and their competitive strategies. Few if any businesses can escape making some effort to use Internet applications to improve their value chain activities. This much is a given—anything less risks competitive disadvantage. Companies across the world are deep into the process of implementing a variety of Internet technology applications; the chief question companies face at this point is what additional Internet technology applications to incorporate into day-to-day operations. But the larger and much tougher *strategic* issue is how to make the Internet a fundamental part of a company's competitive strategy—in particular, how much emphasis to place on the Internet as a distribution channel

> Companies today must wrestle with the issue of how to use the Internet in positioning themselves in the marketplace—whether to use the Internet as just a vehicle for disseminating product information, as a minor distribution channel, as one of several important distribution channels, as the primary distribution channel, or as the company's only distribution channel.

for accessing buyers. *Managers must decide how to use the Internet in positioning the company in the marketplace*—whether to use the Internet as *only a means of disseminating product information* (with traditional distribution channel partners making all sales to end users), as a *secondary* or *minor* channel, as *one of several important distribution channels,* as *the primary distribution channel,* or as *the exclusive channel for accessing customers.*[32] Let's look at each of these strategic options in turn.

Using the Internet Just to Disseminate Product Information

Operating a website that contains extensive product information but that relies on click-throughs to the websites of distribution channel partners for sales transactions (or that informs site users where nearby retail stores are located) is an attractive market positioning option for manufacturers and/or wholesalers that already have retail dealer networks and face nettlesome channel conflict issues if they try to sell online in direct competition with their dealers. A manufacturer or wholesaler that aggressively pursues online sales to end users is signaling both a weak strategic commitment to its dealers and a willingness to cannibalize dealers' sales and growth potential. To the extent that strong partnerships with wholesale and/or retail dealers are critical to accessing end users, selling direct to end-users via the company's website is a very tricky road to negotiate. A manufacturer's efforts to use its website to sell around its dealers is certain to anger its wholesale distributors and retail dealers, who may respond by putting more effort into marketing the brands of rival manufacturers who don't sell online. In sum, the manufacturer may stand to lose more sales through its dealers than it gains from its own online sales effort. Moreover, dealers may be in better position to employ a brick-and-click strategy than a manufacturer is because dealers have a local presence to complement their online sales approach (which consumers may find appealing). Consequently, in industries where the strong support and goodwill of dealer networks is essential, manufacturers may conclude that their website should be designed to partner with dealers rather than compete with them—just as the auto manufacturers are doing with their franchised dealers.

Using the Internet as a Minor Distribution Channel

A second strategic option is to use online sales as a relatively minor distribution channel for achieving incremental sales, gaining online sales experience, and doing marketing research. If channel conflict poses a big obstacle to online sales, or if only a small fraction of buyers can be attracted to make online purchases, then companies are well advised to pursue online sales with the strategic intent of gaining experience, learning more about buyer tastes and preferences, testing reaction to new products, creating added market buzz about their products, and boosting overall sales volume a few percentage points. Nike, for example, has begun selling some of its footwear online, giving buyers the option of specifying certain colors and features. Such a strategy is unlikely to provoke much resistance from dealers and could even prove beneficial to dealers if footwear buyers become enamored with custom-made shoes that can be ordered through and/or picked up at Nike retailers. A manufacturer may be able to glean valuable marketing research data from tracking the browsing patterns of website visitors and incorporating what generates the most interest into its mainstream product offerings. The behavior and actions of Web surfers are a veritable gold mine of information for companies seeking to respond more precisely to buyer preferences.

Brick-and-Click Strategies: An Appealing Middle Ground

Employing a brick-and-click strategy to sell directly to consumers while at the same time utilizing traditional wholesale and retail channels can be an attractive market positioning option in the right circumstances. With a brick-and-click strategy, online sales at a company's website can serve as either one of several important distribution channels through which the company accesses end users or as its primary distribution channel. Software developers, for example, have come to rely on the Internet as a highly effective distribution channel to complement sales through brick-and-mortar wholesalers and retailers. Selling online directly to end users has the advantage of cutting out the costs and margins of software wholesalers and retailers (often 35 to 50 percent of the retail price). In addition, allowing customers to download their software purchases immediately via the Internet eliminates the costs of producing and packaging CDs. However, software developers are still strongly motivated to continue to distribute their products through wholesalers and retailers (to maintain broad access to existing and potential users who, for whatever reason, may be reluctant to buy online).

Despite the channel conflict that exists when a manufacturer sells directly to end users at its website in head-to-head competition with its distribution channel allies, there are three major reasons why manufacturers might want to aggressively pursue online sales and establish the Internet as an important distribution channel alongside traditional channels:

1. The manufacturer's profit margin from online sales is bigger than that from sales through wholesale/retail channels.

2. Encouraging buyers to visit the company's website helps educate them to the ease and convenience of purchasing online, thus encouraging more and more buyers to migrate to buying online (where company profit margins are greater).

3. Selling directly to end users allows a manufacturer to make greater use of build-to-order manufacturing and assembly as a basis for bypassing traditional distribution

channels entirely. Dell Computer, for instance, has used online sales to make build-to-order options a cost-effective reality. Similarly, several motor vehicle companies have initiated actions to streamline build-to-order manufacturing capabilities and reduce delivery times for custom orders from 30–60 days to as few as 5–10 days; most vehicle manufacturers already have software on their websites that permits motor vehicle shoppers to select the models, colors, and optional equipment they would like to have. In industries where build-to-order options can result in substantial cost savings along the industry value chain and permit sizable price reductions to end users, companies have to consider making build-to-order and sell-direct an integral part of their market positioning strategy. Over time, such a strategy could increase the rate at which sales migrate from distribution allies to the company's website.

A combination brick-and-click market positioning strategy is highly suitable when on-line sales have a good chance of *evolving* into a manufacturer's primary distribution channel. In such instances, incurring channel conflict in the short term and competing against traditional distribution allies makes good strategic sense.

Many brick-and-mortar companies can enter online retailing at relatively low cost—all they need is a Web store and systems for filling and delivering individual customer orders. Brick-and-click strategies have two big strategic appeals for whole-sale and retail enterprises: They are an economic means of expanding a company's geographic reach, and they give both existing and potential customers another choice of how to communicate with the company, shop for product information, make purchases, or resolve customer service problems. Brick-and-mortar distributors and retailers (as well as manufacturers with company-owned retail stores) can shift to brick-and-click strategies by using their current distribution centers and/or retail stores for picking orders from on-hand inventories and making deliveries. Walgreen's, a leading drugstore chain, allows customers to order a prescription online and then pick it up at a local store (using the drive-through window, in some cases). In banking, a brick-and-click strategy allows customers to use local branches and ATMs for depositing checks and getting cash while using online systems to pay bills, check account balances, and transfer funds. Many industrial distributors are finding it efficient for customers to place their orders over the Web rather than phoning them in or waiting for salespeople to call in person. Company Spotlight 4.7 describes how Office Depot has successfully migrated from a traditional brick-and-mortar distribution strategy to a combination brick-and-click distribution strategy.

Strategies for Online Enterprises

A company that elects to use the Internet as its exclusive channel for accessing buyers is essentially an online business from the perspective of the customer. The Internet becomes the vehicle for transacting sales and delivering customer services; except for advertising, the Internet is the sole point of all buyer–seller contact. Many so-called pure dot-com enterprises have chosen this strategic approach—prominent examples include eBay, Amazon.com, Yahoo!, Buy.com, and Priceline.com. For a company to succeed in using the Internet as its exclusive distribution channel, its product or service must be one for which buying online holds strong appeal. Furthermore, judging from the evidence thus far, an online company's strategy must incorporate the following features:

■ *The capability to deliver unique value to buyers*—Winning strategies succeed in drawing buyers because of the value being delivered. This means that online businesses must usually attract buyers on the basis of something more than just low

Office Depot's Brick-and-Click Strategy

Office Depot was in the first wave of retailers to adopt a combination brick-and-click strategy. In 1996, it began allowing business customers to use the Internet to place orders. Businesses could thus avoid having to make a call, generate a purchase order, and pay an invoice—while still getting same-day or next-day delivery from one of Office Depot's local stores.

Office Depot built its Internet business around its existing network of 750 retail stores; 30 warehouses; 2,000 delivery trucks; $1.3 billion in inventories; and phone-order sales department, which handled large business customers. It already had a solid brand name and enough purchasing power with its suppliers to counter discount-minded online rivals trying to attract buyers of office supplies on the basis of superlow prices. Office Depot's incremental investment to enter the e-commerce arena was extremely low since all it needed to add was a website where customers could see pictures and descriptions of the items it carried, their prices, and in-stock availability; its marketing costs to make customers aware of its Web store option ran less than $10 million.

In setting up customized Web pages for 37,000 corporate and educational customers, Office Depot designed sites that allowed the customer's employees varying degrees of freedom to buy supplies. A clerk might be able to order only copying paper, toner cartridges, computer disks, and paper clips up to a preset dollar limit per order, while a vice president might have carte blanche to order any item Office Depot sold. Office Depot's online prices were the same as its store prices; the company's strategy was to promote Web sales on the basis of service, convenience, and lower customer costs for order processing and inventories.

In 2002, over 50 percent of Office Depot's major customers were ordering most of their supplies online because of the convenience and the savings in transactions costs. Bank of America, for example, was ordering 85 percent of its office supplies online from Office Depot.

Customers reported that using the website cut their transaction costs by up to 80 percent; plus, Office Depot's same-day or next-day delivery capability allowed them to reduce the amount of office supplies they kept in inventory.

Website sales cost Office Depot less than $1 per $100 of goods ordered, compared with about $2 for phone and fax orders. And since Web sales eliminate the need to key in transactions, order-entry errors have been virtually eliminated and product returns cut by 50 percent. Billing is handled electronically.

Office Depot's online unit accounted for $1.5 billion in sales in 2001, up sharply from $982 million in 2000. Online sales contributed 14 percent to the company's overall sales and made Office Depot the second-largest online retailer behind Amazon.com. Office Depot's online operations have been profitable from the start. Industry experts believe that Office Depot's success is based on the company's philosophy of maintaining a strong link between the Internet and its stores. "Office Depot gets it," noted one industry analyst. "It used the Net to build deeper relationships with customers."

Sources: "Office Depot's e-Diva," *Business Week Online* (www.businessweek.com), August 6, 2001; Laura Lorek, "Office Depot Site Picks Up Speed," *Interactive Week* (www.zdnet.com/intweek), June 25, 2001; "Why Office Depot Loves the Net," *Business Week*, September 27, 1999, pp. EB 66, EB 68; and *Fortune*, November 8, 1999, p. 17.

price—indeed, many dot-coms are already working to tilt the basis for competing away from low price and toward build-to-order systems, convenience, superior product information, attentive online service, and other ways to attract customers to buying online (as opposed to buying from offline sellers).

- *Deliberate efforts to engineer a value chain that enables differentiation, lower costs, or better value for the money*—For a company to win in the marketplace with an online-only distribution strategy, its value chain approach must hold potential for low-cost leadership, competitively valuable differentiating attributes, or a best-cost provider advantage. If a firm's strategy is to attract customers by selling at cut-rate prices, then it must possess cost advantages in those activities it performs, and it must outsource the remaining activities to low-cost specialists. If an online seller is going to differentiate itself on the basis of a superior buying experience and top-notch customer service, then it needs to concentrate on having an easy-to-navigate website, an array of functions and conveniences for customers, "Web reps" who can answer questions online, and logistical capabilities to deliver products quickly and accommodate returned merchandise. If it is going to deliver more value for the money, then it must manage value chain activities so as to deliver upscale products and services at lower costs than rivals. Absent a value chain that puts the company in an attractive position to compete head-to-head against other online and brick-and-mortar rivals, such a distribution strategy is unlikely to produce attractive profitability.

- *An innovative, fresh, and entertaining website*—Just as successful brick-and-mortar retailers employ merchandising strategies to keep their stores fresh and interesting to shoppers, Web merchandisers must exert ongoing efforts to add innovative site features and capabilities, enhance the look and feel of their sites, heighten viewer interest with audio and video, and have fresh product offerings and special promotions. Web pages need to be easy to read and interesting, with lots of eye appeal. Website features that are distinctive, engaging, and entertaining add value to the experience of spending time at the site and are thus strong competitive assets. This generally means that the company must have strong Internet technology capabilities.

- *A clear focus on a limited number of competencies and a relatively specialized number of value chain activities in which proprietary Internet applications and capabilities can be developed*—Low-value-added activities can be delegated to outside specialists. A strong market position is far more likely to emerge from efforts to develop proprietary Internet applications than from using third-party developers' software packages, which are also readily available to imitative rivals. Outsourcing value chain activities for which there is little potential for proprietary advantage allows an enterprise to concentrate on the ones for which it has the most expertise and through which it can gain competitive advantage.

- *Innovative marketing techniques that are efficient in reaching the targeted audience and effective in stimulating purchases (or boosting ancillary revenue sources like advertising)*—Websites have to be cleverly marketed. Unless Web surfers hear about the site, like what they see on their first visit, and are intrigued enough to return again and again, the site will not generate enough revenue to allow the company to survive. Marketing campaigns that result only in heavy site traffic and lots of page views are seldom sufficient; the best test of effective marketing is the ratio at which page views are converted into revenues (the "look-to-buy" ratio). For example, in 2001 Yahoo!'s site traffic averaged 1.2 *billion* page views daily but generated only about $2 million in daily revenues; in contrast, the traffic at brokerage firm Charles Schwab's website averaged only 40 *million* page views per day but resulted in an average of $5 million daily in online commission revenues.

- *Minimal reliance on ancillary revenues*—Online businesses have to charge fully for the value delivered to customers rather than subsidizing artificially low prices with revenues collected from advertising and other ancillary sources. Companies should view site-advertising revenues and other revenue extras as a way to boost the profitability of an already profitable core businesses, *not* as a means of covering core business losses.

The Issue of Broad versus Narrow Product Offerings   Given that shelf space on the Internet is unlimited, online sellers have to make shrewd decisions about how to position themselves on the spectrum of broad versus narrow product offerings. A one-stop shopping strategy like that employed by Amazon.com has the appealing economics of helping spread fixed operating costs over a wide number of items and a large customer base. Amazon has diversified its product offerings beyond books to include electronics, computers, housewares, music, DVDs, videos, cameras, toys, baby items and baby registry, software, computer and video games, cell phones and service, tools and hardware, travel services, magazine subscriptions, and outdoor-living items; it has also allowed small specialty-item e-tailers to market their products on the Amazon website. The company's tag line "Earth's Biggest Selection" seems accurate: In 2002, Amazon offered some 34 million items at its websites in the United States, Britain, France, Germany, Denmark, and Japan. Other e-tailers, such as Expedia and Hotel.com, have adopted classic focus strategies—building a website aimed at a sharply defined target audience shopping for a particular product or product category. "Focusers" seek to build customer loyalty based on attractively low prices, better value, wide selection of models and styles within the targeted category, convenient service, nifty options, or some other differentiating attribute. They pay special attention to the details that will please their narrow target audience.

The Order Fulfillment Issue   Another big strategic issue for dot-com retailers is whether to perform order fulfillment activities internally or to outsource them. Building central warehouses, stocking them with adequate inventories, and developing systems to pick, pack, and ship individual orders all require substantial start-up capital but may result in lower overall unit costs than would paying the fees of order fulfillment specialists who make a business of providing warehouse space, stocking inventories, and shipping orders for e-tailers. Outsourcing is likely to be economical unless an e-tailer has high unit volume and the capital to invest in its own order fulfillment capabilities. Buy.com, an online superstore consisting of some 30,000 items, obtains products from name-brand manufacturers and uses outsiders to stock and ship those products; thus, its focus is not on manufacturing or order fulfillment but rather on selling.

Choosing Appropriate Functional-Area Strategies

A company's strategy is not complete until company managers have made strategic choices about how the various functional parts of the business—R&D, production, human resources, sales and marketing, finance, and so on—will be managed in support of its basic competitive strategy approach and the other important competitive moves being taken. Normally, functional-area strategy choices rank third on the menu of choosing among the various strategy options, as shown in Figure 4.1. Deciding how to manage specific functions within a company's business hinges on what needs to be done in each area to support and enhance the success of the company's higher-level strategic thrusts. However, *when* functional strategies are chosen is not as important as *what* the strategies are.

Table 4.1 on page 113 indicates what the production and marketing thrusts need to be in supporting each of the five competitive strategies. Beyond these very general prescriptions, it is difficult to say just what the content of the different functional strategies should be without first knowing what higher-level strategic choices a company has made. Suffice it to say here that company personnel—both managers and employees charged with strategy-making responsibility down through the organizational hierarchy—must be told which higher-level strategies have been chosen and then must tailor the company's functional-area strategies accordingly. (To refresh your memory of what is involved here, you may want to reread the sections in Chapter 1 relating to functional-area strategies and the important role they have in a company's overall strategy—see Figure 1.4 and the subsection headed "Who Participates in Crafting a Company's Strategy?")

The Importance of Linking Strategy to Company Values and Ethical Standards

Managers do not dispassionately assess what strategic course to steer. Their choices are typically influenced by their own vision of how to compete, by their own character and ethical standards, by whether they "walk the talk" in displaying the company's stated values and exemplifying its stated business principles, and by how genuinely they strive to balance the best interests of stakeholders—employees, suppliers, customers, shareholders, and society at large. The experiences at Enron, WorldCom, Tyco, HealthSouth, Rite Aid, and several other companies illustrate that when top executives devise shady strategies or wink at unethical behavior, the impact on the company can be devastating.

But tightly linking company strategy to high ethical standards and societal acceptability goes far beyond simply avoiding a corporate black eye from the blow of public disclosure of corporate misdeeds. Ethical strategy making generally begins with two things: (1) managers who themselves have strong character (i.e., who are honest, have integrity, are ethical, and truly care about how they conduct the company's business), and (2) a set of corporate values and ethical standards that genuinely govern a company's strategy and business conduct. Many companies now have a written statement of company values and a code of ethical conduct, both of which are often posted on the company website. But there's a big difference between adopting statements and codes that serve merely as a public smoke screen and developing values and ethical standards that paint the white lines for a company's actual strategy and business conduct. Several top Enron executives made a farce of the company's stated values of "integrity, respect, communication, and excellence"—and destroyed the company in the process. Top executives, directors, and majority shareholders at Adelphia Communications ripped off the company for amounts totaling well over $1 billion and drove it into bankruptcy; their actions, which represent one of the biggest instances of corporate looting and self-dealing in American business, took place despite the company's public pontifications about the principles it would observe in trying to care for customers, employees, stockholders, and the local communities where it operated. Providian Financial Corporation, despite an otherwise glowing record of social responsibility and service to many of its stakeholders, in December 2001 paid $150 million to settle class-action lawsuits alleging that its strategy included attempts to systematically cheat credit card holders.

Boards of directors and top executives must work diligently to see that values statements and ethical codes not only are scrupulously observed in devising strategies and conducting every facet of the company's business but also become a way of life at the company. No company is protected from unethical actions on the part of executives without close monitoring by board members and strong cultural and peer pressures.

However, the recent spate of corporate scandals, which were hatched in the excesses of the late 1990s and which came home to roost in 2001–2003, has resulted in some very positive reforms. Alarmed by the public's loss of confidence in business practices and financial reporting, corporate America has moved to clean up its act (in part, no doubt, because it had little other choice). Outside auditing firms are exercising greater independence than ever before in reviewing their clients' financial statements (rather than turning a blind eye in order to win multimillion-dollar consulting contracts).

Yet it would be unfair and inaccurate to tar all companies and executives as un-ethical merely because of the excesses of a few that made headline news. At an important number of companies, deeply ingrained values and high ethical standards are reflected in their strategic actions. The strategy crafted by Starbucks' CEO, Howard Schultz, mirrors Schultz's insistence on customers having a very positive experience when patronizing a Starbucks store and his desire to "build a company with soul" and make Starbucks a great place to work. Deere & Company has been guided for over 165 years by four core values exhibited by its founder John Deere and long practiced by company managers and employees: quality, innovation, integrity, and commitment. Deere consistently takes top honors in *Fortune* magazine's annual listing of "America's Most Admired Companies" in the industrial and farm equipment category; in June 2002, *Crain's Chicago Business* ranked Deere & Company as the most-trusted Illinois company and gave it the top ranking for product quality. Deere's mission to "Double and Double Again the John Deere Experience of Genuine Value for Employees, Customers, and Shareholders" is pursued via a strategy aimed at rapidly expanding the company's global ability to supply customers at farmsites, worksites, homes, and turfsites with a growing line of farm, lawn and garden, golf and turf, forestry, and construction equipment products. Most companies have strategies that pass the test of being ethical, and most companies are aware that both their reputations and their long-term well-being are tied to conducting their business in a manner that wins the approval of suppliers, employees, investors, and society at large. Company Spotlight 4.8 contains an "ethics quiz" on the strategic practices of several companies—judge for yourself whether these companies measure up.

First-Mover Advantages and Disadvantages

When to make a strategic move is often as crucial as *what* move to make. Timing is especially important when *first-mover advantages* or *disadvantages* exist.[33] Being first to initiate a strategic move can have a high payoff when (1) pioneering helps build a firm's image and reputation with buyers; (2) early commitments to new technologies, new-style components, distribution channels, and so on can produce an absolute cost advantage over rivals; (3) first-time customers remain strongly loyal to pioneering firms in making repeat purchases; and (4) moving first constitutes a preemptive strike, making imitation extra hard or unlikely. The bigger the first-mover advantages, the more attractive making the first move becomes.[34] In the Internet gold-rush era, several companies that were first with a new technology, network solution, or business model enjoyed lasting first-mover advantages in gaining the visibility and reputation needed to emerge as the dominant market leader—America Online, Amazon.com, Yahoo!, eBay, and Priceline.com are cases

> **Core Concept**
>
> Because of first-mover advantages and disadvantages, competitive advantage can spring from *when* a move is made as well as from *what* move is made.

in point. But a first-mover also needs to be a fast learner (so as to sustain any advantage of being a pioneer), and it helps immensely if the first-mover has deep financial pockets, important competencies and competitive capabilities, and high-quality management. Just being a first-mover by itself is seldom enough to yield competitive advantage. The proper target in timing a strategic move is not that of being the first company to do something but rather that of being the first competitor to put together the precise combination of features, customer value, and sound revenue/cost/profit economics that gives it an edge over rivals in the battle for market leadership.[35]

However, being a fast-follower or even a wait-and-see late-mover doesn't always carry a significant or lasting competitive penalty. There are times when a first-mover's skills, know-how, and actions are easily copied or even surpassed, allowing late-movers to catch or overtake the first-mover in a relatively short period. And there are times when there are actually *advantages* to being an adept follower rather than a first-mover. Late-mover advantages (or first-mover disadvantages) arise when (1) pioneering leadership is more costly than imitating followership and only negligible experience or learning-curve benefits accrue to the leader—a condition that allows a follower to end up with lower costs than the first-mover; (2) the products of an innovator are somewhat primitive and do not live up to buyer expectations, thus allowing a clever follower to win disenchanted buyers away from the leader with better-performing products; and (3) technology is advancing rapidly, giving fast-followers the opening to leapfrog a first-mover's products with more attractive and full-featured second- and third-generation products.

In weighing the pros and cons of being a first-mover versus a fast-follower, it is important to discern when the race to market leadership in a particular industry is a marathon rather than a sprint. In marathons, a slow-mover is not unduly penalized—first-mover advantages can be fleeting, and there's ample time for fast-followers to play catch-up.[36] For instance, it took seven years for videocassette recorders to find their way into 1 million U.S. homes but only 18 months for 10 million users to sign up for Hotmail. The lesson here is that there is a market-penetration curve for every emerging opportunity; typically, the curve has an inflection point at which all the pieces of the business model fall into place, buyer demand explodes, and the market takes off. The inflection point can come early on a fast-rising curve or farther on up a slow-rising curve. Any company that seeks competitive advantage by being a first-mover should thus first pose some hard questions: Does market takeoff depend on the development of complementary products or services that currently are not available? Is new infrastructure required before buyer demand can surge? Will buyers need to learn new skills or adopt new behaviors? Will buyers encounter high switching costs? Are there influential competitors in a position to delay or derail the efforts of a first-mover? When the answers to any of these questions are yes, then a company must be careful not to pour too many resources into getting ahead of the market opportunity—the race is likely going to be more of a 10-year marathon than a 2-year sprint. But being first out of the starting block is competitively important if it produces clear and substantial benefits to buyers and competitors will be compelled to follow.

While being an adept fast-follower has the advantages of being less risky and skirting the costs of pioneering, rarely does a company have much to gain from being a slow-follower and concentrating on avoiding the "mistakes" of first-movers. Habitual late-movers, while often able to survive, are usually fighting to retain their customers and scrambling to keep pace with more progressive and innovative rivals. For a habitual late-mover to catch up, it must count on first-movers to be slow learners.

COMPANY SPOTLIGHT 4.8

Ethics Quiz: Do These Companies Have Shady Strategies?

Read the brief description of what each of the following companies is doing and decide whether its strategy is ethical or not. Then ponder how you would answer the four questions that appear below.

- Fleming Companies, the largest U.S. distributor of grocery products, has been accused by dozens of its suppliers of consistently deducting arbitrary sums (amounting to perhaps $100 million annually) from the billings they submit—the practice was said to be a part of Fleming's turnaround strategy to boost its own margins and restore profitability after five money-losing years (1996–2000). According to a food industry consultant who has worked for the company, Fleming's "relationship with vendors is ugly. They deduct and deduct until a vendor cuts them off, then they pay. Then they start deducting again." Former high-level Fleming employees claimed that the company played games with slotting fees, sometimes taking slotting fee deductions form manufacturer billings for products it never stocked in its warehouse or put on retailers' shelves. Fleming enjoys a powerful gatekeeper status because many food manufacturers use a grocery distributor to access small independent grocery chains and because many small grocers get most of their merchandise through a grocery distributor (unlike large chains like Wal-Mart and Safeway that buy directly from the manufacturers). Thus manufacturers that sell through Fleming are hesitant to cut off deliveries to Fleming or protest its deductions too vociferously because they don't have effective alternatives to getting their products to Fleming's grocery customers.

  Relationships with some of Fleming's retail customers, most notably Kmart (its biggest customer) and several small independent supermarkets, were also said to be strained because of recurring service and billing issues.

- At Salomon Smith Barney (a subsidiary of Citigroup), Credit Suisse First Boston (CSFB), and Goldman Sachs (three of the world's most prominent investment banking companies), part of the strategy for securing the investment banking business of large corporate clients (to handle the sale of new stock issues or new bond issues or advise on mergers and acquisitions) involved (1) hyping the stocks of companies that were actual or prospective customers of their investment

banking services, and (2) allocating hard-to-get shares of hot new initial public offerings (IPOs) to select executives and directors of existing and potential client companies, who then made millions of dollars in profits when the stocks went up once public trading began. Former WorldCom CEO Bernie Ebbers reportedly made more than $11 million in trading profits over a four-year period on shares of IPOs received from Salomon Smith Barney; Salomon served as WorldCom's investment banker on a variety of deals during this period. Jack Grubman, Salomon's top-paid research analyst at the time, enthusiastically touted WorldCom stock and was regarded as the company's biggest cheerleader on Wall Street.

  To help draw in business from new or existing corporate clients, CSFB established brokerage accounts for corporate executives who steered their company's investment banking business to CSFB. Apparently, CSFB's strategy for acquiring more business involved promising the CEO and/or CFO of companies about to go public for the first time or needing to issue new long-term bonds that if CSFB was chosen to handle their company's new initial public offering of common stock or a new bond issue, then CSFB would ensure they would be allocated shares at the initial offering price of all subsequent IPOs in which CSFB was a participant. During 1999–2000, it was common for the stock of a hot new IPO to rise 100 to 500 percent above the initial offering price in the first few days or weeks of public trading; the shares allocated to these executives were then sold for a tidy profit over the initial offering price. According to investigative sources, CSFB increased the number of companies whose executives were allowed to participate in its IPO offerings from 26 companies in January 1999 to 160 companies in early 2000; executives received anywhere from 200 to 1,000 shares each of every IPO in which CSFB was a participant in 2000. CSFB's accounts for these executives reportedly generated profits of about $80 million for the participants. Apparently, it was CSFB's practice to curtail access to IPOs for some executives if their companies didn't come through with additional securities business for CSFB or if CSFB concluded that other securities offerings by these companies would be unlikely.

Goldman Sachs also used an IPO-allocation scheme to attract investment banking business, giving shares to executives at 21 companies—among the participants were the CEOs of eBay, Yahoo!, and Ford Motor Company. EBay's CEO was a participant in over 100 IPOs managed by Goldman during the 1996–2000 period and was on Goldman's board of directors part of this time; eBay paid Goldman Sachs $8 million in fees for services during the 1996–2001 period.

- The world's five major music recording studios—Universal, Sony, Time Warner, EMI/Virgin, and Bertlesmann—have incurred the wrath of numerous recording artists and the Recording Artists' Coalition for pursuing strategies calculated to disadvantage musicians who record for them. Most major-label record companies require artists to sign contracts committing them to do six to eight albums, an obligation that some artists say can entail an indefinite term of indentured servitude. Audits routinely detect unpaid royalties to musicians under contract; according to one music industry attorney, record companies misreport and underpay artist royalties by 10 to 40 percent and are "intentionally fraudulent." One music writer was recently quoted as saying the process was "an entrenched system whose prowess and conniving makes Enron look like amateur hour." Royalty calculations are based on complex formulas that are paid only after artists pay for recording costs and other expenses and after any advances are covered by royalty earnings. A *Baffler* magazine article outlined a hypothetical but typical record deal where a promising young band is given a $250,000 royalty advance on a new album, The album subsequently sells 250,000 copies, earning $710,000 for the record company; but the band, after repaying the record company for $264,000 in expenses ranging from recording fees and video budgets to catering, wardrobe, and bus tour costs for promotional events related to the album, ends up $14,000 in the hole, owes the record company money, and is thus paid no royalties on any of the $710,000 in revenues the recording company receives from the sale of the band's music. It is also standard practice in the music industry for recording studios to sidestep payola laws by hiring independent promoters to lobby and compensate radio stations for playing certain records. Record companies are often entitled to damages for undelivered albums if an artist leaves a recording studio for another label after seven years. Record companies also retain the copyrights in perpetuity on all music recorded under contract, a practice that artists claim is unfair. The Dixie Chicks, after a year-long feud with Sony over contract terms, ended up refusing to do another album; Sony sued for breach of contract, prompting a countersuit by the Dixie Chicks charging "systematic thievery" to cheat them out of royalties. The suits were settled out of court. One artist said, "The record companies are like cartels."

  Recording studios defend their strategic practices by pointing out that fewer than 5 percent of the signed artists ever deliver a hit and that they lose money on albums that sell poorly. According to one study, only 1 of 244 contracts signed during 1994–1996 was negotiated without the artists being represented by legal counsel, and virtually all contracts renegotiated after a hit album added terms more favorable to the artist.

Some Questions for You to Consider

- Would you want to be an employee of any of the companies described above? Would you be proud of the company you worked for if you were an employee?

- Would you feel comfortable doing business with any of these companies? Why or why not?

- If you were a top executive of one of these companies, would you be proud to defend your company's actions? Would you want to step forward and take credit for having been a part of the company's strategy-making team?

- If you were a shareholder in any of these companies, would you be pleased with your company's reputation in the business world and the character of its top executives?

Sources: Ann Zimmerman, "Grocery Supplier Squeezes Suppliers at Bill-Paying Time," *The Wall Street Journal*, September 5, 2002, pp. A1, A10; Charles Gasparino, "Salomon Probe Includes Senior Executives," *The Wall Street Journal*, September 3, 2002, p. C1; Randall Smith and Susan Pulliam, "How a Star Banker Pressed for IPOs," *The Wall Street Journal*, September 4, 2002, pp. C1, C14; Randall Smith and Susan Pulliam, "How a Technology-Banking Star Doled Out Shares of Hot IPOs," *The Wall Street Journal*, September 23, 2002, pp. A1, A10; Randall Smith, "Goldman Sachs Faces Scrutiny for IPO-Allocation Practices," *The Wall Street Journal*, October 3, 2002, pp. A1, A6; Edna Gundersen, "Rights Issue Rocks the Music World," *USA Today*, September 16, 2002, pp. D1, D2.

Plus it has to hope that buyers will be slow to gravitate to the products of first-movers, again giving it time to catch up. And it has to have competencies and capabilities that are sufficiently strong to allow it to close the gap fairly quickly once it makes its move. Counting on all first-movers to stumble or otherwise be easily overtaken is usually a bad bet that puts a late-mover's competitive position at risk.

Key Points

A company competing in a particular industry or market has a varied menu of strategy options for seeking and securing a competitive advantage (see Figure 4.1). The first and foremost strategic choice is which of the five basic competitive strategies to employ—overall low-cost, broad differentiation, best-cost, focused low-cost, or focused differentiation.

A strategy of trying to be the industry's low-cost provider works well in situations where:

1. The industry's product is essentially the same from seller to seller (brand differences are minor).

2. Many buyers are price-sensitive and shop for the lowest price.

3. There are only a few ways to achieve product differentiation that have much value to buyers.

4. Most buyers use the product in the same ways and thus have common user requirements.

5. Buyers' costs in switching from one seller or brand to another are low or even zero.

6. Buyers are large and have significant power to negotiate pricing terms.

To achieve a low-cost advantage, a company must become more skilled than rivals in controlling the cost drivers and/or it must find innovative ways to eliminate or bypass cost-producing activities. Successful low-cost providers usually achieve their cost advantages by imaginatively and persistently ferreting out cost savings throughout the value chain. They are good at finding ways to drive costs out of their businesses year after year after year.

Differentiation strategies seek to produce a competitive edge by incorporating attributes and features into a company's product/service offering that rivals don't have. Anything a firm can do to create buyer value represents a potential basis for differentiation. Successful differentiation is usually keyed to lowering the buyer's cost of using the item, raising the performance the buyer gets, or boosting a buyer's psychological satisfaction. To be sustainable, differentiation usually has to be linked to unique internal expertise, core competencies, and resources that translate into capabilities rivals can't easily match. Differentiation tied just to unique features seldom is lasting because resourceful competitors are adept at cloning, improving on, or finding substitutes for almost any feature that appeals to buyers.

Best-cost provider strategies combine a strategic emphasis on low cost with a strategic emphasis on more than minimal quality, service, features, or performance. The aim is to create competitive advantage by giving buyers more value for the money; this is done by matching close rivals on key quality/service/features/performance attributes and beating them on the costs of incorporating such attributes into the product or service. To be successful with a best-cost provider strategy, a company must be able to incorporate upscale product or service attributes at a lower cost than rivals. Sustaining a best-cost provider strategy generally means having the capability to simultaneously manage unit costs down and product/service caliber up.

A focus strategy delivers competitive advantage either by achieving lower costs in serving the target market niche or by developing an ability to offer niche buyers something different from rival competitors. A focused strategy based on either low cost or differentiation becomes increasingly attractive as more of the following conditions are met:

1. The target market niche is big enough to be profitable and offers good growth potential.

2. Industry leaders do not see that having a presence in the niche is crucial to their own success—in which case focusers can often escape battling head-to-head against some of the industry's biggest and strongest competitors.

3. It is costly or difficult for multisegment competitors to put capabilities in place to meet the specialized needs of the target market niche and at the same time satisfy the expectations of their mainstream customers.

4. The industry has many different niches and segments, thereby allowing a focuser to pick a competitively attractive niche suited to its resource strengths and capabilities. Also, with more niches there is more room for focusers to avoid each other in competing for the same customers.

5. Few, if any, other rivals are attempting to specialize in the same target segment—a condition that reduces the risk of segment overcrowding.

6. The focuser can compete effectively against challengers based on the capabilities and resources it has to serve the targeted niche and the customer goodwill it may have built up.

Once a company has selected which of the five basic competitive strategies to employ in its quest for competitive advantage, then it must decide whether to supplement its choice of a basic competitive strategy approach with strategic actions relating to forming alliances and collaborative partnerships, mergers and acquisitions, integration forward or backward, outsourcing certain value chain activities, offensive and defensive moves, and what use to make of the Internet in selling directly to end users, as shown in Figure 4.1.

Many companies are using strategic alliances and collaborative partnerships to help them in the race to build a global market presence and in the technology race. Even large and financially strong companies have concluded that simultaneously running both races requires more diverse and expansive skills, resources, technological expertise, and competitive capabilities than they can assemble and manage alone. Strategic alliances are an attractive, flexible, and often cost-effective means by which companies can gain access to missing technology, expertise, and business capabilities. The competitive attraction of alliances is to bundle competencies and resources that are more valuable in a joint effort than when kept separate. Competitive advantage emerges when a company acquires valuable resources and capabilities through alliances that it could not otherwise obtain on its own and that give it an edge over rivals.

Mergers and acquisitions are another attractive strategic option for strengthening a firm's competitiveness. Companies racing for global market leadership frequently make acquisitions to build a market presence in countries where they currently do not compete. Similarly, companies racing to establish attractive positions in the industries of the future merge or make acquisitions to close gaps in resources or technology, build important technological capabilities, and move into position to launch next-wave products and services. When the operations of two companies are combined via merger or acquisition, the new company's competitiveness can be enhanced in any of several ways—lower costs; stronger technological skills; more or better competitive capabilities; a more attractive lineup of products and services; wider geographic coverage; and/or greater financial resources with which to invest in R&D, add capacity, or expand into new areas.

Vertically integrating forward or backward makes strategic sense only if it strengthens a company's position via either cost reduction or creation of a differentiation-based advantage. Otherwise, the drawbacks of vertical integration (increased investment, greater business risk, increased vulnerability to technological changes, and less flexibility in making product changes) outweigh the advantages (better coordination of production flows and technological know-how from stage to stage, more specialized use of technology, greater internal control over operations, greater scale economies, and matching production with sales and marketing). Collaborative partnerships with suppliers and/or distribution allies often permit a company to achieve the advantages of vertical integration without encountering the drawbacks.

Outsourcing pieces of the value chain formerly performed in-house can enhance a company's competitiveness whenever (1) an activity can be performed better or more cheaply by outside specialists; (2) the activity is not crucial to the firm's ability to achieve sustainable competitive advantage and won't hollow out its core competencies, capabilities, or technical know-how; (3) it reduces the company's risk exposure to changing technology and/or changing buyer preferences; (4) it streamlines company operations in ways that improve organizational flexibility, cut cycle time, speed decision making, and reduce coordination costs; and/or (5) it allows a company to concentrate on its core business and do what it does best. In many situations outsourcing is a superior strategic alternative to vertical integration.

A variety of offensive strategic moves can be used to secure a competitive advantage. Strategic offensives can be aimed either at competitors' strengths or at their weaknesses; they can involve end runs or grand offensives on many fronts; they can be designed as guerrilla actions or as preemptive strikes; and the target of the offensive can be a market leader, a runner-up firm, or the smallest and/or weakest firms in the industry.

Defensive strategies to protect a company's position usually take the form of making moves that put obstacles in the path of would-be challengers and fortify the company's present position while undertaking actions to dissuade rivals from even trying to attack (by signaling that the resulting battle will be more costly to the challenger than it is worth).

One of the most pertinent strategic issues that companies face is how to use the Internet in positioning the company in the marketplace—whether to use the Internet as *only a means of disseminating product information* (with traditional distribution channel partners making all sales to end users), as a *secondary* or *minor* channel, as *one of several important* distribution channels, as the company's *primary distribution channel,* or as the company's *exclusive channel for accessing customers.*

Once all the higher-level strategic choices have been made, company managers can turn to the task of crafting functional and operating-level strategies to flesh out the details of the company's overall business and competitive strategy.

The timing of strategic moves also has relevance in the quest for competitive advantage. Because of the competitive importance that is sometimes associated with when a strategic move is made, company managers are obligated to carefully consider the advantages or disadvantages that attach to being a first-mover versus a fast-follower versus a wait-and-see late-mover. At the end of the day, though, the proper objective of a first-mover is that of being the first competitor to put together the precise combination of features, customer value, and sound revenue/cost/profit economics that puts it ahead of the pack in capturing an attractive market opportunity. Sometimes the company that first unlocks a profitable market opportunity is the first-mover and sometimes it is not—but the company that comes up with the key is surely the smart mover.

Exercises

1. Log on to www.business-ethics.com and review which companies are on the latest list of the 100 Best Corporate Citizens. Also review the criteria for earning a spot on this list. Are these criteria sound? Is there ample reason to believe that the 100 companies on this list pursue strategies that are ethical? Why or why not?

2. Go to www.google.com and do a search for "low-cost producer." See if you can identify five companies that are pursuing a low-cost strategy in their respective industries.

3. Using the advanced search engine function at www.google.com, enter "best-cost producer" in the exact phrase box and see if you can locate three companies that indicate they are employing a best-cost producer strategy.

CHAPTER 5

Competing in Foreign Markets

You have no choice but to operate in a world shaped by globalization and the information revolution. There are two options: Adapt or die.
—Andrew S. Grove, Chairman, Intel Corporation

You do not choose to become global. The market chooses for you; it forces your hand.
—Alain Gomez, CEO, Thomson, S.A.

[I]ndustries actually vary a great deal in the pressures they put on a company to sell internationally.
—Niraj Dawar and Tony Frost, Professors, Richard Ivey School of Business

A_{ny} company that aspires to industry leadership in the 21st century must think in terms of global, not domestic, market leadership. The world economy is globalizing at an accelerating pace as countries heretofore closed to foreign companies open up their markets; as the Internet shrinks the importance of geographic distance; and as ambitious, growth-minded companies race to build stronger competitive positions in the markets of more and more countries. Companies in industries that are already globally competitive or are in the process of globalizing are under the gun to come up with a strategy for competing successfully in foreign markets.

This chapter focuses on strategy options for expanding beyond domestic boundaries and competing in the markets of either a few or a great many countries. The spotlight will be on four strategic issues unique to competing multinationally:

1. Whether to customize the company's offerings in each different country market to match the tastes and preferences of local buyers or offer a mostly standardized product worldwide.

2. Whether to employ essentially the same basic competitive strategy in all countries or modify the strategy country by country.

3. Where to locate the company's production facilities, distribution centers, and customer service operations so as to realize the greatest locational advantages.

4. How to efficiently transfer the company's resource strengths and capabilities from one country to another in an effort to secure competitive advantage.

In the process of exploring these issues, we will introduce a number of core concepts—multicountry competition, global competition, profit sanctuaries, and cross-market subsidization. The chapter includes sections on cross-country differences in cultural, demographic, and market conditions; strategy options for entering and competing in foreign markets; the growing role of alliances with foreign partners; the importance of locating operations in the most advantageous countries; and the special circumstances of competing in such emerging markets as China, India, and Brazil.

Why Companies Expand into Foreign Markets

A company may opt to expand outside its domestic market for any of four major reasons:

1. *To gain access to new customers*—Expanding into foreign markets offers potential for increased revenues, profits, and long-term growth and becomes an especially attractive option when a company's home markets are mature. Firms like Cisco Systems, Intel, Sony, Nokia, Avon, and Toyota, which are racing for global leadership in their respective industries, are moving rapidly and aggressively to extend their market reach into all corners of the world.

2. *To achieve lower costs and enhance the firm's competitiveness*—Many companies are driven to sell in more than one country because domestic sales volume is not large enough to fully capture manufacturing economies of scale or learning-curve

effects and thereby substantially improve a firm's cost competitiveness. The relatively small size of country markets in Europe explains why companies like Michelin, BMW, and Nestlé long ago began selling their products all across Europe and then moved into markets in North America and Latin America.

3. *To capitalize on its core competencies*—A company may be able to leverage its competencies and capabilities into a position of competitive advantage in foreign markets as well as just domestic markets. Nokia's competencies and capabilities in mobile phones have propelled it to global market leadership in the wireless telecommunications business.

4. *To spread its business risk across a wider market base*—A company spreads business risk by operating in a number of different foreign countries rather than depending entirely on operations in its domestic market. Thus, if the economies of certain Asian countries turn down for a period of time, a company with operations across much of the world may be sustained by buoyant sales in Latin America or Europe.

In a few cases, companies in natural resource–based industries (e.g., oil and gas, minerals, rubber, and lumber) often find it necessary to operate in the international arena because attractive raw material supplies are located in foreign countries.

The Difference between Competing Internationally and Competing Globally

Typically, a company will *start* to compete internationally by entering just one or maybe a select few foreign markets. Competing on a truly global scale comes later, after the company has established operations on several continents and is racing against rivals for global market leadership. Thus, there is a meaningful distinction between the competitive scope of a company that operates in a select few foreign countries (with perhaps modest ambitions to expand further) and a company that markets its products in 50 to 100 countries and is expanding its operations into additional country markets annually. The former is most accurately termed an **international competitor,** while the latter qualifies as a **global competitor.** In the discussion that follows, we'll continue to make a distinction between strategies for competing internationally and strategies for competing globally.

Cross-Country Differences in Cultural, Demographic, and Market Conditions

Regardless of a company's motivation for expanding outside its domestic markets, the strategies it uses to compete in foreign markets must be *situation-driven*. Cultural, demographic, and market conditions vary significantly among the countries of the world. Cultures and lifestyles are the most obvious areas in which countries differ; market demographics are close behind. Consumers in Spain do not have the same tastes, preferences, and buying habits as consumers in Norway; buyers differ yet again in Greece, in Chile, in New Zealand, and in Taiwan. Less than 10 percent of the populations of Brazil, India, and China have annual purchasing power equivalent to $20,000. Middle-class consumers represent a much smaller portion of the population in these and other emerging countries than in North America, Japan, and much of Europe.[1] Sometimes, product designs suitable in one country are inappropriate in another—for example, in the United States electrical devices run on 110-volt electrical systems, but in some European countries the standard is a 240-volt electric system, necessitating the use of different electrical designs and components. In France consumers prefer top-loading washing machines, while in most other European countries consumers prefer front-loading machines. Northern Europeans want large refrigerators because they tend to shop once a week in supermarkets; southern Europeans can get by on small refrigerators because they shop daily. In parts of Asia refrigerators are a status symbol and may be placed in the living room, leading to preferences for stylish designs and colors—in India bright blue and red are popular colors. In other Asian countries, household space is constrained and many refrigerators are only four feet high so that the top can be used for storage. In Hong Kong the preference is for compact European-style appliances, but in Taiwan large American-style appliances are more popular.

Similarly, market growth varies from country to country. In emerging markets like India, China, Brazil, and Malaysia, market growth potential is far higher than in the more mature economies of Britain, Denmark, Canada, and Japan. In automobiles, for example, the potential for market growth is explosive in China, where sales amount to only 1 million vehicles annually in a country with 1.3 billion people. In India there are efficient, well-developed national channels for distributing trucks, scooters, farm equipment, groceries, personal care items, and other packaged products to the country's 3 million retailers, whereas in China distribution is primarily local and there is no national network for distributing most products. The marketplace is intensely competitive in some countries and only moderately contested in others. Industry driving forces may be one thing in Italy, quite another in Canada, and different yet again in Israel or Argentina or South Korea.

One of the biggest concerns of companies competing in foreign markets is whether to customize their offerings in each different country market to match the tastes and preferences of local buyers or whether to offer a mostly standardized product worldwide. While the products of a company that is responsive to local tastes will appeal to local buyers, customizing a company's products country by country *may* have the effect of raising production and distribution costs due to the greater variety of designs and components, shorter production runs, and the complications of added inventory handling and distribution logistics. Greater standardization of the company's product offering, on the other hand, can lead to scale economies and learning-curve effects, thus contributing to the achievement of a low-cost advantage. The tension between the market pressures to customize and the competitive pressures to lower costs is one of the big strategic issues that participants in foreign markets have to resolve.

Aside from the basic cultural and market differences among countries, a company also has to pay special attention to locational advantages that stem from country-to-country variations in manufacturing and distribution costs, the risks of fluctuating exchange rates, and the economic and political demands of host governments.

The Potential for Locational Advantages

Differences in wage rates, worker productivity, inflation rates, energy costs, tax rates, government regulations, and the like create sizable variations in manufacturing costs from country to country. Plants in some countries have major manufacturing cost advantages because of lower input costs (especially labor), relaxed government regulations, the proximity of suppliers, or unique natural resources. In such cases, the low-cost countries become principal production sites, with most of the output being exported to markets in other parts of the world. Companies that build production facilities in low-cost countries (or that source their products from contract manufacturers in these countries) have a competitive advantage over rivals with plants in countries where costs are higher. The competitive role of low manufacturing costs is most evident in low-wage countries like Taiwan, South Korea, China, Singapore, Malaysia, Vietnam, Mexico, and Brazil, which have become production havens for goods with high labor content. Likewise, concerns about short delivery times and low shipping costs make some countries better locations than others for establishing distribution centers.

The quality of a country's business environment also offers locational advantages—the governments of some countries are anxious to attract foreign investments and go all-out to create a business climate that outsiders will view as favorable. A good example is Ireland, which has one of the world's most pro-business environments, offering very low corporate tax rates, a government that is responsive to the needs of industry, and a policy of aggressively recruiting high-tech manufacturing facilities and multinational companies. Such policies were a significant force in making Ireland the most dynamic, fastest-growing nation in Europe during the 1990s. The single biggest foreign investment in Ireland's history is Intel's largest non-U.S. chip manufacturing plant, a $2.5 billion facility employing over 4,000 people. Another locational advantage is the clustering of suppliers of components and capital equipment; infrastructure suppliers (universities, vocational training providers, research enterprises); trade associations; and makers of complementary products in a geographic area—such clustering can be an important source of cost savings in addition to facilitating close collaboration with key suppliers.

The Risks of Adverse Exchange Rate Fluctuations

The volatility of exchange rates greatly complicates the issue of geographic cost advantages. Currency exchange rates often fluctuate 20 to 40 percent annually. Changes of this magnitude can either totally wipe out a country's low-cost advantage or transform a former high-cost location into a competitive-cost location. For instance, in the mid-1980s, when the dollar was strong relative to the Japanese yen (meaning that $1 would purchase, say, 125 yen as opposed to only 100 yen), Japanese heavy-equipment maker Komatsu was able to undercut U.S.-based Caterpillar's prices by as much as 25 percent, causing Caterpillar to lose sales and market share. But starting in 1985, when exchange rates began to shift and the dollar grew steadily weaker against the yen (meaning that $1 was worth fewer and fewer yen), Komatsu had to raise its prices six times over two years, as its yen-based costs in terms of dollars soared. Caterpillar's competitiveness against Komatsu was restored and it regained sales and lost market share. The lesson of fluctuating exchange rates is that companies that export goods to foreign countries always gain in competitiveness when the currency of the country in which the goods are manufactured is weak. Exporters are disadvantaged when the currency of the country where goods are being manufactured grows stronger. Sizable long-term shifts in exchange rates thus shuffle the global cards of which rivals have the upper hand in the marketplace and which countries represent the low-cost manufacturing location.

As a further illustration of the risks associated with fluctuating exchange rates and how they can alter the advantages of manufacturing goals in a particular country, consider the case of a U.S. company that has located manufacturing facilities in Brazil (where the currency is *reals*) and that exports most of the Brazilian-made goods to markets in European Union (where the currency is *euros*). To keep the numbers simple, assume that the exchange rate is 4 Brazilian reals for 1 euro and that the product being made in Brazil has a manufacturing cost of 4 Brazilian reals (or 1 euro). Now suppose that for some reason the exchange rate shifts from 4 reals per euro to 5 reals per euro (meaning that the real has declined in value and that the euro is stronger). Making the product in Brazil is now more cost-competitive because a Brazilian good costing 4 reals to produce has fallen to only 0.8 euros at the new exchange rate. On the other hand, if the value of the Brazilian real grows stronger in relation to the euro—resulting in an exchange rate of 3 reals to 1 euro—the same good costing 4 reals to produce now has a cost of 1.33 euros. Clearly, the attraction of manufacturing a good in Brazil and selling it in Europe is far greater when the euro is strong (an exchange rate of 1 euro for 5 Brazilian reals) than when the euro is weak and exchanges for only 3 Brazilian reals.

> Companies with manufacturing facilities in Brazil are more cost-competitive in exporting goods to world markets when the Brazilian real is weak; their competitiveness erodes when the Brazilian real grows stronger relative to the currencies of the countries where the Brazilian-made goods are being sold.

To put it another way, declines in the value of the dollar against foreign currencies reduce or eliminate whatever cost advantage foreign manufacturers might have over U.S. manufacturers and can even prompt foreign companies to establish production plants in the United States. Likewise, a weak euro enhances the cost-competitiveness of companies manufacturing goods in Europe for export to foreign markets; a strong euro versus other currencies weakens the cost-competitiveness of European plants that manufacture goods for export.

In 2002, when the Brazilian real declined in value by about 25 percent against the dollar, the euro, and several other currencies, the ability of companies with manufacturing plants in Brazil to compete in world markets was greatly enhanced—of course, in the future years this windfall gain in cost advantage might well be eroded by sustained rises in the value of the Brazilian real against these same currencies. Herein lies the risk: Currency exchange rates are rather unpredictable, swinging first one way and then another way, so the competitiveness of any company's facilities in any country is partly dependent on whether exchange rate changes over time have a favorable or unfavorable cost impact. Companies making goods in one country for export to foreign countries always gain in competitiveness as the currency of that country grows weaker. Exporters are disadvantaged when the currency of the country where goods are being manufactured grows stronger. From a different perspective, though, domestic companies that are under pressure from lower-cost imported goods gain in competitiveness when their currency grows weaker in relation to the currencies of the countries where the imported goods are made.

> **Core Concept**
>
> Fluctuating exchange rates pose significant risks to a company's competitiveness in foreign markets. Exporters win when the currency of the country where goods are being manufactured grows weaker, and they lose when the currency grows stronger. Domestic companies under pressure from lower-cost imports are benefited when their government's currency grows weaker in relation to the countries where the imported goods are being made.

Host Government Restrictions and Requirements

National governments enact all kinds of measures affecting business conditions and the operation of foreign companies in their markets. Host governments may set local content requirements on goods made inside their borders by foreign-based companies, put restrictions on exports to ensure adequate local supplies, regulate the prices of imported and locally produced goods, and impose tariffs or quotas on the imports of certain goods—until 2002, when it joined the World Trade Organization, China imposed a 100 percent tariff on motor vehicles. Governments may have burdensome tax structures or they may not. In addition, outsiders may face a web of regulations regarding technical standards, product certification, prior approval of capital spending projects, withdrawal of funds from the country, and required minority (sometimes majority) ownership of foreign company operations by local citizens. A few governments may be hostile to or suspicious of foreign companies operating within their borders. Some governments provide subsidies and low-interest loans to domestic companies to help them compete against foreign-based companies. Other governments, anxious to obtain new plants and jobs, offer foreign companies a helping hand in the form of subsidies, privileged market access, and technical assistance. All of these possibilities argue for taking a close look at a country's politics and policies toward business in general, and foreign companies in particular, in deciding which country markets to participate in and which ones to avoid.

The Concepts of Multicountry Competition and Global Competition

Core Concept

Multicountry competition exists when competition in one national market is not closely connected to competition in another national market—there is no global or world market, just a collection of self-contained country markets.

There are important differences in the patterns of international competition from industry to industry.[2] At one extreme is **multicountry competition,** in which there's so much cross-country variation in market conditions and in the companies contending for leadership that the market contest among rivals in one country is not closely connected to the market contests in other countries. The standout features of multicountry competition are that (1) buyers in different countries are attracted to different product attributes, (2) sellers vary from country to country, and (3) industry conditions and competitive forces in each national market differ in important respects. Take the banking industry in Italy, Brazil, and Japan as an example—the requirements and expectations of banking customers vary among the three countries, the lead banking competitors in Italy differ from those in Brazil or in Japan, and the competitive battle going on among the leading banks in Italy is unrelated to the rivalry taking place in Brazil or Japan. Thus, *with multicountry competition, rival firms battle for national championships and winning in one country does not necessarily signal the ability to fare well in other countries.* In multicountry competition, the power of a company's strategy and resource capabilities in one country may not enhance its competitiveness to the same degree in other countries where it operates. Moreover, any competitive advantage a company secures in one country is largely confined to that country; the spillover effects to other countries are minimal to nonexistent. Industries characterized by multicountry competition include radio and TV broadcasting; consumer banking; life insurance; apparel; metals fabrication; many types of food products (coffee, cereals, breads, canned goods, frozen foods); and retailing.

At the other extreme is **global competition,** in which prices and competitive conditions across country markets are strongly linked and the term *global* or *world market* has true meaning. In a globally competitive industry, much the same group of rival companies competes against each other in many different countries, but especially so in countries where sales volumes are large and where having a competitive presence is strategically important to building a strong global position in the industry. Thus, a company's competitive position in one country both affects and is affected by its position in other countries. In global competition, a firm's overall competitive advantage grows out of its entire worldwide operations; the competitive advantage it creates at its home base is supplemented by advantages growing out of its operations in other countries (having plants in low-wage countries, being able to transfer expertise from country to country, having the capability to serve customers who also have multinational operations, and brand-name recognition in many parts of the world). *Rival firms in globally competitive industries vie for worldwide leadership.* Global competition exists in motor vehicles, television sets, tires, mobile phones, personal computers, copiers, watches, digital cameras, bicycles, and commercial aircraft.

> **Core Concept**
> **Global competition** exists when competitive conditions across national markets are linked strongly enough to form a true international market and when leading competitors compete head to head in many different countries.

An industry can have segments that are globally competitive and segments in which competition is country by country.[3] In the hotel/motel industry, for example, the low- and medium-priced segments are characterized by multicountry competition—competitors mainly serve travelers within the same country. In the business and luxury segments, however, competition is more globalized. Companies like Nikki, Marriott, Sheraton, and Hilton have hotels at many international locations, use worldwide reservation systems, and establish common quality and service standards to gain marketing advantages in serving businesspeople and other travelers who make frequent international trips. In lubricants, the marine engine segment is globally competitive—ships move from port to port and require the same oil everywhere they stop. Brand reputations in marine lubricants have a global scope, and successful marine engine lubricant producers (Exxon Mobil, BP Amoco, and Shell) operate globally. In automotive motor oil, however, multicountry competition dominates—countries have different weather conditions and driving patterns, production of motor oil is subject to limited scale economies, shipping costs are high, and retail distribution channels differ markedly from country to country. Thus, domestic firms—like Quaker State and Pennzoil in the United States and Castrol in Great Britain—can be leaders in their home markets without competing globally.

It is also important to recognize that an industry can be in transition from multicountry competition to global competition. In a number of today's industries—beer and major home appliances are prime examples—leading domestic competitors have begun expanding into more and more foreign markets, often acquiring local companies or brands and integrating them into their operations. As some industry members start to build global brands and a global presence, other industry members find themselves pressured to follow the same strategic path—especially if establishing multinational operations results in important scale economies and a powerhouse brand name. As the industry consolidates to fewer players, such that many of the same companies find themselves in head-to-head competition in more and more country markets, global competition begins to replace multicountry competition.

At the same time, consumer tastes in a number of important product categories are converging across the world. Less diversity of tastes and preferences opens the way for companies to create global brands and sell essentially the same products in most all countries of the world. Even in industries where consumer tastes remain fairly diverse, companies are learning to use custom mass production to economically create different versions of a product and thereby satisfy the tastes of people in different countries.

In addition to noting the obvious cultural and political differences between countries, a company should shape its strategic approach to competing in foreign markets according to whether its industry is characterized by multicountry competition, global competition, or is transitioning from multicountry competition to global competition.

Strategy Options for Entering and Competing in Foreign Markets

There are a host of generic strategic options for a company that decides to expand outside its domestic market and compete internationally or globally:

1. *Maintain a national (one-country) production base and export goods to foreign markets,* using either company-owned or foreign-controlled forward distribution channels.

2. *License foreign firms to use the company's technology or to produce and distribute the company's products.*

3. *Employ a franchising strategy.*

4. *Follow a multicountry strategy,* varying the company's strategic approach (perhaps a little, perhaps a lot) from country to country in accordance with local conditions and differing buyer tastes and preferences.

5. *Follow a global strategy,* using essentially the same competitive strategy approach in all country markets where the company has a presence.

6. *Use strategic alliances or joint ventures with foreign companies as the primary vehicle for entering foreign markets* and perhaps also using them as an ongoing strategic arrangement aimed at maintaining or strengthening its competitiveness.

The following sections discuss each of these six options in more detail.

Export Strategies

Using domestic plants as a production base for exporting goods to foreign markets is an excellent *initial strategy* for pursuing international sales. It is a conservative way to test the international waters. The amount of capital needed to begin exporting is often quite minimal; existing production capacity may well be sufficient to make the goods for export. With an export strategy, a manufacturer can limit its involvement in foreign markets by contracting with foreign wholesalers experienced in importing to handle the entire distribution and marketing function in their countries or regions of the world. If it is more advantageous to maintain control over these functions, however, a manufacturer can establish its own distribution and sales organizations in some or all of the target foreign markets. Either way, a home-based production and export strategy helps the firm minimize its direct investments in foreign countries. Such strategies are commonly favored by Chinese, Korean, and Italian companies—products are designed and manufactured at home and then distributed through local channels in the importing countries; the primary functions performed abroad relate chiefly to establishing a network of distributors and perhaps conducting sales promotion and brand awareness activities.

Whether an export strategy can be pursued successfully over the long run hinges on the relative cost-competitiveness of the home-country production base. In some industries, firms gain additional scale economies and learning-curve benefits from centralizing production in one or several giant plants whose output capability exceeds demand in any one country market; obviously, to capture such economies a company must export. However, an export strategy is vulnerable when (1) manufacturing costs in the home country are substantially higher than in foreign countries where rivals have plants, (2) the costs of shipping the product to distant foreign markets are relatively high, or (3) adverse fluctuations occur in currency exchange rates. Unless an exporter can both keep its production and shipping costs competitive with rivals and successfully hedge against unfavorable changes in currency exchange rates, its success will be limited.

Licensing Strategies

Licensing makes sense when a firm with valuable technical know-how or a unique patented product has neither the internal organizational capability nor the resources to enter foreign markets. Licensing also has the advantage of avoiding the risks of committing resources to country markets that are unfamiliar, politically volatile, economically unstable, or otherwise risky. By licensing the technology or the production rights to foreign-based firms, the firm does not have to bear the costs and risks of entering foreign markets on its own, yet it is able to generate income from royalties. The big disadvantage of licensing is the risk of providing valuable technological know-how to foreign companies and thereby losing some degree of control over its use; monitoring licensees and safeguarding the company's proprietary know-how can prove quite difficult in some circumstances. But if the royalty potential is considerable and the companies to whom the licenses are being granted are both trustworthy and reputable, then licensing can be a very attractive option.

Franchising Strategies

While licensing works well for manufacturers, franchising is often better suited to the global expansion efforts of service and retailing enterprises. McDonald's, Tricon Global Restaurants (the parent of Pizza Hut, Kentucky Fried Chicken, and Taco Bell), and Hilton Hotels have all used franchising to build a presence in foreign markets. Franchising has much the same advantages as licensing. The franchisee bears most of the costs and risks of establishing foreign locations; a franchiser has to expend only the resources to recruit, train, support, and monitor franchisees. The big problem a franchiser faces is maintaining quality control; foreign franchisees do not always exhibit strong commitment to consistency and standardization, especially when the local culture does not stress the same kinds of quality concerns. Another problem that can arise is whether to allow foreign franchisees to make modifications in the franchisor's product offering so as to better satisfy the tastes and expectations of local buyers. Should McDonald's allow its franchised units in Japan to modify Big Macs slightly to suit Japanese tastes? Should the franchised Kentucky Fried Chicken units in China be permitted to substitute spices that are more appealing to Chinese consumers or should the same menu offerings be rigorously and unvaryingly required of all franchisees worldwide?

A Multicountry Strategy or a Global Strategy?

The need for a *multicountry strategy* derives from the sometimes vast differences in cultural, economic, political, and competitive conditions in different countries. The more diverse national market conditions are, the stronger the case for a multicountry strategy, in which the company tailors its strategic approach to fit each host country's market situation. Usually, but not always, companies employing a multicountry strategy use the same basic competitive theme (low-cost, differentiation, or best-cost) in each country, making whatever country-specific variations are needed to best satisfy customers and to position themselves against local rivals. They may aim at broad market targets in some countries and focus more narrowly on a particular niche in others. The bigger the country-to-country variations, the more a company's overall international strategy becomes a collection of its individual country strategies. But country to country variations still allow room to connect the strategies in different countries by making an effort to transfer ideas, technologies, competencies, and capabilities that work successfully in one country market to other fairly similar country markets. Toward this end, it is useful to view operations in each country as experiments that result in learning and in capabilities that may merit transfer to other country markets.[4]

While multicountry strategies are best suited for industries where multicountry competition dominates and a fairly high degree of local responsiveness is competitively imperative; *global strategies* are best suited for globally competitive industries.

> A multicountry strategy is appropriate for industries where multicountry competition dominates and local responsiveness is essential. A global strategy works best in markets that are globally competitive or beginning to globalize.

A global strategy is one in which the company's approach is *predominantly the same* in all countries. Although relatively *minor* country-to-country differences in a company's global strategy may be incorporated to accommodate specific situations in a few host countries, the company's fundamental competitive approach (low-cost, differentiation, best-cost, or focused) remains very much intact worldwide. Moreover, a global strategy involves (1) integrating and coordinating the company's strategic moves worldwide, and (2) selling in many if not all nations where there is significant buyer demand.

Figure 5.1 provides a point-by-point comparison of multicountry versus global strategies. *The issue of whether to employ essentially the same basic competitive strategy in the markets of all countries or whether to vary the company's competitive approach to fit specific market conditions and buyer preferences in each host country is perhaps the foremost strategic issue firms face when they compete in foreign markets.*

The strength of a multicountry strategy is that it matches the company's competitive approach to host-country circumstances and accommodates the differing tastes and expectations of buyers in each country. A multicountry strategy is essential when there are significant country-to-country differences in customers' needs and buying habits (see Global Spotlight 5.1), when buyers in a country insist on special-order or highly customized products; when host governments enact regulations requiring that products sold locally meet strict manufacturing specifications or performance standards; and when the trade restrictions of host governments are so diverse and complicated that they preclude a uniform, coordinated worldwide market approach. However, a multicountry strategy has two big drawbacks: It hinders transfer of a company's competencies and resources across country boundaries (since different competencies and capabilities may be used in different host countries), and it does not promote building a single, unified competitive advantage—especially one based on low cost. Companies employing a multicountry strategy face big hurdles in achieving low-cost leadership unless they find ways to customize their products and still be in position to capture scale economies and learning-curve effects—the capability to implement mass customization assembly at relatively low cost (as Dell and Toyota have demonstrated) greatly facilitates effective use of a multicountry approach.

Figure 5.1   How a Multicountry Strategy Differs from a Global Strategy

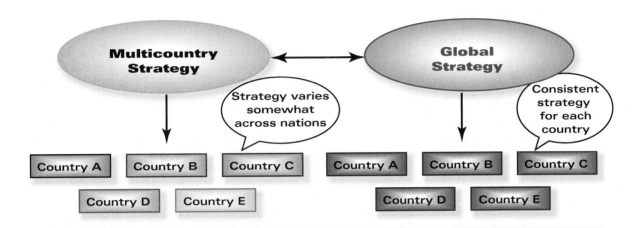

Multicountry Strategy	Global Strategy
■ Customize the company's competitive approach as needed to fit market and business circumstances in each host country—strong responsiveness to local conditions.	■ Pursue same basic competitive strategy worldwide (low-cost, differentiation, best-cost, focused low-cost, focused differentiation) —with minimal responsiveness to local conditions.
■ Sell different product versions in different countries under different brand names—adapt product attributes to fit buyer tastes and preferences country by country.	■ Sell same products under same brand name worldwide.
■ Scatter plants across many host countries, each producing product versions for local markets.	■ Locate plants on basis of maximum locational advantage, usually in countries where production costs are lowest; but plants may be scattered if shipping costs are high or other locational advantages dominate.
■ Preferably use local suppliers (some local sources may be required by host government).	■ Use best suppliers from anywhere in the world.
■ Adapt marketing and distribution to local customs and cultures.	■ Coordinate marketing and distribution worldwide; make minor adaptations to local countries where needed.
■ Transfer some competencies and capabilities from country to country where feasible.	■ Compete on basis of same technologies, competencies, and capabilities worldwide; stress rapid transfer of new ideas, products, and capabilities to other countries.
■ Give country managers fairly wide strategy-making latitude and autonomy.	■ Coordinate major strategic decisions worldwide; expect local managers to stick close to global strategy.

GLOBAL SPOTLIGHT 5.1
Microsoft, McDonald's, and Nestlé: Users of Multicountry Strategies

Microsoft's Multicountry Strategy in PC Software

In order to best serve the needs of users in foreign countries, Microsoft localizes many of its software products to reflect local languages. In France, for example, all user messages and documentation are in French and all monetary references are in euros. In the United Kingdom, monetary references are in British pounds and user messages and documentation reflect certain British conventions. Various Microsoft products have been localized into more than 30 languages.

McDonald's Multicountry Strategy in Fast Food

McDonald's has been highly successful in markets outside the United States, partly because it has been adept in altering its menu offerings to cater to local tastes. In Taiwan and Singapore, McDonald's outlets offer a bone-in fried chicken dish called Chicken Mc-Crispy. In Great Britain, there's McChicken Tikka Naan to appeal to British cravings for Indian food. In India, McDonald's features the Maharajah Mac sandwich (an Indian version of the Big Mac); in Japan, there's the Chicken Tatsuta sandwich and a Teriyaki Burger sandwich; in Australia, there's a McOz Burger. However, the infrastructure and operating systems that are employed in the outlets are largely the same, enabling McDonald's to achieve low-cost leadership status once it builds volume up at its outlets (sometimes a 5-year process) and once it has enough outlets operating in a country to achieve full economies of scale (sometimes a 5- to 10-year process in the largest foreign markets).

Nestlé's Multicountry Strategy in Instant Coffee

Swiss-based Nestlé, the largest food company in the world, is also the largest producer of coffee. With a total workforce of 22,541 people operating in nearly 480 factories in 100 countries, Nestlé's presence is clearly multinational. Chief executive Peter Brabeck-Letmathe advocates understanding the distinctions between the cultures in which Nestlé markets its products. "[If] you are open to new languages, you are also open to new cultures," he explains. Thus, instant coffee names like Nescafé, Taster's Choice, Ricore, and Ricoffy line grocery shelves in various countries. If customers prefer roast or ground coffee, they can purchase Nespresso, Bonka, Zoegas, or Loumidis, depending on where they live.

Nestlé produces 200 types of instant coffee, from lighter blends for the U.S. market to dark espressos for Latin America. To keep its instant coffees matched to consumer tastes in different countries (and areas within some countries), Nestlé operates four coffee research labs that experiment with new blends in aroma, flavor, and color. The strategy is to match the blends marketed in each country to the tastes and preferences of coffee drinkers in that country, introducing new blends to develop new segments when opportunities appear and altering blends as needed to respond to changing tastes and buyer habits. In Britain, Nescafé was promoted extensively to build a wider base of instant-coffee drinkers. In Japan, where Nescafé was considered a luxury item, the company made its Japanese blends available in fancy containers suitable for gift-giving.

Sources: Nestlé website (www.nestle.com), accessed August 15, 2001; "Nestlé S.A.," Hoover's Online (www.hoovers.com), accessed August 15, 2001; Tom Mudd, "Nestlé Plays to Global Audience," *Industry Week* (www.industryweek.com), August 13, 2001; company annual reports; Shawn Tully, "Nestlé Shows How to Gobble Markets," *Fortune*, January 16, 1989, pp. 74–78; and "Nestlé: A Giant in a Hurry," *Business Week*, March 22, 1993, pp. 50–54.

As a rule, most multinational competitors endeavor to employ as global a strategy as customer needs permit. Philips N.V., the Netherlands-based electronics and consumer products company, operated successfully with a multicountry strategy for many years but has recently begun moving more toward a unified strategy within the European Union and within North America.[5] A global strategy can concentrate on building the resource strengths to secure a sustainable low-cost or differentiation-based competitive advantage over both domestic rivals and global rivals racing for world market leadership. Whenever country-to-country differences are small enough to be accommodated within the framework of a global strategy, a global strategy is preferable to a multi-country strategy because of the value of creating both a uniform brand offering and strong competencies and capabilities not readily matched by rivals.

The Quest for Competitive Advantage in Foreign Markets

There are three ways in which a firm can gain competitive advantage (or offset domestic disadvantages) by expanding outside its domestic market.[6] One way exploits a multinational or global competitor's ability to deploy R&D, parts manufacture, assembly, distribution centers, sales and marketing, customer service centers, and other activities among various countries in a manner that lowers costs or achieves greater product differentiation. A second way involves efficient and effective transfer of competitively valuable competencies and capabilities from its domestic markets to foreign markets. A third way draws on a multinational or global competitor's ability to deepen or broaden its resource strengths and capabilities and to coordinate its dispersed activities in ways that a domestic-only competitor cannot.

Using Location to Build Competitive Advantage

To use location to build competitive advantage, a company must consider two issues: (1) whether to concentrate each activity it performs in a few select countries or to disperse performance of the activity to many nations, and (2) in which countries to locate particular activities. Companies tend to concentrate their activities in a limited number of locations in the following circumstances:

- *When the costs of manufacturing or other activities are significantly lower in some geographic locations than in others*—For example, much of the world's athletic footwear is manufactured in Asia (China and Korea) because of low labor costs; much of the production of motherboards for PCs is located in Taiwan because of both low costs and the high-caliber technical skills of the Taiwanese labor force.

> Companies can pursue competitive advantage in world markets by locating activities in the most advantageous nations; a domestic-only competitor has no such opportunities.

- *When there are significant scale economies in performing the activity*—The presence of significant economies of scale in components production or final assembly means that a company can gain major cost savings from operating a few superefficient plants as opposed to a host of small plants scattered across the world. Important marketing and distribution economies associated with multinational operations can also yield low-cost leadership. In situations where some competitors are intent on global dominance, being the worldwide low-cost provider is a powerful competitive advantage. Achieving low-cost provider status often requires a company to have the largest worldwide *manufacturing share,* with production centralized in one or a few world-scale plants in low-cost locations and often using the capacity of these plants to manufacture units sold under the brand names of rivals. Manufacturing share (as distinct from brand share or market share) is significant because it provides more certain access to production-related scale economies. Japanese makers of VCRs, microwave ovens, TVs, and DVD players have used their large manufacturing share to establish a low-cost advantage over rivals.[7]

- *When there is a steep learning curve associated with performing an activity in a single location*—In some industries learning-curve effects in parts manufacture or assembly are so great that a company establishes one or two large plants from which it serves the world market. The key to riding down the learning curve and achieving lower costs is to concentrate production in a few locations to increase the accumulated volume at a plant (and thus the experience of the plant's workforce) as rapidly as possible.

- *When certain locations have superior resources, allow better coordination of related activities, or offer other valuable advantages*—A research unit or a sophisticated production facility may be situated in a particular nation because of its pool of technically trained personnel. Samsung became a leader in memory chip technology by establishing a major R&D facility in Silicon Valley and transferring the know-how it gained back to headquarters and its plants in South Korea. Where just-in-time inventory practices yield big cost savings and/or where the assembly firm has long-term partnering arrangements with its key suppliers, parts manufacturing plants may be clustered around final assembly plants. An assembly plant may be located in a country in return for the host government's allowing freer import of components from large-scale, centralized parts plants located elsewhere. A customer service center or sales office may be opened in a particular country to help cultivate strong relationships with pivotal customers located nearby.

However, in several instances, *dispersing activities is more advantageous than concentrating them.* Buyer-related activities—such as distribution to dealers, sales and advertising, and after-sale service—usually must take place close to buyers. This means physically locating the capability to perform such activities in every country market where a global firm has major customers (unless buyers in several adjoining countries can be served quickly from a nearby central location). For example, firms that make mining and oil-drilling equipment maintain operations in many international locations to support customers' needs for speedy equipment repair and technical assistance. The four biggest public accounting firms have numerous international offices to service the foreign operations of their multinational corporate clients. A global competitor that effectively disperses its buyer-related activities can gain a service-based competitive edge in world markets over rivals whose buyer-related activities are more concentrated—this is one reason the Big Four public accounting firms (PricewaterhouseCoopers, KPMG, Deloitte & Touche, and Ernst & Young) have been so successful relative to second-tier firms. Dispersing activities to many locations is also competitively advantageous when high transportation costs, diseconomies of large size, and trade barriers make it too expensive to operate from a central location. Many companies distribute their products from multiple locations to shorten delivery times to customers. In addition, it is strategically advantageous to disperse activities to hedge against the risks of fluctuating exchange rates; supply interruptions (due to strikes, mechanical failures, and transportation delays); and adverse political developments. Such risks are greater when activities are concentrated in a single location.

The classic reason for locating an activity in a particular country is low cost.[8] Even though multinational and global firms have strong reason to disperse buyer-related activities to many international locations, such activities as materials procurement, parts manufacture, finished goods assembly, technology research, and new product development can frequently be decoupled from buyer locations and performed wherever advantage lies. Components can be made in Mexico; technology research done in Frankfurt; new products developed and tested in Phoenix; and assembly plants located in Spain, Brazil, Taiwan, or South Carolina. Capital can be raised in whatever country it is available on the best terms.

Using Cross-Border Transfers of Competencies and Capabilities to Build Competitive Advantage

Expanding beyond domestic borders is a way for companies to leverage their core competencies and resource strengths, using them as a basis for competing successfully in additional country markets and growing sales and profits in the process. Transferring competencies, capabilities, and resource strengths from country to country contributes to the development of broader or deeper competencies and capabilities— ideally helping a company achieve *dominating depth* in some competitively valuable area. Dominating depth in a competitively valuable capability or resource or value chain activity is a strong basis for sustainable competitive advantage over other multinational or global competitors and especially so over domestic-only competitors. A one-country customer base is too small to support the resource buildup needed to achieve such depth; this is particularly true when the market is just emerging and sophisticated resources have not been required.

Wal-Mart is slowly but forcefully expanding its operations into other parts of the world with a strategy that involves transferring its considerable domestic expertise in distribution and discount retailing to other countries. Its status as the largest, most resource-deep, and most sophisticated user of distribution-retailing know-how has served it well in building its foreign sales and profitability. But Wal-Mart is not racing madly to position itself in many foreign markets very quickly; rather, it is establishing a strong presence in select country markets and learning how to be successful in these before tackling entry into other major markets.

However, cross-border resource transfers are not a guaranteed recipe for succeeding in entering foreign markets. Amsterdam-based Philips Electronics sells more color TVs and DVD recorders in Europe than any other company does; its biggest technological breakthrough was the compact disc, which it invented in 1982. Philips has worldwide sales of about €32 billion, but as of 2002 Philips had lost money for 15 consecutive years in its U.S. consumer electronics business. In the United States, the company's color TVs and DVD recorders (sold under the Magnavox and Philips brands) are slow sellers. Philips is notoriously slow in introducing new products into the U.S. market and has been struggling to develop an able sales force that can make inroads with U.S. electronics retailers and change Philips' image as a clunky brand.

Using Cross-Border Coordination to Build Competitive Advantage

Coordinating company activities across different countries contributes to sustainable competitive advantage in several different ways. Multinational and global competitors can choose where and how to challenge rivals. They may decide to retaliate against an aggressive rival in the country market where the rival has its biggest sales volume or its best profit margins in order to reduce the rival's financial resources for competing in other country markets. They may also decide to wage a price-cutting offensive against weak rivals in their home markets, capturing greater market share and subsidizing any short-term losses with profits earned in other country markets.

If a firm learns how to assemble its product more efficiently at, say, its Brazilian plant, the accumulated expertise can be easily transferred via the Internet to assembly plants in other world locations. Knowledge gained in marketing a company's product in Great Britain can readily be exchanged with company personnel in New Zealand or Australia. A company can shift production from one country to another to take advantage of exchange rate fluctuations, to enhance its leverage with host country governments, and to respond to changing wage rates, components shortages, energy costs, or changes in tariffs and quotas. Production schedules can be coordinated worldwide; shipments can be diverted from one distribution center to another if sales rise unexpectedly in one place and fall in another.

Using Internet technology applications, companies can collect ideas for new and improved products from customers and sales and marketing personnel all over the world, permitting informed decisions about what can be standardized and what should be customized. Likewise, Internet technology can be used to involve the company's best design and engineering personnel (wherever they are located) in collectively coming up with next-generation products—it is becoming increasingly easy for company personnel in one location to use the Internet to collaborate closely with personnel in other locations in performing strategically relevant activities. Efficiencies can also be achieved by shifting workloads from where they are unusually heavy to locations where personnel are underutilized.

A company can enhance its brand reputation by consistently incorporating the same differentiating attributes in its products in the various worldwide markets where it competes. The reputation for quality that Honda established worldwide first in motorcycles and then in automobiles gave it competitive advantage in positioning Honda lawn mowers at the upper end of the U.S. outdoor power equipment market—the Honda name gave the company instant credibility with U.S. buyers.

Profit Sanctuaries, Cross-Market Subsidization, and Global Strategic Offensives

Profit sanctuaries are *country markets in which a company derives substantial profits because of its strong or protected market position.* Japan, for example, is a profit sanctuary for most Japanese companies because trade barriers erected around Japanese industries by the Japanese government effectively block foreign companies from competing for a large share of Japanese sales. Protected from the threat of foreign competition in their home market, Japanese companies can safely charge somewhat higher prices to their Japanese customers and thus earn attractively large profits on sales made in Japan. In most cases, a company's biggest and most strategically crucial profit sanctuary is its home market, but international and global companies may also enjoy profit sanctuary status in other nations where they have a strong competitive position, big sales volume, and attractive profit margins. Companies that compete globally are likely to have more profit sanctuaries than companies that compete in just a few country markets; a domestic-only competitor, of course, can have only one profit sanctuary (see Figure 5.2).

Core Concept

Companies with large, protected **profit sanctuaries** have competitive advantage over companies that don't have a protected sanctuary. Companies with multiple profit sanctuaries have a competitive advantage over companies with a single sanctuary.

Figure 5.2   Profit Sanctuary Potential of Domestic-Only, International, and Global Competitors

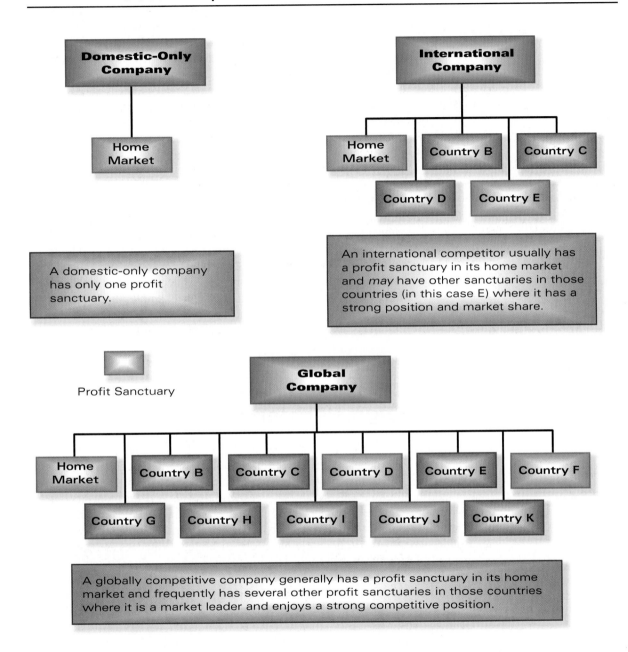

Using Cross-Market Subsidization to Wage a Strategic Offensive

Profit sanctuaries are valuable competitive assets, providing the financial strength to support strategic offensives in selected country markets and aid a company's race for global market leadership. The added financial capability afforded by multiple profit sanctuaries gives a global or multicountry competitor the financial strength to wage a market offensive against a domestic competitor whose only profit sanctuary is its home market. Consider the case of a purely domestic company in competition with a company that has multiple profit sanctuaries and that is racing for global market leadership. The global company has the flexibility of lowballing its prices in the domestic company's home market and grabbing market share at the domestic company's expense, subsidizing razor-thin margins or losses with the healthy profits earned in its sanctuaries—a practice called **cross-market subsidization.** The global company can adjust the depth of its price-cutting to move in and capture market share quickly, or it can shave prices slightly to make gradual market inroads (perhaps over a decade or more) so as not to threaten domestic firms precipitously or trigger protectionist government actions. If the domestic company retaliates with matching price cuts, it exposes its entire revenue and profit base to erosion; its profits can be squeezed substantially and its competitive strength sapped, even if it is the domestic market leader.

> **Core Concept**
>
> **Cross-market subsidization**—supporting competitive offensives in one market with resources and profits diverted from operations in other markets—is a powerful competitive weapon.

There are numerous instances across the world where domestic companies, rightly or wrongly, have accused foreign competitors of "dumping" goods at unreasonably low prices to put the domestic firms in dire financial straits or drive them out of business. Many governments have antidumping laws aimed at protecting domestic firms from unfair pricing by foreign rivals. In 2002, for example, the U.S. government imposed tariffs of up to 30 percent on selected steel products that Asian and European steel manufacturers were said to be selling at ultralow prices in the U.S. market.

Strategic Alliances and Joint Ventures with Foreign Partners

Strategic alliances and cooperative agreements of one kind or another with foreign companies are a favorite and potentially fruitful means for entering a foreign market or strengthening a firm's competitiveness in world markets. Historically, export-minded firms in industrialized nations sought alliances with firms in less-developed countries to import and market their products locally—such arrangements were often necessary to win approval for entry from the host country's government. More recently, companies from different parts of the world have formed strategic alliances and partnership arrangements to strengthen their mutual ability to serve whole continents and move toward more global market participation. Both Japanese and American companies are actively forming alliances with European companies to strengthen their ability to compete in the 15-nation European Union and to capitalize on the opening up of Eastern European markets. Many U.S. and European companies are allying with Asian companies in their efforts to enter markets in China, India, and other Asian countries.

> Strategic alliances can help companies in globally competitive industries strengthen their competitive positions while still preserving their independence.

Of late, the number of alliances, joint ventures, and other collaborative efforts has exploded. Cooperative arrangements between domestic and foreign companies have strategic appeal for reasons besides gaining wider access to attractive country markets.[9] One is to capture economies of scale in production and/or marketing—cost reduction can be the difference that allows a company to be cost-competitive. By joining forces in producing components, assembling models, and marketing their products, companies can realize cost savings not achievable with their own small volumes. A second reason is to fill gaps in technical expertise and/or knowledge of local markets (buying habits and product preferences of consumers, local customs, and so on). Allies learn much from one another in performing joint research, sharing technological know-how, studying one another's manufacturing methods, and understanding how to tailor sales and marketing approaches to fit local cultures and traditions. A third reason is to share distribution facilities and dealer networks, thus mutually strengthening their access to buyers. Fourth, allied companies can direct their competitive energies more toward mutual rivals and less toward one another; teaming up may help them close the gap on leading companies. Fifth, companies opt to form alliances with local companies (even where not legally required) because of the partner's local market knowledge and working relationships with key officials in the host country government.[10] And, finally, alliances can be a particularly useful way to gain agreement on important technical standards—they have been used to arrive at standards for videocassette recorders, assorted PC devices, Internet-related technologies, and mobile phones and other wireless communications devices.

The Risks of Strategic Alliances with Foreign Partners

Alliances and joint ventures have their pitfalls, however. Achieving effective collaboration between independent companies, each with different motives and perhaps conflicting objectives, is not easy.[11] It requires many meetings of many people working in good faith over a period of time to iron out what is to be shared, what is to remain proprietary, and how the cooperative arrangements will work. Cross-border allies typically have to overcome language and cultural barriers; the communication, trust-building, and coordination costs are high in terms of management time. Often, once the bloom is off the rose, partners with conflicting objectives and strategies discover they have deep differences of opinion about how to proceed. Tensions build up, working relationships cool, and the hoped-for benefits never materialize.[12]

Another major problem is getting alliance partners to make decisions fast enough to respond to rapidly advancing technological developments. Large telecommunications companies striving to achieve "global connectivity" have made extensive use of alliances and joint ventures with foreign counterparts, but they are encountering serious difficulty in reaching agreements on which of several technological approaches to employ and how to adapt to the swift pace at which all of the alternatives are advancing. AT&T and British Telecom, which formed a $10 billion joint venture to build an Internet-based global network linking 100 major cities, took eight months to find a CEO to head the project and even longer to come up with a name; the joint venture was abandoned in 2002.

Many times allies find it difficult to collaborate effectively in competitively sensitive areas, thus raising questions about mutual trust and forthright exchanges of information and expertise. There can also be clashes of egos and company cultures. The key people on whom success or failure depends may have little personal chemistry, be unable to work closely together or form a partnership, or be unable to come to consensus. For example, an alliance between Northwest Airlines and KLM Royal Dutch Airlines linking their hubs in Detroit and Amsterdam resulted in a bitter feud among both companies' top officials (who, according to some reports, refused to speak to each other) and precipitated a battle for control of

> Strategic alliances are more effective in helping establish a beachhead of new opportunity in world markets than in achieving and sustaining global leadership.

Northwest Airlines engineered by KLM. The dispute was rooted in a clash of business philosophies (the American way versus the European way), basic cultural differences, and an executive power struggle.[13]

Another danger of collaborative partnerships is that of becoming overly dependent on another company for essential expertise and capabilities over the long term. To be a serious market contender, a company must ultimately develop internal capabilities in all areas important to strengthening its competitive position and building a sustainable competitive advantage. When learning from allies holds only limited potential (because those allies guard their most valuable skills and expertise), acquiring or merging with a company possessing the desired know-how and resources is a better solution. If a company is aiming for global market leadership, then cross-border merger or acquisition may be a better alternative than cross-border alliances or joint ventures. Global Spotlight 5.2 relates the experiences of various companies with cross-border strategic alliances.

Making the Most of Strategic Alliances with Foreign Partners

Whether a company realizes the potential of alliances and collaborative partnerships with foreign enterprises seems to be a function of six factors:[14]

1. *Picking a good partner*—A good partner not only has the desired expertise and capabilities but also shares the company's vision about the purpose of the alliance. Experience indicates that it is generally wise to avoid partnering with foreign companies where there is strong potential of direct competition because of overlapping product lines or other conflicting interests—agreements to jointly market each other's products hold much potential for conflict unless the products are complements rather than substitutes and unless there is good chemistry among key personnel.

2. *Being sensitive to cultural differences*—Unless the outsider exhibits respect for the local culture and local business practices, productive working relationships are unlikely to emerge.

3. *Recognizing that the alliance must benefit both sides*—Information must be shared as well as gained, and the relationship must remain forthright and trustful. Many alliances fail because one or both partners grow unhappy with what they are learning. Also, if either partner plays games with information or tries to take advantage of the other, the resulting friction can quickly erode the value of further collaboration.

4. *Ensuring that both parties live up to their commitments*—Both parties have to deliver on their commitments for the alliance to produce the intended benefits. The division of work has to be perceived as fairly apportioned, and the caliber of the benefits received on both sides has to be perceived as adequate.

5. *Structuring the decision-making process so that actions can be taken swiftly when needed*—In many instances, the fast pace of technology and competitive changes dictates an equally fast decision-making process. If the parties get bogged down in discussions among themselves or in gaining internal approval from higher-ups, the alliance can turn into an anchor of delay and inaction.

6. *Managing the learning process and then adjusting the alliance agreement over time to fit new circumstances*—In today's fast-moving markets, few alliances can succeed by holding only to initial plans. One of the keys to long-lasting success is learning to adapt to change; the terms and objectives of the alliance must be adjusted as needed.

GLOBAL SPOTLIGHT 5.2

Cross-Border Strategic Alliances: The New Shape of Global Business

As the chairman of British Aerospace recently observed, a strategic alliance with a foreign company is "one of the quickest and cheapest ways to develop a global strategy." Cross-border strategic alliances are influencing competition in world markets, pitting one group of allied global companies against other groups of allied global companies. High-profile global alliances include the following:

- Airbus Industrie, one of the world's two leading makers of commercial aircraft, was formed by an alliance of aerospace companies from Britain, Spain, Germany, and France that included British Aerospace, Daimler-Benz Aerospace, and Aerospatiale. Airbus and Boeing vie for world leadership in large commercial aircraft (over 100 passengers).

- General Electric and SNECMA, a French maker of jet engines, have had a longstanding 50–50 partnership to make jet engines to power aircraft made by Boeing and Airbus Industrie. Their partnership company is called CFM International. The GE/SNECMA alliance is regarded as a model because it has enjoyed great success since the 1970s, winning market shares for aircraft with 100+ passengers of about 35 percent through the 1980s and market shares approaching 50 percent since 1995. CFM International had approximately 200 customers worldwide using its engines as of 2002.

- Two struggling auto firms, Renault of France and Nissan of Japan, formed a global partnership aimed at making them more competitive with DaimlerChrysler, General Motors, Ford, and Toyota, all of which were engaged in numerous alliances of their own. Since the early 1990s, hundreds of strategic alliances have been formed in the motor vehicle industry as both car and truck manufacturers and automotive parts suppliers moved aggressively to strengthen the ability to compete globally. Not only have there been joint production and marketing alliances between automakers strong in one region of the world and automakers strong in another region, but there have also been strategic alliances between vehicle makers and parts suppliers.

- Vodaphone AirTouch PLC and Bell Atlantic Corporation in 1999 agreed to from a partnership to create a wireless business with a single brand and common digital technology covering the entire U.S. market and to work together on global business synergies in handset and equipment purchases, global corporate account programs, global roaming agreements, and the development of new products and technologies. The new business, known as Verizon Wireless, combined the domestic U.S. operations of Bell Atlantic Mobile, AirTouch Communications, and PrimeCo Personal Communications LP. Shortly thereafter, Verizon Wireless was further strengthened by the addition of GTE's domestic wireless properties, as part of the Bell Atlantic/GTE merger. At the time of the initial partnership in 1999, Vodaphone AirTouch, based in Great Britain, was the world's largest mobile communications company, and Bell Atlantic was completing a merger with GTE to make the new company, Verizon, one of the premier telecommunications service providers in the United States and a participant in the global telecommunications market, with operations and investments in 25 countries.

- Toyota and First Automotive Works, China's biggest automaker, entered into an alliance in 2002 to make luxury sedans, sport-utility vehicles, and minivehicles for the Chinese market. The intent was to make as many as 400,000 vehicles annually by 2010, an amount equal to the number that Volkswagen, the company with the largest share of the Chinese market, was making as of 2002. The alliance envisioned a joint investment of about $1.2 billion. At the time of the announced alliance, Toyota was lagging behind Honda, General Motors, and Volkswagen in setting up production facilities in China. Capturing a bigger share of the Chinese market was seen as crucial to Toyota's success in achieving its strategic objective of having a 15 percent share of the world's automotive market by 2010.

Source: Company websites and press releases; Yves L. Doz and Gary Hamel, *Alliance Advantage: The Art of Creating Value through Partnering* (Boston, MA: Harvard Business School Press, 1998).

Most alliances with foreign companies that aim at technology-sharing or providing market access turn out to be temporary, fulfilling their purpose after a few years because the benefits of mutual learning have occurred and because the businesses of both partners have developed to the point where they are ready to go their own ways. In such cases, it is important for the company to learn thoroughly and rapidly about a partner's technology, business practices, and organizational capabilities and then transfer valuable ideas and practices into its own operations promptly. Although long-term alliances sometimes prove mutually beneficial, most partners don't hesitate to terminate the alliance and go it alone when the payoffs run out.

Alliances are more likely to be long-lasting when (1) they involve collaboration with suppliers or distribution allies and each party's contribution involves activities in different portions of the industry value chain, or (2) both parties conclude that continued collaboration is in their mutual interest, perhaps because new opportunities for learning are emerging or perhaps because further collaboration will allow each partner to extend its market reach beyond what it could accomplish on its own.

Competing in Emerging Foreign Markets

Companies racing for global leadership have to consider competing in *emerging markets* like China, India, Brazil, Indonesia, and Mexico—countries where the business risks are considerable but where the opportunities for growth are huge, especially as economies and living standards increase toward levels in the developed world.[15] With the world now comprising more than 6 billion people—fully one-third of whom are in India and China, and hundreds of millions more in other less-developed countries of Asia and Latin America—a company that aspires to world market leadership (or to sustained rapid growth) cannot ignore the market opportunities or the base of technical and managerial talent such countries offer. This is especially true given that once-high protectionist barriers in most of these countries are in the process of crumbling. Coca-Cola, for example, has predicted that its $2 billion investment in China, India, and Indonesia—which together hold 40 percent of the world's population—can produce sales in those countries that double every three years for the foreseeable future (compared to a modest 4 percent growth rate that Coca-Cola averaged in the United States during the 1990s and to only 1–2 percent U.S. growth in 2000–2002).[16]

Tailoring products for these big emerging markets often involves more than making minor product changes and becoming more familiar with their local cultures.[17] Ford's attempt to sell a Ford Escort in India at a price of $21,000—a luxury-car price, given that India's best-selling Maruti-Suzuki model sold at the time for $10,000 or less, and that fewer than 10 percent of Indian households have annual purchasing power greater than $20,000—met with a less-than-enthusiastic market response. McDonald's has had to offer vegetable burgers in parts of Asia and to rethink its prices, which are often high by local standards and affordable only by the well-to-do. Kellogg has struggled to introduce its cereals successfully because consumers in many less-developed countries do not eat cereal for breakfast—changing habits is difficult and expensive. In several emerging countries, Coca-Cola has found that advertising its world image does not strike a chord with the local populace. Single-serving packages of detergents, shampoos, pickles, cough syrup, and cooking oils are very popular in India because they allow buyers to conserve cash by purchasing only what they need immediately.

Strategy Implications   Consumers in emerging markets are highly focused on price, in many cases giving local low-cost competitors the edge. Companies wishing to succeed in these markets have to attract buyers with bargain prices as well as better products—an approach that can entail a radical departure from the strategy used in other parts of the world. If building a market for the company's products is likely to be a long-term process and involve reeducation of consumers, a company must not only be patient with regard to sizable revenues and profits but also prepared in the interim to invest sizable sums to alter buying habits and tastes. Also, specially designed or packaged products may be needed to accommodate local market circumstances. For example, when Unilever entered the market for laundry detergents in India, it realized that 80 percent of the population could not afford the brands it was selling to affluent consumers there (as well as in wealthier countries). To compete against a very low-priced detergent made by a local company, Unilever came up with a low-cost formula that was not harsh to the skin, constructed new low-cost production facilities, packaged the detergent (named Wheel) in single-use amounts so that it could be sold very cheaply, distributed the product to local merchants by hand carts, and crafted an economical marketing campaign that included painted signs on buildings and demonstrations near stores—the new brand captured $100 million in sales in a relatively short period of time. Unilever later replicated the strategy in South America with a brand named Ala.

> Profitability in emerging markets rarely comes quickly or easily—new entrants have to be very sensitive to local conditions, be willing to invest in developing the market for their products over the long term, and be patient in earning a profit.

Because managing a new venture in an emerging market requires a blend of global knowledge and local sensitivity to the culture and business practices, the management team must usually consist of a mix of expatriate and local managers. Expatriate managers are needed to transfer technology, business practices, and the corporate culture and serve as conduits for the flow of information between the corporate office and local operations; local managers bring needed understanding of the area's nuances and deep commitment to its market.

Strategies for Local Companies in Emerging Markets

If large, opportunity-seeking, resource-rich companies are looking to enter emerging markets, what strategy options can local companies use to survive? As it turns out, the prospects for local companies facing global giants are by no means grim. Their optimal strategic approach hinges on (1) whether their competitive assets are suitable only for the home market or can be transferred abroad, and (2) whether industry pressures to move toward global competition are strong or weak. The four generic options are shown in Figure 5.3.

Using Home-Field Advantages

When the pressures for global competition are low and a local firm has competitive strengths well suited to the local market, a good strategy option is to concentrate on the advantages enjoyed in the home market, cater to customers who prefer a local touch, and accept the loss of customers attracted to global brands.[18] A local company may be able to astutely exploit its local orientation—its familiarity with local preferences, its expertise in traditional products, its long-standing customer relationships. A local company, in

Figure 5.3   Strategy Options for Local Companies in Competing against Global Companies

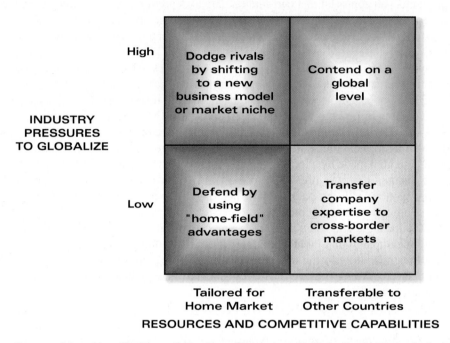

INDUSTRY PRESSURES TO GLOBALIZE

High
- Dodge rivals by shifting to a new business model or market niche
- Contend on a global level

Low
- Defend by using "home-field" advantages
- Transfer company expertise to cross-border markets

Tailored for Home Market   Transferable to Other Countries

RESOURCES AND COMPETITIVE CAPABILITIES

Source: Adapted from Niroj Dawar & Tony Frost, "Competing with Giants: Survival Strategies for Local Companies in Emerging Markets," *Harvard Business Review* 77, no. 1 (January–February 1999), p. 122.

many cases, enjoys a significant cost advantage over global rivals (perhaps because of simpler product design, lower operating and overhead costs), allowing it to compete on the basis of a lower price. Its global competitors often aim their products at upper- and middle-income urban buyers, who tend to be more fashion-conscious, more willing to experiment with new products, and more attracted to global brands. Bajaj Auto, India's largest producer of scooters, has defended its turf against Honda (which entered the Indian market with a local joint venture partner to sell scooters, motorcycles, and other vehicles on the basis of its superior technology, quality, and brand appeal) by focusing on buyers who wanted low-cost, durable scooters and easy access to maintenance in the countryside. Bajaj designed a rugged, cheap-to-build scooter for India's rough roads, increased its investments in R&D to improve reliability and quality, and created an extensive network of distributors and roadside-mechanic stalls, a strategic approach that served it well—while Honda captured about an 11 percent market share, Bajaj maintained a share above 70 percent, close to its 77 percent share prior to Honda's entry. In the fall of 1998, Honda announced it was pulling out of its scooter manufacturing joint venture with its Indian partner.

Transferring the Company's Expertise to Cross-Border Markets

When a company has resource strengths and capabilities suitable for competing in other country markets, launching initiatives to transfer its expertise to cross-border markets becomes a viable strategic option.[19] Televisa, Mexico's largest media company, used its expertise in Spanish culture and linguistics to become the world's most prolific producer of Spanish-language soap operas. Jollibee Foods, a family-owned company with 56 percent of the fast-food business in the Philippines, combated McDonald's entry first by upgrading service and delivery standards and then by using its expertise in seasoning hamburgers with garlic and soy sauce and making noodle and rice meals with fish to open outlets catering to Asian residents in Hong Kong, the Middle East, and California.

Shifting to a New Business Model or Market Niche

When industry pressures to globalize are high, any of three options make the most sense: (1) shift the business to a piece of the industry value chain where the firm's expertise and resources provide competitive advantage, (2) enter into a joint venture with a globally competitive partner, or (3) sell out to (be acquired by) a global entrant into the home market who concludes the company would be a good entry vehicle.[20] When Microsoft entered China, local software developers shifted from cloning Windows products to developing Windows application software customized to the Chinese market. When the Russian PC market opened to IBM, Compaq, and Hewlett-Packard, local Russian PC maker Vist focused on assembling very low-cost models, marketing them through exclusive distribution agreements with selected local retailers, and opening company-owned full-service centers in dozens of Russian cities. Vist focused on providing low-cost PCs, giving lengthy warranties, and catering to buyers who felt the need for local service and support. Vist's strategy allowed it to remain the market leader, with a 20 percent share.

Contending on a Global Level

If a local company in an emerging market has transferable resources and capabilities, it can sometimes launch successful initiatives to meet the pressures for globalization head-on and start to compete on a global level itself.[21] When General Motors decided to outsource the production of radiator caps for all of its North American vehicles, Sundaram Fasteners of India pursued the opportunity; it purchased one of GM's radiator cap production lines, moved it to India, and became GM's sole supplier of radiator caps in North America—at 5 million units a year. As a participant in GM's supplier network, Sundaram learned about emerging technical standards, built its capabilities, and became one of the first Indian companies to achieve QS 9000 certification, a quality standard that GM now requires for all suppliers. Sundaram's acquired expertise in quality standards enabled it then to pursue opportunities to supply automotive parts in Japan and Europe.

Key Points

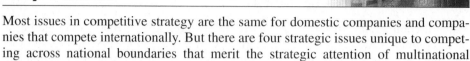

Most issues in competitive strategy are the same for domestic companies and companies that compete internationally. But there are four strategic issues unique to competing across national boundaries that merit the strategic attention of multinational companies:

1. Whether to customize the company's offerings in each different country market to match the tastes and preferences of local buyers or offer a mostly standardized product worldwide.

2. Whether to employ essentially the same basic competitive strategy in all countries or modify the strategy country by country to fit the specific market conditions and competitive circumstances it encounters.

3. Where to locate the company's production facilities, distribution centers, and customer service operations so as to realize the greatest locational advantages.

4. Whether and how to efficiently transfer the company's resource strengths and capabilities from one country to another in an effort to secure competitive advantage.

Companies opt to expand outside their domestic market for any of four major reasons: to gain access to new customers for their products or services, to achieve lower costs and become more competitive on price, to leverage their core competencies, and to spread their business risk across a wider market base. A company is an *international* or *multinational competitor* when it competes in several foreign markets; it is a *global competitor* when it has or is pursuing a market presence in virtually all of the world's major countries.

The strategies a company uses to compete in foreign markets have to be *situation-driven*—cultural, demographic, and market conditions vary significantly among the countries of the world. One of the biggest concerns of competing in foreign markets is whether to customize the company's offerings to cater to the tastes and preferences of local buyers in each different country market or whether to offer a mostly standardized product worldwide. While being responsive to local tastes makes a company's products more appealing to local buyers, customizing a company's products country by country may have the effect of raising production and distribution costs due to the greater variety of designs and components, shorter production runs, and the complications of added inventory handling and distribution logistics. Greater standardization of the company's product offering, on the other hand, enhances the capture of scale economies and experience curve effects, contributing to the achievement of a low-cost advantage. The tension between the market pressures to customize and the competitive pressures to lower costs is one of the big strategic issues that participants in foreign markets have to resolve.

Multicountry competition exists when competition in one national market is independent of competition in another national market—there is no "international market," just a collection of self-contained country markets. *Global competition* exists when competitive conditions across national markets are linked strongly enough to form a true world market and when leading competitors compete head-to-head in many different countries. A multicountry strategy is appropriate for industries where multicountry competition dominates, but a global strategy works best in markets that are globally competitive or beginning to globalize. Other strategy options for competing in world markets include maintaining a national (one-country) production base and exporting goods to foreign markets, licensing foreign firms to use the company's technology or produce and distribute the company's products, employing a franchising strategy, and using strategic alliances and collaborative partnerships to enter a foreign market or strengthen a firm's competitiveness in world markets.

The number of global strategic alliances, joint ventures, and collaborative arrangements has exploded in recent years. Cooperative arrangements with foreign partners have strategic appeal from several angles: gaining wider access to attractive country markets, allowing capture of economies of scale in production and/or marketing, filling gaps in technical expertise and/or knowledge of local markets, saving on costs by sharing distribution facilities and dealer networks, helping gain agreement on important technical standards, and helping combat the impact of alliances that rivals have formed. Cross-border strategic alliances are fast reshaping competition in world markets, pitting one group of allied global companies against other groups of allied global companies.

There are three ways in which a firm can gain competitive advantage (or offset domestic disadvantages) in global markets. One way involves locating various value chain activities among nations in a manner that lowers costs or achieves greater product differentiation. A second way involves efficient and effective transfer of competitively valuable competencies and capabilities from its domestic markets to foreign markets. A third way draws on a multinational or global competitor's ability to deepen or broaden its resource strengths and capabilities and to coordinate its dispersed activities in ways that a domestic-only competitor cannot.

Profit sanctuaries are country markets in which a company derives substantial profits because of its strong or protected market position. They are valuable competitive assets, providing the financial strength to support competitive offensives in one market with resources and profits diverted from operations in other markets, and aid a company's race for global market leadership. The *cross-subsidization capabilities* provided by multiple profit sanctuaries gives a global or international competitor a powerful offensive weapon. Companies with large, protected profit sanctuaries have competitive advantage over companies that don't have a protected sanctuary. Companies with multiple profit sanctuaries have a competitive advantage over companies with a single sanctuary.

Companies racing for global leadership have to consider competing in *emerging markets* like China, India, Brazil, Indonesia, and Mexico—countries where the business risks are considerable but the opportunities for growth are huge. To succeed in these markets, it is usually necessary to attract buyers with bargain prices as well as better products—an approach that can entail a radical departure from the strategy used in other parts of the world. Moreover, building a market for the company's products in these markets is likely to be a long-term process, involving the investment of sizable sums to alter buying habits and tastes and reeducate consumers. Profitability is unlikely to come quickly or easily.

The outlook for local companies in emerging markets wishing to survive against the entry of global giants is by no means grim. The optimal strategic approach hinges on whether a firm's competitive assets are suitable only for the home market or can be transferred abroad and on whether industry pressures to move toward global competition are strong or weak. Local companies can compete against global newcomers by (1) defending on the basis of home-field advantages, (2) transferring their expertise to cross-border markets, (3) dodging large rivals by shifting to a new business model or market niche, or (4) launching initiatives to compete on a global level themselves.

Exercises

1. Log on to www.caterpillar.com and search for information about Caterpillar's strategy in foreign markets. Is it pursuing a global strategy or a multicountry strategy? Support your answer.

2. Assume you are in charge of developing the strategy for a multinational company selling products in some 50 different countries around the world. One of the issues you face is whether to employ a multicountry strategy or a global strategy.

   (a) If your company's product is personal computers, do you think it would make better strategic sense to employ a multicountry strategy or a global strategy? Why?

   (b) If your company's product is dry soup mixes and canned soups, would a multicountry strategy seem to be more advisable than a global strategy? Why?

   (c) If your company's product is mobile phones, would it seem to make more sense to pursue a multicountry strategy or a global strategy? Why?

   (d) If your company's product is basic work tools (hammers, screwdrivers, pliers, wrenches, saws), would a multicountry strategy or a global strategy seem to have more appeal? Why?

CHAPTER 6

Diversification

Strategies for Managing a Group of Businesses

To acquire or not to acquire: that is the question.
—Robert J. Terry

Fit between a parent and its businesses is a two-edged sword: a good fit can create value; a bad one can destroy it.
—Andrew Campbell, Michael Goold, and
  Marcus Alexander

Achieving superior performance through diversification is largely based on relatedness.
—Philippe Very

Make winners out of every business in your company. Don't carry losers.
—Jack Welch, former CEO, General Electric

We measure each of our businesses against strict criteria: growth, margin, and return-on-capital hurdle rate, and does it have the ability to become number one or two in its industry? We are quite pragmatic. If a business does not contribute to our overall vision, it has to go.
—Richard Wambold, CEO, Pactiv

In this chapter, we move up one level in the strategy making hierarchy, from strategy making in a single-business enterprise to strategy making in a diversified enterprise. Because a diversified company is a collection of individual businesses, the strategy-making task is a more complicated exercise than crafting strategy for a single-business enterprise. In a one-business company, managers have to contend with assessing only one industry environment and the question of how to compete successfully in it—the result is what we labeled in Chapter 1 as *business strategy* (or *business-level strategy*). But in a diversified company, the strategy making challenge involves assessing multiple industry environments and coming up with a *set* of business strategies, one for each industry arena in which the diversified company operates. And top executives at a diversified company must still go one step further and devise a companywide or *corporate strategy* for improving the attractiveness and performance of the company's overall business lineup and for making a rational business whole out of its collection of individual businesses.

In most diversified companies, corporate-level executives delegate considerable strategy-making authority to the heads of each business, usually giving them the latitude to craft a business strategy suited to their particular industry and competitive circumstances and holding them accountable for producing good results. But the task of crafting a diversified company's overall or corporate strategy falls squarely in the lap of top-level executives.

Devising a corporate strategy covering multiple businesses has four distinct facets:

1. *Picking new industries to enter and deciding on the means of entry*—The first concerns in diversifying are what new industries to get into and whether to enter by starting a new business from the ground up, acquiring a company already in the target industry, or forming a joint venture or strategic alliance with another company. A company can diversify narrowly into a few industries or broadly into many industries. The choice of whether to enter an industry via a start-up operation; a joint venture; or the acquisition of an established leader, an up-and-coming company, or a troubled company with turnaround potential shapes what position the company will initially stake out for itself.

2. *Initiating actions to boost the combined performance of the businesses the firm has entered*—As positions are created in the chosen industries, corporate strategists typically zero in on ways to strengthen the long-term competitive positions and profits of the businesses the firm has invested in. Corporate parents can help their business subsidiaries by providing financial resources, by supplying missing skills or technological know-how or managerial expertise to better perform key value chain activities, and by providing new avenues for cost reduction. They can also acquire another company in the same industry and merge the two operations into a stronger business, or acquire new businesses that strongly complement existing businesses. Typically, a company will pursue rapid-growth strategies in its most promising businesses, initiate turnaround efforts in weak-performing businesses with potential, and divest businesses that are no longer attractive or that don't fit into management's long-range plans.

3. *Pursuing opportunities to leverage cross-business value chain relationships and strategic fits into competitive advantage*—A company that diversifies into businesses with related value chain activities (pertaining to technology, supply chain logistics, production, overlapping distribution channels, or common customers) gains competitive advantage potential not open to a company that diversifies into businesses whose value chains are totally unrelated. Related diversification presents

opportunities to transfer skills, share expertise, share facilities, or share a common brand name, thereby reducing overall costs, strengthening the competitiveness of some of the company's products, and enhancing the capabilities of particular business units.

4. *Establishing investment priorities and steering corporate resources into the most attractive business units*—A diversified company's different businesses are usually not equally attractive from the standpoint of investing additional funds. It is incumbent on corporate management to (a) decide on the priorities for investing capital in the company's different businesses, (b) channel resources into areas where earnings potentials are higher and away from areas where they are lower, and (c) divest business units that are chronically poor performers or are in an increasingly unattractive industry. Divesting poor performers and businesses in unattractive industries frees up unproductive investments either for redeployment to promising business units or for financing attractive new acquisitions.

The demanding and time-consuming nature of these four tasks explains why corporate executives generally refrain from becoming immersed in the details of crafting and implementing business-level strategies, preferring instead to delegate lead responsibility for business strategy to the heads of each business unit.

In the first portion of this chapter we describe the various paths through which a company can become diversified and explain how a company can use diversification to create or compound competitive advantage for its business units. In the second part of the chapter, we will examine the techniques and procedures for assessing the strategic attractiveness of a diversified company's business portfolio and survey the strategic options open to already-diversified companies.

When to Diversify

So long as a company has its hands full trying to capitalize on profitable growth opportunities in its present industry, there is no urgency to pursue diversification. Companies that concentrate on a single business can achieve enviable success over many decades without relying on diversification to sustain their growth—good examples include McDonald's, Southwest Airlines, Coca-Cola, Domino's Pizza, Apple Computer, Wal-Mart, Federal Express, Hershey, Timex, Anheuser-Busch, Xerox, Gerber, and Ford Motor Company. In the nonprofit sector, continued emphasis on a single activity has proved successful for the Red Cross, the Salvation Army, the Christian Children's Fund, the Girl Scouts, Phi Beta Kappa, and the American Civil Liberties Union. Concentrating on a single line of business (totally or with a small dose of diversification) has important advantages. A single-business company has less ambiguity about who it is, what it does, and where it is headed. It can devote the full force of its resources to improving its competitiveness, expanding into geographic markets it doesn't serve, and responding to changing market conditions and evolving customer preferences. The more successful a single-business enterprise is, the more able it is to parlay its accumulated know-how, competitive capabilities, and reputation into a sustainable position as a leading firm in its industry.

The big risk of a single-business company, of course, is having all of the firm's eggs in industry basket. If the market is eroded by the appearance of new technologies, new products, or fast-shifting buyer preferences, or if it otherwise becomes competitively unattractive, then a company's prospects can quickly dim. Consider, for example, what digital cameras are doing to the market for film and film processing, what CD and DVD technology has done to the market for cassette tapes and 3.5-inch disks, and what mobile phones are doing to the long-distance business and the need for ground-line telephones in homes. Where there are substantial risks that a single business company's market may dry up or when opportunities to grow revenues and earnings in the company's mainstay business begin to peter out, managers usually have to put diversifying into other businesses on the front-burner for consideration.

Factors That Signal It Is Time to Diversify

Diversification merits strong consideration whenever a single-business company is faced with diminishing market opportunities and stagnating sales in its principal business. But there are four other instances in which a company becomes a prime candidate for diversifying:

1. When it can expand into industries whose technologies and products complement its present business.

2. When it can leverage existing competencies and capabilities by expanding into businesses where these same resource strengths are key success factors and valuable competitive assets.

3. When diversifying into closely related businesses opens new avenues for reducing costs.

4. When it has a powerful and well-known brand name that can be transferred to the products of other businesses and thereby used as a lever for driving up the sales and profits of such businesses.

As part of the decision to diversify, the company must ask itself, "What kind and how much diversification?" The strategic possibilities are wide open. A company can diversify into closely related businesses or into totally unrelated businesses. It can diversify its present revenue and earning base to a small extent (such that new businesses account for less than 15 percent of companywide revenues and profits) or to a major extent (such that new businesses produce 30 or more percent of revenues and profits). It can move into one or two large new businesses or a greater number of small ones. It can achieve diversification by acquiring an existing company already in a business it wants to enter, starting up a new business subsidiary from scratch, or entering into a joint venture.

There's no tried-and-true method for determining when its time for a company to diversify. Judgments about the timing of a company's diversification effort are best made case by case, according to the company's own unique situation.

Building Shareholder Value: The Ultimate Justification for Diversifying

Diversification must do more for a company than simply spreading its business risk across various industries. Shareholders can easily diversify risk on their own by purchasing stock in companies in different industries or investing in mutual funds, so they don't need a company to diversify merely to spread their risk across different industries. In principle, diversification makes good strategic and business sense only if it results in added shareholder value—value that shareholders cannot capture through their ownership of different companies in different industries.

For there to be reasonable expectations that a company can produce added value for shareholders, through its own diversification efforts, a diversification move must pass three tests:[1]

1. *The industry attractiveness test*—The industry chosen for diversification must be attractive enough to yield consistently good returns on investment. Whether an industry is attractive depends chiefly on the presence of favorable competitive conditions and a market environment conducive to earning as good or better profits and return on investment than the company is earning in its present business(es). And certainly it is hard to imagine declaring an industry to be attractive if profit expectations are *lower* than in the company's present businesses.

2. *The cost-of-entry test*—The cost to enter the target industry must not be so high as to erode the potential for good profitability. A catch-22 can prevail here, however. The more attractive an industry's prospects are for growth and good long-term profitability, the more expensive it can be to get into. Entry barriers for start-up companies are likely to be high in attractive industries; were barriers low, a rush of new entrants would soon erode the potential for high profitability. And buying a well-positioned company in an appealing industry often entails a high acquisition cost. Paying too much to acquire a company in an attractive industry reduces a company's rate of return on the acquisition price and erodes the potential for enhanced shareholder value.

3. *The better-off test*—Diversifying into a new business must offer potential for the company's existing businesses and the new business to perform better together under a single corporate umbrella than they would perform operating as independent, stand-alone businesses. For example, let's say that company A diversifies by purchasing company B in another industry. If A and B's consolidated profits in the years to come prove no greater than what each could have earned on its own, then A's diversification won't provide its shareholders with added value. Company A's shareholders could have achieved the same $1 + 1 = 2$ result by merely purchasing stock in company B. Shareholder value is not created by diversification unless it produces a $1 + 1 = 3$ effect where sister businesses perform better together as part of the same firm than they could have performed as independent companies. The best chance of a $1 + 1 = 3$ outcome occurs when a company diversifies into businesses that have competitively important value chain matchups with its existing businesses—matchups that offer opportunities to reduce costs, to transfer skills or technology from one business to another, to create valuable new competencies and capabilities, or to leverage existing resources (such as brand-name reputation). Absent such strategic fits, a firm ought to be skeptical about the potential for the businesses to perform better together than apart.

Diversification moves that satisfy all three tests have the greatest potential to grow shareholder value over the long term. Diversification moves that can pass only one or two tests are suspect.

Strategies for Entering New Businesses

Entry into new businesses can take any of three forms: acquisition, internal start-up, or joint ventures/strategic partnerships.

Acquisition of an Existing Business

Acquisition is the most popular means of diversifying into another industry. Not only is it quicker than trying to launch a brand-new operation but it also offers an effective way to hurdle such entry barriers as acquiring technological know-how, establishing supplier relationships, becoming big enough to match rivals' efficiency and unit costs, having to spend large sums on introductory advertising and promotions, and securing adequate distribution. Whether friendly or hostile,[2] acquisitions allow the acquirer to move directly to the task of building a strong market position in the target industry, rather than getting bogged down in going the internal start-up route and trying to develop the knowledge, resources, scale of operation, and market reputation necessary to become an effective competitor within a few years.

However, finding the right kind of company to acquire sometimes presents a challenge.[3] The big dilemma an acquisition-minded firm faces is whether to pay a premium price for a successful company or to buy a struggling company at a bargain price. If the buying firm has little knowledge of the industry but ample capital, it is often better off purchasing a capable, strongly positioned firm—unless the price of such an acquisition is prohibitive and flunks the cost-of-entry test. However, when the acquirer sees promising ways to transform a weak firm into a strong one and has the resources, the know-how, and the patience to do it, a struggling company can be the better long-term investment.

The cost-of-entry test requires that the expected profit stream of an acquired business provide an attractive return on the total acquisition cost and on any new capital investment needed to sustain or expand its operations. A high acquisition price can make meeting that test improbable or difficult. For instance, suppose that the price to purchase a company is $3 million and that the company is earning after-tax profits of $200,000 on an equity investment of $1 million (a 20 percent annual return). Simple arithmetic requires that the profits be tripled if the purchaser (paying $3 million) is to earn the same 20 percent return. Building the acquired firm's earnings from $200,000 to $600,000 annually could take several years—and require additional investment on which the purchaser would also have to earn a 20 percent return. Since the owners of a successful and growing company usually demand a price that reflects their business's profit prospects, it's easy for such an acquisition to fail the cost-of-entry test. A would-be diversifier can't count on being able to acquire a desirable company in an appealing industry at a price that still permits attractive returns on investment.

Internal Start-Up

Achieving diversification through *internal start-up* involves building a new business subsidiary from scratch. This entry option takes longer than the acquisition option and poses some hurdles. A newly formed business unit not only has to overcome entry barriers but also has to invest in new production capacity, develop sources of supply, hire and train employees, build channels of distribution, grow a customer base, and so on. Generally, forming a start-up subsidiary to enter a new

> The biggest drawbacks to entering an industry by forming an internal start-up are the costs of overcoming entry barriers and the extra time it takes to build a strong and profitable competitive position.

business has appeal only when (1) the parent company already has in-house most or all of the skills and resources it needs to piece together a new business and compete effectively; (2) there is ample time to launch the business; (3) internal entry has lower costs than entry via acquisition; (4) the targeted industry is populated with many relatively small firms such that the new start-up does not have to compete head-to-head against larger, more powerful rivals; (5) adding new production capacity will not adversely impact the supply–demand balance in the industry; and (6) incumbent firms are likely to be slow or ineffective in responding to a new entrant's efforts to crack the market.[4]

Joint Ventures and Strategic Partnerships

Joint ventures typically entail forming a new corporate entity owned by the partners, whereas strategic partnerships represent a collaborative arrangement that usually can be terminated whenever one of the partners so chooses. Most joint ventures involve two partners and, historically, were formed to pursue opportunities that were somewhat peripheral to the strategic interests of the partners; very few companies have used joint ventures to enter new industries central to their diversification strategy. In recent years, strategic partnerships/alliances have replaced joint ventures as the favored mechanism for joining forces to pursue strategically important diversification opportunities because they can readily accommodate multiple partners and are more adaptable to rapidly changing technological and market conditions than a formal joint venture.

A strategic partnership or joint venture can be useful in at least three types of situations.[5] First, a strategic alliance/joint venture is a good way to pursue an opportunity that is too complex, uneconomical, or risky for a single organization to pursue alone. Second, strategic alliances/joint ventures make sense when the opportunities in a new industry require a broader range of competencies and know-how than any one organization can marshal. Many of the opportunities in satellite-based telecommunications, biotechnology, and network-based systems that blend hardware, software, and services call for the coordinated development of complementary innovations and integrating a host of financial, technical, political, and regulatory factors. In such cases, pooling the resources and competencies of two or more independent organizations is essential to generate the capabilities needed for success.

Third, joint ventures are sometimes the only way to gain entry into a desirable foreign market, especially when the foreign government requires companies wishing to enter the market to secure a local partner; for example, the Chinese government closed entry in the automotive industry to all but a few select automakers, and in the elevator industry it originally permitted only Otis, Schindler, and Mitsibushi to establish joint ventures with local partners. Although permission was later granted to other companies, the three early entrants were able to retain a market advantage.[6] Alliances with local partners have become a favorite mechanism for global companies not only to establish footholds in desirable foreign country markets but also to surmount tariff barriers and import quotas. Local partners offer outside companies the benefits of local knowledge about market conditions, local customs and cultural factors, and customer buying habits; they can also be a source of managerial and marketing personnel and provide access to distribution outlets. The foreign partner's role is usually to provide specialized skills, technological know-how, and other resources needed to crack the local market and serve it efficiently.

However, like alliances, joint ventures have their difficulties, often posing complicated questions about how to divide efforts among the partners and about who has effective control.[7] Conflicts between foreign and domestic partners can arise over whether to use local sourcing of components, how much production to export, whether operating procedures should conform to the local partner's or the foreign company's standards, and the extent to which the local partner is entitled to make use of the foreign partner's technology and intellectual property. As the foreign partner acquires experience and confidence in the local market, its need for the local partner typically diminishes, posing the strategic issue of whether the partnership/joint venture should be dissolved. This happens frequently in alliances between global manufacturers and local distributors.[8] Joint ventures are generally the least durable of the entry options, usually lasting only until the partners decide to go their own ways. Japanese automakers have abandoned their European distribution partners and set up their own dealer networks; BMW did the same in Japan. However, the temporary character of joint ventures is not always bad. Several ambitious local partners have used their alliances with global companies to master technologies and build key competitive skills, then capitalized on the acquired know-how to launch their own entry into the international arena. Taiwan's Acer Computer Group used its alliance with Texas Instruments as a stepping-stone for entering the world market for desktop and laptop computers.

Choosing the Diversification Path: Related versus Unrelated Businesses

Once the decision is made to pursue diversification, the firm must choose whether to diversify into **related businesses, unrelated businesses,** or some mix of both (see Figure 6.1). *Businesses are said to be related when their value chains possess competitively valuable relationships that present opportunities to transfer resources from one business to another, combine similar activities and reduce costs, share a common brand name, or create mutually useful resource strengths and capabilities.* The appeal of related diversification is exploiting these value chain matchups to realize a $1 + 1 = 3$ performance outcome and thus build shareholder value from operating separate businesses under a common corporate umbrella. *Businesses are said to be unrelated when the activities comprising their respective value chains are so dissimilar that no competitively valuable cross-business relationships are present.*

> **Core Concept**
>
> **Related businesses** possess competitively valuable cross-business value chain matchups; **unrelated businesses** have dissimilar value chains, containing no competitively useful cross-business relationships.

Most companies favor related diversification strategies because of the performance-enhancing potential of cross-business synergies. However, some companies have, for one reason or another, opted to try to build shareholder value with unrelated diversification strategies. And a few have diversified into both related and unrelated businesses. The next two sections explore the ins and outs of related and unrelated diversification.

The Case for Diversifying into Related Businesses

A related diversification strategy involves building the company around businesses whose value chains possess competitively valuable strategic fits, as shown in Figure 6.2. **Strategic fit** exists whenever one or more activities comprising the value chains

Figure 6.1   Strategy Alternatives for a Company Looking to Diversify

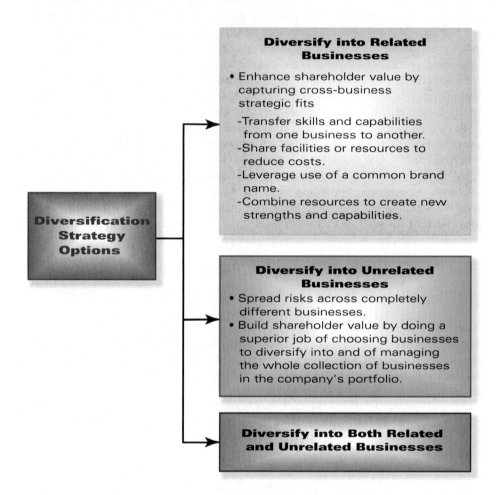

Diversification Strategy Options

Diversify into Related Businesses

- Enhance shareholder value by capturing cross-business strategic fits
  - Transfer skills and capabilities from one business to another.
  - Share facilities or resources to reduce costs.
  - Leverage use of a common brand name.
  - Combine resources to create new strengths and capabilities.

Diversify into Unrelated Businesses

- Spread risks across completely different businesses.
- Build shareholder value by doing a superior job of choosing businesses to diversify into and of managing the whole collection of businesses in the company's portfolio.

Diversify into Both Related and Unrelated Businesses

Core Concept

Strategic fit exists when the value chains of different businesses present opportunities for cross-business resource transfer, lower costs through combining the performance of related value chain activities, cross-business use of a potent brand name, and cross-business collaboration to build new or stronger competitive capabilities.

of different businesses are sufficiently similar as to present opportunities for:[9]

- Transferring competitively valuable expertise, technological know-how, or other capabilities from one business to another.

- Combining the related activities of separate businesses into a single operation to achieve lower costs.

- Exploiting common use of a well-known brand name.

- Cross-business collaboration to create competitively valuable resource strengths and capabilities.

Related diversification thus has strategic appeal from several angles. It allows a firm to reap the competitive advantage benefits of skills transfer, lower costs, common brand names, and/or stronger competitive

Figure 6.2   Related Businesses Possess Related Value Chain Activities and Competitively Valuable Strategic Fits

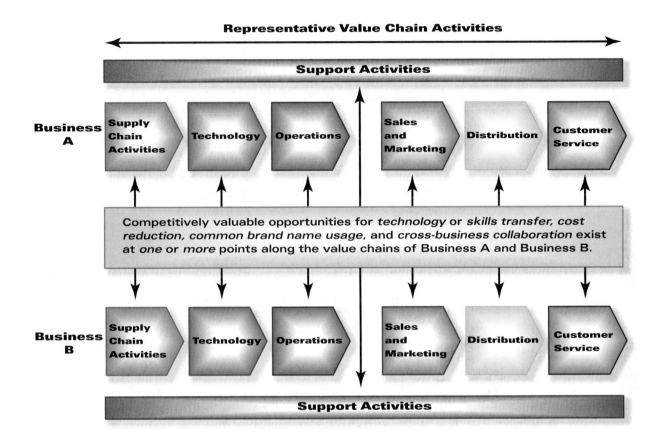

capabilities and still spread investor risks over a broad business base. Furthermore, the relatedness among the different businesses provides sharper focus for managing diversification and a useful degree of strategic unity across the company's various business activities.

Cross-Business Strategic Fits along the Value Chain

Cross-business strategic fits can exist anywhere along the value chain—in R&D and technology activities, in supply chain activities and relationships with suppliers, in manufacturing, in sales and marketing, in distribution activities, or in administrative support activities.[10]

Strategic Fits in R&D and Technology Activities   Diversifying into businesses where there is potential for sharing common technology, exploiting the full range of business opportunities associated with a particular technology and its derivatives, or transferring technological know-how from one business to another has considerable appeal. Businesses with technology-sharing benefits can perform better together than apart because of potential cost savings in R&D and potentially shorter times in getting new products to market; also, technological advances in one business can lead to increased sales for both. Technological innovations have been the driver behind the efforts of cable TV companies to diversify into high-speed Internet access (via the use of cable modems) and, further, to explore providing local and long-distance telephone service to residential and commercial customers in a single wire.

Strategic Fits in Supply Chain Activities   Businesses that have supply chain strategic fits can perform better together because of the potential for skills transfer in procuring materials, greater bargaining power in negotiating with common suppliers, the benefits of added collaboration with common supply chain partners, and/or added leverage with shippers in securing volume discounts on incoming parts and components. Dell Computer's strategic partnerships with leading suppliers of microprocessors, motherboards, disk drives, memory chips, monitors, modems, flat-panel displays, long-life batteries, and other desktop and laptop components have been an important component of the company's strategy to diversify into servers and data storage devices—products that include many components common to PCs and that can be sourced from the same strategic partners that provide Dell with PC components.

Manufacturing-Related Strategic Fits   Cross-business strategic fits in manufacturing-related activities can represent an important source of competitive advantage in situations where a diversifier's expertise in quality manufacture and cost-efficient production methods can be transferred to another business. When Emerson Electric diversified into the chain-saw business, it transferred its expertise in low-cost manufacture to its newly acquired Beaird-Poulan business division; the transfer drove Beaird-Poulan's new strategy—to be the low-cost provider of chain-saw products—and fundamentally changed the way Beaird-Poulan chain saws were designed and manufactured. Another benefit of value chain matchups in production may involve cost-saving opportunities stemming from the ability to perform manufacturing or assembly activities jointly in the same facility rather than independently, thus making it feasible to consolidate production into a smaller number of plants and significantly reduce overall production costs. When snowmobile maker Bombardier diversified into motorcycles, it was able to set up motorcycle assembly lines in the same manufacturing facility where it was assembling snowmobiles.

Distribution-Related Strategic Fits   Businesses with closely related distribution activities can perform better together than apart because of potential cost savings in sharing the same distribution facilities or using many of the same wholesale distributors and retail dealers to access customers. When Sunbeam acquired Mr. Coffee, it was able to consolidate its own distribution centers for small household appliances with those of Mr. Coffee, thereby generating considerable cost savings. Likewise, since Sunbeam products were sold to many of the same retailers as Mr. Coffee products (Wal-Mart, Kmart, department stores, home centers, hardware chains, supermarket chains, and drugstore chains), Sunbeam was able to convince many of the retailers carrying Sunbeam appliances to also take on the Mr. Coffee line and vice versa.

Strategic Fits in Sales and Marketing Activities   Various cost-saving opportunities spring from diversifying into businesses with closely related sales and marketing activities. Sales costs can often be reduced by using a single sales force for the products of both businesses rather than having separate sales forces for each business. When the products are distributed through many of the same wholesale and retail dealers or are sold directly to the same customers, it is usually feasible to give one salesperson the responsibility for handling the sales of both products (rather than have two different salespeople call on the same customer). The products of related businesses can be promoted at the same website, and included in the same media ads and sales brochures. After-sale service and repair organizations for the products of closely related businesses can often be consolidated into a single operation. There may be opportunities to reduce costs by coordinating delivery and shipping, consolidating order processing and billing, and using common promotional tie-ins (cents-off couponing, free samples and trial offers, seasonal specials, and the like). When global power-tool maker Black & Decker acquired General Electric's domestic small household appliance business, it was able to use its own global sales force and distribution facilities to sell and distribute toasters, irons, mixers, and coffeemakers because the types of customers that carried its power tools (discounters like Wal-Mart and Kmart, home centers, and hardware stores) also stocked small appliances. The economies Black & Decker achieved for both product lines were substantial.

A second category of benefits arises when different businesses use similar sales and marketing approaches; in such cases, there may be competitively valuable opportunities to transfer selling, merchandising, advertising, and product differentiation skills from one business to another. Procter & Gamble's product lineup includes Folgers coffee, Tide laundry detergent, Crest toothpaste, Ivory soap, Charmin toilet tissue, and Head & Shoulders shampoo. All of these have different competitors and different supply chain and production requirements, but they all move through the same wholesale distribution systems, are sold in common retail settings to the same shoppers, are advertised and promoted in much the same ways, and require the same marketing and merchandising skills.

A third set of benefits arises from related sales and marketing activities when a company's brand name and reputation in one business is transferable to other businesses. Honda's name in motorcycles and automobiles gave it instant credibility and recognition in entering the lawn-mower business, allowing it to achieve a significant market share without spending large sums on advertising to establish a brand identity for its lawn mowers. Canon's reputation in photographic equipment was a competitive asset that facilitated the company's diversification into copying equipment. Panasonic's name in consumer electronics (radios, TVs) was readily transferred to microwave ovens, making it easier and cheaper for Panasonic to diversify into the microwave oven market.

Strategic Fits in Managerial and Administrative Support Activities   Often, different businesses require comparable types of skills, competencies, and managerial know-how, thereby allowing know-how in one line of business to be transferred to another. At General Electric (GE), managers who were involved in GE's expansion into Russia were able to expedite entry because of information gained from GE managers involved in expansions into other emerging markets. The lessons GE managers learned in China were passed along to GE managers in Russia, allowing them to anticipate that the Russian government would demand that GE build production capacity in the country rather than enter the market through exporting or licensing. In addition, GE's managers in Russia were better able to develop realistic performance expectations and make tough upfront decisions since experience in China and elsewhere

Five Companies That Have Diversified into Related Businesses

Gillette

- Blades and razors
- Toiletries (Right Guard, Foamy, Dry Idea, Soft & Dry, White Rain)
- Oral-B toothbrushes
- Braun shavers, coffeemakers, alarm clocks, mixers, hair dryers, and electric toothbrushes
- Duracell batteries

Darden Restaurants

- Olive Garden restaurant chain (Italian-themed)
- Red Lobster restaurant chain (seafood-themed)
- Bahama Breeze restaurant chain (Caribbean-themed)

L'Oréal

- Maybelline, Lancôme, Helena Rubenstein, Kiehl's, Garner, and Shu Uemura cosmetics
- L'Oréal and Soft Sheen/Carson hair care products
- Redken, Matrix, L'Oréal Professional, and Kerastase Paris professional hair care and skin care products
- Ralph Lauren and Giorgio Armani fragrances
- Biotherm skincare products
- La Roche–Posay and Vichy Laboratories dermocosmetics

Johnson & Johnson

- Baby products (powder, shampoo, oil, lotion)
- Band-Aids and other first-aid products
- Women's health and personal care products (Stayfree, Carefree, Sure & Natural)
- Neutrogena and Aveeno skin care products
- Nonprescription drugs (Tylenol, Motrin, Pepcid AC, Mylanta, Monistat)
- Prescription drugs
- Prosthetic and other medical devices
- Surgical and hospital products
- Accuvue contact lenses

PepsiCo, Inc.

- Soft drinks (Pepsi, Diet Pepsi, Pepsi One, Mountain Dew, Mug, Slice)
- Fruit juices (Tropicana and Dole)
- Sports drinks (Gatorade)
- Other beverages (Aquafina bottled water, SoBe, Lipton ready-to-drink tea, Frappucino—in partnership with Starbucks, international sales of 7UP)
- Snack foods (Fritos, Lay's, Ruffles, Doritos, Tostitos, Santitas, Smart Food, Rold Gold pretzels, Chee-tos, Grandma's cookies, Sun Chips, Cracker Jack, Frito-Lay dips and salsas)
- Cereals, rice, and breakfast products (Quaker oatmeal, Cap'n Crunch, Life, Rice-A-Roni, Quaker rice cakes, Aunt Jemima mixes and syrups, Quaker grits)

Source: Company annual reports.

---

warned them (1) that there would likely be increased short-term costs during the early years of start-up and (2) that if GE committed to the Russian market for the long term and aided the country's economic development it could eventually expect to be given the freedom to pursue profitable penetration of the Russian market.[11]

Likewise, different businesses sometimes use the same sorts of administrative support facilities. For instance, an electric utility that diversifies into natural gas, water, appliance sales and repair services, and home security services can use the same customer data network, the same customer call centers and local offices, the same billing and customer accounting systems, and the same customer service infrastructure to support all of its products and services.

Company Spotlight 6.1 lists the businesses of five companies that have pursued a strategy of related diversification.

Strategic Fit, Economies of Scope, and Competitive Advantage

What makes related diversification an attractive strategy is the opportunity to convert the strategic fit between the value chains of different businesses into a competitive advantage over business rivals that have not diversified or that have diversified in ways that don't give them access to such strategic-fit benefits. The greater the relatedness among the businesses of a diversified company, the greater the opportunities for skills transfer and/or combining related value chain activities to achieve lower costs and/or leveraging use of a well-respected brand name and/or collaborating to create new resource strengths and capabilities. The more competitively important the strategic fit relationships across related businesses, the bigger the window for converting strategic fits into competitive advantage over rivals lacking comparable strategic fits in their own operations.

Economies of Scope: A Path to Competitive Advantage   One of the most important competitive advantages that a related diversification strategy can produce is lower costs than competitors. Related businesses often present opportunities to consolidate certain value chain activities or use common resources, and thereby eliminate costs. Such cost savings are termed **economies of scope**—a concept distinct from *economies of scale*. Economies of *scale* are cost savings that accrue directly from a larger-sized operation; for example, unit costs may be lower in a large plant than in a small plant, lower in a large distribution center than in a small one, lower for large-volume purchases of components than for small-volume purchases. Economies of *scope*, however, stem directly from cost-saving strategic fits along the value chains of related businesses; such economies are open only to a multibusiness enterprise and are very much a phenomenon of related diversification. Most usually, economies of scope are the result of two or more businesses sharing technology, performing R&D together, using common manufacturing or distribution facilities, sharing a common sales force or distributor/dealer network, using the same established brand name, and/or sharing the same administrative infrastructure. *The greater the economies associated with cost-saving strategic fits, the greater the potential for a related diversification strategy to yield a competitive advantage based on lower costs.*

> **Core Concept**
>
> **Economies of scope** are cost reductions that flow from operating in multiple businesses; such economies stem directly from strategic fit efficiencies along the value chains of related businesses.

From Competitive Advantage to Added Profitability and Gains in Shareholder Value   Armed with the competitive advantages that come from economies of scope and the capture of other strategic-fit benefits, a company with a portfolio of related businesses is poised to achieve $1 + 1 = 3$ financial performance and the hoped-for gains in shareholder value. The strategic and business logic is compelling: A company that succeeds in capturing strategic fits along the value chains of its related businesses has a clear path to achieving competitive advantage over undiversified competitors and competitors whose own diversification efforts don't offer equivalent strategic-fit benefits. With such competitive advantage, a company then has a dependable basis for earning better-than-average profits—in particular, profits and a return on investment that exceed what the company's businesses could earn as stand-alone enterprises. In turn, above-average profitability is what fuels $1 + 1 = 3$ gains in

> **Core Concept**
>
> A company that leverages the strategic fit of its related businesses into competitive advantage has a clear avenue to producing gains in shareholder value.

shareholder value—the necessary outcome for satisfying the better-off test and proving the business merit of a company's diversification effort.

Consequently, a strategy of diversifying into related businesses where competitively valuable strategic fit benefits can be captured has strong potential for putting sister businesses in position to perform better financially as part of the same company than they could have performed as independent enterprises. This makes a strategy of related diversification a very appealing vehicle for building shareholder value in ways that shareholders cannot undertake by simply owning a portfolio of stocks of companies in different industries. The capture of strategic-fit benefits is possible only via a strategy of related diversification.[12]

A Word of Caution   Diversifying into related businesses is no guarantee of gains in shareholder value. Many companies have stumbled with related diversification because they overpaid for the acquired companies, failing the cost-of-entry test. And two problems commonly arise in passing the better-off test: One occurs when the likely cost savings of combining related value chain activities and capturing economies of scope are overestimated; in such cases, the realized cost savings and gains in profitability prove too small to justify the acquisition-price premium. The second occurs when transferring resources from one business to another is fraught with unforeseen obstacles that delay or diminish the strategic-fit benefits actually captured. Experience indicates that it is easy to be overly optimistic about the value of the cross-business synergies—realizing them is harder than first meets the eye.

The Case for Diversifying into Unrelated Businesses

A strategy of diversifying into unrelated businesses discounts the value and importance of the strategic-fit benefits associated with related diversification and instead focuses on building and managing a portfolio of business subsidiaries capable of delivering good financial performance in their respective industries. Companies that pursue a strategy of unrelated diversification generally exhibit a willingness to diversify into *any industry* where there's potential for a company to realize consistently good financial results. Decisions to diversify into one industry versus another are the product of an opportunistic search for good companies to acquire—*the basic premise of unrelated diversification is that any company that can be acquired on good financial terms and that has satisfactory earnings potential represents a good acquisition.* While companies pursuing unrelated diversification may well look for companies that can satisfy the industry attractiveness and cost-of-entry tests, they either disregard the better-off test or relegate it to secondary status. *A strategy of unrelated diversification involves no deliberate effort to seek out businesses having strategic fit with the firm's other businesses* (see Figure 6.3). Rather, the company spends much time and effort screening new acquisition candidates and deciding whether to keep or divest existing businesses, using such criteria as:

- Whether the business can meet corporate targets for profitability and return on investment.

- Whether the business will require substantial infusions of capital to replace out-of-date plants and equipment, fund expansion, and provide working capital.

- Whether the business is in an industry with significant growth potential.

Figure 6.3   Unrelated Businesses Have Unrelated Value Chains and No Strategic Fits

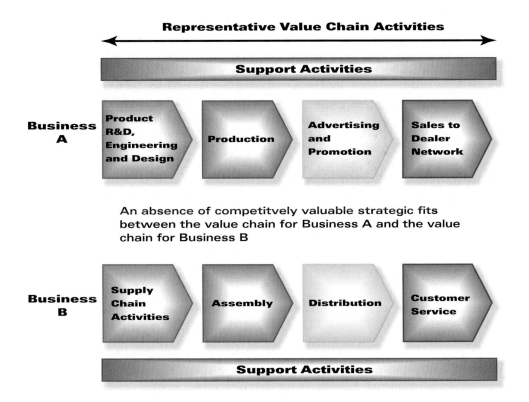

Representative Value Chain Activities

Support Activities

Business A
Product R&D, Engineering and Design → Production → Advertising and Promotion → Sales to Dealer Network

An absence of competitvely valuable strategic fits between the value chain for Business A and the value chain for Business B

Business B
Supply Chain Activities → Assembly → Distribution → Customer Service

Support Activities

- Whether the business is big enough to contribute *significantly* to the parent firm's bottom line.
- Whether there is a potential for union difficulties or adverse government regulations concerning product safety or the environment.
- Whether there is industry vulnerability to recession, inflation, high interest rates, or shifts in government policy.

Some acquisition candidates offer quick opportunities for financial gain because of their "special situation." Three types of businesses may hold such attraction:

- *Companies whose assets are undervalued*—Opportunities may exist to acquire undervalued companies and resell their assets for more than the acquisition costs.
- *Companies that are financially distressed*—Businesses in financial distress can often be purchased at a bargain price, their operations turned around with the aid of the parent company's financial resources and managerial know-how, and then either held as long-term investments in the acquirer's business portfolio (because of their strong earnings or cash flow potential) or sold at a profit, whichever is more attractive.
- *Companies that have bright growth prospects but are short on investment capital*—Cash-poor, opportunity-rich companies are usually coveted acquisition candidates for a financially strong opportunity-seeking firm.

Companies that pursue unrelated diversification nearly always enter new businesses by acquiring an established company rather than by forming a start-up subsidiary within their own corporate structures. The premise of acquisition-minded corporations is that growth by acquisition can deliver enhanced shareholder value through upward trending corporate revenues and earnings and a stock price that *on average* rises enough year after year to amply reward and please shareholders.

A key issue in unrelated diversification is how wide a net to cast in building a portfolio of unrelated businesses. In other words, should a company pursuing unrelated diversification seek to have few or many unrelated businesses? How much business diversity can corporate executives successfully manage? A reasonable way to resolve the issue of how much diversification comes from answering two questions: "What is the least diversification it will take to achieve acceptable growth and profitability?" and "What is the most diversification that can be managed, given the complexity it adds?"[13] The optimal amount of diversification usually lies between these two extremes.

Company Spotlight 6.2 lists the businesses of five companies that have pursued unrelated diversification. Such companies are frequently labeled *conglomerates* because their business interests range broadly across diverse industries.

The Merits of an Unrelated Diversification Strategy

A strategy of unrelated diversification has appeal from several angles:

1. Business risk is scattered over a set of truly *diverse* industries. In comparison to related diversification, unrelated diversification more closely approximates *pure* diversification of financial and business risk because the company's investments are spread over businesses whose technologies and value chain activities bear no close relationship and whose markets are largely disconnected.[14]

2. The company's financial resources can be employed to maximum advantage by investing in *whatever industries* offer the best profit prospects (as opposed to considering only opportunities in industries with related value chain activities). Specifically, cash flows from company businesses with lower growth and profit prospects can be diverted to acquiring and expanding businesses with higher growth and profit potentials.

3. To the extent that corporate managers are exceptionally astute at spotting bargain-priced companies with big upside profit potential, shareholder wealth can be enhanced by buying distressed businesses at a low price, turning their operations around fairly quickly with infusions of cash and managerial know-how supplied by the parent company, and then riding the crest of the profit increases generated by the newly acquired businesses.

4. Company profitability may prove somewhat more stable over the course of economic upswings and downswings because market conditions in all industries don't move upward or downward simultaneously—in a broadly diversified company, there's a chance that market downtrends in some of the company's businesses will be partially offset by cyclical upswings in its other businesses, thus producing somewhat less earnings volatility. (In actual practice, however, there's no convincing evidence that the consolidated profits of firms with unrelated diversification strategies are more stable or less subject to reversal in periods of recession and economic stress than the profits of firms with related diversification strategies.)

Five Companies That Have Diversified into Unrelated Businesses

United Technologies, Inc.

- Pratt & Whitney aircraft engines
- Carrier heating and air-conditioning equipment
- Otis elevators
- Sikorsky helicopters
- Hamilton Substrand aerospace subsystems and components

The Walt Disney Company

- Theme parks
- Disney Cruise Line
- Resort properties
- Movie, video, and theatrical productions (for both children and adults)
- Television broadcasting (ABC, Disney Channel, Toon Disney, Classic Sports Network, ESPN and ESPN2, E!, Lifetime, and A&E networks)
- Radio broadcasting (Disney Radio)
- Musical recordings and sales of animation art
- Anaheim Mighty Ducks NHL franchise
- Anaheim Angels major league baseball franchise (25 percent ownership)
- Books and magazine publishing
- Interactive software and Internet sites
- The Disney Store retail shops

Cooper Industries

- Crescent wrenches, pliers, and screwdrivers
- Nicholson files and saws
- Diamond horseshoes and farrier tools
- Lufkin measuring and layout products
- Gardner-Denver electric power tools
- Electrical construction materials
- Lighting fixtures, fuses, and circuit protection devices
- Electric utility products (transformers, relays, capacitor controls, switches)
- Emergency lighting, fire detection, and security systems

Textron, Inc.

- Bell helicopters
- Cessna Aircraft
- E-Z-Go golf carts
- Textron Automotive (instrument panels, plastic fuel tanks, plastic interior and exterior trim)
- Textron Fastening Systems (the global leader)
- Fluid and power systems
- Textron Financial Services
- Jacobsen turf care equipment
- Ransomes turf care and utility vehicles
- Tools and testing equipment for the wire and cable industry

American Standard

- Trane and American Standard furnaces, heat pumps, and air conditioners
- Plumbing products (American Standard, Ideal Standard, Standard, Porcher lavatories, toilets, bath tubs, faucets, whirlpool baths, and shower basins)
- Automotive products (commercial and utility vehicle braking and control systems)
- Medical systems (DiaSorin disease assessment and management products)

Source: Company annual reports.

Unrelated diversification can be appealing in several other circumstances. It certainly merits consideration when a firm needs to diversify away from an endangered or unattractive industry and has no distinctive competencies or capabilities it can transfer to an adjacent industry. There's also a rationale for unrelated diversification to the extent that owners have a strong preference for spreading business risks widely and not restricting themselves to investing in a family of closely related businesses.

Building Shareholder Value via Unrelated Diversification
Building shareholder value via unrelated diversification is predicated on executive skill in managing a group of unrelated businesses. For a strategy of unrelated diversification to generate gains in shareholder value, corporate-level managers must produce companywide financial results above and beyond what business-level managers could produce if the businesses operated as stand-alone entities. Corporate executives add value to a diversified enterprise by shrewdly deciding which businesses to get into and which ones to get out of, cleverly allocating the corporate parent's financial resources to businesses with the best profit potential, and consistently providing high-caliber decision-making guidance to the general managers of the company's business subsidiaries. In more specific terms, this means corporate-level executives must:

- Do a superior job of diversifying into new businesses that can produce consistently good earnings and returns on investment (thereby satisfying the attractiveness test).

- Do an excellent job of negotiating favorable acquisition prices (thereby satisfying the cost-of-entry test).

- Discern when it is the "right" time to sell a particular business (sensing when a business subsidiary is on the verge of confronting adverse industry and competitive conditions and probable declines in long-term profitability) and also selling it at the "right" price, ideally for more than the company's net investment in the business.

- Shift corporate financial resources out of businesses where profit opportunities are dim and into businesses with the potential for above-average earnings growth and returns on investment.

- Do such a good job overseeing the firm's business subsidiaries and contributing to how they are managed—by providing expert problem-solving skills, creative strategy suggestions, decision-making guidance to business-level managers, and needed infusions of investment capital—that the subsidiaries perform at a higher level than they would otherwise be able to do (a possible way to satisfy the better-off test).

To the extent that corporate executives are able to craft and execute a strategy of unrelated diversification that produces enough of the above outcomes to produce a stream of dividends and capital gains for stockholders greater than a $1 + 1 = 2$ outcome, a case can be made that shareholder value has truly been enhanced.

The Drawbacks of Unrelated Diversification

Unrelated diversification strategies have two important negatives that undercut the pluses: very demanding managerial requirements and limited competitive advantage potential.

Demanding Managerial Requirements Successfully managing a set of fundamentally different businesses operating in fundamentally different industry and competitive environments is a very challenging and exceptionally difficult proposition for corporate-level managers. It is difficult because key executives at the corporate level, while perhaps having personally worked in one or two of the company's businesses, cannot possibly have in-depth familiarity with each of the company's businesses—the prevailing competitive market

Core Concept

The two biggest drawbacks to unrelated diversification are the difficulties of competently managing many different businesses and being without the added source of competitive advantage that cross-business strategic fit provides.

conditions, driving forces, industry key success factors, each business's competitive strengths and weaknesses, and so on. The greater the number of businesses a company is in and the more diverse they are, the harder it is for corporate managers to (1) stay abreast of what's happening in each industry and each subsidiary and thus judge whether a particular business has bright prospects or is headed for trouble, (2) know enough about the issues and problems facing each subsidiary to pick business-unit heads having the requisite combination of managerial skills and know-how, (3) be able to tell the difference between those strategic proposals of business-unit managers that are prudent and those that are risky or unlikely to succeed, and (4) know what to do if a business unit stumbles and its results suddenly head downhill.[15]

In a company like Walt Disney (see Company Spotlight 6.2) or Tyco International (which acquired over 1,000 companies during the 1990–2001 period), corporate executives are constantly scrambling to stay on top of fresh industry developments and the strategic progress and plans of each subsidiary, often depending on briefings by business-level managers for many of the details. As a rule, the more unrelated businesses that a company has diversified into, the more corporate executives are reduced to "managing by the numbers"—that is, keeping a close track on the financial and operating results of each subsidiary and assuming that everything is under control in a business as long as the latest key financial and operating measures look good. Managing by the numbers can work if the heads of the various business units are quite capable, but there's still ample room for strategic issues to be glossed over and impending downturns in some of the company's key businesses to go unnoticed. Just one or two unforeseen declines or big strategic mistakes (misjudging the importance of certain competitive forces or the impact of driving forces or key success factors, encountering unexpected problems in a newly acquired business, or being too optimistic about turning around a struggling subsidiary) can cause a precipitous drop in corporate earnings and crash the parent company's stock price. As the former chairman of a Fortune 500 company advised, "Never acquire a business you don't know how to run." Because every business tends to encounter rough sledding, a good way to gauge the merits of acquiring a company in an unrelated industry is to ask, "If the business got into trouble, is corporate management likely to know how to bail it out?" When the answer is no (or even a qualified yes or maybe), growth via acquisition into unrelated businesses is a chancy strategy.[16]

Hence, while overseeing a set of widely diverse businesses may sound doable, it can turn out to be much harder than it sounds. In practice, comparatively few companies have proved that they have top management capabilities that are up to the task. There are far more companies that have tried unrelated diversification and failed than there are companies that have tried it and succeeded. It is simply very difficult for corporate executives to build shareholder value based on their expertise in (*a*) picking which industries to diversify into and which companies in these industries to acquire, (*b*) shifting resources from low-performing business into high performing businesses, and (*c*) giving high-caliber decision-making guidance to the general managers of their business subsidiaries. Instead of achieving 1 + 1 = 3 gains in shareholder value, the odds are that the result of unrelated diversification will be 1 + 1 = 2 or less.

> Relying solely on the expertise of corporate executives to wisely manage a set of unrelated businesses is *a much weaker foundation for enhancing sharehold value* than is a strategy of related diversification where corporate performance can be boosted by expert corporate-level management.

Limited Competitive Advantage Potential   The second big negative is that *unrelated diversification offers no potential for competitive advantage beyond* *that of what each individual business can generate on its own.* Unlike a related diversification strategy, there are no cross-business strategic fits to draw on for reducing costs, beneficially transferring skills and technology, leveraging use of a powerful brand name, or collaborating to build mutually beneficial competitive capabilities and thereby *adding to any competitive advantage possessed by individual businesses.* Yes, a cash-rich corporate parent can provide its subsidiaries with much-needed capital, and there are times when a corporate parent may have the managerial know-how to help resolve problems in particular business units. But, otherwise, a corporate parent pursuing unrelated diversification has little to offer in the way of enhancing the competitive strength of its individual business units. *Without the competitive advantage potential of strategic fits, consolidated performance of an unrelated group of businesses stands to be little or no better than the sum of what the individual business units could achieve if they were independent,* and it may be worse to the extent that corporate managers do a poor job of supervising certain business subsidiaries or hamstringing them with questionable corporate policies. In trying to manage a set of unrelated businesses, the value added by corporate managers depends primarily on how good they are at deciding what new businesses to add, which ones to get rid of, how best to deploy the parent company's financial resources in supporting the needs of its business units and boosting overall corporate performance, and the quality of the decision-making guidance they give to the managers of their business subsidiaries.

Combination Related–Unrelated Diversification Strategies

There's nothing to preclude a company from diversifying into both related and unrelated businesses. Indeed, in actual practice the business makeup of diversified companies varies considerably. Some diversified companies are really *dominant-business enterprises*—one major "core" business accounts for 50 to 80 percent of total revenues and a collection of small related or unrelated businesses accounts for the remainder. Some diversified companies are *narrowly diversified* around a few (two to five) related or unrelated businesses. Others are *broadly diversified* around a wide-ranging collection of related businesses, unrelated businesses, or a mixture of both. And a number of multibusiness enterprises have diversified into unrelated areas but have a collection of related businesses within each area—thus giving them a business portfolio consisting of *several unrelated groups of related businesses.* There's ample room for companies to customize their diversification strategies to incorporate elements of both related and unrelated diversification, as may suit their own risk preferences and strategic vision.

Figure 6.4 indicates what to look for in identifying the main elements of a company's diversification strategy. Having a clear fix on the company's current corporate strategy sets the stage for evaluating how good the strategy is and proposing strategic moves to boost the company's performance.

Evaluating the Strategy of a Diversified Company

Strategic analysis of diversified companies builds on the concepts and methods used for single-business companies. But there are some additional aspects to consider and a

Figure 6.4   Identifying a Diversified Company's Strategy

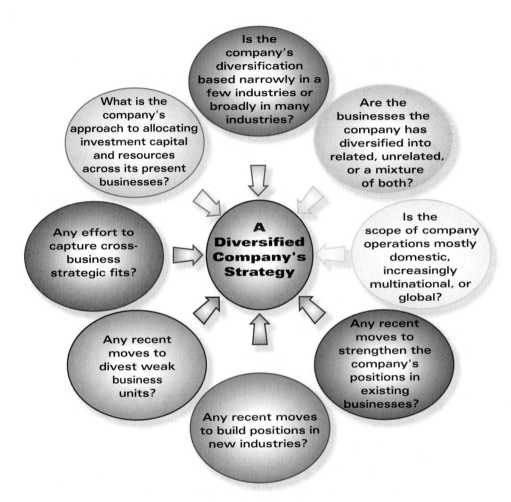

couple of new analytical tools to master. The procedure for evaluating the pluses and minuses of a diversified company's strategy and deciding what actions to take to improve the company's performance involves six steps:

1. Assessing the attractiveness of the industries the company has diversified into, both individually and as a group.

2. Assessing the competitive strength of the company's business units and determining how many are strong contenders in their respective industries.

3. Checking the competitive advantage potential of cross-business strategic fits among the company's various business units.

4. Checking whether the firm's resources fit the requirements of its present business lineup.

5. Ranking the performance prospects of the businesses from best to worst and determining what the corporate parent's priority should be in allocating resources to its various businesses.

6. Crafting new strategic moves to improve overall corporate performance.

The core concepts and analytical techniques underlying each of these steps merit further discussion.

Step 1: Evaluating Industry Attractiveness

A principal consideration in evaluating a diversified company's business makeup and the caliber of its strategy is the attractiveness of the industries in which it has business operations. Answers to several questions are required:

1. *Does each industry the company has diversified into represent a good business for the company to be in?* Ideally, each industry in which the firm operates will pass the attractiveness test.

2. *Which of the company's industries are most attractive and which are least attractive?* Comparing the attractiveness of the industries and ranking them from most to least attractive is a prerequisite to deciding how to allocate corporate resources across the various businesses.

3. *How appealing is the whole group of industries in which the company has invested?* The answer to this question points to whether the group of industries holds promise for attractive growth and profitability or whether the company may be in too many slow-growing, intensely competitive, highly cyclical businesses. A company whose revenues and profits come chiefly from businesses in relatively unattractive industries probably needs to look at building positions in additional industries that qualify as highly attractive.

The more attractive the industries (both individually and as a group) a diversified company is in, the better its prospects for good long-term performance.

Calculating Industry Attractiveness Scores for Each Industry into Which the Company Has Diversified   A simple and reliable analytical tool involves calculating quantitative industry attractiveness scores, which can then be used to gauge each industry's attractiveness, rank the industries from most to least attractive, and make judgments about the attractiveness of all the industries as a group. A sample calculation is shown in Table 6.1. The following measures of industry attractiveness are likely to come into play for most companies:

- *Market size and projected growth rate*—Big industries are more attractive than small industries, and fast-growing industries tend to be more attractive than slow-growing industries, other things being equal.

- *The intensity of competition*—Industries where competitive pressures are relatively weak are more attractive than industries where competitive pressures are strong.

- *Emerging opportunities and threats*—Industries with promising opportunities and minimal threats on the near horizon are more attractive than industries with modest opportunities and imposing threats.

- *The presence of cross-industry strategic fits*—The more the industry's value chain and resource requirements match up well with the value chain activities of other industries in which the company has operations, the more attractive the industry is to a firm pursuing related diversification. However, cross-industry strategic fits may be of no consequence to a company committed to a strategy of unrelated diversification.

Table 6.1   CALCULATING WEIGHTED INDUSTRY ATTRACTIVENESS SCORES

Industry Attractiveness Measure	Importance Weight	Industry A Rating/ Score	Industry B Rating/ Score	Industry C Rating/ Score	Industry D Rating/ Score
Market size and projected growth rate	0.10	8/0.80	5/0.50	7/0.70	3/0.30
Intensity of competition	0.25	8/2.00	7/1.75	3/0.75	2/0.50
Emerging opportunities and threats	0.10	2/0.20	9/0.90	4/0.40	5/0.50
Cross-industry strategic fits	0.20	8/1.60	4/0.80	8/1.60	2/0.40
Resource requirements	0.10	9/0.90	7/0.70	10/1.00	5/0.50
Seasonal and cyclical influences	0.05	9/0.45	8/0.40	10/0.50	5/0.25
Societal, political, regulatory, and environmental factors	0.05	10/1.00	7/0.70	7/0.70	3/0.30
Industry profitability	0.10	5/0.50	10/1.00	3/0.30	3/0.30
Industry uncertainty and business risk	0.05	5/0.25	7/0.35	10/0.50	1/0.05
Sum of the assigned weights	1.00				
Overall industry attractiveness scores		7.70	7.10	5.45	3.10

Rating scale: 1 = Very unattractive to company; 10 = Very attractive to company

- *Resource requirements*—Industries having resource requirements within the company's reach are more attractive than industries where capital and other resource requirements could strain corporate financial resources and organizational capabilities.

- *Seasonal and cyclical factors*—Industries where buyer demand is relatively steady year-round and not unduly vulnerable to economic ups and downs tend to be more attractive than industries where there are wide swings in buyer demand within or across years. However, seasonality may be a plus for a company that is in several seasonal industries, if the seasonal highs in one industry correspond to the lows in another industry, thus helping even out monthly sales levels. Likewise, cyclical market demand in one industry can be attractive if its up-cycle runs counter to the market down-cycles in another industry where the company operates, thus helping reduce revenue and earnings volatility.

- *Social, political, regulatory, and environmental factors*—Industries with significant problems in such areas as consumer health, safety, or environmental pollution or that are subject to intense regulation are less attractive than industries where such problems are not burning issues.

- *Industry profitability*—Industries with healthy profit margins and high rates of return on investment are generally more attractive than industries where profits have historically been low or unstable.

- *Industry uncertainty and business risk*—Industries with less uncertainty on the horizon and lower overall business risk are more attractive than industries whose prospects for one reason or another are quite uncertain, especially when the industry has formidable resource requirements.

After settling on a set of attractiveness measures that suit a diversified company's circumstances, each attractiveness measure is assigned a weight reflecting its relative importance in determining an industry's attractiveness—it is weak methodology to assume that the various attractiveness measures are equally important. The intensity of competition in an industry should nearly always carry a high weight (say, 0.20 to 0.30). Strategic-fit considerations should be assigned a high weight in the case of companies with related diversification strategies; but, for companies with an unrelated diversification strategy, strategic fits with other industries may be given a low weight or even dropped from the list of attractiveness measures altogether. Seasonal and cyclical factors generally are assigned a low weight (or maybe even eliminated from the analysis) unless a company has diversified into industries strongly characterized by seasonal demand and/or heavy vulnerability to cyclical upswings and downswings. The importance weights must add up to 1.0. Next, each industry is rated on each of the chosen industry attractiveness measures, using a rating scale of 1 to 10 (where a *high* rating signifies *high* attractiveness and a *low* rating signifies *low* attractiveness). Keep in mind here that the more intensely competitive an industry is, the *lower* the attractiveness rating for that industry. Likewise, the higher the capital and resource requirements associated with being in a particular industry, the lower the attractiveness rating. And an industry subject to stringent pollution control regulations or that causes societal problems (like cigarettes or alcoholic beverages) should be given a low attractiveness rating. Weighted attractiveness scores are then calculated by multiplying the industry's rating on each measure by the corresponding weight. For example, a rating of 8 times a weight of 0.25 gives a weighted attractiveness score of 2.00. The sum of the weighted scores for all the attractiveness measures provides an overall industry attractiveness score.

There are two hurdles to using this method of evaluating industry attractiveness. One is deciding on appropriate weights for the industry attractiveness measures. Not only may different analysts have different views about which weights are appropriate for the different attractiveness measures but also different weightings may be appropriate for different companies—based on their strategies, performance targets, and financial circumstances. For instance, placing a low weight on industry resource requirements may be justifiable for a cash-rich company, whereas a high weight may be more appropriate for a financially strapped company. The second hurdle is getting reliable data for use in assigning accurate and objective ratings. Without good information, the ratings necessarily become subjective, and their validity hinges on whether management has probed industry conditions sufficiently to make reliable judgments. Generally, a company can come up with the statistical data needed to compare its industries on such factors as market size, growth rate, seasonal and cyclical influences, and industry profitability. Cross-industry fits and resource requirements are also fairly easy to judge. But the attractiveness measure where judgment weighs most heavily is that of intensity of competition. It is not always easy to conclude whether competition in one industry is stronger or weaker than in another industry because of the different types of competitive influences that prevail and the differences in their relative importance. In the event that the available information is too skimpy to confidently assign a rating value to an industry on a particular attractiveness measure, then it is usually best to use a score of 5, which avoids biasing the overall attractiveness score either up or down.

Nonetheless, industry attractiveness scores are a reasonably reliable method for ranking a diversified company's industries from most to least attractive—quantitative ratings like those shown for the four industries in Table 6.1 tell a valuable story about just how and why some of the industries a company has diversified into are more attractive than others.

Interpreting the Industry Attractiveness Scores   Industries with a score much below 5.0 probably do not pass the attractiveness test. If a company's industry attractiveness scores are all above 5.0, it is probably fair to conclude that the group of industries the company operates in is attractive as a whole. But the group of industries takes on a decidedly lower degree of attractiveness as the number of industries with scores below 5.0 increases, especially if industries with low scores account for a sizable fraction of the company's revenues.

For a diversified company to be a strong performer, a substantial portion of its revenues and profits must come from business units with relatively high attractiveness scores. It is particularly important that a diversified company's principal businesses be in industries with a good outlook for growth and above-average profitability. Having a big fraction of the company's revenues and profits come from industries with slow growth, low profitability, or intense competition tends to drag overall company performance down. Business units in the least attractive industries are potential candidates for divestiture, unless they are positioned strongly enough to overcome the unattractive aspects of their industry environments or they are a strategically important component of the company's business makeup.

Step 2: Evaluating Business-Unit Competitive Strength

The second step in evaluating a diversified company is to appraise how strongly positioned each of its business units are in their respective industry. Doing an appraisal of each business unit's strength and competitive position in its industry not only reveals its chances for industry success but also provides a basis for ranking the units from competitively strongest to competitively weakest and sizing up the competitive strength of all the business units as a group.

Calculating Competitive Strength Scores for Each Business Unit   Quantitative measures of each business unit's competitive strength can be calculated using a procedure similar to that for measuring industry attractiveness (see Table 6.2). There are a host of measures that can be used in assessing the competitive strength of a diversified company's business subsidiaries:

- *Relative market share*—A business unit's **relative market share** is defined as the ratio of its market share to the market share held by the largest rival firm in the industry, with market share measured in unit volume, not dollars. For instance, if business A has a market-leading share of 40 percent and its largest rival has 30 percent, A's relative market share is 1.33. (Note that only business units that are market share leaders in their respective industries can have relative market shares greater then 1.0.) If business B has a 15 percent market share and B's largest rival has 30 percent, B's relative market share is 0.5. The further below 1.0 a business unit's relative market share is, the weaker its competitive strength and market position vis-à-vis rivals. *Using relative market share is analytically superior to using straight-percentage market share to measure competitive strength.* A 10 percent market share, for example, does not signal much competitive strength if the leader's share is 50 percent (a 0.20 relative market share), but a 10 percent share is actually quite strong if the leader's share is 12 percent (a 0.83 relative market share).

- *Costs relative to competitors' costs*—Business units that have low costs relative to key competitors' costs tend to be more strongly positioned in their industries than

Table 6.2   CALCULATING WEIGHTED COMPETITIVE STRENGTH SCORES FOR THE BUSINESS UNITS

Competitive Strength Measure	Importance Weight	Business A in Industry A Rating/ Score	Business B in Industry B Rating/ Score	Business C in Industry C Rating/ Score	Business D in Industry D Rating/ Score
Relative market share	0.15	10/1.50	1/0.15	6/0.90	2/0.30
Costs relative to competitors' costs	0.20	7/1.40	2/0.40	5/1.00	3/0.60
Ability to match or beat rivals on key product attributes	0.05	9/0.45	4/0.20	8/0.40	4/0.20
Ability to benefit from strategic fits with sister businesses	0.20	8/1.60	4/0.80	8/0.80	2/0.60
Bargaining leverage with suppliers/ buyers; caliber of alliances	0.05	9/0.90	3/0.30	6/0.30	2/0.10
Brand image and reputation	0.10	9/0.90	2/0.20	7/0.70	5/0.50
Competitively valuable capabilities	0.15	7/1.05	2/0.20	5/0.75	3/0.45
Profitability relative to competitors	0.10	5/0.50	1/0.10	4/0.40	4/0.40
Sum of the assigned weights	1.00				
Overall industry attractiveness scores		8.30	2.35	5.25	3.15

Rating scale: 1 = Very weak; 10 = Very strong

business units struggling to maintain cost parity with major rivals. Assuming that the prices charged by industry rivals are about the same, there's reason to expect that business units with higher relative market shares have lower unit costs than competitors with lower relative market shares because their greater unit sales volumes offer the possibility of economies from larger-scale operations and the benefits of any experience or learning-curve effects. On the other hand, a business unit with higher costs than its key rivals is likely to be competitively vulnerable unless its product is strongly differentiated from rivals and its customers are willing to pay premium prices for the differentiating features. Another indicator of low cost can be a business unit's supply chain management capabilities.

- *Ability to match or beat rivals on key product attributes*—A company's competitiveness depends in part on being able to satisfy buyer expectations with regard to features, product performance, reliability, service, and other important attributes.

- *Ability to benefit from strategic fits with sister businesses*—Strategic fits with other businesses within the company enhance a business unit's competitive strength and may provide a competitive edge.

- *Ability to exercise bargaining leverage with key suppliers or customers*—Having bargaining leverage signals competitive strength and can be a source of competitive advantage.

- *Caliber of alliances and collaborative partnerships with suppliers and/or buyers*—Well-functioning alliances and partnerships may signal a potential competitive advantage vis-à-vis rivals and thus add to a business's competitive strength. Alliances with key suppliers are often the basis for competitive strength in supply chain management.

- *Brand image and reputation*—A strong brand name is a valuable competitive asset in most industries.

- *Competitively valuable capabilities*—Business units recognized for their technological leadership, product innovation, or marketing prowess are usually strong competitors in their industry. Skills in supply chain management can generate valuable cost or product differentiation advantages. So can unique production capabilities. Sometimes a company's business units gain competitive strength because of their knowledge of customers and markets and/or their proven managerial capabilities. *An important thing to look for here is how well a business unit's competitive assets match industry key success factors.* The more a business unit's resource strengths and competitive capabilities match the industry's key success factors, the stronger its competitive position tends to be.

- *Profitability relative to competitors*—Business units that consistently earn above-average returns on investment and have bigger profit margins than their rivals usually have stronger competitive positions than business units with below-average profitability for their industry. Moreover, above-average profitability signals competitive advantage, while below-average profitability usually denotes competitive disadvantage.

After settling on a set of competitive strength measures that are well matched to the circumstances of the various business units, weights indicating each measure's importance need to be assigned. A case can be made for using different weights for different business units whenever the importance of the strength measures differs significantly from business to business, but otherwise it is simpler just to go with a single set of weights and avoid the added complication of multiple weights. As before, the importance weights must add up to 1.0. Each business unit is then rated on each of the chosen strength measures, using a rating scale of 1 to 10 (where a *high* rating signifies competitive *strength* and a *low* rating signifies competitive *weakness*). In the event that the available information is too skimpy to confidently assign a rating value to a business unit on a particular strength measure, then it is usually best to use a score of 5, which avoids biasing the overall score either up or down. Weighted strength ratings are calculated by multiplying the business unit's rating on each strength measure by the assigned weight. For example, a strength score of 6 times a weight of 0.15 gives a weighted strength rating of 0.90. The sum of weighted ratings across all the strength measures provides a quantitative measure of a business unit's overall market strength and competitive standing.

Interpreting the Competitive Strength Scores   Business units with competitive strength ratings above 6.7 (on a scale of 1 to 10) are strong market contenders in their industries. Businesses with ratings in the 3.3 to 6.7 range have moderate competitive strength vis-à-vis rivals. Businesses with ratings below 3.3 are in competitively weak market positions. If a diversified company's business units all have competitive strength scores above 5.0, it is fair to conclude that its business units are all fairly strong market contenders in their respective industries. But as the number of business units with scores below 5.0 increases, there's reason to question whether the company can perform well with so many businesses in relatively weak competitive positions. This concern takes on even more importance when business units with low scores account for a sizable fraction of the company's revenues.

Using a Nine-Cell Matrix to Simultaneously Portray Industry Attractiveness and Competitive Strength   The industry attractiveness and business strength scores can be used to portray the strategic positions of each business in a diversified company. Industry attractiveness is plotted on the vertical axis, and competitive strength on the horizontal axis. A nine-cell grid emerges from dividing the vertical axis into three regions (high, medium, and low attractiveness) and the horizontal axis into three regions (strong, average, and weak competitive strength). As shown in Figure 6.5, high attractiveness is associated with scores of 6.7 or greater on a rating scale of 1 to 10, medium attractiveness to scores of 3.3 to 6.7, and low attractiveness to scores below 3.3. Likewise, high competitive strength is defined as a score greater than 6.7, average strength as scores of 3.3 to 6.7, and low strength as scores below 3.3. *Each business unit is plotted on the nine-cell matrix according to its overall attractiveness score and strength score, and then shown as a "bubble."* The size of each bubble is scaled to what percentage of revenues the business generates relative to total corporate revenues. The bubbles in Figure 6.5 were located on the grid using the attractiveness scores from Table 6.1 and the strength scores for the four business units in Table 6.2.

The locations of the business units on the attractiveness–strength matrix provide valuable guidance in deploying corporate resources to the various business units. In general, *a diversified company's prospects for good overall performance are enhanced by concentrating corporate resources and strategic attention on those business units having the greatest competitive strength and positioned in highly attractive industries*— specifically, businesses in the three cells in the upper left portion of the attractiveness-strength matrix, where industry attractiveness and competitive strength/market position are both favorable. The general strategic prescription for businesses falling in these three cells (for instance, business A in Figure 6.5) is "grow and build," with businesses in the high–strong cell standing first in line for resource allocations by the corporate parent.

> **Core Concept**
>
> In a diversified company, businesses having the greatest competitive strength and positioned in attractive industries should generally have top priority in allocating corporate resources.

Next in priority come businesses positioned in the three diagonal cells stretching from the lower left to the upper right (businesses B and C in Figure 6.5). Such businesses usually merit medium or intermediate priority in the parent's resource allocation ranking. However, some businesses in the medium-priority diagonal cells may have brighter or dimmer prospects than others. For example, a small business in the upper right cell of the matrix (like business B), despite being in a highly attractive industry, may occupy too weak a competitive position in its industry to justify the investment and resources needed to turn it into a strong market contender and shift its position leftward in the matrix over time. If, however, a business in the upper right cell has attractive opportunities for rapid growth and a good potential for winning a much stronger market position over time, it may merit a high claim on the corporate parent's resource allocation ranking and be given the capital it needs to pursue a grow-and-build strategy—the strategic objective here would be to move the business leftward in the attractiveness–strength matrix over time.

Businesses in the three cells in the lower right corner of the matrix typically are weak performers and have the lowest claim on corporate resources. Most such

Figure 6.5   A Nine-Cell Industry Attractiveness–Competitive Strength Matrix

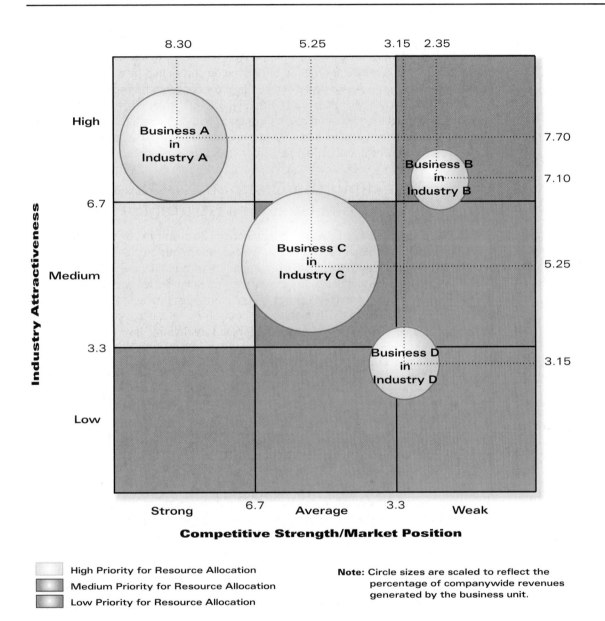

businesses are good candidates for being divested (sold to other companies) or else managed in a manner calculated to squeeze out the maximum cash flows from operations—the cash flows from low-performing/low-potential businesses can then be diverted to financing expansion of business units with greater market opportunities. In exceptional cases where a business located in the three lower-right cells is nonetheless fairly profitable (which it might be if it is in the low–average cell) or has the potential for good earnings and return on investment, the business merits retention and the allocation of sufficient resources to achieve better performance.

The contribution of the nine-cell attractiveness–strength matrix is the clarity and strong logic it provides for why a diversified company needs to consider both industry attractiveness and business strength in allocating resources and investment capital to its different businesses. A good case can be made for concentrating resources in those businesses that enjoy higher degrees of attractiveness and competitive strength, being very selective in making investments in businesses with intermediate positions on the grid, and withdrawing resources from businesses that are lower in attractiveness and strength unless they offer exceptional profit or cash flow potential.

Step 3: Checking the Competitive Advantage Potential of Cross-Business Strategic Fits

A company's related diversification strategy derives its power in large part from competitively valuable strategic fits among its businesses. While step 3 in the evaluation process can be bypassed for diversified companies whose business are all unrelated (since, by design, no strategic fits are present), a high potential for converting strategic fits into competitive advantage is central to concluding just how good a company's related diversification strategy is. Checking the competitive advantage potential of cross-business strategic fits involves searching for and evaluating how much benefit a diversified company can gain from four types of value chain matchups:

1. *Opportunities to combine the performance of certain activities,* thereby reducing costs. Potential value chain matchups where economies of scope can be realized include purchasing (where combining materials purchases could lead to greater bargaining leverage with suppliers); manufacturing (where it may be possible to share manufacturing facilities); or distribution (where it may be possible to share warehousing, sales forces, distributors, dealers, online sales channels, and after-sale service activities).

2. *Opportunities to transfer skills, technology, or intellectual capital from one business to another*, thereby leveraging use of existing resources. Good candidates for transfer include speed in bringing new products to market, proven R&D skills in generating new products or improving existing technologies, organizational agility in responding to shifting market conditions and emerging opportunities, and state-of-the-art systems for doing business via the Internet.

3. *Opportunities to share use of a well-respected brand name*, thereby gaining credibility with brand-conscious buyers and perhaps commanding prominent display space with retailers.

4. *Opportunities for businesses to collaborate in creating valuable new competitive capabilities* (enhanced quality control capabilities, quicker first-to-market capabilities, greater product innovation capabilities).

Figure 6.6 illustrates the process of searching for competitively valuable cross-business strategic fits and value chain matchups. *But more than just strategic fit identification is needed. The real test is what competitive value can be generated from these fits.* To what extent can cost savings be realized? How much competitive value will come from cross-business transfer of skills, technology, or intellectual capital? Will

Figure 6.6   Identifying the Competitive Advantage Potential of Cross-Business Strategic Fits

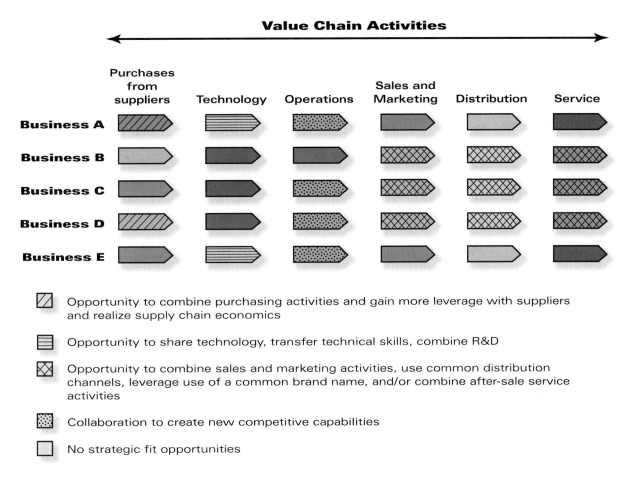

Opportunity to combine purchasing activities and gain more leverage with suppliers and realize supply chain economics

Opportunity to share technology, transfer technical skills, combine R&D

Opportunity to combine sales and marketing activities, use common distribution channels, leverage use of a common brand name, and/or combine after-sale service activities

Collaboration to create new competitive capabilities

No strategic fit opportunities

transferring a potent brand name to the products of sister businesses grow sales significantly? Will cross-business collaboration to create or strengthen competitive capabilities lead to significant gains in the marketplace or in financial performance? Absent significant strategic fits and dedicated company efforts to capture the benefits, one has to be skeptical about the potential for a diversified company's businesses to perform better together than apart.

> **Core Concept**
>
> The greater the value of cross-business strategic fits in enhancing a company's performance in the marketplace or on the bottom line, the more competitively powerful is its strategy of related diversification.

Step 4: Checking for Resource Fit

The businesses in a diversified company's lineup need to exhibit good *resource fit* as well as good strategic fit. Resource fit exists when (1) businesses add to a company's resource strengths, either financially or strategically, and (2) a company has the resources to adequately support its businesses as a group without spreading itself too thin. One important dimension of resource fit concerns whether a diversified company has the financial strength to satisfy the cash flow and investments of its different businesses.

Financial Resource Fits: Cash Cows versus Cash Hogs   Different businesses have different cash flow and investment characteristics. For example, business units in rapidly growing industries are often **cash hogs**—so labeled because the cash flows they are able to generate from internal operations aren't big enough to fund their expansion. To keep pace with rising buyer demand, rapid-growth businesses frequently need sizable annual capital investments—for new facilities and equipment, for new product development or technology improvements, and for additional working capital to support inventory expansion and a larger base of operations. A business in a fast-growing industry becomes an even bigger cash hog when it has a relatively low market share and is pursuing a strategy to become an industry leader. Because a cash hog's financial resources must be provided by the corporate parent, corporate managers have to decide whether its investment requirements are strategically and financially worthwhile.

> **Core Concept**
>
> A **cash hog** is a business whose internal cash flows are inadequate to fully fund its needs for working capital and new capital investment.

In contrast, business units with leading market positions in mature industries may, however, be **cash cows**—businesses that generate substantial cash surpluses over what is needed for capital reinvestment and competitive maneuvers to sustain their present market position. Market leaders in slow-growth industries often generate sizable positive cash flows *over and above what is needed for reinvestment in operations* because their industry-leading positions tend to give them the sales volumes and reputation to earn attractive profits and because the slow-growth nature of their industry often entails relatively modest annual investment requirements. Cash cows, though not always attractive from a growth standpoint, are valuable businesses from a financial resource perspective. The surplus cash flows they generate can be used to pay corporate dividends, finance acquisitions, and provide funds for investing in the company's promising cash hogs. It makes good financial and strategic sense for diversified companies to keep cash cows in healthy condition, fortifying and defending their market position so as to preserve their cash-generating capability over the long term and thereby have an ongoing source of financial resources to deploy elsewhere.

> **Core Concept**
>
> A **cash cow** is a business that generates cash flows over and above its internal requirements, thus providing a corporate parent with funds for investing in cash hog businesses, financing new acquisitions, or paying dividends.

Viewing a diversified group of businesses as a collection of cash flows and cash requirements (present and future) is a major step forward in understanding what the financial ramifications of diversification are and why having businesses with good financial resource fit is so important. For instance, a diversified company's businesses exhibit good financial resource fit when the excess cash generated by its cash cow businesses is sufficient to fund the investment requirements of promising cash hog businesses. Ideally, such investment over time results in growing the hogs to become self-supporting "stars" having strong or market-leading competitive positions in attractive, high-growth markets and high levels of profitability. *Star businesses* are often the cash cows of the future—when the markets of star businesses begin to mature and their growth slows, their competitive strength should produce self-generated cash flows more than sufficient to cover their investment needs. The "success sequence" is thus cash hog to young star (but perhaps still a cash hog) to self-supporting star to cash cow.

If, however, a cash hog has questionable promise (either because of low industry attractiveness or a weak competitive position), then it becomes a logical candidate for divestiture. Pursuing an aggressive invest-and-expand strategy for cash hog with an uncertain future seldom makes sense because it requires the corporate parent to keep pumping more capital into the business with only a dim hope of eventually turning the cash hog into a future star and realizing a good return on its investments. Such businesses are a financial drain and fail the resource fit test because they strain the corporate parent's ability to adequately fund its other businesses. Divesting a less attractive cash hog business is usually the best alternative unless (1) it has valuable strategic fits with other business units or (2) the capital infusions needed from the corporate parent are modest relative to the funds available and there's a decent chance of growing the business into a solid bottom-line contributor yielding a good return on invested capital.

Aside from cash flow considerations, a business has good financial fit when it contributes to the achievement of corporate performance objectives (growth in earnings per share, above-average return on investment, recognition as an industry leader, etc.) and when it materially enhances shareholder value via helping drive increases in the company's stock price. A business exhibits poor financial fit if it soaks up a disproportionate share of the company's financial resources, makes subpar or inconsistent bottom-line contributions, is unduly risky and failure would jeopardize the entire enterprise, or remains too small to make a material earnings contribution even though it performs well.

A diversified company's strategy also fails the resource fit test when its financial resources are stretched across so many businesses that its credit rating is impaired. Severe financial strain sometimes occurs when a company borrows so heavily to finance new acquisitions that it has to trim way back on capital expenditures for existing businesses and use the big majority of its financial resources to meet interest obligations and to pay down debt. Some diversified companies have found themselves so financially overextended that they have had to sell off certain businesses to raise the money to meet existing debt obligations and fund essential capital expenditures for the remaining businesses.

Competitive and Managerial Resource Fits   A diversified company's strategy must aim at producing a good fit between its resource capability and the competitive and managerial requirements of its businesses.[17] Diversification is more likely to enhance shareholder value when the company has or can develop strong competitive and managerial capabilities. Sometimes the resource strengths crucial to succeeding in one particular business are a poor match with the key success factors in other businesses. For instance, BTR, a multibusiness company in Great Britain, discovered that the company's resources and managerial skills were quite well suited for parenting industrial manufacturing businesses but

> A close match between industry key success factors and company resources and capabilities is a solid sign of good resource fit.

not for parenting its distribution businesses (National Tyre Services and Texas-based Summers Group); as a consequence, BTR decided to divest its distribution businesses and focus exclusively on diversifying around small industrial manufacturing.[18] One company with businesses in restaurants and retailing decided that its resource capabilities in site selection, controlling operating costs, management selection and training, and supply chain logistics would enable it to succeed in the hotel business and in property management; but what management missed was that these businesses had some significantly different key success factors—namely, skills in controlling property development costs, maintaining low overheads, product branding (hotels), and ability to recruit a sufficient volume of business to maintain high levels of facility utilization.[19] A mismatch between the company's resource strengths and the key success factors in a particular business can be serious enough to warrant divesting an existing business or not acquiring a new business. In contrast, when a company's resources and capabilities are a good match with the key success factors of industries it is not presently in, it makes sense to take a hard look at acquiring companies in these industries and expanding the company's business lineup.

A second instance in which a diversified company can fail the resource fit test is by not having sufficient *resource depth* to support all of its businesses. A diversified company has to guard against stretching its resource base too thin and trying to do too many things. The broader the diversification, the greater the concern about whether the company has sufficient managerial depth to cope with the diverse range of operating problems its wide business lineup presents (plus those it may be contemplating getting into). The more a company's diversification strategy is tied to leveraging its resources and capabilities in new businesses, the more it has to develop a big enough and deep enough resource pool to supply these businesses with sufficient capability to create competitive advantage.[20] Otherwise its strengths end up being stretched too thin across too many businesses and the opportunity for competitive advantage is lost.

A Note of Caution   Just because a company has hit a home run in one business doesn't mean it can easily enter a new business with similar resource requirements and hit a second home run.[21] Noted British retailer Marks & Spencer, despite possessing a range of impressive resource capabilities (ability to choose excellent store locations, having a supply chain that gives it both low costs and high merchandise quality, loyal employees, an excellent reputation with consumers, and strong management expertise) that have made it one of Britain's premier retailers for 100 years, has failed repeatedly in its efforts to diversify into department store retailing in the United States. Even though Philip Morris (now named Altria) had built powerful consumer marketing capabilities in its cigarette and beer businesses, it floundered in soft drinks and ended up divesting its acquisition of 7UP after several frustrating years of competing against strongly entrenched and resource-capable rivals like Coca-Cola and PepsiCo.

Step 5: Ranking the Business Units on the Basis of Performance and Priority for Resource Allocation

Once a diversified company's strategy has been evaluated from the perspective of industry attractiveness, competitive strength, strategic fit, and resource fit, the next step is to rank the performance prospects of the businesses from best to worst and determine which businesses merit top priority for new investments by the corporate parent.

The most important considerations in judging business-unit performance are sales growth, profit growth, contribution to company earnings, and return on capital invested in the business. (As we noted in Chapter 1, more and more companies are evaluating business performance on the basis of economic value added—the return on invested capital over and above the firm's cost of capital.) Sometimes, cash flow is a big consideration. Information on each business's past performance can be gleaned from a company's financial records. While past performance is not necessarily a good predictor of future performance, it does signal whether a business is in a strong position or a weak one.

The industry attractiveness/business strength evaluations provide a basis for judging a business's prospects. Normally, strong business units in attractive industries have significantly better prospects than weak businesses in unattractive industries. And, normally, the revenue and earnings outlook for businesses in fast-growing industries is better than for businesses in slow-growing industries—one important exception is when a business has the competitive strength to draw sales and market share away from its rivals and thus achieve much faster growth than the industry as whole. As a

Figure 6.7   The Chief Strategic and Financial Options for Allocating a Diversified Company's Financial Resources

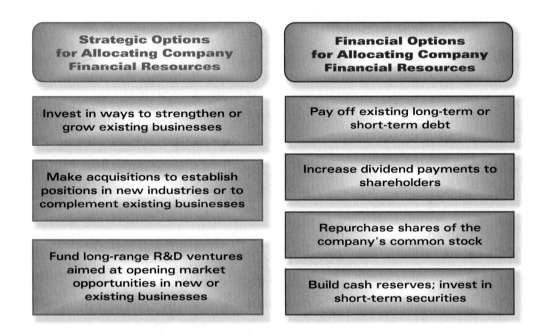

rule, the prior analyses, taken together, signal which business units are likely to be strong performers on the road ahead and which are likely to be laggards. And it is a short step from ranking the prospects of business units to drawing conclusions about whether the company as a whole is capable of strong, mediocre, or weak performance in upcoming years.

The rankings of future performance generally determine what priority the corporate parent should give to each business in terms of resource allocation. The task here is to decide which business units should have top priority for corporate resource support and new capital investment and which should carry the lowest priority. *Business subsidiaries with the brightest profit and growth prospects and solid strategic and resource fits generally should head the list for corporate resource support.* However, corporate executives need to give special attention to whether and how corporate resources and capabilities can be used to enhance the competitiveness of particular business units. Opportunities for resource transfer, activity combining, or infusions of new financial capital become especially important when improvement in some key success area could make a big difference to a particular business unit's performance.

For a company's diversification strategy to generate ever-higher levels of performance, corporate managers have to do an effective job of steering resources out of low-opportunity areas into high-opportunity areas. Divesting marginal businesses is one of the best ways of freeing unproductive assets for redeployment. Surplus funds from cash cows also add to the corporate treasury. Figure 6.7 shows the chief strategic and financial options for allocating a diversified company's financial resources. Ideally, a company will have enough funds to do what is needed, both strategically and financially. If not, strategic uses of corporate resources should usually take precedence unless there is a compelling reason to strengthen the firm's balance sheet or divert financial resources to pacify shareholders.

Step 6: Crafting New Strategic Moves to Improve Overall Corporate Performance

The diagnosis and conclusions flowing from the five preceding analytical steps set the agenda for crafting strategic moves to improve a diversified company's overall performance. The strategic options boil down to five broad categories of actions:

1. Sticking closely with the existing business lineup and pursuing the opportunities it presents.
2. Broadening the company's business scope by making new acquisitions in new industries.
3. Divesting certain businesses and retrenching to a narrower base of business operations.
4. Restructuring the company's business lineup and putting a whole new face on the company's business makeup.
5. Pursuing multinational diversification and striving to globalize the operations of several of the company's business units.

The option of sticking with the current business lineup makes sense when the company's present businesses offer attractive growth opportunities and can be counted on to generate dependable earnings and cash flows. As long as the company's set of existing businesses puts it in good position for the future and these businesses have good strategic and/or resource fits, then rocking the boat with major changes in the company's business mix is usually unnecessary. Corporate executives can concentrate their attention on getting the best performance from each of its businesses, steering corporate resources into those areas of greatest potential and profitability. The specifics of "what to do" to wring better performance from the present business lineup have to be dictated by each business's circumstances and the preceding analysis of the corporate parent's diversification strategy.

However, in the event that corporate executives are not entirely satisfied with the opportunities they see in the company's present set of businesses and conclude that changes in the company's direction and business makeup are in order, they can opt for any of the four other strategic alternatives listed above. These options are discussed in the following section.

After a Company Diversifies: The Four Main Strategy Alternatives

Diversifying is by no means the final chapter in the evolution of a company's strategy. Once a company has diversified into a collection of related or unrelated businesses and concludes that some overhaul is needed in the company's present lineup and diversification strategy, there are four main strategic paths it can pursue (see Figure 6.8). To more fully understand the strategic issues corporate managers face in the ongoing process of managing a diversified group of businesses, we need to take a brief look at the central thrust of each of the four post-diversification strategy alternatives.

Figure 6.8   A Company's Four Main Strategic Alternatives after It Diversifies

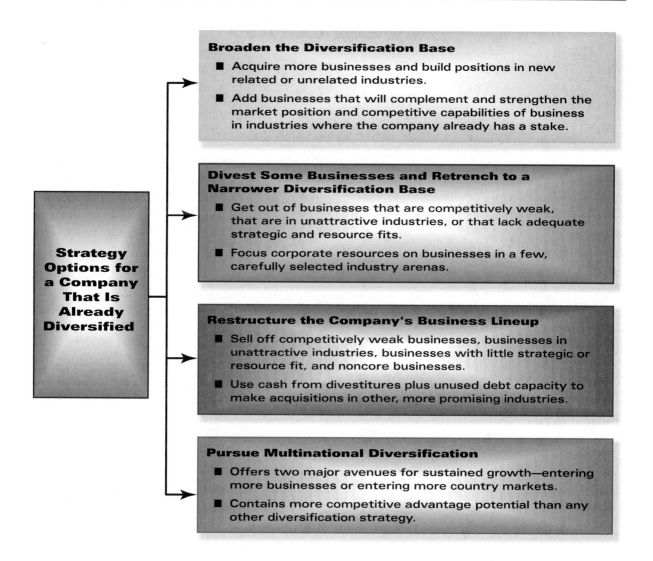

Strategy Options for a Company That Is Already Diversified

Broaden the Diversification Base
- Acquire more businesses and build positions in new related or unrelated industries.
- Add businesses that will complement and strengthen the market position and competitive capabilities of business in industries where the company already has a stake.

Divest Some Businesses and Retrench to a Narrower Diversification Base
- Get out of businesses that are competitively weak, that are in unattractive industries, or that lack adequate strategic and resource fits.
- Focus corporate resources on businesses in a few, carefully selected industry arenas.

Restructure the Company's Business Lineup
- Sell off competitively weak businesses, businesses in unattractive industries, businesses with little strategic or resource fit, and noncore businesses.
- Use cash from divestitures plus unused debt capacity to make acquisitions in other, more promising industries.

Pursue Multinational Diversification
- Offers two major avenues for sustained growth—entering more businesses or entering more country markets.
- Contains more competitive advantage potential than any other diversification strategy.

Strategies to Broaden a Diversified Company's Business Base

Diversified companies sometimes find it desirable to build positions in new industries, whether related or unrelated. There are several motivating factors. One is sluggish growth that makes the potential revenue and profit boost of a newly acquired business look attractive. A second is vulnerability to seasonal or recessionary influences or to threats from emerging new technologies. A third is the potential for transferring resources and capabilities to other related or complementary businesses. A fourth is rapidly changing conditions in one or more of a company's core businesses brought on by technological, legislative, or new product innovations that alter buyer requirements and preferences. For instance, the passage of legislation in the United States allowing banks, insurance companies, and stock brokerages to enter each other's businesses spurred a raft of acquisitions and mergers to create full-service financial enterprises capable of meeting the multiple financial needs of customers. Citigroup, already the largest U.S. bank with a global banking franchise, acquired Salomon Smith Barney to position itself in the investment banking and brokerage business and acquired insurance giant Travelers Group to enable it to offer customers insurance products.

A fifth, and often very important, motivating factor for adding new businesses is to complement and strengthen the market position and competitive capabilities of one or more of its present businesses. Viacom's acquisition of CBS strengthened and extended Viacom's reach into various media businesses—it was the parent of Paramount Pictures, an assortment of cable TV networks (UPN, MTV, Nickelodeon, VH1, Showtime, The Movie Channel, Comedy Central), Blockbuster video stores, two movie theater chains, and 19 local TV stations. Unilever, a leading maker of food and personal care products, expanded its business lineup by acquiring SlimFast, Ben & Jerry's Homemade Ice Cream, and Best Foods (whose brands included Knorr's soups, Hellman's mayonnaise, Skippy peanut butter, and Mazola cooking oils). Unilever saw these businesses as giving it more clout in competing against such other diversified food and household products companies as Nestlé, Kraft, Procter & Gamble, and Danone.

Usually, expansion into new businesses is undertaken by acquiring companies already in the target industry. Some companies depend on new acquisitions to drive a major portion of their growth in revenues and earnings, and thus are always on the acquisition trail. Cisco Systems built itself into a worldwide leader in networking systems for the Internet by making 75 technology-based acquisitions during 1993–2002 to extend its market reach from routing and switching into voice and video over Internet protocol, optical networking, wireless, storage networking, security, broadband, and content networking. Tyco International, recently beset with charges of looting on the part of several top executives, transformed itself from an obscure company in the early 1990s into a $36 billion global manufacturing enterprise with operations in over 100 countries as of 2002 by making over 1,000 acquisitions; the company's far-flung diversification includes businesses in electronics, electrical components, fire and security systems, health care products, valves, undersea telecommunications systems, plastics, and adhesives. Tyco made over 700 acquisitions of small companies in the 1999–2001 period alone.

Divestiture Strategies Aimed at Retrenching to a Narrower Diversification Base

A number of diversified firms have had difficulty managing a diverse group of businesses and have elected to get out of some of them. Retrenching to a narrower diversification base is usually undertaken when top management concludes that its diversification strategy has ranged too far afield and that the company can improve long-term performance by concentrating on building stronger positions in a smaller number of core businesses and industries. Hewlett-Packard spun off its testing and measurement businesses into a stand-alone company called Agilent Technologies so that it could better concentrate on its PC, workstation, server, printer and peripherals, and electronics businesses. PepsiCo divested its cash-hog

> Focusing corporate resources on a few core and mostly related businesses avoids the mistake of diversifying so broadly that resources and management attention are stretched too thin.

group of restaurant businesses, consisting of Kentucky Fried Chicken, Pizza Hut, Taco Bell, and California Pizza Kitchens, to provide more resources for strengthening its soft-drink business (which was losing market share to Coca-Cola) and growing its more profitable Frito-Lay snack foods business. Kmart divested OfficeMax, Sports Authority, and Borders Bookstores in order to refocus management attention and all of the company's resources on restoring luster to its distressed discount retailing business, which was (and still is) being totally outclassed in the marketplace by Wal-Mart and Target.

But there are other important reasons for divesting one or more of a company's present businesses. Sometimes divesting a business has to be considered because market conditions in a once-attractive industry have badly deteriorated. A business can become a prime candidate for divestiture because it lacks adequate strategic or resource fit, because it is a cash hog with questionable long-term potential, or because it is weakly positioned in its industry with little prospect the corporate parent can realize a decent return on its investment in the business. Sometimes a company acquires businesses that, down the road, just do not work out as expected even though management has tried all it can think of to make them profitable—mistakes cannot be completely avoided because it is hard to foresee how getting into a new line of business will actually work out. Subpar performance by some business units is bound to occur, thereby raising questions of whether to divest them or keep them and attempt a turnaround. Other business units, despite adequate financial performance, may not mesh as well with the rest of the firm as was originally thought.

On occasion, a diversification move that seems sensible from a strategic-fit standpoint turns out to be a poor *cultural fit.*[22] Several pharmaceutical companies had just this experience. When they diversified into cosmetics and perfume, they discovered their personnel had little respect for the "frivolous" nature of such products compared to the far nobler task of developing miracle drugs to cure the ill. The absence of shared values and cultural compatibility between the medical research and chemical-compounding expertise of the pharmaceutical companies and the fashion/marketing orientation of the cosmetics business was the undoing of what otherwise was diversification into businesses with technology-sharing potential, product-development fit, and some overlap in distribution channels.

Recent research indicates that pruning businesses and narrowing a firm's diversification base improves corporate performance.[23] Corporate parents often end up selling off businesses too late and at too low a price, sacrificing shareholder value.[24] A useful guide to determine whether or when to divest a business subsidiary is to ask, "If we were not in this business today, would we want to get into it now?"[25] When the answer is no or probably not, divestiture should be considered. Another signal that a business should become a divestiture candidate is whether it is worth more to another company than to the present parent; in such cases, shareholders would be well served if the company sells the business and collects a premium price from the buyer for whom the business is a valuable fit.[26]

The Two Options for Divesting a Business: Selling It or Spinning It Off as an Independent Company Selling a business outright to another company is far and away the most frequently used option for divesting a business. But sometimes a business selected for divestiture has ample resource strengths to compete successfully on its own. In such cases, a corporate parent may elect to spin the unwanted business off as a financially and managerially independent company, either by selling shares to the investing public via an initial public offering or by distributing shares in the new company to existing shareholders of the corporate parent. When a corporate parent decides to spin off one of its businesses as a separate company, there's the issue of whether or not to retain partial ownership. Retaining partial ownership makes sense when the business to be divested has a hot product or technological capabilities that give it good profit prospects. When 3Com elected to divest its PalmPilot business, which investors then saw as having very promising profit potential, it elected to retain a substantial ownership interest so as to provide 3Com shareholders a way of participating in whatever future market success that PalmPilot (now Palm, Inc.) might have on its own.

Selling a business outright requires finding a buyer. This can prove hard or easy, depending on the business. As a rule, a company selling a troubled business should not ask, "How can we pawn this business off on someone, and what is the most we can get for it?"[27] Instead, it is wiser to ask, "For what sort of company would this business be a good fit, and under what conditions would it be viewed as a good deal?" Enterprises for which the business is a good fit are likely to pay the highest price. Of course, if a buyer willing to pay an acceptable price cannot be found, then a company must decide whether to keep the business until a buyer appears; spin it off as a separate company; or, in the case of a crisis-ridden business that is losing substantial sums, simply close it down and liquidate the remaining assets. Liquidation is obviously a last resort.

Strategies to Restructure a Company's Business Lineup

Restructuring strategies involve divesting some businesses and acquiring others so as to put a whole new face on the company's business lineup. Performing radical surgery on the group of businesses a company is in becomes an appealing strategy alternative when a diversified company's financial performance is being squeezed or eroded by:

> **Core Concept**
>
> **Restructuring** involves divesting some businesses and acquiring others so as to put a whole new face on the company's business lineup.

- Too many businesses in slow-growth, declining, low-margin, or otherwise unattractive industries (a condition indicated by the number and size of businesses with industry attractiveness ratings below 5 and located on the bottom half of the attractiveness–strength matrix—see Figure 6.5).
- Too many competitively weak businesses (a condition indicated by the number and size of businesses with competitive strength ratings below 5 and located on the right half of the attractiveness–strength matrix).
- Ongoing declines in the market shares of one or more major business units that are falling prey to more market-savvy competitors.
- An excessive debt burden with interest costs that eat deeply into profitability.
- Ill-chosen acquisitions that haven't lived up to expectations.

Restructuring can also be mandated by the emergence of new technologies that threaten the survival of one or more of a diversified company's important businesses or by the appointment of a new CEO who decides to redirect the company. On occasion, restructuring can be prompted by special circumstances—like when a firm has a unique opportunity to make an acquisition so big and important that it has to sell several existing business units to finance the new acquisition or when a company needs to sell off some businesses in order to raise the cash for entering a potentially big industry with wave-of-the-future technologies or products.

Candidates for divestiture in a corporate restructuring effort typically include not only weak or up-and-down performers or those in unattractive industries but also business units that lack strategic fit with the businesses to be retained, businesses that are cash hogs or that lack other types of resource fit, and businesses incompatible with the company's revised diversification strategy (even though they may be profitable or in an attractive industry). As businesses are divested, corporate restructuring generally involves aligning the remaining business units into groups with the best strategic fits and then redeploying the cash flows from the divested business to either pay down debt or make new acquisitions to strengthen the parent company's business position in the industries it has chosen to emphasize.[28]

Over the past decade, corporate restructuring has become a popular strategy at many diversified companies, especially those that had diversified broadly into many different industries and lines of business. For instance, one struggling diversified company over a two-year period divested four business units, closed down the operations of four others, and added 25 new lines of business to its portfolio (16 through acquisition and 9 through internal start-up). During Jack Welch's first four years as CEO of General Electric (GE), the company divested 117 business units, accounting for about 20 percent of GE's assets; these divestitures, coupled with several important acquisitions, provided GE with 14 major business divisions and led to Welch's challenge to the managers of GE's divisions to become number one or number two in their industry. Ten years after Welch became CEO, GE was a different company, having divested operations worth $9 billion, made new acquisitions totaling $24 billion, and cut its workforce by 100,000 people. Then, during the 1990–2001 period, GE continued to reshuffle its business lineup, acquiring over 600 new companies, including 108 in 1998 and 64 during a 90-day period in 1999. Most of the new acquisitions were in Europe, Asia, and Latin America and were aimed at transforming GE into a truly global enterprise. PerkinElmer used a series of divestitures and new acquisitions to transform itself from a supplier of low-margin services sold to the government agencies into an innovative high-tech company with operations in over 125 countries and businesses in four industry groups—life sciences (drug research and clinical screening), optoelectronics, instruments, and fluid control and containment (for customers in aerospace, power generation, and semiconductors).

Several broadly diversified companies have pursued restructuring by splitting into two or more independent companies. In 1996, AT&T divided itself into three companies—one (that retained the AT&T name) for long-distance and other telecommunications services, one (called Lucent Technologies) for manufacturing telecommunications equipment, and one (called NCR) for computer systems that essentially represented the divestiture of AT&T's earlier acquisition of National Cash Register. A few years after the split-up, AT&T acquired TCI Communications and MediaOne, both leading cable TV providers, in an attempt to restructure itself into a new-age telecommunications company offering bundled local and long-distance service, cable TV, and high-speed Internet access. In 2000, after its bundled services concept flopped and its debt had become excessive, AT&T proposed splitting itself once again, this time into four businesses—AT&T Comcast (formed by the 2002 merger of Comcast and AT&T's cable TV operations), AT&T Consumer, AT&T Business, and AT&T Wireless. Before beginning a restructuring effort in 1995, British-based Hanson PLC owned companies with more than $20 billion in revenues in industries as diverse as beer, exercise equipment, tools, construction cranes, tobacco, cement, chemicals, coal mining, electricity, hot tubs and whirlpools, cookware, rock and gravel, bricks, and asphalt. By early 1997, Hanson had restructured itself into a $3.8 billion enterprise focused more narrowly on gravel, crushed rock, cement, asphalt, bricks, and construction cranes; the remaining businesses were divided into four groups and divested.

In a study of the performance of the 200 largest U.S. corporations from 1990 to 2000, McKinsey & Company found that those companies that actively managed their business portfolios through acquisitions and divestitures created substantially more shareholder value than those that kept a fixed lineup of businesses.[29]

Multinational Diversification Strategies

The distinguishing characteristics of a multinational diversification strategy are a *diversity of businesses* and a *diversity of national markets*.[30] Such diversity makes multinational diversification a particularly challenging and complex strategy to conceive and execute. Managers have to develop business strategies for each industry (with as many multinational variations as conditions in each country market dictate). Then, they have to pursue and manage opportunities for cross-business and cross-country collaboration and strategic coordination in ways calculated to result in competitive advantage and enhanced profitability.

Moreover, the geographic operating scope of individual businesses within a diversified multinational company (DMNC) can range from one country only to several countries to many countries to global. Thus, each business unit within a DMNC often competes in a somewhat different combination of geographic markets than the other businesses do—adding another element of strategic complexity, and perhaps an element of opportunity.

Global Spotlight 6.3 shows the scope of four prominent DMNCs.

The Appeal of Multinational Diversification: More Opportunities for Sustained Growth and Maximum Competitive Advantage Potential   Despite their complexity, multinational diversification strategies have great appeal. They contain *two major avenues* for growing revenues and profits: One is to grow by entering additional businesses, and the other is to grow by extending the operations of existing businesses into additional country markets. Moreover, a strategy of multinational diversification also contains six attractive paths to competitive advantage, *all of which can be pursued simultaneously*:

1. *Full capture of economies of scale and experience and learning-curve effects.* In some businesses, the volume of sales needed to realize full economies of scale and/or benefit fully from experience and learning-curve effects is rather sizable, often exceeding the volume that can be achieved operating within the boundaries of a single country market, especially a small one. *The ability to drive down unit costs by expanding sales to additional country markets is one reason why a diversified multinational may seek to acquire a business and then rapidly expand its operations into more and more foreign markets.*

2. *Opportunities to capitalize on cross-business economies of scope.* Diversifying into related businesses offering economies of scope can drive the development of a low-cost advantage over less diversified rivals. For example, a DMNC that uses mostly the same distributors and retail dealers worldwide can diversify into new businesses using these same worldwide distribution channels at relatively little incremental expense. The cost savings of piggybacking distribution activities can be substantial. Moreover, with more business selling more products in more countries, a DMNC acquires more bargaining leverage in its purchases from suppliers and more bargaining leverage with retailers in securing attractive display space for

GLOBAL SPOTLIGHT 6.3

The Global Scope of Four Prominent Diversified Multinational Corporations

Company	Global Scope	Businesses into Which the Company Has Diversified
Sony	Operations in more than 100 countries and sales offices in more than 200 countries	▪ Televisions, VCRs, DVD players, radios, CD players and home stereos, digital cameras and video equipment, PCs and Trinitron computer monitors ▪ PlayStation game consoles and video game software ▪ Columbia, Epic, and Sony Classical prerecorded music ▪ Columbia TriStar motion pictures, syndicated television programs ▪ Other businesses (insurance, financing, entertainment complexes, Internet-related businesses)
Nestlé	Operations in 70 countries and sales offices in more than 200 countries	▪ Beverages (Nescafé and Taster's Choice coffees, Nestea, Perrier, Arrowhead, & Calistoga mineral and bottled waters) ▪ Milk products (Carnation, Gloria, Neslac, Coffee Mate, Nestlé ice cream and yogurt) ▪ Pet foods (Friskies, Alpo, Fancy Feast, Mighty Dog) ▪ Contadina, Libby's, and Stouffer's food products and prepared dishes ▪ Chocolate and confectionery products (Nestlé Crunch, Smarties, Baby Ruth, Butterfinger, KitKat) ▪ Pharmaceuticals (Alcon ophthalmic products, Galderma dermatological products)
Siemens	Operations in 160 countries and sales offices in more than 190 countries	▪ Electrical power generation, transmission, and distribution equipment and products ▪ Manufacturing automation systems, industrial motors, industrial computers, industrial machinery, industrial tools, plant construction and maintenance ▪ Information and communications (solutions and services needed for corporate communication networks, telephones, PCs, mainframes, computer network products, consulting services) ▪ Mass transit and light rail systems, rail cars, locomotives ▪ Medical equipment, health care management services ▪ Semiconductors, memory components, microcontrollers, capacitors, resistors ▪ Lighting (bulbs, lamps, theater and television lighting systems) ▪ Home electronics, large home appliances, vacuum cleaners ▪ Financial services (commercial lending, pension administration, venture capital) ▪ Procurement and logistics services, business consulting services
Samsung	Operations in more than 60 countries and sales in more than 200 countries	▪ Electronics (computers, peripherals, displays, televisions, telecommunications equipment, semiconductors, memory chips, circuit boards, capacitors, information technology services, systems integration) ▪ Machinery and heavy industry (shipbuilding, oil and gas storage tank construction, marine engines, aircraft and aircraft parts, gas turbines, military hardware, industrial robots, factory automation systems) ▪ Automotive (passenger cars, commercial trucks) ▪ Chemicals (general chemicals, petrochemicals, fertilizers) ▪ Financial services (insurance, credit card services, securities trading, consumer credit services, trust management) ▪ Other affiliated companies (theme parks, hotels, medical centers, apparel, professional sports teams, film, music, and television production)

Source: Company annual reports and websites.

its products. Consider, for example, the competitive power that Sony derived from these very sorts of economies of scope when it decided to diversify into the video game business with its PlayStation product line. Sony had in-place capability to go after video game sales in all country markets where it presently did business in other product categories (TVs, computers, DVD players, VCRs, radios, CD players, and digital and video cameras). And it had the marketing clout and brand-name credibility to persuade retailers to give Sony's PlayStation products prime shelf space and visibility. These strategic-fit benefits helped Sony quickly overtake longtime industry leaders Nintendo and Sega and (so far, as of this writing) fortify its position against Microsoft's new Xbox offerings.

3. *Opportunities to transfer competitively valuable resources both from one business to another and from one country to another.* A company pursuing related diversification can gain a competitive edge over less diversified rivals by transferring competitively valuable resources from one business to another; a multinational company can gain competitive advantage over rivals with narrower geographic coverage by transferring competitively valuable resources from one country to another. But a strategy of multinational diversification enables simultaneous pursuit of both sources of competitive advantage.

4. *Ability to leverage use of a well-known and competitively powerful brand name.* Diversified multinational companies whose businesses have brand names that are well known and respected across the world possess a valuable strategic asset with competitive advantage potential. For example, Sony's well-established global brand-name recognition gives it an important marketing and advertising advantage over rivals with lesser-known brands. When Sony goes into a new marketplace with the stamp of the Sony brand on new businesses or product families, it can command prominent display space with retailers. It can expect to win sales and market share simply on the confidence that buyers place in products carrying the Sony name. While Sony may spend money to make consumers aware of the availability of its new products, it does not have to spend nearly as much on achieving brand recognition and market acceptance as would a lesser-known competitor looking at the marketing and advertising costs of entering the same new product/business/country markets and trying to go head-to-head against Sony. Further, if Sony moves into a new country market for the first time and does well selling Sony PlayStations and video games, it is easier to sell consumers in that country Sony TVs, digital cameras, PCs, and so on—plus, the related advertising costs are likely to be less than they would be without having already established the Sony brand strongly in the minds of buyers.

> **Core Concept**
>
> Transferring a powerful brand name from one product or business to another can usually be done very economically.

5. *Ability to capitalize on opportunities for cross-business and cross-country collaboration and strategic coordination.*[31] A multinational diversification strategy allows competitively valuable cross-business and cross-country coordination of certain value chain activities. For instance, by channeling corporate resources directly into a combined R&D/technology effort for all related businesses, as opposed to letting each business unit fund and direct its own R&D effort however it sees fit, a DMNC can merge its expertise and efforts *worldwide* to advance core technologies, expedite cross-business and cross-country product improvements, speed the development of new products that complement existing products, and pursue promising technological avenues to create altogether new businesses—all significant contributors to competitive advantage and better corporate performance.[32] Honda has been

very successful in building R&D expertise in gasoline engines and transferring the resulting technological advances to its businesses in automobiles, motorcycles, outboard engines, snow blowers, lawn mowers, garden tillers, and portable power generators. Further, a DMNC can reduce costs through cross-business and cross-country coordination of purchasing and procurement from suppliers, from collaborative introduction and shared use of e-commerce technologies and online sales efforts, and from coordinated product introductions and promotional campaigns. Firms that are less diversified and less global in scope have less such cross-business and cross-country collaborative opportunities.

6. *Opportunities to use cross-business or cross-country subsidization to outcompete rivals.* A financially successful DMNC has potentially valuable organizational resources and multiple profit sanctuaries in both certain country markets and certain business that it can draw on to wage a market offensive. In comparison, a one-business domestic company has only one profit sanctuary—its home market. A diversified one-country competitor may have profit sanctuaries in several businesses, but all are in the same country market. A one-business multinational company may have profit sanctuaries in several country markets, but all are in the same business. All three are vulnerable to an offensive in their more limited profit sanctuaries by an aggressive DMNC willing to lowball its prices and/or spend extravagantly on advertising to win market share at their expense. A DMNC's ability to keep hammering away at competitors with low prices year after year may reflect either a cost advantage growing out of its related diversification strategy or a willingness to accept low profits or even losses in the market being attacked because it has ample earnings from its other profit sanctuaries. For example, Sony's global-scale diversification strategy gives it unique competitive strengths in outcompeting Nintendo and Sega, neither of which are diversified. If need be, Sony can maintain low prices on its PlayStations or fund high-profile promotions for its latest video game products, using earnings from its other business lines to fund its offensive to wrest market share away from Nintendo and Sega in video games. At the same time, Sony can draw on its considerable resources in R&D, its ability to transfer electronics technology from one electronics product family to another, and its expertise in product innovation to introduce better and better video game players, perhaps players that are multifunctional and do more than just play video games. Such competitive actions not only enhance Sony's own brand image but also make it very tough for Nintendo and Sega to match Sony's prices, advertising, and product development efforts and still earn acceptable profits.

The Combined Effects of These Advantages Is Potent   A strategy of diversifying into *related* industries and then competing *globally* in each of these industries thus has great potential for being a winner in the marketplace because of the long-term growth opportunities it offers and the multiple corporate-level competitive advantage opportunities it contains. Indeed, *a strategy of multinational diversification contains more competitive advantage potential* (above and beyond what is achievable through a particular business's own competitive strategy) *than any other diversification strategy.* The strategic key to maximum competitive advantage is for a DMNC to concentrate its diversification efforts in those industries where there are resource-sharing and resource-transfer opportunities and where there are important economies of scope and brand name benefits. The more a company's diversification strategy yields these kinds

> **Core Concept**
>
> A strategy of multinational diversification has more built-in potential for competitive advantage than any other diversification strategy.

of strategic-fit benefits, the more powerful a competitor it becomes and the better its profit and growth performance is likely to be.

However, it is important to recognize that while a DMNC's cross-subsidization capabilities are a potent competitive weapon in theory, in actual practice cross-subsidization can only be used sparingly. It is one thing to *occasionally* divert a portion of the profits and cash flows from existing businesses to help fund entry into a new business or country market or wage a competitive offensive against select rivals. It is quite another thing to *regularly* use cross-subsidization tactics and thereby weaken overall company performance. A DMNC is under the same pressures as any other company to demonstrate consistently acceptable profitability across its whole operation. At some juncture, every business and every country market needs to make a profit contribution or become a candidate for abandonment. As a general rule, *cross-subsidization tactics are justified only when there is a good prospect that the short-term impairment to corporate profitability will be offset by stronger competitiveness and better overall profitability over the long term.*

> **Core Concept**
>
> Although cross-subsidization is a potent competitive weapon, it can only be used infrequently because of its adverse impact on overall corporate profitability.

Key Points

Most companies have their business roots in a single industry. Even though they may have since diversified into other industries, a substantial part of their revenues and profits still usually comes from the original or core business. Diversification becomes an attractive strategy when a company runs out of profitable growth opportunities in its original business. The purpose of diversification is to build shareholder value. Diversification builds shareholder value when a diversified group of businesses can perform better under the auspices of a single corporate parent than they would as independent, stand-alone businesses—the goal is to achieve not just a $1 + 1 = 2$ result but rather to realize important $1 + 1 = 3$ performance benefits. Whether getting into a new business has potential to enhance shareholder value hinges on whether a company's entry into that business can pass the attractiveness test, the cost-of-entry test, and the better-off test.

Entry into new businesses can take any of three forms: acquisition, internal start-up, or joint venture/strategic partnership. Each has its pros and cons, but acquisition is the most frequently used; internal start-up takes the longest to produce home-run results, and joint venture/strategic partnership, though used second most frequently, is the least durable.

There are two fundamental approaches to diversification—into related businesses and into unrelated businesses. The rationale for *related* diversification is *strategic:* Diversify into businesses with strategic fits along their respective value chains, capitalize on strategic-fit relationships to gain competitive advantage, and then use competitive advantage to achieve the desired $1 + 1 = 3$ impact on shareholder value. Businesses have strategic fit when their value chains offer potential (1) for realizing economies of scope or cost-saving efficiencies associated with sharing technology, facilities, functional activities, distribution outlets, or brand names; (2) for competitively valuable cross-business transfers of technology, skills, know-how, or other resource capabilities; (3) for leveraging use of a well-known and trusted brand name, and (4) for competitively valuable cross-business collaboration to build new or stronger resource strengths and competitive capabilities.

The basic premise of unrelated diversification is that any business that has good profit prospects and can be acquired on good financial terms is a good business to diversify into. Unrelated diversification strategies surrender the competitive advantage potential of strategic fit in return for such advantages as (1) spreading business risk over a variety of industries and (2) providing opportunities for financial gain (if candidate acquisitions have undervalued assets, are bargain-priced and have good upside potential given the right management, or need the backing of a financially strong parent to capitalize on attractive opportunities). In theory, unrelated diversification also offers greater earnings stability over the business cycle (a third advantage), but this advantage is very hard to realize in actual practice. The greater the number of businesses a conglomerate is in and the more diverse these businesses are, the harder it is for corporate executives to select capable managers to run each business, know when the major strategic proposals of business units are sound, or decide on a wise course of recovery when a business unit stumbles. Unless corporate managers are exceptionally shrewd and talented, unrelated diversification is a dubious and unreliable approach to building shareholder value when compared to related diversification.

Analyzing how good a company's diversification strategy is a six-step process:

Step 1: *Evaluate the long-term attractiveness of the industries into which the firm has diversified.* Industry attractiveness needs to be evaluated from three angles: the attractiveness of each industry on its own, the attractiveness of each industry relative to the others, and the attractiveness of all the industries as a group. Quantitative measures of industry attractiveness tell a valuable story about just how and why some of the industries a company has diversified into are more attractive than others. The two hardest parts of calculating industry attractiveness scores are deciding on appropriate weights for the industry attractiveness measures and knowing enough about each industry to assign accurate and objective ratings.

Step 2: *Evaluate the relative competitive strength of each of the company's business units.* Again, quantitative ratings of competitive strength are preferable to subjective judgments. The purpose of rating the competitive strength of each business is to gain clear understanding of which businesses are strong contenders in their industries, which are weak contenders, and the underlying reasons for their strength or weakness. The conclusions about industry attractiveness can be joined with the conclusions about competitive strength by drawing an industry attractiveness–competitive strength matrix displaying the positions of each business on a nine-cell grid. The attractiveness–strength matrix helps identify the prospects of each business and what priority each business should be given in allocating corporate resources and investment capital.

Step 3: *Check for cross-business strategic fits.* A business is more attractive strategically when it has value chain relationships with sister business units that present opportunities to transfer skills or technology, reduce overall costs, share facilities, or share a common brand name—any of which can represent a significant avenue for producing competitive advantage beyond what any one business can achieve on its own. The more businesses with competitively valuable strategic fits, the greater a diversified company's potential for achieving economies of scope, enhancing the competitive capabilities of particular business units, and/or strengthening the competitiveness of its product and business lineup, thereby realizing a combined performance greater than the units could achieve operating independently.

Step 4:   *Check whether the firm's resource strengths fit the resource requirements of its present business lineup.* Resource fit exists when (1) businesses add to a company's resource strengths, either financially or strategically; (2) a company has the resources to adequately support the resource requirements of its businesses as a group without spreading itself too thin; and (3) there are close matches between a company's resources and industry key success factors. One important test of resource fit concerns whether the company's business lineup is well matched to its financial resources. Assessing the cash requirements of different businesses in a diversified company's portfolio and determining which are cash hogs and which are cash cows highlights opportunities for shifting corporate financial resources between business subsidiaries to optimize the performance of the whole corporate portfolio, explains why priorities for corporate resource allocation can differ from business to business, and provides good rationalizations for both invest-and-expand strategies and divestiture.

Step 5:   *Rank the performance prospects of the businesses from best to worst and determine what the corporate parent's priority should be in allocating resources to its various businesses.* The most important considerations in judging business-unit performance are sales growth, profit growth, contribution to company earnings, and the return on capital invested in the business. Sometimes, cash flow generation is a big consideration. Normally, strong business units in attractive industries have significantly better performance prospects than weak businesses or businesses in unattractive industries. Information on each business's past performance can be gleaned from a company's financial records. While past performance is not necessarily a good predictor of future performance, it does signal which businesses have been strong performers and which have been weak performers. The industry attractiveness–competitive strength evaluations provide a basis for judging future prospects. Normally, strong business units in attractive industries have significantly better prospects than weak businesses in unattractive industries. And, normally, the revenue and earnings outlook for businesses in fast-growing industries is better than for businesses in slow-growing industries. The rankings of future performance generally determine what a business unit's priority for resource allocation by the corporate parent should be. Business subsidiaries with the brightest profit and growth prospects and solid strategic and resource fits generally should head the list for corporate resource support.

Step 6:   *Crafting new strategic moves to improve overall corporate performance.* This step entails using the results of the preceding analysis as the basis for devising actions to strengthen existing businesses, make new acquisitions, divest weak-performing and unattractive businesses, restructure the company's business lineup, expand the scope of the company's geographic reach multinationally or globally, and otherwise steer corporate resources into the areas of greatest opportunity.

Once a company has diversified, corporate management's task is to manage the collection of businesses for maximum long-term performance. There are four different strategic paths for improving a diversified company's performance: (1) broadening the firm's business base by diversifying into additional businesses, (2) retrenching to a narrower diversification base by divesting some of its present businesses, (3) corporate restructuring, and (4) multinational diversification.

Broadening the diversification base is attractive when growth is sluggish and the company needs the revenue and profit boost of a newly acquired business, when it has resources and capabilities that are eminently transferable to related or complementary businesses, or when the opportunity to acquire an attractive company unexpectedly lands on its doorstep. Furthermore, there are occasions when a diversified company makes new acquisitions to complement and strengthen the market position and competitive capabilities of one or more of its present businesses.

Retrenching to a narrower diversification base is usually undertaken when corporate management concludes that the firm's diversification efforts have ranged too far afield and that the best avenue for improving long-term performance is to concentrate on building strong positions in a smaller number of businesses. Retrenchment is usually accomplished by divesting businesses that are no longer deemed suitable for the company to be in. A business can become a prime candidate for divestiture because market conditions in a once attractive industry have badly deteriorated, because it lacks adequate strategic or resource fit, because it is a cash hog with questionable long-term potential, or because it is weakly positioned in its industry with little prospect for earning a decent return on investment. Sometimes a company acquires businesses that just do not work out as expected even though management has tried all it can think of to make them profitable. Divesting such businesses frees resources that can be used to reduce debt, to support expansion of the remaining businesses, or to make acquisitions that materially strengthen the company's competitive position in one or more of the remaining core businesses. Most of the time, companies divest businesses by selling them to another company, but sometimes they spin them off as financially and managerially independent enterprises in which the parent company may or may not retain an ownership interest.

Corporate restructuring strategies involve divesting some businesses and acquiring new businesses so as to put a whole new face on the company's business makeup. Performing radical surgery on the group of businesses a company is in becomes an appealing strategy alternative when a diversified company's financial performance is being squeezed or eroded by (1) too many businesses in slow-growth or declining or low-margin or otherwise unattractive industries, (2) too many competitively weak businesses, (3) ongoing declines in the market shares of one or more major business units that are falling prey to more market-savvy competitors, (4) an excessive debt burden with interest costs that eat deeply into profitability, or (5) ill-chosen acquisitions that haven't lived up to expectations.

Multinational diversification strategies feature a diversity of businesses and a diversity of national markets. Despite the complexity of having to devise and manage so many strategies (at least one for each industry, with as many variations for country markets as may be needed), multinational diversification strategies have considerable appeal. They offer two avenues for long-term growth in revenues and profitability—one is to grow by entering additional businesses and the other is to grow by extending the operations of existing businesses into additional country markets. Moreover, multinational diversification offers six ways to build competitive advantage: (1) full capture of economies of scale and experience or learning-curve effects, (2) opportunities to capitalize on cross-business economies of scope, (3) opportunity to transfer competitively valuable resources from one business to another and from one country to another, (4) ability to leverage use of a well-known and competitively powerful brand name, (5) ability to capitalize on opportunities for cross-business and cross-country collaboration and strategic coordination, and (6) opportunities to use cross-business or cross-country subsidization to wrest sales and market share from rivals. A strategy of multinational diversification contains more competitive advantage potential than any other diversification strategy.

 # Exercises

1. What do you see as the strategic fits that exist among the value chains of the diversified companies listed in Company Spotlight 6.1?

2. Consider the business lineup of the Walt Disney Company shown in Company Spotlight 6.2. What problems do you think the top executives at Disney would encounter in trying to stay on top of all the businesses the company is in? How might they decide the merits of adding new businesses or divesting poorly performing businesses? What types of advice might they give to the general managers of each of Disney's business units?

CHAPTER 7

Building a Capable Organization

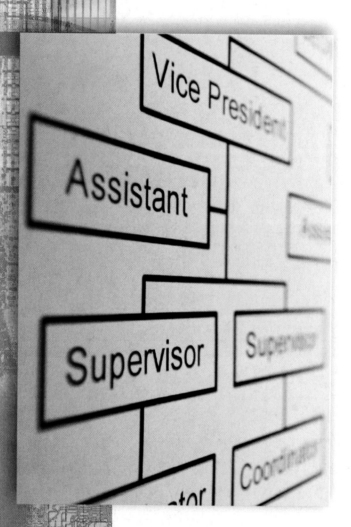

The best game plan in the world never blocked or tackled anybody.
—Vince Lombardi

Strategies most often fail because they aren't executed well.
—Larry Bossidy, CEO Honeywell International, and
    Ram Charan, author and consultant

Organizing is what you do before you do something, so that when you do it, it is not all mixed up.
—A. A. Milne

Once managers have decided on a strategy, the emphasis turns to converting it into actions and good results. Putting the strategy into place and getting the organization to execute it well call for different sets of managerial skills. Whereas crafting strategy is largely a market-driven activity, implementing and executing strategy is primarily an operations-driven activity revolving around the management of people and business processes. Whereas successful strategy making depends on business vision, solid industry and competitive analysis, and shrewd market positioning, successful strategy execution depends on doing a good job of working with and through others, building and strengthening competitive capabilities, motivating and rewarding people in a strategy-supportive manner, and instilling a discipline of getting things done. Executing strategy is an action-oriented, make-things-happen task that tests a manager's ability to direct organizational change, achieve continuous improvement in operations and business processes, create and nurture a strategy-supportive culture, and consistently meet or beat performance targets.

Experienced managers are emphatic in declaring that it is a whole lot easier to develop a sound strategic plan than it is to execute the plan and achieve the desired outcomes. According to one executive, "It's been rather easy for us to decide where we wanted to go. The hard part is to get the organization to act on the new priorities."[1] What makes executing strategy a tougher, more time-consuming management challenge than crafting strategy is the wide array of managerial activities that have to be attended to, the many ways managers can proceed, the demanding people-management skills required, the perseverance necessary to get a variety of initiatives launched and moving, the number of bedeviling issues that must be worked out, the resistance to change that must be overcome, and the difficulties of integrating the efforts of many different work groups into a smoothly functioning whole.

Just because senior managers announce a new strategy doesn't mean that organizational members will agree with it or enthusiastically move forward in implementing it. Senior executives cannot simply tell their immediate subordinates to undertake new strategic initiatives and expect the needed actions and changes to occur in rapid-fire fashion and deliver the intended results. Some managers and employees may be skeptical about the merits of the strategy, seeing it as contrary to the organization's best interests, unlikely to succeed, or threatening to their departments or careers. Moreover, different employees may interpret the new strategy differently or have different ideas about what internal changes are needed to execute it. Long-standing attitudes, vested interests, inertia, and ingrained organizational practices don't melt away when managers decide on a new strategy and begin efforts to implement it—especially when only comparatively few people have been involved in crafting the strategy and when the rationale for strategic change has to be sold to enough organizational members to root out the status quo. It takes adept managerial leadership to convincingly communicate the new strategy and the reasons for it, overcome pockets of doubt and disagreement, secure the commitment and enthusiasm of concerned parties, identify and build consensus on all the hows of implementation and execution, and move forward to get all the pieces into place. Depending on how much consensus building, motivating, and organizational change is involved, the process of implementing strategy changes can take several months to several years.

Like crafting strategy, executing strategy is a job for the whole management team, not just a few senior managers. While an

> ### Core Concept
> All managers have strategy-executing responsibility in their areas of authority, and all employees are participants in the strategy execution process.

organization's chief executive officer and the heads of major units (business divisions, functional departments, and key operating units) are ultimately responsible for seeing that strategy is executed successfully, the process typically affects every part of the firm, from the biggest operating unit to the smallest frontline work group. Top-level managers have to rely on the active support and cooperation of middle and lower managers to push strategy changes into functional areas and operating units and to see that the organization actually operates in accordance with the strategy on a daily basis. Middle and lower-level managers not only are responsible for initiating and supervising the execution process in their areas of authority but also are instrumental in getting subordinates to continuously improve on how strategy-critical value chain activities are being performed and in producing the operating results that allow company performance targets to be met—their role on the company's strategy execution team is by no means minimal. *Strategy execution thus requires every manager to think through the answer to "What does my area have to do to implement its part of the strategic plan, and what should I do to get these things accomplished?"*

A Framework for Executing Strategy

Implementing and executing strategy both entail figuring out all the hows—the specific techniques, actions, and behaviors that are needed for a smooth strategy-supportive operation—and then following through to get things done and deliver results. The idea is to make things happen and make them happen right. The first step in implementing strategic changes is for management to communicate the case for organizational change so clearly and persuasively to organizational members that a determined commitment takes hold throughout the ranks to find ways to put the strategy into place, make it work, and meet performance targets. The ideal condition is for managers to arouse enough enthusiasm for the strategy to turn the implementation process into a companywide crusade. *Management's handling of the strategy implementation process can be considered successful if and when the company achieves the targeted strategic and financial performance and shows good progress in making its strategic vision a reality.*

The specific hows of executing a strategy—the exact items that need to be placed on management's action agenda—always have to be customized to fit the particulars of a company's situation. Making minor changes in an existing strategy differs from implementing radical strategy changes. The hot buttons for successfully executing a low-cost provider strategy are different from those in executing a high-end differentiation strategy. Implementing and executing a new strategy for a struggling company in the midst of a financial crisis is a different job than improving strategy execution in a company where the execution is already pretty good. Moreover, some managers are more adept than others at using this or that approach to achieving the desired kinds of organizational changes. Hence, there's no definitive 10-step checklist or managerial recipe for successful strategy execution that cuts across all company situations and all types of strategies or that works for all types of managers. The hows of implementing and executing strategy require a customized approach—one based on individual company situations and circumstances, the strategy implementer's best judgment, and the implementer's ability to use particular organizational change techniques effectively.

Figure 7.1   The Eight Components of the Strategy Execution Process

The Principal Managerial Components of the Strategy Execution Process

While a company's strategy-executing approaches always have to be tailored to the company's situation, certain managerial bases that have to be covered no matter what the circumstances. Eight managerial tasks crop up repeatedly in company efforts to execute strategy (see Figure 7.1).

1. Building an organization with the competencies, capabilities, and resource strengths to execute strategy successfully.
2. Allocating ample resources to strategy-critical activities.
3. Ensuring that policies and procedures facilitate rather than impede strategy execution.
4. Instituting best practices and pushing for continuous improvement in how value chain activities are performed.

5. Installing information and operating systems that enable company personnel to carry out their strategic roles proficiently.

6. Typing rewards directly to the achievement of strategic and financial targets and to good strategy execution.

7. Shaping the work environment and corporate culture to fit the strategy.

8. Exerting the internal leadership needed to drive implementation forward and keep improving on how the strategy is being executed.

How well managers perform these eight tasks has a decisive impact on whether the outcome is a spectacular success, a colossal failure, or something in between. Moreover, the nature of just what needs to be accomplished on these eight fronts, as determined by the particulars of a company's situation, drives the action priorities on management's agenda and shapes its implementation/execution process.

In devising an action agenda for implementing and executing strategy, the place for managers to start is with *a probing assessment of what the organization must do differently and better to carry out the strategy successfully.* They should then consider *precisely how to make the necessary internal changes* as rapidly as possible. Successful strategy implementers have a knack for diagnosing what their organizations need to do to execute the chosen strategy well and figuring out how to get things done—they are masters in promoting results-oriented behaviors on the part of company personnel and following through on making the right things happen.[2]

> When strategies fail, it is often because of poor execution—things that were supposed to get done slip through the cracks.

In big organizations with geographically scattered operating units, the action agenda of senior executives mostly involves communicating the case for change to others, building consensus for how to proceed, installing strong allies in positions where they can push implementation along in key organizational units, urging and empowering subordinates to keep the process moving, establishing measures of progress and deadlines, recognizing and rewarding those who achieve implementation milestones, directing resources to the right places, and personally leading the strategic change process. Thus, the bigger the organization, the more successful strategy execution depends on the cooperation and implementing skills of operating managers who can push needed changes at the lowest organizational levels and deliver results. In small organizations, top managers can deal directly with frontline managers and employees, personally orchestrating the action steps and implementation sequence, observing firsthand how implementation is progressing, and deciding how hard and how fast to push the process along. Regardless of the organization's size and whether implementation involves sweeping or minor changes, the most important leadership traits are a strong, confident sense of what to do and how to do it. Having a strong grip on these two things comes from understanding the circumstances of the organization and the requirements for effective strategy execution. Then it remains for those managers and company personnel in strategy-critical areas to step up to the plate and produce the desired results.

Managing the Strategy Execution Process: What's Covered in Chapters 7, 8, and 9   In the remainder of this chapter and the next two chapters, we will discuss what is involved in managing the process of implementing and executing strategy. The discussion of executing strategy in Chapters 7, 8, and 9 is framed around the eight managerial tasks shown in Figure 7.1 and the most common issues associated with each. This chapter explores building a capable organization. Chapter 8 looks at budgets, allocating establishing strategy-facilitating policies and procedures, instituting best practices, installing operating systems, and tying rewards to achievement. Chapter 9 deals with creating a strategy-supportive corporate culture and exercising appropriate strategic leadership.

Building a Capable Organization

Proficient strategy execution depends heavily on competent personnel, better-than-adequate competitive capabilities, and effective internal organization. Building a capable organization is thus always a top priority in strategy execution. As shown in Figure 7.2, three types of organization-building actions are paramount:

1. *Staffing the organization*—putting together a strong management team, and recruiting and retaining employees with the needed experience, technical skills, and intellectual capital.

2. *Building core competencies and competitive capabilities* that will enable good strategy execution and updating them as strategy and external conditions change.

3. *Structuring the organization and work effort*—organizing value chain activities and business processes and deciding how much decision-making authority to push down to lower-level managers and frontline employees.

Figure 7.2   The Three Components of Building a Capable Organization

Staffing the Organization
- Putting together a strong management team
- Recruiting and retaining talented employees

Building Core Competencies and Competitive Capabilities
- Developing a set of competencies and capabilities suited to the current strategy
- Updating and revising this set as external conditions and strategy change
- Training and retraining employees as needed to maintain skills-based competencies

Structuring the Organization and Work Effort
- Designing an organization structure that facilitates good strategy execution
- Deciding how much decision-making authority to push down to lower-level managers and front line employees

A Company with the Organizational Capability Needed for Proficient Strategy Execution

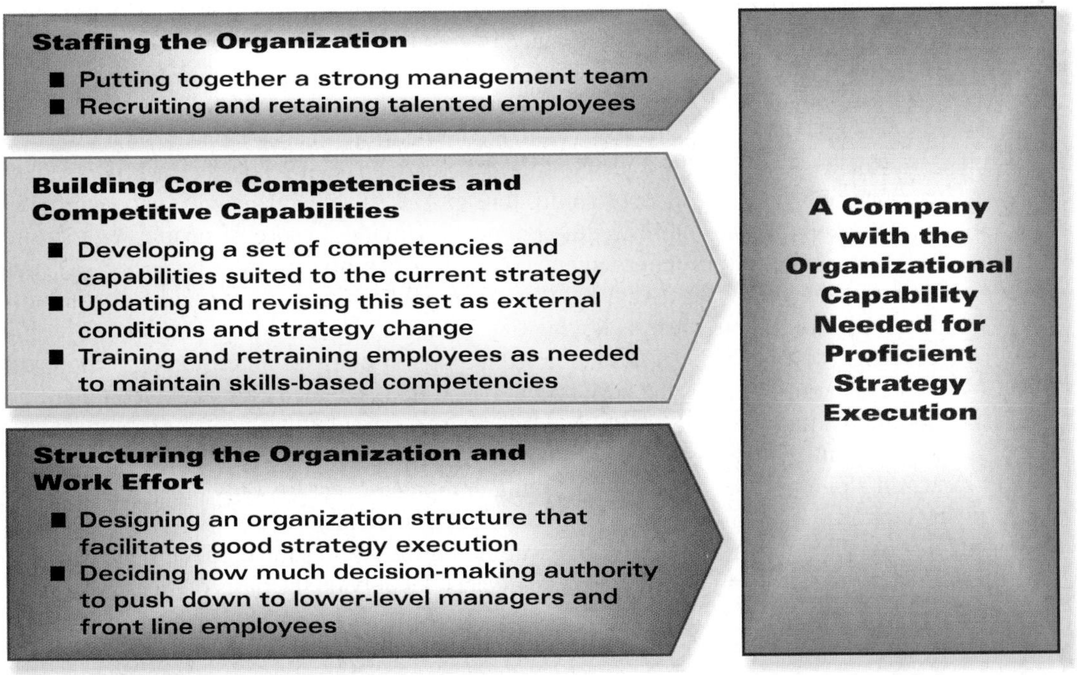

Staffing the Organization

No company can hope to perform the activities required for successful strategy execution without attracting capable managers and without employees that give it a suitable knowledge base and portfolio of intellectual capital.

Putting Together a Strong Management Team

Assembling a capable management team is a cornerstone of the organization-building task.[3] Different strategies and company circumstances often call for different mixes of backgrounds, experiences, know-how, values, beliefs, management styles, and personalities. The personal chemistry among the members of the management team needs to be right, and the talent base needs to be appropriate for the chosen strategy. But the most important condition is to fill key managerial slots with people who can be counted on to get things done; otherwise the implementation-execution process can't proceed at full speed. Sometimes the existing management team is suitable; at other times it may need to be strengthened or expanded by promoting qualified people from within or by bringing in outsiders whose experience, skills, and leadership styles better suit the situation. In turnaround and rapid-growth situations, and in instances when a company doesn't have insiders with the requisite experience or know-how, filling key management slots from the outside is a fairly standard organization-building approach. Company Spotlight 7.1 describes General Electric's widely acclaimed approach to developing a high-caliber management team.

> **Core Concept**
>
> Putting together a talented management team with the right mix of skills and experiences is one of the first strategy-implementing steps.

Recruiting and Retaining Capable Employees

Assembling a capable management team is not enough. Staffing the organization with the right kinds of people must go much deeper than managerial jobs in order to build an organization capable of effective strategy execution. Companies like Electronic Data Systems (EDS), McKinsey & Company, Cisco Systems, Southwest Airlines, Procter & Gamble, PepsiCo, Nike, Microsoft, and Intel make a concerted effort to recruit the best and brightest people they can find and then retain them with excellent compensation packages, opportunities for rapid advancement and professional growth, and challenging and interesting assignments. Having a cadre of people with strong skill sets and budding management potential is essential to their business. EDS requires college graduates to have at least a 3.5 grade point average (on a 4.0 scale) just to qualify for an interview, believing that having a high-caliber pool of employees is crucial to operating the information technology systems of its customers. Microsoft makes a point of hiring the very brightest and most talented programmers it can find and motivating them with both good monetary incentives and the challenge of working on cutting-edge software design projects. McKinsey & Company, one of the world's premier management consulting companies, recruits only cream-of-the-crop MBAs at the nation's top 10 business schools; such talent is essential to McKinsey's strategy of performing high-level consulting for the world's top corporations. The leading global accounting firms screen candidates not only on the basis of their accounting expertise but also on whether they possess the people skills needed to relate well with clients and colleagues. Southwest Airlines goes to considerable lengths to hire people who can have fun and be fun on the job; it uses special interviewing and screening

How General Electric Develops a Talented and Deep Management Team

General Electric is widely considered to be one of the best-managed companies in the world, partly because of its concerted effort to develop outstanding managers. For starters, GE strives to hire talented people with high potential for executive leadership; it then goes to great lengths to expand the leadership, business, and decision-making capabilities of all its managers. Four key elements undergird GE's efforts to build a talent-rich stable of managers:

1. GE makes a practice of transferring managers across divisional, business, or functional lines for sustained periods of time. Such transfers allow managers to develop relationships with colleagues in other parts of the company, help break down insular thinking in business "silos," and promote the sharing of cross-business ideas and best practices. There is an enormous emphasis at GE on transferring ideas and best practices from business to business and making GE a "boundaryless" company.

2. In selecting executives for key positions, GE is strongly disposed to candidates who exhibit what are called the four E's—enormous personal *energy,* the ability to motivate and *energize* others, *edge* (a GE code word for instinctive competitiveness and the ability to make tough decisions in a timely fashion, saying yes or no, and not maybe), and *execution* (the ability to carry things through to fruition).

3. All managers are expected to be proficient at what GE calls *workout*—a process in which managers and employees come together to confront issues as soon as they come up, pinpoint the root cause of the issues, and bring about quick resolutions so the business can move forward. Workout is GE's way of training its managers to diagnose what to do and how to do it.

4. Each year GE sends about 10,000 newly hired and longtime managers to its Leadership Development Center (generally regarded as one of the best corporate training centers in the world), for a three-week course on the company's six sigma quality initiative. More than 5,000 "Master Black Belt" and "Black Belt" six sigma experts have graduated from the program to drive forward thousands of quality initiatives throughout GE. Six sigma training is an ironclad requirement for promotion to any professional and managerial position and any stock option award. GE's Leadership Development Center also offers advanced courses for senior managers that may focus on a single management topic for a month. All classes involve managers from different GE businesses and different parts of the world. Some of the most valuable learning comes in between formal class sessions when GE managers from different businesses trade ideas about how to improve processes and better serve the customer. This knowledge sharing not only spreads best practices throughout the organization but also improves each GE manager's knowledge.

Each of GE's 85,000 managers and professionals is graded in an annual process that divides them into five tiers: the top 10 percent, the next 15 percent, the middle 50 percent, the next 15 percent, and the bottom 10 percent. Everyone in the top tier gets stock options, nobody in the fourth tier gets options, and most of those in the fifth tier become candidates for being weeded out. Business heads are pressured to wean out "C" players. GE's CEO personally reviews the performance of the top 3,000 managers. Senior executive compensation is heavily weighted toward six sigma commitment and producing successful business results.

According to Jack Welch, GE's CEO from 1980 to 2001, "The reality is, we simply cannot afford to field anything but teams of 'A' players."

Sources: 1998 annual report; www.ge.com; John A. Byrne, "How Jack Welch Runs GE," *Business Week,* June 8, 1998, p. 90; Miriam Leuchter, "Management Farm Teams," *Journal of Business Strategy,* May 1998, pp. 29–32; and "The House That Jack Built, *The Economist,* September 18, 1999.

methods to gauge whether applicants for customer-contact jobs have outgoing personality traits that match its strategy of creating a high-spirited, fun-loving, in-flight atmosphere for passengers; it is so selective that only about 3 percent of the people who apply are offered jobs.

In high-tech companies, the challenge is to staff work groups with gifted, imaginative, and energetic people who can bring life to new ideas quickly and inject into the organization what one Dell Computer executive calls "hum."[3] The saying "People are our most important asset" may seem hollow, but it fits high-technology companies dead-on. Besides checking closely for functional and technical skills, Dell Computer tests applicants for their tolerance of ambiguity and change, their capacity to work in teams, and their ability to learn on the fly. Companies like Amazon.com and Cisco Systems have broken new ground in recruiting, hiring, cultivating, developing, and retaining talented employees—most all of whom are in their 20s and 30s. Cisco goes after the top 10 percent, raiding other companies and endeavoring to retain key people at the companies it acquires so as to maintain a cadre of star engineers, programmers, managers, salespeople, and support personnel in executing its strategy to remain the world's leading provider of Internet infrastructure products and technology.

> **Core Concept**
>
> In many industries adding to a company's talent base and building intellectual capital is more important to good strategy execution than additional investments in capital projects.

Where intellectual capital is crucial in building a strategy-capable organization, companies have instituted a number of practices in staffing their organizations and developing a strong knowledge base:

1. Spending considerable effort in screening and evaluating job applicants, selecting only those with suitable skill sets, energy, initiative, judgment, and aptitudes for learning and adaptability to the company's work environment and culture.

2. Putting employees through training programs that continue throughout their careers.

3. Providing promising employees with challenging, interesting, and skill-stretching assignments.

4. Rotating people through jobs that not only have great content but also span functional and geographic boundaries. Providing people with opportunities to gain experience in a variety of international settings is increasingly considered an essential part of career development in multinational or global companies.

5. Encouraging employees to be creative and innovative, to challenge existing ways of doing things and offer better ways, and to submit ideas for new products or businesses. Progressive companies work hard at creating an environment in which ideas and suggestions bubble up from below rather than proceed from the top down. Employees are made to feel that their opinions count.

6. Fostering a stimulating and engaging work environment such that employees will consider the company a great place to work.

7. Exerting efforts to retain high-potential, high-performing employees with salary increases, performance bonuses, stock options and equity ownership, and other long-term incentives.

8. Coaching average performers to improve their skills and capabilities, while weeding out underperformers and benchwarmers.

Building Core Competencies and Competitive Capabilities

High among the organization-building priorities in the strategy implementing/executing process is the need to build and strengthen competitively valuable core competencies and organizational capabilities. Whereas managers identify the desired competencies and capabilities in the course of crafting strategy, good strategy execution requires putting the desired competencies and capabilities in place, upgrading them as needed, and then modifying them as market conditions evolve. Sometimes a company already has the needed competencies and capabilities, in which case managers can concentrate on nurturing them to promote better strategy execution. More usually, however, company managers have to add new competencies and capabilities to implement strategic initiatives and promote proficient strategy execution.

A number of prominent companies have succeeded in establishing core competencies and capabilities that have been instrumental in making them winners in the marketplace. Honda's core competence is its depth of expertise in gasoline engine technology and small engine design. Intel's is in the design of complex chips for personal computers. Procter & Gamble's core competencies reside in its superb marketing/distribution skills and its R&D capabilities in five core technologies—fats, oils, skin chemistry, surfactants, and emulsifiers. Sony's core competencies are its expertise in electronic technology and its ability to translate that expertise into innovative products (cutting-edge video game hardware, miniaturized radios and video cameras, TVs and DVDs with unique features, attractively designed PCs). Dell Computer has the capabilities to deliver state-of-the-art products to its customers within days of next-generation components coming available—and to do so at attractively low costs (it has leveraged its collection of competencies and capabilities into being the global low-cost leader in PCs).

The Three-Stage Process of Developing and Strengthening Competencies and Capabilities

Building core competencies and competitive capabilities is a time-consuming, managerially challenging exercise. While some organization-building assist can be gotten from discovering how best-in-industry or best-in-world companies perform a particular activity, trying to replicate and then improve on the competencies and capabilities of others is, however, much easier said than done—for the same reasons that one is unlikely to ever become a good golfer just by studying what Tiger Woods does. Putting a new capability in place is more complicated than just forming a new team or department and charging it with becoming highly competent in performing the desired activity, using whatever it can learn from other companies having similar competencies or capabilities. Rather, it takes a series of deliberate and well orchestrated organizational steps to achieve mounting proficiency in performing an activity. The capability-building process has three stages:

Stage 1—First, the organization must develop the *ability* to do something, however imperfectly or inefficiently. This entails selecting people with the requisite skills and experience, upgrading or expanding individual abilities as needed, and then molding the efforts and work products of individuals into a collaborative effort to create organizational ability.

Stage 2—As experience grows and company personnel learn how to perform the activity *consistently well and at an acceptable cost*, the ability evolves into a tried-and-true *competence* or *capability*.

Stage 3—Should the organization continue to polish and refine its know-how and otherwise sharpen its performance such that it becomes *better than rivals* at performing the activity, the core competence rises to the rank of a *distinctive competence* (or the capability becomes a competitively superior capability), thus providing a path to competitive advantage.

Many companies manage to get through stages 1 and 2 in performing a strategy-critical activity, but comparatively few achieve sufficient proficiency in performing strategy-critical activities to qualify for the third stage.

Managing the Process   Four traits concerning core competencies and competitive capabilities are important in successfully managing the organization-building process:[4]

1. *Core competencies and competitive capabilities are bundles of skills and know-how that most often grow out of the combined efforts of cross-functional work groups and departments performing complementary activities at different locations in the firm's value chain.* Rarely does a core competence or capability consist of narrow skills attached to the work efforts of a single department. For instance, a core competence in speeding new products to market involves the collaborative efforts of personnel in R&D, engineering and design, purchasing, production, marketing, and distribution. Similarly, the capability to provide superior customer service is a team effort among people in customer call centers (where orders are taken and inquiries are answered), shipping and delivery, billing and accounts receivable, and after-sale support. Complex activities (like designing and manufacturing a sports-utility vehicle or creating the capability for secure credit card transactions over the Internet) usually involve a number of component skills, technological disciplines, competencies, and capabilities—some performed in-house and some provided by suppliers/allies. An important part of the organization-building function is to think about which activities of which groups need to be linked and made mutually reinforcing and then to forge the necessary collaboration both internally and with outside resource providers.

2. *Normally, a core competence or capability emerges incrementally* out of company efforts either to bolster skills that contributed to earlier successes or to respond to customer problems, new technological and market opportunities, and the competitive maneuverings of rivals. Migrating from the one-time ability to do something up the ladder to a core competence or competitively valuable capability is usually an organization-building process that takes months and often years to accomplish—it is definitely not an overnight event.

3. The key to leveraging a core competence into a distinctive competence (or a capability into a competitively superior capability) is *concentrating more effort and more talent than rivals on deepening and strengthening the competence or capability, so as to achieve the dominance needed for competitive advantage.* This does not necessarily mean spending more money on such activities than competitors, but it does mean consciously focusing more talent on them and striving for best-in-industry, if not best-in-world, status. To achieve dominance on lean financial resources, companies like Cray in large computers and Honda in gasoline engines have leveraged the expertise of their talent pool by frequently re-forming high-intensity teams and reusing key people on special projects. The experiences of these and other companies indicate that the usual keys to successfully building core competencies and valuable capabilities are superior employee selection, thorough training and retraining, powerful cultural influences, effective cross-functional collaboration, empowerment, motivating incentives, short deadlines, and good databases—not big operating budgets.

4. Evolving changes in customers' needs and competitive conditions often require *tweaking and adjusting a company's portfolio of competencies and intellectual capital to keep its capabilities freshly honed and on the cutting edge.* This is particularly important in high-tech industries and fast-paced markets where important developments occur weekly. As a consequence, wise company managers work at anticipating changes in customer-market requirements and staying ahead of the curve in proactively building a package of competencies and capabilities that can win out over rivals.

Managerial actions to develop core competencies and competitive capabilities generally take one of two forms: either strengthening the company's base of skills, knowledge, and intellect, or coordinating and networking the efforts of the various work groups and departments. Actions of the first sort can be undertaken at all managerial levels, but actions of the second sort are best orchestrated by senior managers who not only appreciate the strategy-executing significance of strong competencies/capabilities but also have the clout to enforce the necessary networking and cooperation among individuals, groups, departments, and external allies.

One organization-building question is whether to develop the desired competencies and capabilities internally or to outsource them by partnering with key suppliers or forming strategic alliances. The answer depends on what can be safely delegated to outside suppliers or allies versus what internal capabilities are key to the company's long-term success. Either way, though, calls for action. Outsourcing means launching initiatives to identify the most attractive providers and to establish collaborative relationships. Developing the capabilities in-house means marshaling personnel with relevant skills and experience, collaboratively networking the individual skills and related cross-functional activities to form organizational capability, and building the desired levels of proficiency through repetition (practice makes perfect).[5]

Sometimes the tediousness of internal organization building can be shortcut by buying a company that has the requisite capability and integrating its competencies into the firm's value chain. Indeed, a pressing need to acquire certain capabilities quickly is one reason to acquire another company—an acquisition aimed at building greater capability can be every bit as competitively valuable as an acquisition aimed at adding new products or services to the company's business lineup. Capabilities-motivated acquisitions are essential (1) when a market opportunity can slip by faster than a needed capability can be created internally, and (2) when industry conditions, technology, or competitors are moving at such a rapid clip that time is of the essence. But usually there's no good substitute for ongoing internal efforts to build and strengthen the company's competencies and capabilities in performing strategy-critical value chain activities.

Updating and Reshaping Competencies and Capabilities as External Conditions and Company Strategy Change   Even after core competencies and competitive capabilities are in place and functioning, company managers can't relax. Competencies and capabilities that grow stale can impair competitiveness unless they are refreshed, modified, or even phased out and replaced in response to ongoing market changes and shifts in company strategy. Indeed, the buildup of knowledge and experience over time, coupled with the imperatives of keeping capabilities in step with ongoing strategy and market changes, makes it appropriate to view a company as *a bundle of evolving competencies and capabilities.* Management's organization-building challenge is one of deciding when and how to recalibrate existing competencies and capabilities, and when and how to develop new ones. Although the task is formidable, ideally it produces a dynamic organization with "hum" and momentum as well as a distinctive competence.

From Competencies and Capabilities to Competitive Advantage

While strong core competencies and competitive capabilities are a major assist in executing strategy, they are an equally important avenue for securing a competitive edge over rivals in situations where it is relatively easy for rivals to copy smart strategies. Any time rivals can readily duplicate successful strategy features, making it difficult or impossible to outstrategize rivals and beat them in the marketplace with a superior

> ### Core Concept
>
> Building competencies and capabilities has a huge payoff—improved strategy execution and a potential for competitive advantage.

strategy, the chief way to achieve lasting competitive advantage is to outexecute them (beat them by performing certain value chain activities in superior fashion). Building core competencies, resource strengths, and organizational capabilities that rivals can't match is thus one of the best and most reliable ways to outexecute them. Moreover, cutting-edge core competencies and organizational capabilities are not easily duplicated by rival firms; thus, any competitive edge they produce is likely to be sustainable, paving the way for above-average organizational performance.

The Strategic Role of Employee Training

Training and retraining are important when a company shifts to a strategy requiring different skills, competitive capabilities, managerial approaches, and operating methods. Training is also strategically important in organizational efforts to build skills-based competencies. And it is a key activity in businesses where technical know-how is changing so rapidly that a company loses its ability to compete unless its skilled people have cutting-edge knowledge and expertise. Successful strategy implementers see to it that the training function is both adequately funded and effective. If the chosen strategy calls for new skills, deeper technological capability, or building and using new capabilities, training should be placed near the top of the action agenda.

The strategic importance of training has not gone unnoticed. Over 600 companies have established internal "universities" to lead the training effort, facilitate continuous organizational learning, and help upgrade company competencies and capabilities. Many companies conduct orientation sessions for new employees, fund an assortment of competence-building training programs, and reimburse employees for tuition and other expenses associated with obtaining additional college education, attending professional development courses, and earning professional certification of one kind or another. A number of companies offer online, just-in-time training courses to employees around the clock. Increasingly, employees at all levels are expected to take an active role in their own professional development, assuming responsibility for keeping their skills and expertise up-to-date and in sync with the company's needs.

Matching Organization Structure to Strategy

There are few hard-and-fast rules for organizing the work effort to support strategy. Every firm's organization chart is partly a product of its particular situation, reflecting prior organizational patterns, varying internal circumstances, executive judgments about reporting relationships, and the politics of who gets which assignments. Moreover, every strategy is grounded in its own set of key success factors and value chain

Figure 7.3   Structuring the Work Effort to Promote Successful Strategy Execution

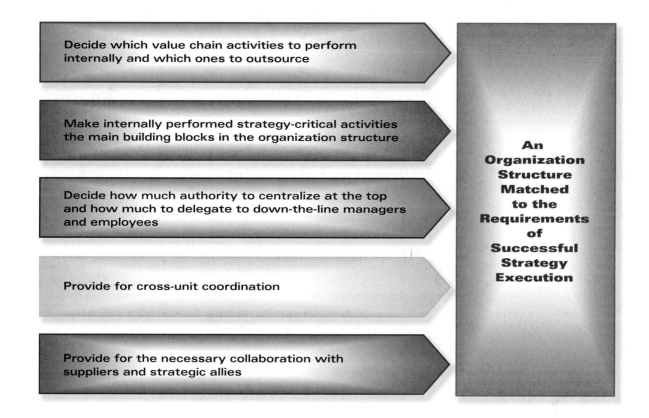

activities. But some considerations are common to all companies. These are summarized in Figure 7.3 and discussed in turn in the following sections.

Deciding Which Value Chain Activities to Perform Internally and Which to Outsource

In any business, some activities in the value chain are always more critical to strategic success and competitive advantage than others. Among the primary value chain activities are certain crucial business processes that have to be performed either exceedingly well or in closely coordinated fashion for the organization to deliver on the capabilities needed for strategic success. For instance, hotel/motel enterprises have to be good at fast check-in/check-out, room maintenance, food service, and creating a pleasant ambience. For a manufacturer of chocolate bars, buying quality cocoa beans at low prices is vital and reducing production costs by a fraction of a cent per bar can mean a seven-figure improvement in the bottom line. In discount stock brokerage, the strategy-critical activities are fast access to information, accurate order execution, efficient record keeping and transactions processing, and good customer service. In specialty chemicals, the critical activities are R&D, product innovation, getting new products onto the market quickly, effective marketing, and expertise in assisting customers. In consumer electronics, where advancing technology drives new product innovation, rapidly getting cutting-edge, next-generation products to market is a critical organizational capability.

As a general rule, strategy-critical activities need to be performed internally so that management can directly control their performance. Less important activities—like routine administrative housekeeping (doing the payroll, administering employee benefit programs, providing corporate security, managing stockholder relations, maintaining fleet vehicles) and some support functions (information technology and data processing, training, public relations, market research, legal and legislative affairs)—may be strong candidates for outsourcing. Two questions help pinpoint an organization's strategy-critical activities: "What functions or business processes have to be performed extra well or in timely fashion to achieve sustainable competitive advantage?" and "In what value chain activities would poor execution seriously impair strategic success?"[6] However, a number of companies have found ways to successfully rely on outside components suppliers, product designers, distribution channels, advertising agencies, and financial services firms to perform strategically significant value chain activities.[7] For years Polaroid Corporation bought its film from Eastman Kodak, its electronics from Texas Instruments, and its cameras from Timex and others, while it concentrated on producing its unique self-developing film packets and designing its next-generation cameras and films. Nike concentrates on design, marketing, and distribution to retailers, while outsourcing virtually all production of its shoes and sporting apparel. Likewise, a number of PC manufacturers outsource assembly, concentrating their energies instead on product design, sales and marketing, and distribution. So while performing strategy-critical activities in-house normally makes good sense, there can be times when outsourcing some of them works to good advantage.

The Merits of Outsourcing Noncritical Value Chain Activities

Managers too often spend inordinate amounts of time, mental energy, and financial resources wrestling with functional support groups and other internal bureaucracies, which diverts their attention from the company's strategy-critical activities. One way to reduce such distractions is to cut the number of internal staff support activities and instead rely on outside vendors with specialized expertise to supply such noncritical support services as website operations, data processing, fringe benefits management, and training. An outsider, by concentrating specialists and technology in its area of expertise, can frequently perform certain services as well or better, and often more cheaply, than a company that performs these services only for itself. Many mining companies outsource geological work, assaying, and drilling. E. & J. Gallo Winery outsources 95 percent of its grape production, letting farmers take on the weather and other grape-growing risks while it concentrates on wine production and sales.[8] Eastman Kodak, Ford, Exxon Mobil, Merrill Lynch, and Chevron have outsourced their data processing activities to computer service firms, believing that outside specialists can perform the needed services at lower costs and equal or better quality. A relatively large number of companies outsource the operation of their websites to Web design and hosting enterprises.

But besides less internal hassle and lower costs there are other strong reasons to consider outsourcing. Approached from a strategic point of view, outsourcing noncrucial support activities can decrease internal bureaucracies, flatten the organization structure, speed decision making, heighten the company's strategic focus, improve its innovative capacity (through interaction with best-in-world suppliers),

Core Concept

Outsourcing has many strategy-executing advantages—lower costs, less internal bureaucracy, speedier decision-making, and heightened strategic focus.

and increase competitive responsiveness.[9] Outsourcing has considerable merit when it allows a company to concentrate its own energies and resources on those value chain activities for which it can create unique value and thus become best in the industry (or, better still, best in the world). It also has merit when the company needs strategic control to build core competencies, achieve competitive advantage, and manage key customer–supplier–distributor relationships.

The Merits of Partnering with Others to Gain Added Competitive Capabilities   There is another, equally important reason to look outside for resources to compete effectively aside from just the cost savings and agility that outsourcing can permit. *Partnerships can add to a company's arsenal of capabilities and contribute to better strategy execution.* By building, continually improving, and then leveraging partnerships, a company enhances its overall organizational capabilities and builds resource strengths—strengths that deliver value to customers and consequently pave the way for competitive success.

Automobile manufacturers work closely with their suppliers to advance the design and functioning of parts and components, to incorporate new technology, to better integrate individual parts and components to form engine cooling systems, transmission systems, electrical systems, and so on—all of which helps shorten the cycle time for new models, improve the quality and performance of those models, and lower overall production costs. Prior to merging with Germany's Daimler-Benz, Chrysler transformed itself from a high-cost producer into a low-cost producer by abandoning internal production of many parts and components and instead outsourcing them from more efficient parts/components suppliers; greater reliance on outsourcing enabled Chrysler to shorten its design-to-market cycle for new models and drive down its production costs. Soft-drink and beer manufacturers all cultivate their relationships with their bottlers and distributors to strengthen access to local markets and build the loyalty, support, and commitment for corporate marketing programs,

> **Core Concept**
> Strategic partnerships, alliances, and close collaboration with suppliers, distributors, and makers of complementary products, and even competitors all make good strategic sense whenever the result is to enhance organizational resources and capabilities.

without which their own sales and growth are weakened. Similarly, fast-food enterprises like McDonald's and Taco Bell find it essential to work hand-in-hand with franchisees on outlet cleanliness, consistency of product quality, in-store ambience, courtesy and friendliness of store personnel, and other aspects of store operations. Unless franchisees continuously deliver sufficient customer satisfaction to attract repeat business, a fast-food chain's sales and competitive standing will suffer quickly. Companies like Ford, Boeing, Aerospatiale, AT&T, BMW, and Dell Computer have learned that their central R&D groups cannot begin to match the innovative capabilities of a well-managed network of supply chain partners having the ability to advance the technology, lead the development of next-generation parts and components, and supply them at a relatively low price.[10]

The Dangers of Excessive Outsourcing   Critics contend that *a company can go overboard on outsourcing and so hollow out its knowledge base and capabilities as to leave itself at the mercy of outside suppliers and short of the resource strengths to be master of its own destiny.*[11] The point is well taken. Outsourcing strategy-critical activities must be done judiciously and with safeguards against losing control over the performance of key value chain activities and becoming overly dependent on outsiders. Thus, many companies refuse to source key components from a single supplier, opting to use two or three suppliers as a way of becoming overly dependent on any one supplier and giving any one supplier too much bargaining power. Moreover, they regularly evaluate their suppliers, looking not only at the supplier's overall performance but also at whether they should switch to another supplier or even bring the activity back in-house. To avoid loss of control, companies typically work closely with key suppliers, endeavoring to make sure that suppliers' activities are closely integrated with their own requirements and expectations. Most companies appear alert to the primary danger of excessive outsourcing: being caught without the internal strengths and capabilities needed to protect their well-being in the marketplace.

Making Strategy-Critical Activities the Main Building Blocks of the Organization Structure

The rationale for making strategy-critical activities the main building blocks in structuring a business is compelling: If activities crucial to strategic success are to have the resources, decision-making influence, and organizational impact they need, they have to be centerpieces in the organizational scheme. Plainly, implementing a new or changed strategy is likely to entail new or different key activities, competencies, or capabilities and therefore to require new or different organizational arrangements. If workable organizational adjustments are not forthcoming, the resulting mismatch between strategy and structure can open the door to execution and performance problems.[12] Hence, attempting to carry out a new strategy with an old organizational structure is usually unwise.

> **Core Concept**
>
> Just as a company's strategy evolves to stay in tune with changing external circumstances, so must an organization's structure evolve to fit shifting requirements for proficient strategy execution.

Although the stress here is on designing the organization structure around the needs of effective strategy execution, it is worth noting that structure can and does influence the choice of strategy. A good strategy must be doable. When an organization's present structure is so far out of line with the requirements of a particular strategy that the organization would have to be turned upside down to implement it, the strategy may not be doable and should not be given further consideration. In such cases, structure shapes the choice of strategy. The thing to remember, however, is that *once a strategy is chosen, structure must be modified to fit the strategy if, in fact, an approximate fit does not already exist.* Any influences of structure on strategy should, logically, come before the point of strategy selection rather than after it.

The Primary Building Blocks of the Organization Structure

The primary organizational building blocks within a business are usually *traditional functional departments* (R&D, engineering and design, production and operations, sales and marketing, information technology, finance and accounting, and human resources) and *process-complete departments* (supply chain management, filling customer orders, customer service, quality control, direct sales via the company's website).[13] In enterprises with operations in various countries around the world (or with geographically scattered organizational units within a country), the basic building blocks may also include *geographic organizational units*, each of which has profit/loss responsibility for its assigned geographic area. In vertically integrated firms, the major building blocks are *divisional units performing one or more of the major processing steps along the value chain* (raw materials production, components manufacture, assembly, wholesale distribution, retail store operations); each division in the value chain may operate as a profit center for performance measurement purposes.

The typical building blocks of a diversified company are its *individual businesses*, with each business unit usually operating as an independent profit center and with corporate headquarters performing assorted support functions for all of its business units.

Why Functional Organization Structures Often Impede Strategy Execution   A big weakness of traditional functionally organized structures is that pieces of strategically relevant activities and capabilities often end up scattered across many departments, with the result that no one group or manager is accountable. Consider, for example, how a functional structure results in fragmented performance of the following strategy-critical activities:

- *Filling customer orders accurately and promptly*—a process that cuts across sales (which wins the order); finance (which may have to check credit terms or approve special financing); production (which must produce the goods and replenish warehouse inventories as needed); warehousing (which has to verify whether the items are in stock, pick the order from the warehouse, and package it for shipping); and shipping (which has to choose a carrier to deliver the goods and release the goods to the carrier).[14]

- *Fast, ongoing introduction of new products*—a cross-functional process involving personnel in R&D, engineering, purchasing, manufacturing, and sales and marketing.

- *Improving product quality*—a process that often involves the collaboration of personnel in R&D, engineering and design, components purchasing from suppliers, in-house components production, manufacturing, and assembly.

- *Supply chain management*—a collaborative process that cuts across such functional areas as purchasing, engineering and design, components purchasing, inventory management, manufacturing and assembly, and warehousing and shipping.

- *Building the capability to conduct business via the Internet*—a process that involves personnel in information technology, supply chain management, production, sales and marketing, warehousing and shipping, customer service, finance, and accounting.

- *Obtaining feedback from customers and making product modifications to meet their needs*—a process that involves personnel in customer service and after-sale support, R&D, engineering and design, components purchasing, manufacturing and assembly, and marketing research.

Handoffs from one department to another lengthen completion time and frequently drive up administrative costs, since coordinating the fragmented pieces can soak up hours of effort on the parts of many people.[15] This is not a fatal flaw of functional organization—organizing around specific functions has worked to good advantage in support activities like finance and accounting, human resource management, and engineering, and in such primary activities as R&D, manufacturing, and marketing. But fragmentation is an important weakness of functional organization, accounting for why we indicated that a company's competencies and capabilities are usually cross-functional and don't reside in the activities of a single functional department.

Increasingly during the past decade, companies have found that rather than continuing to scatter related pieces of a strategy-critical business process across several functional departments and scrambling to integrate their efforts, it is better to reengineer the

Core Concept

Business process reengineering involves pulling the pieces of a strategy-critical process out of various functional departments and integrating them into a streamlined, cohesive series of work steps performed within a single work unit.

work effort and create *process departments*. This is done by pulling the people who performed the pieces in functional departments into a group that works together to perform the whole process. Pulling the pieces of strategy-critical processes out of the functional silos and creating process departments or cross-functional work groups charged with performing all the steps needed to produce a strategy-critical result has been termed **business process reengineering.**

In the electronics industry, where product life cycles run three to six months due to the speed of advancing technology, companies have formed process departments charged with cutting the time it takes to bring new technologies and products to commercial fruition. Northwest Water, a British utility, used business process reengineering to eliminate 45 work depots that served as home bases to crews who installed and repaired water and sewage lines and equipment.[16] Now crews work directly from their vehicles, receiving assignments and reporting work completion from computer terminals in their trucks. Crew members are no longer employees but contractors to Northwest Water. These reengineering efforts not only eliminated the need for the work depots but also allowed Northwest Water to eliminate a big percentage of the bureaucratic personnel and supervisory organization that managed the crews. At acute care hospitals such as Lee Memorial in Fort Myers, Florida, and St. Vincent's in Melbourne, Australia, medical care has been reengineered so that it is delivered by interdisciplinary teams of health care professionals organized around the needs of the patients and their families rather than around functional departments within the hospital. Both hospitals created treatment-specific focused care wards within the hospital to handle most of a patient's needs, from admission to discharge. Patients are no longer wheeled from department to department for procedures and tests; instead, teams have the equipment and resources within each focused care unit to provide total care for the patient. While the hospitals had some concern about functional inefficiency in the use of some facilities, process organization has resulted in substantially lower operating costs, faster patient recovery, and greater satisfaction on the part of patients and caregivers.

Reengineering strategy-critical business processes to reduce fragmentation across traditional departmental lines and cut bureaucratic overhead has proved to be a legitimate organization design tool, not a passing fad. Process organization is every bit as valid an organizing principle as functional specialization. Strategy execution is improved when the pieces of strategy-critical activities and core business processes performed by different departments are properly integrated and coordinated.

Companies that have reengineered some of their business processes have ended up compressing formerly separate steps and tasks into jobs performed by a single person and integrating jobs into team activities. Reorganization then follows as a natural consequence of task synthesis and job redesign. When done properly, reengineering can produce dramatic gains in productivity and organizational capability. In the order-processing section of General Electric's circuit breaker division, elapsed time from order receipt to delivery was cut from three weeks to three days by consolidating six production units into one, reducing a variety of former inventory and handling steps, automating the design system to replace a human custom-design process, and cutting the organizational layers between managers and workers from three to one. Productivity rose 20 percent in one year, and unit manufacturing costs dropped 30 percent.[17]

Table 7.1   ADVANTAGES AND DISADVANTAGES OF CENTRALIZED VERSUS DECENTRALIZED DECISION-MAKING

Centralized Organizational Structures	Decentralized Organizational Structures
Basic Tenets	**Basic Tenets**
■ Decisions on most matters of importance should be pushed to managers up the line who have the experience, expertise, and judgment to decide what is the wisest or best course of action. ■ Frontline supervisors and rank-and-file employees can't be relied on to make the right decisions—because they seldom know what is best for the organization and because they do not have the time or the inclination to properly manage the tasks they are performing (letting them decide what to do is thus risky).	■ Decision-making authority should be put in the hands of the people closest to and most familiar with the situation, and these people should be trained to exercise good judgment. ■ A company that draws on the combined intellectual capital of all its employees can outperform a command-and-control company.
Chief Advantage	**Chief Advantages**
■ Tight control from the top allows for accountability.	■ Encourages lower-level managers and rank-and-file employees to exercise initiative and act responsibly. ■ Promotes greater motivation and involvement in the business on the part of more company personnel. ■ Spurs new ideas and creative thinking. ■ Allows fast response times. ■ Reduces layers of management.
Primary Disadvantages	**Primary Disadvantages**
■ Slows response times because management bureaucracy must decide on a course of action. ■ Does not encourage responsibility among lower-level managers and rank-and-file employees. ■ Discourages lower-level managers and rank-and-file employees from exercising any initiative—they are expected to wait to be told what to do.	■ Puts the organization at risk if many bad decisions are made at lower levels. ■ Impedes cross-unit coordination and capture of strategic fits.

Determining the Degree of Authority and Independence to Give Each Unit and Each Employee

In executing the strategy and conducting daily operations, companies must decide how much authority to delegate to the managers of each organization unit—especially the heads of business subsidiaries, functional and process departments, and plants, sales offices, distribution centers and other operating units—and how much decision-making latitude to give individual employees in performing their jobs. The two extremes are to *centralize decision making* at the top (the CEO and a few close lieutenants) or to *decentralize decision making* by giving managers and employees considerable decision-making latitude in their areas of responsibility. As shown in Table 7.1, the two approaches are based on sharply different underlying principles and beliefs, with each having its pros and cons.

Centralized Decision-Making   *In a highly centralized organization structure, top executives retain authority for most strategic and operating decisions and keep a tight rein on business-unit heads, department heads, and the managers of key operating units; comparatively little discretionary authority is granted to frontline supervisors and rank-and-file employees.* The command-and-control paradigm of centralized structures is based on the underlying assumption that frontline personnel have neither the time nor the inclination to direct and properly control the work they are

There are serious disadvantages to having a small number of top-level managers micromanage the business by personally making decisions or by requiring they approve the recommendations of lower-level subordinates before actions can be taken.

performing, and that they lack the knowledge and judgment to make wise decisions about how best to do it—hence the need for managerially prescribed policies and procedures, close supervision, and tight control. The thesis underlying authoritarian structures is that strict enforcement of detailed procedures backed by rigorous managerial oversight is the most reliable way to keep the daily execution of strategy on track.

The big advantage of an authoritarian structure is tight control by the manager in charge—it is easy to know who is accountable when things do not go well. But there are some serious disadvantages. Hierarchical command-and-control structures make an organization sluggish in responding to changing conditions because of the time it takes for the review/approval process to run up all the layers of the management bureaucracy. Furthermore, to work well, centralized decision making requires top-level managers to gather and process whatever information is relevant to the decision. When the relevant knowledge resides at lower organizational levels (or is technical, detailed, or hard to express in words), it is difficult and time-consuming to get all of the facts and nuances in front of a high-level executive located far from the scene of the action—full understanding of the situation cannot be readily copied from one mind to another. Hence, centralized decision making is often impractical—the larger the company and the more scattered its operations, the more that decision-making authority has to be delegated to managers closer to the scene of the action.

Decentralized Decision-Making *In a highly decentralized organization, decision-making authority is pushed down to the lowest organizational level capable of making timely, informed, competent decisions.* The objective is to put adequate decision-making authority in the hands of the people closest to and most familiar with the situation and train them to weigh all the factors and exercise good judgment. The case for empowering down-the-line managers and employees to make decisions related to daily operations and executing the strategy is based on the belief that a company that draws on the combined intellectual capital of all its employees can outperform a command-and-control company. Decentralized decision making means, for example, that in a diversified company the various business-unit heads have broad authority to execute the agreed-on business strategy with comparatively little interference from corporate headquarters; moreover, the business-unit heads delegate considerable decision-making latitude to functional and process department heads and the heads of the various operating units (plants, distribution centers, sales offices) in implementing and executing their pieces of the strategy. In turn, work teams may be empowered to manage and improve their assigned value chain activity, and employees with customer contact may be empowered to do what it takes to please customers. At Starbucks, for example, employees are encouraged to exercise initiative in promoting customer satisfaction—there's the story of a store employee who, when the computerized cash register system went offline, enthusiastically offered free coffee to waiting customers.[18] With decentralized decision making, top management maintains control by limiting empowered managers' and employees' discretionary authority and holding people accountable for the decisions they make.

The ultimate goal of decentralized decision making is not to push decisions down to lower levels but to put decision-making authority in the hands of those persons or teams closest to and most knowledgeable about the situation.

Decentralized organization structures have much to recommend them. Delegating greater authority to subordinate managers and employees creates a more horizontal organization structure with fewer management layers. Whereas in a centralized vertical structure managers and workers have to go up the ladder of authority for an answer, in a decentralized horizontal structure they develop their own answers and action plans—making decisions in their areas of responsibility and being accountable for results is an integral part of their job. Pushing decision-making authority down to middle and lower-level managers and then further on to work teams and individual employees shortens organizational response times and spurs new ideas, creative thinking, innovation, and greater involvement on the part of subordinate managers and employees. In worker-empowered structures, jobs can be defined more broadly, several tasks can be integrated into a single job, and people can direct their own work. Fewer managers are needed because deciding how to do things becomes part of each person's or team's job. Further, today's electronic communication systems make it easy and relatively inexpensive for people at all organizational levels to have direct access to data, other employees, managers, suppliers, and customers. They can access information quickly (via the Internet or company intranet), readily check with superiors or whomever else as needed, and take responsible action. Typically, there are genuine gains in morale and productivity when people are provided with the tools and information they need to operate in a self-directed way. Decentralized decision making can not only shorten organizational response times but also spur new ideas, creative thinking, innovation, and greater involvement on the part of subordinate managers and employees.

Insofar as all five tasks of strategic management are concerned, a decentralized approach to decision making means that the managers of each organizational unit should not only lead the crafting of their unit's strategy but also lead the decision making on how to execute it. Decentralization thus requires selecting strong managers to head each organizational unit and holding them accountable for crafting and executing appropriate strategies for their units. Managers who consistently produce unsatisfactory results have to be weeded out.

The past decade has seen a growing shift from authoritarian, multilayered hierarchical structures to flatter, more decentralized structures that stress employee empowerment. There's strong and growing consensus that authoritarian, hierarchical organization structures are not well suited to implementing and executing strategies in an era when extensive information and instant communication are the norm and when a big fraction of the organization's most valuable assets consists of intellectual capital and resides in the knowledge and capabilities of its employees. Many companies have therefore begun empowering lower-level managers and employees throughout their organizations, giving them greater discretionary authority to make strategic adjustments in their areas of responsibility and to decide what needs to be done to put new strategic initiatives into place and execute them proficiently.

Maintaining Control in a Decentralized Organization Structure Pushing decision-making authority deep down into the organization structure and empowering employees presents its own organizing challenge: *how to exercise adequate control over the actions of empowered employees so that the business is not put at risk at the same time that the benefits of empowerment are realized.*[19] Maintaining adequate organizational control over empowered employees is generally accomplished by placing limits on the authority that empowered personnel can exercise, holding people accountable for their decisions, instituting compensation incentives that reward people for doing their jobs in a manner to contributes to good company performance, and creating a corporate culture where there's strong peer pressure on individuals to act responsibly.

Capturing Strategic Fits in a Decentralized Structure   Diversified companies striving to capture cross-business strategic fits have to beware of giving business heads full rein to operate independently when cross-business collaboration is essential in order to gain strategic fit benefits. Cross-business strategic fits typically have to be captured either by enforcing close cross-business collaboration or by centralizing performance of functions having strategic fits at the corporate level.[20] For example, if businesses with overlapping process and product technologies have their own independent R&D departments—each pursuing their own priorities, projects, and strategic agendas—it's hard for the corporate parent to prevent duplication of effort, capture either economies of scale or economies of scope, or broaden the company's R&D efforts to embrace new technological paths, product families, end-use applications, and customer groups. Where cross-business R&D fits exist, the best solution is usually to centralize the R&D function and have a coordinated corporate R&D effort that serves both the interests of individual business and the company as a whole. Likewise, centralizing the related activities of separate businesses makes sense when there are opportunities to share a common sales force, use common distribution channels, rely on a common field service organization to handle customer requests for technical assistance or provide maintenance and repair services, use common e-commerce systems and approaches, and so on.

The point here is that efforts to decentralize decision making and give organizational units leeway in conducting operations have to be tempered with the need to maintain adequate control and cross-unit coordination—decentralization doesn't mean delegating authority in ways that allow organization units and individuals to do their own thing. There are numerous instances when decision-making authority must be retained at high levels in the organization and ample cross-unit coordination strictly enforced.

Providing for Internal Cross-Unit Coordination

The classic way to coordinate the activities of organizational units is to position them in the hierarchy so that the most closely related ones report to a single person (a functional department head, a process manager, a geographic area head, a senior executive). Managers higher up in the ranks generally have the clout to coordinate, integrate, and arrange for the cooperation of units under their supervision. In such structures, the chief executive officer, chief operating officer, and business-level managers end up as central points of coordination because of their positions of authority over the whole unit. When a firm is pursuing a related diversification strategy, coordinating the related activities of independent business units often requires the centralizing authority of a single corporate-level officer. Also, diversified companies commonly centralize such staff support functions as public relations, finance and accounting, employee benefits, and information technology at the corporate level both to contain the costs of support activities and to facilitate uniform and coordinated performance of such functions within each business unit.

But, as explained earlier, the functional organization structures employed in most businesses often result in fragmentation. Close cross-unit collaboration is usually needed to build core competencies and competitive capabilities in such strategically important activities as speeding new products to market and providing superior customer service. To combat fragmentation and achieve the desired degree of cross-unit cooperation and collaboration, most companies supplement their functional organization structures. Sometimes this takes the form of creating process departments to bring together the pieces of strategically important activities previously performed in

COMPANY SPOTLIGHT 7.2

Cross-Unit Coordination on Technology at 3M Corporation

At 3M, technology experts in more than 100 laboratories around the world have come to work openly and cooperatively without resorting to turf-protection tactics or not-invented-here mindsets. 3M management has been successful in creating a collegial working environment that results in the scientists calling on one another for assistance and advice and in rapid technology transfer.

Management formed a Technical Council, composed of the heads of the major labs; the council meets monthly and has a three-day annual retreat to discuss ways to improve cross-unit transfer of technology and other issues of common interest. In addition, management created a broader-based Technical Forum, composed of scientists and technical experts chosen as representatives, to facilitate grassroots communication among employees in all the labs.

One of the forum's responsibilities is to organize employees with similar technical interests from all the labs into chapters; chapter members attend regular seminars with experts from outside the company. There's also an annual three-day technology fair at which 3M scientists showcase their latest findings for colleagues and expand their network of acquaintances.

As a result of these collaborative efforts, 3M has developed a portfolio of more than 100 technologies and created the capability to routinely use these technologies in product applications in three different divisions that each serve multiple markets.

Source: Adapted from Sumantra Ghoshal and Christopher A. Bartlett, "Changing the Role of Top Management: Beyond Structure to Process," *Harvard Business Review* 73, no. 1 (January–February 1995), pp. 93–94.

---

separate functional units. And sometimes the coordinating mechanisms involve the use of cross-functional task forces, dual reporting relationships, informal organizational networking, voluntary cooperation, incentive compensation tied to group performance measures, and strong executive-level insistence on teamwork and cross-department cooperation (including removal of recalcitrant managers who stonewall collaborative efforts). At one European-based company, a top executive promptly replaced the managers of several plants who were not fully committed to collaborating closely on eliminating duplication in product development and production efforts among plants in several different countries. Earlier, the executive, noting that negotiations among the managers had stalled on which labs and plants to close, had met with all the managers, asked them to cooperate to find a solution, discussed with them which options were unacceptable, and given them a deadline to find a solution. When the asked-for teamwork wasn't forthcoming, several managers were replaced.

See Company Spotlight 7.2 for how 3M Corporation puts the necessary organizational arrangements into place to create worldwide coordination on technology matters.

Providing for Collaboration with Outside Suppliers and Strategic Allies

Someone or some group must be authorized to collaborate as needed with each major outside constituency involved in strategy execution. Forming alliances and cooperative relationships presents immediate opportunities and opens the door to future possibilities, but nothing valuable is realized until the relationship grows, develops, and blossoms. Unless top management sees that constructive organizational bridge-building with strategic partners occurs and that productive working relationships emerge, the value of alliances is lost and the company's power to execute its strategy is weakened. If close working relationships with suppliers are crucial, then supply chain management must be given formal status on the company's organization chart and a significant position in the pecking order. If distributor/dealer/franchisee relationships are important, someone must be assigned the task of nurturing the relationships with forward channel allies. If working in parallel with providers of complementary products and services contributes to enhanced organizational capability, then cooperative organizational arrangements have to be put in place and managed to good effect.

Building organizational bridges with external allies can be accomplished by appointing "relationship managers" with responsibility for making particular strategic partnerships or alliances generate the intended benefits. Relationship managers have many roles and functions: getting the right people together, promoting good rapport, seeing that plans for specific activities are developed and carried out, helping adjust internal organizational procedures and communication systems, ironing out operating dissimilarities, and nurturing interpersonal cooperation. Multiple cross-organization ties have to be established and kept open to ensure proper communication and coordination.[21] There has to be enough information sharing to make the relationship work and periodic frank discussions of conflicts, trouble spots, and changing situations.[22]

Perspectives on the Organization-Building Effort

All organization designs have their strategy-related strengths and weaknesses. To do a good job of matching structure to strategy, strategy implementers first have to pick a basic design and modify it as needed to fit the company's particular business lineup.

| There is no perfect or ideal organization structure. |

They must then (1) supplement the design with appropriate coordinating mechanisms (cross-functional task forces, special project teams, self-contained work teams, and so on), and (2) institute whatever networking and communication arrangements it takes to support effective execution of the firm's strategy. While companies may not set up "ideal" organizational arrangements to avoid disturbing certain existing reporting relationships or to accommodate other situational idiosyncrasies, they must work toward the goal of building a competitively capable organization.

The ways and means of developing stronger core competencies and organizational capabilities (or creating altogether new ones) have to fit a company's own circumstances. Not only do different companies and executives tackle the capabilities-building challenge in different ways, but the task of building different capabilities requires

| Organizational capabilities emerge from a process of consciously knitting together the efforts of different work groups, departments, and external allies, not from how the boxes on the organization chart are arranged. |

different organizing techniques. Thus, generalizing about how to build capabilities has to be done cautiously. What can be said unequivocally is that building a capable organization entails a process of consciously knitting together the efforts of individuals and groups. Competencies and capabilities emerge from establishing and nurturing cooperative working relationships among people and groups to perform activities in a more customer-satisfying fashion, not from rearranging boxes on an organization chart. Furthermore, organization building is a task in which senior management must be deeply involved. Indeed, effectively managing both internal organization processes and external collaboration to create and develop competitively valuable competencies and capabilities is a top challenge for senior executives in today's companies.

Organizational Structures of the Future

Many of today's companies are winding up the task of remodeling their traditional hierarchical structures once built around functional specialization and centralized authority. Much of the corporate downsizing movement in the late 1980s and early 1990s was aimed at recasting authoritarian, pyramidal organizational structures into flatter, decentralized structures. The change was driven by growing realization that command-and-control hierarchies were proving a liability in businesses where customer preferences were shifting from standardized products to custom orders and special features, product life cycles were growing shorter, custom mass production methods were replacing standardized mass production techniques, customers wanted to be treated as individuals, technological change was ongoing, and market conditions were fluid. Layered management hierarchies with lots of checks and controls that required people to look upward in the organizational structure for answers and approval were failing to deliver responsive customer service and timely adaptations to changing conditions. Likewise, functional silos, task-oriented work, and fragmentation of strategy-critical activities further contributed to an erosion of competitiveness in fluid or volatile business environments.

> Revolutionary changes in how companies are organizing the work effort have been occurring since the early 1990s.

The organizational adjustments and downsizing of companies in 2001–2002 brought further refinements and changes to streamline organizational activities and shake out inefficiencies. The goals have been to make the organization leaner, flatter, and more responsive to change. Many companies are drawing on five tools of organizational design: (1) managers and workers empowered to act on their own judgments, (2) reengineered work processes, (3) self-directed work teams, (4) rapid incorporation of Internet technology applications, and (5) networking with outsiders to improve existing organization capabilities and create new ones. Considerable management attention is being devoted to building a company capable of outcompeting rivals on the basis of superior resource strengths and competitive capabilities—capabilities that are increasingly based on intellectual capital.

The organizations of the future will have several new characteristics:

- Fewer barriers between different vertical ranks, between functions and disciplines, between units in different geographic locations, and between the company and its suppliers, distributors/dealers, strategic allies, and customers.

- A capacity for change and rapid learning.

- Collaborative efforts among people in different functional specialties and geographic locations—essential to create organization competencies and capabilities.

- Extensive use of Internet technology and e-commerce business practices—real-time data and information systems, greater reliance on online systems for transacting business with suppliers and customers, and Internet-based communication and collaboration with suppliers, customers, and strategic partners.

Key Points

The job of strategy implementation and execution is to convert strategic plans into actions and good results. The test of successful strategy execution is whether actual organization performance matches or exceeds the targets spelled out in the strategic plan. Shortfalls in performance signal weak strategy, weak execution, or both.

In deciding how to implement a new or revised strategy, managers have to determine what internal conditions are needed to execute the strategic plan successfully. Then they must create these conditions as rapidly as practical. The process of implementing and executing strategy involves:

1. Building an organization with the competencies, capabilities, and resource strengths to execute strategy successfully.

2. Allocating ample resources to strategy-critical activities.

3. Ensuring that policies and procedures facilitate rather than impede strategy execution.

4. Instituting best practices and pushing for continuous improvement in how value chain activities are performed.

5. Installing information and operating systems that enable company personnel to carry out their strategic roles proficiently.

6. Tying rewards and incentives directly to the achievement of strategic and financial targets and to good strategy execution.

7. Shaping the work environment and corporate culture to fit the strategy.

8. Exerting the internal leadership needed to drive implementation forward and to keep improving on how the strategy is being executed.

The place for managers to start in implementing and executing a new or different strategy is with *a probing assessment of what the organization must do differently and better to carry out the strategy successfully.* They should then consider *precisely how to make the necessary internal changes* as rapidly as possible. Successful strategy implementers have a knack for diagnosing what their organizations need to do to execute the chosen strategy well and figuring out how to get things done—they are masters in promoting results-oriented behaviors on the part of company personnel and following through on making the right things happen.

Like crafting strategy, executing strategy is a job for a company's whole management team, not just a few senior managers. Top-level managers have to rely on the active support and cooperation of middle and lower managers to push strategy changes into functional areas and operating units and to see that the organization actually operates in accordance with the strategy on a daily basis. Middle and lower-level managers not only are responsible for initiating and supervising the execution process in their areas of authority but also are instrumental in getting subordinates to continuously improve on how strategy-critical value chain activities are being performed and in producing the operating results that allow company performance targets to be met. Thus, all managers have to consider what actions to take in their areas to achieve the intended results in executing strategy—they each need *an action agenda.*

Building a capable organization is always a top priority in strategy execution; three types of organization-building actions are paramount:

1. *Staffing the organization*—putting together a strong management team, and recruiting and retaining employees with the needed experience, technical skills, and intellectual capital.

2. *Building core competencies and competitive capabilities* that will enable good strategy execution and updating them as strategy and external conditions change.

3. *Structuring the organization and work effort*—organizing value chain activities and business processes and deciding how much decision-making authority to push down to lower-level managers and frontline employees.

Selecting able people for key positions tends to be one of the earliest strategy implementation steps. No company can hope to perform the activities required for successful strategy execution without attracting capable managers and without employees that give it a suitable knowledge base and portfolio of intellectual capital.

Building core competencies and competitive capabilities is a time-consuming, managerially challenging exercise that involves three stages: (1) developing the *ability* to do something, however imperfectly or inefficiently, by selecting people with the requisite skills and experience, upgrading or expanding individual abilities as needed, and then molding the efforts and work products of individuals into a collaborative group effort; (2) coordinating group efforts to learn how to perform the activity *consistently well and at an acceptable cost*, thereby transforming the ability into a tried-and-true *competence* or *capability*; and (3) continuing to polish and refine the organization's know-how and otherwise sharpen performance such that it becomes *better than rivals* at performing the activity, thus raising the core competence (or capability) to the rank of a *distinctive competence* (or competitively superior capability) and opening an avenue to competitive advantage. Many companies manage to get through stages 1 and 2 in performing a strategy-critical activity but comparatively few achieve sufficient proficiency in performing strategy-critical activities to qualify for the third stage.

Managerial actions to develop core competencies and competitive capabilities generally take one of two forms: either strengthening the company's base of skills, knowledge, and intellect, or coordinating and networking the efforts of the various work groups and departments. Actions of the first sort can be undertaken at all managerial levels, but actions of the second sort are best orchestrated by senior managers who not only appreciate the strategy-executing significance of strong competencies/capabilities but also have the clout to enforce the necessary networking and cooperation among individuals, groups, departments, and external allies.

Strong core competencies and competitive capabilities are an important avenue for securing a competitive edge over rivals in situations where it is relatively easy for rivals to copy smart strategies. Any time rivals can readily duplicate successful strategy features, making it difficult or impossible to outstrategize rivals and beat them in the marketplace with a superior strategy, the chief way to achieve lasting competitive advantage is to outexecute them (beat them by performing certain value chain activities in superior fashion). Building core competencies, resource strengths, and organizational capabilities that rivals can't match is one of the best and most reliable ways to outexecute them.

Structuring the organization and organizing the work effort in a strategy-supportive fashion has five aspects:

1. Deciding which value chain activities to perform internally and which ones to outsource.

2. Making internally performed strategy-critical activities the main building blocks in the organization structure.

3. Deciding how much authority to centralize at the top and how much to delegate to down-the-line managers and employees.

4. Providing for internal cross-unit coordination and collaboration to build and strengthen internal competencies/capabilities.

5. Providing for the necessary collaboration and coordination with suppliers and strategic allies.

The primary organizational building blocks within a business are usually *traditional functional departments* and *process-complete departments*. In enterprises with operations in various countries around the world (or with geographically scattered organizational units within a country), the basic building blocks may also include *geographic organizational units*, each of which has profit/loss responsibility for its assigned geographic area. In vertically integrated firms, the major building blocks are *divisional units performing one or more of the major processing steps along the value chain* (raw materials production, components manufacture, assembly, wholesale distribution, retail store operations); each division in the value chain may operate as a profit center for performance measurement purposes. The typical building blocks of a diversified company are its *individual businesses*, with each business unit usually operating as an independent profit center and with corporate headquarters performing assorted support functions for all the businesses.

Whatever basic structure is chosen, it usually has to be supplemented with interdisciplinary task forces, incentive compensation schemes tied to measures of joint performance, empowerment of cross-functional and/or self-directed work teams to perform and unify fragmented processes and strategy-critical activities, special project teams, relationship managers, and special top management efforts to knit the work of different individuals and groups into valuable competitive capabilities.

In more and more companies, efforts to match structure to strategy involve fewer layers of management authority; managers and workers are empowered to act on their own judgment; work processes are being reengineered to reduce cross-department fragmentation; collaborative partnerships exist with outsiders (suppliers, distributors/dealers, companies with complementary products/services, and even select competitors); and there's increased outsourcing of selected value chain activities, leaner staffing of internal support functions, and rapidly growing use of Internet technology applications to streamline operations and expedite cross-unit communication.

Exercise

As the new owner of a local ice cream store located in a strip mall adjacent to a university campus, you are contemplating how to organize your business—whether to make your ice cream in-house or outsource its production to a nearby ice cream manufacturer whose brand is in most of the local supermarkets, and how much authority to delegate to the two assistant store managers and to employees working the counter and the cash register. You plan to sell 20 flavors of ice cream. (a) What are the pros and cons of contracting with the local company to custom-produce your product line? (b) Since you do not plan to be in the store during all of the hours it is open, what specific decision-making authority would you delegate to the two assistant store managers? (c) To what extent, if any, should store employees—many of whom will be university students working part-time—be empowered to make decisions relating to store operations (opening and closing, keeping the premises clean and attractive, keeping the work area behind the counter stocked with adequate supplies of cups, cones, napkins, and so on)? (d) Should you create a policies and procedures manual for the assistant managers and employees, or should you just give oral instructions and have them learn their duties and responsibilities on the job? (e) How can you maintain control during the times you are not in the store?

CHAPTER 8

Managing Internal Operations
Actions That Facilitate Strategy Execution

Winning companies know how to do their work better.
—Michael Hammer and James Champy

If you talk about change but don't change the reward
and recognition system, nothing changes.
—Paul Allaire, former CEO, Xerox Corporation

If you want people motivated to do a good job, give
them a good job to do.
—Frederick Herzberg

You ought to pay big bonuses for premier performance
. . . Be a top payer, not in the middle or low end of the
pack.
—Lawrence Bossidy, CEO, Honeywell International

In Chapter 7 we emphasized the importance of building organization capabilities and structuring the work effort so as to perform strategy-critical activities in a coordinated and highly competent manner. In this chapter we discuss five additional managerial actions that facilitate the success of a company's strategy execution efforts:

1. Marshaling resources to support the strategy execution effort.
2. Instituting policies and procedures that facilitate strategy execution.
3. Adopting best practices and striving for continuous improvement in how value chain activities are performed.
4. Installing information and operating systems that enable company personnel to better carry out their strategic roles proficiently.
5. Tying rewards and incentives directly to the achievement of strategic and financial targets and to good strategy execution.

Marshaling Resources to Support the Strategy Execution Effort

Early in the process of implementing and executing a new or different strategy managers need to identify the resource requirements of each new strategic initiative and then consider whether the current pattern of resource allocation and the budgets of the various subunits are suitable. Plainly, organizational units must have the budgets and resources for executing their parts of the strategic plan effectively and efficiently. Developing a strategy-driven budget requires top management to determine what funding is needed to execute new strategic initiatives and to strengthen or modify the company's competencies and capabilities. This includes careful screening of requests for more people and more or better facilities and equipment, approving those that hold promise for making a cost-justified contribution to strategy execution, and turning down those that don't. Should internal cash flows prove insufficient to fund the planned strategic initiatives, then the company must be in a financial position to raise additional funds through borrowing or selling additional shares of stock to willing investors.

A company's ability to marshal the resources needed to support new strategic initiatives and steer them to the appropriate organizational units has a major impact on the strategy execution process. Too little funding (stemming either from constrained financial resources or from sluggish management action to adequately increase the budgets of strategy-critical organizational units) slows progress and impedes the efforts of organizational units to execute their pieces of the strategic plan proficiently. Too much funding wastes organizational resources and reduces financial performance. Both outcomes argue for managers to be deeply involved in reviewing budget proposals and directing the proper kinds and amounts of resources to strategy-critical organization units.

A change in strategy nearly always calls for budget reallocations. Units important in the prior strategy but having a lesser role in the new strategy may need downsizing. Units that now have a bigger and more critical strategic role may need more people, new equipment, additional facilities, and above-average increases in their operating

Core Concept

The funding requirements of a new strategy must drive how capital allocations are made and the size of each unit's operating budgets. Underfunding organizational units and activities pivotal to strategic success impedes execution and the drive for operating excellence.

budgets. Strategy implementers need to be active and forceful in shifting resources, downsizing some areas and upsizing others, to not only amply fund activities with a critical role in the new strategy but also avoid inefficiency and achieve profit projections. They have to exercise their power to put enough resources behind new strategic initiatives to make things happen and make the tough decisions to kill projects and activities that are no longer justified.

Visible actions to reallocate operating funds and move people into new organizational units signal a determined commitment to strategic change and frequently are needed to catalyze the implementation process and give it credibility. Microsoft has made a practice of regularly shifting hundreds of programmers to new high-priority programming initiatives within a matter of weeks or even days. At Harris Corporation, where the strategy was to diffuse research ideas into areas that were commercially viable, top management regularly shifted groups of engineers out of government projects and into new commercial venture divisions. Fast-moving developments in many markets are prompting companies to abandon traditional annual or semiannual budgeting and resource allocation cycles in favor of cycles that match the strategy changes a company makes in response to newly developing events. Annual or semiannual budget and resource reallocation reviews do not work when companies make strategic shifts weekly. Bluefly.com, a discount Internet retailer of designer brands, revises its budgets and shifts resources weekly. Bluefly.com's CEO observed, "For us, 11 months is long-term planning."[1]

Just fine-tuning the execution of a company's existing strategy, however, seldom requires big movements of people and money from one area to another. The desired improvements can usually be accomplished through above-average budget increases to organizational units where new initiatives are contemplated and below-average increases (or even small cuts) for the remaining organizational units. The chief exception occurs where a prime ingredient of strategy is to create altogether new capabilities or to generate fresh products and business opportunities within the existing budget. Then, as proposals and business plans worth pursuing bubble up from below, managers have to decide where the needed capital expenditures, operating budgets, and personnel will come from. Companies like 3M, General Electric, and Boeing shift resources and people from area to area as needed to support the launch of new products and new business ventures. They empower "product champions" and small bands of would-be entrepreneurs by giving them financial and technical support and by setting up organizational units and programs to help new ventures blossom more quickly.

Instituting Policies and Procedures That Facilitate Strategy Execution

Core Concept

Well-conceived policies and procedures aid strategy execution; out-of-sync ones are barriers.

Changes in strategy generally call for some changes in work practices and internal operations. Asking people to alter established procedures always upsets the internal order of things. It is normal for pockets of resistance to develop and for people to exhibit some degree of stress and anxiety about how the changes will affect them, especially when the changes may eliminate jobs. Questions are also likely to arise over what activities need to be rigidly prescribed and where there ought to be leeway for independent action.

Figure 8.1   How Prescribed Policies and Procedures Facilitate Strategy Execution

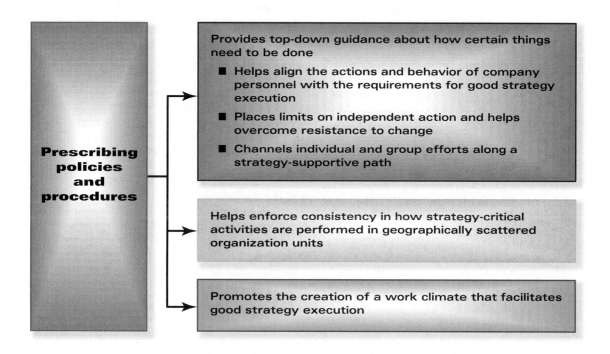

As shown in Figure 8.1, prescribing new policies and operating procedures designed to facilitate strategy execution has merit from several angles:

1. It *provides top-down guidance regarding how certain things now need to be done.* New policies and operating practices can help align actions with strategy throughout the organization, placing limits on independent behavior and channeling individual and group efforts along a path in tune with the new strategy. They also help counteract tendencies for some people to resist change—most people refrain from violating company policy or going against recommended practices and procedures without first gaining clearance or having strong justification.

2. It *helps enforce needed consistency in how particular strategy-critical activities are performed in geographically scattered operating units.* Eliminating significant differences in the operating practices of different plants, sales regions, customer service centers, or the individual outlets in a chain operation is frequently desirable to avoid sending mixed messages to internal personnel and to customers who do business with the company at multiple locations.

3. It *promotes the creation of a work climate that facilitates good strategy execution.* Because dismantling old policies and procedures and instituting new ones invariably alter the internal work climate, strategy implementers can use the policy-changing process as a powerful lever for changing the corporate culture in ways that produce a stronger fit with the new strategy.

Company managers therefore need to be inventive in devising policies and practices that can provide vital support to effective strategy implementation and execution.

Graniterock's "Short Pay" Policy: An Innovative Way to Promote Strategy Execution

In 1987, the owners of Graniterock, a 100-plus-year-old supplier of crushed gravel, sand, concrete, and asphalt in Watsonville, California, set two big, hairy, audacious goals (BHAGs) for the company: total customer satisfaction and a reputation for service that met or exceeded that of Nordstrom, the upscale department store famous for pleasing its customers. To drive the internal efforts to achieve these two objectives, top management instituted "short pay," a policy designed to signal both employees and customers that Graniterock was deadly serious about its two strategic commitments. At the bottom of every Graniterock invoice was the following statement:

> If you are not satisfied for any reason, don't pay us for it. Simply scratch out the line item, write a brief note about the problem, and return a copy of this invoice along with your check for the balance.

Customers did not have to call and complain and were not expected to return the product. They were given complete discretionary power to decide whether and how much to pay based on their satisfaction level.

The policy has worked exceptionally well, providing unmistakable feedback and spurring company managers to correct any problems quickly in order to avoid repeated short payments. Graniterock has enjoyed market share increases, while charging a 6 percent price premium for its commodity products in competition against larger rivals. Its profit margins and overall financial performance have improved. Graniterock won the prestigious Malcolm Baldrige National Quality Award in 1992, about five years after instituting the policy. *Fortune* rated Graniterock as one of the 100 best companies to work for in America in 2001 (ranked 17th) and 2002 (ranked 16th). Company employees receive an average of 43 hours of training annually. Entry-level employees, called job owners, start at $16 an hour and progress to such positions as "accomplished job owner" and "improvement champion" (base pay of $26 an hour). The company has a no-layoff policy, provides employees with 12 massages a year, and sends positive customer comments about employees home for families to read.

Source: Based on information in Jim Collins, "Turning Goals into Results: The Power of Catalytic Mechanisms," *Harvard Business Review* 77, no. 4 (July–August 1999), pp. 72–73; and Robert Levering and Milton Moskowitz, "The 100 Best Companies to Work For," *Fortune,* February 4, 2002, p. 73.

In an attempt to steer "crew members" into stronger quality and service behavior patterns, McDonald's policy manual spells out procedures in detail; for example, "Cooks must turn, never flip, hamburgers. If they haven't been purchased, Big Macs must be discarded in 10 minutes after being cooked and French fries in 7 minutes. Cashiers must make eye contact with and smile at every customer." Hewlett-Packard requires R&D people to make regular visits to customers to learn about their problems, talk about new product applications, and in general keep the company's R&D programs customer-oriented. Mrs. Fields Cookies has a policy of establishing hourly sales quotas for each store outlet; furthermore, it is company policy that cookies not sold within two hours after being baked have to be removed from the case and given to charitable organizations. Company Spotlight 8.1 describes how Graniterock's "short pay" policy spurs employee focus on providing total customer satisfaction and building the company's reputation for superior customer service.

Thus, there is a definite role for new and revised policies and procedures in the strategy implementation process. Wisely constructed policies and procedures help channel actions, behavior, decisions, and practices in directions that promote good strategy execution. When policies and practices aren't strategy-supportive, they become a barrier to the kinds of attitudinal and behavioral changes strategy implementers are trying to promote. Sometimes people hide behind or vigorously defend long-standing policies and operating procedures in an effort to stall implementation or force it along a different route. Anytime a company alters its strategy, managers should review existing policies and operating procedures, proactively revise or discard those that are out of sync, and formulate new ones to facilitate execution of new strategic initiatives.

None of this implies that companies need thick policy manuals to direct the strategy execution process and prescribe exactly how daily operations are to be conducted. Too much policy can erect as many obstacles as wrong policy or be as confusing as no policy. There is wisdom in a middle approach: *Prescribe enough policies to give organization members clear direction in implementing strategy and to place desirable boundaries on their actions; then empower them to act within these boundaries however they think makes sense.* Allowing company personnel to act anywhere between the "white lines" is especially appropriate when individual creativity and initiative are more essential to good strategy execution than standardization and strict conformity. Instituting strategy-facilitating policies can therefore mean more policies, fewer policies, or different policies. It can mean policies that require things to be done a certain way or policies that give employees leeway to do activities the way they think best.

Adopting Best Practices and Striving for Continuous Improvement

Company managers can significantly advance the cause of competent strategy execution by pushing organization units and company personnel to identify and adopt the best practices for performing value chain activities and, further, insisting on continuous improvement in how internal operations are conducted. One of the most widely used and effective tools for gauging how well a company is executing pieces of its strategy entails benchmarking a company's performance of particular activities and business processes against "best-in-industry" and "best-in-world" performers.[2] It can also be useful to look at "best-in-company" performers of an activity if a company has a number of different organizational units performing much the same function at different locations. Identifying, analyzing, and understanding how top companies or individuals perform particular value chain activities and business processes provides useful yardsticks for judging the effectiveness and efficiency of internal operations and setting performance standards for organization units to meet or beat.

> **Core Concept**
>
> Managerial efforts to identify and adopt **best practices** are a powerful tool for promoting operating excellence and better strategy execution.

How the Process of Identifying and Incorporating Best Practices Works

A **best practice** is a technique for performing an activity or business process that at least one company has demonstrated works particularly well. To qualify as a legitimate best practice, the technique must have a proven record in significantly lowering costs, improving quality or performance, shortening time requirements, enhancing safety, or delivering some other highly positive operating outcome. Best practices thus identify a path to operating excellence. For a best practice to be valuable and transferable, it must demonstrate success over time, deliver quantifiable and highly positive results, and be repeatable.

> **Core Concept**
>
> A **best practice** is any practice that at least one company has proved works particularly well.

Benchmarking is the backbone of the process of identifying, studying, and implementing outstanding practices. A company's benchmarking effort looks outward to

Figure 8.2   From Benchmarking and Best-Practice Implementation to Operating Excellence

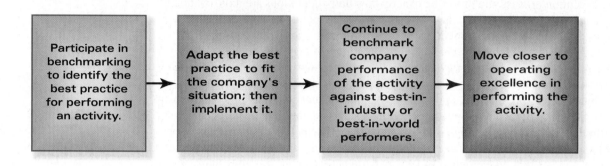

find best practice and then proceeds to develop the data for measuring how well a company's own performance of an activity stacks up against the best-practice standard. Informally, benchmarking involves being humble enough to admit that others have come up with world-class ways to perform particular activities yet wise enough to try to learn how to match, and even surpass, them at it. But, as shown in Figure 8.2, the payoff of benchmarking comes from applying the top-notch approaches pioneered by other companies in the company's own operation and thereby spurring dramatic improvements in the proficiency with which value chain tasks are performed. The goal of benchmarking is to promote the achievement of operating excellence in a variety of strategy-critical and support activities.

However, benchmarking is more complicated than simply identifying which companies are the best performers of an activity and then trying to exactly copy other companies' approaches—especially if these companies are in other industries. Normally, the outstanding practices of other organizations have to be adapted to fit the specific circumstances of a company's own business and operating requirements. Since most companies believe "our work is different" or "we are unique", the telling part of any best-practice initiative is how well the company puts its own version of the best practice into place and makes it work. Indeed, a best practice remains little more than an interesting success story unless company personnel buy into the task of translating what can be learned from other companies into real action and results. The agents of change must be frontline employees who are convinced of the need to abandon the old ways of doing things and switch to a best practice mindset. The more that organizational units utilize best practices in performing their work, the closer a company moves toward performing its value chain activities as effectively and efficiently as possible. This is what operational excellence is all about.

Legions of companies across the world now engage in benchmarking to improve their strategy execution efforts and, ideally, gain a strategic, operational, and financial advantage over rivals. A survey of over 4,000 managers in 15 countries indicated that over 85 percent were using benchmarking to measure the efficiency and effectiveness of their internal activities.[3] Since 1990, the number of companies instituting best-practice programs as an integral part of their efforts to improve strategy execution has grown significantly. Scores of trade associations and special interest organizations have undertaken efforts to collect best-practice data relevant to a particular industry or business function and make their databases available online to members. Benchmarking and best-practice implementation have clearly emerged as legitimate and valuable managerial tools for promoting operational excellence.

TQM and Six Sigma Quality Programs: Tools for Promoting Operational Excellence

Best-practice implementation has stimulated greater management awareness of the importance of business process reengineering, total quality management (TQM) programs, Six Sigma quality control techniques, and other continuous improvement methods. Indeed, quality improvement processes of one kind or another have become globally pervasive management tools for implementing strategies keyed to defect-free manufacture, superior product quality, superior customer service, and total customer satisfaction. The following paragraphs describe two specific types of programs and then discuss the difference between process reengineering and continuous improvement.

Total Quality Management Programs *Total quality management (TQM) is a philosophy of managing a set of business practices that emphasizes continuous improvement in all phases of operations, 100 percent accuracy in performing tasks, involvement and empowerment of employees at all levels, team-based work design, benchmarking, and total customer satisfaction.*[4] While TQM concentrates on the production of quality goods and fully satisfying customer expectations, it achieves its biggest successes when it is also extended to employee efforts in *all departments*—human resources, billing, R&D, engineering, accounting and records, and information systems—that may lack pressing,

> **Core Concept**
> TQM entails creating a total quality culture bent on continuously improving the performance of every task and value chain activity.

customer-driven incentives to improve. It involves re-forming the corporate culture and shifting to a total quality/continuous improvement business philosophy that permeates every facet of the organization.[5] TQM aims at instilling enthusiasm and commitment to doing things right from top to bottom of the organization. It entails a restless search for continuing improvement, the little steps forward each day that the Japanese call *kaizen*. TQM is thus a race without a finish. The managerial objective is to kindle a burning desire in people to use their ingenuity and initiative to progressively improve on how tasks and value chain activities are performed. TQM doctrine preaches that there's no such thing as "good enough" and that everyone has a responsibility to participate in continuous improvement.

Six Sigma Quality Control *Six sigma quality control consists of a disciplined, statistics-based system aimed at producing not more than 3.4 defects per million iterations for any business process—from manufacturing to customer transactions.* The six sigma process of define, measure, analyze, improve, and control (DMAIC) is an improvement system for existing processes falling below specification and needing incremental improvement. The six sigma process of define, measure, analyze, design, and verify (DMADV) is an improvement system used to develop new processes or products at six sigma quality levels. Both six sigma processes are executed by personnel who have earned six sigma "green belts" and six sigma "black belts," and are overseen by personnel who have completed six sigma "master black belt" training. According to the Six Sigma Academy, personnel with black belts can save companies approximately $230,000 per project and can complete four to six projects a year.[6] General Electric (GE), one of the most successful companies implementing six sigma training and pursuing six sigma perfection, estimated benefits on the order of $10 billion during the first five years of implementation. GE first began six sigma in 1995 after Motorola and Allied Signal blazed the six sigma trail. Since the mid-1990s, thousands of companies around the world have discovered the far reaching benefits of six sigma. Consultants proficient in six sigma techniques have developed proprietary methodologies for implementing six sigma quality for clients, using various change management tools and applications.

The Difference between Process Reengineering and Continuous Improvement Programs   Business process reengineering and continuous improvement efforts like TQM and six sigma quality programs both aim at improved efficiency and reduced costs, better product quality, and greater customer satisfaction. The essential difference between business process reengineering and continuous improvement programs is that reengineering aims at *quantum gains* on the order of 30 to 50 percent or more whereas total quality programs stress *incremental progress*, striving for inch-by-inch gains again and again in a never-ending stream. The two approaches to improved performance of value chain activities and operating excellence are not mutually exclusive; it makes sense to use them in tandem. Reengineering can be used first to produce a good basic design that yields dramatic improvements in performing a business process fairly quickly. Total quality programs can then be used as a follow-on to reengineering and/or best-practice implementation, delivering gradual improvements by fine-tuning and honing how particular activities are performed over time. Such a two-pronged approach to implementing operational excellence is like a marathon race in which you run the first four laps as fast as you can, then gradually pick up speed the remainder of the way.

> Business process reengineering aims at one-time quantum improvement; TQM and six sigma aim at ongoing incremental improvements.

Capturing the Benefits of Best-Practice and Continuous Improvement Programs

Research indicates that some companies benefit from reengineering and continuous improvement programs (like TQM and six sigma) and some do not.[7] Usually, the biggest beneficiaries are companies that view such programs not as ends in themselves but as tools for implementing and executing company strategy more effectively. The skimpiest payoffs from best practices, TQM, six sigma, and reengineering occur when company managers seize them as something worth trying—novel ideas that could improve things. In most such instances, they result in strategy-blind efforts to simply manage better. There's an important lesson here. Best practices, TQM, six sigma quality, and reengineering all need to be seen and used as part of a bigger-picture effort to execute strategy proficiently. Only strategy can point to which value chain activities matter and what performance targets make the most sense. Absent a strategic framework, managers lack the context in which to fix things that really matter to business-unit performance and competitive success.

To get the most from programs for facilitating better strategy execution, managers have to start with a clear fix on the indicators of successful strategy execution—what specific outcomes really matter? Examples of such performance indicators include a six sigma defect rate (fewer than 3.4 defects per million), on-time delivery percentages, low overall costs relative to rivals, data indicating high percentages of pleased customers and few customer complaints, shorter cycle times, and a higher percentage of revenues coming from recently introduced products. Benchmarking best-in-industry and best-in-world performance of most or all value chain activities provides a realistic basis for setting internal performance milestones and longer-range targets.

Then comes the managerial task of building a total quality culture and instilling the necessary commitment to achieving the targets and performance measures that the strategy requires. Managers can take the following action steps to realize full value from TQM or six sigma initiatives:[8]

- Visible, unequivocal, and unyielding commitment to total quality and continuous improvement, including a quality vision and specific, measurable objectives for boosting quality and making continuous improvement.

- Nudging people toward TQM-supportive behaviors by:
  - Screening job applicants rigorously and hiring only those with attitudes and aptitudes right for quality-based performance.
  - Providing quality training for most employees.
  - Using teams and team-building exercises to reinforce and nurture individual effort (expansion of a TQM culture is facilitated when teams become more cross-functional, multitask, and increasingly self-managed).
  - Recognizing and rewarding individual and team efforts regularly and systematically.
  - Stressing prevention (doing it right the first time), not inspection (instituting ways to correct mistakes).

- Empowering employees so that authority for delivering great service or improving products is in the hands of the doers rather than the overseers.

- Using online systems to provide all relevant parties with the latest best practices and actual experiences with them, thereby speeding the diffusion and adoption of best practices throughout the organization and also allowing them to exchange data and opinions about how to upgrade the prevailing best practices.

- Preaching that performance can, and must, be improved because competitors are not resting on past laurels and customers are always looking for something better.

If the targeted performance measures are appropriate to the strategy and if all organizational members (top executives, middle managers, professional staff, and line employees) buy into the process of continuous improvement, then the work climate becomes decidedly more conducive to proficient strategy execution.

When used effectively, TQM, six sigma and other similar continuous improvement techniques can greatly enhance a company's product design, cycle time, production cost, product quality, service, customer satisfaction, and other operating capabilities—and it can even deliver competitive advantage.[9] Not only do ongoing incremental improvements add up over time and strengthen organizational capabilities but continuous improvement programs have hard-to-imitate aspects. While it is relatively easy for rivals to undertake benchmarking, process improvement, and quality training, it is much more difficult and time-consuming for them to instill a total quality culture (as occurs when TQM or six sigma techniques are religiously employed) and generate lasting management commitment to operational excellence throughout their organizations. Successfully implementing TQM or six sigma initiatives requires a substantial investment of management time and effort; some managers and employees resist such techniques, viewing them as overly ideological, burdensome, or faddish. Both TQM and six sigma are expensive in terms of training and meetings. TQM takes a fairly long time to show significant results—very little benefit emerges within the first six months. The long-term payoff of TQM, if it comes, depends heavily on management's success in implanting a culture within which TQM philosophies and practices can thrive.

Installing Information and Operating Systems

Company strategies can't be implemented or executed well without a number of internal systems for business operations. Southwest, American, Northwest, Delta, and other major airlines cannot hope to provide passenger-pleasing service without a user-friendly online reservation system, an accurate and expeditious baggage handling system, and a strict aircraft maintenance program that minimizes equipment failures requiring at-the-gate service and delaying plane departures. Federal Express (FedEx) has internal communication systems that allow it to coordinate its nearly 60,000 vehicles in handling an average of 5.2 million packages per day. Its leading-edge flight operations systems allow a single controller to direct as many as 200 of FedEx's 650-plus aircraft simultaneously, overriding their flight plans should weather or other special emergencies arise. In addition, FedEx has created a series of e-business tools for customers that allow them to ship and track packages online (either at FedEx's website or on their own company intranets or websites), create address books, review shipping history, generate custom reports, simplify customer billing, reduce internal warehousing and inventory management costs, purchase goods and services from suppliers, and respond quickly to changing customer demands. All of FedEx's systems support the company's strategy of providing businesses and individuals with a broad array of package delivery services (from premium next-day to economical five-day deliveries) and boosting its competitiveness against United Parcel Service, Airborne Express, and the U.S. Postal Service.

Otis Elevator has a 24-hour centralized communications center called OtisLine to coordinate its maintenance efforts in North America.[10] Trained operators take all trouble calls, input critical information on a computer screen, and dispatch people directly via a beeper system to the local trouble spot. Also, much of the information needed for repairs is provided directly from faulty elevators through internally installed microcomputer monitors, helping keep the outage time on Otis elevators and escalators to less than two and a half hours. From the trouble-call inputs, problem patterns across North America are identified and the information communicated to design and manufacturing personnel, allowing them to quickly alter design specifications or manufacturing procedures when needed to correct recurring problems.

Wal-Mart is generally considered to have the most sophisticated retailing systems of any company in the world. For example, Wal-Mart's computers transmit daily sales data to Wrangler, a supplier of blue jeans; Wrangler then uses a model that interprets the data, and software applications that act on these interpretations, in order to ship specific quantities of specific sizes and colors to specific stores from specific warehouses—the system lowers logistics and inventory costs and leads to fewer stockouts.[11] Domino's Pizza has computerized systems at each outlet to facilitate ordering, inventory, payroll, cash flow, and work control functions, thereby freeing managers to spend more time on supervision, customer service, and business development activities.[12] Most telephone companies, electric utilities, and TV broadcasting systems have online monitoring systems to spot transmission problems within seconds and increase the reliability of their services. At eBay, there are systems for real-time monitoring of new listings, bidding activity, website traffic, and page views. Many companies have cataloged best-practice information on their company intranets to promote faster transfer and implementation organizationwide.[13]

Well-conceived state-of-the-art operating systems not only enable better strategy execution but also strengthen organizational capabilities—perhaps enough to provide a competitive edge over rivals. For example, a company with a differentiation strategy based on superior quality has added capability if it has systems for training personnel in quality techniques, tracking product quality at each production step, and ensuring that all goods shipped meet quality standards. A company striving to be a low-cost provider is competitively stronger if it has a benchmarking system that identifies opportunities to implement best practices and drive costs out of the business. Fast-growing companies get an important assist from having capabilities in place to recruit and train new employees in large

> **Core Concept**
>
> State-of-the-art support systems can be a basis for competitive advantage if they give a firm capabilities that rivals can't match.

numbers and from investing in infrastructure that gives them the capability to handle rapid growth as it occurs. It is nearly always better to put infrastructure and support systems in place before they are actually needed than to have to scramble to catch up to customer demand. In businesses such as public accounting and management consulting, where large numbers of professional staff need cutting-edge technical know-how, companies need well-functioning systems for training and retraining employees regularly and keeping them supplied with up-to-date information. Companies that rely on empowered customer service employees to act promptly and creatively in pleasing customers need state-of-the-art information systems that put essential data in front of employees with a few keystrokes, allowing them to handle inquiries and transactions expeditiously.

Instituting Adequate Information Systems, Performance Tracking, and Controls

Accurate and timely information about daily operations is essential if managers are to gauge how well the strategy execution process is proceeding. Information systems need to cover five broad areas: (1) customer data, (2) operations data, (3) employee data, (4) supplier/partner/collaborative ally data, and (5) financial performance data. All key strategic performance indicators have to be tracked and reported as often as practical. Monthly profit-and-loss statements and monthly statistical summaries, long the norm, are fast being replaced by daily statistical updates and even up-to-the-minute performance monitoring that online technology makes possible. Many retail companies have automated online systems that generate daily sales reports for each store and maintain up-to-the-minute inventory and sales records on each item. Manufacturing plants typically generate daily production reports and track labor productivity on every shift. Many retailers and manufacturers have online data systems connecting them with their suppliers that monitor the status of inventories, track shipments and deliveries, and measure defect rates.

Real-time information systems permit company managers to stay on top of implementation initiatives and daily operations, and to intervene if things seem to be drifting off course. Tracking key performance indicators, gathering information from operating personnel, quickly identifying and diagnosing problems, and taking corrective actions are all integral pieces of the process of managing strategy implementation and execution and exercising adequate organization control. Telephone companies have elaborate information systems to measure signal quality, connection times, interrupts, wrong connections, billing errors, and other measures of reliability that affect customer service and satisfaction. To track and manage the quality of passenger service, airlines have information systems to monitor gate delays, on-time departures and arrivals, baggage handling times, lost baggage complaints, stockouts on meals and drinks, overbookings, and maintenance delays and failures. Virtually all companies now provide customer-contact personnel with computer access to customer databases so that they can respond effectively to customer inquiries and deliver personalized customer service.

Statistical information gives managers a feel for the numbers; briefings and meetings provide a feel for the latest developments and emerging issues; and personal contacts add a feel for the people dimension. All are good barometers. Managers have to identify problem areas and deviations from plan before they can take actions to get the organization back on course, either by improving the approaches to strategy execution or fine-tuning the strategy.

> **Core Concept**
>
> Having good information systems and operating data are integral to the managerial task of executing strategy successfully and achieving greater operating excellence.

Exercising Adequate Controls over Empowered Employees

Another important aspect of effectively managing and controlling the strategy execution process is monitoring the performance of empowered workers to see that they are acting within the specified limits.[14] Leaving empowered employees to their own devices in meeting performance standards without appropriate check and balances can expose an organization to excessive risk.[15] Instances abound where employees' decisions or behavior have gone awry, sometimes costing a company huge sums or producing lawsuits aside from just generating embarrassing publicity.

Managers can't devote big chunks of their time to making sure that the decisions and behavior of empowered employees are between the white lines—this would defeat the major purpose of empowerment and, in effect, lead to the reinstatement of a managerial bureaucracy engaged in constant over-the-shoulders supervision. Yet management has a clear responsibility to exercise sufficient control over empowered employees to protect the company against out-of-bounds behavior and unwelcome surprises. Management scrutiny of daily and weekly operating statistics is one of the important ways to monitor the results that flow from the actions of empowered subordinates—if the operating results flowing from the actions of empowered employees look good, then it is reasonable to assume that empowerment is working.

One of the main purposes of tracking daily operating performance is to relieve managers of the burden of constant over-the-shoulders supervision and give them time for other issues. But managerial control is only part of the answer. Another valuable lever of control in companies that rely on empowered employees, especially in those that use self-managed work groups or other such teams, is peer-based control.[16] The big majority of team members feel responsible for the success of the whole team and tend to be relatively intolerant of any team member's behavior that weakens team performance or puts team accomplishments at risk. Because peer evaluation is such a powerful control device, companies organized into teams can remove some layers of the management hierarchy. This is especially true when a company has the information systems capability to closely monitor team performance.

Tying Rewards and Incentives Directly to Good Strategy Execution

It is important for both organization subunits and individuals to be enthusiastically committed to executing strategy and achieving performance targets. Company managers typically use an assortment of motivational techniques and rewards to enlist organizationwide commitment to executing the strategic plan. A manager has to do more than just talk to everyone about how important new strategic practices and performance targets are to the organization's well-being. No matter how inspiring, talk seldom commands people's best efforts for long. *To get employees' sustained, energetic commitment, management has to be resourceful in designing and using motivational incentives—both monetary and nonmonetary.* The more a manager understands what motivates subordinates and the

> **Core Concept**
>
> A properly designed reward structure is management's most powerful tool for mobilizing organizational commitment to successful strategy execution.

more he or she relies on motivational incentives as a tool for achieving the targeted strategic and financial results, the greater will be employees' commitment to good day-in, day-out execution of the company's strategic plan.

Strategy-Facilitating Motivational Practices

Financial incentives generally head the list of motivating tools for trying to gain wholehearted employee commitment to good strategy execution and operating excellence. Monetary rewards generally include some combination of base pay increases, performance bonuses, profit sharing plans, stock options, company contributions to employee 401(k) or retirement plans, and piecework incentives (in the case of production workers). But successful companies and managers normally make extensive use of such nonmonetary carrot-and-stick incentives as frequent words of praise (or constructive criticism), special recognition at company gatherings or in the company newsletter, more (or less) job security, stimulating assignments, opportunities to transfer to attractive locations, increased (or decreased) autonomy, and rapid promotion (or the risk of being sidelined in a routine or dead-end job). In addition, companies use a

> **Core Concept**
>
> One of management's biggest strategy-executing challenges is to employ motivational techniques that build wholehearted commitment to operating excellence and winning attitudes among employees.

host of other motivational approaches to spur stronger employee commitment to the strategy execution process; the following are some of the most important:[17]

- *Providing attractive perks and fringe benefits*—The various options here include full coverage of health insurance premiums; full tuition reimbursement for work on college degrees; paid vacation time of three or four weeks; on-site child care at major facilities; on-site gym facilities and massage therapists; getaway opportunities at company-owned recreational facilities (beach houses, ranches, resort condos); personal concierge services; subsidized cafeterias and free lunches; casual dress every day; personal travel services; paid sabbaticals; maternity leaves; paid leaves to care for ill family members; telecommuting; compressed workweeks (four 10-hour days instead of five 8-hour days); reduced summer hours; college scholarships for children; on-the-spot bonuses for exceptional performance; and relocation services.

- *Relying on promotion from within whenever possible*—This practice helps bind workers to their employer and employers to their workers; plus, it is an incentive for good performance. Promotion from within also helps ensure that people in positions of responsibility actually know something about the business, technology, and operations they are managing.

- *Making sure that the ideas and suggestions of employees are valued and respected*—Research indicates that the moves of many companies to push decision making down the line and empower employees increases employee motivation and satisfaction, as well as boosting their productivity. The use of self-managed teams has much the same effect.

- *Creating a work atmosphere where there is genuine sincerity, caring, and mutual respect among workers and between management and employees*—A "family" work environment where people are on a first-name basis and there is strong camaraderie promotes teamwork and cross-unit collaboration.

- *Stating the strategic vision in inspirational terms that make employees feel they are a part of doing something very worthwhile in a larger social sense*—There's strong motivating power associated with giving people a chance to be part of something exciting and personally satisfying. Jobs with noble purpose tend to turn employees on. At Medtronic, Merck, and most other pharmaceutical companies, it is the notion of helping sick people get well and restoring patients to full life. At Whole Foods Market (a natural foods grocery chain), it is helping customers discover good eating habits and thus improving human health and nutrition.

- *Sharing information with employees about financial performance, strategy, operational measures, market conditions, and competitors' actions*—Broad disclosure and prompt communication send the message that managers trust their workers. Keeping employees in the dark denies them information useful to performing their job, prevents them from being "students of the business," and usually turns them off.

- *Having knockout facilities*—An impressive corporate facility for employees to work in usually has decidedly positive effects on morale and productivity.

- *Being flexible in how the company approaches people management (motivation, compensation, recognition, recruitment) in multinational, multicultural environments*—Managers and employees in countries whose customs, habits, values, and business practices vary from those at the home office often become frustrated with insistence on consistent people-management practices worldwide. But the one area where consistency is essential is conveying the message that the organization values people of all races and cultural backgrounds and that discrimination of any sort will not be tolerated.

For specific examples of the motivational tactics employed by several prominent companies, see Company Spotlight 8.2.

Striking the Right Balance between Rewards and Punishment　While most approaches to motivation, compensation, and people management accentuate the positive, companies also embellish positive rewards with the risk of punishment. At General Electric, McKinsey & Company, several global public accounting firms, and other companies that look for and expect top-notch individual performance, there's an "up-or-out" policy—managers and professionals whose performance is not good enough to warrant promotion are first denied bonuses and stock options and eventually weeded out. A number of companies deliberately give employees heavy workloads and tight deadlines—personnel are pushed hard to achieve "stretch" objectives and expected to put in long hours (nights and weekends if need be). At most companies, senior executives and key personnel in underperforming units are under the gun to boost performance to acceptable levels and keep it there or risk being replaced.

As a general rule, it is unwise to take off the pressure for good individual and group performance or play down the stress, anxiety, and adverse consequences of shortfalls in performance. There is no evidence that a no-pressure/no-adverse-consequences work environment leads to superior strategy execution or operating excellence. As the CEO of a major bank put it, "There's a deliberate policy here to create a level of anxiety. Winners usually play like they're one touchdown behind."[18] *High-performing organizations nearly always have a cadre of ambitious people who relish the opportunity to climb the ladder of success, love a challenge, thrive in a performance-oriented environment, and find some competition and pressure useful to satisfy their own drives for personal recognition, accomplishment, and self-satisfaction.*

However, if an organization's motivational approaches and reward structure induce too much stress, internal competitiveness, job insecurity, and unpleasant consequences, the impact on workforce morale and strategy execution can be counterproductive. Evidence shows that managerial initiatives to improve strategy execution should incorporate more positive than negative motivational elements because when cooperation is positively enlisted and rewarded, rather than strong-armed by orders and threats (implicit or explicit), people tend to respond with more enthusiasm, dedication, creativity, and initiative. Something of a middle ground is generally optimal—not only handing out decidedly positive rewards for meeting or beating performance targets but also imposing sufficiently negative consequences (if only withholding rewards) when actual performance falls short of the target. But the negative consequences of underachievement should never be so severe or demoralizing as to impede a renewed and determined effort to overcome existing obstacles and hit the targets in upcoming periods.

Linking the Reward System to Strategically Relevant Performance Outcomes

The most dependable way to keep people focused on strategy execution and the achievement of performance targets is to *generously* reward and recognize individuals and groups who meet or beat performance targets and deny rewards and recognition to those who don't. *The use of incentives and rewards is the single most powerful tool management has to win strong employee commitment to diligent, competent strategy execution and operating excellence.* Decisions on salary increases, incentive compensation, promotions, key assignments, and the ways and means of awarding praise and recognition are potent attention-getting, commitment-generating devices. Such decisions seldom escape the closest employee scrutiny, saying more about what is expected and who is considered to be doing a good job than any other factor. Hence, when achievement of the targeted strategic and financial outcomes become *the dominating basis* for designing incentives, evaluating individual and group efforts, and handing out rewards, company personnel quickly grasp that it is in their own self-interest to do their best in executing the strategy competently and achieving key performance targets.[19] Indeed, it is usually through the company's system of incentives and rewards that workforce members emotionally ratify their commitment to the company's strategy execution effort.

> **Core Concept**
>
> A properly designed reward system aligns the well-being of organization members with their contributions to competent strategy execution and the achievement of performance targets.

Strategy-driven performance targets need to be established for every organization unit, every manager, every team or work group, and perhaps every employee—targets that measure whether strategy execution is progressing satisfactorily. If the company's strategy is to be a low-cost provider, the incentive system must reward actions and achievements that result in lower costs. If the company has a differentiation strategy predicated on superior quality and service, the incentive system must reward such outcomes as six sigma defect rates, infrequent need for product repair, low numbers of customer complaints, and speedy order processing and delivery. If a company's growth is predicated on a strategy of new product innovation, incentives should be tied to factors such as the percentages of revenues and profits coming from newly introduced products.

Company Spotlight 8.3 provides two vivid examples of how companies have designed incentives linked directly to outcomes reflecting good strategy execution.

The Importance of Basing Incentives on Achieving Results, Not on Performing Assigned Functions To create a strategy-supportive system of rewards and incentives, a company must emphasize rewarding people for accomplishing results, not for just dutifully performing assigned functions. Focusing jobholders' attention and energy on what to *achieve* as opposed to what to *do* makes the work environment results-oriented. It is flawed management to tie incentives and rewards to satisfactory performance of duties and activities in hopes that the by-products will be the desired business outcomes and company achievements.[20] In any job, performing assigned tasks is not equivalent to achieving intended outcomes. Diligently attending to assigned duties does not, by itself, guarantee results. (As any student knows, just because an instructor teaches and students go to class doesn't mean students are learning. Teaching and going to class are activities, and learning is a result. The enterprise of education would no doubt take on a different character if teachers were rewarded for the result of student learning rather than the activity of teaching.)

> It is folly to reward one outcome in hopes of getting another outcome.

twice the average incomes of sales employees at competing stores. Nordstrom's rules for employees are simple: "Rule #1: Use your good judgment in all situations. There will be no additional rules." Nordstrom is widely regarded for its superior in-house customer service experience.

■ Cisco Systems offers on-the-spot bonuses of up to $2,000 for exceptional performance; Kimberly-Clark spends about $6 million annually on events to celebrate employee successes; and FedEx gives out awards to employees whose job performance is above and beyond expectations (in 2001 the company spent over $13 million on such awards).

■ Lincoln Electric, a company deservedly famous for its piecework pay scheme and incentive bonus plan, rewards individual productivity by paying workers for each nondefective piece produced. Workers have to correct quality problems on their own time—defects in products used by customers can be traced back to the worker who caused them. Lincoln's piecework plan motivates workers to pay attention to both quality and volume produced. In addition, the company sets aside a substantial portion of its profits above a specified base for worker bonuses. To determine bonus size, Lincoln Electric rates each worker on four equally important performance measures: dependability, quality, output, and ideas and cooperation. The higher a worker's

merit rating, the higher the incentive bonus earned; the highest rated workers in good profit years receive bonuses of as much as 110 percent of their piecework compensation.

■ Monsanto, FedEx, AT&T, Whole Foods Markets, Advanced Micro Devices, and W. L. Gore & Associates (the maker of Gore-Tex) have tapped into the motivational power of self-managed teams, recognizing that team members put considerable peer pressure on coworkers to pull their weight and help achieve team goals and expectations. At W. L. Gore (a regular member on annual listings of the 100 best companies to work for), each team member's compensation is based on other team members' rankings of his or her contribution to the enterprise.

■ GE Medical Systems has a program called Quick Thanks!, in which an employee can nominate any colleague to receive a $25 gift certificate in appreciation of a job well done. Employees often hand out the award personally to deserving coworkers. In one 12-month period, over 10,000 Quick Thanks! awards were presented.

Sources: Jeffrey Pfeffer and John F. Veiga, "Putting People First for Organizational Success," *Academy of Management Executive* 13, no. 2 (May 1999), pp. 40–42; *Fortune*'s lists of the 100 best companies to work for in America—see the January 12, 1998; January 10, 2000, and February 4, 2002, issues; Jeffrey Pfeffer, "Producing Sustainable Competitive Advantage through the Effective Management of People," *Academy of Management Executive* 9, no. 1 (February 1995), pp. 59–60; and Steven Kerr, "Risky Business: The New Pay Game," *Fortune*, July 22, 1996, p. 95.

Incentive compensation for top executives is typically tied to company profitability (earnings growth, return on equity investment, return on total assets, economic value added); the company's stock price performance; and perhaps such measures as market share, product quality, or customer satisfaction. However, incentives for department heads, teams, and individual workers may be tied to performance outcomes more closely related to their strategic area of responsibility. In manufacturing, incentive compensation may be tied to unit manufacturing costs, on-time production and shipping, defect rates, the number and extent of work stoppages due to labor disagreements and equipment breakdowns, and so on. In sales and marketing, there may be incentives for achieving dollar sales or unit volume targets, market share, sales penetration of each target customer group, the fate of newly introduced products, the frequency of customer complaints, the number of new accounts acquired, and customer satisfaction. Which performance measures to base incentive compensation on depends on the situation—the priority placed on various financial and strategic objectives, the requirements for strategic and competitive success, and what specific results are needed in different facets of the business to keep strategy execution on track.

> **Core Concept**
>
> The role of the reward system is to align the well-being of organization members with realizing the company's vision, so that organization members benefit by helping the company execute its strategy competently and fully satisfy customers.

Guidelines for Designing Incentive Compensation Systems

The concepts and company experiences discussed above yield the following prescriptive

COMPANY SPOTLIGHT 8.3

COMPANY SPOTLIGHT 8.3

Nucor and Bank One: Two Companies That Tie Incentives Directly to Strategy Execution

The strategy at Nucor Corporation, now the biggest steel producer in the United States, is to be *the* low-cost producer of steel products. Because labor costs are a significant fraction of total cost in the steel business, successful implementation of Nucor's low-cost leadership strategy entails achieving lower labor costs per ton of steel than competitors' costs. Nucor management uses an incentive system to promote high worker productivity and drive labor costs per ton below rivals'. Each plant's workforce is organized into production teams (each assigned to perform particular functions), and weekly production targets are established for each team. Base pay scales are set at levels comparable to wages for similar manufacturing jobs in the local areas where Nucor has plants, but workers can earn a 1 percent bonus for each 1 percent that their output exceeds target levels. If a production team exceeds its weekly production target by 10 percent, team members receive a 10 percent bonus in their next paycheck; if a team exceeds its quota by 20 percent, team members earn a 20 percent bonus. Bonuses, paid every two weeks, are based on the prior two weeks' actual production levels measured against the targets.

Nucor's piece-rate incentive plan has resulted in labor productivity levels 10 to 20 percent above the average of the unionized workforces of large, integrated steel producers like U.S. Steel and Bethlehem Steel, given Nucor a cost advantage over most rivals, and made Nucor workers among the best-paid in the U.S. steel industry.

At Bank One (one of the 10 largest U.S. banks and also one of the most profitable based on return on assets), operating in a manner that produces consistently high levels of customer satisfaction makes a big competitive difference in how well the company fares against rivals; customer satisfaction ranks high on Bank One's list of strategic priorities. To enhance employee commitment to the task of pleasing customers, Bank One ties the pay scales in each branch office to that branch's customer satisfaction rating—the higher the branch's ratings, the higher that branch's pay scales. By shifting from a theme of equal pay for equal work to one of equal pay for equal performance, Bank One has focused the attention of branch employees on the task of pleasing, even delighting, their customers.

---

guidelines for creating an incentive compensation system to help drive successful strategy execution:

1. *The performance payoff must be a major, not minor, piece of the total compensation package.* Payoffs must be at least 10 to 12 percent of base salary to have much impact. Incentives that amount to 20 percent or more of total compensation are big attention-getters, likely to really drive individual or team effort; incentives amounting to less than 5 percent of total compensation have comparatively weak motivational impact. Moreover, the payoff for high-performing individuals and teams must be meaningfully greater than the payoff for average performers, and the payoff for average performers meaningfully bigger than for below-average performers.

2. *The incentive plan should extend to all managers and all workers, not just top management.* It is a gross miscalculation to expect that lower-level managers and employees will work their hardest to hit performance targets just so a few senior executives can get lucrative rewards.

3. *The reward system must be administered with scrupulous care and fairness.* If performance standards are set unrealistically high or if individual/group performance evaluations are not accurate and well documented, dissatisfaction with the system will overcome any positive benefits.

4. *The incentives should be based only on achieving performance targets spelled out in the strategic plan.* Incentives should not be linked to outcomes that get thrown in because they are thought to be nice. Performance evaluation based on factors not

tightly related to good strategy execution signal that either the strategic plan is incomplete (because important performance targets were left out) or management's real agenda is something other than the stated strategic and financial objectives.

5. *The performance targets each individual is expected to achieve should involve outcomes that the individual can personally affect.* The role of incentives is to enhance individual commitment and channel behavior in beneficial directions. This role is not well served when the performance measures by which an individual is judged are outside his or her arena of influence.

6. *Keep the time between the performance review and payment of the reward short.* A lengthy interval between review and payment breeds discontent and works against reinforcing cause and effect. Companies like Nucor and Continental Airlines have discovered that weekly or monthly payments for good performance work much better than annual payments. Nucor pays weekly bonuses based on prior-week production levels; Continental awards employees a monthly bonus for each month that on-time flight performance meets or beats a specified percentage companywide.

7. *Make liberal use of nonmonetary rewards; don't rely solely on monetary rewards.* When used properly, money is a great motivator, but there are also potent advantages to be gained from praise, special recognition, handing out plum assignments, and so on.

8. *Absolutely avoid skirting the system to find ways to reward effort rather than results.* Whenever actual performance falls short of targeted performance, there's merit in determining whether the causes are attributable to subpar individual/group performance or to circumstances beyond the control of those responsible. An argument can be made that exceptions should be made in giving rewards to people who've tried hard, gone the extra mile, yet still come up short because of circumstances beyond their control. The problem with making exceptions for unknowable, uncontrollable, or unforeseeable circumstances is that once good excuses start to creep into justifying rewards for subpar results, the door is open for all kinds of reasons why actual performance failed to match targeted performance. By and large, a "no excuses" standard is more evenhanded and certainly easier to administer.

Once the incentives are designed, they have to be communicated and explained. Everybody needs to understand how their incentive compensation is calculated and how individual/group performance targets contribute to organizational performance targets. The pressure to achieve the targeted strategic and financial performance and continuously improve on strategy execution should be unrelenting, with few (if any) loopholes for rewarding shortfalls in performance. People at all levels have to be held accountable for carrying out their assigned parts of the strategic plan, and they have to understand their rewards are based on the caliber of results that are achieved. But with the pressure to perform should come meaningful rewards. Without an ample payoff, the system breaks down, and managers are left with the less workable options of barking orders, trying to enforce compliance, and depending on the good will of employees.

Core Concept

The unwavering standard for judging whether individuals, teams, and organizational units have done a good job must be whether they achieve performance targets consistent with effective strategy execution.

Performance-Based Incentives and Rewards in Multinational Enterprises   In some foreign countries, incentive pay runs counter to local customs and cultural norms. Professor Steven Kerr cites the time he lectured an executive education class on the need for more performance-based pay and a Japanese manager protested, "You shouldn't bribe your children to do their homework, you shouldn't bribe your wife to prepare dinner, and you shouldn't bribe your employees to work for the company."[21] Singling out individuals and commending them for unusually good effort can also be a problem; Japanese culture considers public praise of an individual an affront to the harmony of the group. In some countries, employees have a preference for nonmonetary rewards—more leisure time, important titles, access to vacation villages, and nontaxable perks. Thus, multinational companies have to build some degree of flexibility into the design of incentives and rewards in order to accommodate cross-cultural traditions and preferences.

Key Points

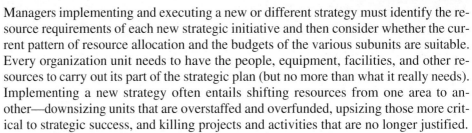

Managers implementing and executing a new or different strategy must identify the resource requirements of each new strategic initiative and then consider whether the current pattern of resource allocation and the budgets of the various subunits are suitable. Every organization unit needs to have the people, equipment, facilities, and other resources to carry out its part of the strategic plan (but no more than what it really needs). Implementing a new strategy often entails shifting resources from one area to another—downsizing units that are overstaffed and overfunded, upsizing those more critical to strategic success, and killing projects and activities that are no longer justified.

Anytime a company alters its strategy, managers should review existing policies and operating procedures, proactively revise or discard those that are out of sync, and formulate new ones to facilitate execution of new strategic initiatives. Prescribing new or freshly revised policies and operating procedures aids the task of strategy execution (1) by providing top-down guidance to operating managers, supervisory personnel, and employees regarding how certain things need to be done and what the boundaries are on independent actions and decisions; (2) by enforcing consistency in how particular strategy-critical activities are performed in geographically scattered operating units; and (3) by promoting the creation of a work climate and corporate culture that promotes good strategy execution. Thick policy manuals are usually unnecessary. Indeed, when individual creativity and initiative are more essential to good execution than standardization and conformity, it is better to give people the freedom to do things however they see fit and hold them accountable for good results rather than try to control their behavior with policies and guidelines for every situation.

Competent strategy execution entails visible, unyielding managerial commitment to best practices and continuous improvement. Benchmarking, the discovery and adoption of best practices, reengineering core business processes, and continuous improvement initiatives like total quality management (TQM) or six sigma programs, all aim at improved efficiency, lower costs, better product quality, and greater customer satisfaction. *These initiatives are important tools for learning how to execute a strategy more proficiently.* Benchmarking, part of the process of discovering best practices, provides a realistic basis for setting performance targets. Instituting "best-in-industry" or "best-in-world" operating practices in most or all value chain activities provide a means for taking strategy execution to a higher plateau of competence and nurturing a high-performance work environment. Business process reengineering is a way to make quantum progress toward becoming a world-class organization, while TQM and six sigma programs instill a commitment to continuous improvement and operating excellence. An organization bent on continuous improvement is a valuable competitive asset—one that, over time, can yield important competitive capabilities (in reducing costs, speeding new products to market, or improving product quality, service, or customer satisfaction) and be a source of competitive advantage.

Company strategies can't be implemented or executed well without a number of support systems to carry on business operations. Well-conceived state-of-the-art support systems cannot only facilitate better strategy execution but also strengthen organizational capabilities enough to provide a competitive edge over rivals. In the age of the Internet, real-time information and control systems, growing use of e-commerce technologies and business practices, company intranets, and wireless communications capabilities, companies can't hope to outexecute their competitors without cutting-edge information systems and technologically sophisticated operating capabilities that enable fast, efficient, and effective organization action.

Strategy-supportive motivational practices and reward systems are powerful management tools for gaining employee commitment. The key to creating a reward system that promotes good strategy execution is to make strategically relevant measures of performance *the dominating basis* for designing incentives, evaluating individual and group efforts, and handing out rewards. Positive motivational practices generally work better than negative ones, but there is a place for both. There's also a place for both monetary and nonmonetary incentives.

For an incentive compensation system to work well (1) the monetary payoff should be a major percentage of the compensation package, (2) the use of incentives should extend to all managers and workers, (3) the system should be administered with care and fairness, (4) the incentives should be linked to performance targets spelled out in the strategic plan, (5) each individual's performance targets should involve outcomes the person can personally affect, (6) rewards should promptly follow the determination of good performance, (7) monetary rewards should be supplemented with liberal use of nonmonetary rewards, and (8) skirting the system to reward nonperformers or subpar results should be scrupulously avoided.

Exercises

1. Go to www.google.com and, using the advanced search feature, enter "best practices." Browse through the search results to identify at least five organizations that have gathered a set of best practices and are making the best practices library they have assembled available to members. Explore at least one of the sites to get an idea of the kind of best practice information that is available.

2. Using the Internet search engine at www.google.com, do a search on "six sigma" quality programs. Browse through the search results and (*a*) identify several companies that offer six sigma training and (*b*) find lists of companies that have implemented six sigma programs in their pursuit of operational excellence. In particular, you should go to www.isixsigma.com and explore the Six Sigma Q&A menu option.

3. Using the Internet search engine at www.google.com, do a search on "total quality management." Browse through the search results and (*a*) identify companies that offer TQM training, (*b*) identify some books on TQM programs, and (*c*) find lists of companies that have implemented TQM programs in their pursuit of operational excellence.

4. Consult the latest issue of *Fortune* containing the annual "100 Best Companies to Work For" (usually a late-January or early-February issue) and identify at least 5 (preferably 10) compensation incentives that these companies use to enhance employee motivation and reward them for good strategic and financial performance.

CHAPTER 9

Corporate Culture and Leadership

An organization's capacity to execute its strategy depends on its "hard" infrastructure—its organizational structure and systems—and on its "soft" infrastructure—its culture and norms.
—Amar Bhide

Weak leadership can wreck the soundest strategy; forceful execution of even a poor plan can often bring victory.
—Sun Zi

Leadership is accomplishing something through other people that wouldn't have happened if you weren't there . . . Leadership is being able to mobilize ideas and values that energize other people . . . Leaders develop a story line that engages other people.
—Noel Tichy

The biggest levers you've got to change a company are strategy, structure, and culture. If I could pick two, I'd pick strategy and culture.
—Wayne Leonard, CEO, Entergy

In the previous two chapters we examined six of the managerial tasks that are important to good strategy execution and operating excellence—building a capable organization, marshaling the needed resources and steering them to strategy-critical operating units, establishing policies and procedures that facilitate good strategy execution, adopting best practices and pushing for continuous improvement in how value chain activities are performed, creating internal operating systems that enable better execution, and employing motivational practices and compensation incentives that gain wholehearted employee commitment to the strategy execution process. In this chapter we explore the two remaining managerial tasks that shape the outcome of efforts to execute a company's strategy: creating a strategy-supportive corporate culture and exerting the internal leadership needed to drive the implementation of strategic initiatives forward and achieve higher plateaus of operating excellence.

Building a Corporate Culture That Promotes Good Strategy Execution

Every company has its own unique culture. The character of a company's culture or work climate is a product of the core values and business principles that executives espouse, the standards of what is ethically acceptable and what is not, the behaviors that define "how we do things around here", and the stories that get told over and over to illustrate and reinforce the company's values and business practices, approach to people management, and internal politics. The meshing together of stated beliefs, business principles, style of operating, ingrained behaviors and attitudes, and work climate define a company's **corporate culture.**

> **Core Concept**
>
> **Corporate culture** refers to the character of a company's internal work climate and personality—as shaped by its core values, beliefs, business principles, traditions, ingrained behaviors, and style of operating.

The cultures of different companies vary widely. For instance, the bedrock of Wal-Mart's culture is dedication to customer satisfaction, zealous pursuit of low costs and frugal operating practices, a strong work ethic, ritualistic Saturday-morning headquarters meetings to exchange ideas and review problems, and company executives' commitment to visiting stores, listening to customers, and soliciting suggestions from employees. At Nordstrom, the corporate culture is centered on delivering exceptional service to customers; the company's motto is "Respond to unreasonable customer requests"—each out-of-the-ordinary request is seen as an opportunity for a "heroic" act by an employee that can further the company's reputation for a customer-pleasing shopping environment. Nordstrom makes a point of promoting employees noted for their heroic acts and dedication to outstanding service; the company motivates its salespeople with a commission-based compensation system that enables Nordstrom's best salespeople to earn more than double what other department stores pay. General Electric's culture is founded on a hard-driving, results-oriented atmosphere (where all of the company's business divisions are held to a standard of being number one or two in their industries as well as achieving good business results); extensive cross-business sharing of ideas, best practices, and learning; the reliance on "workout sessions" to identify, debate, and resolve burning issues; a commitment to six sigma quality; and globalization of the company. At Microsoft, there are stories of the long hours programmers put in,

COMPANY SPOTLIGHT 9.1

The Culture at Alberto-Culver

The Alberto-Culver Company, with 2002 revenues of about $2.7 billion and over 13,000 employees worldwide, is the producer and marketer of Alberto VO5 hair care products; St. Ives skin care, hair care, and facial care products; and such brands as Molly McButter, Mrs. Dash, Consort, Just for Me, TRE-Semmé, and Static Guard. Alberto-Culver brands are sold in 120 countries. The company's Sally Beauty Company has 2,700 stores in five countries and is the world's largest distributor of professional salon products.

At the careers section of its website, the company described its culture in the following words:

Building careers is as important to us at Alberto-Culver as building brands. We believe in a values-based workplace. We believe in the importance of families and a life/family balance. We believe in in-your-face-honesty without the taint of corporate politics. There's no talk behind your back. If there are issues you'll know, face-to-face. We believe the best ideas make their way—quickly—up an organization, not down. We believe that we should take advantage of every ounce of your talent, not just assign you to a box. We believe in celebrating our victories. We believe in open communication. We believe you can improve what you measure, so we survey and spot check all the time. For that same reason, everyone has specific goals so that their expectations are in line with their managers and the company. We believe that victory is a team accomplishment. We believe in personal development. We believe if you talk with us, you will catch our enthusiasm and want to be part of us.

Source: Alberto-Culver website, December 2, 2002.

---

the emotional peaks and valleys in encountering and overcoming coding problems, the exhilaration of completing a complex program on schedule, the satisfaction of working on cutting-edge projects, the rewards of being part of a team responsible for a popular new software program, and the tradition of competing aggressively. Enron's collapse in 2001 was partly the product of a flawed corporate culture—one based on the positives of product innovation, aggressive risk-taking, and a driving ambition to lead global change in the energy business but also on the negatives of arrogance, ego, greed, deliberately obscure accounting practices, and an "ends-justify-the-means" mentality in pursuing stretch revenue and profitability targets. In the end, Enron came unglued because a few top executives chose unethical and illegal paths to pursue corporate revenue and profitability targets—in a company that publicly preached integrity and other notable corporate values but was lax in making sure that key executives walked the talk.

Company Spotlight 9.1 presents Alberto-Culver's description of its corporate culture.

What to Look for in Identifying a Company's Corporate Culture

The taproot of corporate culture is the organization's beliefs and philosophy about how its affairs ought to be conducted—the reasons why it does things the way it does. A company's culture is manifested in the values and business principles that management preaches and practices, in official policies and procedures, in its revered traditions and oft-repeated stories, in the attitudes and behaviors of employees, in the peer pressures that exist to display core values, in the organization's politics, in its approaches to people management and problem solving, in its relationships with external stakeholders (particularly vendors and the communities in which it operates), and in the "chemistry" and the "personality" that permeates its work environment. Some of these sociological forces are readily apparent, and others operate quite subtly.

The values, beliefs, and practices that undergird a company's culture can come from anywhere in the organization hierarchy, sometimes representing the philosophy of an influential executive and sometimes resulting from exemplary actions on the part of a specific employee, work group, department, or division.[1] Very often, key elements of the culture originate with a founder or certain strong leaders who articulated them as a set of business principles, company policies, or ways of dealing with employees, customers, vendors, shareholders, and the communities in which it operated. Over time, these cultural underpinnings take root, become embedded in how the company conducts its business, come to be accepted and shared by company managers and employees, and then persist as new employees are encouraged to adopt and follow the professed values and practices.

The Role of Stories Frequently, a significant part of a company's culture is captured in the stories that get told over and over again to illustrate to newcomers the importance of certain values and the depth of commitment that various company personnel have displayed. One of the folktales at FedEx, world renowned for the reliability of its next-day package delivery guarantee, is about a deliveryman who had been given the wrong key to a FedEx drop box. Rather than leave the packages in the drop box until the next day when the right key was available, the deliveryman unbolted the drop box from its base, loaded it into the truck, and took it back to the station. There, the box was pried open and the contents removed and sped on their way to their destination the next day. Nordstrom keeps a scrapbook commemorating the heroic acts of its employees and uses it as a regular reminder of the above-and-beyond-the-call-of-duty behaviors that employees are encouraged to display. At Frito-Lay, there are dozens of stories about truck drivers who went to extraordinary lengths in overcoming adverse weather conditions in order to make scheduled deliveries to retail customers and keep store shelves stocked with Frito-Lay products. Such stories serve the valuable purpose of illustrating the kinds of behavior the company encourages and reveres. Moreover, each retelling of a legendary story puts a bit more peer pressure on company personnel to go an extra step when the opportunity presents itself and do their part in making company traditions live on and to display core values.

Perpetuating the Culture Once established, company cultures are perpetuated in six important ways: (1) by screening and selecting new employees that will mesh well with the culture, (2) by systematic indoctrination of new members in the culture's fundamentals, (3) by the efforts of senior group members to reiterate core values in daily conversations and pronouncements, (4) by the telling and retelling of company legends, (5) by regular ceremonies honoring members who display desired cultural behaviors, and (6) by visibly rewarding those who display cultural norms and penalizing those who don't.[2] The more that new employees are being brought into the organization the more important it becomes to screen job applicants every bit as much for how well their values, beliefs, and personalities match up with the culture as for their technical skills and experience. For example, a company that stresses operating with integrity and fairness has to hire people who themselves have integrity and place a high value on fair play. A company whose culture revolves around creativity, product innovation, and leading change has to screen new hires for their ability to think outside the box, generate new ideas, and thrive in a climate of rapid change and ambiguity. Southwest Airlines, whose two core values "LUV" and fun permeate the work environment and whose objective is to ensure that passengers have a positive and enjoyable flying experience, goes to considerable lengths to hire flight attendants and gate personnel who are witty, cheery, and outgoing and who display "whistle while you work" attitudes. Fast-growing companies risk creating a culture by chance rather than by design if they rush to hire employees mainly for their talents and credentials and neglect to screen out candidates whose values, philosophies, and personalities aren't a good fit with the organizational character, vision, and strategy being articulated by the company's senior executives.

As a rule, companies are attentive to the task of hiring people who will fit in and who will embrace the prevailing culture. And, usually, job seekers lean toward accepting jobs at companies where they feel comfortable with the atmosphere and the people they will be working with. Employees who don't hit it off at a company tend to leave quickly, while employees who thrive and are pleased with the work environment stay on, eventually moving up the ranks to positions of greater responsibility. The longer people stay at an organization, the more that they come to embrace and mirror the corporate culture—their values and beliefs tend to be molded by mentors, fellow workers, company training programs, and the reward structure. Normally, employees who have worked at a company for a long time play a major role in indoctrinating new employees into the culture.

Forces That Cause a Company's Culture to Evolve   However, even stable cultures aren't static—just like strategy and organization structure, they evolve. New challenges in the marketplace, revolutionary technologies, and shifting internal conditions—especially eroding business prospects, an internal crisis, or top executive turnover—tend to breed new ways of doing things and, in turn, cultural evolution. An incoming CEO who decides to shake up the existing business and take it in new directions often triggers a cultural shift, perhaps one of major proportions. Likewise, diversification into new businesses, expansion into foreign countries, rapid growth, an influx of new employees, and merger with or acquisition of another company can all precipitate cultural changes of one kind or another.

Company Subcultures: The Problems Posed by New Acquisitions and Multinational Operations   Although it is common to speak about corporate culture in the singular, companies typically have multiple cultures (or subcultures).[3] Values, beliefs, and practices within a company sometimes vary significantly by department, geographic location, division, or business unit. A company's subcultures can clash, or at least not mesh well, if they embrace conflicting business philosophies or operating approaches, or if key executives employ different approaches to people management or if important differences between a company's culture and those of recently acquired companies have not yet been ironed out. *Global and multinational companies tend to be at least partly multicultural* because cross-country organization units have different operating histories and work climates, as well as members who have grown up under different social customs and traditions and who have different sets of values and beliefs. The human resources manager of a global pharmaceutical company who took on an assignment in the Far East discovered, to his surprise, that one of his biggest challenges was to persuade his company's managers in China, Korea, Malaysia, and Taiwan to accept promotions—their cultural values were such that they did not believe in competing with their peers for career rewards or personal gain, nor did they relish breaking ties to their local communities to assume cross-national responsibilities.[4] Many companies that have merged with or acquired foreign companies have to deal with language- and custom-based cultural differences.

Nonetheless, the existence of subcultures does not preclude important areas of commonality and compatibility. For example, General Electric's cultural traits of boundarylessness, workout, and six sigma quality can be implanted and practiced successfully in different countries. AES, a global power company with operations in over 20 countries, has found that the four core values of integrity, fairness, fun, and social responsibility underlying its culture are readily embraced by people in most countries. Moreover, AES tries to define and practice its cultural values the same way in all of its locations while still being sensitive to differences that exist among various people groups across the world; top managers at AES express the views that people across the world are more similar than different and that the company's culture is as meaningful in Buenos Aires or Kazakhstan as in Virginia.

In today's globalizing world, multinational companies are learning how to make strategy-critical cultural traits travel across country boundaries and create a workably uniform culture worldwide. Likewise, company managements are quite alert to the importance of cultural compatibility in making acquisitions and the need to address how to merge and integrate the cultures of newly acquired companies—cultural due diligence is often as important as financial due diligence in deciding whether to go forward on an acquisition or merger. On a number of occasions, companies have decided to pass on acquiring particular companies because of culture conflicts that they believed would be hard to resolve.

Culture: Ally or Obstacle to Strategy Execution?

A company's present culture and work climate may or may not be compatible with what is needed for effective implementation and execution of the chosen strategy. *When a company's present work climate promotes attitudes and behaviors that are well suited to first-rate strategy execution, its culture functions as a valuable ally in the strategy execution process.* When the culture is in conflict with some aspect of the company's direction, performance targets, or strategy, the culture becomes a stumbling block.[5]

How Culture Can Promote Better Strategy Execution   A culture grounded in strategy-supportive values, practices, and behavioral norms adds significantly to the power and effectiveness of a company's strategy execution effort. For example, a culture where frugality and thrift are values widely shared by organizational members nurtures employee actions to identify cost-saving opportunities—the very behavior needed for successful execution of a low-cost leadership strategy. A culture built around such business principles as pleasing customers, fair treatment, operating excellence, and employee empowerment promotes employee behaviors and an esprit de corps that facilitate execution of strategies keyed to high product quality and superior customer service. A culture in which taking initiative, challenging the status quo, exhibiting creativity, embracing change, and collaborative teamwork pervade the work climate promotes creative collaboration on the part of employees and organization drive to lead market change—outcomes that are very conducive to successful execution of product innovation and technological leadership strategies.[6]

A tight culture–strategy alignment furthers a company's strategy execution effort in two ways:[7]

1. *A culture that encourages actions supportive of good strategy execution not only provides company personnel with clear guidance regarding what behaviors and results constitute good job performance but also produces significant peer pressure*

from coworkers to conform to culturally acceptable norms. The tighter the strategy–culture fit, the more that the culture pushes people to display behaviors and observe operating practices that are conducive to good strategy execution. A strategy-supportive culture thus funnels organizational energy toward getting the right things done and delivering positive organizational results. In a company where strategy and culture are misaligned, some of the very behaviors needed to execute strategy successfully run contrary to the behaviors and values imbedded in the prevailing culture. Such a clash nearly always produces resistance from employees who have strong allegiance to the present culture. Culture-bred resistance to the actions and behaviors needed for good execution, if strong and widespread, poses a formidable hurdle that has to be cleared for strategy execution to get very far.

2. *A culture imbedded with values and behaviors that facilitate strategy execution promotes strong employee identification with and commitment to the company's vision, performance targets, and strategy.* When a company's culture is grounded in many of the needed strategy-executing behaviors, employees feel genuinely better about their jobs, the company they work for, and the merits of what the company is trying to accomplish. As a consequence, company personnel are more inclined to exhibit some passion and exert their best efforts in making the strategy work, trying to achieve the targeted performance, and moving the company closer to realizing its strategic vision.

> **Core Concept**
>
> Because culturally approved behavior thrives, while culturally disapproved behavior gets squashed and often penalized, a culture that supports and encourages the behaviors conducive to good strategy execution is a matter that merits the full attention of company managers.

This says something important about the task of managing the strategy executing process: *Closely aligning corporate culture with the requirements for proficient strategy execution merits the full attention of senior executives.* The managerial objective is to create and nurture a work culture that mobilizes organizational energy squarely behind efforts to execute strategy. A good job of culture-building on management's part promotes can-do attitudes and acceptance of change, instills strong peer pressures for behaviors conducive to good strategy execution, and enlists more enthusiasm and dedicated effort among company personnel for achieving company objectives.

The Perils of Strategy–Culture Conflict   Conflicts between behaviors approved by the culture and behaviors needed for good strategy execution send mixed signals to organization members, forcing an undesirable choice. Should organization members be loyal to the culture and company traditions (as well as to their own personal values and beliefs, which are likely to be compatible with the culture) and thus resist or be indifferent to actions and behaviors that will promote better strategy execution? Or should they support the strategy execution effort and engage in actions and behaviors that run counter to the culture?

When a company's culture is out of sync with what is needed for strategic success, the culture has to be changed as rapidly as can be managed—this, of course, presumes that it is one or more aspects of the culture that are out of whack rather than the strategy. While correcting a strategy–culture conflict can occasionally mean revamping strategy to produce cultural fit, more usually it means revamping the mismatched cultural features to produce strategy fit. The more entrenched the mismatched aspects of the culture, the greater the difficulty of implementing new or different strategies until better strategy–culture alignment emerges. A sizable and prolonged strategy–culture conflict weakens and may even defeat managerial efforts to make the strategy work.

Strong versus Weak Cultures

Company cultures vary widely in the degree to which they are embedded in company practices and behavioral norms. Strongly embedded cultures go directly to a company's heart and soul; those with shallow roots provide little in the way of a definable corporate character.

Strong-Culture Companies A company's culture can be strong and cohesive in the sense that the company conducts its business according to a clear and explicit set of principles and values, that management devotes considerable time to communicating these principles and values to organization members and explaining how they relate to its business environment, and that the values are shared widely across the company—by senior executives and rank-and-file employees alike.[8] Strong-culture companies have a well-defined corporate character, typically underpinned by a creed or values statement. Executives regularly stress the importance of using company values and business principles as the basis for decisions and actions taken throughout the organization. In strong-culture companies, values and behavioral norms are so deeply rooted that they don't change much when a new CEO takes over—although they can erode over time if the CEO ceases to nurture them. And they may not change much as strategy evolves and the organization acts to make strategy adjustments, either because the new strategies are compatible with the present culture or because the dominant traits of the culture are somewhat strategy-neutral and compatible with evolving versions of the company's strategy.

> In a strong-culture company, values and behavioral norms are like crabgrass: deeply rooted and hard to weed out.

Three factors contribute to the development of strong cultures: (1) a founder or strong leader who establishes values, principles, and practices that are consistent and sensible in light of customer needs, competitive conditions, and strategic requirements; (2) a sincere, long-standing company commitment to operating the business according to these established traditions, thereby creating an internal environment that supports decision making and strategies based on cultural norms; and (3) a genuine concern for the well-being of the organization's three biggest constituencies—customers, employees, and shareholders. Continuity of leadership, small group size, stable group membership, geographic concentration, and considerable organizational success all contribute to the emergence and sustainability of a strong culture.[9]

During the time a strong culture is being implanted, there's nearly always a good strategy–culture fit (which partially accounts for the organization's success). Mismatches between strategy and culture in a strong-culture company tend to occur when a company's business environment undergoes significant change, prompting a drastic strategy revision that clashes with the entrenched culture. A strategy–culture clash can also occur in a strong-culture company whose business has gradually eroded; when a new leader is brought in to revitalize the company's operations, he or she may push the company in a strategic direction that requires substantially different cultural and behavioral norms. In such cases, a major culture-changing effort has to be launched.

One of the best examples of an industry in which strategy changes have clashed with deeply implanted cultures is the electric utility industry. Most electric utility companies, long used to operating as slow-moving regulated monopolies with captive customers, are now confronting the emergence of a vigorously competitive market in wholesale power generation and growing freedom on the part of industrial, commercial, and residential customers to choose their own energy supplier (in much the same way as customers choose their long-distance telephone carriers—an industry that once was a heavily regulated market). These new market circumstances are prompting electric companies to shift away from cultures predicated on risk avoidance, centralized control of decision making, and the politics of regulatory relationships toward cultures aimed at entrepreneurial risk taking, product innovation, competitive thinking, greater attention to customer service, cost reduction, and competitive pricing.

Weak-Culture Companies   In direct contrast to strong-culture companies, weak-culture companies are fragmented in the sense that no one set of values is consistently preached or widely shared, few behavioral norms are evident in operating practices, and few traditions are widely revered or proudly nurtured by company personnel. Because top executives don't repeatedly espouse any particular business philosophy or exhibit longstanding commitment to particular values or extol particular operating practices and behavioral norms, organization members at weak-culture companies typically lack any deeply felt sense of corporate identity. While employees may have some bonds of identification with and loyalty toward their department, their colleagues, their union, or their boss, a weak company culture breeds no strong employee allegiance to what the company stands for or to operating the business in well-defined ways. Such lack of a definable corporate character results in many employees viewing their company as just a place to work and their job as just a way to make a living—there's neither passion about the company nor emotional commitment to what it is trying to accomplish. Very often, cultural weakness stems from moderately entrenched subcultures that block the emergence of a well-defined companywide work climate.

As a consequence, *weak cultures provide little or no strategy-implementing assistance* because there are no traditions, beliefs, values, common bonds, or behavioral norms that management can use as levers to mobilize commitment to executing the chosen strategy. While a weak culture does not usually pose a strong barrier to strategy execution, it also provides no support. Absent a work climate that channels organizational energy in the direction of good strategy execution, managers are left with the options of either using compensation incentives and other motivational devices to mobilize employee commitment or trying to establish cultural roots that will in time start to nurture the strategy execution process.

Unhealthy Cultures

The distinctive characteristic of an unhealthy corporate culture is the presence of counterproductive cultural traits that adversely impact the work climate and company performance.[10] The following three traits are particularly unhealthy:

1. A highly politicized internal environment in which many issues get resolved and decisions made on the basis of which individuals or groups have the most political clout to carry the day.

2. Hostility to change and a general wariness of people who champion new ways of doing things.

3. A "not-invented-here" mindset that makes company personnel averse to looking outside the company for best practices, new managerial approaches, and innovative ideas.

What makes a politicized internal environment so unhealthy is that political infighting consumes a great deal of organizational energy, often with the result that what's best for the company takes a backseat to political maneuvering. In companies where internal politics pervades the work climate, empire-building managers jealously guard their decision-making prerogatives. They have their own agendas and operate the work units under their supervision as autonomous "fiefdoms," and the positions they take on issues is usually aimed at protecting or expanding their turf. Collaboration with other organizational units is viewed with suspicion (What are "they" up to? How can "we" protect "our" flanks?), and cross-unit cooperation occurs grudgingly. When an important proposal moves to the front burner, advocates try to ram it through and opponents try to alter it in significant ways or else kill it altogether. The support or opposition of politically influential executives and/or coalitions among departments with vested interests in a particular outcome typically weigh heavily in deciding what actions the company takes. All this maneuvering takes away from efforts to execute strategy with real proficiency and frustrates company personnel who are less political and more inclined to do what is in the company's best interests.

In less-adaptive cultures where skepticism about the importance of new developments and resistance to change are the norm, managers prefer waiting until the fog of uncertainty clears before steering a new course, making fundamental adjustments to their product line, or embracing a major new technology. They believe in moving cautiously and conservatively, preferring to follow others rather than take decisive action to be in the forefront of change. Change-resistant cultures place a premium on not making mistakes, prompting managers to lean toward safe, don't-rock-the-boat options that will have only a ripple effect on the status quo, protect or advance their own careers, and guard the interests of their immediate work groups.

Change-resistant cultures encourage a number of undesirable or unhealthy behaviors—avoiding risks, not making bold proposals to pursue emerging opportunities, a lax approach to both product innovation and continuous improvement in performing value chain activities, and following rather than leading market change. In change-resistant cultures, word quickly gets around that proposals to do things differently face an uphill battle and that people who champion them may be seen as either something of a nuisance or a troublemaker. Executives who don't value managers or employees with initiative and new ideas put a damper on product innovation, experimentation, and efforts to improve. At the same time, change-resistant companies have little appetite for being first-movers or fast-followers, believing that being in the forefront of change is too risky and that acting too quickly increases vulnerability to costly mistakes. They are more inclined to adopt a wait-and-see posture, carefully analyze several alternative responses, learn from the missteps of early movers, and then move forward cautiously and conservatively with initiatives that are deemed safe. Hostility to change is most often found in companies with multilayered management bureaucracies that have enjoyed considerable market success in years past and that are wedded to the "We have done it this way for years" syndrome.

When such companies encounter business environments with accelerating change, going slow on altering traditional ways of doing things can be become a liability rather than an asset. General Motors, IBM, Sears, and Eastman Kodak are classic examples of companies whose change-resistant bureaucracies were slow to respond to fundamental changes in their markets; clinging to the cultures and traditions that made them successful, they were reluctant to alter operating practices and modify their business approaches. As strategies of gradual change won out over bold innovation and being an early mover, all four lost market share to rivals that quickly moved to institute changes more in tune with evolving market conditions and buyer preferences. These companies are now struggling to recoup lost ground with cultures and behaviors more suited to market success—the kinds of fit that caused them to succeed in the first place.

The third unhealthy cultural trait—the not-invented-here mindset—tends to develop when a company reigns as an industry leader or enjoys great market success for so long that its personnel start to believe they have all the answers or can develop them on their own. Such confidence in the correctness of how it does things and in the company's skills and capabilities breeds arrogance—there's a strong tendency for company personnel to discount the merits or significance of what outsiders are doing and what can be learned by studying best-in-class performers. Benchmarking and a search for the best practices of outsiders are seen as offering little payoff. Any market share gains on the part of up-and-coming rivals are regarded as temporary setbacks, soon to be reversed by the company's own forthcoming initiatives. Insular thinking, internally driven solutions, and a must-be-invented-here mindset come to permeate the corporate culture. An inwardly focused corporate culture gives rise to managerial inbreeding and a failure to recruit people who can offer fresh thinking and outside perspectives. The big risk of insular cultural thinking is that the company can underestimate the competencies and accomplishments of rival companies and overestimate its own progress—with a resulting loss of competitive advantage over time.

Unhealthy cultures typically impair company performance. Avon, BankAmerica, Citicorp, Coors, Ford, General Motors, Kmart, Kroger, Sears, and Xerox are examples of companies whose unhealthy cultures during the late 1970s and early 1980s contributed to ho-hum performance on the bottom line and in the marketplace.[11] General Motors, Kmart, and Sears are still struggling to uproot problematic cultural traits and replace them with behaviors having a more suitable strategy–culture fit.

Adaptive Cultures

The hallmark of adaptive corporate cultures is willingness on the part of organizational members to accept change and take on the challenge of introducing and executing new strategies.[12] Company personnel share a feeling of confidence that the organization can deal with whatever threats and opportunities come down the pike; they are receptive to risk taking, experimentation, innovation, and changing strategies and practices. In direct contrast to change-resistant cultures, adaptive cultures are very supportive of managers and employees at all ranks who propose or help initiate useful change. Internal entrepreneurship on the part of individuals and groups is encouraged and rewarded. Senior executives seek out, support, and promote individuals who exercise initiative, spot opportunities for improvement, and display the skills to implement them. Managers habitually fund product development initiatives, evaluate new ideas openly, and take prudent risks to create new business positions. As a consequence, the company exhibits a proactive approach to identifying issues, evaluating the implications and options, and implementing workable solutions. Strategies and traditional operating practices are modified as needed to adjust to or take advantage of changes in the business environment.

Core Concept

In adaptive cultures, there's a spirit of doing what's necessary to ensure long-term organizational success provided the new behaviors and operating practices that management is calling for are seen as legitimate and consistent with the core values and business principles underpinning the culture.

But why is change so willingly embraced in an adaptive culture? Why are organization members not fearful of how change will affect them? Why does an adaptive culture not become unglued with ongoing changes in strategy, operating practices, and behavioral norms? The answers lie in two distinctive and dominant traits of an adaptive culture: (1) Any changes in operating practices and behaviors must *not* compromise core values and long-standing business principles, and

(2) the changes that are instituted must satisfy the legitimate interests of stakeholders—customers, employees, shareowners, suppliers, and the communities where the company operates.[13] In other words, what sustains an adaptive culture is that organization members perceive the changes that management is trying to institute as legitimate and in keeping with the core values and business principles that form the heart and soul of the culture.

Thus, for an adaptive culture to remain intact over time, top management must orchestrate the responses in a manner that demonstrates genuine care for the well-being of all key constituencies and tries to satisfy all their legitimate interests simultaneously. Unless fairness to all constituencies is a decision-making principle and a commitment to doing the right thing is evident to organization members, the changes are not likely to be seen as legitimate and thus be readily accepted and implemented.[14] Making changes that will please customers and/or that protect, if not enhance, the company's long-term well-being are generally seen as legitimate and are often seen as the best way of looking out for the interests of employees, stockholders, suppliers, and communities where the company operates. At companies with adaptive cultures, management concern for the well-being of employees is nearly always a big factor in gaining employee support for change—company personnel are usually receptive to change as long as employees understand that changes in their job assignments are part of the process of adapting to new conditions and that their employment security will not be threatened unless the company's business unexpectedly reverses direction. In cases where workforce downsizing becomes necessary, management concern for employees dictates that separation be handled humanely, making employee departure as painless as possible. Management efforts to make the process of adapting to change fair and equitable for customers, employees, stockholders, suppliers, and communities where the company operates, keeping adverse impacts to a minimum insofar as possible, breeds acceptance of and support for change among all organization stakeholders.

Technology companies, software companies, and today's dot-com companies are good illustrations of organizations with adaptive cultures. Such companies thrive on change—driving it, leading it, and capitalizing on it (but sometimes also succumbing to change when they make the wrong move or are swamped by better technologies or the superior business models of rivals). Companies like Microsoft, Intel, Nokia, Amazon.com, and Dell Computer cultivate the capability to act and react rapidly. They are avid practitioners of entrepreneurship and innovation, with a demonstrated willingness to take bold risks to create altogether new products, new businesses, and new industries. To create and nurture a culture that can adapt rapidly to changing to shifting business conditions, they make a point of staffing their organizations with people who are proactive, who rise to the challenge of change, and who have an aptitude for adapting.

In fast-changing business environments, a corporate culture that is receptive to altering organizational practices and behaviors is a virtual necessity. However, adaptive cultures work to the advantage of all companies, not just those in rapid-change environments. Every company operates in a market and business climate that is changing to one degree or another and that, in turn, requires internal operating responses and new behaviors on the part of organization members. As a company's strategy evolves, an adaptive culture is a definite ally in the strategy-implementing, strategy-executing process as compared to cultures that have to be coaxed and cajoled to change. This constitutes a good argument for why managers should strive to build a strong, adaptive corporate culture.

> A good case can be made that a strongly planted, adaptive culture is the best of all corporate cultures.

Creating a Strong Fit between Strategy and Culture

It is the *strategy maker's* responsibility to select a strategy compatible with the sacred or unchangeable parts of the organization's prevailing corporate culture. It is the *strategy implementer's* task, once strategy is chosen, to change whatever facets of the corporate culture hinder effective execution.

Changing a Problem Culture   Changing a company's culture to align it with strategy is among the toughest management tasks because of the heavy anchor of deeply held values and habits—people cling emotionally to the old and familiar. It takes concerted management action over a period of time to replace an unhealthy culture with a healthy culture or to root out certain unwanted behaviors and instill ones that are more strategy-supportive. *The single most visible factor that distinguishes successful culture-change efforts from failed attempts is competent leadership at the top.* Great power is needed to force major cultural change—to overcome the springback resistance of entrenched cultures—and great power normally resides only at the top.

> Once a culture is established, it is difficult to change.

The first step in fixing a problem culture is to identify those facets of the present culture that are dysfunctional and explain why they pose obstacles to executing new strategic initiatives and achieving company performance targets. Second, managers have to clearly define the desired new behaviors and specify the key features of the culture they want to create. Third, managers have to talk openly and forthrightly to all concerned about problematic aspects of the culture and why and how new behaviors will improve company performance—the case for cultural change has to be persuasive and the benefits of a reformed culture made convincing to all concerned. Finally, and most important, the talk has to be followed swiftly by visible, aggressive actions to promote the desired new behaviors—actions that everyone will understand are intended to produce behaviors and practices conducive to good strategy execution.

The menu of actions management can take to change a problem culture includes the following:[15]

- Making a compelling case for why the company's new direction and a different cultural atmosphere are in the organization's best interests and why individuals and groups should commit themselves to making it happen despite the obstacles. Skeptics have to be convinced that all is not well with the status quo. This can be done by:

  - Challenging the status quo with very basic questions: Are we giving customers what they really need and want? Why aren't we taking more business away from rivals? Why do our rivals have lower costs than we do? How can we drive costs out of the business and be more competitive on price? Why can't design-to-market cycle time be halved? Why aren't we moving faster to make better use of the Internet and e-commerce technologies and practices? How can we grow company revenues at 15 percent instead of 10 percent? What can we do to speed up our decision making and shorten response times?

  - Creating events where everyone in management is forced to listen to angry customers, dissatisfied strategic allies, alienated employees, or disenchanted stockholders.

- Repeating at every opportunity the messages of why cultural change is good for company stakeholders (particularly customers, employees, and shareholders).

Effective culture-change leaders are good at telling stories to convey new values and connect the case for change to organization members.

- Visibly praising and generously rewarding people who display newly advocated cultural norms and who participate in implementing the desired kinds of operating practices.

- Altering incentive compensation to reward the desired cultural behavior and deny rewards to those who resist change.

- Recruiting and hiring new managers and employees who have the desired cultural values and can serve as role models for the desired cultural behavior.

- Replacing key executives who are strongly associated with the old culture.

- Revising policies and procedures in ways that will help drive cultural change.

Only with bold leadership and concerted action on many fronts can a company succeed in tackling so large and difficult a task as major cultural change. When only strategic fine-tuning is being implemented, it takes less time and effort to bring values and culture into alignment with strategy, but there is still a lead role for the manager to play in communicating the need for new cultural behaviors and personally launching actions to prod the culture into better alignment with strategy.

Symbolic Culture-Changing Actions   Managerial actions to tighten the strategy–culture fit need to be both symbolic and substantive. Symbolic actions are valuable for the signals they send about the kinds of behavior and performance strategy implementers wish to encourage. The most important symbolic actions are those that top executives take to *lead by example*. For instance, if the organization's strategy involves a drive to become the industry's low-cost producer, senior managers must display frugality in their own actions and decisions: inexpensive decorations in the executive suite, conservative expense accounts and entertainment allowances, a lean staff in the corporate office, scrutiny of budget requests, few executive perks, and so on. If the culture change imperative is to be more responsive to customers' needs and to pleasing customers, the CEO can instill greater customer awareness by requiring all officers and executives to spend a significant portion of each week talking with customers about their needs.

Another category of symbolic actions includes the ceremonial events organizations hold to designate and honor people whose actions and performance exemplify what is called for in the new culture. Many universities give outstanding teacher awards each year to symbolize their commitment to good teaching and their esteem for instructors who display exceptional classroom talents. Numerous businesses have employee-of-the-month awards. The military has a long-standing custom of awarding ribbons and medals for exemplary actions. Mary Kay Cosmetics awards an array of prizes—from ribbons to pink automobiles—to its beauty consultants for reaching various sales plateaus.

The best companies and the best executives expertly use symbols, role models, ceremonial occasions, and group gatherings to tighten the strategy–culture fit. Low-cost leaders like Wal-Mart and Nucor are renowned for their spartan facilities, executive frugality, intolerance of waste, and zealous control of costs. Nucor executives make a point of flying coach class and using taxis at airports rather than limousines. Executives sensitive to their role in promoting strategy–culture fits make a habit of appearing at ceremonial functions to praise individuals and groups that get with the program. They honor individuals who exhibit cultural norms and reward those who achieve strategic milestones. They participate in employee training programs to stress strategic priorities, values, ethical principles, and cultural norms. Every group gathering is seen as an opportunity to repeat and ingrain values, praise good deeds, reinforce cultural norms, and promote changes that assist strategy execution. Sensitive executives make sure that current decisions and policy changes will be construed by organizational members as consistent with cultural values and supportive of the company's new strategic direction.[16]

Substantive Culture-Changing Actions While symbolically leading the push for new behaviors and communicating the reasons for new approaches is crucial, strategy implementers have to convince all those concerned that the culture-changing effort is more than cosmetic. Talk and symbolism have to be complemented by substantive actions and real movement. The actions taken have to be credible, highly visible, and unmistakably indicative of the seriousness of management's commitment to new strategic initiatives and the associated cultural changes. There are several ways to accomplish this. One is to engineer some quick successes that highlight the benefits of the proposed changes, thus making enthusiasm for them contagious. However, instant results are usually not as important as having the will and patience to create a solid, competent team psychologically committed to pursuing the strategy in a superior fashion. The strongest signs that management is truly committed to creating a new culture include replacing old-culture traditionalist managers with new-breed managers, changing dysfunctional policies and operating practices, instituting new compensation incentives visibly tied to the achievement of freshly set performance targets, and making major budgetary reallocations that shift substantial resources from old-strategy projects and programs to new-strategy projects and programs.

Implanting the needed culture-building values and behavior depends on a sincere, sustained commitment by the chief executive coupled with extraordinary persistence in reinforcing the culture at every opportunity through both word and deed. Neither charisma nor personal magnetism is essential. However, personally talking to many departmental groups about the reasons for change *is* essential; organizational changes are seldom accomplished successfully from an office. Moreover, creating and sustaining a strategy-supportive culture is a job for the whole management team. Major cultural change requires many initiatives from many people. Senior officers, department heads, and middle managers have to reiterate valued behaviors and translate the organization's core values and business principles into everyday practice. In addition, for the culture-building effort to be successful, strategy implementers must enlist the support of frontline supervisors and employee opinion leaders, convincing them of the merits of practicing and enforcing cultural norms at the lowest levels in the organization. Until a big majority of employees join the new culture and share an emotional commitment to its basic values and behavioral norms, there's considerably more work to be done in both instilling the culture and tightening the strategy–culture fit.

Changing culture to support strategy is not a short-term exercise. It takes time for a new culture to emerge and prevail. Overnight transformations simply don't occur. The bigger the organization and the greater the cultural shift needed to produce a strategy–culture fit, the longer it takes. In large companies, fixing a problem culture and instilling a new set of attitudes and behaviors can take two to five years. In fact, it is usually tougher to reform an entrenched problematic culture than it is to instill a strategy-supportive culture from scratch in a brand new organization. Sometimes executives succeed in changing the values and behaviors of small groups of managers and even whole departments or divisions, only to find the changes eroded over time by the actions of the rest of the organization—what is communicated, praised, supported, and penalized by an entrenched majority undermines the new emergent culture and halts its progress. Executives, despite a series of well-intended actions to reform a problem culture, are likely to fail at weeding out embedded cultural traits when widespread employee skepticism about the company's new directions and culture-change effort spawns covert resistance to the cultural behaviors and operating practices advocated by top management. This is why management must take every opportunity to convince employees of the need for culture change and communicate to them how new attitudes, behaviors, and operating practices will benefit the interests of organizational stakeholders.

A company that has done a good job of fixing its problem culture is Alberto-Culver—see Company Spotlight 9.2.

Grounding the Culture in Core Values and Ethics

A corporate culture grounded in socially approved values and ethical business principles is a vital ingredient in a company's long-term strategic success.[17] Unless a company's executives genuinely care about how the company's business affairs are conducted, the company's reputation and ultimately its performance are put at risk. One need look no further than the scandals at companies like Enron, WorldCom, and HealthSouth to see the damage that occurs when the public spotlight is trained on a company's shady business practices and unethical behavior.

While there's no doubt that some companies and some company personnel knowingly engage in shady business practices and have little regard for ethical standards, one must be cautious about assuming that a company's core values and ethical standards are meaningless window dressing. Executives at many companies genuinely care about the values and ethical standards that company personnel exhibit in conducting the company's business; they are aware that their own reputations, as well as the company's reputation, hangs on whether outsiders see the company's actions as ethical or honest or socially acceptable. At such companies, values statements and codes of ethics matter, and they are ingrained to one degree or another in the company's culture—see Table 9.1 for the kinds of topics that are commonly found in values statements and codes of ethics.

Indeed, at companies where executives are truly committed to practicing the values and ethical standards that have been espoused, *the stated core values and ethical principles are the cornerstones of the corporate culture*. As depicted in Figure 9.1, a company that works hard at putting its stated core values and ethical principles into practice fosters a work climate where company personnel share common convictions about how the company's business is to be conducted and where they are expected to act in accord with stated values and ethical standards. By promoting behaviors that mirror the values and ethics standards, a company's stated values and ethical standards nurture the corporate culture in

> A company's values statement and code of ethics communicate expectations of how employees should conduct themselves in the workplace.

three highly positive ways: (1) they communicate the company's good intentions and validate the integrity and above-board character of its business principles and operating methods, (2) they steer company personnel toward both doing the right thing and doing things right, and (3) they establish a "corporate conscience" and provide yardsticks for gauging the appropriateness of particular actions, decisions, and policies (see Figure 9.2).[18]

COMPANY SPOTLIGHT 9.2

The Culture-Change Effort at Alberto-Culver's North American Division

In 1993, Carol Bernick—vice chairperson of Alberto-Culver, president of its North American division, and daughter of the company's founders—concluded that her division's existing culture had four problems: Employees dutifully waited for marching orders from their bosses, workers put pleasing their bosses ahead of pleasing customers, some company policies were not family-friendly, and there was too much bureaucracy and paperwork. What was needed, in Bernick's opinion, was a culture in which company employees had a sense of ownership and an urgency to get things done, welcomed innovation, and were willing to taking risks.

To change the culture, Alberto-Culver's management undertook a series of actions:

- In 1993, a new position, called growth development leader (GDL), was created to help orchestrate the task of fixing the culture deep in the ranks (there were 70 GDLs in Alberto-Culver's North American division). GDLs came from all ranks of the company's managerial ladder and were handpicked for such qualities as empathy, communication skills, positive attitude, and ability to let their hair down and have fun. GDLs performed their regular jobs in addition to taking on the GDL roles; it was considered an honor to be chosen. Each GDL mentored about 12 people from both a career and a family standpoint. GDLs met with senior executives weekly, bringing forward people's questions and issues and then, afterward, sharing with their groups the topics and solutions that were discussed. GDLs brought a group member as a guest to each meeting. One meeting each year is devoted to identifying "macros and irritations"—attendees are divided into four subgroups and given 15 minutes to identify the company's four biggest challenges (the macros) and the four most annoying aspects of life at the company (the irritations); the whole group votes on which four deserve the company's attention. Those selected are then addressed, and assignments made for follow-up and results.

- Changing the culture was made an issue across the company, starting in 1995 with a two-hour State of the Company presentation to employees covering where the company was and where it wanted to be. The State of the Company address was made an annual event.

- Management created ways to measure the gains in changing the culture. One involved an annual all-employee survey to assess progress against cultural goals and to get 360-degree feedback—the 2000 survey had 180 questions, including 33 relating to the performance of each respondent's GDL. A bonfire celebration was held in the company parking lot to announce that paperwork would be cut 30 percent.

- A list of 10 cultural imperatives was formalized in 1998—honesty, ownership, trust, customer orientation, commitment, fun, innovation, risk taking, speed and urgency, and teamwork. These imperatives came to be known internally as HOT CC FIRST.

- Instituting extensive celebrations and awards programs. Most celebrations are scheduled, but some are spontaneous (an impromptu thank-you party for a good fiscal year). Business Builder Awards (initiated in 1997) are given to individuals and teams that make a significant impact on the company's growth and profitability. The best-scoring GDLs on the annual employee surveys are awarded shares of company stock. The company notes all work anniversaries and personal milestones with "Alberto-appropriate" gifts; appreciative company employees sometimes give thank-you gifts to their GDLs. According to Carol Bernick, "If you want something to grow, pour champagne on it. We've made a huge effort—maybe even an over-the-top effort—to celebrate our successes and, indeed, just about everything we'd like to see happen again."

The culture change effort at Alberto-Culver North America was viewed as a major contributor to improved performance. From 1993, when the effort first began, to 2001, the division's sales increased from just under $350 million to over $600 million and pretax profits rose from $20 million to almost $50 million.

Source: Carol Lavin Bernick, "When Your Culture Needs a Makeover," *Harvard Business Review* 79, no. 6 (June 2001), p. 61.

Table 9.1   THE CONTENT OF COMPANY VALUE STATEMENTS AND CODES OF ETHICS

Topics Commonly Appearing in Values Statements	Topics Commonly Appearing in Codes of Ethics
▪ Commitment to such outcomes as customer satisfaction and customer service, quality, product innovation, and/or technological leadership ▪ Commitment to achievement, excellence, and results ▪ Importance of demonstrating such qualities as honesty, integrity, trust, fairness, quality of life, pride of workmanship, and ethics ▪ Importance of creativity, taking initiative, and accepting responsibility ▪ Importance of teamwork and a cooperative attitude ▪ Importance of Golden Rule behavior and respect for coworkers ▪ Making the company a great place to work ▪ Importance of having fun and creating a fun work environment ▪ Duty to stakeholders—customers, employees, suppliers, shareholders, communities where the company operates, and society at large ▪ Commitment to exercising social responsibility and being a good community citizen ▪ Commitment to protecting the environment ▪ Commitment to workforce diversity	▪ A mandate that company personnel will behave with honesty and integrity ▪ An expectation that all company personnel will comply fully with all laws and regulations, specifically: • Antitrust laws prohibiting anticompetitive practices, conspiracies to fix prices, or attempts to monopolize • Foreign Corrupt Practices Act • Securities laws and prohibitions against insider trading • Environmental and workplace safety regulations • Discrimination and sexual harassment regulations ▪ Prohibitions against accepting bribes or making payments to obtain business ▪ Avoiding conflicts of interest ▪ Fairness in selling and marketing practices ▪ Supplier relationships and procurement practices ▪ Acquiring and using competitively sensitive information about rivals and others ▪ Political activities and lobbying ▪ Avoiding use of company assets, resources, and property for personal or other inappropriate purposes ▪ Responsibility to protect proprietary information

Figure 9.1   The Two Culture-Building Roles of a Company's Core Values and Ethical Standards

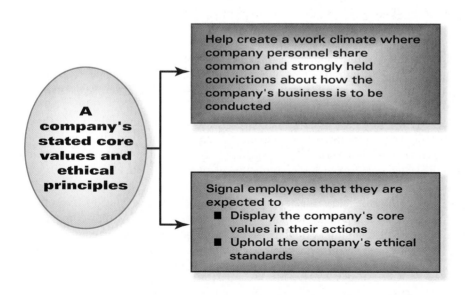

Figure 9.2   How the Practice of Stated Core Values and Ethical Principles Positively Impact the Corporate Culture

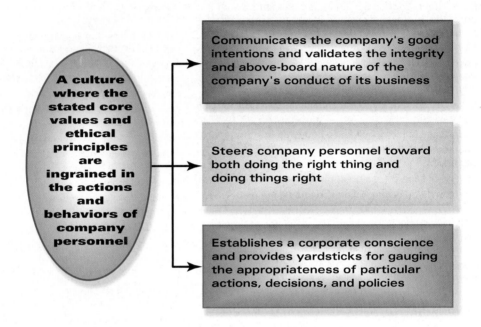

Companies ingrain their values and ethical standards in a number of different ways.[19] Tradition-steeped companies with a rich folklore rely heavily on word-of-mouth indoctrination and the power of tradition to instill values and enforce ethical conduct. But many companies today convey their values and codes of ethics to stakeholders and interested parties in their annual reports, on their websites, and in internal communications to all employees. The standards are hammered in at orientation courses for new employees and in training courses for managers and employees. The trend of making stakeholders aware of a company's commitment to core values and ethical business conduct is attributable to three factors: (1) greater management understanding of the role these statements play in culture building, (2) a renewed focus on ethical standards stemming from the corporate scandals that came to light in 2001–2002, and (3) the growing numbers of consumers who prefer to patronize ethical companies with ethical products.

However, there is a considerable difference between saying the right things (having a well-articulated corporate values statement or code of ethics) and truly managing a company in an ethical and socially responsible way. Companies that are truly committed to the stated core values and to high ethical standards make ethical behavior *a fundamental component of their corporate culture.* They put a stake in the ground, making it unequivocally clear that company personnel are expected to live up to the company's values and ethical standards—how well individuals display core values and adhere to ethical standards is often part of their job performance evaluations. Peer pressures to conform to cultural norms are quite strong, acting as an important deterrent to outside-the-lines behavior. Moreover, values statements and codes of ethical conduct are used as benchmarks for judging the appropriateness of company policies and operating practices.

At Darden Restaurants—a $4.5 billion casual dining company with over 1,200 company-owned Red Lobster, Olive Garden, Bahama Breeze, and Smokey Bones BBQ Sports Bar restaurants—the core values are operating with integrity, treating people fairly, and welcoming and celebrating workforce diversity; the company's practice of these values has been instrumental in creating a culture characterized by trust, exciting jobs and career opportunities for employees, and a passion to be the best in casual dining.[20]

Once values and ethical standards have been formally adopted, they must be institutionalized in the company's policies and practices and ingrained in the conduct of company personnel. Imbedding the values and code of ethics entails several actions:

- Incorporation of the statement of values and the code of ethics into employee training and educational programs.

- Explicit attention to values and ethics in recruiting and hiring to screen out applicants who do not exhibit compatible character traits.

- Frequent reiteration of company values and ethical principles at company events and internal communications to employees.

- Active management involvement, from the CEO down to frontline supervisors, in stressing the importance of values and ethical conduct and in overseeing the compliance process.

- Ceremonies and awards for individuals and groups who display the values.

- Instituting ethics enforcement procedures.

In the case of codes of ethics, special attention must be given to sections of the company that are particularly vulnerable—procurement, sales, and political lobbying. Employees who deal with external parties are in ethically sensitive positions and often are drawn into compromising situations. Company personnel assigned to subsidiaries in foreign countries can find themselves trapped in ethical dilemmas if bribery and corruption of public officials are common practices or if suppliers or customers are accustomed to kickbacks of one kind or another. Mandatory ethics training for such personnel is usually desirable.

As a test of your ethics, take the quiz on page 314.

Structuring the Ethics Enforcement Process   If a company's executives truly aspire for company personnel to behave ethically, then procedures for enforcing ethical standards and handling potential violations have to be developed. Even in an ethically strong company, there can be bad apples—and some of the bad apples may even rise to the executive ranks. So it is not enough to rely on an ethically-strong culture to produce ethics compliance.

The compliance effort must permeate the company, extending to every organizational unit. The attitudes, character, and work history of prospective employees must be scrutinized. Every employee must receive adequate training. Line managers at all levels must give serious and continuous attention to the task of explaining how the values and ethical code apply in their areas. In addition, they must insist that company values and ethical standards become a way of life. In general, instilling values and insisting on ethical conduct must be looked on as a continuous culture-building, culture-nurturing exercise. Whether the effort succeeds or fails depends largely on how well corporate values and ethical standards are visibly integrated into company policies, managerial practices, and actions at all levels.

A TEST OF YOUR BUSINESS ETHICS

As a gauge of your own ethical and moral standards, take the following quiz and see how you stack up against other members of your class. For the test to be valid, you need to answer the questions candidly and not on the basis of what you think the right answer is. When you finish the test, you should compare your answers to how your future employer would likely want you to answer each of these questions. Which are likely to be considered vital?

1. Is it unethical to make up data to justify the introduction of a new product if, when you start to object, your boss tells you, "Just do it"?
____Yes ____No ____Unsure (it depends) ____Need more information

2. Do you think that it is acceptable to give your boss a $100 gift to celebrate a birthday or holiday?
____Yes ____No ____Unsure (it depends) ____Need more information

3. Would it be wrong to accept a $100 gift from your boss (who is of the opposite sex) to celebrate your birthday?
____Yes ____No ____Unsure (it depends) ____Need more information

4. Is it unethical to accept an invitation from a supplier to spend a holiday weekend skiing at the supplier company's resort home in Colorado? (Would your answer be different if you were presently considering a proposal from that supplier to purchase $1 million worth of components?)
____Yes ____No ____Unsure (it depends) ____Need more information

5. Is it unethical to give a customer company's purchasing manager free tickets to the Super Bowl if he or she is looking for tickets and is likely to make a large purchase from your company?
____Yes ____No ____Unsure (it depends) ____Need more information

6. Is it unethical to use sick days provided in your company benefits plan as personal days so that you can go attend a family event or leave early for a weekend vacation?
____Yes ____No ____Unsure (it depends) ____Need more information

7. Would it be wrong to keep quiet if you, as a junior financial analyst, had just calculated that the projected return on a possible project was 18 percent and your boss (a) informed you that no project could be approved without the prospect of a 25 percent return and (b) told you to go back and redo the numbers and "get them right"?
____Yes ____No ____Unsure (it depends) ____Need more information

8. Would it be unethical to allow your supervisor to believe that you were chiefly responsible for the success of a new company initiative if it actually resulted from a team effort or major contributions by a coworker?
____Yes ____No ____Unsure (it depends) ____Need more information

9. Is it unethical to fail to come forward to support an employee wrongfully accused of misconduct if that person is a source of aggravation for you at work?
____Yes ____No ____Unsure (it depends) ____Need more information

10. Is it wrong to use your employer's staff to prepare invitations for a party that you will give when clients or customers are among those invited?
____Yes ____No ____Unsure (it depends) ____Need more information

11. Is it wrong to browse the Internet while at work if all your work is done and there is otherwise nothing you ought to be doing? (Would your answer be the same if the websites you visited were pornographic?)
____Yes ____No ____Unsure (it depends) ____Need more information

12. Is it unethical to keep quiet if you are aware that a coworker is being sexually harassed by his or her boss?
____Yes ____No ____Unsure (it depends) ____Need more information

13. Is there an ethical problem with using your employer's copier to make a small number of copies for personal use (for example, your tax returns, your child's school project, or personal correspondence)?
____Yes ____No ____Unsure (it depends) ____Need more information

14. Is it unethical to install company-owned software on your home computer without the permission of your supervisor and the software vendor?
____Yes ____No ____Unsure (it depends) ____Need more information

15. Is it unethical to okay the shipment of products to a customer that do not meet the customer's specifications without first checking with the customer?
____Yes ____No ____Unsure (it depends) ____Need more information

ANSWERS: We think a strong case can be made that the answers to questions 1, 3, 4, 5, 6, 7, 8, 9, 10, 11, 12, 13, 14, and 15 are yes and that the answer to question 2 is no. Most employers would consider the answers to questions 10 and 13 to be yes unless company policy allows personal use of company resources under certain specified conditions.

If a company is really serious about enforcing ethical behavior, it probably needs to do two things:

1. Conduct an annual audit of each manager's efforts to uphold ethical standards and require formal reports on the actions taken by managers to remedy deficient conduct.

2. Require all employees to sign a statement annually certifying that they have complied with the company's code of ethics.

While these actions may seem extreme or objectionable, they leave little room to doubt the seriousness of a company's commitment to ethics compliance. And most company personnel will think twice about knowingly engaging in unethical conduct when they know their actions will be audited and/or when they have to sign statements certifying compliance with the company's code of ethics.

Establishing a Strategy–Culture Fit in Multinational and Global Companies

In multinational and global companies, where some cross-border diversity in the corporate culture is normal, efforts to establish a tight strategy–culture fit is complicated by the diversity of societal customs and lifestyles from country to country. Company personnel in different countries sometimes fervently insist on being treated as distinctive individuals or groups, making a one-size-fits-all culture potentially inappropriate. Leading cross-border culture-change initiatives requires sensitivity to prevailing cultural differences; managers must discern when diversity has to be accommodated and when cross-border differences can be and should be narrowed.[21] Cross-country cultural diversity in a multinational enterprise is more tolerable if the company is pursuing a multicountry strategy and if the company's culture in each country is well aligned with its strategy in that country. But significant cross-country differences in a company's culture are likely to impede execution of a global strategy and have to be addressed.

As discussed earlier in this chapter, the trick to establishing a workable strategy–culture fit in multinational and global companies is to ground the culture in strategy-supportive values and operating practices that travel well across country borders and strike a chord with managers and workers in many different areas of the world, despite the diversity of local customs and traditions. A multinational enterprise with a misfit between its strategy and culture in certain countries where it operates can attack the problem by reinterpreting or deemphasizing or even abandoning those values and cultural traits which it finds inappropriate for some countries where it operates. Problematic values and operating principles can be replaced with values and operating approaches that travel well across country borders but that are still strategy supportive. Many times a company's values statement only has to be reworded so as to express existing values in ways that have more universal appeal. Sometimes certain offending operating practices can be modified to good advantage in all locations where the company operates.

Aside from trying to ground the culture in a set of core values and operating principles that have universal appeal, management can seek to minimize the existence of subcultures and cross-country cultural diversity by:

- Instituting training programs to communicate the meaning of core values and explain the case for common operating principles and practices.

- Drawing on the full range of motivational and compensation incentives to induce personnel to adopt and practice the desired behaviors.

▨ Allowing some leeway for certain core values and principles to be interpreted and applied somewhat differently, if necessary, to accommodate local customs and traditions.

Generally, a high degree of cross-country cultural homogeneity is desirable and has to be pursued. Having too much variation in the culture from country to country not only makes it difficult to use the culture in helping drive the strategy execution process but also works against the establishment of a one-company mindset and a consistent corporate identity.

Leading the Strategy Execution Process

The litany of managing the strategy process is simple enough: Craft a sound strategic plan, implement it, execute it to the fullest, adjust it as needed, and win! But the leadership challenges are significant and diverse. Exerting take-charge leadership, being a "spark plug," ramrodding things through, and achieving results thrusts a manager into a variety of leadership roles in managing the strategy execution process: resource acquirer and allocator, capabilities builder, motivator, policymaker, policy enforcer, head cheerleader, crisis solver, decision maker, and taskmaster, to mention a few. There are times when leading the strategy execution process entails being authoritarian and hardnosed, times when it is best to be a perceptive listener and a compromising decision maker, times when matters are best delegated to people closest to the scene of the action, and times when being a coach is the proper role. Many occasions call for the manager in charge to assume a highly visible role and put in long hours guiding the process, while others entail only a brief ceremonial performance with the details delegated to subordinates.

For the most part, leading the strategy execution process has to be top-down and driven by mandates to get things done and show good results. Just how to go about the specifics of leading organization efforts to put a strategy in place and deliver the intended results has to start with understanding the requirements for good strategy execution, followed by a diagnosis of the organization's capabilities and preparedness to execute the necessary strategic initiatives, and then decisions as to which of several ways to proceed to get things done and achieve the targeted results.[22] In general, leading the drive for good strategy execution and operating excellence calls for several actions on the part of the manager-in-charge:

1. Staying on top of what is happening, closely monitoring progress, ferreting out issues, and learning what obstacles lie in the path of good execution.

2. Putting constructive pressure on the organization to achieve good results.

3. Keeping the organization focused on operating excellence.

4. Leading the development of stronger core competencies and competitive capabilities.

5. Exercising ethics leadership and insisting that the company conduct its affairs like a model corporate citizen.

6. Pushing corrective actions to improve strategy execution and achieve the targeted results.

Staying on Top of How Well Things Are Going

To stay on top of how well the strategy execution process is going, a manager needs to develop a broad network of contacts and sources of information, both formal and informal. The regular channels include talking with key subordinates, attending presentations and meetings, reading reviews of the latest operating results, talking to customers, watching the competitive reactions of rival firms, exchanging e-mail and holding telephone conversations with people in outlying locations, making onsite visits, and listening to rank-and-file employees. However, some information is more trustworthy than the rest, and the views and perspectives offered by different people can vary widely. Presentations and briefings by subordinates may not represent the whole truth. Bad news or problems may be minimized or in some cases not reported at all as subordinates delay conveying failures and problems in hopes that they can turn things around in time. Hence, strategy managers have to make sure that they have accurate information and a feel for the existing situation. They have to confirm whether things are on track, identify problems, learn what obstacles lie in the path of good strategy execution, and develop a basis for determining what, if anything, they can personally do to move the process along.

One of the best ways for executives in charge of strategy execution to stay on top of things is by making regular visits to the field and talking with many different people at many different levels—a technique often labeled **managing by walking around (MBWA).** Wal-Mart executives have had a long-standing practice of spending two to three days every week visiting Wal-Mart's stores and talking with store managers and employees. Sam Walton, Wal-Mart's founder, insisted, "The key is to get out into the store and listen to what the associates have to say." Jack Welch, the highly effective CEO of General Electric (GE) from 1980 to 2001, not only spent several days each month personally visiting GE operations and talking with major customers but also arranged his schedule so that he could spend time exchanging information and ideas with GE

> **Core Concept**
>
> **Management by walking around (MBWA)** is one of the techniques that effective leaders use to stay informed about how well the strategy execution process is progressing.

managers from all over the world who were attending classes at the company's leadership development center near GE's headquarters. Some companies have weekly get-togethers in each division (often on Friday afternoons), attended by both executives and employees, to create a regular opportunity for tidbits of information to flow freely between down-the-line employees and executives. Many manufacturing executives make a point of strolling the factory floor to talk with workers and meeting regularly with union officials. Some managers operate out of open cubicles in big spaces populated with open cubicles for other personnel so that they can interact easily and frequently with coworkers.

Most managers rightly attach great importance to spending time with people at various company facilities and gathering information and opinions firsthand from diverse sources about how well various aspects of the strategy execution process are going. Such contacts give managers a feel for what progress is being made, what problems are being encountered, and whether additional resources or different approaches may be needed. Just as important, MBWA provides opportunities for managers to talk informally to many different people at different organizational levels, give encouragement, lift spirits, shift attention from the old to the new priorities, and create some excitement—all of which generate positive energy and help mobilize organizational efforts behind strategy execution.

Putting Constructive Pressure on the Organization to Achieve Good Results

Managers have to be out front in mobilizing organizational energy behind the drive for good strategy execution and operating excellence. Part of the leadership requirement here entails nurturing a results-oriented work climate. A culture where there's constructive pressure to achieve good results is a valuable contributor to good strategy-execution and operating excellence. Results-oriented cultures are permeated with a spirit of achievement and have a good track record in meeting or beating performance targets. If management wants to drive the strategy execution effort by instilling a results-oriented work climate, then senior executives have to take the lead in promoting certain enabling cultural drivers: a strong sense of involvement on the part of company personnel, emphasis on individual initiative and creativity, respect for the contribution of individuals and groups, and pride in doing things right.

Organizational leaders who succeed in creating a results-oriented work climate typically are intensely people-oriented, and they are skilled users of people-management practices that win the emotional commitment of company personnel and inspire them to do their best.[23] They understand that treating employees well generally leads to increased teamwork, higher morale, greater loyalty, and increased employee commitment to making a contribution. All of these foster an esprit de corps that energizes organizational members to contribute to the drive for operating excellence and proficient strategy execution.

Successfully leading the effort to instill a spirit of high achievement into the culture generally entails such leadership actions and managerial practices as:

- Treating employees with dignity and respect. This often includes a strong company commitment to training each employee thoroughly, providing attractive career opportunities, emphasizing promotion from within, and providing a high degree of job security. Some companies symbolize the value of individual employees and the importance of their contributions by referring to them as cast members (Disney), crew members (McDonald's), coworkers (Kinko's and CDW Computer Centers), job owners (Graniterock), partners (Starbucks), or associates (Wal-Mart, Lenscrafters, W. L. Gore, Edward Jones, Publix Supermarkets, and Marriott International). At a number of companies, managers at every level are held responsible for developing the people who report to them.

- Making champions out of the people who turn in winning performances—but doing so in ways that promote teamwork and cross-unit collaboration as opposed to spurring an unhealthy footrace among employees to best one another.

- Encouraging employees to use initiative and creativity in performing their work.

- Setting stretch objectives and clearly communicating an expectation that company personnel are to give their best in achieving performance targets.

- Granting employees enough autonomy to stand out, excel, and contribute.

- Using the full range of motivational techniques and compensation incentives to inspire company personnel, nurture a results-oriented work climate, and enforce high-performance standards.

- Celebrating individual, group, and company successes. Top management should miss no opportunity to express respect for individual employees and their appreciation of extraordinary individual and group effort.[24] Companies like Mary Kay Cosmetics, Tupperware, and McDonald's actively seek out reasons and opportunities to give pins, buttons, badges, and medals for good showings by average performers—the idea being to express appreciation and give a motivational boost to people who stand out in doing ordinary jobs. General Electric and 3M Corporation make a point of ceremoniously honoring individuals who believe so strongly in their ideas that they take it on themselves to hurdle the bureaucracy, maneuver their projects through the system, and turn them into improved services, new products, or even new businesses.

While leadership efforts to instill a results-oriented culture usually accentuate the positive, there are negative reinforcers too. Managers whose units consistently perform poorly have to be replaced. Low-performing workers and people who reject the results-oriented cultural emphasis have to be weeded out or at least moved to out-of-the-way positions. Average performers have to be candidly counseled that they have limited career potential unless they show more progress in the form of more effort, better skills, and ability to deliver better results.

Keeping the Internal Organization Focused on Operating Excellence

Another leadership dimension of the drive for good strategy execution is keeping the organization bubbling with fresh supplies of ideas and suggestions for improvement. Managers cannot mandate innovative improvements by simply exhorting people to "be creative," nor can they make continuous progress toward operating excellence with directives to "try harder." Rather, they have to foster a culture where innovative ideas and experimentation with new ways of doing things can blossom and thrive. There are several actions that organizational leaders can take to promote new ideas for improving the performance of value chain activities:

▨ *Encouraging individuals and groups to brainstorm, let their imaginations fly in all directions, and come up with proposals for improving how things are done*—Operating excellence requires that everybody be expected to contribute ideas, exercise initiative, and pursue continuous improvement. The leadership trick is to keep a sense of urgency alive in the business so that people see change and innovation as necessities. One year after taking charge at Siemens-Nixdorf Information Systems, Gerhard Schulmeyer produced the first profit in the merged company, which had been losing hundreds of millions of dollars annually since 1991; he credited the turnaround to the creation of 5,000 "change agents," almost 15 percent of the workforce, who volunteered for active roles in the company's change agenda while continuing to perform their regular jobs.

▨ *Taking special pains to foster, nourish, and support people who are eager for a chance to try turning their ideas into better ways of operating*—People with maverick ideas or out-of-the-ordinary proposals have to be tolerated and given room to operate. Above all, would-be champions who advocate radical or different ideas must not be looked on as disruptive or troublesome. The best champions and change agents are persistent, competitive, tenacious, committed, and fanatic about seeing their idea through to success.

▨ *Ensuring that the rewards for successful champions are large and visible and that people who champion an unsuccessful idea are not punished or sidelined but rather encouraged to try again*—Encouraging lots of "tries" is important since many ideas won't pan out.

- *Using all kinds of ad hoc organizational forms to support ideas and experimentation*—Venture teams, task forces, "performance shootouts" among different groups working on competing approaches, and informal "bootleg" projects composed of volunteers are just a few of the possibilities.

- *Using the tools of benchmarking, best practices, business process reengineering, TQM, and six sigma quality to focus attention on continuous improvement*—These are proven approaches to getting better operating results and facilitating better strategy execution.

Leading the Development of Better Competencies and Capabilities

A third avenue to better strategy execution and operating excellence is proactively strengthening organizational competencies and competitive capabilities. Senior management usually has to lead the strengthening of core competencies and competitive capabilities because they typically reside in the combined efforts of different work groups, departments, and strategic allies. Stronger competencies and capabilities can not only lead to better performance of value chain activities but also to a competitive edge over rivals that paves the way for better bottom-line results.

Exercising Ethics Leadership and Insisting on Good Corporate Citizenship

For an organization to avoid the pitfalls of scandal and disgrace and consistently display the intent to conduct its business in a socially acceptable manner, the CEO and those around the CEO must be openly and unequivocally committed to ethical conduct and socially redeeming business principles and values. It is never enough for senior executives to assume that all of the company's business activities are being conducted ethically, nor can it be assumed that employees understand how to handle situations that are in ethically gray areas.

Leading the enforcement of ethical behavior has four pieces. First and foremost, the CEO and other senior executives must set an excellent example in their own ethical behavior and demonstrate integrity in their actions and decisions. Company decisions have to be seen as ethical—actions speak louder than words. Second, company personnel have to be educated about what is ethical and what is not; the company may have to establish ethics training programs and discuss what to do in gray areas. Everyone must be encouraged to raise issues with ethical dimensions, and such discussions should be treated as a legitimate topic. Third, top management should regularly declare unequivocal support of the company's ethical code and take a strong stand on expecting all company personnel to conduct themselves in an ethical fashion at all times. This means iterating and reiterating to employees that it is their duty to observe the company's ethical codes. Ideally, the company's commitment to its stated values and ethical principles will instill not only a corporate conscience but also a conscience on the part of company personnel that prompts them to report possible ethical violations. While ethically conscious companies have provisions for disciplining violators, *the main purpose of enforcement is to encourage compliance rather than administer punishment.* Thus, the motive for reporting possible ethical violations is not so much to get someone in trouble as to prevent further damage and heighten awareness of operating within ethical bounds. Fourth, top management must be prepared to act as the final ar-

Lockheed Martin's Corrective Actions after Violating U.S. Antibribery Laws

Lockheed Martin Corporation is among the world's leading producers of aeronautics and space systems, with 2002 sales of $26 billion. The company designed and built the P-38 fighter, B-29 bomber, U-2 and SR-71 reconnaissance aircraft, C-130 cargo planes, F-104 Starfighter, F-16 Fighting Falcon, F-22 Raptor, and Titan and Trident missiles. It has been a major contractor on the Mercury, Gemini, Apollo, Skylab, and shuttle space programs.

Lockheed Martin's status as a U.S. government contractor was jeopardized in 1995 when company officials admitted that the company had conspired to violate U.S. antibribery laws. The infraction occurred in 1990 when Lockheed Martin paid an Egyptian lawmaker $1 million to help the company secure a contract to supply Egypt with C-130 cargo planes. The U.S. government fined Lockheed Martin $24.8 million and placed it on three-year probation during which further ethics violations could bar the company from bidding on government contracts.

After the conviction, Lockheed Martin's CEO and other senior executives put a comprehensive ethics compliance program in place to guard against subsequent violations. Completion of an online ethics training course was made mandatory for all employees; the course covered Lockheed Martin's code of ethics and business conduct. The online software system records when employees complete online sessions on such topics as sexual harassment, security, software-license compliance, labor charging, insider trading, and gratuities. It also gives the company the capability to conduct up-to-the-minute ethics audits to determine how many hours of training have been completed by each of Lockheed Martin's 170,000 employees.

Lockheed Martin's ethics software programs provide company managers with a variety of statistics related to ethics violations that do occur at the company—like the number of detected violations of misuse of company resources, conflicts of interest, and security breaches. In addition, the system gives an accounting of the number of Lockheed Martin employees discharged, suspended, and reprimanded for ethics violations. Lockheed Martin managers and the U.S. government use the database to assess the state of business ethics at the company.

Lockheed Martin's renewed commitment to honesty, integrity, respect, trust, responsibility, and citizenship—along with its method for monitoring ethics compliance—paved the way for the company to receive the 1998 American Business Ethics Award. Upon receiving the award, the company's chairman and CEO, Vance Coffman, said, "At Lockheed Martin, we have stressed that the first and most important unifying principle guiding us is ethical conduct, every day and everywhere we do business. Receiving the American Business Ethics Award is a strong signal that we are achieving our goal of putting our Corporation on a firm ethical foundation for the challenges of the 21st century."

Sources: Lockheed Martin website and *The Wall Street Journal*, October 21, 1999, p. B1.

---

biter on hard calls; this means removing people from key positions or terminating them when they are guilty of a violation. It also means reprimanding those who have been lax in monitoring and enforcing ethical compliance. Failure to act swiftly and decisively in punishing ethical misconduct is interpreted as a lack of real commitment.

See Company Spotlight 9.3 for a discussion of the actions Lockheed Martin's top executives took when the company faced a bribery scandal.

Corporate Citizenship and Social Responsibility: Another Dimension of Model Ethical Behavior Strong enforcement of a corporate code of ethics by itself is not sufficient to make a company a good corporate citizen. Business leaders who want their companies to be regarded as exemplary corporate citizens must not only see that their companies operate ethically but also display a social conscience in decisions that affect stakeholders, especially employees, the communities in which they operate, and society at large. Corporate citizenship and socially responsible decision making are demonstrated in a number of ways: having family-friendly employment practices, operating a safe workplace, taking special pains to protect the environment (beyond what is required by law), taking an active role in community affairs, interacting with community officials to minimize the impact of layoffs or hiring large numbers of new employees (which could put a strain on local schools and utility services), and being a generous supporter of charitable causes and projects that benefit society. For example, Chick-Fil-A, an Atlanta-based fast-food chain with 700 outlets, has a charitable foundation, supports 10 foster homes and a summer camp, funds two scholarship programs, and participates in a number of one-on-one programs with children.[25] Toys "R" Us supports initiatives addressing the issues of child labor and fair labor practices around the world. Community Pride Food Stores is assisting in revitalizing the inner city of Richmond, Virginia, where the company is based. The owner of Malden Mills Industries in Malden, Massachusetts, kept employees on the company's payroll for months while a fire-razed plant was rebuilt.

What separates companies that make a sincere effort to carry their weight in being good corporate citizens from companies that are content to do only what is legally required of them are company leaders who believe strongly in good corporate citizenship. Companies with socially conscious strategy leaders and a core value of corporate social responsibility are the most likely to conduct their affairs in a manner befitting a good corporate citizen.

Leading the Process of Making Corrective Adjustments

The leadership challenge of making corrective adjustments is twofold: deciding when adjustments are needed and deciding what adjustments to make. Both decisions are a normal and necessary part of managing the strategy execution process, since no scheme for implementing and executing strategy can foresee all the events and problems that will arise. There comes a time at every company when managers have to fine-tune or overhaul the approaches to strategy execution and push for better results. Clearly, when a company's strategy execution effort is not delivering good results and making measure progress toward operating excellence, it is the leader's responsibility to step forward and push corrective actions.

The *process* of making corrective adjustments varies according to the situation. In a crisis, it is typical for leaders to have key subordinates gather information, identify and evaluate options (crunching whatever numbers may be appropriate), and perhaps prepare a preliminary set of recommended actions for consideration. The organizational leader then usually meets with key subordinates and personally presides over extended discussions of the proposed responses, trying to build a quick consensus among members of the executive inner circle. If no consensus emerges and action is required immediately, the burden falls on the manager in charge to choose the response and urge its support.

When the situation allows managers to proceed more deliberately in deciding when to make changes and what changes to make, most managers seem to prefer a process of incrementally solidifying commitment to a particular course of action.[26] The process that managers go through in deciding on corrective adjustments is essentially the same for both proactive and reactive changes: They sense needs, gather information, broaden and deepen their understanding of the situation, develop options and explore their pros and cons, put forth action proposals, generate partial (comfort-level) solutions, strive for a consensus, and finally formally adopt an agreed-on course of action.[27] The time frame for deciding what corrective changes to initiate can take a few hours, a few days, a few weeks, or even a few months if the situation is particularly complicated.

Success in initiating corrective actions usually hinges on thorough analysis of the situation, the exercise of good business judgment in deciding what actions to take, and good implementation of the corrective actions that are initiated. Successful managers are skilled in getting an organization back on track rather quickly; they (and their staffs) are good at discerning what actions to take and in ramrodding them through to a successful conclusion. Managers that struggle to show measurable progress in generating good results and improving the performance of strategy-critical value chain activities are candidates for being replaced.

The challenges of leading a successful strategy execution effort are, without question, substantial.[28] But the job is definitely doable. Because each instance of executing strategy occurs under different organizational circumstances, the managerial agenda for executing strategy always needs to be situation-specific—there's no neat generic procedure to follow. And, as we said at the beginning of Chapter 7, executing strategy is an action-oriented, make-the-right-things-happen task that challenges a manager's ability to lead and direct organizational change, create or reinvent business processes, manage and motivate people, and achieve performance targets. If you now better understand what the challenges are, what approaches are available, which issues need to be considered, and why the action agenda for implementing and executing strategy sweeps across so many aspects of administrative and managerial work, then we will look on our discussion in Chapters 7–9 as a success.

A Final Word on Managing the Process of Crafting and Executing Strategy   In practice, it is hard to separate the leadership requirements of executing strategy from the other pieces of the strategy process. As we said in Chapter 1, the job of crafting, implementing, and executing strategy is a five-task process with much looping and recycling to fine-tune and adjust strategic visions, objectives, strategies, capabilities, implementation approaches, and cultures to fit one another and to fit changing circumstances. The process is continuous, and the conceptually separate acts of crafting and executing strategy blur together in real-world situations. The best tests of good strategic leadership are whether the company has a good strategy and whether the strategy execution effort is delivering the hoped-for results. If these two conditions exist, the chances are excellent that the company has good strategic leadership.

Key Points

A company's culture is manifested in the values and business principles that management preaches and practices, in the tone and philosophy of official policies and procedures, in its revered traditions and oft-repeated stories, in the attitudes and behaviors of employees, in the peer pressures that exist to display core values, in the organization's politics, in its approaches to people management and problem solving, in its relationships with external stakeholders (particularly vendors and the communities in which it operates), and in the atmosphere that permeates its work environment. Culture thus concerns the personality a company has and the style in which it does things.

Very often, the elements of company culture originate with a founder or other early influential leaders who articulate the values, beliefs, and principles to which the company should adhere. These elements then get incorporated into company policies, a creed or values statement, strategies, and operating practices. Over time, these values and practices become shared by company employees and managers. Cultures are perpetuated as new leaders act to reinforce them, as new employees are encouraged to adopt and follow them, as stories of people and events illustrating core values and practices are told and retold, and as organization members are honored and rewarded for displaying cultural norms.

Company cultures vary widely in strength and in makeup. Some cultures are strongly embedded, while others are weak or fragmented. Some cultures are unhealthy, often dominated by self-serving politics, resistance to change, and inward focus. Unhealthy cultural traits are often precursors to declining company performance. In adaptive cultures, the work climate is receptive to new ideas, experimentation, innovation, new strategies, and new operating practices provided the new behaviors and operating practices that management is calling for are seen as legitimate and consistent with the core values and business principles underpinning the culture. An adaptive culture is a terrific managerial ally, especially in fast-changing business environments, because company personnel are receptive to risk taking, experimentation, innovation, and changing strategies and practices—there's a feeling of confidence that the organization can deal with whatever threats and opportunities come down the pike. In direct contrast to change-resistant cultures, adaptive cultures are very supportive of managers and employees at all ranks who propose or help initiate useful change; indeed, there's a proactive approach to identifying issues, evaluating the implications and options, and implementing workable solutions.

A culture grounded in values, practices, and behavioral norms that match what is needed for good strategy execution helps energize people throughout the company to do their jobs in a strategy-supportive manner, adding significantly to the power of a company's strategy execution effort and the chances of achieving the targeted results. But when the culture is in conflict with some aspect of the company's direction, performance targets, or strategy, the culture becomes a stumbling block. Thus, an important part of the managing the strategy execution process is establishing and nurturing a good fit between culture and strategy.

Changing a company's culture, especially a strong one with traits that don't fit a new strategy's requirements, is one of the toughest management challenges. Changing a culture requires competent leadership at the top. It requires symbolic actions and substantive actions that unmistakably indicate serious commitment on the part of top management. The more that culture-driven actions and behaviors fit what's needed for good strategy execution, the less managers have to depend on policies, rules, procedures, and supervision to enforce what people should and should not do.

Healthy corporate cultures are grounded in ethical business principles, socially approved values, and socially responsible decision making. One has to be cautious in jumping to the conclusion that a company's stated values and ethical principles are mere window dressing. While some companies display low ethical standards, many companies are truly committed to the stated core values and to high ethical standards, and they make ethical behavior *a fundamental component of their corporate culture*. If management practices what it preaches, a company's core values and ethical standards nurture the corporate culture in three highly positive ways: (1) they communicate the company's good intentions and validate the integrity and above-board character of its business principles and operating methods, (2) they steer company personnel toward both doing the right thing and doing things right, and (3) they establish a corporate conscience that gauges the appropriateness of particular actions, decisions, and policies. Companies that really care about how they conduct their business put a stake in the ground, making it unequivocally clear that company personnel are expected to live up to the company's values and ethical standards—how well individuals display core values and adhere to ethical standards is often part of the job performance evaluations. Peer pressures to conform to cultural norms are quite strong, acting as an important deterrent to outside-the-lines behavior.

To be effective, corporate ethics and values programs have to become a way of life through training, strict compliance and enforcement procedures, and reiterated management endorsements. Moreover, top managers must practice what they preach, serving as role models for ethical behavior, values-driven decision making, and a social conscience.

Successful managers have to do several things in leading the drive for good strategy execution and operating excellence. First, they stay on top of things. They keep a finger on the organization's pulse by spending considerable time outside their offices, listening and talking to organization members, coaching, cheerleading, and picking up important information. Second, they are active and visible in putting constructive pressure on the organization to achieve good results. Generally, this is best accomplished by promoting an esprit de corps that mobilizes and energizes organizational members to execute strategy in a competent fashion and deliver the targeted results. Third, they keep the organization focused on operating excellence by championing innovative ideas for improvement and promoting the use of best practices and benchmarking to measure the progress being made in performing value chain activities in first-rate fashion. Fourth, they exert their clout in developing competencies and competitive capabilities that enable better execution. Fifth, they serve as a role model in displaying high ethical standards and insist that company personnel conduct the company's business ethically and in a socially responsible manner. They demonstrate unequivocal and visible commitment to the ethics enforcement process. And, finally, when a company's strategy execution effort is not delivering good results and the organization is not making measure progress toward operating excellence, it is the leader's responsibility to step forward and push corrective actions.

Exercises

1. Go to www.hermanmiller.com and read what the company has to say about its corporate culture in the careers sections of the website. Do you think this statement is just nice window dressing, or, based on what else you can learn about the Herman Miller Company from browsing this website, is there reason to believe that management has truly built a culture that makes the stated values and principles come alive? Explain.

2. Go to the careers section at www.qualcomm.com and see what Qualcomm, one of the most prominent companies in mobile communications technology, has to say about "life at Qualcomm." Is what's on this website just recruiting propaganda, or does it convey the type of work climate that management is actually trying to create? If you were a senior executive at Qualcomm, would you see merit in building and nurturing a culture like what is described in the section on "life at Qualcomm?" Would such a culture represent a tight fit with Qualcomm's high-tech business and strategy (you can get an overview of the Qualcomm's strategy by exploring the section for investors and some of the recent press releases)? Is your answer consistent with what is presented in the "Awards and Honors" menu selection in the "About Qualcomm" portion of the website?

3. Go to www.jnj.com, the website of Johnson & Johnson and read the "J&J Credo," which sets forth the company's responsibilities to customers, employees, the community, and shareholders. Then read the "Our Company" section. Why do you think the credo has resulted in numerous awards and accolades that recognize the company as a good corporate citizen?

4. Do some research on the Internet and see if you can identify five specific examples of unethical conduct on the part of Enron personnel that contributed to the company's downfall.

5. Do a web search on Dennis Kozlowski, former CEO of Tyco International, and gather information on what unethical actions he is alleged to have engaged in during his tenure as the company's CEO. How serious do you think the alleged misconduct is? What sort of ethical climate do you think prevailed at Tyco while Kozlowski was CEO? If you had been an employee of Tyco under Kozlowski, what would your opinion be of his leadership qualities (keeping in mind that the company's financial performance during his tenure was quite good)?

Strategy as Balance
From "Either-Or" to "And"

Costas Markides
London Business School

Differences in opinion on the content and process of developing strategy are passionately argued. They often seem rampant and huge—particularly to the protagonists. Yet these debates are mostly little more than "academic." They cease to matter when we realise that: (1) strategy needs to be approached from a variety of perspectives; and (2) rather than adopt a single perspective at the expense of all others, good strategies have to achieve a fine balance between seemingly divergent views.

What issues should senior executives consider in thinking about a new strategy and how should they think about them? Despite the apparent simplicity of this question, it is one of the most controversial in the field of management. People seem to disagree about almost everything contained in this question: about what issues are relevant; about the process that a manager should go through to develop strategy; and about the actual physical output that should emerge at the end of a strategy process. Sometimes, they even disagree as to whether we can actually "think" about strategy at all.

As with most academic debates, when one probes below the surface, the apparently-divergent points of view are in fact amazingly similar. And even when views are not so similar, it does not mean that one is superior to another. Further analysis reveals that rather than depend on one perspective at the expense of all others, good strategies encompass elements from all the different perspectives and points of view. Yet, the academic debates continue to rage on like uncontrolled forest fires, spreading confusion among both academics and managers. In this article, I identify the three main areas of "controversy" and discuss how strategy must achieve a fine balance between these "different" points of view. The three main areas of controversy are:

- What constitutes the content and process of strategy.
- Strategy as analysis or as creativity.
- Strategy dynamics.

Problem One: The Content and Process of Strategy

There is general agreement that every company needs a strategy—either explicit or implicit. Yet, there is surprisingly little agreement as to what strategy *really* is. Within both business and academic circles, it is not easy to identify two people who share the same definition of strategy. For example, consider the numerous ways that academics have defined strategy over the years: as positioning the company in its industry environment; as a collection of a few simple rules; as hustle; as stretch and leverage; as the embodiment of a company's values; and so on. Add to these the plethora of other possible definitions currently making the rounds (definitions which might include such "hot" concepts as strategic intent, vision, core competences, breaking the rules, learning, systems thinking and so on) and you begin to understand why even *The Economist* has claimed that "nobody really knows what strategy is." (20.3.93, p. 106).

Similar confusion and disagreements also exist on the process by which good strategies are developed. According to Gary Hamel (1998), we are all experts after the fact in identifying companies with superior strategies but we have little to say on how these superior strategies were created in the first place or how other companies could develop similarly innovative strategies. Along similar lines, the big debate that ensued following the publication of Michael Porter's 1996 *Harvard Business Review* (HBR) article: "What is Strategy?" was whether a company can choose its strategy through a rational thinking process or whether the strategy really "emerges" through a process of experimentation.

Let us first consider the debate on the content of strategy. Beyond the rhetoric, we can identify two main schools of thought on what strategy is. The more "Porterian" view of strategy emphasizes the positioning elements of strategy. This school views strategy primarily as positioning the company in its industry environment. This is another way of saying that strategy is all about *choosing a good game to play* (Porter 1980). The other main school of thought considers positioning to be "static" and old news. Proponents of this school encourage us to embrace the "new" and more "dynamic" view of strategy which emphasizes outplaying and out-manoeuvering our competitors, no matter what game they are playing. According to this way of thinking, strategy is more about *how you play the game* than about choosing what game to play (D'Aveni 1994, Kay 1994).

> *It is true that most managers are preoccupied with the 'How' question.*

It should be quite obvious to all that strategy is *both* of these things: strategy must decide what game we want to play and then determine how to play that game well. Both are important decisions and both belong to strategy. Deciding on what game to play boils down to making choices on two dimensions: who to target as customers and what to offer them. Determining how to play this game requires us to decide what value-chain activities we will perform (and what not to). Put the two together and it becomes quite clear that strategy is all about finding answers to three interrelated questions: *Who* will be my targeted customers? *What* products and services should I be offering? And *How* should I offer these products and services to my targeted customers in an efficient and innovative way (Markides 2000)?

Strategy in Practice: The Nespresso Example

In early 1988, Mr. Jean-Paul Gaillard had just taken over the Nespresso subsidiary which, despite selling one of Nestlé's most innovative new products, was facing serious financial problems. He therefore had to decide how to rejuvenate the subsidiary's financial fortunes by developing a new strategy.

The Nespresso product was a system which allowed the consumer to produce a fresh cup of espresso coffee at home. Though simple in appearance and use, it took Nestlé more than ten years to develop it. The system consisted of two parts: a coffee capsule and a machine. The coffee capsule was hermetically sealed in aluminum and contained 5g of roast and ground coffee. The machine consisted of four parts—a handle, a water container, a pump and an electrical heating system. These four parts were cast into a body and formed the machine.

The use of the Nespresso system was straightforward. The coffee capsule was placed in the handle which was then inserted into the machine. The act of inserting the handle into the machine pierced the coffee capsule at the top. At the press of a button, pressurized, steamed water was passed through the capsule. The result was a creamy, foamy and high-quality cup of espresso coffee.

The new product was introduced in 1986. The original strategy adopted by Nestlé was to set up a joint venture with a Swiss-based distributor called Sobal to sell the new product. This joint venture (named Sobal-Nespresso) was supposed to purchase the machines from another Swiss Company (called Turmix), the coffee capsules from Nestlé and then distribute and sell everything as a system—one product, one price. Offices and restaurants were targeted as the customers and a separate unit called Nespresso SA was set up within Nestlé to support the joint venture and to service and maintain the machines.

By 1988, it was clear that the new product was not living up to its promise. Sales were well below budget and quality problems were driving costs through the roof. Nestlé headquarters was considering freezing the operation when Jean-Paul Gaillard took over. He had to decide whether and how to strategically reposition the subsidiary.

But which way should he go? At the top of his "to-do" list were questions such as: "Should we continue targeting offices and restaurants as our customer or should we focus on upper-income households and individuals?" "Should we continue focusing our activities in Switzerland or should we expand in other espresso-friendly countries?" "Should we stick to our current strategy of selling both the coffee and the machines as a system or should we just concentrate on coffee?" "Does our current distribution policy make sense or should we choose an alternative distribution method such as the Internet or mail order?"

These were not easy questions and the answers were not immediately obvious. Yet, these questions had to be asked, possible alternatives identified and specific choices made. In fact, going through the process of asking these questions and then making difficult choices (which may turn out to be wrong) is what strategy is all about.

As it turned out, Jean-Paul Gaillard chose correctly for Nespresso. He changed the targeted customer from offices to high-income households and the distribution of the coffee capsules from the joint venture to mail order (through the "Nespresso Club"). As a result of these choices and other strategic decisions, Nespresso grew tremendously in the next five years. The main point of this story is simple: the heart and soul of strategy is asking the "who-what-how" questions, developing alternatives, and choosing what to do and what not to do.

Let me therefore repeat my main point: strategy is all about deciding what game we want to play **and** then playing that game well. Both are important decisions and both belong to strategy. Both require the company to make choices—often painful ones. A company that fails to make choices abdicates one of its most important responsibilities.

To see how these three decisions combine to form an organization's strategy, consider the situation facing the newly appointed CEO of the Nestlé subsidiary, Nespresso, in 1988 (see box). Note in particular how this manager had to make some difficult choices on all three of these parameters.

The "New" Challenge: Competing for the Future

As if the confusion generated from the two schools of thought identified above was not bad enough, we now have a new challenge to strategy. In their best-selling book *Competing for the Future,* Gary Hamel and C. K. Prahalad (1994) have argued that the prevailing view of strategy is flawed. Their main criticism is that as practised today, strategy is preoccupied with fixing the problems in the *existing* business rather than thinking about *future* businesses. To them, strategy is not about deciding on "What game to play?" or "How to play the game?" because both of these issues emphasize how to win in the current business. For them, the essence of a good strategy is to create new markets, new products, new industries, new "white spaces." This leads them to their position that strategy should be about competing for the industries of the future rather than competing for market share in the industries of today.

It is hard to argue with the need to focus the organization's attention on discovering new markets. But this should not come at the expense of today's businesses. Sure, every company needs to worry about the future and every company should attempt to create the industries of the future. But in the meantime, a company must also ensure that it is still making money in its existing markets. After all, without making sure that we are winning in the markets of today, there will be *no* future for us to worry about!

Therefore, the key question for any company is not whether it should try to create the industries of the future but how to take care of its existing business *while at the same time* attempting to create the industries of the future. This means that strategy is more than just deciding what game we want to play and playing that game well. While doing this, every company should also prepare for an unknown future—either by trying to create this new future itself or by creating the conditions that will allow it to exploit the future when this unfolds.

A company can do this in two basic ways. The first way is simple enough: once it has settled on a "Who/What/How" position in its existing business, a company must repeatedly revisit these choices and continuously question the answers it has given to these three questions. Strategic planning, if done properly, should primarily be about challenging and questioning the answers that a company has given to the "Who-What-How" questions in previous years.

The new definition must include not only a consideration of what game to play and how to play it, but also a consideration of how our company can attempt to create, or at least prepare for, the industries of the future while taking care of its existing business.

The second way that a company can take care of its existing business while attempting to create the industries of the future is to accept that in all likelihood, that company will *not* be the one that comes up with the new innovation that creates a new industry. In most cases, the best that the company can do is to be ready to take advantage of an innovation when somebody else develops it. But what exactly does it mean "to be ready"?

Research shows that most established companies fail when a new technological innovation invades their market (e.g., Cooper and Smith 1992; Cooper and Schendel 1976). But the reason they fail is not because they neglect to adopt the new technology but because: (1) they do not have the necessary core competences to take advantage of it; (2) they wait too long before adopting it and they abandon it with the first sign of trouble; (3) they are trapped in their ways of competing so that their past core competences have become core rigidities; and (4) even when adopting a new technology, they do not manage the organizational transition from the "old" to the "new" as effectively as they should.

What all this means is that for an organization "to be ready" for the inevitable innovation that would disrupt its market, it has to:

- Build internal variety that would allow it to develop competences even before it knows which competences will be needed.

- Institutionalize continuous innovation in its culture and values.

- Develop a culture that continuously questions the established status quo and encourages experimentation and change.

- Develop an early monitoring system that warns it of what Intel's Andy Grove called "inflexion points" in its future—well in advance.

- Continuously challenge and update its capabilities so as prevent core competences from becoming core rigidities.

- Organize itself to be effective in a dying business while making the transition to the new market.

This discussion suggests that we need to broaden our definition of strategy. The new definition must include not only a consideration of what game to play and how to play it, but also a consideration of how our company can attempt to create, or at least prepare for, the industries of the future while taking care of its existing business.

More Confusion: The Making of Strategy

The discussion so far has focused on the question: "what is strategy?" It is obvious that differences of opinion exist on the answer to this question. Unfortunately, similar confusion and disagreements also exist on the process by which good strategies are developed. As argued by Gary Hamel (1996): ". . . the *practice* of strategy must be re-invented. Sorry, did I say *re*-invent? Let's not pretend. There's little that's worth *re*-inventing. Surely we're not going to start with the traditional planning process in our quest to increase the value-added of strategy! No, we must start from scratch."

The big disagreements on the process of creating strategy revolve around two issues:

- Can we plan for strategy—or do good strategies emerge through experimentation and trial and error (the "Design versus Emergent" schools of thought)?

- In developing strategy do we start with an analysis of the market and then think what we need to do in this market or do we start with an analysis of our existing core competences and think how to build competitive advantage on the back of these competences (the "Industrial Organization" school versus the "Resource-based" view of the firm).

(1) Can We Plan Strategy? A marvellous articulation of the first debate (i.e., can we plan for strategy?) is found in the exchange of letters between Michael Porter and Ian MacMillan/Rita Gunther McGrath (1997), following Porter's article in HBR. Whereas Porter seems to imply that strategy can be a well-thought-out plan of action, MacMillan and McGrath argue that strategy is nothing more than the final outcome of a process of trial-and-error and learning by doing.

As before, the answer to this debate lies somewhere in the middle of these two extreme points of view: strategy must encompass both ends of this spectrum. On the one hand, it has to be thought out and planned at a general level; on the other hand, it must remain flexible and adaptable to new learning and changes in the market. Although analysis will not produce a full-fledged strategy ready to be implemented, *it does help us narrow the options.* Experimentation can then follow on a limited number of options so that the dead ends can be identified and the "unexpected" opportunities uncovered. It would take a hopelessly romantic planner to argue that in-depth analysis alone is what creates masterful strategies. However, it would be equally silly to pretend that analysis or thinking are not necessary ingredients and that trial and error alone will give rise to a winning strategy. Both are essential elements of strategy: analysis sketches the "skeleton" of a possible strategy; experimentation allows us to refine, add or change altogether our original skeleton.

To see this point in action, consider once again the case of Nespresso. There is no question that the strategy adopted by Jean-Paul Gaillard at Nespresso was a winning strategy. By targeting households instead of offices as his customers; by unbundling the coffee machines and their servicing from the sale of coffee; by developing two separate selling and distribution methods—one for the coffee and one for the machines; and by developing an "aura" of exclusivity through the "Nespresso Club," Gaillard rejuvenated the fortunes of Nespresso and turned a dying operation into a growing unit within Nestlé.

But how did Jean-Paul Gaillard come up with his brilliant strategy? Did he really plan for all this or did the ideas somehow "emerge" over time through trial and error? According to Gaillard, it was a mixture of both. When he joined Nespresso, it was clear that the existing strategy was not working. Based on the situation he inherited and using his past experience as a guide, he made certain decisions—like the decision to change the targeted customer focus from offices to households and the decision to separate the coffee from the machine side of operations. According to Gaillard: *"I knew in my guts that these were the correct decisions. But you are not 100 percent sure. So you try them out in a limited way; and you learn as you go along. . ."*

> *It would take a hopelessly romantic planner to argue that in-depth analysis alone is what creates masterful strategies.*

The Nespresso example demonstrates a simple but powerful point: *the process of developing superior strategies is part planning, part trial and error, until you hit upon something that works.* Sometimes you start with the planning part and then adjust what you have through trial and error. Other times you start with trial and error and then use planning to fine-tune the system.

Strategy-making must encompass both elements. This point must be emphasized because it has become fashionable lately for people to argue that, in today's volatile environment, planning is useless: by the time you decide on a plan, the claim goes, the environment has changed so much that your plan is no longer valid. The best you can do is develop an organizational environment that allows superior ideas and strategies to emerge through day-to-day experimentation by everybody in the organization (Hamel 1998).

Without denying the importance of developing such an organizational environment, I argue that this is not enough. A company that relies only on trial and error to develop its strategy is like a rudderless ship being torn apart in the middle of the ocean.

The parameters within which the firm will operate *must* be developed before experimentation is allowed to take place; and these parameters can only be developed by top management—not by just anybody in the organization. Experimentation without clear boundaries will lead to chaos, confusion and ultimately a demotivated workforce. Similarly, top managers that shy away from deciding the parameters within which their people can manoeuver (in the name of democracy and flexibility) are abdicating one of the most crucial responsibilities of leadership.

Therefore, to repeat my main point, the ideas that make up a strategy (such as what customers to target or what products to sell) can emerge through careful planning or after experimentation. Anybody in the organization can come up with these ideas, but it is the responsibility of top management to decide what will be implemented and what will be discarded.

(2) Where Do We Start Our Analysis?   The second debate on creating strategy stems not so much from real disagreements as from differences in emphasis: should we start our strategy process by analysing the external market or should we start by building on our existing competencies? The first approach emphasises an external orientation while the second approach stresses an internal one.

Needless to say, consideration of both the outside market and the inside competences must underpin any strategy development—after all, the goal is to discover a *fit* between the inside and the outside so consideration must be given to both. However, how we decide to start will ultimately determine how creative we are thinking of strategic options.

This is because most companies have a *dominant* way of thinking about strategy. Some start with the outside market and try to decide what to do while others start with their internal competences and try to leverage them. The problem is that after following the dominant way of thinking a few times, people become comfortable in that way of thinking and passive thinking sets in. As a result, we don't really think about the issues in a creative way. For this to happen, people must become "uncomfortable."

Therefore, innovations in strategy take place when a company is able to switch from its dominant way of thinking to an alternative way. It is this continuous switching from one way of thinking to another and the continuous switching from one sequence of questions to another that "wakes up" the mind and prompts active thinking. And it is active thinking that leads to strategic innovation. This implies that sometimes a company must start its strategy process with an external orientation and then switch to an internal orientation. At other times, it should start with an internal orientation and then switch to an external one. It is the continuous switching from one to the other which is crucial—not picking one of them as the "right" one.

A fascinating illustration of the power of switching the starting point of our thinking was recently articulated by Hal Rosenbluth, the president and CEO of Rosenbluth Travel. In describing how he managed to transform the company from a $20m business in 1978 to a $1.3bn global travel management company by 1990, he argues that: "*. . . our biggest advantage was to understand that as deregulation changed the rules of travel, we were no longer in the travel business so much as we were in the information business*" [emphasis added]. This fundamental re-thinking of what business the company was in led Rosenbluth to initiate a series of actions (such as acquisitions of computers and airline reservation systems, the development of a private reservation data system, the development of relational databases, etc.) which to an outside observer must have seen, at the very least, "strange." But to Rosenbluth, these actions made perfect sense: if you are in the travel information business, this is what you need to be successful. Hal Rosenbluth claims that the company had undergone a similar transformation in 1892, when his great-grandfather had an insight into the business. He realized that "... *he wasn't just in travel, selling tickets to people who wanted to cross the Atlantic. He was in family immigration, getting whole clans of people successfully settled in America.*"

Such redefinition of the business is at the heart of strategic innovation. It is truly re-markable how many of today's strategic innovators started out on their revolutionary journey by first redefining the business they were in. Thus, Howard Schultz, president of Starbucks, does not believe he is in the coffee business. Instead, he is in the business of creating a consumption experience, of which coffee is a part. Thus, a visit to one of his stores is "... romance, theatrics, community—the totality of the coffee experience" (*Wall Street Journal,* 8.1.93, p. B2). It goes without saying that if you think you are in the "ex-perience" business rather than the coffee business, you will behave very differently from any competitor who thinks he/she is in the coffee business. Not better, just differently.

Such redefinition of the business is possible only if the question "What business are we really in" is asked. It does not mean that by asking the question a new or even better definition will be discovered. But even a remote possibility of discovering some-thing new will never come up if the question is never asked.

Problem Two: Strategy as Analysis Rather than Creativity

The second major problem with strategy today is that we often confuse tools and frame-works with the strategy itself, while rational analysis of data has become the accepted way to develop strategy. Strategic thinking and strategic planning in the modern corpo-ration have degenerated into a search for "the formulae of success" where wishful think-ing (i.e., stargazing), sexy slogans (i.e., vision statements) and/or non-thinking and logical analysis of data have replaced true strategic thinking. In many companies, strate-gic planning takes the form of mindless number crunching and endless projections whose ultimate purpose is to prepare huge reports that nobody would read.

Inevitably, there has been a justifiable backlash against such waste of company time and resources. One response has been to get rid of the "strategic planning" de-partment and to abandon "strategic planning" altogether. Another response has been to emphasize the importance of "emergent" strategies over "planned" ones—that is, strategies that apparently emerge over time through experimentation and trial and error. Yet another response has been the recent rise of the "democratic" way to develop strategy—where everybody in the organization is expected to put on their army-general hats and contribute to the development of the company's strategy. My position is that all these reactions are unnecessary and the wrong response to the problem.

Strategy should be a mixture of rational thinking and creativity; of analysis and ex-perimentation; of planning and learning. Researchers who have examined how the eyes of chess masters move during a competitive game have found that, once their op-ponent has made a move, the chess master's eyes will go straight to the best move pos-sible 75 percent of the time. However, after this initial reaction, the chess master's eyes will evaluate other possible moves before eventually returning (75 percent of the time) to the original best move. This suggests that chess masters rise to the top on the basis of creativity ***and*** analysis. Strategy should not be any different.

To be effective, strategic thinking should be creative and intuitive (rather than just rational) and should be supported (but not substituted) by analysis. Effective strategic thinking is a process of continuously asking questions and thinking through the issues in a creative way. Thus, correctly formulating the questions is often more important than finding a "solution"; thinking through an issue from a variety of angles is often more productive than collecting and analysing unlimited data; and actually experimenting with new ideas is often more critical than scientific analysis and discussion.

> *There has been a justifiable backlash against such waste of company time and resources.*

Unfortunately, as Kenichi Ohmae (1982) has commented in his book *The Mind of the Strategist,* the culture of the modern corporation exalts logic and rationality. Hence, it is analysts rather than innovators who tend to get ahead.

To be effective, strategic thinking should be *a creative thinking process based on real facts and analysis which tries to combine the rational with the emotional.* Thus, the essence of effective strategic thinking is (1) to think through the issues in a creative way; and (2) to not only come up with innovative new ideas but to generate the necessary emotional commitment on the part of the organization that will result in the people actually changing their behaviours to effectively implement these new ideas. A good strategy must, therefore, balance:

- the emotional with the logical and rational;
- the thinking process with the application and implementation of ideas;
- the creative jumps with the analysis of facts.

Consider, for example, what the CEO of the small Danish bank Lån & Spar had to say upon the successful implementation of a radical new strategy at the bank in the early 1990s: "*. . . I have been in the banking industry since the age of 16. By the time I moved to Lån & Spar as the CEO, I had already thought about the issues and I had pretty much decided on the main elements of our new strategy. In fact, I had tested this concept in a limited way in my previous bank. However, I had to go slow at first. We had to try out some of these things first before rolling them out full scale. . . . *"

Most strategy books and most teaching on strategy tend to focus on the techniques and the analytical tools that people can use in developing strategy, forgetting that tools are not a substitute for thinking. Any manager entrusted with developing strategy must understand that the *thinking process* that they go through is more important than finding "the answer"; and that strategy is based more on creativity than analysis.

A major reason for the current sad state of affairs is the way strategy is taught at most business schools. When one looks at how companies actually develop strategy, the process that they use (either formally or in the CEO's head) is one of trying to find answers to specific questions, such as: who are my competitors and how can I position myself relative to them? Who are my customers and how can I satisfy their needs? What are the key success factors in this business and what can I do to develop a competitive advantage? What changes are taking place in my business and how should I react to them?

Yet, when one opens any strategy book (which supposedly aims to help managers develop a strategy), you very rarely find the book devoted to helping managers ask and find answers to these questions. What you find instead is a book with chapter titles such as "Cost and Differentiation Strategies" or "Analyzing the Environment." In other words, we do not structure our books in the way a manager thinks of strategy but in self-contained chunks of knowledge which we then expect the manager to integrate and put together so as to develop a strategy.

This implies that the strategy field is in need of process re-engineering. We business schools never look at the issue of "how to develop strategy" from the customer's point of view. We are—like every other organization in this world—supply-driven. We therefore teach our MBA students a course on Marketing, a course on Finance and a course on OB and we then expect *them* to do the integration. Our strategy books provide the intellectual inputs that go into a strategy but we then leave it up to the customer to put it all together and develop the strategy.

However, our customers do not think like this. They have certain questions to answer, such as: "who are my competitors and what shall I do to gain competitive advantage over them?" In answering this question, they have to use some knowledge from Marketing and some from OB. But they do not care if we call some of this knowledge Marketing and some OB. Just like a customer who doesn't care if it is the front desk or the room service people who messed up his stay at the hotel, the customer of strategy is not interested in the labels we put on our different inputs. What they want is a "total" service from us. Thus, to be truly customer-driven, business schools need to identify all the relevant questions that a manager needs to address and then help this manager think through these questions.

The worst side-effect of our tendency to be supply-driven rather than customer-driven is the chasm that has been created between strategy formulation and implementation. We have very little to say to our customers about how to do anything. We have been preoccupied with telling them how to *think* about something and we left them to do it as they saw fit. It is only when we think in terms of the questions that they themselves think that it becomes impossible for us not to think of the implementation issues as well. It is only when we look at the issues as they (the customers) see them that formulation and implementation cease to be two separate entities and, as if by magic, fuse into one.

Problem Three: The Dynamic Elements of Strategy

The third and final problem with strategy today is that it is *a*historical—that is, it does not place a company in its historical context. Yet, what a company needs to do and what strategy it needs to follow is often contingent on where in its evolution that company is. For example, whether a company should "stick to its knitting" or diversify out of its core depends to a large extent on whether a technological innovation is about to destroy the company's core. Similarly, whether a company should try to be "better" than its competitors or try instead to be "different" by breaking the rules of the game depends primarily on where in its evolution that company's industry is located.

Failure to think of companies in a dynamic way has resulted in two major problems. The first and more apparent problem is the conflicting and contradictory advice given to companies by academics or consultants. Examples abound:

■ Following the success of the book *In Search of Excellence* by Peters and Waterman (1982), companies were advised to "stick to their knitting." Yet another consultant (Richard Foster) from the same firm (McKinsey) in his study of technological innovations (Foster 1986) suggested that the last thing a company wants to do in times of technological upheaval is stick to its knitting.

▪ Similarly, Ted Levitt (1960) argued in his influential HBR article *Marketing Myopia* that companies should define their business according to the underlying functionality of their products. Yet, Hermann Simon (1996), in his study of German success stories (*Hidden Champions*) found that these German companies succeeded by defining their business narrowly, according to the product they were selling.

▪ Finally, a well-known dictum from Marketing is that companies should stay close to and listen to their customers. Yet, the article that won the McKinsey award in the 1995 HBR argued that companies which pay too much attention to their existing customers at times of technological change will fail (Bower and Christensen 1995).

All these examples are meant to show that no advice—however sound and practical—will apply to all the firms all the time. What a firm should do depends on its own particular circumstances which are in turn determined by where in its evolution that company is in. Strategic advice that fails to put the company in its historical context runs the risk of being dangerous advice.

A less obvious problem with being ahistorical is the failure of strategy to consider how a company's past as well as its (still to unfold) *future* influence its strategic choices of *today*. What the company does today will determine what options the company has tomorrow. This should have an effect on what the company decides to do. Similarly, just because the future has not happened yet, it does not mean that a company cannot do anything today to prepare for things to come. For example, every company ought to know that its product will eventually mature and will most likely be replaced by another product made possible by a technological innovation. This will happen sometime in the future but surely the company's strategy today ought to take this into consideration. It should therefore ask: "What can I do today to make sure that when the 'death' of my product arrives, I am ready for it?" It should not wait for this to happen before doing anything.

The Future of Strategy

For any company, success stems from the exploitation of a distinctive or unique strategy. As I argued here, this strategy is nothing more than the answers we have given to the "Who-What-How" questions. Unfortunately, no strategic position will remain unique or attractive forever! Not only do attractive positions get imitated by aggressive competitors but also—and perhaps more importantly—*new* strategic positions keep emerging all the time. A new strategic position is simply a new viable Who-What-How combination—perhaps a new customer segment (a new Who), or a new value proposition (a new What), or a new way of distributing or manufacturing the product (a new How). Over time, these new positions may grow to challenge the attractiveness of our own position.

No advice—however sound and practical—will apply to all the firms all the time.

You see this happening in industry after industry: once-formidable companies that built their success on what seemed to be unassailable strategic positions find themselves humbled by relatively unknown companies who base their attacks on creating and exploiting new strategic positions in the industry.

New strategic positions—that is, new Who-What-How combinations—emerge all around us all the time. As industries change, new strategic positions emerge to challenge existing positions for supremacy. Changing industry conditions, changing customer needs or preferences, countermoves by competitors and a company's own evolving competences give rise to new opportunities and the potential for new ways of playing the game. Unless a company continuously questions its accepted norms and behaviours, it will never discover what else has become available. It will miss these new combinations and other, more agile players will jump in and exploit the gaps left behind.

Therefore, a company must never settle for what it has. While fighting it out in its current position, it must continuously search for new positions to colonize and new opportunities to take advantage of. Simple as this may sound, it contrasts sharply with the way most competitors compete in their industries: most of them take the established rules of the game as given and spend all their time trying to become *better* than each other in their existing positions—usually through cost or differentiation strategies. Little or no emphasis is placed at becoming *different* from competitors. The majority of companies which strategically innovate by breaking the rules of the game tend to be small niche players or new market entrants. It is indeed rare to find a strategic innovator who is also an established industry big player—a fact which hints at the difficulties of risking the sure thing for something uncertain.

There are many reasons why established companies find it hard to become strategic innovators. Compared to new entrants or niche players, leaders are weighed down by *structural* and *cultural* inertia, internal politics, complacency, fear of cannibalising existing products, fear of destroying existing competences, satisfaction with the status quo, and a general lack of incentives to abandon a certain present for an uncertain future. In addition, since there are fewer industry leaders than potential new entrants, the chances that the innovator will emerge from the ranks of the leaders is unavoidably small.

Despite such obstacles, established companies cannot afford not to strategically innovate. As already pointed out, dramatic shifts in company fortunes can only take place if a company succeeds in not only playing its game better than its rivals but in also designing and playing a different game from its competitors. Strategic innovation has the potential to take third-rate companies and elevate them to industry leadership status; and it can take established industry leaders and destroy them in a short period of time. Even if the established players do not want to strategically innovate (for fear of destroying their existing profitable positions), somebody else will. Established players might as well pre-empt that from happening.

The culture that established players must develop is that strategies are not cast in concrete. A company needs to remain flexible and ready to adjust its strategy if the feedback from the market is not favourable. More importantly, a company needs to continuously question the way it operates in its current position while still fighting it out in its current position against existing competitors.

Continuously questioning one's accepted strategic position serves two vital purposes: first, it allows a company to identify early enough whether its current position in the business is losing its attractiveness to others (and so decide what to do about it); second and more importantly, it gives the company the opportunity to proactively explore the emerging terrain and hopefully be the first to discover new and attractive strategic positions to take advantage of. This is no guarantee: questioning one's accepted answers will not automatically lead to new unexploited goldmines. But even a remote possibility of discovering something new will never come up if the questions are never asked.

Selected References*

Bower, J. and Christensen, C. (1995) Disruptive Technologies: Catching the Wave, *Harvard Business Review,* January–February, pp43–53.

Cooper, A. and Smith, C. (1992) How Established Firms Respond to Threatening Technologies, *Academy of Management Executive,* Vol. 6, No. 2, pp55–70.

Cooper, A. and Schendel, D. (1976) Strategic Responses to Technological Threats, *Business Horizons,* February, pp61–69.

Foster, R. (1986): *Innovation: The Attacker's Advantage,* New York: Summit Books.

Hamel, G. (1996) *The Search for Strategy,* working paper, London Business School.

Kay, J. (1994) *The Foundations of Corporate Success,* Oxford: OUP.

MacMillan, I. and McGrath, R. (1997) Letter published in *Harvard Business Review,* January–February 1997, pp154–156.

Ohmae, K. (1982) *The Mind of the Strategist,* New York: McGraw Hill.

Rosenbluth, H. (1991) Tales from a nonconformist company, *Harvard Business Review,* July–August, pp26–36.

---

*For the full list of references, see www.london.edu/bsr and click on "references."

READING

2

Has Strategy Changed?

Kathleen M. Eisenhardt
Stanford University

The powerful forces of globalization are fundamentally
changing the nature and dimensions of strategy.

Has strategy changed in the wake of the recent economic frenzy and subsequent downturn? Is the New Economy finished? Has the Old Economy returned? At this point, most managers understand what the advent of the Internet implies—operating efficiency for most companies, a terrific channel for some, and a fundamentally new business opportunity for only a few. So is it back to "strategy as usual"?

The answer is no. While many executives were focused on the implications of the Internet, a more powerful force was quietly transforming the economic playing field. Globalization. Massive in scope, deep in impact—and ironically, almost unmanaged—globalization is the increasingly deep interrelationship among countries, companies and individuals. The connections may be cultural, as in the case of global brands like Sony, or environmental, as in global climate change and overfishing of the oceans. The connections may be technical, as in the case of the Web and wireless communication, or financial, as in the linking of major stock exchanges and the proliferation of NAFTA-like trade agreements. Globalization, not the Internet, is the fundamental driver of the real New Economy.

Instability

Density of connections throughout the world affects corporations by amplifying instability. Even small events in one location can affect events in another, in often oblique and nonlinear fashion. Cold weather means increased coal usage in England that can trigger acid rain in Ukraine. Economies of scale at a smattering of Australian wineries can affect life in rural France. AIDS activists in South Africa can threaten the profits of the pharmaceuticals industry. The scale and pace of change are particularly challenging to predict. Wall Street expected that a correction would follow dot-com mania, but no one anticipated the correction's magnitude and speed.

The international power structure, or lack of one, further amplifies instability. For almost five decades, the geopolitics of the post–World War II era were shaped by the two principal Cold War combatants. Today, although the United States is dominant and the European Union is asserting a more unified point of view, free trade and transparent

Reprinted from *MIT Sloan Management Review*, Vol. 42, No. 2, Winter 2002, pp. 88–91 by permission of publisher. Copyright © 2002 Massachusetts Institute of Technology. All rights reserved. The author is grateful for the wisdom, counsel and creativity of Chris Bingham, Shona Brown, Charlie Galunic, Jeff Martin, Filipe Santos and Don Sull in helping to shape the ideas expressed.

markets are the forces shaping commerce, not any one nation. The Internet speeds communication. Invention spreads almost overnight. Yet no one is in charge. In the era of globalization, it is not obvious whether major political leaders, such as British Prime Minister Tony Blair, or business leaders, such as AOL Time Warner's Steve Case, have much economic clout. Perhaps both types will take a back seat to some single-issue global crusader. Adding to the instability is a strong and often thoughtful backlash to globalization among an unlikely coalition of trade unionists, environmentalists, and cultural nationalists.

At the same time, industries with strong network effects (for example, telecommunications), in which standards can take hold rapidly, and industries such as software, which depend on the economics of information rather than the economics of things, have further destabilized the predictable world of business. Globalization, together with those forces, has created a new economic playing field. The play on that field is high-velocity with strikingly nonlinear instability, unpredictability and ambiguity. No wonder that the principal theme of the January 2002 gathering of the economic and political elite at the World Economic Forum in New York City is designated as "coping with fragility."

New Economics, New Strategy

Does the new economic playing field imply throwing out traditional economics? No, but it does suggest that the belief in equilibrium and the naïve understanding of (or perhaps lack of interest in) the internal workings of corporations that characterize traditional economics render its paradigms less germane. Rather, a new economics—or more accurately, an *old* new economics pioneered by Frank Knight, Friedrich Hayek, and Joseph Schumpeter—is coming into its own. This latter form of economics is entrepreneurial in its riveted focus on disequilibrium, the capture of fleeting opportunities and the relentless cycle of wealth creation and destruction.

The new economic playing field also suggests a fresh view of strategy. During conversations on our collective work, Donald N. Sull of Harvard Business School struck upon a military analogy that graphically conveys the point. Military leaders often fight traditional wars in the map room by locating defensible positions and then fortifying them. In the same way, executives plan their strategic positions and defend them with carefully intertwined activity systems.

Sometimes a traditional war is fought in the storeroom, with leaders amassing stockpiles of specific weapons such as tanks and then deploying them wherever the battle may be. Similarly, executives may formulate resource-based strategy and then leverage their related core competencies in many markets.

But as we know, there are wars in which the enemy is difficult to engage, battle dynamics fluctuate, and the terrain is treacherous and unknown. Here, the strategy of choice is guerilla warfare—moving quickly, taking advantage of opportunity and rapidly cutting losses. That kind of entrepreneurial strategy always makes sense for underdog companies because they lack resources and position. But in unstable, unpredictable, and ambiguous terrain like the new economic playing field, entrepreneurial strategy is attractive for large companies as well. The fundamental precept that "strategy is about being different" continues to be true. But what constitutes that strategy has changed. The new strategy watchwords are simplicity, organization and timing.

Strategy Is Simple

First and foremost, strategy on the new economic playing field has to be simple. Complicated, intertwined activity systems or elaborately planned leveraging of core competencies make sense in slower and more-linear situations. On the new high-velocity playing field, they are cumbersome and glacially slow. Managers now must jump into uncertain situations because that is where the opportunities are most abundant. They must capture and exploit promising opportunities or drop them rapidly if they fail to develop. Counterintuitively, complicated markets demand simple, back-to-basics strategy.

Simple strategy means using one or two critical strategic processes and the handful of unique rules that guide them. The critical processes are those that put the corporation into the flow of the most promising opportunities and therefore will differ company to company. For consumer-products giant Colgate-Palmolive, global product management is a key strategic process. Product managers follow a few simple precepts, such as "maintain the brand" and "keep relative product positioning stable." But within those rules, Colgate managers around the globe have considerable freedom. For example, while maintaining the defined brand image of toothpaste and its relative positioning against other Colgate dental-care products, managers can alter the flavor, change the packaging, create locally tailored advertising, tinker with the ingredients, shift prices and more. Within a few parameters, managers move as they see fit.

Another example is Netherlands-based Ispat International, one of the fastest-growing steel companies in the world. Throughout the 1990s, the Ispat strategy was centered on the acquisition process and a few simple guidelines for two aspects of that process: first, which acquisition opportunities to pick (state-owned companies, companies in which costs could be reduced, companies with direct-reduction or electric-arc technologies); second, how to integrate the acquisitions (always retain existing top managers, insist on daily meetings and reporting). But within the guidelines, Ispat managers could buy companies from Germany to Kazakhstan and run them in accordance with the changing flow of opportunities.

In contrast, complicated and richly resourced strategies often do not work. Take Pandesic, the joint venture for 3-commerce services that Intel and SAP launched in 1997 and that folded in 2000. Too much effort went into a strategic plan that was overly complex and difficult to revise. Too many people were assigned to execute the plan. Pandesic executives had too many resources and an overly defined strategic position. What they did not have was simplicity. As the real market opportunity unfolded, they needed a simple focus in order to adjust flexibly.

Strategy Is Organizational

Programming the strategy from the top and then figuring out an organization to implement it may work in slow-moving markets. It's the signature approach of strategists who simplistically think of organizations in terms of control and alignment of management incentives. In high-velocity markets, that approach won't work. In such circumstances, strategy consists of choosing an excellent team, picking the right roles for team members, and then letting their moves emerge. It's like basketball. Los Angeles Lakers' coach Phil Jackson does not mastermind the moves of Kobe Bryant and Shaquille O'Neal. Rather, he puts the right personnel in a triangle offense and lets them play. To the uninformed, the moves seem to flow from an elaborate playbook, but the astute fan understands that the organization itself is the strategy.

For companies, organizational strategy is the unique mapping (often termed patching) of modular businesses onto specific market opportunities. Think Velcro. Organizational strategy is firm and clear at any point in time but also is able to change quickly. A prime example: Hewlett-Packard's wildly successful strategy in the mid-1980s to mid-1990s, which led to domination of the global printer industry.

H-P executives focused their business-unit teams—whether in Spain, Italy, Idaho, Colorado or Singapore—on clearly defined product and market targets. The teams' assignment was to "take the hill." They were guided by a few simple rules—for example, never spend money on an activity if someone else can do it. But the real key to the strategy was organizational. The quarterly realignment of the businesses against the shifting pattern of emerging, colliding, splitting, and declining market and product opportunities defined the H-P strategy. As the markets changed, H-P executives added businesses, such as scanners and printer cartridges. They split off businesses, including removing the deskjet business from LaserJets. Sometimes they combined businesses (the dot-matrix and network-printing businesses). Occasionally, they exited a business. The repatching of businesses was rarely reported in the media, because the moves were usually small and even routine. Nonetheless, the frequent realignment of business units was the central feature of H-P's enormously successful printer strategy.

Most subtly, organizational strategy involves choosing the business scale, not just the focus, that is uniquely suited to the velocity of each market. Dell managers operate their businesses at the scale of about $1 billion. As businesses grow beyond that size, they are broken into smaller modules. Microsoft managers often operate their businesses at the scale of about 200 programmers.

The Economist magazine embodies a particularly strategic use of modularity and scale. From the outside, the weekly publication's strategy seems to be to leverage a core competence in writing and to position itself as a magazine for the sophisticated reader. From the inside, the strategy is the organization. Editors at *The Economist* give their writers unusually large swaths of territory and considerable freedom in choosing what to cover. The organizational strategy not only gives writers greater scope to develop stories, it enables senior editors to hire fewer (and, presumably, better) writers and compensate them more, both with money and with unfettered, interesting work. The resulting product is more creative than that of other news magazines and has the greater depth that appeals particularly to the upmarket reader.

Strategy Is Temporal

Finally, strategy is temporal. In traditional strategy, time is not part of the strategic equation. After all, markets are assumed to move slowly and predictably, if at all. In contrast, time is crucial on the new high-velocity playing field. The easiest way to think about temporal strategy is through understanding the concept of corporate genes. A corporation's unique mix of genes is its combined products, brand, technology, manufacturing capabilities, geographic locations and so on. Managers using temporal strategy conduct a kind of genetic engineering, pursuing a series of unique strategic moves in which one or more genes are changed. They may introduce a new technology, change a brand, enter a new

> *Although most executives would like sustained advantage, they are forced to operate as if it does not exist. The challenge is coping with not knowing whether such an advantage actually exists—except in retrospect.*

country or drop a manufacturing competence. They are constantly splicing in new genes or cutting out others to engineer genetic evolution.

The best temporal strategies also exhibit a pattern that occurs in the natural world of earthquakes and tropical storms: the inverse power law. That is, small events are common, midsize events occur occasionally, and large events are rare. Good temporal strategies are unique combinations of small, incremental changes plus midsize changes and large, radical changes. Most of the time, temporal strategy should feature safe, small changes that elaborate on aspects of the core business. But temporal strategy needs to include medium-scale moves occasionally and, even more occasionally, large-scale moves that reinvent significant portions of the corporation. This also means that the dichotomy of "stick to the core" versus "creative destruction" is a false one. Effective managers pursue both approaches.

EBay offers an excellent example of temporal strategy. The Internet star was launched as a website where traders of collectibles could congregate and trade. It morphed into an auction, added other kinds of merchandise (such as cars and fine art), branched beyond the auction format to fixed-price markets and expanded into numerous countries. It became what the business-to-business exchange was to have been. Most often, eBay's changes were small. Occasionally they were large. There was always a mix of large and small changes, with varying emphasis on changing the genes of country, merchandise, business model or auction format. EBay managers also sometimes added rhythm to their temporal strategy by pacing the evolution more rapidly or more slowly as the opportunity for advantage dictated. As a result, eBay managers evolved their businesses through varying moves—and created the Internet's most durable star.

Sustainable Competitive Advantage?

Is sustained competitive advantage still relevant? Sometimes long-term competitive advantage and its attendant creation of wealth can occur on the new economic playing field. More often, they cannot. The more salient point is, however, that the duration of competitive advantage is unpredictable. It may last 10 minutes, 10 months or 10 years. So although most executives would like sustained advantage, they are forced to operate as if it does not exist. The challenge is, therefore, not so much achieving sustainable advantage as it is coping with not knowing whether such an advantage actually exists—except in retrospect.

Strategy is still about being different. But today, the way in which strategy is different is itself different. Globalization is rearranging the turf. The speed of play on the field is lightning fast. The scale and pace of change are unpredictable. The economics of disequilibrium and information have moved to center stage. As a result, the recipe for effective strategy must now focus on unique strategic processes with simple rules, on the modular patching of businesses to fleeting market opportunities and on evolutionary timing for ongoing strategic moves. In other words, we are not back to "strategy as usual." Whether we like it or not, strategy has changed.

READING

3

A Fresh Look at Industry and Market Analysis

Stanley F. Slater
University of Washington, Bothell

Eric M. Olson
University of Colorado–Colorado Springs

In 1980, Michael Porter introduced the Five Forces Model of Industry Competition and forever changed how managers, consultants, and academics would view competitive environments. His basic premises were that the collective strength of five basic competitive forces determine the return on capital potential in an industry and influence the strategies available to firms in the industry. The competitive forces are: (1) threat of new entry into an industry; (2) intensity of rivalry among existing competitors; (3) pressure from substitute products; (4) bargaining power of buyers; and (5) bargaining power of suppliers.

Since the introduction of this model, a substantial body of research has been compiled that either supports or complements the basic premises set forth by Porter. However, industry dynamics have evolved in subtle and not so subtle ways over the past two decades. We have moved closer to a global marketplace in many industries; technology has advanced rapidly and in unforeseen ways; deregulation has opened the door for aggressive forms of entrepreneurship; and the Internet has created an entirely new way to do business.

How can we augment Porter's Five Forces Model to reflect these and other developments? We can begin by examining its basic underlying premises:

1. Industry Is the Appropriate Unit of Analysis

Industries are frequently identified by two- or four-digit SIC (Standard Industrial Classification) codes. But this is too broad a definition to be valuable for meaningful analysis. Porter attempts to bring more precision to the issue of what constitutes an industry by defining it as "the group of firms producing products that are close substitutes for each other." However, this is still rather vague in that it leaves the definition of "close substitutes" open. Are minivans close substitutes for sport utility vehicles? Are frozen vegetables substitutes for fresh vegetables? Is an industrial strength adhesive a close substitute for a nut and bolt or a rivet? Porter provides us with no clear-cut way to answer these questions.

We prefer a customer-oriented, demand-side definition of industry to the more traditional, production-oriented, supply-side definition. We also prefer the term "market" to "industry." A market is where buyers and sellers meet to execute an exchange. More precisely, it is where buyers who have similar needs meet sellers who have "products"

Reprinted from *Business Horizons,* Vol. 45, No. 1, January–February 2002, pp. 15–22.

that provide benefits to satisfy this need. (For convenience here, we use "product" to represent products and/or services.) This distinction between industries and markets, though subtle, suggests different mental models for managers. Mental models shape the way we perceive and process information. Markets as a mental model are less likely to produce rigid thinking.

The first step in an analysis, then, is to define a group of buyers who have a relatively homogeneous need. Standard market research techniques such as focus groups, survey research, and conjoint analysis, among others, are appropriate for this task. The potential demand in the market must be assessed to determine whether a strategy for creating superior value for this set of buyers is economically feasible. Finally, the market must be strategically distinctive for product development and communication purposes. If a market is not determined to be strategically distinctive, it should be combined with a related market.

2. Industry Factors Determine the Average Return on Capital in an Industry

This topic has been the subject of research in both economics and strategic management, and the results largely conform with Porter's position. An analysis of businesses in the PIMS (Profit Impact of Market Strategies) database by Buzzell and Gale (1987) indicated that the average pretax ROI for businesses competing in unattractive markets was 13.4 percent, compared to 31.3 percent for those competing in attractive markets. Schmalensee's (1985) analysis of FIC Line of Business data showed that industry effects accounted for about 75 percent of the difference in industry returns. Rumelt's (1991) more conservative analysis of the same data showed that industry effects still account for about 40 percent of the differences among industries.

Two influences are at work here that need to be considered. The first is that both stable and transient forces affect ROI. Stable forces, such as the value of brand names or patents, typically do not change rapidly. The exception might be when a catastrophic event occurs similar to what recently happened with Firestone tires. In contrast, transient forces, such as the number of potential buyers for full-sized cars, can change dramatically from year to year based on demographic shifts or changes in fuel prices. Thus, market analysis must consider the rate and unpredictability of change because these will influence profitability, strategy formulation, and strategy content. We will return to the influence of market change when we present the augmented model.

The second influence is that the collective strength of market forces has much greater influence on average returns than on the ROI for a specific business. The research cited above shows that there is substantial variation within an industry—or market—around its average ROI. This means that even firms in unattractive markets can achieve exceptional rates of return by developing the appropriate configuration of physical assets, intangible assets, and capabilities, and by deploying them in an integrated strategy. The U.S. Forest and Paper Products Industry had a median ROI of 3.7 percent in 1999, but the ROIs for individual companies ranged from 1 percent for International Paper to 18 percent for Chesapeake.

3. Industry Factors Influence Competitive Strategy

A common meaning of competitive strategy is that it is the set of actions, including the development and deployment of resources, that position the business to both exploit opportunities and avoid threats in its markets. While this meaning would make the premise true by definition, there is substantial evidence that some strategies are more effective than others in particular industry environments. Several studies have found that, in turbulent environments, companies that attempt to be first to market with innovative product concepts are less successful than those with more conservative strategies. It is not our purpose here to explain these results. Rather, we merely point out that industry factors do influence the selection of strategies and their effectiveness.

Our conclusion is that Porter's basic premises are indeed valid. However, we believe the Five Forces model is an incomplete representation of the market factors that influence industry and business performance. So we turn now to the development of an augmented model.

An Augmented Model for Market Analysis

Figure 1 presents our augmented model, which reconfigures Porter's five original forces without removing any of them. For instance, we now combine substitutes and threat of new entry with traditional competitors into a single category we refer to as the "composite competitive rivalry force." There are four other major revisions of note. First, the model explicitly considers the role of "complementors." A market participant is a complementor if buyers value a company's product more highly when they have access to the complementor's product than if they do not. Second, we consider the impact of changing market conditions—specifically, market turbulence and market growth—on profitability and strategy. Third, we now explicitly consider the impact of market structure on the risk profiles of companies competing in a market. Risk, in this context, is the variability of returns in a market. Anticipated variability of returns for a firm influences shareholder value creation. The greater the anticipated variability, the greater the risk premium investors will demand. Finally, we bring the results of recent research and thinking to bear in our discussion of the original forces.

In presenting this model, we stress that the vast majority of Porter's conclusions are as valid today as they were 20 years ago. Thus, we do not challenge the points he has made so effectively. Instead, we concentrate on forces that were not elements in the Five Forces Model, as well as on new ways of thinking about the original forces.

Composite Competitive Rivalry

Competitive rivalry is a force that appears to have the greatest influence on both ROI potential and business-specific risk. We include competition by producers of substitute products and the threat posed by potential entrants in our consideration of rivalry. Rather than separating them into distinctive forces, we combine them because they are so highly interrelated. Separating them could obscure the interrelationships.

Porter suggests that rivalry can be portrayed as falling on a continuum from civilized to cutthroat. Cutthroat competition is often characterized by price wars, which, though good for buyers, are very damaging to industry profitability. Because of price wars, the U.S. airline industry lost more money in the early 1990s than it had earned in the preceding five decades. In 1999, the median return on sales (ROS) for the U.S. *Fortune* 500 was 5 percent. A 2 percent price cut would produce an ROS of 3.5 percent (assuming a 30 percent tax rate), resulting in 30 percent less total profit if no additional sales were generated. The average company would require a 40 percent sales increase

Figure 1   Market Influences on Profitability, Risk, and Strategy

*Subsumes direct competition and threats from substitutes and potential entrants.

to compensate for the reduction. Because price cuts can be quickly, if painfully, invoked, they can be quickly matched, which gives the firm initiating the cut only a temporary advantage and market share increase. After price cuts are matched by competitors, total industry demand would have to increase by the entire 40 percent. Few industries have such elastic demand.

Porter characterizes nonprice-competitive tactics like product development or advertising as more civilized rivalry. This begs the question, though: How civilized is such rivalry? To answer it we must consider the firm's objectives. The financial objective is to produce a return on capital that exceeds the cost of capital, thereby creating shareholder value. This can be done consistently only when the firm has a position of sustainable competitive advantage—creating more value for buyers than competitors can, and in a way that is difficult to imitate. However, all a firm can really hope to do is impede imitation because in the long run any product, asset, or capability can be imitated or innovated around.

Innovation, whether in products or processes, is the key to achieving and sustaining competitive advantage. There are two generic types of innovation. *Disruptive innovations,* according to Christensen and Bower (1996), are the stuff of which Schumpeter's "creative destruction" is made. These innovations happen rarely but have the potential to destroy incumbent products and businesses. The advent of the compact disc player destroyed the majority of the market for turntables and many of the companies that manufactured them. Digital photography represents another disruptive innovation that poses a substantial threat to manufacturers and developers of 35mm film, such as Kodak.

In contrast, *sustaining innovations* are the type of innovations we associate with continuous improvement. An example is the Iomega 250M Zip drive. The basic technology is not substantially different from that found in the company's 100M Zip drive. However, the sustaining innovation of a 150 percent increase in storage capacity allows for the convenient backing up of memory-hungry video files that have become more and more popular with the advent of increased PC processing power and more user-friendly video-editing software.

Innovation is at least as much of a competitive threat as price competition. Unless a competitor has developed a new process that dramatically lowers cost, price competition is easily matched. While a price cut may damage industry profitability in the short run, it is not likely to cause an industry to become irrelevant. In contrast, introducing a disruptive innovation can be very damaging or even fatal to a firm or industry's fiscal viability. At the introduction of a disruptive innovation, incumbent firms may actually realize short-term victories as innovators find it difficult to motivate customer buying due to relatively high prices and possible switching costs. Because of their installed base and substantial investment, incumbents are highly motivated to protect their markets. However, if the innovation truly has merit, price disadvantages will be overcome. The end result for incumbents is that short-term gains will not be sustained; ultimately they will experience long-term market share and financial losses.

A major reason we include substitutes and new entrants here is that these market players often instigate disruptive innovation. Incumbents must be alert to the threats posed by innovations coming from outside the market. In the long run, disruptive innovations have a greater potential to destroy incumbents' profitability, if not the incumbents themselves.

Even the development of sustaining innovations poses risks and is a substantial threat to profitability. Procter & Gamble and Unilever are currently locked in a war for increased market share in the slow-growth laundry detergent business. Brooker (2001) recently noted that "the real genius of Tide's strategy is its relentless stream of new and improved products. Each year Procter & Gamble spends close to $2 billion on research and development, a large portion of which goes toward developing new formulations of Tide." Between the massive amounts spent on marketing and R&D, the financial performance of both firms has suffered.

Complementors

Brandenburger and Nalebuff (1996) coined the term "complementor" based on a branch of economics that is concerned with the impact of network effects on market evolution. Network effects occur when the value of or demand for a product rises with the number of complementary products and the extent of their availability. Microsoft's Windows operating system is valuable to buyers partly because of the many applications that run on it. In this case, we have a wide variety of products that complement Windows and are readily available.

Microsoft's symbiotic relationships with application developers and Intel are the most visible examples of positive network effects. However, network effects are important in low-tech markets as well. The demand for shaving cream is loosely linked to the demand for safety razors, and the demand for safety razors is related to improvements in the quality of shaving cream. These products complement one another; the value of either is dependent on the usefulness of the other.

A subtle but important distinction can be made between complementary products and products whose demand is derived simply from the demand for other products. Diesel truck engines are bought largely because of new trucks. In this case, the diesel engine is a purchased component that will stimulate very little increased demand for the final product category even if it is substantially improved. In contrast, final demand for PCs is likely to increase if an improvement in microprocessor technology enables users to perform a new task or to perform a current task much more effectively. It is important for producers to recognize these different demand situations and understand their position in the network.

Network effects can also lead to increasing returns—that is, the tendency for products that have been accepted as the standard to continue to get farther ahead. Thus, once the VHS recording system established itself as the standard over Sony's Betamax, it achieved an unassailable position. However, its position is assured only until a disruptive innovation comes along. Such an innovation may be the Personal Video Recorder (PVR), which uses large hard disks and computer circuitry inside a set-top box to digitally record anything broadcast over cable or satellite systems. As such, PVRs pose a substantial threat to VCRs and even DVD players. Network effects lead to increasing returns only to the point at which an innovative substitute is developed and introduced to the market.

Customer Power

The bargaining power of customers determines their influence on the selling industry's profitability. Traditional economics tells us that customers have the greatest bargaining power when they are large, few in number, and able to switch easily to alternate suppliers. The question, then, is: How does a seller demonstrate to powerful customers why they should be willing to pay a premium price for its product? There are two common responses to this question. The first is to accept the power imbalance and the reduced profitability that accompanies it. Most firms that adopt this philosophy accept rates of return on capital that approximate their cost of capital. A second response is to find some means for raising the costs customers incur when they switch from one seller to another. Although this is a laudable objective, it is difficult for small sellers to achieve because most customers recognize that their degrees of freedom will be reduced if they become locked in to a particular seller.

Given that the second response, though difficult, is generally considered the preferable option, the question then becomes: How do sellers increase customer commitment while preserving customer choice? The answer is to create customer loyalty, which comes from providing more value to the customer than competitors provide. This can be accomplished in one of three ways. The first is to increase benefits, such as quality or service, to the customer. The second is to reduce non-price costs for the customer, such as adopting a JIT delivery system to help reduce the customer's inventory carrying costs. A third, though potentially self-defeating, approach is to lower prices. If competitors match reduced prices, as frequently happens, this approach will only motivate short-term brand switching, fail to create customer loyalty, and ultimately result in lower profitability for the entire industry.

Supplier Power

Most buyers seek a bargaining advantage relative to suppliers. The forces that lead to more supplier power are the same as those that lead to more customer power. Suppliers have the greatest bargaining power when they are large, few in number, and can sell easily to alternate customers. Traditionally, supplier power has been seen as greater when the product provided represents a low percentage of the buyer's total costs. But this last guideline is no longer true.

In recent years, most buyers have come to appreciate the substantial profitability improvement that a 1 or 2 percent reduction in the cost of purchased products or services can yield. This explains the popularity of reengineering programs. Reengineering begins with the firm's customer value proposition and aligns all internal processes to deliver this value at the lowest cost, which is achieved through efficient processes and inexpensive purchases.

There are two issues here: (1) How can firms successfully bargain with powerful suppliers? and (2) Should buyers attempt to negotiate the lowest prices from weaker suppliers? With regard to the first issue, buyers can bargain for either lower prices or additional benefits. Powerful suppliers are inclined to offer lower prices when they believe it is in their long-run best interests to do so. This may be because they see the buyer as a more important partner in the future and they want to establish a relationship today. Or the buyer may offset some of the supplier's power by entering into a long-term contract. On the other hand, suppliers may hold firm on price but provide additional benefits to buyers. This can be a win-win situation, preserving the revenue stream of the seller while providing additional value to buyers.

> *Once the VHS recording system established itself as the standard over Sony's Betamax system, it achieved an unassailable position. However, its position is assured only until a disruptive innovation comes along.*

With regard to the second issue, powerful buyers should wield their power in a thoughtful manner. Buyers depend on suppliers that can provide high-quality and innovative raw materials, components, and professional services. Innovation requires investment derived from a strong and stable stream of cash flows. Such cash flows require a fair price that produces an adequate return on capital. Firms that view relations with suppliers as transactions to be exploited for maximum gain may be short-sighted. Good relationships with strong suppliers have the greatest potential for creating additional value for ultimate customers—value for which customers will be willing to pay a premium price.

Market Change: Growth and Turbulence

Market growth occurs as the result of growth in the number of market members, more purchases by the members, or the creation of a solution to a latent need (one that is evolving or unexpressed) in the market. An example of the latter situation is IBM's development of the Advanced Dictation System, which enabled traveling managers to relay correspondence to their secretaries. Neither managers nor secretaries found it acceptable as a dictation system, but managers did start to use it to leave messages for the secretaries. In the early 1970s, the system was modified and became the Speech Filing System, the precursor to today's voice mail.

The first two situations are not as disruptive as the development of solutions to latent needs because they can be anticipated more easily and so do not have as substantial an effect on profitability, risk, or strategy. However, the development of new solutions to needs that are not obvious has the potential to alter market structure significantly. This is where we now turn our attention.

Such growth stems from satisfying the pent-up or developing demand for a product that provides the solution to a latent need. The conventional wisdom is that such growth markets are attractive, but this may be a dangerous assumption for several reasons. At best, they represent a classic case of the risk/return trade-off. At worst, the uncertainty surrounding them leads to poor decisions that are precipitated by the desire to achieve or sustain a strong market position.

What are the threats posed by rapid market growth? Growth starts with the introduction of an innovative product that addresses a latent need. Early adopters who embrace risk to gain advantage over users of the old solution are the first to embrace innovations. They are willing to accept a partial but potentially superior solution from the seller and work closely with the seller to refine the product to meet their needs. These early adopters are often small—individually and collectively—with respect to the potential market. But they are the true lead users (customers or potential customers who have advanced needs compared to other market members and who expect to benefit significantly from a solution to those needs), so sellers expend considerable effort to identify and work closely with members of this market segment to develop and refine the concept.

This is a critical step in the product's commercialization as the solution embraced by the early adopters becomes the core of the product that will be adopted by early majority buyers. The greatest risk, says Moore (1991, 1995), lies in the ability of sellers to cross this "chasm" between the early adopters and the early majority. This latter is composed of pragmatists who require a clear understanding of how adopting the new product will create value for them.

> The presence of durable barriers to imitation is the most powerful deterrent to destructive turbulence.

Pragmatists require the supplier to produce a whole solution that is more effective or efficient than the buyers' current solution. They often are reluctant adopters because of the cost of switching from the traditional solution to the innovation. However, industry average returns on capital are most likely to exceed the cost of capital when sellers address the needs of the early majority. Although high growth rates may have occurred during the phase when early adopters accepted and used the innovation, much of the growth will be unprofitable.

Moreover, as the early majority of buyers begin to show interest in the product concept, risk-averse competitors will start to take interest in the market. These fast followers enter a market when the concept has been largely proven. They have the ability to assess the likelihood of success or failure in the market, to learn how the product concept might be improved from that market intelligence, and to rapidly develop and introduce an improved version of the product. This is one reason why only a small percentage of firms that pioneered a new product concept are still market leaders by the time late majority buyers have entered the market. Ironically, it is the entry of new competitors that legitimizes the product concept and demonstrates its acceptability to pragmatic buyers.

As new competitors enter the market during its growth stage, the market will become saturated. Most firms have a minimum efficient operating scale that is required for them to be profitable. The invalid assumption made too often is that market growth rates achieved in the early and middle stages of a market's development are sustainable. If these rates are the basis for investment in R&D or facilities, an adequate ROI may not be realized. The softness of demand in the PC market at the end of 2000, even with faster microprocessors from Intel and AMD, shows both that market growth will slow and that the market will not be able to sustain the profitable operation of all competitors. The concern in this situation is that competitors will lower prices to raise demand and reach a break-even volume. This returns us to the proposition that lower prices decrease margins, raise break-even volume, and, because they are easily matched, provide little hope of accomplishing the objective of substantially raising demand.

While turbulence is a common characteristic of growth markets, it is also likely to characterize slower growing markets. The discussion of turbulence can be simplified by classifying it into one of two broad types: *market turbulence* and *competitive turbulence.* Market turbulence concerns primarily the rate of change in customers' needs and preferences and in the composition of the served market. Competitive turbulence concerns the rate at which other firms change their competitive methods, including the development and introduction of technological innovations.

In growth markets, sellers quickly discover that the needs of early majority buyers differ from those of early adopters. Moreover, as the product concept matures, the requirements of early adopters evolve as well. In mature markets, late majority buyers continuously press for additional benefits at the same or lower prices. In growth markets, little is certain about buyer preferences. Thus, competitors frequently enhance the product and non-product portions of their value propositions. In mature markets, they seek to enhance their value proposition to avoid price competition.

Not all markets are equal in their susceptibility to the disruptions caused by market or competitive turbulence. The presence of durable barriers to limitation is the most powerful deterrent to destructive turbulence. These barriers include patents, strong brand names, access to critical resources, scale economies, competencies that span numerous parts of the firm, and relationships with key suppliers or customers. They protect sellers from price competition and lead to a position of sustainable competitive advantage and the superior profitability that accrues to it.

Industries may be portrayed on a continuum based on the height of the barriers to imitation. Those with high barriers, such as pharmaceuticals and the beverage industry, typically face lower turbulence and achieve consistently higher profitability. Industries with lower barriers to imitation face higher turbulence, particularly competitive turbulence, and their profitability varies more over time.

Strategic Positioning in Competitive Markets

So how might firms reduce the pressure of the competitive forces in their markets? Several suggestions follow. Of course, no single strategy exists that is appropriate for all firms in a market. The result of strategic homogeneity will be intense, head-to-head competition. Ultimately, meaningful differentiation is the key to competitive advantage and superior performance.

Moreover, markets do not look the same to all competitors. Different firms in a market will have different levels of power, depending on their resources and capabilities. Strategy formulation must be based on a firm's market position, not on some generic assessment of market structure.

Create a Market-Focused Organization

To stay even with or ahead of developments in their markets, firms must develop a market sensing capability, commonly referred to as a *market orientation.* Fundamental to such an orientation is organizational learning—a firm continuously generating knowledge about its target markets and reflecting that knowledge in its market behavior.

There are many ways in which businesses can draw useful inferences about customer needs. They can often discover latent needs by observing customers' use of products or services in various contexts. They can also monitor data on customer complaints, product returns, and warranty claims—all of which may reveal information about customers' product knowledge, ease of use, and product maintenance.

Market-oriented firms scan the market broadly, have a long-term focus, and work closely with lead users. Because the future is so uncertain in a turbulent market, they conduct small-scale market experiments, learn from the results, and modify their offerings based on this new knowledge and insight.

Thus, a market orientation is reflected in behaviors that enable the business to learn from current and potential customers about their existing and latent needs, and to act in an entrepreneurial manner to create superior customer value. The capabilities inherent in a market orientation enable the business to discover customer need opportunities in unserved markets as well as in the markets it serves.

Establish Relationships with Key Customers and Suppliers

The development of strong relationships with key customers and suppliers follows naturally as a firm becomes market-focused. The most valuable and enduring relationships are built on a foundation of trust and common interest. Obviously, not all buyers and sellers are similarly inclined toward establishing relationships. Buyers of commodity-like products, for example, may not see much value in it because they have many suppliers from which to choose. On the other hand, buyers of specialized or customized products will tend to seek sellers with whom they can work comfortably for a long period of time. They make substantial investments of time, information, and money, and they want to see a return on that investment.

The challenge, then, is to be able to demonstrate the value of a relationship, even if the seller's product is commodity-like. One natural resource-based firm we have worked with has been able to accomplish this by providing services that augment the value of its products. Sophisticated, key customers are willing to pay premium prices for the seller's products and accompanying services. Its competitors target price-sensitive customers, charge lower prices, and earn lower returns—business in which the seller is not interested.

Create New Market Space

One way to avoid head-to-head competition is by finding new market space that represents a new opportunity to create customer value. This is accomplished by closely examining all the key influences in the market's structure for hidden opportunities, influences such as strategic groups, buyer networks, complementors, substitute industries, and time.

Strategic groups are clusters of firms that have similar value propositions. There are generally four to six groups competing in a market. The challenge is to identify a value proposition that none of these groups has adopted. Home Depot slipped in between traditional hardware and building supply stores that catered to do-it-yourselfers with some expertise and buyers with little expertise who hired contractors to do their remodeling. It did this by providing classes for novice, would-be remodelers.

> *Strategy formulation must be based on a firm's market position, not on some generic assessment of market structure.*

Buyer networks include actual purchasers, users, and other important influencers. Chuck E. Cheese Restaurants assembled a value proposition that was fun for kids, took some of the burden off parents, and was reasonably priced. For more than 30 years gas stations have sold a wide variety of drinks, snacks, and other appropriate impulse items. Barnes & Noble booksellers enhanced the buying experience for their customers by having coffee shops on the premises to encourage longer browsing.

Is there a member of the buying network in our market whose needs are not being adequately addressed? Looking at your business from a buyer's perspective, what are natural complements to your offering that you could provide within the scope of your core competencies?

Maybe the key priority is to develop a sense of the future. What trends are taking place that have the potential to be the foundation for new value propositions? In many cases this requires the ability to anticipate which disruptive technologies have the greatest potential to alter the value equation. In many electronics markets, innovations that enable a seller to make the product smaller, faster, or less expensive will often have substantial potential. Often, however, they will make the seller's current product obsolete as well.

Conceive of Strategy as a Series of Real Options

It is incumbent on managers to invest in innovative strategic initiatives that create substantial opportunities for future growth and profitability and that balance the created opportunity with the underlying risk. Traditional approaches to financial analysis have placed too great an emphasis on risk reduction. Consequently, many businesses invest primarily in incremental product modifications and market expansion. Although the initial results from this investment strategy may be acceptable, these initiatives do little to position the firm for the long term.

Strategic options analysis takes a broader and more realistic view of the investment decision. It recognizes that investments may be delayed or reconfigured as conditions change or new information becomes available. More important, it recognizes that managers are active decision-makers both when a project is authorized and as it is implemented. Combining the qualitative insights from strategic options analysis with the quantitative outputs from a discounted cash flow analysis gives managers a rich body of information upon which to make decisions. There will be times when the results from the two analyses will conflict. This should be expected and should be viewed as an opportunity for frank discussions of the direction to take. In the quest for competitive advantage, innovative strategy development driven by adaptability and flexibility is probably the most critical activity for all businesses, and should not be hampered by improper use of the standard analytical and evaluation techniques in use today.

Most scholars and consultants agree that the effective creation and deployment of company-specific resources and capabilities has greater influence on company profitability than does industry membership. However, this should not be interpreted to mean that an understanding of market forces should be relegated to secondary importance. Market forces determine which resources and capabilities have the potential to be a source of competitive advantage. The current and anticipated actions of competitors, customers, suppliers, and complementors should shape the actions of the seller firm. Our goal here has been to complement, not replace, Porter's Five Forces Model. We suggest that, taken together, these works provide a framework for market analysis and the development of a strategy for competitive advantage.

Selected References

Amram, M., and N. Kulatilaka. 1999. Disciplined decisions: Aligning strategy with the financial markets. *Harvard Business Review* (January–February): 95–104.

Anderson, J., and J. Narus. 1991. Partnering as a focused market strategy. *California Management Review* (Spring): 95–113.

Brandenburger, A., and B. Nalebuff. 1996. *Co-opetition.* New York: Currency Doubleday.

Brooker, K. 2001. A game of inches. *Fortune* (5 February): 98–100.

Buzzell, R., and B. Gale. 1987. *The PIMS principles.* New York: Free Press.

Christensen, C., and J. Bower. 1996. Customer power, strategic investment, and the failure of leading firms. *Strategic Management Journal* (March): 197–218.

Golder, P., and G. Tellis. 1993. Pioneer advantage: Marketing logic or marketing legend? *Journal of Marketing Research* (May): 158–170.

Kim, W. C., and R. Mauborgne. 1999. Creating new market space. *Harvard Business Review* (January–February): 83–93.

Moore, G. 1991. *Crossing the chasm.* New York: HarperBusiness.

———. 1995. *Inside the tornado.* New York: HarperBusiness.

Porter, M. 1980. *Competitive strategy.* New York: Free Press.

Rumelt, R. 1991. How much does industry matter? *Strategic Management Journal* (March): 167–186.

Schmalensee, R. 1985. Do markets differ much? *American Economic Review* (June): 341–351.

Slater, S., and J. Narver. 1995. Market orientation and the learning organization. *Journal of Marketing* (July): 63–74.

———. 1998. Customer-led and market-oriented: Let's not confuse the two. *Strategic Management Journal* (October): 1,001–1,006.

The Science, *Not Art,* of Business Intelligence

Michael C. O'Guin
Knowledge Link

Timothy Ogilvie
Brivo Systems

The intelligence process starts with management articulating the need for information that will allow it to make a critical decision. As our case study demonstrates, effective business intelligence results not from luck, but from a systematic process. The intelligence analyst deduces a target's most likely actions or intentions using a hypothesis-based approach. This approach allows the analyst to form and test a theory about the target's actions. Testing a set of hypotheses causes the analysis to identify, plan, and seek out market signals that betray a competitor's actions. By implementing the intelligence plan, the analyst is able to collect the necessary facts to deduce a competitor's actions, allowing his or her company a decisive advantage in the marketplace.

While no great general goes into battle without knowing the size, composition, location, weaponry, and tactics of the enemy, many captains of industry do. Many executives embark upon costly competitions for vital business without considering the enemy's capabilities and possible strategies. Just as in combat, this lack of intelligence frequently leads to defeat. This was a key finding of a strategic benchmarking survey of 24 aerospace and defense (A&D) companies (see O'Guin, 1994). The study uncovered a direct relationship between a company's knowledge of its competitor's approach and its success at winning contracts.

However, most companies gather competitor information in an ad hoc manner—they take what they can get, when and where they can get it. They think of business intelligence as an unaffordable luxury and its practice as a mystical art of dubious repute. As a result, their haphazard collection of data fails to provide insight of much value.

Reprinted from *Competitive Intelligence Review,* Vol. 12, No. 4 (4th Quarter 2001), pp. 15–24. This material is used by permission of John Wiley & Sons, Inc.

However, the companies with the highest success rates at winning new business have found that business intelligence is not a mystical art, it is a science whose ethical practice readily impacts a company's top and bottom lines.

The winners use business intelligence methodically to collect and organize information about the external world. They systematically develop intelligence that reveals their competitor's strategies, provides performance benchmarks, and illuminates changing customer preferences and needs. Business intelligence systems allow companies to anticipate and adapt to changing market conditions by providing them with early warning of emerging technologies, new regulations, market entrants, and other forces.

The following disguised case study illustrates how business intelligence (BI) professionals systematically collect and analyze information that affects critical business decisions. This article shows how the BI professional plans, collects, and analyzes information to enable a company to compete successfully.

Business Intelligence—The Framework

Providing executives with knowledge or foreknowledge of a competitor's (or customer's, or regulator's) actions does not happen by accident. A compelling business case results from a carefully constructed and executed business intelligence plan. This plan follows a familiar framework—the scientific method. After studying the universe, the scientist reasons both deductively and inductively, searching for an explanation of his or her observations, and develops a series of hypotheses to explain the behavior of nature. The scientist then constructs an experiment or series of experiments to test the hypotheses. The collection of this data either confirms or denies the hypotheses.

Business intelligence (BI) follows the same process. When management needs to understand a target's actions, it tasks the business intelligence professional for answers. From their observations, the BI analyst develops a series of hypotheses regarding the target's actions. But the BI professional lacks the luxury of staging a controlled experiment (however attractive it would be to put your competitor's executives in a maze searching for a piece of cheese). So, the professional must observe how the target organization interacts with the external environment. These interactions broadcast signals that reveal a target's intentions. For example, to introduce a new product, a company conducts market studies, files for trademarks, hires key skills, contracts for laboratory test time, installs new equipment, develops advertising, designs new packaging, and lines up launch customers. Each of these actions creates subtle signals in the marketplace.

The BI professional seeks out a set of signals consistent with their hypotheses covering the various marketing, technical, product line, manufacturing, and service options open to the target. The presence or absence of these signals indicates whether or not the hypothesis is true. The professional crafts an intelligence plan to prove (or, by default, disprove) each hypothesis through planned, proactive, and focused data collection of these signals. After seeking out and analyzing this data, the professional synthesizes and packages the accumulated evidence into an intelligence product that allows management to reach a decision and take action.

Implementing the intelligence plan consists of the following steps:

1. Determine the business decision that you must make.

2. Identify the specific questions you need answered to reach a decision.

3. Develop specific hypotheses about the answer to each question.

4. Identify the signals the target would emit if the hypothesis were true.

5. Identify sources that would see these signals.

6. Develop data collection plan to contact those sources and look for the anticipated signals.

7. Collect the data.

8. Analyze the data, reach a conclusion and report your findings.

To illustrate this process, we will describe each step and then how it was implemented in a case study.

Step 1. Determine the Business Decision You Must Make

Intelligence is "actionable" information. It is information, about the external environment, which management requires to make an effective business decision. It is not "nice-to-have," it is "must-have" information. Intelligence can focus on a competitor, customer, regulator, teammate, acquisition candidate, market, or any other external influence. Therefore, the first step in any intelligence project is defining the business decision management must make.

> **Case Study: Freebird's Global Pursuit.** Recently, an electronics manufacturer used business intelligence to determine the competition's offering for a large aircraft contract. The company, which we will call Freebird, was competing for the navigation system on a new passenger aircraft being developed by Global Aerospace. The navigation system provides the air crew with the aircraft's position, flight path, arrival times, and other navigation information. The system integrates a guidance computer and cockpit display with such sensors as a rate gyro, Global Positioning System (GPS) receiver, and inertial measuring unit (IMU).
>
> *Freebird's business decision was: What strategy should they propose to win the Global contract and still achieve an attractive financial return?*

Step 2. Identify the Specific Questions You Need Answered to Reach a Decision

For each critical business decision, an intelligence analyst must define exactly what information will be required to take decisive action. Complex questions with many dimensions must be dissected into a set of discrete, specific questions. Therefore, the intelligence professional breaks down the information requirements into manageable questions with discrete answers.

> **Case study:** Freebird knew that its principal competitor, AirLink, would also bid on the contract. While the Request for Proposal (RFP) was scheduled for release more than a year in the future, Freebird needed to craft its win strategy and begin developing and positioning its solution. Freebird's executives knew that effective win strategies are based on selecting a solution which is clearly differentiated as superior to the competition on those factors most important to the customer.
>
> *Foreknowledge of AirLink's approach would allow Freebird to select an effective win strategy which: (1) emphasized its strengths, (2) minimized its*

weaknesses, (3) highlighted AirLink's weaknesses, and (4) neutralized AirLink's strengths. Therefore, Freebird's management needed discrete answers to the following questions:

- *What are the customer's most important values?*
- *What technical solution will AirLink propose?*
- *What price will AirLink bid?*
- *How will they structure their offer with financing, design assistance, etc.?*

The rest of the article will focus on the techniques used by Freebird to decipher AirLink's solution.

Step 3. Develop Specific Hypotheses about the Answer to Each Question

For each specific question, you analyze your observations of the target and their available alternatives. Using this data you develop a hypothesis about what you think the target is doing or will do. You consciously try to avoid your own prejudices by viewing the customer and market from the target's perspective. A good strategy is to pick the competitor's most aggressive or threatening option to you as your hypothesis. From brainstorming of this type, you develop a set of hypotheses about the target's likely actions, then devise ways to test each hypothesis.

The greater your initial knowledge of the target, the more accurate and detailed your initial hypotheses can be. However, experience has shown that correct initial hypotheses are unnecessary and, in practice, usually wrong. The hypotheses, correct or not, lead you to identify a comprehensive set of signals, and the sources who will see them. If the intelligence plan is executed effectively across a broad spectrum of sources, your sources will spot signals of every major competitor action, even those that are unanticipated. Uncovering conflicting data may disprove some of your hypotheses and lead you to formulate new hypotheses and retest them. This iterative process leads you to develop an accurate picture of the competition's strategy without its foreknowledge.

In addition, the hypotheses can and are developed at multiple levels: The top-level hypothesis determines whether or not a competitor is developing a product and subsequent analysis examines the various possible features of the new product.

> **Case study:** To develop a hypothesis, Freebird assessed AirLink's strengths and weaknesses versus the customer's most important values. They found that Global's most important values for the navigation system were:
>
> - *light weight*
> - *navigation accuracy*
> - *low life-cycle cost*

In addition, this new program was putting a severe strain on Global's engineering staff and they would probably welcome any approaches that reduced their engineering content.

Historically, AirLink sold individual components that were renowned for their outstanding field reliability. AirLink's customer, the aircraft manufacturer, integrated these components into navigation system. AirLink's high reliability resulted in a low life-cycle cost, but to achieve Global's required navigation accuracy, AirLink would have to propose a solution that included some of their larger and heavier sensors.

From this assessment, Freebird identified two alternative strategies for AirLink to satisfy Global's needs: (1) continue to offer individual components but repackage them to reduce their weight or (2) integrate the various components using software into a smaller and lighter assembly.

AirLink had few successful programs based on software integration (source: their Annual Reports and marketing literature, bidders conferences, *Commerce Business Daily* contract listings, and copies of past contracts obtained through the Freedom of Information Act [FOIA]). However, they had recently told a Wall Street financial analysts meeting of their initiative into this higher value-added segment of the business (source: industry analyst). In addition, AirLink had recently hired a senior vice president with a software integration background (source: local paper).

Freebird's management believed that an integrated solution would be AirLink's most formidable offering. Not only would this approach significantly lower the system's weight, but also it had the added benefit of reducing the workload on Global's already thin engineering staff. Therefore, based on their observations, Freebird would test the hypothesis that AirLink was developing an integrated navigation system for the Global contract.

Step 4. Identify the Signals the Target Would Emit if the Hypothesis Were True

No organization functions in isolation. Every action an organization takes emits signals into its environment. These signals potentially betray the target's intentions, if systematically collected and analyzed. However, most of the time these signals are drowned out by the background noise in the market. The intelligence plan tasks your employees to seek out these signals. The presence or absences of signals are facts. By piecing these facts together, the intelligence analyst assembles the puzzle that is the competitor's offering.

The search for meaningful signals starts by identifying all of the actions the target would be taking if your hypothesis were correct. Typically, you use a brainstorming meeting with your internal functional experts—marketing, sales, engineering, human resources, quality, service personnel, purchasing, manufacturing, and facilities for this process. In many cases, it is productive and appropriate to involve outside partners in this effort—trusted consultants, teammates, supplier representatives, etc.

Each expert provides his or her perspective on the competitor's situation and possible actions. As you attempt to identify the competitor's actions, it is helpful to use your own company as a model. If your company were developing an integrated navigation system, what actions would you have to take? Then, consider how your target is different. The greater your initial knowledge of the target's capabilities and processes, the more focused and precise the list of potential actions will be. Using this approach, you identify all of their critical configuration choices the target can make in developing their solution. These key product, technology, supplier, distribution, and manufacturing choices shape their offering to the customer.

Case study: If AirLink were developing a new product some actions would be obvious. They would conduct market studies, develop advertising, and float their new product ideas by the customer. However, developing a new product is a complex undertaking. For the analyst to systematically and comprehensively identify all of the actions required, Freebird's technical experts decomposed an integrated navigation system engineering project into its work breakdown

Figure 1   Work Breakdown Structure of an Integrated Navigation System Project

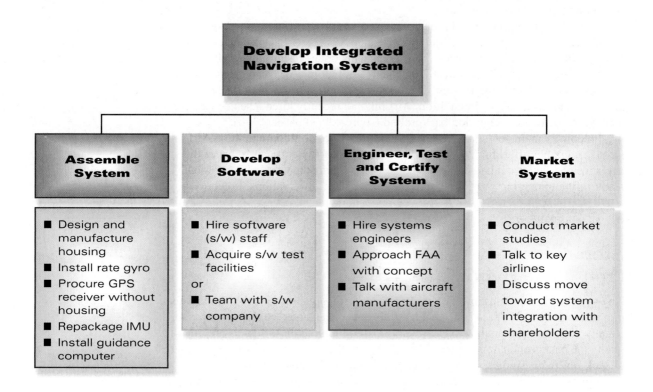

structure. By breaking the product into discrete tasks (shown in Figure 1) it is easier to identify the actions AirLink must take. Freebird identified the following signals for AirLink's introduction of an integrated navigation system.

- *AirLink would have to buy a GPS receiver. Currently AirLink does not sell any products requiring a GPS receiver. In addition, if AirLink bought a GPS receiver for this purpose, they would try to procure it without its housing since it would be integrated into a single sensor assembly with its own packaging.*
- *AirLink would also have to repackage its Inertial Measuring Unit (IMU) to fit into the integrated sensor assembly.*
- *Given AirLink's limited software capability, they would either have to team with a software integration company or significantly enhance their current capabilities. Each of these actions would give off clear signals. Developing internal software capability, on the other hand, might emit different signals, including hiring new staff, buying or building a software integration test facility, and applying for a higher Software Engineering Institute (SEI) certification rating.*
- *To conduct the necessary trade studies, simulation and other system engineering activities, AirLink would need to hire some senior systems engineers with navigation experience.*

Table 1   AIRLINK ACTIONS AND SIGNALS

Actions	Signals
Buy a GPS receiver without housing	AirLink requests quotes from GPS suppliers
Repackage Inertial Measuring Unit	AirLink requests quote from casting house
Team with a software integration company	■ AirLink explores software integration and navigation experience with software companies ■ AirLink conducts teaming negotiations with software integration companies
Enhance current software development capabilities	■ Advertising for senior software integration expert ■ Filing a building permit for a software integration test facility ■ Hiring a Software Engineering Institute (SEI) certification consultant
Hire systems engineers	■ Places ads in local papers ■ Places ads in system engineering journals ■ Has job openings for system engineering listed on their website ■ Participates in local job fairs looking for systems engineers

Once you identify the actions the target must take if they are following your hypothesis, you identify the corresponding signals these actions would emit into the marketplace (see Table 1). An action may result in one or more signals. For example, to build a new software integration test facility creates a large number of signals from acquiring property, to filing building permits, to procuring test equipment. However, engineering a new sensor assembly may be done entirely in-house with existing resources and emit no signals to the market place.

Step 5. Identify Sources Who Would See These Signals

After identifying the hypothesis' signals, you brainstorm with your team to identify sources that would see these signals. Suppliers would see components being bought. Key customers would see marketing studies being conducted. The Environmental Protection Agency might see new production processes being installed, and so on.

Many times it is your own internal experts who see the signals. Your sales force hears of competitor marketing studies and picks up the competitor's product literature at a trade show. Your engineering staff frequently learns from conferences and personal networks about the technologies your competition is working on.

Do not limit your research to either primary (interviewing people) or secondary sources (published materials). Likewise, do not limit yourself to those sources that will directly see the signals. Industry watchers such as consultants, academics, financial analysts, trade officials, and journal editors follow the industry and frequently know what the major players are working on. In addition, you should identify sources that have direct knowledge of the target, including former or current employees of the target. A cross-functional team with significant industry experience, effectively facilitated, can usually identify 50 or more sources.

Case study: In AirLink's case, some of the sources identified to spot key moves:

- **Buying a GPS receiver.** There are only three GPS receiver manufacturers that build units suitable for the Global program.
- **Repackage IMU.** Accurate Casting currently supplies AirLink's IMU housings. If AirLink were repackaging their IMU, Accurate would be the logical choice to provide the sensor assembly housing.
- **Teaming with a software company.** There are only two software companies with navigation systems experience capable of developing the integration software AirLink requires.
- **Hiring systems engineers.** AirLink would probably try to find systems engineers either through the International Society of Systems Engineers, advertising in the *Journal of Systems Engineering,* or going to one of the few technical specialist search firms.

Some signals are easier to observe than others. For example, the company president's announcement to her shareholders that the company intends to enter the system integration business is both a well-publicized (e.g., easy to spot) and clear signal. A good signal is a clear signal—its meaning is unambiguous. In this case, the president's statement is public and directed to shareholders, and therefore it is a highly credible signal.

On the other hand, trying to hire a software integration expert, unless you are in a very small field, tends to be an action that is done very discreetly, making it a difficult signal to observe.

Step 6. Develop a Data Collection Plan

The next step is to develop a data collection plan. This plan guides the effort by defining the sources and questions to be asked. The sources on the data collection plan are sequenced from the outside of the "intelligence onion" to the inside (see Figure 2). In this way the easiest and most accessible sources—literature searches and talking to your internal experts—are tapped first. As the plan is implemented, your knowledge grows. The more knowledge you have, the more detail you can solicit from a source. Therefore, you are able to approach the most difficult and expensive sources for only the most valuable information.

For example, you should not waste the time of the country's foremost authority on navigation systems by asking her what an IMU (inertial measuring unit) does. However, you might ask her whether companies are moving toward developing integrated navigation systems for military aircraft. Since she has a close relationship with Air-Link, she is liable to hint that she knows of a company working on an integrated system, or she might come out and tell you they are, or she could tell you those developments are still years away. The most difficult or valuable sources (such as competitor employees) are used only for the most difficult information. However, accessible sources are not necessarily less valuable than hard to access ones.

The plan ensures accountability for data collection by identifying a responsible individual and due date for each piece of information (see Table 2). Preferably, the person assigned responsibility for the information already knows the source and contacts them as a regular part of his or her job. If the source is a supplier, the plan designates a buyer, if it is a customer, a salesman will contact them, etc. The comments column should note helpful information, any concerns, or suspected biases for a given source.

Figure 2 The "Intelligence Onion" of Sources

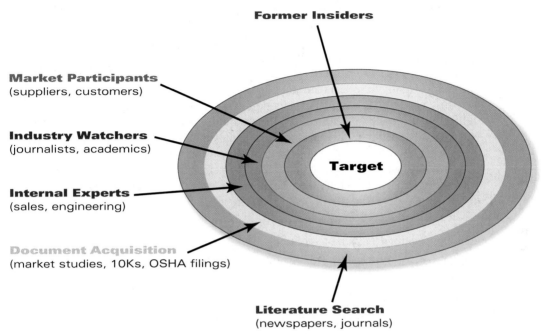

Former Insiders

Market Participants
(suppliers, customers)

Industry Watchers
(journalists, academics)

Internal Experts
(sales, engineering)

Document Acquisition
(market studies, 10Ks, OSHA filings)

Target

Literature Search
(newspapers, journals)

Source: The Futures Group.

Table 2 EXCERPT FROM A DATA COLLECTION PLAN

Questions Asked/ Data Required	Source	Comments	Responsible Individual	Date
Names of industry experts	Database search of technical journals for last 3 years		J. Russell	11/1
Is AirLink trying to hire systems engineers with navigation experience?	Advertising manager, *Journal of Systems Engineering*		J. Russell	11/1
Is AirLink buying a GPS receiver? When do they want delivery? Without a housing?	Acme Electronics— Bill Lehman, Sales Manager, 212-555-1213	Sells GPS receivers. Worked with Gary Larsons on TSEC project	T. Britton	11/2
Is AirLink repackaging their IMU for a new sensor assembly?	Accurate Casting— Julie Rosen, Plant Manager	Supplies AirLink's IMU housings	C. Russ	11/3
Is AirLink in discussions about developing an integrated solution?	Beth Wilkinson— Cybersoft, S/W Engineering Dir. 714-732-8432	S/W integration house. Likes to talk about new technology	J. Ness	11/5
What market niches is AirLink targeting? Was AirLink interested in developing an integrated solution?	Scott Van Sooy, Mesa Electronics 619-234-5654	Ex-AirLink engineer, hates AirLink, knows J. Ness	J. Ness	11/9

Step 7. Collect the Data

You contact sources looking for the presence or absence of signals. Planning is critical to optimize every source. Prior to calling or meeting with a source, you should define exactly what information is needed, information you are willing to share, the sequence of the questions, and the exact phrasing. The intent is to drive the conversation from general questions to more specific ones. Trained data collectors ask open-ended questions that prompt descriptive and detailed responses, offering each source the maximum opportunity to reveal their knowledge.

Just as scientists base their methodology and findings on facts, so do business intelligence professionals. Therefore, the data collector must assess the validity of the source's information by understanding how they obtained it. Did the source see it first hand, hear about it from a reliable source or hear a third-hand rumor? Although opinions are not facts, they are recorded. The collector attempts to prompt the source for underlying facts upon which their opinions are based by asking for examples and details. Three types of facts will be uncovered:

1. Observations that tend to support or confirm your hypotheses;

2. Observations that tend to contradict or disprove your hypotheses; and

3. Observations that introduce completely new possibilities, suggesting new hypotheses.

Your search must be open to each type of fact. The analysis of a robust fact set will permit your organization to iterate the data collection process until you are reasonably certain of the target's actions and intentions.

The success of this step relies on the use of skilled, well-trained, and unbiased data collectors to contact sources. It is relatively easy to structure a conversation to probe a source for an anticipated signal. However, collecting unanticipated signals requires experienced data collectors. It takes significant skill to ask broad enough questions and listen for subtle clues that lead a data collector to probe for unanticipated signals, because you do not necessarily know in advance what questions to ask. Yet, these signals are the most valuable because they indicate unforeseen strategies and actions that can cause you to reconsider your hypotheses.

The importance of executing this step well cannot be overstated. Mistakes are rarely made in analysis. Intelligence failures almost always result from failing either to collect or to synthesize pertinent data. Likewise, it is important to remember the objective of the data collection process is *not to prove your hypotheses.* Just as with the scientist, the BI professional seeks to collect facts—not opinions or the proof of some preconceived notion. A professional draws conclusions by analyzing a set of facts. Intelligence professionals rely on the maxim: **weigh facts, not experts.**

You will find a wealth of information in some surprising places and some promising sources will yield nothing. To maintain the integrity of your process, it is critical when approaching all sources that you identify yourself and your employer and that you specifically state that you do not seek any proprietary information. From each contact, you should try to obtain referrals to additional sources. In this way, the intelligence plan is a living document, with new sources and questions being continuously added or subtracted. After the conclusion of the interview, the results are recorded as soon as possible.

Case study: A typical abbreviated interview follows below:

Charlie Russ: Hi, this is Charlie Russ with Knowledge Link. We're conducting a market study for Freebird Aerospace of particular aspects of the aerospace industry; we are specifically interested in shifts to "smaller-lighter-faster" systems. Bill Lehman of Acme Electronics referred me to you. He said you make a lot of components for the industry and have an excellent perspective on industry trends. Do you have a few minutes to talk with me?

Julie Rosen: A few. What's your research about?

Charlie Russ: Well, part of my research shows that the shift to integrated systems is coming at the expense of high reliability. So companies are staying with older, heavier components longer than they thought.

Julie Rosen: Hmm, I don't think that's quite true. I don't think it's a question of reliability as much as a lack of systems engineering capability at the components houses. However, the components houses would probably say it is a reliability issue. As a matter of fact, I've got one components customer who is trying to flow down warranty coverage to me in their contract. Apparently, they are trying to go for a very low life-cycle cost.

Charlie Russ: Well, that might be true for valves or fuel assemblies, but that wouldn't be true for something complex like a navigation system would it?

Julie Rosen: As a matter of fact, the product I just mentioned is a navigation system.

Step 8. Analyze the Data, Reach a Conclusion, and Report Your Findings

Executing the intelligence plan provides the data to assess your hypotheses. However, some data will conflict. Following good intelligence tradecraft, you should consider a data point valid only if it is confirmed by two independent sources or it has been confirmed by a proven source of high reliability with first-hand knowledge.

As you receive, analyze, and consolidate the data, you assess each hypothesis. In many cases, the facts you uncover will conclusively prove your hypothesis is true. Likewise, in other cases, you confirm an absence of any signals consistent with your hypothesis, indicating the hypothesis is false. However, in most cases, you obtain imperfect knowledge—a mix of confirming and disconfirming signals. Where conflicting data exist, the BI professional, unlike the scientist, applies the analytical standard called "a preponderance of the evidence," which is the standard lawyers use in civil proceedings. Specifically, they make a decision with the rationale that "it is more likely than not that the hypothesis is true."

The more varied the sources, facts and data, the less likely you are to draw an erroneous conclusion. Although, in intelligence, quality is always more important than quantity, most business intelligence professionals agree with Joseph Stalin when he said, "Quantity has a quality all of its own." Therefore, they rely on the *Law of Large Numbers.* By using well-trained researchers to saturate the target with 150 to 200 focused interviews, rarely does an intelligence effort miss any pertinent signals. In this way, rarely do any "unanticipated signals" slip by undetected.

Analysis of your hypotheses should tell a story. Much like a game of "20 Questions," the proving or disproving of your series of hypotheses should lead you to a conclusion. The conclusion must be fact based and structured so that management is driven to take action. In fact, experience has shown that greatest benefit of intelligence is its ability to provide management with the **confidence** to take decisive action. Ignorance and doubt breed inaction.

Case study: In Freebird's case, the competitive analysis:

■ *Proved*—The hypothesis that AirLink is targeting the Global program as a "must-win." The program plays a critical role in AirLink's market strategy and will receive significant investment resources.

■ *Disproved*—The hypothesis that AirLink is going to offer an integrated system. They have not established any teaming agreements with software companies nor were they acquiring software test facilities, hiring system engineering staff, or buying any GPS receivers, and the Software Engineering Institute (SEI) never heard of AirLink.

■ *Proved*—The subsequent hypothesis that AirLink was going to compete on low life-cycle cost. This hypothesis was developed after the researchers discovered a number of unanticipated signals. In discussions with AirLink's suppliers, it was discovered that AirLink was trying to flow down performance warranties to their suppliers. The conclusion that AirLink was going to propose a longer and more extensive warranty (no company offered such warranties in this market) on their products was validated by industry observers and discussions with key customers.

In addition, Freebird uncovered that Airlink was redesigning its components' packaging to reduce weight and make the products easier to install in aircraft. The conclusion was that AirLink would propose a solution focusing on a low life-cycle cost through ease of installation and high component reliability, guaranteed with a warranty.

Another surprising finding was that AirLink was making significant R&D investments at a research lab and university in micromachining technology. Apparently, they were actively working on developing a "sensor system on a board." Although commercial applications were at least four to five years away, such a development would reduce navigation costs and weight by a 100–1 ratio and dramatically change Freebird's marketplace. Now, Freebird was warned and alert.

After Freebird completed this analysis, they established a program to monitor AirLink's progress on a continuous basis. Freebird is aware that competitors sometimes change their offering at the last minute (however, this is not typically a winning tactic). They did not want AirLink to surprise them. So they planned to be in regular contact with their sources looking for new or inconsistent signals.

This competitive intelligence allowed Freebird to craft a win strategy that clearly differentiated their offering vis-à-vis AirLink, as well as transform the competition. Freebird decided to develop an integrated solution and lobby for a sole-source contract award. Freebird's integrated solution would provide significant weight reductions, improved accuracy, and improved reliability. In addition, Freebird designed their solution to ensure that it overcame or at least neutralized AirLink's advantages in life-cycle cost. Freebird designed their system for ease of installation, modular component replacement and self-diagnostics. Freebird crafted a plan to convince Global that:

▨ They offered a clearly superior solution compared to AirLink's.

▨ An integrated solution would significantly reduce Global's engineering workload.

▨ Foregoing a competition would save Global time and money on this critical program.

In this case, business intelligence not only allowed the company to craft a superior solution, it provided them the knowledge and confidence to proactively "change the rules of the game."

Summary

The intelligence process starts with management articulating the need for information that will allow them to make a critical decision. Effective business intelligence results not from luck, but from the same careful planning, discipline, and systematic process that scientists employ. The intelligence analyst deduces a target's most likely actions or intentions using the scientific method. The analyst forms and tests a theory about the target's actions, complete with a set of hypotheses that are consistent with the overall theory. However, instead of crafting an experiment like a scientist, the business intelligence looks for observations consistent or inconsistent with their hypothesis. The analyst constructs an intelligence plan to seek signals about the target's actions in the marketplace. The presence or absence of these signals betrays a target's intentions.

This process is so effective that there is very, very little that the skilled business intelligence professional cannot find out legally and ethically. The only requirements are the will to win and willingness to commit the resources. Conducting the Freebird analysis took five trained professionals two months full-time. While such intelligence is not inexpensive, it does result in a decisive competitive advantage.

Reference

O'Guin, M. (1994). Competitive intelligence and superior business performance: A strategic benchmarking study. *Competitive Intelligence Review,* 5(2), 4–12.

READING 5

The Past and Future of Competitive Advantage

Clayton M. Christensen
Harvard Business School

$\Large Competitive$ advantage is a concept that often inspires in strategists a form of idol worship—a desire to imitate the strategies that make the most successful companies successful. It is interesting, however, that strategists have viewed precisely *opposite* factors to be sources of competitive advantage at different points in the histories of a number of industries. For example, Henry Ford's emphasis on focus has been touted right next to General Motors' product-line breadth as the key to success. Today, the outsourcing flexibility inherent in the nonintegrated business models of Cisco Systems and Dell Computer is held up as a model for all to emulate, whereas a generation ago IBM's vertical integration was widely considered an unassailable source of competitive advantage. In the 1980s, power-tool maker Black & Decker aggressively consolidated its diffused international-manufacturing infrastructure into a few global-scale facilities so that it could counter the aggressive market-share gains that Makita had logged by serving the world market from a single plant in Japan. At that very time, Makita was moving aggressively toward manufacturing in smaller-scale local facilities around the world.

Indeed, strategists whose anecdotal understanding of competitive advantage runs only as deep as "If it's good for Cisco, it must be good for everybody" at best are likely to succeed in building yesterday's competitive advantages. If history is any guide, the practices and business models that constitute advantages for today's more successful companies confer those advantages only because of particular factors at work under particular conditions at this particular time.

Historically, several factors have conferred powerful advantages on the companies that possessed them—economies of scale and scope, integration and nonintegration, and process-based core competencies. What are the circumstances that cause each factor to be a competitive advantage? How and why do competitive actions erode the underpinnings of those advantages? Strategists need to peel away the veneer of *what* works, and understand more deeply *why* and under *what conditions* certain practices lead to advantage. In so doing, they might begin to predict successfully which of today's powerful competitive advantages are likely to erode and what might cause new sources of advantage to emerge in the future. (Many of the insights presented here are rooted in work on disruptive innovation presented in my 1997 book *The Innovator's Dilemma: When New Technologies Cause Great Firms to Fail.*)

Reprinted from *MIT Sloan Management Review,* Vol. 42, No. 2, Winter 2001, pp. 105–109 by permission of publisher. Copyright © 2001 by the Massachusetts Institute of Technology. All rights reserved.

Historical Disruptions in Retailing

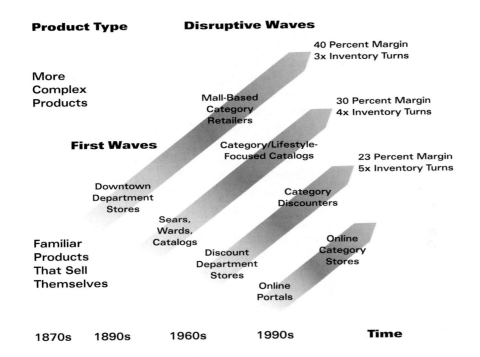

Product Type

Disruptive Waves

40 Percent Margin
3x Inventory Turns

More
Complex
Products

Mall-Based
Category
Retailers

30 Percent Margin
4x Inventory Turns

First Waves

Category/Lifestyle-
Focused Catalogs

23 Percent Margin
5x Inventory Turns

Downtown
Department
Stores

Category
Discounters

Sears,
Wards,
Catalogs

Online
Category
Stores

Familiar
Products
That Sell
Themselves

Discount
Department
Stores

Online
Portals

1870s   1890s   1960s   1990s   **Time**

Economies of Scale

In the 1960s and 1970s, concepts of competitive advantage often were predicated upon steep scale economics, and many tools of strategic analysis were built upon those economics (for example, growth-share matrices, experience curves and industry-supply curves). Indeed, scale allowed successful companies such as General Motors and IBM to enjoy lower costs than their competitors. IBM, with 70 percent market share, earned 95 percent of the mainframe-computer industry's profits; General Motors, with 55 percent market share, earned 80 percent of the automobile industry's profits. Today steep scale economics explain the profits and dominant market shares of companies such as Intel, Boeing and Microsoft.

Steep economies of scale exist when there are high fixed vs. variable costs in the predominant business model. Large organizations can amortize the fixed costs over greater volumes, condemning small competitors to playing the game on an adversely sloped playing field.

However, Toyota taught the Western world that many fixed costs aren't ordained by nature but are artifacts of specific technological and managerial solutions to problems. By reducing in-process inventories, setup times for machinery, and the overhead costs inherent in an inventory-intensive batch-manufacturing process, Toyota flattened the scale economics of assembling a car. CAD (computer-aided-design) systems had a similar effect on reducing the fixed, upfront cost of designing a new model. As a result, there is now no relationship between an auto producer's market share and its profitability. Analogous innovations have flattened scale economics in steel, electric-power generation and computers—and rendered transitory what were once thought to be sustainable advantages.

Strategists in industries that today see leading companies enjoying scale-based competitive advantage ought to ask themselves if the fundamental trade-offs that create today's high fixed costs might change—leveling the playing field in even more situations. Consider Intel. A barrier to potential competitors is the $700 million cost to design a new family of microprocessors and the $3 billion needed to build a new fabrication facility. However, disruptive technologies such as Tensilica's modular microprocessor architecture are flattening the scale economics of design. And small fabrication facilities, or minifabs, could reduce the fixed costs of production. Such technologies take root at the low end of the market first, but they are marching relentlessly up the performance spectrum.

In the pharmaceutical industry, megamergers have created $100 billion behemoths. The logic behind those mergers has been that the huge fixed costs and extraordinary uncertainty associated with clinical trials for new drugs confer ever greater advantages on ever larger companies. Historically, that has indeed been the case. But could something change the underpinnings of those high fixed costs?

Understanding of the human genome will flatten the scale economics in clinical trials. For example, we now understand that there are at least six distinctly different diseases that were once thought to be one disease—leukemia. Each of the six is associated with a specific, unique treatment protocol, and each can be precisely diagnosed through a characteristic pattern among about 50 genes. We now realize that in the past, most of the patients in a clinical trial for a new leukemia treatment didn't have the specific disease being studied. Compounds worked for some patients and not for others; and to determine clinical efficacy with satisfactory statistical results, large numbers of patients needed to be enrolled for long clinical trails. That created huge, front-end fixed costs and steepened the scale economics.

Now, however, a technician can draw a blood sample and compare the pattern in the patient's genes with a template and diagnose specifically which leukemia is present. In the future, 100 percent of the patients in a clinical trial will have the specific disease being studied, and smaller, faster trails will achieve clearer clinical outcomes. Scale will no longer confer superior profits upon larger companies; it will be an albatross. Today's merging companies are moving exactly in the wrong direction at exactly the wrong time because their strategists (and investment bankers) have not thought deeply about cause and effect in competitive advantage.

Economies of Scope

A second source of competitive advantage, intertwined with scale economics, has been product-line breadth. For example, through the 1970s, Caterpillar's scope gave the company an unassailable advantage in construction equipment against smaller competitors such as Komatsu. Only Caterpillar was large enough to absorb the complexity-driven overhead costs of developing, manufacturing and distributing a full product line. Caterpillar's dealers did not need to carry equipment from other manufacturers in order to offer customers whatever they needed. Caterpillar's huge installed base of equipment in the field meant its dealers, who were the largest dealers in each market, could afford to stock the parts necessary to offer 24-hour delivery of any spare part to any Caterpillar owner. No competitor could match that—until the underpinnings of the trade-offs inherent in the advantages changed.

Caterpillar's economies of scope had pinned Komatsu into a niche position, until Toyota's methods for reducing fixed costs in design and assembly came to construction equipment. That allowed Komatsu to produce a broader range of products in its existing plants without a ballooning of changeover, scheduling, inventory, expediting costs and quality costs that historically had plagued less focused factories. Furthermore, the advent of overnight air-delivery services meant that local dealers did not need to stock a complete inventory of spare parts in order to equal Caterpillar's service. Such factors leveled the playing field.

Retailing is an industry in which competitive advantages have waxed and waned. In fact, four waves of disruptive technology have swept through the industry. In the first wave were downtown department stores such as Marshall Field's, which came to prominence in the early 1870s. The second wave consisted of mail-order catalogs such as Sears, Roebuck in the 1890s. In the early 1960s, the third disruptive wave broke, and discount department stores such as Kmart and Wal-Mart emerged. Online retailing is the latest wave.

Two patterns have recurred in these waves. First, the disruptive retailers survived on much lower gross margins than the established retailers and earned acceptable returns by turning inventories faster. At the outset, because their salespeople had less product expertise than salespeople in the prior wave, the disruptive retailers could sell only simple products that were familiar in use, such as hardware, paint and kitchen utensils. In each instance, the retailers subsequently migrated upmarket toward more complex, nonstandard products, such as clothing and home furnishings.

A second pattern was that in each instance, the dominant disrupters at the outset were broad-line department stores, or portals, whose scope conferred powerful competitive advantages. Marshall Field's, for example, was the portal of the 1870s. Before Marshall Field's, consumers didn't know where to go to get what they needed. But people walking through the new portal realized that what they wanted was probably in there somewhere. The Sears catalog served as a portal to rural Americans. Discount department stores also were portals, selling a little bit of everything. In each of the prior waves of disruption, however, the portals were preempted by retailers focusing on a product category or a lifestyle. Focused retailers had a similar financial model (measured by typical margins and inventory turns), but their focus simplified the shopping experience and enabled a deeper product line and better service. Hence, mall-based retailers such as Banana Republic and Williams-Sonoma have largely preempted department stores. Specialized catalogs such as L.L. Bean have preempted full-line catalogs. Focused discounters such as Circuit City, Toys "R" Us, Home Depot and Staples are supplanting discount department stores. When customers learn where to go to get what they need, the portals' competitive advantage of scope becomes a disadvantage.

Online retailing appears to be following the same pattern. Portal envy afflicts many venture capitalists and dot-com entrepreneurs because the most valuable real estate on the Internet has been claimed by America Online, Yahoo! and Amazon.com. Nevertheless, history may prove the portals' current advantages transitory.

Vertical Integration and Nonintegration as a Competitive Advantage

It was not that long ago that the ability to do everything internally at IBM, General Motors, Standard Oil, Alcoa and AT&T was viewed as a powerful competitive advantage.

What Determines Competitive Advantage?

Performance

Beat Competitors with Functionality

> **Sustaining Technology**
> Companies with Integral Architectures

Beat Competitors with Speed and Customization

> **Disruptive Technology**
> Companies with Modular Architectures

Time

Now the tables seem to have turned, and vertical integration seems to slow companies down. Cisco and other nonintegrated companies, which outsource much of their manufacturing and product development to partners or startup companies they subsequently acquire, have the model that is the envy of today's corporate strategists. But what are the circumstances that confer advantage upon integrated and nonintegrated companies, and what could cause those circumstances to change?

Every product or service is produced in a chain of value-added activities. To be successful at outsourcing a piece of that chain to a supplier, a company must meet three conditions. First, it must be able to specify what attributes it needs. Second, the technology to measure those attributes must be reliably and conveniently accessible, so that both the company and the supplier can verify that what is being provided is what is needed. And third, if there is any variation in what the supplier delivers, the company needs to know what else in the system must be adjusted. The company needs to understand how the supplier's contribution will interact with other elements of the system so that the company can take what it procures and plug it into the value chain with predictable effect. If those three conditions are met, then it is possible to outsource a value-added activity.

Markets work when there is adequate information—and the three classes above constitute the information that is necessary and sufficient for markets to emerge between stages of value-added activity. But what about the innumerable situations in which market-enabling information does *not* exist—for example, when truly new technologies emerge? IBM's development of magnetoresistive (MR) disk-drive recording heads in the early 1990s is such an example. MR heads can increase a disk drive's data-storage capacity by a factor of 10—and yet achieving that increase is not an easy feat. A drive maker cannot simply outsource the heads and plug them into a product that was designed using conventional algorithms. The design of the disks, the actuator mechanisms, the error-correction software and dozens of other aspects of the product need to be interactively modified as the MR heads are incorporated. MR technology is not yet understood well enough for engineers to specify to suppliers which attributes are most critical. Technology to measure those attributes is not well developed, and engineers can't predict accurately how variability in the properties of a head might affect the performance of the system. Nor do they understand how changes in product design might affect manufacturability or how subtle changes in manufacturing methods might affect product performance. Manufacturing therefore *must* be done in-house. When necessary and sufficient information doesn't exist at critical interfaces, integration is imperative.

In general, vertical integration is an advantage when a company is competing for the business of customers whose needs have not yet been satisfied by the functionality of available products. Integrated companies are able to design interactively each of the major subsystems of a product or service, efficiently extracting the most performance possible out of the available technology.

When the prevailing functionality of products has overshot what customers can utilize, however, then the way companies compete must change. Making even better products no longer yields superior profits. Instead, innovations that enhance a company's abilities to bring products rapidly to market—and responsively and conveniently to customize offerings—become the mechanisms for achieving advantage. When the basis of competition evolves thus, then modular, industry-standard interfaces among the major subsystems of a product become defined, enabling nonintegrated, focused companies to emerge and provide specific pieces of value-added activity. Focused companies can operate on much lower overhead costs, and standard interfaces enable product designers and assemblers to mix and match components to tailor features and functions to the needs of specific customers. Hence, in tiers of a market in which customers are overserved by the functionality of available products, nonintegration is an advantage: A population of nonintegrated companies that interface through market mechanisms is faster and more flexible than an integrated company. (Supporting data appear in a Harvard Business School working paper the author and M. Verlinden wrote last year, "Disruption, Dis-Integration and the Dissipation of Differentiability.")

The opposite extremes of the computer industry illustrate the advantages of each structure. Machines that push the bleeding edge of performance, such as mission-critical servers, often combine nonstandard components designed and manufactured within integrated companies such as Hewlett-Packard. Machines not targeted at the frontiers of performance can be made more effectively in a nonintegrated model such as Dell's.

Cisco, which exploited the modular architecture of its routers to disrupt the telecommunications switching business from the low end, established in the minds of many the standard for a New Economy company. Cisco has efficiently outsourced much of its manufacturing to suppliers in its network and much of its new-product development to the startups it acquires. However, as Cisco has moved up into the most performance-demanding tiers of its markets—particularly optical networks—it is being forced to integrate, performing many more product-design and manufacturing activities internally than was necessary when it competed at greater distances from the bleeding edge. Cisco's competitors, such as Corning, JDS Uniphase, Nortel Networks and Lucent Technologies, also are finding that they have to become more integrated—*less* outsourced—in order to compete.

Hence, if customer needs go beyond the current technology, vertical integration constitutes a competitive advantage. If the technology is well established, integration is an albatross. Today's strategists must strive to understand the circumstances in which a company and its business model compete and whether the model puts the company at a competitive advantage or disadvantage.

Core Competence and Competitive Advantage

Some types of competitive advantage, such as those associated with the economics of scale and scope, are rooted in market positions. Others are rooted in business models; still others in the processes or competencies of organizations. Although the value of market positions and the relevance of business models can wax and wane, "tacit" competencies—internal processes—have been thought to be more enduring because they are harder to copy. Nevertheless, it turns out that competence residing in proprietary processes is also built upon temporary underpinnings.

DuPont, for example, enjoyed years of unparalleled capability to formulate new organic compounds. Its scientists did their work through collaborative trial and error. A scientists would mix and heat things in a beaker, draw a fiber out and then consult with colleagues who had expertise in various dimensions of organic chemistry about what the material might do, and how it could be improved. Over time, however, DuPont's strength, which had resided in the patterns of interaction and collaboration among its scientists, came to be embodied in quantum theory. Now that the science of how atoms combine in molecular structures to create materials with particular properties is well defined, success is open to all. Any company can specify the properties needed in a material and then use theory-based algorithms to determine which atoms need to bond with which atoms in which patterns.

Similarly, a company such as BMW might say that its competitive advantage resides in its internal processes for designing unique automobiles. Indeed, there has been a "BMW-ness" to its designs that other companies' processes have not successfully replicated. The process of designing a new automobile is fixed-cost intensive and historically has entailed extensive interaction and collaboration among large groups of engineers. However, in order to reduce costs and improve its ability to design safe automobiles, BMW recently has created a system that enables its engineers to use computer simulations to crash-test the cars they design—before physical models are built. The simulations enable BMW's engineers to observe the crashes carefully and to improve designs—a wonderful system. But a capability that formerly resided in the interaction among the company's engineers is not embodied in algorithms—which not only flatten the scale economics associated with product design, but could make BMW's core competence more broadly available. In general, scientific progress that results in deeper, more fundamental understanding transforms into explicit, codified and replicable knowledge many things that once were accomplished only through proprietary problem-solving routines.

Every competitive advantage is predicated upon a particular set of conditions that exist at a particular point in time for particular reasons. Many of history's seemingly unassailable advantages have proved transitory because the underlying factors changed. The very existence of competitive advantage sets in motion creative innovations that, as competitors strive to level the playing field, cause the advantage to dissipate. That does not mean the search for competitive advantage is futile. Rather, it suggests that successful strategists need to cultivate a deep understanding of the processes of competition and progress and of the factors that undergird each advantage. Only thus will they be able to see when old advantages are poised to disappear and how new advantages can be built in their stead.

READING

6

Sowing Growth in Your Own Backyard

Bob Lurie
Market2Customer and Monitor Group

Toby Thomas
Market2Customer

Growing a business seems next to impossible in tough economic times. Your customers aren't buying as much or as frequently as they used to, and the usual programs don't seem to work as well anymore. And that's frustrating, because the benefits of growing your core business are clear. Nothing creates greater shareholder value or builds a more vibrant organization than generating higher and higher levels of growth in your principal business.

But sowing growth in your own backyard is hard to do—really hard to do. Even talented and seasoned managers blessed with boom times have toiled with this problem year after year. They have broken their analytical picks trying to make sense of the complexities of their market, they have harvested all the low-hanging fruit, and even when they do spot promising new opportunities, their organization often rejects them in favor of business-as-usual programs. The reward for their hard work: frustration and tepid growth.

And yet, even in really tough times, and perhaps especially in tough times, there lies a golden opportunity. Slowdowns compel managers to take a hard look at their organizations, to challenge conventional wisdom, and to reconnect with their markets (lest they fall further out of step with them). To make the most of the unfreezing of the way their company thinks and acts, they need a fertile, concrete approach to guide their thinking. Actually finding golden opportunities doesn't require access to a silver bullet, just the discipline of employing the tried and true growth principles that deliver in good times and in bad. In fact, these principles consistently serve to double and triple growth rates. Throw out the fads and begin the hard work—a cornucopia lies in your own backyard.

Take a Closer Look

The first step is to look more carefully at the parts of your core market in which you have not traditionally participated. You may find the most attractive sources of growth in places where you haven't looked before, or where you've looked but haven't seen. Managers often fail to notice all the potential sources of growth in a business. No surprises here. Every company has its reflexes, its biases. It looks at the sources of growth that have worked in the past—say, poaching new customers from bit competitors—not

Reprinted from *Journal of Business Strategy*, Vol. 23, No. 1, January–February 2002, pp. 20–23.

necessarily at those holding the most promise for the future—for instance, stimulating existing customers to use more of the product.

For example, in the late 1980s, Fujitsu had an active business customizing its PCs for sales-force automation tasks at companies that sold big-ticket, information-intensive products. Salespeople at these firms would typically make two or three sales calls a day; then, at five o'clock, they'd enter the day's activity into their home PCs, using Fujitsu's software.

But this method made little sense for the salespeople who supplied, say, snack foods to convenience stores and might make as many as 70 sales calls a day. They couldn't possibly sit down at a PC and write memos about each call. And in the late-1980s many of them didn't own PCs and were unaccustomed to using them. Fujitsu helped address the problem by building a portable, task-specific computer for Frito-Lay's sales force. Ultimately, this gave rise to a huge new product category: hand-held devices for sales and delivery workers, used routinely today by such companies as FedEx and UPS.

Break the Mold

Top managers need to undertake a careful, disciplined search for every opportunity to expand sales in the company's core market. To lend structure to this task, we've divided all growth opportunities into five types. Running through this list one by one, and writing down as many growth opportunities as possible of each type, can help you break out of tradition-constrained thinking. The five types of growth opportunity are:

1. Retaining uses by existing customers (reducing attrition is the same as growth);
2. Stimulating more uses by existing customers seeking to satisfy the same basic needs as they have in the past;
3. Generating new uses by existing customers seeking to satisfy new needs or a different combination of needs;
4. Stealing new customers from your competitors; and
5. Bringing in customers who are totally new to the product category.

To see how the categories work, consider the case of Cobra Golf. In the early 1990s, Cobra doubled its sales in just three years, by recognizing huge growth opportunities in categories 3 and 5—while other golf club manufacturers continued playing a zero-sum game in category 4. First, Cobra's managers observed that many women were taking up golf, but Cobra's competitors were focused on their traditional market of young and middle-aged men. So Cobra redesigned its clubs to suit the needs of novice women and enjoyed considerable success. This was a type-5 growth opportunity.

Around the same time, Cobra introduced an oversized club with a graphite shaft, which helped older golfers drive balls as far as they had when they were younger. Customers who had bought new clubs mainly when the old ones wore out suddenly started buying clubs to satisfy a new need: the need to continue playing their old game after reaching a certain age. As a result, Cobra enjoyed sales growth of type 3.

Whatever you do, when you look at categories 1 through 5, don't limit your thinking to the growth opportunities that seem most "realistic" based on past experience. The whole idea is to transcend your experience, so write down all growth opportunities that occur to you.

Focus on a Specific Goal

You will need to figure out how much effort (or, equivalently, money) it would take to realize each of these opportunities. Here, it's important to focus on the specific customer behaviors that would have to change if each opportunity were to be realized—because no matter what, the problem always boils down to getting a particular customer segment to change its behavior in a particular way.

For instance, Listerine's current ad campaign tells customers to "use Listerine for 30 seconds two times a day." This is much more effective than just telling them to "use Listerine to have fresher breath and fight plaque," because it identifies a desired behavior and tells customers why they should adopt this behavior. Similarly, if you are selling Internet connectivity to businesses, then trying to get your customer's IT manager to give everyone at his company Internet access is much better than lecturing him in general terms about the benefits of TI lines. Again, it aims for a particular type of behavior.

A word of warning here: You may find that your company lacks the kind of data on customers and end-users that would enable you to figure out which of their behaviors will result in the most growth. Either your data will not be sufficiently detailed, or you will have detailed data on customers and on end-users, but no way of matching the two up so that you can see all the way down the distribution pipe.

For example, say you're a manager at Xerox, interested in improving sales of your company's premier optical character recognition software. You may see an opportunity to bundle your OCR software into fax/printer peripherals manufactured by companies like HP. You may already have detailed data on HP—from previous interactions with that company. But that's not enough. You must also collect detailed data on HP's customers, and on how each customer segment uses HP's fax/printer bundle. If you can convince HP that some of its customers would be more likely to buy the HP peripheral if OCR software was a part of a bundle, then you can convince HP to change its behavior—by bundling your OCR software with a particular line of products, by advertising the OCR feature, and by working to make it more compatible with HP machines.

In short, you may have to identify a desired change in the end-user's behavior if you hope to promote some other behavioral change in your direct customer. And you can't do this unless you know which end-user segments go with which direct customers, and vice-versa.

Set Priorities

Let's assume that you've managed to get detailed data on your own market segments, and on the corresponding end-user segments. Now you should be able to pair each growth opportunity on your list with one or more specific changes in behavior—changes in your customers' behavior, and in some cases corresponding changes in their customers' behavior.

Against each of these behavioral changes you will find that there are barriers. These could be internal barriers within your company, or they could be practical barriers in the outside world, such as existing customer preferences or the lack of a distribution channel to reach the desired customer segment. And,

Organize your market research, your customer profiles, and your growth strategies around segments that your company can somehow act on.

of course, overcoming each barrier will take effort and cost a certain amount of money. Thus, one can assemble a cost/benefit analysis for each growth opportunity: (1) Here's how much growth I can expect, and (2) Here's how much it will cost to remove the barriers that now stand in the way of the behavior change that will trigger that growth.

You can assign probabilities, take expectation values, construct decision trees, and so on. But ultimately, the goal is to use some sort of cost/benefit analysis to prioritize your list of growth opportunities. And if one or two on your list have a huge demonstrable upside, you may find that your organization is suddenly willing to do what it takes to topple the barriers preventing you from realizing those opportunities.

Know Your Customers Inside and Out

Many companies, even if they do identify great growth opportunities, have a dreadful time trying to capture them. The problem here is often the lack of a fine-grained understanding of customers—which is indispensable if one hopes to influence particular customer behaviors.

You can address this problem by crafting an in-depth picture of the type of person who comprises a certain customer segment. The process starts with a description of that customer's social, organizational, and physical environment. What constraints and opportunities set the context for this person's behavior? Is she in a hurry? Is she at leisure? Is she with a family member? And so on. Next, we try to describe the desired experience that this customer associates with a particular product or service, bearing in mind that people really buy "bundles of experiences" more than they buy products. For instance, affluent teenage boys might visit Barnes & Noble not so much to purchase books as to be seen purchasing certain books—say, books by Albert Camus, Ayn Rand, and the like. And Barnes & Noble would want to be aware of this if these boys comprised a significant customer segment. Finally, it is helpful to assemble a profile of the customer's beliefs—beliefs about himself, about the relevant product category, and even about particular products.

These three factors—the customer's environment, the sort of experience he is seeking, and his beliefs—combine to form a concrete explanation of his behaviors: why he buys what he buys, and why he does not buy what he does not buy.

Tell the Whole Story

The goal is to investigate your customer segments so thoroughly that you can truly "crawl inside the heads" of their constituent members. Managers at Barnes & Noble discussing "the segment of affluent teenage boys" should all be able to envision the 17-year-old budding intellectual as if he were sitting right across the table from them. They should recognize this young man in their friends' kids, in their own kids—perhaps in themselves. They should know him not just in broad generalities, but in intimate detail. He spends weekday afternoons in a coffee shop (the local chain, not Starbucks). He supports environmental causes. He listens to Korn. He resents being under the thumb of his banal high-school teachers and fantasizes about the independence that will come with college admission. And what about his books? Well, they are not merely his "pastime," they are his badge of alienation, of independence, of his status as an intellectual.

If Barnes & Noble managers can see this customer, and the segment he represents, at that level of detail, then they will know how to market to him. For instance, they might want to promote CDs by college bands near the store's philosophy section. And if you as a manager can picture this kid, then the people who run your marketing, sales, and operations will be able to picture him as well. Everyone at the company will be working in unison, because they'll all have the same understanding of the sheepish, alienated, spoiled-rebellious teen who finds himself in your marketplace.

So ask yourself: Can you tell this kind of story about your customers? Can you relate to them, spot them at trade shows, guess what kind of bank they might use? If not, you may have trouble inducing the sorts of behavioral changes you will need to generate growth. Behavioral change is an intimate business. It occurs at the level of the human being, not at the level of "men between the ages of 27 and 35."

This lesson applies to those who sell to businesses, as surely as it applies to those who sell to consumers. Consider the gas pipeline business. Pipeline operators sell long- and short-term contracts that give their customers the right to use their pipe capacity to transport gas from point A to point B. Simple enough. You might imagine that this is a pure commodity business, in which the sale always goes to the pipeline operator with the lowest price. Well, it can be that sort of business, but it doesn't have to be—not if you're a pipeline operator who has a nuanced understanding of his customer segments.

For instance, think about the segment of "arbitrage marketers." These professional traders buy, re-sell, and deliver gas to their customers when they see a higher than normal price imbalance in the market. If the price of gas in Eastern Ohio is 20 basis points lower than it is in Upstate New York, an arbitrage marketer knows, if he's quick enough, he can make money. In a matter of minutes, he must find someone who will sell him the gas, persuade someone else to buy the gas, and then contract with a third person to transport the gas. If he's not quick enough, gas companies might adjust their price, or worse still, a competitor will beat him to the punch. Arbitrage marketers need information about gas availability and pipeline capacity and to talk to a decision maker at the pipeline company who can quickly say yes or no to a contract.

Traditionally pipeline companies have regarded arbitrage marketers as nuisances and have been slow to respond to their requests, focusing instead on established relationships and long-term contracts with local distribution companies. A pipeline operator who takes the time to understand the arbitrage marketer might behave differently. He would learn how much time arbitragers spend trying to find the market information they need to concoct the deal. He would learn that most of the arbitrager's requests come first thing in the morning, precisely when the pipeline operator typically holds his staff meetings. He would also realize that if you tell an arbitrage marketer "I have to check with our gas control people, we will let you know later this afternoon," the arbitrager will hang up, hit the speed dial button, and contact a competitor. He would also understand how much the arbitrage marketers resent the way most pipeline companies treat them.

If the pipeline operator acts on this insight and does an about-face, giving the arbitrage traders more information than they ever could have hoped for and making key decision makers available when the arbitragers call, he wins their business then and there. In the long run, the pipeline operator will be the first number the arbitrager will call, enabling him to sell more of his excess capacity, translating into higher margins—effectively a price premium relative to competitors.

Create Meaningful and Actionable Segmentations

Traditional market segmentation can succeed in identifying groups of customers who share the same basic needs and beliefs, but it's often done in such a way that no one can ever find them. For instance, say you commission a study that concludes that "You have tremendous growth potential among 'feel-gooder' types," or "You need to use a different pricing strategy on 'self-assured' young women." Well, these assertions may be quite accurate, and "feel-gooders" and "self-assureds" may be perfectly well defined groups in a laboratory setting. But many managers will sensibly ask: "Where does a feel-gooder shop?" "What advertisements do self-assureds see?" In short: How do I find these people? Too often the answer is, "We don't know," and the manager is left with an honorary Ph.D. in psychology rather than a growth strategy.

The lesson here is always to organize your market research, your customer profiles, and your growth strategies around segments that your company can somehow act on. If your company and its distribution channels cannot isolate a particular type of customer—speak to him, market to him, and price to him—you're never going to influence his behavior, no matter how intimately you understand him. The game is to find customer segments that are relevant to the realities of your company—its organizational structure, sales capabilities, distribution channels, and so on—and also economically well-defined, in the sense that all members of the same segment have similar needs and experiences concerning your product. In other words, your customer segments must be both meaningful—in that those customers exhibit distinct behaviors, needs, and beliefs—and actionable, in that your company can conceivably do something to affect their behavior. One of these without the other won't work.

No matter what, the problem always boils down to getting a particular customer segment to change its behavior in a particular way.

The right customer segments are not always the obvious ones. For instance, studios that make animated films for children often gather their market data according to standard demographic categories, such as "mothers with young children." But it turns out that this segmentation is not meaningful: The movie-going needs of a working mother and a stay-at-home mother are so different that they render a single customer profile useless. In particular, the life of a working mother is often filled with notions of being tired, feelings of guilt toward her children, and a desire to share with them special, potentially educational experiences, such as going to see an animated movie. The stay-at-home mother spends half her life carting her kids from one activity to the next, and regards children's movies as no more than a discretionary diversion. Subdividing the segment into "working moms" and "stay-at-home moms," gives you categories that are far more meaningful, but still actionable. Why actionable? Well, it turns out that working moms are far more likely to show up in the opening weeks of a movie's run, while stay-at-home moms, spared the guilt that plagues working mothers, save the movie for a rainy day. The lesson: If you want to get people to attend the first run, pitch your message at working moms; target stay-at-home moms for later-run shows. Who would have guessed?

Align Your Organization for Growth

You also need to design your organization itself for growth. Every department of your company—marketing, product design, even finance—must target the desired customer behaviors. Internal factors that can retard growth range from organizational structures that focus on products rather than customer needs, to inconsistent reward-systems, to a growth-averse company culture.

It's also helpful to organize your company's growth budget just as you would organize your growth plan itself: around particular behavior changes in particular customer segments. You start by budgeting specific amounts of money to change behaviors: "$2.8 million to persuade the segment of office secretaries to buy their office supplies online." Only later do you allocate that money to particular departments and product lines. Finally, if you lack data on key customer segments, you may have to seek out data specifically on those segments. Packaged-goods makers have reams of scanner data from large retailers, but if the people in the chosen market segment do their shopping at mom-and-pop stores, the companies might as well use their scanner data to paper a birdcage.

To summarize, if you want to generate superior growth year after year in your traditional lines of business, you need to do the following things:

1. Divide your market into segments that are both actionable and meaningful;

2. Use the five types of growth—1 through 5 above—to help identify the most important growth opportunities;

3. Make sure you understand all the economic activity of each segment;

4. Focus on customer behaviors you need to change to take advantage of those opportunities, and on the barriers that you must overcome to effect the desired behavior changes;

5. Create a holistic, fine-grained picture of the relevant customer segments, to bring the customers to life for the whole organization;

6. Insure that your organization has a growth-oriented structure and mind-set.

Successful growth-oriented firms work on all of these tasks at all times and know how to integrate them so they work in harmony. Hard work? It certainly is. But it's well worth the effort.

Internationalization, Globalization, and Capability-Based Strategy

Stephen Tallman
University of Utah

Karin Fladmoe-Lindquist
University of Utah

Globalization is often presented as the strategic effort to treat the world, or a significant part of it, as a single market in which to do business. However, it is also potentially a single research and development laboratory, a single production center, a single logistics network, and a single headquarters site. For example, many of the major pharmaceutical firms, such as Merck or Johnson & Johnson, conduct major research in numerous research facilities located around the globe, and the international networking of these firms in research, production, and marketing have placed most of their activities into global contexts. If we look at the potential for competitive advantage through globalization from a strategic perspective, all of the value-adding activities of a business, not just the delivery of the product to the customer, may benefit dramatically from a "one-world" view. From this perspective, the world becomes an important source for new knowledge as well as new markets.

Traditional market-focused models of multinational strategy may be inadequate to represent the activities of the firm in the global arena. Newer models of strategy driven by the search for sustained competitive advantage derived from the internal knowledge resources or capabilities of the firm rather than from its market position offer advantages in understanding strategy and structure among global firms. Strategists believe that sustained competitive advantage is found in the strategic resources of the firm, specifically in both the organizational knowledge and the capabilities of the firm. Capability-based frameworks have been found to have much power as general models of strategy and organization.[1] However, their application to multinational firms and their strategies has been limited.[2] This article integrates the various findings of recent empirical and conceptual studies of capability development in multinational firms (and their subsidiaries) with traditional approaches to foreign direct investment, licensing, and exports that focus primarily on market-oriented strategies. The resulting framework is a useful guide to both academics and managers interested in global strategy.

A concise example of the gap that needs to be bridged can be seen in two now-classic articles by Gary Hamel and C. K. Prahalad. The first proclaims that competitive advantage accrues to those multinational firms that have been able to extend their product lines into open market niches in foreign markets, take advantage of global economies and opportunities to tie markets together through cross-subsidies, and then extend their product lines globally.[3] The later article explains that competitive advantage is the consequence of holding and combining unique resources and capabilities and creating a strategic architecture that can apply the resulting core capabilities across product and business lines.[4] While their examples in the latter case include companies from around the world, they do not make an explicit connection to their earlier work on multinational strategy processes. If we reconsider the multinational story in the light of these new organizational capability-driven models, then we will be able to improve our understanding of the drivers of competitive advantage in global markets.

The framework presented here shows how multinational firms can gain sustained competitive advantage in the global marketplace by basing their strategies on building and leveraging their unique internal capabilities. The "dynamic capabilities" perspective presents an explicit argument for the importance to sustainable competitive advantage of both exploiting current capabilities and developing new capabilities.[5] Applied to the activities of multinational firms, the perspective considers the different ways in which international market expansion and global integration of operations work to enhance long-term performance. It also reveals why multinational firms might *not* be successful in all cases, as various combinations of capabilities and environments might require particular strategies and organizations for success.

Capability-Driven Strategies and the Global Firm

The major current models of the multinational firm[6] might be described as *capability-recognizing* in that they assume multinational firms possess some unique knowledge-based resources. These resources typically are treated as home-country based and fixed over time for any multinational firm. The multinational firm's international strategies then are determined either by external industry conditions or by internal demands for efficiency. These models recognize that the firm may engage in resource-seeking strategies, but these are targeted at acquiring local complementary resources for market entry or at accessing location-bound natural or technological resources.[7] A few newer models have addressed the possibilities of foreign national units taking a major strategic role within the multinational firm, whether from the corporate perspective[8] or from the national subsidiary point of view.[9] These models, though, focus on specific aspects of the subsidiary role rather than on an overall theory of multinational strategy based on resource and capability opportunities and needs.

On the other hand, our *capability-driven* framework of the multinational firm considers the firm's attempts to build, protect, and exploit a set of unique capabilities and resources as the key factors that determine performance levels and the key forces that drive firms into international and global strategies. Our focus is on how firms can create new value for themselves to increase their long-term profitability, rather than on how to divide markets and share profits among a group of undifferentiated, static companies.[10] The framework provides explicit mechanisms that drive international expansion and integration and that build and leverage capabilities. The model begins by defining component or business-level capabilities and architectural or corporate-level capabilities as sources of competitive advantage (see Figure 1). These firm-specific complex resources are built and leveraged for long-term success in worldwide markets through strategies of international expansion and global integration.

Figure 1   Capabilities and Multinational Strategy

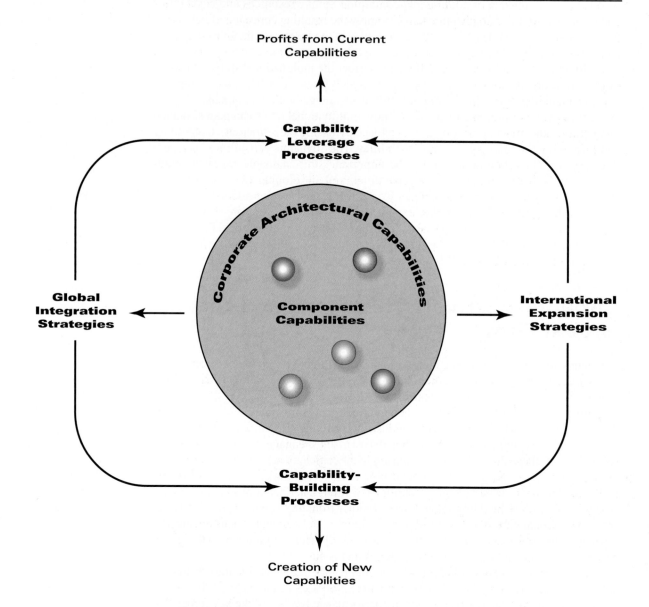

Capabilities and Knowledge in the Global Firm

Capability-based and related strategy frameworks suggest that the competitive advantage of firms results from their possession of unique internal resources and capabilities and their ability to apply these resources in the marketplace to earn superior profits.[11] From this perspective, the multinational firm gains advantage internationally if it possesses unique resources that can be leveraged in foreign markets. Further, the multinational firm will sustain its competitive advantage only if it can continue to develop new capabilities in the face of changing environments and evolving competition. Two general types of resource-related capabilities in multinational firms are particularly relevant to internationalization of strategy: business-level component capabilities and corporate-level architectural capabilities.

Business-Level Component Capabilities This type of capability relates to the competitive advantage of the firm in its business area or areas and includes its ability to produce better products, devise superior processes, and generate more effective marketing. These "doing business" concerns have been described as competencies, capabilities, or skills, depending on the level of specificity.[12] Such capabilities are defined by the idea of "component knowledge"[13] The components of a business's knowledge involve the various complex but identifiable skills and activities needed to operate the business and constitute the bundles of strategic resources and capabilities that are unique to the firm.[14] Component capabilities go beyond the realm of pure knowledge to include the broader set of actions and structures that are critical to competitive advantage and to multinational strategy. For example, 3M is widely viewed as having strong routines and capabilities for remaining innovative in a wide variety of products and businesses. From the perspective of the multinational corporation, its business-level component capabilities would be the larger, but still identifiable, skills of its business units.[15]

Corporate-Level Architectural Capabilities Architectural capabilities are defined as organization-wide routines for integrating the components of the organization to productive purposes.[16] They are the sources of the organizational synergies at the core of the firm.[17] In the multinational corporation, architectural capabilities involve identifying, replicating, integrating, and otherwise managing hard assets and business-level component capabilities effectively and efficiently. These capabilities are developed in the process of operating the firm, so they are strictly firm-specific and tied closely to the administrative history of the firm. Wal-Mart is widely regarded as a firm that has superior architectural capabilities. It has managed to grow from a small firm in Arkansas to the position of global retailer based on its abilities to coordinate and integrate its (equally strong) component capabilities. Internationally, Wal-Mart did have some initial difficulties in its entry into some South American markets; however, its strong architectural capabilities allowed it to revise and adjust its local strategies rapidly. McDonald's is another example of a firm that has been able to develop an extensive global empire based on capabilities for identifying, replicating, integrating, and managing assets globally.

Corporate-level architectural capabilities allow the incorporation of new, even foreign-based, assets and capabilities while maintaining efficient management. At the same time, architectural knowledge coordinates the employment of pieces of component knowledge in ways that are newly effective—truly adding value, not just preventing its erosion. These capabilities relate to the ability of the firm to organize so as to function competitively in different contexts and apply its component capabilities in ways that successfully attain the firm's goals. This "macro-level" organizational knowledge[18] is not simply a way to reduce opportunistic risk through less costly governance of transactions, but enhances the profit potential of the firm's component capabilities. Because these resources involve structures and action as well as know-how and understanding, we characterize them as architectural capabilities, not as pure knowledge.

Capability Processes and Competitive Advantage in Multinational Firms

The two key processes of capability leverage and capability building provide the essential mechanisms to drive a capability-based strategy.[19] A capability-driven strategy is fueled by the leverage or exploitation of its current capabilities and resources to earn superior profits, and it is maintained into the future through the continuous building or development of new competitive resources and capabilities as investments in future profits. Although leverage and building processes commonly are associated with market-seeking and asset-seeking strategies tied to real resources, their real benefits for sustained advantage arise when they are addressed to complex knowledge resources—i.e., to capabilities.

Capability Leverage   Capability leverage processes are those efforts the firm makes to gain competitive advantage (and superior profits) from the exploitation of its existing capabilities in the marketplace. Leveraging capabilities developed in the home market, or in previous international forays, is of great importance to the multinational firm. Even in a globalizing world, most firms move initially into foreign markets on the strength of apparent competitive advantage based on business-level component capabilities from the home market. All firms rely on their existing capabilities to gain the profits needed to provide returns to investors, to pay for further expansion, and to finance new assets and capabilities. Multinationals simply pursue these same leverage objectives across borders. As Kogut and Zander note, "the primary explanation for direct investment is the possession of . . . superior capabilities . . . responsible for the growth of the firm across international borders."[20] Ferdows's framework of the strategic roles of foreign factories reflects this capability leverage concept.[21] Factory types such as Offshore, Outpost, and Server—with their need for lower site competencies and transfer of home-country skills—are examples of multinational firms' efforts to exploit existing capabilities.

The leverage concept is most easily understood with respect to business-level component capabilities. Returns on investments in the combinations of resources and skills involved in business capabilities improve if the cost base established for the domestic market can be exploited in the broader international marketplace. Products and processes, brand names, marketing schemes, advertising programs, and other business-related resources and skills often can be leveraged across borders with minimal changes—enough to fit the local context, but not typically so much as to change the basic capability.[22] Coca-Cola has been a classic example of a firm that excels at capability leverage. Traditionally, Coca-Cola took pride in its one world approach to its products and its marketing schemes, with some minor local adaptation. Interestingly, the most recent changes in the corporate approach to global systems allow much more local decision making on new product development along with very locally oriented advertising and marketing campaigns. Whether the company can maintain its success with this new strategy remains an open question today.

Leveraging corporate-level architectural capabilities and appropriating their value added can drive international expansion as well.[23] Resource-based models place great emphasis on managerial capabilities for organizing component knowledge into profit-generating bundles as drivers of firm expansion. New models of technological development in multinational firms treat architectural capabilities as essential to the coordination of technological efforts across boundaries. Architectural knowledge gained in managing multi-business domestic corporations can be extended to managing multi-country operations in international markets more effectively.[24] In addition, corporate-level architectural capabilities appear likely to enhance the value of leveraging component knowledge by improving efficiency and effectiveness in sharing technical or other business-specific knowledge.[25]

Capability Building   If leveraging capabilities in the marketplace is to continue generating competitive advantage and superior profits over time, new capabilities must be created as old ones are compromised. Building capabilities and developing resources must continue for the life of the firm. While capability-building strategies are not directly addressed by most models of the multinational firm, multinationals cannot rely solely on home-country-derived capabilities to operate global networks.[26] A focus on "the world as a single market" marginalizes new technical and managerial knowledge to the role of overcoming "the liability of foreignness," making the application of "real knowledge" from the home market more efficient in earning new profits from old capabilities. Capability building has been treated as an outcome of home-country conditions of competition, factor availability, and consumption.[27] The multinational is assumed to be able to carry its strategic resources and capabilities into international markets, but not to be overly concerned with creating them "out there."

However, both business-level and corporate-level capabilities are subject to improvement, discovery, re-creation, and innovation through global learning. Forward-looking firms are finding that no region or country has a monopoly on business-level component capabilities and firms that actively seek the latest resources and skills from around the world can build superior component knowledge. Strategy analysts have shown technological and business skills can be developed through international diversification into multiple markets[28] and by emphasizing strategic leadership roles for national subsidiaries.[29] Porter[30] and others find that the ability of multinational firms to access foreign-based clusters of excellence is a clear source of advantage in gaining component knowledge-based advantage. Combined with complementary resources based in their home countries, such technical know-how may have profit-earning potential in excess of what the local embers of the regional cluster can generate. The development of foreign manufacturing facilities to take advantage of high levels of local site competencies is a key step in this process. Hewlett-Packard's effort to upgrade its Singapore operations is a good example of the capability-building process. The factory began as a simple production facility for basic calculators and is now responsible for all aspects, including basic design, of portable printers.[31] This process reflects the historical process of asset-seeking foreign direct investment, but with a focus on business-related knowledge, rather than natural resources or other location-bound hard assets. The entire image of the national subsidiary as a simple conduit for home-country-based knowledge is being reworked in favor of one as potential strategic site and source of new capabilities.

Corporate-level architectural capabilities must also undergo a process of capability building. Companies may learn new ways of organizing, rewarding, and communicating in foreign or international markets. A more important influence, though, seems to be the need to create new internal systems as the strict relationships or hierarchies prove unable to handle the complex, changing environment characteristic of global businesses. The architectural knowledge needed to identify, leverage, and build new component capabilities requires a level of managerial sophistication that moves the firm toward real globalization—seeing one world, not just one world market. ABB, for example, had to develop entirely new internal processes for coordinating its global businesses during its transformation, including strategic human resource policies, accounting systems, and the creation of a new organizational culture.[32]

Multinational Strategies and Capability Processes

Component and architectural capabilities lead to both international expansion and global integration in the process of building and leveraging capabilities. International expansion (*internationalization*) refers to a strategy of greater presence in international locations. Global integration (*globalization*) involves a strategy of consolidating international markets and operations into a single worldwide strategic entity. Most existing models of international expansion and consolidation are driven by industry characteristics.[33] However, in resource-based strategic models, industry characteristics are treated as the consolidated outcome of multiple firm-level decisions in an environment consisting of other firms, suppliers, and customers, not of a pre-existing competitive landscape. Thus, while the overall competitive conditions of an industry may influence multinational strategy decisions, capability-based models suggest that individual firms respond successfully to industry pressures only within their own set of capabilities.

International Expansion   The process of building an operational presence in foreign locations is the primary concern of traditional market power and internalization models of the multinational firm.[34] Early models that focused on large multinational firms viewed the market power of the large multinational as a means of gaining advantage. They treated increasing internationalization as a way to leverage existing power, to gain new market power by increasing size, and to exploit existing power in a wider market.[35] As an alternative, internalization models suggested that international activities, once brought under the management of the firm, would provide the most efficient means of extending existing knowledge resources to overseas markets.[36] With an efficient transmission mechanism, international expansion provided increasing economies of scope in applying the unique private capabilities of the firm.[37] The newer international diversification literature takes a capability-based approach by which firms can appropriate additional profits through operations in multiple national markets.[38]

In the area of capability building, firms can tap competitive clusters in other countries either through acquisition of or alliance with a cluster member or through a start-up in a highly advantaged region (as was done, for instance, by Motorola Semiconductor as it developed "smartcard" technology in France). Multinationals are no longer doomed to possess only technical competitive advantages developed back in the home market, but can uncover and incorporate new component capabilities from abroad. These new and traditional approaches to the multinational firm suggest that existing capabilities can be leveraged and enhanced through greater international presence. Most resource and capability building through increased international market scope must derive from access to new component knowledge—firms can access strategic know-how as well as complementary skills, but it still most often has to do with improving in a particular business or business activity. Corporate-level architectural knowledge is more likely to be tied to managing market integration.

Global Integration   Globalization is the managerial process of integrating worldwide activities into a single world strategy by managing a network of differentiated but integrated subsidiaries, affiliates, alliances, and associations. Porter[39] and Doz[40] treat globalization of strategy as a response to industry pressures toward ever increasing efficiency through economies of scale and scope. However, researchers have begun to move away from treating industry as the single driver of multinational strategy and toward identifying internal processes critical to the development of transnational (global) competitive advantage in many industries. In Bartlett and Ghoshal's Transnational Model, with its focus on the firm rather than the industry, globalization leads to integrating strategic demands for worldwide efficiency, local market responsiveness, and world-class technology across all national markets.[41] The Transnational

Model also addresses the need for an organizational structure that is capable of controlling this integration without losing the unique qualities of the individual firm. Capability-based models show that advantage comes to the global firm that is able to decentralize operational responsibilities in differentiated subsidiaries while supporting strong integration among all affiliates.[42] This process dramatically reduces the "command and control" role of the corporate center in favor of "coordination and coaching." Clearly, there has been an evolution of thinking about multinational firms from an industry-driven set of similar organizations to a resource- or capability-type model in which unique heritage and idiosyncratic capabilities are reflected in firms facing similar market demands but meeting these with individual responses.

Leverage of capabilities is assisted by coordinating activities across multiple markets.[43] Global flexibility, arbitrage possibilities, and cost optimization are all improved if the firm has integrated its activities and its decision-making apparatus. In a multi-market but not integrated company, new component knowledge is likely to stay in the country where it develops. An integrated global architecture, on the other hand, can spread new technical capabilities throughout the worldwide firm, exploiting new assets while they are still unique. Research into international knowledge flows[44] shows that cross-border movement of knowledge, especially tacit knowledge, is possible but not easy, and it is significantly assisted by formal and informal corporate mechanisms for integration. Building architectural capabilities through integration may come from internal synergies in re-bundling business-level component knowledge and complementary assets from various units of the company. It also may come from improved architectural knowledge of how to find such opportunities. "Global network" type firms, such as Hewlett-Packard or DuPont, add value by stimulating the exchange and recombination of resources in such a way that new capabilities are incorporated into the fabric of the network—effectively generating profits from architectural knowledge. The process of creating architectural knowledge regarding efficient and effective operations in an integrated global organization must be understood as an idiosyncratic process tied closely to the historical order of events and decisions in the firm. Understanding these aspects of the modern multinational firm requires an explicitly capability-driven strategic approach.

Capability Strategies and Multinational Competition: Implications and Practice

Successful organizational structure, systems, cultures, and other manifested characteristics are contingent on the interaction of the different aspects of capabilities and strategy. Our framework considers capability types, capability processes, and international strategies and suggests the contingent consequences of these forces on observable organizational characteristics. This section provides a model specifying possible organizational responses of multinational firms to the strategic pressures of component versus architectural capabilities, leveraging versus building capability processes, and expansion versus integration-oriented multinational strategies. The model is formalized with a set of propositions that are tied to the contingency framework as shown in Table 1.

Table 1   CONTINGENT STRATEGIES OF MULTINATIONAL FIRMS

	Leverage Processes		Building Processes	
	Intl. Expansion	Global Integration	Intl. Expansion	Global Integration
Business-Level Component Capabilities	■ Global product divisions ■ Export strategies using global production platforms ■ Local skills used in sales and marketing ■ Internal trade of final goods mostly one direction from parent to subsidiary	■ Home-based global product divisions ■ High levels of two-way internal trade of intermediate goods between parent and subsidiaries	■ Frequent use of MN—local joint ventures ■ Acquisition of local firms with unique capabilities in foreign regional clusters	■ Heavy use of strategic alliances with other MNEs ■ Worldwide internal joint ventures and alliances
Corporate-Level Architectural Capabilities	■ Geographically based organization and multi-local approaches ■ Expansion primarily through greenfield and wholly owned subsidiaries ■ Replication of home-country corporate systems	■ Worldwide functional and product divisions ■ Foreign-based product divisions ■ Extensive financial cross-subsidy ■ Considerable direct intersubsidiary trade	■ Merger with or acquisition of other multinational firms or their subsidiaries and management as new independent business units ■ Holding company	■ Use of differentiated network organization ■ Highly decentralized and geographically dispersed operations ■ Multiple strategic leader subsidiaries

Leverage Strategies and the Multinational Firm

Leverage strategies are at the core of most existing models of the multinational firm.[45] Internalization models assume that firms have useful component knowledge and examine the most efficient means of exploiting these capabilities in international markets, looking to efficient architecture to minimize the cost of this leverage.[46] On the other hand, market power models treat the exploitation of architectural capabilities as a direct source of advantage for multinational firms in foreign markets.[47]

From a capability-driven perspective, leverage concerns have specific identifiable consequences for the multinational firm as it devises its strategy, whether involving business-level components or corporate-level architectural capabilities. First, leverage implies static sources of advantage.[48] International markets represent opportunities to further leverage assets and capabilities that have exhausted the capacity of the home market but which are essentially unchanged. Second, a preference for whole ownership is implied to protect the firm-specific, but contestable, knowledge of these firms from prying partners or incompetent middlemen and to permit the maximum strategic freedom to apply component capabilities in the "approved" manner. Third, larger companies are generally implied, as they have the managerial and financial assets to build an organization of wholly owned subsidiaries over time and the existing market power to move product on the basis of low price while fighting to counter imitative competition. Fourth, new product development in the home market or strategic stronghold is also implied, as this provides the best protection for skills in research and design. Learning in foreign locations is focused primarily on acquiring or developing complementary skills about the local market and business practices, very much in the "exploitative learning" mode.[49] Finally, specific practices of multinational firms in organization and control will be oriented toward efficiency in "know-how logistics," the ability to transmit specialized knowledge. Fixed sources of advantage must be exploited by the most efficient architecture in order to generate advantage, as all firms in an industry will eventually converge on the same basic component knowledge.

Leverage and International Expansion   The most obvious benefits of leverage through internationalization occur with component capabilities. Business-level component capabilities can be incorporated into products and exported, often are transmissible through licenses or management contracts, and are straightforward drivers of direct investment. Static component knowledge, however, is also the resource most subject to opportunistic behavior, the key consideration of transaction cost models of the multinational.[50] Particularly relevant when seeking profitability from technical resources are: decisions about protecting key skills from opportunism in the market or from partners; organizing to maximize efficiency in selling established technology; and appropriating as much of the value-added chain as possible through internalization. Also most apparent when focused on leveraging component knowledge are: market power strategies, enhancing oligopolistic worldwide industry structures, leveraging financial strength, exploiting brand names, and overwhelming, acquiring, or co-opting local competitors. For example, DuPont's initial motivation to move into Europe was the exploitation of U.S.-developed technical skills and capabilities to extend current competitive advantage in a larger market. Essentially, most of this firm's overseas activities related initially to strategies of exploiting component capabilities developed in the U.S. Accordingly, firms leveraging *business-level component* capabilities internationally are most likely to organize into global product divisions with export strategies based on global production platforms while seeking local skills only in sales and marketing. Internal trade will be one-way from the parent to subsidiaries and will focus on final goods.

Most leverage strategies appear to focus on component capabilities, but the corporate-level architectural capabilities developed in home markets also may be leveraged in international expansion. Worldwide export strategies that exploit size advantages benefit from skills in the management of ever-larger plants, complex distribution, and cost-based marketing. The "mini-parent firm" structures found in multi-domestic firms with independent subsidiaries reflect the organizational strategies and structures of the home country (even when not strictly appropriate). Multi-country operations are, to a certain extent, an extension of multi-plant management problems in the home country. Many of the problems of running a large domestic company can be extended to international markets,[51] and traditional models of the multinational firm assume that such firms are, in most cases, large firms. For example, in 1996, Amoco's commodity chemical group had moved its products, processes, human resource, marketing, and sales strategies to Europe in their totality. Its international capability strategy was to leverage capabilities developed in the United States. To accommodate this purpose, the architectural capabilities of the American parent were followed in detail despite the lack of local fit. For this company, internationalization provided a broader scope for the application of capabilities learned at home, as when it decided to use stock options to reward European workers and managers, despite tax disadvantages not present in the United States. Firms leveraging home-country-based *corporate-level architectural* capabilities through international expansion are more likely to use a geographically based organization and a multi-local strategy based on greenfield startups and whole owner-ship in an effort to reproduce home-country corporate structures and systems exactly.

Leverage and Global Integration   Leverage is enhanced by the integra-tion of markets. Not only are existing capabilities extended to foreign markets, they are applied to a world market. Given the need to adapt somewhat to local conditions,[52] core capabilities that can be targeted at global markets gain maximum benefits to size and market strength. Global integration permits each process technology to be pushed to its limit, global products provide the returns needed to push technology and quality as far as possible, and brand names take on a larger-than-life aura. Kogut describes ad-vantages of matching competitive and comparative advantage and of arbitraging across markets and leveraging advantages from one market into another.[53] Similarly, Hamel and Prahalad suggest that leveraging brand names, distribution capabilities, and finan-cial resources are the key characteristics of global strategy.[54] Matching component ca-pabilities to local economic conditions by differentiating activities across national locations and coordinating the value chain worldwide is the hallmark of the global firm. For example, Caterpillar has had extensive experience in international markets for fifty years as a dominant competitor in heavy equipment. As a result, it has consid-erable expertise in sourcing high-value components from the U.S. and less critical parts in low-cost areas, while focusing on local assembly and downstream activities. Firms leveraging *business-level component* capabilities globally are most likely to or-ganize into home-based global product divisions that split their value-added activities across markets based on matching firm-specific capabilities and location-specific re-sources. These firms will demonstrate high levels of two-way internal trade in inter-mediate goods between subsidiaries and the center.

Leveraging component knowledge globally requires sophisticated capabilities in splitting and coordinating value-added activities, implying the need to replicate archi-tectural capabilities. Managing a product-diversified domestic firm can be leveraged into managing an internationally diversified and globally integrated firm.[55] It would seem that functional management skills, much as functional technical skills, can be brought from national to international to global competition through extension and ex-ploitative learning.[56] Managers must learn to do what they do better, larger, faster, more efficiently, but do not really need to learn to do new things. The management systems of Matsushita have been leveraged globally, with coordination of the worldwide value chain looking much like that in Japan. Capabilities developed over the years in provid-ing high quality goods, superior asset management, and highly competitive prices quickly and accurately were leveraged into all of the firm's worldwide markets.[57] Ulti-mately, firms leveraging *corporate-level architectural* capabilities globally are most likely to extend their primary functional or product division structure globally. How-ever, such firms are more likely to base product divisions abroad, to use financial cross-subsidies, and to engage in inter-subsidiary trade (activities that require high levels of coordinating capabilities) than are firms leveraging component capabilities.

Building Strategies and the Multinational Firm

Multinational firms must build new capabilities as well as leveraging existing ones if they intend to find sustained advantage in worldwide markets.[58] Porter suggests that firms can tap into location-tied skills through direct investment.[59] Birkinshaw and Hood address capability building and its relationship to strategic change at the level of the single subsidiary, which can provide considerable technical skill if given some independence.[60] Bartlett and Ghoshal describe "strategic leader" subsidiaries that provide both component and architectural skills to the entire multinational network.[61] Certain consequences for the strategic configuration of the multinational firm also can be drawn at the corporate level from the demands of capability building. First, advantage is dynamic, based on ability to create the new, not to exploit the old. Second, this implies the extensive use of joint ventures, alliances, and acquisitions to explore for new knowledge rather than a focus on whole ownership to protect old knowledge. Third, as component capabilities can best be developed where the local business environment favors them, a global search for new products and processes suggests product divisions based around the world, not controlled from home. Finally, component capabilities in leading firms must be shared inside as well as outside the firm to make use of them before new learning makes them obsolete. This implies that internal networks are critical, providing a much more active role for the subsidiaries and affiliates of the firm in working together directly. The central headquarters must develop skills at coordinating, not controlling, on a global basis. Thus, it becomes responsible for setting standards and building frameworks rather than actively managing operations on a daily basis. As a result, the corporate headquarters must know when to set standards (such as information systems and financial reporting) and when to stay out of transactions (as when subsidiaries share technology). While component capabilities can be found in new places and created by new combinations, architectural capabilities in integrating networks of differentiated affiliates must be built by managing such a network.[62]

To a large extent, the very characteristics of successful leverage strategies create barriers to building innovative strategies.[63] Often firms seems to either focus on exploiting parent capabilities or on incorporating the rich experiences of newly developed networks. Where both strategies exist, they are tied to very distinct business areas that appeared to offer little support for one another. In 1996, Manpower International, a large multinational promoter of personnel services, continued to provide its traditional, very locally organized, personnel services through one SBU, based in the U.S. At the same time, a separate division, headquartered in Europe and founded only a few years earlier, offered globally integrated services of greater variety to large, multinational, corporate accounts.

Capability Building and International Expansion   If capability leverage strategies seem most intensely tied to component capabilities and internationalization, capability building among multinationals appears to be more closely tied to globalization efforts and architectural capabilities. Internalization of significant new skills, while feasible, is not described commonly in the international business literature. Rather, home-country-derived tacit knowledge most often is treated as the strength of the firm.[64] However, internationalization certainly provides access to new products, processes, and technologies that can be incorporated into the firm's array of technical capabilities. Many firms have come to the U.S. seeking technical skills to either outsource or incorporate in the search for international competitive advantage. However, even firms based in the U.S. are now discovering superior technological capabilities in European, East Asian, even former socialist countries. Global multinationals encourage major new businesses to develop in the most demanding foreign local markets. At the same time, barriers to multinational firms' investing in foreign locations to tap into local clusters of unique skills are diminishing around the world. An acquisition, alliance, or start-up in the right location can access skills and resources unavailable in the home country. Learning through international expansion confronts the problem of "sticky" or location-bound knowledge that multinational firms can incorporate only by establishing new units in the originating location. Stickiness of component capabilities suggests that a critical role for the multinational in the developing information age is to transmit internally information that would be tied to a single location in external market conditions.[65]

For example, both Hewlett-Packard and Motorola Semiconductor have largely shifted from their capability exploitation strategies of earlier times to recently developed searches for new technology *in situ*. They have organized into global product divisions but have based these divisions in various foreign subsidiaries rather than relocating these "headquarters" operations to the United States. This approach is intended to take advantage of local capabilities in particular business areas and bring them into the organization through acquisition, alliance, or start-up. Of course, these firms have also moved to leverage their newly incorporated know-how, but the building strategy is what really distinguishes the internationalizing efforts of technology leaders. In another example, Sony moved to set up data storage labs in the U.S. as American technology surpassed Sony's original Japan-sourced storage technology, and the same company decided to form a joint venture with Qualcomm in San Diego as digital cellular telephone technology began to dominate Sony's original analog technology.[66] As a result, firms building *business-level component* capabilities through international expansion are more likely to acquire local firms or set up joint ventures with local partners in foreign locations that are known to have regional clusters with unique capabilities in that line of business.

Separating component knowledge from architectural knowledge in international expansion is difficult. Building worldwide architectural capabilities is tied more to globalization than to internationalization. From the multinational corporate perspective, most of the skills related to a specific location appear to be components of a specific business. Firms such as DuPont have preferred to build new know-how through greenfield approaches or using alliances, reserving acquisition for major expansions into new business areas, usually buying an existing multinational firm rather than a local operation. Such acquisitions bring in not just technical skills in the new business area, but the industry-specific architectural knowledge of the acquired firm. Primary targets are typically successful international competitors, not struggling takeover candidates, reinforcing the proposition that acquisitions by global firms are for the purpose of building architectural capabilities. Consequently, firms attempting to build *corporate-level architectural* capabilities through international expansion are more likely to acquire other multinational firms or their units rather than foreign local companies. These acquisitions also are more likely to be set up as new business units.

Capability Building and Global Integration   Corporations appear to build most major capabilities in international markets through globalization. It is possible for the integrated global firm to find component and architectural capabilities in foreign locations that would otherwise not be available to the firm and then bring them in to a broader set of corporate skills. As Nohria and Ghoshal observe, "a key advantage of the multinational arises from its ability to create new value through the accumulation, transfer, and integration of different kinds of knowledge, resources, and capabilities across its dispersed organizational units."[67] In common with other studies,[68] these authors see that the organizational changes associated with global integration produce new component capabilities through the vehicle of network structures simultaneously developed for these purposes. Kogut and Zander show that in a final stage of the evolutionary process of international firm growth, "the learning from the foreign market is transferred internationally and influences the accumulation and recombination of knowledge through the network of subsidiaries, including the home market."[69]

Business-level component knowledge is built in global firms through a two-stage process. First, the firm conducts the same sort of search, identification, and incorporation process as noted above for international strategies. The second phase involves a process of combining resources and capabilities taken from various subsidiaries and alliances into new capability bundles not available to any one national affiliate. Thus, building capabilities through globalization is as much a creative process as an accumulation and translation process, which involves devising or acquiring major new technical capabilities and including both exploratory and exploitative learning elements.[70] Building component knowledge through globally integrated activities is perhaps the best use of strategic alliances between multinational partners. Unique capabilities in a particular business area can be shared to the mutual benefit of all of the partners, yet can be exploited separately. Capability bundles that are otherwise not available to any individual firm can be assembled in an efficient and flexible manner through the alliance, where whole ownership would be a slow and expensive path to new capabilities. For example, Hewlett-Packard has set up a system of "internal joint ventures" to create coordinated strategies across several of its highly decentralized and highly specialized business units. In this way, it can present globally unique products and product lines that are unavailable from any single business unit or country unit. Ultimately, firms building *business-level component* capabilities through global integration will use a preponderance of strategic alliances, both external and internal, in their core businesses.

The transfer of knowledge from subsidiary to network is difficult, but it is a key part of the architectural knowledge of the successful multinational network. Global integration is key to the development of new architectural capabilities. Hewlett-Packard's internal joint ventures pulled together component knowledge, but they required unique organizational skills (and most of the time of a corporate vice-president) to arrange. While international diversification appears to require similar elements to product diversification, the complexity of managing an integrated global strategy through a complex firm structure is unique to the global firm. These capabilities are essential to the coordination of the technical capabilities described above, but also produce new methods of structuring all aspects of the firm's activities. Innovation becomes a product of internal R&D, research partnerships with various clients and suppliers, market scanning, and other processes pulled together through the network of relationships of the central firm. Global firms are able to combine products across product lines and business units to offer bundles of products and services around the world that involve intensive coordination, not just international access, and which provide significant competitive advantage over firms which focus on isolated component knowledge.

For both Hewlett-Packard and Motorola Semiconductor, the use of internal and external partnerships was widespread in 1996, new basic research facilities were being added in new regions, and multiple business units spread around the world all retained new product development responsibilities in a decentralized network. Furthermore, production was located where most effective, then coordinated by various processes, including but not limited to hierarchical line management. Hewlett-Packard separated sales and marketing (organized on a geographical and product-line basis) from production and development (organized into independent profit centers) and yet was able to tightly coordinate all these activities. Significantly, this firm showed high levels of intra-firm (but international) movement of knowledge, particularly of tacit, complex knowledge.

NCR and Hewlett-Packard also have been involved in efforts to globalize both their component and architectural capabilities through finding new combinations of businesses and business skills from their subsidiaries and alliances. Both of these firms have transformed some of their production facilities into "Lead" factories with responsibilities to truly innovate and create new technologies, processes, and products.[71] Nohria and Ghoshal's vision of business-related capabilities arising from Schumpeterian insight within the global network firm has been quite evident in these companies.[72] In the process of pursuing these advantages, these firms have been involved in actively pursuing such architectural capabilities as internal joint venture development, corporate specialists in emerging economies, and active technology partnerships with multiple competing customers. In order to do this, decentralization of authority has been a goal of these firms, but continued non-authoritarian interventions by higher central authorities has also been important. Effectively, multinational firms that are building *corporate-level architectural* capabilities in global markets are most likely to be characterized as differentiated networks with "headquarters activities" that are highly decentralized and geographically dispersed—i.e., true transnationals.

Conclusions

Capability-based theory provides a conceptually rigorous approach to the analysis of multinational strategies that can complement and augment transaction-efficiency models and market power models of globalization. Our framework builds a coherent model of international expansion and global integration from two basic types of complex assets (component and architectural capabilities) and two basic capability processes (leverage and building). The influence of these strategic imperatives on decisions to internationalize and globalize in multinational firms is an outcome of organizational strategies based on fundamental drives for expansion of resources and extraction of profits, rather than an unspecified need for integration unique to multinational firms. On the other hand, we also use this inherently firm-level model to predict individual company outcomes that cannot be extracted from the macro-economic or industry-level theories common to foreign direct investment theory.

Leading firms in technology-intensive industries are indeed globalizing, but they are doing so to build or discover new capabilities as much as to further lever their existing assets and skills. Other companies, however, can gain considerable economic benefit from the high leverage and low exploration inherent in more simple international strategies. In mature, cost-competitive industries, the complex organizations and high-opportunity-cost management techniques required to manage global capability building are not able to generate benefits that would justify their costs. One implication often drawn from the current literature is that all firms in all industries are moving toward an integrated global network. However, while of great value in innovation-driven businesses, these network forms are extremely expensive, in both real and opportunity costs, and may offer little value in more traditional cost-driven businesses. Our model provides managers of multinational firms with a framework to decide just how international or how global they might want to be. Ultimately, this decision needs to be based on the situation of the firm, not on generic industry recommendations or on standardized solutions to a complex set of issues.

Notes

1. K. R. Conner, "A Historical Comparison of Resource-Based Theory and Five Schools of Thought within Industrial Organization Economics: Do We Have a New Theory of the Firm?" *Journal of Management,* 17/1 (March 1991): 121–154; J. B. Barney, "Firm Resources and Sustained Competitive Advantage," *Journal of Management,* 17/1 (March 1991): 99–120; D. Teece, G. Pisano, and A. Shuen, "Dynamic Capabilities and Strategic Management," *Strategic Management Journal,* 18/7 (August 1997): 509–533.

2. D. J. Collis, "A Resource-Based Analysis of Global Competition: The Case of the Bearings Industry," *Strategic Management Journal,* 12 (Summer 1991): 49–68; G. Hedlund and J. Ridderstrale, "Toward the N-Form Corporation: Exploitation and Creation in the MNC," Institute of International Business, Stockholm School of Economics, RP 92/15, 1993; K. Fladmoe-Lindquist and S. Tallman, "Resource-Based Strategy and Competitive Advantage among Multinationals," in P. Shrivastava, A. Huff, J. Dutton, eds., *Advances In Strategic Management,* 10 (Greenwich, CT: JAI Press, 1994); B. Kogut, "The Evolutionary Theory of the Multinational Corporation: Within and across Country Options," in B. Toyne and D. Nigh, eds., *International Business: An Emerging Vision* (Columbia, SC: University of South Carolina Press, 1997), pp. 470–488.

3. G. Hamel and C. K. Prahalad, "Do You Really Have a Global Strategy?" *Harvard Business Review,* 63/4 (July/August 1985): 139–148.

4. C. K. Prahalad and G. Hamel, "The Core Competence of the Corporation," *Harvard Business Review,* 68/3 (May/June 1990): 79–91.

5. Teece, Pisano, and Shuen, op. cit.

6. P. Buckley and M. Casson, *The Future of the Multinational Enterprise* (London: MacMillan, 1976); J. Dunning, "The Eclectic Paradigm of International Production: A Restatement," *Journal of International Business Studies,* 19/1 (Spring 1988): 1–32; M. E. Porter, *The Competitive Advantage of Nations* (New York: NY: The Free Press, 1990).

7. Ibid.

8. C. A. Bartlett and S. Ghoshal, *Managing Across Borders: The Transnational Solution* (Boston, MA: Harvard Business School Press, 1989); N. Nohria and S. Ghoshal, *The Differentiated Network* (San Francisco, CA: Jossey-Bass, 1997).

9. H. Bresman, J. Birkinshaw, and R. Nobel, "Knowledge Transfer in International Acquisitions," *Journal of International Business Studies,* 30/3 (1999): 439–462; J. Birkinshaw and N. Hood, "Characteristics of Foreign Subsidiaries in Industry Clusters," *Journal of International Business Studies,* 31/1 (2000): 141–154.

10. Nohria and Ghoshal [op. cit.] discuss value-creation as a key aspect of their differentiated network model, but do not provide an explicit model of the strategic motivations for this reorganization of multinational firms. From our perspective, they have an implicit competence-based strategy model in mind. We make this explicit.

11. Resource-based, knowledge-based, competency-based, and so on.

12. R. Sanchez, A. Heene, and H. Thomas, eds., *Dynamics of Competence-Based Competition* (Oxford: Elsevier Pergamon, 1996), Chapter 1.

13. S. Matusik and C. W. L. Hill, "The Utilization of Contingent Work, Knowledge Creation and Competitive Advantage," *Academy of Management Review,* 23/4 (October 1998): 680—697.

14. T. Chi, "Trading in Strategic Resources: Necessary Conditions, Transaction Cost Problems, and Choice of Exchange Structure," *Strategic Management Journal,* 15/4 (May 1994): 271–290.

15. Prahalad and Hamel, op. cit.

16. Ibid.

17. Conner, op. cit.

18. Sanchez, Heene, and Thomas, op. cit.

19. Teece, Pisano, and Shuen, op. cit.

20. B. Kogut and U. Zander, "Knowledge of the Firm and the Evolutionary Theory of the Multinational Corporation," *Journal of International Business Studies,* 24/4 (1993): 637.

21. K. Ferdows, "Making the Most of Foreign Factories," *Harvard Business Review,* 75/2 (March/April 1997): 74–88.

22. S. B. Tallman, "A Strategic Management Perspective on Host Country Structure of Multinational Enterprises," *Journal of Management,* 18/3 (September 1992): 455–471.

23. Nohria and Ghoshal, op. cit.

24. J. A. Cantwell and L. Piscitello, "Accumulating Technological Competence—Its Changing Impact on Corporate Diversification and Internationalization," Department of Economics Discussion Papers in International Investment and Management, University of Reading, UK, 1997; M. Hitt, R. Hoskisson, and H. Kim, "International Diversification: Effects on Innovation and Firm Performance in Product-Diversified Firms," *Academy of Management Journal,* 40/4 (August 1997): 767–798.

25. Bartlett and Ghoshal, op. cit.; A. K. Gupta and V. Govindarajan, "Knowledge Flows within Multinational Corporations," *Strategic Management Journal,* 21/4 (April 2000): 473–496.

26. Hedlund and Ridderstrale, op. cit.

27. Dunning, op. cit.; Porter (1990), op. cit.

28. Cantwell and Piscitello, op. cit.; K. Ohmae, "Managing in a Borderless World," *Harvard Business Review,* 67/3 (May/June 1989): 152–161.

29. Bartlett and Ghoshal, op. cit.; J. Birkinshaw and N. Hood, "Multinational Subsidiary Evolution: Capability and Charter Change in Foreign-Owned Subsidiary Companies," *Academy of Management Review,* 23/4 (October 1998): 773–795.

30. M. E. Porter, "Clusters and the New Economics of Competition," *Harvard Business Review,* 76/6 (November/December 1998): 77–90.

31. Ferdows, op. cit.
32. K. Barham and C. Heimer, *ABB: the Dancing Giant: Creating the Globally Connected Corporation* (London: Financial Times/Pittman Publishing, 1998).
33. M. E. Porter, "Competition in Global Industries: a Conceptual Framework," in M. E. Porter, ed., *Competition in Global Industries* (Boston, MA: Harvard Business School Press, 1986), pp. 15–60; Y. Doz, *Strategic Management in Multinational Companies* (Oxford: Pergamon Press, 1985).
34. J. A. Cantwell, "A Survey of Theories of International Production," in C. Pitelis and R. Sugden, eds., *The Nature of the Transnational Firm* (London: Routledge, 1991): 18–63.
35. R. Vernon, *Sovereignty at Bay* (New York, NY: Basic Books, 1966); J. Stopford and L. Wells, *Managing the Multinational Enterprise* (New York, NY: Basic Books, 1971).
36. Buckley and Casson, op. cit.
37. R. Caves, "International Corporations: The Industrial Economics of Foreign Investment," *Economica,* 38 (1971): 1–27.
38. M. Hitt, R. Hoskisson, and H. Kim, "International Diversification: Effects on Innovation and Firm Performance in Product-Diversified Firms," *Academy of Management Journal,* 40/4 (August 1997): 767–798; S. Tallman and J. T. Li, "Effects of International Diversity and Product Diversity on the Performance of Multinational Firms," *Academy of Management Journal,* 39/1 (February 1996): 179–196.
39. Porter (1986), op. cit.
40. Doz, op. cit.
41. Bartlett and Ghoshal, op. cit.
42. G. Hedlund, "The Hypermodern MNC—A Heterarchy?" *Human Resource Management,* 25/1 (Spring 1986): 9–35; Nohria and Ghoshal, op. cit.
43. B. Kogut, "Designing Global Strategies: Profiting from Operational Flexibility," *Sloan Management Review,* 27/1 (Fall 1985): 27–38; Hamel and Prahalad, op. cit.
44. Kogut and Zander, op. cit.; A. K. Gupta and V. Govindarajan, "Knowledge Flows within Multinational Corporations," *Strategic Management Journal,* 21/4 (April 2000): 473–496.
45. Hedlund and Ridderstrale, op. cit.
46. P. Buckley, "The Limits of Explanation: Testing the Internalization Theory of the Multinational Enterprise," *Journal of International Business Studies,* 19/2 (Summer 1988): 181–194.
47. Caves, op. cit.
48. Even in a dynamic learning environment, leverage works only with present capabilities rather than future prospects.
49. J. March, "Exploration and Exploitation in Organizational Learning," *Organization Science,* 2/1 (1991): 71–87.
50. Buckley and Casson, op. cit.
51. Hitt, Hoskisson, and Kim, op. cit.
52. Ohmae, op. cit.
53. Kogut (1985), op. cit.
54. Hamel and Prahalad, op. cit.
55. Hitt, Hoskisson, and Kim, op. cit.; Cantwell and Piscitello, op. cit.
56. March, op. cit.
57. Hamel and Prahalad, op. cit.
58. Teece, Pisano, and Shuen, op. cit.
59. Porter (1998), op. cit.
60. Birkinshaw and Hood (1998), op. cit.
61. Bartlett and Ghoshal, op. cit.
62. Hedlund, op. cit.
63. Hedlund and Ridderstrale, op. cit.
64. B. Kogut, "Country Capabilities and the Permeability of Borders," *Strategic Management Journal,* 12 (Summer 1991): 33–48; Porter (1990), op. cit.
65. Kogut and Zander, op. cit.; Hedlund and Ridderstrale, op. cit.
66. M. Peng and Y. Wang, "Innovation Capability and Foreign Direct Investment: Toward a Learning Option Perspective," *Management International Review,* 40 (2000): 79–94.
67. Nohria and Ghoshal, op. cit.
68. Cantwell and Piscitello, op. cit.
69. Kogut and Zander, op. cit., p. 636.
70. March, op. cit.
71. Ferdows, op. cit.
72. Nohria and Ghoshal, op. cit.

Judo Strategy: 10 Techniques for Beating a Stronger Opponent

David B. Yoffie
Harvard Business School

Mary Kwak
Harvard Business School

The idea of judo economics, building on analogies with the sport of judo, has been around for at least 20 years. But taking these ideas further to judo strategy means that a framework of strategic principles can be developed to help companies put stronger opponents on the mat.

Why do some companies succeed in defeating stronger rivals, while others fail? This is a question that all ambitious businesses eventually face. Whether you're a start-up taking on industry giants or a giant moving into markets dominated by powerful incumbents, the basic problem remains the same: how do you compete with opponents who have size, strength, and history on their side?

The answer lies in a simple but powerful lesson: successful challengers use what we call "judo" strategy to prevent opponents from bringing their full strength into play. Judo strategists avoid forms of competition, such as head-to-head struggles, that naturally favour the large and the strong. Instead, they relay on speed, agility, and creative thinking in crafting strategies that make it difficult for powerful rivals to compete.

This is not, of course, an entirely new idea. It has long been recognised, for example, that by first securing a foothold in an undefended market, a company can improve its chances of ultimate success. (In fact, Peter Drucker has labelled this process "entrepreneurial judo.")

We have taken this thinking on unequal competition further.

First, rather than focus on a single insight, such as the importance of niche picking, we provide an overarching framework that ties together a wealth of strategic ideas.

Second, we offer numerous examples of how companies have put these ideas to work, based on our interviews with executives at a broad range of companies—both old and new economy, large and small. (Unless otherwise noted, all quotations are drawn from these interviews.)

Moreover, the judo strategy approach seems particularly timely today. In the go-go years of the Internet boom, tilting with giants was all the rage. But in the vast

Reprinted from *Business Strategy Review,* Vol. 13, Issue 1, March 2002, pp. 20–30. © London Business School. Used with permission.

majority of cases, it was the upstarts, not the incumbents, who found themselves facing defeat. Does this mean that competing with giants is a doomed enterprise? No, but it surely means that would-be challengers must find smarter ways to compete.

What Is Judo Strategy?

Judo strategy is an approach to competition that emphasises skill, rather than size or strength. In developing this framework, we were inspired by the work of two economists, Judith Gelman and Steven Salop, who coined the term "judo economics" to describe a strategy that allows a company to use a larger opponent's size to its advantage.

In their model, a challenger must decide how aggressively to enter a market dominated by an incumbent. Based on some simple assumptions (see box), Gelman and Salop show that if a challenger tries to capture the entire market, the incumbent will fight back—and probably win. However, the challenger can induce the incumbent to accommodate his entry by making a credible commitment to target only a small subset of the market. This approach works because the incumbent is better off ceding a fraction of the market than cutting prices across its entire customer base.

The central idea behind this model—turning an opponent's strength into a disadvantage—has enormous appeal. But judo economics also has important limitations. For example, it's very difficult to implement. It's one thing to say that you won't threaten bigger competitors. It's quite another to convince them that you mean what you say. Moreover, judo economics looks rather less promising once the assumptions behind the original model, such as the prohibition on price discrimination, are relaxed.

But perhaps the most important limitation of judo economics is that it requires an entrant to remain small in order to survive. For most managers and companies, this is not enough. Consequently, judo strategy picks up where judo economics leaves off.

Judo strategy provides a set of tools that allow you to do more than just survive in the face of daunting competition; they show you how to thrive and grow. Building on the insights of both judo economics and judo, its original source, we argue that companies can win against larger or stronger competitors by mastering three core principles: movement, balance and leverage.

In judo, these principles work closely together. As one expert writes: "Through movement the opponent is led into an unbalanced position. Then he is thrown either by some form of leverage or by stopping or sweeping away some part of his body or limbs."

Analogously, through movement managers can seize the lead and make the most of their initial advantage. By maintaining balance, they can successfully engage with opponents and respond to rivals' attacks. And, finally, by exploiting leverage, firms can transform their competitors' strengths into strategic liabilities. By mastering these principles, any company can learn to compete more effectively with stronger opponents.

If a challenger tries to capture the entire market, the incumbent will fight back—and probably win.

Below we discuss 10 core techniques that the companies we studied have used to put these ideas to work. However, it is important to note that this is by no means an exhaustive account. Moreover, judo strategy is not a rigid formula to be followed systematically. Depending on the nature of their competition, firms will combine and implement movement, balance and leverage in different ways.

Judo Economics—A Simple Example

- Assume that an incumbent faces a single challenger, who has no cost advantage; that customers in this market choose their suppliers solely based on price; and that all customers must be charged the same price.
- At the beginning of the game, the incumbent supplies 10 customers with widgets for $50.
- Scenario A: If the challenger offers to supply the entire market at $40, the incumbent will be forced to match the price or lose all of its sales. Eventually, the challenger will be driven from the market.
- Scenario B: If the challenger only invests in enough capacity to sell to one customer, the incumbent will find it more profitable to accommodate his entry by sticking to the original price and selling to the remaining nine.

Mastering Movement

Judo strategy, like judo, begins with movement. In judo, movement serves both offensive and defensive goals. Competitors use their quickness and agility to move into a position of relative strength while evading attack. Judo masters also use movement to take an opponent "out of his game," in the words of Olympic medallist Jimmy Pedro, by preventing him from employing his strongest techniques. Finally, once he's gained an edge, a skilled *judoka* follows through quickly, moving seamlessly from attack to attack. In a sport where advantage can shift in a second, faltering when it comes to the follow-through can be a fatal mistake.

The same tactics can help companies seize and keep the lead away from powerful opponents. Judo strategists learn to implement the "puppy dog ploy" (a term we have borrowed from economists Drew Fudenberg and Jean Tirole), steadily building market momentum while cultivating an unthreatening image in order to avoid provoking an attack. They also move quickly to define the competitive space, challenging competitors to compete by new and unfamiliar rules. And finally, they follow through fast, capitalising on their initial advantage with a well-executed plan of continuous attack.

> *Judo strategy counsels challengers to keep a low profile and avoid head-to-head battles that they're too weak to win.*

Technique No. 1: The "Puppy Dog Ploy"

In any kind of competition, your first goal is to stay in the game. So judo strategy counsels challengers to keep a low profile and avoid head-to-head battles that they're too weak to win. This advice goes against the grain for many managers. In a crowded marketplace, it's often said, you have to shout to be heard. You have to be aggressive to win customers and build value, and often that means attacking giants head-on.

There's a kernel of truth in this argument. In order to make a dent in the market, you do have to attract attention and win credibility among customers, partners and sometimes the media as well. This is particularly true in business-to-business markets and in sectors where network effects are strong. But in most cases, this goal can be accomplished without initiating or provoking a full frontal attack.

For evidence, consider the rapid rise of Capital One, which became one of the biggest and most profitable credit card issuers in the United States in less than 10 years, thanks largely to its ability to remain "extremely confidential and very, very hush-hush," as one former executive explained. By forgoing product announcements and other publicity in favour of direct marketing campaigns, Capital One made it nearly impossible for competitors to imitate its highly targeted products. Consequently, the company faced little direct competition in many of the market segments it pioneered.

Palm Computing, by contrast, was unable to keep its products under wraps. But by downplaying their potential, the company succeeded in temporarily averting a full-scale attack. Unlike earlier handheld players, such as Apple, Palm described its products as companions, not substitutes, for personal computers. In this way, the company hoped to keep competitors like Microsoft and Compaq from identifying Palm as an urgent threat.

In addition, although the Palm operating system was eventually to serve as a launch pad for thousands of applications, Palm tiptoed around Microsoft's greatest area of sensitivity—the potential emergence of competing platform players—by defining the Pilot not as a platform, but as a relatively inoffensive device. As a result, handheld computing remained low on Microsoft's list of priorities for at least two years after the Pilot's debut, giving Palm the opportunity to build a massive installed base.

For a final, cautionary example, we turn to Netscape, which rejected the puppy dog ploy in favour of "mooning the giant," in one senior executive's words. Netscape drew tremendous attention by posing as a giant-killer early in the game—labeling Microsoft "the Death Star" and predicting that the web would make Windows obsolete. This aggressive positioning helped Netscape in the battle for publicity and, for a while, the start-up's fortunes soared. Over the longer run, however, the danger of mooning the giant became clear. The company's bravado helped push the Internet to the top of Bill Gates' list of priorities and secure Netscape's position as enemy number-one.

Technique No. 2: Define the Competitive Space

While the puppy dog ploy is largely about defence, with this next technique, offence comes into play. Here's where you seize the initiative by defining a competitive space where you can take the lead. Most champions rise to the top by learning to excel at a few key skills—shoulder throws, for example, or cutting costs. Competing with a stronger player at what he does best is a losing game, But every champion has areas where he's weak, often precisely because he's invested so heavily in his core strengths. Take advantage of these weak points to define a game you can win.

Intuit chose usability as its battlefield in implementing this technique. When it entered the personal finance software market in the early 1980s, the seven-person start-up found that the usual road to victory lay in packing more and more complicated features into your products with every release. This was a contest that only the resource-rich could win. But by redefining customer expectations, Intuit managed to rise to the top.

Intuit didn't try to out-feature the competition; it didn't even try to match most of the features its rivals already had. Instead, the company picked a short list of functions that consumers used, such as writing cheques and keeping a cheque register and focused on making those things quick and easy to do. Customers flocked to purchase Quicken while the previous market leaders remained locked in the "more is better" mind-set and Intuit vaulted into first place.

In a very different market, Juniper Networks also found the key to competing successfully with Cisco Systems in proactively defining the competitive space. Previous challengers had attacked Cisco on its home turf, selling "the same application to the same customers"—multi-protocol routers to enterprise customers—as Juniper CEO Scott Kriens explained.

Juniper, by contrast, forced Cisco to compete on far less hospitable terrain. The networking start-up targeted the top of the market, where Cisco was relatively weak. Moreover, Juniper broke with Cisco's traditional product architecture in order to meet the performance needs of customers like AT&T. Rather than rely on software to drive its routers, Juniper focused on adding intelligence to the underlying chips. This strategy shifted the battleground from software to silicon, making it even harder for Cisco to match its challenger's moves and opening the way for Juniper to capture nearly 40 per cent of the high-end router market in less than two-and-a-half years.

Technique No. 3: Follow Through Fast

By combining the first two movement techniques, you create a window of opportunity. Next, you need to use this opening to strengthen your position through continuous attack. One day soon—and these days, that's sooner than ever—your competitors will see through the puppy dog ploy, rise to the challenges of a new competitive space and seek to bring the advantages of superior size and strength into play. By following through fast, you can postpone this day of reckoning and make the most of your early lead.

Palm Computing in many ways exemplifies this approach. In order to stay ahead of Microsoft and its allies, Palm turned itself into a moving target, bringing new product generations to market at least once a year. Three key practices helped the company maintain this pace.

First, unlike many high-tech start-ups, Palm avoided rocket science and lengthy wish lists that could delay a launch by months or even years. The company also included manufacturing managers in the design process from the very beginning in order to help keep its engineers' feet on the ground. And Palm relied heavily on outsourcing for non-core tasks, including electrical engineering, mechanical engineering and industrial design, and manufacturing rather than spend scarce time and resources developing these capabilities in-house.

> *One day soon your competitors will see through the puppy dog ploy, rise to the challenges of a new competitive space and seek to bring the advantages of superior size and strength into play.*

While Palm's engineering teams streamlined the development process for speed, the company's marketers focused on reaching critical mass by starting with low prices ($300 as opposed to $500 for a typical Microsoft-based device) and lowering them every year.

Palm also reached out quietly to developers, who could further the company's momentum by creating complementary applications. As early as 1996, Palm took the unusual step of publishing the source code for its basic applications in order to make it easier for developers to create new software. These decisions helped push Palm toward a market share of nearly 80 per cent in less than three years.

But what is perhaps most impressive about Palm's follow-through is the company's ability to speed ahead without losing its balance. Palm constantly faced temptations to extend its brand. "We had people knocking at our door to license this bit or that bit for this thing or the other thing, whether it was for set-top boxes or big-screen phones," CEO Donna Dubinsky later recalled. But in most cases, Palm turned its suitors down.

The company's management realised that even as sales exploded, Palm needed to focus its resources on just one goal: building and selling the best handheld device in the world.

Skilled judo strategists like Dubinsky understand that speed is a means, not an end. While moving quickly, they remain wary of becoming overextended and creating an opening for the competition. Equally important, they realise that speed should never become an obsession to the point where it excludes other critical concerns, such as product quality, customer satisfaction and long-run profitability—a lesson that many humbled new-economy firms would have done well to learn.

Mastering Balance

Movement can help you avoid head-to-head battles with bigger, stronger opponents. Eventually, however, you'll have to meet the competition. In judo strategy, as in judo, you have to learn to engage with opponents in order to win. This is where balance comes into play.

Rather than oppose strength to strength, judo practitioners learn to conserve their resources and maintain their balance by first giving way.

At the beginning of a judo match, each player battles to secure a grip on the other's collar or sleeve with the aim of pushing or pulling his or her opponent into a weakened or unbalanced position. Meanwhile, the recipient of this treatment must follow a simple but counterintuitive rule. Rather than resist, he should give way to his opponent's momentum, pushing when pulled and pulling when pushed. Rather than oppose strength to strength, judo practitioners learn to conserve their resources and maintain their balance by first giving way. Then they use their opponents' momentum to help bring them down.

A similar set of techniques can help companies keep the upper hand in encounters with more powerful competitors. By gripping their opponents, skilled judo strategists maximise their influence over the future course of competition, with the ultimate aim of averting an attack. Should this prove impossible, they can minimise the impact of an opponent's blows by avoiding tit-for-tat. Pushing when pulled takes them one step further by re-channelling an opponent's momentum and turning it against him. And finally, by mastering *ukemi,* judo strategists can remain in control of their future, even in the face of temporary defeat.

Technique No. 4: Grip Your Opponent

By gripping an opponent early, you may succeed in pre-empting competition: securing victory, in essence, by making it unnecessary to fight. You can also build relationships with current or future rivals that limit their room for manoeuvre or allow you to benefit at their expense. Both moves will undercut their future ability to attack.

There are many ways to grip another player. If you want to avoid future combat, give potential competitors a stake in your success through partnerships, joint ventures or equity deals. Alternatively, if you want to limit your rivals' options and reduce their incentives to develop their own capabilities, offer your services or products instead. Several Japanese consumer electronics companies took this route in the 1960s and 1970s, gripping their larger U.S. competitors by producing low-end products that were sold under their rivals' brands. In many cases, these tactics will involve what modern strategy jargon calls "co-opetition": competing and co-operating with other companies at the same time. But keep in mind that the true goal of gripping isn't to make all sides better off; it's to defend and strengthen your competitive position.

RealNetworks, the leader in streaming media software, implemented gripping early in its history through distribution partnerships that fed it customers at its potential competitors' expense. By convincing Microsoft to bundle RealAudio with Internet Explorer, for example, RealNetworks built a devoted installed base that later became one of the obstacles facing Microsoft when it launched its own streaming media products.

While gripping strengthened Real's position vis-à-vis Microsoft, it was unable to eliminate the threat of attack. At eBay, however, the same technique had more lasting results. Beginning in the fall of 1997, eBay executives worked hard to head off the spectre of competition with AOL by negotiating three successive deals. By the spring of 1999, eBay had established a firm grip on AOL, which was left with little incentive to enter its partner's space. In return for payments of $75m over four years, AOL agreed to make eBay the exclusive auction provider on all AOL properties around the world, to co-brand eBay's auctions under the eBay@AOL name, and to sell ads for the co-branded site. In addition, AOL pledged not to enter the auction market for two years.

EBay CEO Meg Whitman recognised that AOL could still decide to enter the auction market on its own. "You never can say never with AOL," she points out. But by providing AOL with an important revenue stream with margins estimated at nearly 98 per cent, eBay was doing its utmost to ensure that AOL would remain on the sidelines of the game.

Technique No. 5: Avoid Tit-for-Tat

Through gripping you can sometimes alter a competitor's incentives sufficiently to head off a battle. Often, however, despite your best efforts, a rival company will eventually decide to attack. Once this happens, keeping your balance is a challenge. Your gut tells you to match every move. Your instinct is to stop your opponent from getting the upper hand. But as a judo strategist, the last thing you want is to get locked into a tit-for-tat struggle or a war of attrition, as tit-for-tat often becomes.

So study your opponent carefully before deciding which attacks to counter and how. "Go to school on your competitors," as Intuit founder Scott Cook likes to say. Figure out what works and what's just a marketing flash in the pan. Separate the truly compelling propositions from the chaff you should ignore. Figure out the moves you can match without getting dragged out of your depth, and craft counter attacks that play to your strength when you can't afford to respond in kind.

Matching an opponent's move makes sense in certain situations: when you can match without provoking an escalatory response, for example, or in cases where you can easily neutralise your opponent's advantage and recapture the lead (often a sign that the enemy has strayed onto your home turf). But if matching means getting dragged into a war of attrition or a pure trial of strength, then resist the temptation to fight tit-for-tat and strike back on your own terms instead.

This is a message that Novell would have done well to heed. As late as 1992, Novell still held onto two-thirds of the market for network operating systems, despite repeated attacks by Microsoft, a company four times it size. But then CEO Ray Noorda made a fateful mistake. Angered by Microsoft's attacks on his core business, Noorda decided to respond in kind, taking the battle to his opponent's home turf. Novell went on an acquisition spree, buying AT&T's UNIX, WordPerfect and Borland's QuattroPro with the goal of storming the markets for operating systems and office productivity suites.

Five years later, the company was in shambles, undone by the unequal struggle and facing its first loss in 14 years. It took a new CEO and a radical new strategy toward the end of the decade to bring Novell back to life.

By contrast, eBay avoided Novell's mistakes. Between the fall of 1998 and the summer of 1999, the company was forced into competition with three of the Internet's powerhouses: Yahoo!, Amazon, and Microsoft (in alliance with Excite). Nonetheless, the company maintained its balance by avoiding tit-for-tat and meeting the competition on its own terms.

> *By incorporating a competitor's products, services or technology into your attack, you can throw him off-balance.*

After careful study of the market, eBay resisted the temptation to reflexively match competitors' moves, such as Yahoo's decision to make its auctions free. Instead, the company responded with moves that played to its strengths—stepping up grassroots marketing, for example, rather than trying pointlessly to match Yahoo!'s marketing on the web. This strategy helped eBay stay firmly in the lead without burning through mountains of cash. By early 2000, eBay was doing more than 25 times as much business as Yahoo!Auctions, and its other competitors trailed even further behind.

Technique No. 6: Push When Pulled

Gripping your opponent and avoiding tit-for-tat help you minimise the prospect or impact of a competitor's attack. With push when pulled, you go one step further by using your opponent's force or momentum to your advantage. By incorporating a competitor's products, services or technology into your attack, you can throw him off-balance and confront him with a painful choice: whether to abandon his initial strategy or to watch it fail.

A classic example of this technique comes from the diaper business, which saw an upstart named Drypers emerge in the 1980s. Drypers challenged market leader Procter & Gamble by offering a branded product at a lower price, giving consumers a choice between no-frills store brands and premium-priced Pampers.

When Drypers entered the market in Texas, P&G responded with unusual vigour, bombarding the state with coupons for $2—more than twice the usual 75 cents. Drypers could not afford to print and distribute coupons all across the state. But CEO

> *Even in temporary or partial defeat, you should give in to your opponent's momentum, rather than resist and risk losing control.*

Dave Pitassi, who had just finished reading a book on judo, came up with a creative response. Rather than try to match P&G's offensive, Drypers piggybacked on its rival's attack. The company launched a statewide advertising campaign to tell consumers that P&G coupons could be used on Drypers and sales shot up. In a matter of weeks, Drypers had added as much as 15 points to its market share in some stores. Within two months, the company was running at full capacity and it was cash-positive for the first time. Thanks to Pitassi's inspired use of judo strategy, P&G's

attack had seriously backfired. By harnessing its competitor's momentum, Drypers had used P&G to underwrite its own promotional campaign.

While Drypers fits the classic start-up profile—small and scrappy—large companies can also push when pulled to powerful effect. Wal-Mart used this technique against Kmart in the 1980s, as it battled to seize the discount-retailing crown. At the time, Wal-Mart's average prices were slightly lower than Kmart's but Kmart aggressively advertised weekly specials in order to pull customers into its stores. Wal-Mart was reluctant to match Kmart's advertising and promotional strategy because its business model relied on low costs and "Everyday Low Prices."

So managers in several stores used judo strategy instead. They posted Kmart's weekly circular at the front of their stores and promised that Wal-Mart would match or beat any of the advertised deals. This move created a real dilemma for Kmart: just like P&G, the more it advertised, the more it drove customers to the competition.

Technique No. 7: Practice *Ukemi*

In judo, *ukemi* is the technique of falling safely and with minimal loss of advantage in order to return more effectively to the fight. In other words, even in temporary or partial defeat, you should give in to your opponent's momentum, rather than resist and risk losing control.

Ukemi is the first thing that new students of judo learn, and it is a critical discipline in judo strategy as well. No matter how skilled you are as a strategist, you are unlikely to win every skirmish. But losing a battle need not lead to defeat in the war. By beating a strategic retreat, you can conserve your resources and regroup in better position for the confrontations ahead.

Microsoft absorbed this lesson in the mid-1990s when it decided to walk away from its efforts to establish the Microsoft Network (MSN) as a proprietary online service—a project that soaked up nearly $1bn in company resources—and relaunched its service on the web. A few years later, Charles Schwab took a similar step by integrating eSchwab into its core discount brokerage business, at a short-term cost of $125m in revenues.

Larger companies, of course, have both the organisational resources and the deep pockets that are often necessary to absorb a temporary loss. But while harder to implement, *ukemi* can be even more critical for smaller firms facing determined opponents, as the history of Dublin-based Ryanair shows.

Cathal and Declan Ryan started Ryanair with a single 44-seat turboprop plane in 1986. The brothers' strategy was to build a beachhead by offering better service and simplified pricing on the London–Dublin route. But this plan soon came to an end when British Airways and Aer Lingus launched a full-scale price war, dropping fares by 20 per cent. By 1991, facing mounting losses, Ryanair was on the verge of bankruptcy.

That's when the company's founders decided they had to give up the struggle and find another strategy. They dropped the effort to match BA and Aer Lingus on service and made price the focus of their offering. In a Herculean effort, all unnecessary expenses were eliminated, including in-flight food and pens for headquarters staff.

With its new cost and fare structure, Ryanair returned to profitability in 1992 and remained there throughout the 1990s. After losing their balance in an initial battle, the Ryan brothers had learned the same lesson as Bill Gates and Schwab: rather than fight a losing battle, it is better to fall of your own accord and rebuild momentum.

Mastering Leverage

By mastering movement, you improve your chances of building a strong initial position and getting ahead of competitors before they respond. The techniques of balance, in turn, allow you to engage bigger or stronger rivals without getting knocked down. In some cases, by making the most of these two principles, you can build and consolidate an insurmountable lead. In most cases, however, you will need leverage to score a win. As an old judo master said: that one does not fall in a bout means that one is not beaten; it doesn't mean that you've won.

By avoiding a fall, you've hung on for another round or another day—or another few seconds in an actual match. But in order to win, you need to take your opponent to the mat. And that's where leverage comes into play.

In judo, your opponent's body becomes a lever in your hands. In judo strategy, a competitor's assets, partners and rivals can all play a similar role. By leveraging your opponent's assets, you can transform a competitor's strengths into sources of weakness. Similarly, by leveraging your opponent's partners, you can turn an opponent's allies into brakes on his ability to respond. Finally, by leveraging your opponent's competitors, you can confront a rival with a double challenge: first deciding to co-operate with his competitors and then convincing them to co-operate with him.

Technique No. 8: Leverage Your Opponent's Assets

It may sound trite, but a company's greatest assets can often become its greatest liabilities. Whether intangible, like brand names and intellectual property, or tangible, like property and plant, "assets collect risks around them in one form or another," as Michael Dell, Dell Computer's chairman and CEO has said. Anything that represents a significant investment can become a barrier to change. And by exploiting these barriers, you can find the leverage you need to win.

In implementing this technique, your goal is to find moves that shift your opponents' assets to the other side of the ledger, as Sega did by leveraging Nintendo's investments in technology and marketing in the early 1990s. At the beginning of the decade, Nintendo dominated the U.S. home video game market with an 80 per cent share to Sega's seven per cent. Yet three years later, the two companies were locked in a dead heat.

Sega owed much of its success to two deft judo strategy moves. In hardware, it leveraged Nintendo's near-monopoly in eight-bit technology by launching faster, 16-bit machines. In software, it leveraged Nintendo's brand equity by targeting an older, hipper audience with game titles containing generous doses of sex and gore.

Both moves turned Nintendo's investments into hostages: forcing the company to decide between destroying its own assets (by matching Sega's moves) and losing share (by failing to respond). If Nintendo brought out its own 16-bit machine, it would accelerate the cannibalisation of its highly profitable eight-bit business. Similarly, by following Sega into the teen and adult market, Nintendo would undercut its image as a trustworthy, family-entertainment brand.

Faced with this dilemma, Nintendo froze. It took two years to update its hardware and even

Anything that represents a significant investment can become a barrier to change. And by exploiting these barriers, you can find the leverage you need to win.

longer to revamp its image by issuing unsanitised versions of games like Mortal Kombat. In the meantime, Sega forged ahead, capturing 50 per cent of the market by 1993.

Sega used leverage to give itself a short-term boost. Once Nintendo resigned itself to destroying its own assets, Sega's leverage lost its force. But in other contexts, leverage can do more than impose a one-time hit. It can also make it difficult for an opponent to compete effectively, even after he's made the decision to match an attack. Delta and United found this to be true, for example, when they tried to fight back against Southwest Airlines, which also used leverage to underpin its attack.

The Texas-based airline rose to prominence thanks to an interlocking set of policies—smaller airports, no connecting flights, no assigned seating, no meals, and an all-737 fleet—that made it possible to slash costs to the bone and keep fares 50 per cent to 60 per cent below competitors' rates. The major carriers might try to match Southwest's fares on selected routes, but only at the cost of cannibalising their own sales. Moreover, even if they were willing to make this sacrifice, Southwest's rivals were at a permanent disadvantage in competing head-to-head. They could never match Southwest's profitability if they charged the same prices due to the cost of maintaining the assets—the big-city terminals, complex reservations systems, and mixed fleets—that had originally underwritten their strength.

> *By 1999 consumers could choose from nearly 3,000 PlayStation titles, more than 10 times the number available for Nintendo 64, and Sony had sold more than 50 million PlayStations.*

Technique No. 9: Leverage Your Opponent's Partners

In addition to investing in valuable assets, many powerful competitors have built up networks of suppliers, distributors and "complementors" who are a significant source of strength. But by exploiting differences among them, you can turn a rival's partners into false friends. Using the old tactic of divide and conquer, sow dissension within the opposing camp. Set old allies at odds by creating situations where their interests are no longer aligned. You may have to look carefully but on close inspection even the most solid-looking bloc is likely to yield up a fissure you can exploit.

Back in the 1930s, Pepsi-Cola used this technique to pose its first successful challenge to Coke. By offering consumers "12 full ounces" (in the words of the once-ubiquitous jingle) for the same price as a six-and-one-half ounce Coke, Pepsi turned Coca-Cola's army of franchised bottlers—who had millions of dollars invested in six-and-one-half ounce bottles—into a force that helped significantly delay Coke's response.

While Pepsi found leverage in its rival's dependence on its bottlers, Sony took advantage of its competitors' efforts to dominate their partners, using a divide-and-conquer strategy to seize the lead in home video games in the second half of the 1990s. When Sony entered the market, Nintendo and Sega were accustomed to keeping partners on a tight leash, charging steep royalties and allowing only a limited number of independent developers to produce games for their machines.

In addition to allowing them to control game quality, this approach ensured that Nintendo and Sega would be able to keep a healthy share of the games market for themselves.

However, this strategy also created an opening for Sony to hold its competitors hostage to their own success. Rather than dictate to games developers, Sony gave them free rein, making PlayStation development tools widely available and cutting licensing fees. As a result, by 1999 consumers could choose from nearly 3,000 PlayStation titles, more than 10 times the number available for Nintendo 64, and Sony had sold more than 50 million PlayStations, generating over a billion dollars in profit in a single year.

Technique No. 10: Leverage Your Opponent's Competitors

Compared to the first two leverage techniques, this one sounds like child's play. What could be easier and more natural than allowing your competitor's competitors to wear him down? After all, as the old saying has it, "the enemy of my enemy is my friend." But judo strategists don't just sit back and let someone else do the job. By staying on the offensive you can craft a strategy using an opponent's competitors that he'll be hard-pressed to match.

There are many ways to leverage an opponent's competitors. You can add value on top of his competitors' products, as Netscape did by developing software that ran on UNIX, the chief competitor to Microsoft's industrial-strength Windows NT. You can build coalitions with his competitors, a tactic that JVC used to beat Sony, a much stronger company, in the race to set standards in the market for VCRs. Or you can serve as a distributor for his competitors, as Charles Schwab has done to powerful effect.

In the early 1990s, Schwab decided to become a major player in the mutual fund business. Senior executives at the discount brokerage knew that they lacked the resources to compete head-to-head with entrenched opponents like Fidelity by launching their own funds. However, by rewriting the rules of fund distribution, Schwab could take a big bite out of Fidelity's business.

Schwab's innovation was to make mutual fund transactions free. Rather than collect commissions from customers, Schwab's OneSource, which launched in July 1992, charged fund families a fee of 25 basis points on invested assets. Fidelity, in an impressive demonstration of strategic flexibility, soon matched Schwab's move. In July 1993, the mutual fund giant, which had been operating its own multifamily fund supermarket since mid-1989, eliminated transactions fees on 195 competitor-run funds. Nonetheless, due to Schwab's continuing leverage, Fidelity's third-party fund distribution remained a fraction of Schwab's.

Many fund companies were slow to join forces with Fidelity. As a senior executive at Invesco told *The New York Times* in 1994, "We don't sell our funds through Fidelity. It goes to a competitive issue. Their interest is in selling customers Fidelity funds." (Invesco later rethought its position and signed on.) In addition, competitors were unhappy about Fidelity's ability to monopolise communications with customers—a sacrifice that Schwab made more palatable by declining to offer its own actively managed funds.

But the biggest brakes on the growth of Fidelity's supermarket came from within Fidelity, where executives were keenly aware that every dollar taken in by another fund family was, to some extent, at their expense. As a result, backers of third-party distribution often found themselves on the losing side of battles over strategy, and Fidelity's FundsNetwork was unable to copy some of Schwab's most successful moves, such as the Mutual Fund Select List, a quarterly list of recommended funds that based its picks on a combination of risk and return.

By the end of the decade, Fidelity had overcome some of its internal resistance. In fact, for a few fund families, Fidelity was outselling OneSource. Yet from Schwab's perspective, this was a win-win situation. As long as Fidelity held back, Schwab could count on the lead. But when Fidelity put its muscle behind third-party distribution, Schwab would still gain.

As one Schwab executive pointed out: "If we force Fidelity to offer third-party mutual funds at 25 basis points instead of 125 basis points [the fee Fidelity collected on in-house funds], they have fewer bullets in their cannon to aim our way."

Conclusion: Judo Strategy in Action

In this article, we've analysed judo strategy as a series of individual techniques. This approach has two advantages. Treating each technique in isolation makes it easier to identify both the similarities and the differences in how various companies have put it to work. In addition, this approach gives us the opportunity to suggest judo strategy's range by profiling 15 companies in nearly as many industries.

However, without two important caveats, this discussion would be incomplete.

First, although we've focused on illustrating individual techniques, the most effective judo strategists rely on a combination of different techniques and principles. The puppy dog ploy, for example, becomes much more effective when used in conjunction with defining the competitive space and follow through fast—as a more extended discussion of Palm Computing would show.

Similarly, when it comes to the core judo strategy principles, at any one time, one of the three may play a particularly important role. In the early days, before the contours of the competitive landscape have been fully defined, movement is often the principle most critical to success. Balance takes over as competitors start to pay attention and pre-

> *The most effective judo strategists rely on a combination of different techniques and principles.*

pare to attack. And finding and applying leverage usually become crucial once you aim to knock a serious competitor down.

Winning over the long run, however, requires you to master a much larger portfolio of judo techniques. A true master of judo strategy must possess a rich repertoire of skills while at the same time being constantly prepared to learn new ways to win.

Our second caveat picks up on this point. By delineating 10 core techniques, we've tried to make the concepts of movement, balance, and leverage more concrete. But it would be a mistake to see this menu of choices as a definitive account of judo strategy. No listing can capture the potential richness of this approach.

At its heart, judo strategy is about developing a deep understanding of your competitors and espying the potential weaknesses that lurk among their strengths. This is no science. There are no easy formulas for victory. Instead, judo strategy demands discipline, creativity and the flexibility to mix and match techniques. But the power and promise of this approach are equal to the investment it demands, for by mastering the principles behind judo strategy, you can use your competitors' strength to bring them down.

Resources

Brandenburger, A. and Nalebuff, B. (1996) *Co-opetition,* New York, Doubleday.
Cusumano, M. A. and Yoffie D. B. (1998) *Competing on Internet Time: Lessons from Netscape and Its Battle with Microsoft,* New York, Free Press.
Dell, M. (1998) The Power of Virtual Integration, *Harvard Business Review,* 76, 2.

Drucker, P. (1985) *Innovation and Entrepreneurship: Practice and Principles,* New York, Harper & Row.

Fulford, B. (1999) Leisure Killer Sequel, *Forbes,* April 5.

Gelman, J. R. and Salop, S. C. (1983) Judo Economics: Capacity Limitation and Coupon Competition, *Rand Journal of Economics,* 14, 2.

Posner, B. (1993) Targeting the Giant, *Inc,* 15, 10.

Rivkin, J. W. (2000) Dogfight Over Europe: Ryanair (A), Boston, Harvard Business School.

Tedlow, R. (1996) *New and Improved: The Story of Mass Marketing in America,* Boston, Harvard Business School Press.

Tomiki, K. (1959) *Judo,* Tokyo, Japan Travel Bureau.

Wayne, L. (1994) The Next Giant in Mutual Funds? *The New York Times,* 20 March.

Yerkow, C. (1942) *Modern Judo: The Complete Ju-Jutsu Library,* Harrisburg, The Military Service Publishing Co.

READING

9

Controlling International Expansion

Freek Vermeulen
London Business School

Despite the apparently inexorable march of globalization, many firms struggle for long periods to make their foreign ventures a success. Sometimes they fail altogether. This article argues that the key to success is to stay in control of the process of internationalization. To achieve this, firms need to follow a set of basic principles that will cause their expansion to unfold in a consistent pattern. They should build on the company's existing knowledge base, give priority to expansion via greenfield investment (not acquisition), avoid home-grown mental inertia, and match the pace of their expansion with their capacity to assimilate.

Direct investment in foreign countries continues to rise and will soon reach over a trillion dollars per annum, according to United Nations forecasts. But the performance of firms outside their domestic borders is decidedly mixed. Some firms achieve huge profit gains while others seem to accumulate mounting losses.

Consider Ahold, a large retailer from the Netherlands, which has successfully concentrated on operating high-quality supermarkets. About a decade ago, Ahold decided to expand abroad. It targeted the United States, where it acquired TOPS markets and, later, continued to grow through the takeover of chains such as Stop & Shop and Giant Landover. Today, turnover in the United States alone is over $20bn, representing 60 percent of the company's total sales. The company also set up operations in a number of countries in Latin America, and in Southern and Eastern Europe, all of them profitable. Recently, it has set foot in the Far East. The share price has tripled over the last five years.

Around the same time, HBG, another large company from the Netherlands, also decided to expand abroad. HBG had built up superior technological skills in the area of construction works, dredging, civil and maritime engineering. It started ambitiously, acquiring large companies in various countries, and especially in Germany. HBG, however, has been struggling with its affiliates ever since, forced to report huge losses on foreign operations year after year, giving its shareholders no increase in share price at all. Finally, HBG terminated many of its foreign ventures.

Why is one company so successful while another one, in comparable circumstances, fails big? To answer this question, I collected data on the foreign expansion of 25 Dutch multinationals—including Ahold and HBG—and analyzed them using various statistical techniques. From these analyses, a remarkable conclusion emerged. It was not that the unsuccessful companies like HBG had made bad individual decisions: considered in isolation their decisions made good sense and were generally well thought through. The problem consisted in how these decisions related to one another: all of them were treated as *individual* moves. Successful companies like Ahold, by contrast, revealed clear and consistent patterns in their expansion over time.

Why do firms need to expand by means of a consistent pattern, rather than through individual, ad-hoc ventures? A strange, foreign country requires a firm to adopt many new skills and develop additional knowledge. In this article, I argue that these new skills and additional knowledge can be obtained and fully exploited only if a firm expands systematically. Each step must follow logically from the prior one. If treated in isolation, a firm will not be able to grasp the new experiences presented by a foreign venture and, as a consequence, will not be able to manage it.

Firms have to expand following a logical path, where established affiliates act as stepping-stones from which to launch further expansions.

Therefore, firms have to expand following a logical path, where established affiliates act as stepping-stones from which to launch further expansions (see also Yip *et al.* 1998).

Does this mean that a firm needs to plan ahead its entire path of international expansion? Certainly not. The dynamics of the international arena require a firm to be flexible in responding to opportunities and threats when and wherever they emerge. Instead, what a firm needs to do, when assessing its (next) foreign venture, is to follow a number of basic rules. These principles, that serve as "footholds" for international market entry, will restrain a young internationalizing firm from overburdening its capacity to learn, and will cause an expansion path to unfold in a consistent and coherent manner. My research revealed a series of four rules, summarized in the figure.

Build on the Company's Existing Knowledge Base

The first principle when setting up a subsidiary in a foreign country is to establish the venture based on what the company already knows. This means that the firm should try to minimize everything that is new about a venture, on top of the unfamiliar circumstances created by the fact that the venture in taking place in a strange country.

It is easy to underestimate the number of things that one does not know about doing business in another country. Cultural differences, language barriers, infrastructure, institutional and legislative differences, different consumer preferences, competitors with a different repertoire, and so forth. Together they form what is often referred to as "the liability of foreignness"; a foreign company has a fundamental disadvantage compared to its local competitors, who do know all these things.

Hence, if a firm wants to beat its competitors, it needs something—some competence, resource, or skill—that helps it to overcome the liability of foreignness. Therefore,

Successful International Expansion: Four Steps

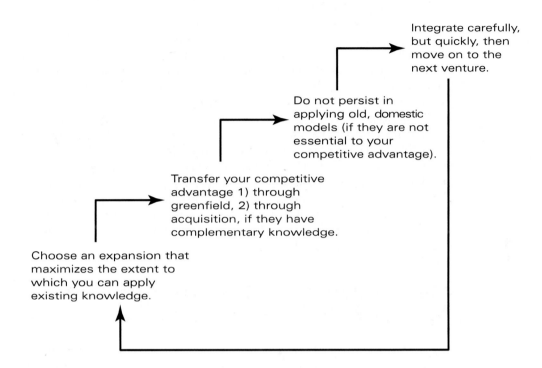

Integrate carefully, but quickly, then move on to the next venture.

Do not persist in applying old, domestic models (if they are not essential to your competitive advantage).

Transfer your competitive advantage 1) through greenfield, 2) through acquisition, if they have complementary knowledge.

Choose an expansion that maximizes the extent to which you can apply existing knowledge.

when a company seeks to expand abroad it should identify its strongest competitive advantage and select the country where this can best be applied.

Ahold, for instance, first expanded abroad in the supermarket business. This was sensible. A company's best bet is usually in its core business. Only after getting to know how to operate in its core business in the new country with all of its idiosyncrasies (in this case the United States), can a firm start to conquer adjoining markets. Now that Ahold has learned how to manage supermarkets in the United States, it is moving into online ordering—for example through the acquisition of the internet grocer Peapod—and business-to-business deliveries—for example through the recent acquisition of US Foodservice.

Moreover, a company's best opportunity usually lies in a country that is culturally similar to its home market. It is here that its competitive advantage is most likely to catch on. A major temporary employment agency from the Netherlands, for example, based its competitive advantage on its ability to operate in close co-operation with unions, employers, and legislators. One of its first ventures, in Russia, did not become a success. The institutional framework in Russia appeared so different that it did not support the application of a Dutch-grown competitive advantage. Indeed, research indicates that companies that sequentially enter countries with increasing cultural distance outperform companies that take large leaps into the unknown (Barkema *et al* 1996). Organizations need to gradually build up their capacity to operate abroad.

Market knowledge is not the only area where firms should carefully build on their existing capabilities. Partnering is another one. Often, when firms want to set foot in a foreign market, they decide to do it through a joint venture. They figure: "We have the knowledge about the product and the business, but lack the skills to operate in this country. They have the knowledge about the local market, but could use some keen production skills." And forces are joined.

Partnerships might work. However, they often don't. It is easy to overlook that partnering is a skill in itself. According to the chairman of Corning Glass, partnering skills include "the ability to cope with the constant compromise and give-and-take that successful joint ventures require," and the ability, when necessary, to "sit back and let someone else be in the driver's seat." Partnering is never easy. But partnering with a firm from a strange foreign culture is particularly intricate.

A joint venture with a local partner will work only if the firm has a lot of experience co-operating—perhaps in its home country—or when the firm is already familiar with the foreign market. If a firm lacks both types of experience, it is a hazardous enterprise (Barkema *et al* 1997). For example, some time ago, Peugeot saw itself forced to wind down its joint ventures in both India and China. Yet, the failure of these ventures did not come as a surprise: Peugeot was neither used to sharing control over its manufacturing plants, nor did it have much experience in the region. If co-operating with a foreign partner is not related to anything an organization has dealt with before, it will not be able to grasp what it takes to make the venture work.

Make Greenfield Investment, Not Acquisition, the Default Option

A greenfield investment forces you to exactly define what is likely to give you your competitive advantage.

Once decided what sort of a subsidiary the company wants and where—given its current knowledge base—the second rule is to first consider building it up from scratch. Only if a company feels it is in need of something that it cannot develop itself should it consider taking over an existing firm. Making an acquisition on the basis that "I will turn it around, infuse it with my own superior knowledge, and boost its performance" is a perilous affair.

Often, when managers have set their mind on a certain market, they start searching for a suitable acquisition candidate. Why? Because a greenfield operation can be superficially more intimidating than an acquisition. Greenfield involves building from scratch. This is laborious, may take many years to come to fruition (perhaps beyond retirement), and looks like a risky undertaking.

There are two reasons why a company should first consider the feasibility of greenfield rather than acquisition when expanding into a new foreign market. First a greenfield investment forces you to exactly define what is likely to give you your competitive advantage. Second, a competitive advantage is often much more difficult to exploit through an acquisition.

Consider the position of Cisco Systems when planning its biggest foreign expansion ever, in Amsterdam. The affiliate is meant to enable Cisco to further apply and exploit its current capabilities in the European market. For this purpose, Cisco does not acquire another company; it builds up the entire affiliate from scratch, including the hiring and training of about 5,000 people, the entire infrastructure, and accommodation. Doing this enables Cisco to incorporate its firm-specific advantages from the outset, which is grounded in a complex combination of technology, culture, and management practice.

The Research

The propositions put forward in this paper are based on research over the past five years on the development paths of 25 Dutch multinationals. All the foreign expansions of these firms during the last three decades—acquisitions, greenfield investment, and joint ventures, a total of 829 cases—were analyzed in terms of a number of indicators, such as their success rate, timing, business domain, and geographical location. In addition, these indicators were related to the overall performance of the expanding companies. What resulted were clear patterns of (un)successful expansion. The results are supplemented with insights from the research of others who have uncovered similar patterns for American and Japanese firms (Chang 1995, Li 1995).

Building up a new affiliate stimulates a firm to define what the precise basis of its company advantage is, and forces it to translate and transfer it to the foreign setting. Yet, doing so will also clarify what it is the firm should *not* transfer to the subsidiary. As a result, it becomes clear what the local affiliate needs to do to adapt to local circumstances (Das 1993). Yahoo!'s webpages, for example, have a similar design everywhere, and they offer the same services, but the content is carefully tuned to local needs. Likewise for Compuserve and, nowadays, Amazon. These companies have created foreign subsidiaries that are based on the same business concept and technology, but where local employees tailor content, marketing, and customer service.

Acquisition, on the other hand, is a daunting operation to transfer competitive advantages to a strange, foreign market. Changing an acquired organization is always a complicated and lengthy process even in a domestic context—one that is often underestimated. Trying to change an established company from an unfamiliar culture in such a way that it can be infused with the (superior) technology and work methods of an alien, acquiring firm is far more so: integration problems will grow exponentially. HBG found this out during its (failed) attempts to make its German subsidiary profitable. A foreign firm simply lacks the in-depth knowledge of the local context necessary to make such a complicated process work.

So, when should a firm acquire? An acquisition *can* be very useful, but only if done because it has something to offer that the expanding firm cannot feasibly develop by itself. For example, the only reason why Cisco engages in acquisitions is to obtain new capabilities. Likewise, a foreign company should not be acquired to change it into the spitting image of the acquiring firm by installing all sorts of home-grown methods and routines. Then you are better-off with greenfield. It should be acquired precisely because of its own, current capabilities: the marketing knowledge to reach specific local customers, the human resource skills necessary to attract and manage a local workforce, or the connections with local government, suppliers, and institutions. Thus, an acquisition in a strange country should never be done out of superiority, but solely from a mind-set to learn from the acquire (Vermeulen and Barkema 2001a).

Ahold, the Dutch multinational retailer, has been a favorite of analysts and investors on the Amsterdam Stock Exchange for many years, largely because of its remarkably successful acquisition record. Ahold, however, does not set out to take over underperforming firms. As Cees van der Hoeven, CEO of Ahold puts it: "We don't fancy poorly running companies, but want companies with good management and good performance." The attitude is to engage in an exchange of knowledge, and to learn from each other: "Our people are trained not to say 'we know everything better.' Rather they are expected to learn from it."

And this might work. A diversity of subsidiaries within one organization may prove to be fertile soil for the development of innovative ideas and competencies (Barkema and Vermeulen 1998). The different subsidiaries may learn from each other what their specific setting has inspired them to do best. Certain strengths, developed in a local setting inspired by specific circumstances, may prove to be of value in other parts of the organization. Ahold, for instance, found that Dutch supermarkets had developed superior skills regarding the efficient use of shop-space and shelving. This is not surprising given the smallness of the shops in the Dutch cities and communities. American supermarkets appeared to have superior skills in managing customer relations, because of the service-oriented nature of the U.S. market. U.S. supermarkets now adopt Dutch-grown routines on the use of shop-space, while Dutch supermarkets adopt U.S. routines on the maintenance of customer relations, such as the use of customer-cards.

In sum, I do *not* argue against all use of acquisitions in foreign expansion; I caution that foreign acquisitions rarely work out if they concern underperforming companies that are expected to boost their performance through the adoption of the acquirer's work methods. If mere expansion and exploitation of existing competencies is what you have in mind, you are much better off with greenfield investments. Acquisitions may succeed, however, if one adopts the attitude to learn from them, and seeks to engage in a mutual exchange of knowledge.

Avoid Home-Grown Mental Inertia

Once established, a foreign subsidiary is often granted quite a lot of autonomy. Sometimes it is attached to the parent company as a separate unit or division. Some practices may be transferred to the affiliate, and financial controls will be implemented, but considerable freedom is given to it, and its initial financial performance is treated with tolerance. This stage is referred to as "the honeymoon": things are new, things are exciting, and we are of good cheer.

What happens when the honeymoon is over? After a while, when performance is consistently below expectations, top management at headquarters begins to wonder what is wrong, and sets out to investigate, often to discover that the foreign subsidiary does not quite follow company prescriptions on how to produce, manage, and market.

The result is a foregone conclusion. The way things are organized and managed in the home country are the result of years of experience, and have brought the firm (and its directors) success and prosperity. Hence, top management takes control. It orders the subsidiary to clearly follow company regulations, and to produce and market following the proven formula. New management may be sent to the affiliate and new, strict directives will be issued. This time, they think, we will make it work.

But often it doesn't, as BMW found when it tried to impose its working methods onto Rover, or as Lincoln Electric discovered persistently when it tried to transfer its incentive system to various countries. Despite the considerable efforts and strict procedures, performance does not pick up. What is worse, it may actually drop, sometimes quite dramatically. What is going wrong? What prevents the old models from working?

For sure, the company is trying hard enough. But it is doing the wrong things. It is trying to apply beliefs and practices from its own home country in a strange foreign setting. The old home-grown models simply do not work in the new situation. Incentive schemes from one country may not work in another, due to cultural differences; supplier schedules may not be workable in a country with a different infrastructure;

and marketing campaigns may not appeal to people from a different culture. What is more, trying harder will just make things worse.

Consider the example of a German bank that set up a subsidiary in Singapore. It had prepared well, for example issuing clear descriptions of the financial products and services to be brought to the market, and how. What it had overlooked is that the Singaporean market is in many respects very different from the German one. The employees in the subsidiary, however, found this out quickly. They turned to sell their products through local intermediaries, who helped patch things up and make services more in tune with the local situation. Despite this palliative, the financial performance of the subsidiary was lagging behind expectations at German headquarters. Yet, headquarters' response was not to question the effectiveness of its products in the Singaporean market, but to issue the directive that all use of intermediaries was to be stopped.

> *Trying harder will just make things worse.*

The example represents a typical response for an internationalizing company in distress, and a sort of organizational behavior well known to management researchers. It is related to a phenomenon known as "the success trap"; when successful organizations are confronted with the failure of their established models, they do not respond by developing new ones, but by myopically trying to extend their existing ones (Hastings 1999, Sull 1999). But this actually aggravates the situation. In trying to dig themselves out of the hole, they just deepen it. Firms often set up foreign subsidiaries with the idea of further applying and exploiting what they have been doing so well in their own country. This is a good idea: they *should* build on their existing knowledge base. But it does not mean that they should do everything exactly the same as in their home country. A different country means a different context, and in a different context one should do things differently. If the established models do not result in the same positive performance as back home—which is far from unlikely—the firm should not respond by trying harder, by taking control, and becoming stricter than ever. Its response should be to question and investigate what aspects of "the old way of doing things" can and should be preserved and which ones should be altered and adapted to the local circumstances (e.g., James 1994).

How can companies avoid failures? The first answer is that they can't. At least, not entirely. And that is an important lesson in itself. You can't learn to ride a bicycle and expect to never fall off. Likewise, you can't expand abroad and expect to get it right the first and every time. Organizations venturing abroad should be well prepared. This includes having the leeway to make mistakes and fail. Firms should reckon with foreign ventures not working out, at least not immediately. This also implies having the financial means to handle failure, and to forgo returns for some period of time.

But although organizations will not be able to avoid all mistakes, they are, of course, hoping to minimize their probability. The way to do that is to maximize learning from prior experiences. That is what the principles described in this article help to do. They make actions and experiences interpretable. As such, firms should try to avoid failures by learning from them. *If* a mistake is made, the firm should carefully reflect, question, and interpret what caused it to happen. Too often, failures are denied, with "external circumstances" being held accountable. If failure occurs, it should be treated as an opportunity for learning. It may tell you how things should not be done and, hence, how you should do things differently the next time.

> *Too often, failures are denied, with "external circumstances" being held accountable.*

Match the Pace of Expansion with the Capacity to Assimilate

The final principle when expanding abroad is to carefully assimilate the subsidiary and, hence, not expand faster than you are able to assimilate. Firms should realize that a multinational organization is not something you can (quickly) assemble, and that an international posture is not a position you simply choose and take up. A profitable multinational firm is a diverse yet coherent system, which consists of different, interacting elements. This is something you have to build one step at a time (Bartlett and Ghoshal 1989, Vermeulen and Barkema 2001b).

How much can you do? Consider Randstad. Randstad is the biggest temporary employment agency in the Netherlands (which has the most advanced temporary employment market in the world). Randstad has been very successful in its international expansion—a reason why its share price is now five times what it was five years ago. Randstad selects a country, penetrates it through a greenfield or an acquisition (dependent on local circumstances and the availability of high-quality candidates), and subsequently invests in its organic growth. When the company has established a strong foothold in the foreign market, it moves on to the next one. Moreover, it doesn't stop. It has upheld its pace for many years.

What makes Randstad successful is focus and patience. Entering a new market takes effort and time. The organization needs to invest in it, in terms of managerial attention and finance. Simultaneously expanding into a large number of countries scatters these efforts, which causes the subsidiaries to lack critical mass for too long. This is also true if one enters a country in very different lines of business at the same time. There is just so much an organization and its management team can grasp and accomplish. An organization cannot integrate large numbers of new elements *and* keep up its performance. It has to be able to assimilate them one by one.

Integration is necessary. If you do not integrate a company, you cannot learn from it, and if it doesn't get assimilated, it cannot benefit from you. In addition to the idea that an acquisition must have new knowledge to offer, Cisco uses three other criteria to judge whether a company is a suitable candidate for takeover:

- It must be relatively small;
- It must be comparable in organizational culture; and
- It must be physically close to one of its existing affiliates.

All these rules of thumb exist to smooth the company's integration process. Likewise for Ahold and Randstad. These companies pay great attention to the careful integration of their newly formed foreign subsidiaries.

HBG on the other hand, the Dutch hi-tech construction company, made a big acquisition in Germany. But it left the new subsidiary largely autonomous (it even had its own foreign operations)—and it is not difficult to see why: the integration process of a large acquisition can lame an entire firm. The result, however, was unsatisfactory. The German affiliate never got to learn HBG's skills, and HBG never got to grips with the German venture. Currently, HBG is assimilating the parts of the subsidiary that it did not divest.

Certainly, you can quickly buy and start up a number of foreign subsidiaries. But for them to co-operate, interact, and benefit from each other as a coherent, integrated, international organization is something else again. It simply takes time and effort to assimilate newly formed subsidiaries. What successfully expanding companies such as

Footholds for International Expansion

Build on the Company's Existing Knowledge Base

- Look for the country that most resembles yours
- Let the new country be the only thing that is new about the venture
- Expand in a familiar business
- Use a (local) partner only if you have experience with partnering in your own country

Make Greenfield Investment, Not Acquisition, the Default Option

- Grow through greenfield investments if you seek to transfer and exploit a complex competitive advantage
- Do not acquire companies which you have to change extensively
- Explicitly set out to learn from each other—acquisition from acquirer *and* vice versa.

Avoid Home-Grown Mental Inertia

- Failures will be inevitable
- Do not automatically blame failure on external circumstances
- Interpret failure as an indication that you are doing the wrong things, rather than as an indication that you are not doing things well enough
- Question whether your old models are entirely appropriate in the new setting
- Adapt home-grown models to the local setting

Match Expansion Pace with Capacity to Assimilate

- Don't be seduced by opportunities in many countries; do not scatter your efforts, but focus your capacity to expand
- Treat subsidiaries as elements of a system; add them one by one, assimilate them carefully
- Expand at a constant, rhythmic pace
- Don't set too fast a pace

Cisco, Ahold, and Randstad have in common is that they focus their efforts on a reasonably-sized venture, assimilate it, and then move on, without losing momentum.

Conclusion

When a firm decides that it wants to grow beyond the borders of its home country, it needs clear principles that will guide it through the expansion process. Setting up ventures in strange countries in a brash and precipitate manner will inevitably lead to failure (Monti and Yip 2000). The firm will simply not be able to interpret its experiences, and improve its actions in turn. This may ultimately force a firm to withdraw from foreign operations entirely, leaving it with a heavy debt burden, if it survives the adventure at all.

The principles described in this article and summarized in the box can assist a firm to make consistent choices on the time, place, and mode of its international ventures. Following these steps or "footholds" will constitute a coherent pattern, where one venture is the logical ramification of the prior one. This will enable a firm to grasp the challenges it faces, and keep it from straining its current abilities, thus putting it on a path of progressing international growth.

Together, the four principles comprise a logic for international expansion. They describe how to grow as a young multinational organization. Setting up ventures in a strange foreign country coerces a firm to learn new things. New models have to be adopted and hence, old domestic ones unlearned. Therefore, an international firm has to expand incrementally, forming and adding elements in a clear and ongoing fashion, building on, and incorporating its experiences. In this manner, a company gradually masters how to operate and prosper abroad.

References

Barkema, H. G., Bell, J. H. J., and J. M. Pennings (1996) Foreign entry, cultural barriers, and learning, *Strategic Management Journal,* 17, pp151–166.

Barkema, H. G. and Vermeulen, F. (1998) International expansion through start-up or acquisition: A learning perspective, *Academy of Management Journal,* 41, pp7–26.

Barkema, H. G., Shenkar, O., Vermeulen, F., and Bell, J. H. J. (1997) Working abroad, working with others: How firms learn to operate international joint ventures, *Academy of Management Journal,* 40, pp426–442.

Bartlett C. A., and Ghoshal, S. (1989) *Managing across borders: The transnational solution,* Cambridge: Harvard Business School Press.

Chang, S. J. (1995) International expansion strategy of Japanese firms: Capability building through sequential entry, *Academy of Management Journal,* 38, pp383–407.

Das, G. (1993) Local memoirs of a global manager, *Harvard Business Review,* 71, March–April, pp38–47.

Hastings, D. F. (1999) Lincoln Electric's harsh lessons from international expansion, *Harvard Business Review,* 77, May–June, pp163–178.

James, B. (1994) EuroDisney throws the book away, *International Herald Tribune,* October 20, pp9–11.

Li, J. (1995) Foreign entry and survival: Effects of strategic choices on performance in international markets, *Strategic Management Journal,* 16, pp333–351.

Monti, J. A., and Yip, G. S. (2000) Taking the high road when going international, *Business Horizons,* July–August, pp65–72.

Sull, D. N. (1999) Why good companies go bad, *Harvard Business Review,* 77, July–August, pp42–52.

Vermeulen, F., and Barkema, H. G. (2001a) Learning through acquisitions, *Academy of Management Journal,* 44,1.

Vermeulen, F., and Barkema, H. G. (2001b) Pace, rhythm, and scope: Process dependence in building a profitable multinational corporation, *Strategic Management Journal,* (forthcoming)

Yip, G. S., Biscarri, J. G., and Monti, J. A. (1998) The role of the internationalization process in the performance of newly internationalizing firms, *Journal of International Marketing,* 8, pp10–35.

READING 10

Outsourcing: A Core or Non-Core Strategic Management Decision?

Jussi Heikkilä,
Helsinki University of Technology

Carlos Cordon,
International Institute for Management Development

▪ *Practicing managers often use the idea of core competence as one of the principal guidelines for making decisions about outsourcing. Managers of large corporations commonly support their outsourcing decisions with the familiar argument that 'We keep core competences in-house, and we outsource non-core activities.'*

▪ *This paper questions the usefulness of the 'non-core competence' concept for practical decision making. It reviews and discusses a comprehensive list of drivers for outsourcing decisions as well as the potential risks related to outsourcing initiatives.*

▪ *Instead of taking the simplistic 'core or non-core' approach, the paper suggests a more creative way to evaluate a larger variety of competencies. The business contexts of four successful companies are described and several examples of their outsourcing/insourcing decisions are presented.*

▪ *Examples show that poor implementation undermines decisions that are based on even the most imaginative definition of competence structures. Successful outsourcing depends on the outsourcing relationship well after the decision is made.*

The oft-heard justification for outsourcing decisions is: 'We keep core competencies in-house, and we outsource non-core activities.' However, the question remains: what is 'core' and what is 'non-core'? Typical managerial answers are 'Well, that depends on how we define our business.' Or 'Obviously, if we plan to continue this activity in-house, it should be a core competence.' Granted, the process of defining a company's core competence is important but the non-core realm also offers a wide spectrum of choices.

Corporate Dilemmas

Corporations are increasing their outsourcing significantly. The drive to increase shareholder value and focus on core business is pushing companies to continuously assess outsourcing opportunities. In 1997, a survey of large European corporations (Vollmann *et al.,* 1997) revealed that 52 percent of the responding companies expected to increase their levels of outsourcing activity. This is what we saw during the last years of the 1990s. For example, in the electronics and telecommunications industries, the electronics manufacturing services (EMS) providers, such as Solectron, Flextronics, SCI Systems, Jabil Circuit, Celestica, ACT Manufacturing, Plexus, and Sanmina were growing faster than their customers, the major original equipment manufacturers (OEMs) like Dell, Compaq, Sony, Philips, Cisco, Nokia, Motorola, and Ericsson. From 1996 to 2000, the combined capital expenditures of the above-mentioned EMS firms grew eleven-fold, revenues increased almost 400 percent and the annual growth rate of the market capitalization was 87 percent. Solectron alone made 27 acquisitions in 2000.

The year 2001 saw a change in the business cycle of high-tech industries. OEM sales volume growth stopped, which caused scaled-down manufacturing volumes, lay-offs and growing inventories at both the OEMs and EMS. OEMs needed to rethink their outsourcing strategies.

Evaluating and implementing outsourcing decisions are challenging. Many corporations are facing a situation where the very activities they outsource in one business unit are considered fundamental in another (and are therefore not outsourced). Different sets of competencies in similar businesses create among the corporate strategy makers the suspicion that some business units may be misaligned. Line managers face the dual pressures of both making efficient use of resources and resolving the recurring question of whether to outsource or not. The decision to outsource or keep in-house seems, in many cases, to be situation-dependent rather than strategy driven. Therefore, if companies choose to follow the dictum of insourcing core activities and outsourcing non-core activities, they may well end up with either:

Evaluating and implementing outsourcing decisions is challenging.

- Outsourcing too many activities, or
- A tortuous and unhelpful definition of their core competencies that confuses rather than clarifies the outsourcing decision.

Non-Core Activities Require Accurate Classification

Classifying an activity as 'non-core' may lead to serious oversimplification of the complexity of the real business situation. The concept of core competence, as coined by Prahalad and Hamel (1990), is widely used as an essential element in formulating global company strategy and it has proven useful in that process. Prahalad and Doz (1987) use an example of core competence from Honda. The authors of this paper see the internal combustion engine as Honda's core competence, because engines are the common core ingredient of Honda's diversity of products that include cars, motorcycles, lawnmowers, power generators, outboard motors, snowmobiles, snow blowers, and garden tillers, Originally, Prahalad and Hamel developed their core competence concept as an alternative to Strategic Business Unit (SBU) thinking. They criticized the SBU organization format of poor resource allocation because it does not allow diversified multinational corporations to allocate resources to core technologies, distribution, and brand development, all of which can cut across several SBUs.

The core competence concept can help an organization focus on the key strategic actions it needs to take in order to maintain its special expertise. We wish to emphasize however, that classifying an activity as 'non-core' should not be meant to imply or support the argument that 'non-core' equals 'unimportant.' The Honda example clarifies the many-faceted role of 'non-core' activities. During the 1980s, Honda was extremely successful. From 1980 to 1988, the company grew 200 percent. Focusing on the internal combustion engine, the company's core competence was an important factor in this success. Honda established a worldwide reputation for quality, first in motorcycles, and then in automobiles. A slowdown of the motorcycle business in the 1980s encouraged Honda to look to other markets to maintain full use of their production facilities. The company identified outdoor power equipment (OPE) as an appropriate new business opportunity. In many respects, OPE products represented a natural business diversification for Honda. After all, the company had originally been founded in 1948 to produce small internal combustion engines.

How did Honda enter the OPE business? By manufacturing engines and outsourcing the rest? The answer is not that simple. The strength of Honda's products stemmed from its extensive R&D expenditures and its speedy incorporation of cutting-edge technological developments. Honda marketed its products with the aid of extensive advertising and promotion and priced them competitively. Until 1984, Honda lawnmowers bound for the USA had been manufactured in Japan. When U.S. sales reached a level at which it made sense economically to establish a production base in the USA, Honda built a manufacturing plant for engines and lawnmowers in Swepsonville, North Carolina. Honda was also one of the few companies in the OPE industry in the USA that vertically integrated backward into components. In addition to engines the plant made housings, frames and components (Hoffman *et al.,* 1996). Thus Honda did not concentrate on core competencies only and outsource the rest. Instead the company saw good strategic reasons for backward integration.

Honda's quick access to the OPE business can be attributed (in addition to their superiority in engines) to their well-known brand. But manufacturing components also made economic sense. Although making components might not have reflected a core competence, it did allow Honda to reach its objectives *and* do good business.

Reasons to Outsource

If the 'core or non-core' distinction is insufficient, how do managers decide what to outsource? One conceptual framework for understanding the configuration and coordination of a firm's activities is the firm's value chain and its place in the larger stream of activities in the industry's value system (Porter, 1985). Analyzing the firm's value chain reveals the value created by the various activities in its chain. It also reveals how activities are linked to each other and to other activities in the whole value system. The management of the linkages among activities in the system is essential to creating and sustaining competitive advantage.

Outsourcing, the management of virtual organizations, developing supplier networks and partnerships in various industry environments have all been comprehensively researched (Alexander, 1997; Dyer, 1996; Insinga and Werle, 2000; Lambert *et al.*, 1996; Upton and McAfee, 1996). We started building our outsourcing decision-making framework from observations made during case research. According to much of the literature and observations from research on case studies, the most common outsourcing drivers are:

- **Scarcity of capital.** Fast-growing companies often have insufficient capital to fund all the activities they could profitably develop. Outsourcing some activities reduces the capital required.

- **Lack of know-how.** In many cases, other firms know how to perform certain activities better. Lack of knowledge is often related to the difficulty of developing competencies in-house fast enough.

- **Flexibility and the need for quick response or small production.** Some companies specialize in being able to quickly increase production to support the marketplace.

- **Speed or time to market.** In many cases, outsourcing development activities to key suppliers allows a company to bring products to market or enter a new geographical area much faster than they could by doing everything internally.

- **Asset utilization or spare capacity.** Many chemical companies require a minimum level of asset utilization to justify an investment. If this minimum is not reached, production is often outsourced, in some cases even to competitors who have free capacity.

- **Economies of scale.** Personal computer manufacturers used to undertake many more assembly activities internally. Now specialized contract manufacturers carry out assembly for several companies, obtaining economies of scale that a single company could not obtain on its own. As a consequence, the cost of assembly has been reduced significantly.

At the same time, several potential drawbacks to outsourcing initiatives have also become apparent:

- **Transfer of know-how that encourages new competitors.** In the 1980s in order to reduce manufacturing costs, many American businesses outsourced activities to Asian manufacturers, only to see these manufacturers emerge years later as their toughest competitors.

- **Changes in the balance of power in the industry.** IBM's decision in the 1980s to outsource its microprocessor to Intel and its operating system to Microsoft set the destiny of the entire industry for years to come.

- **Dependency, confidentiality and security issues.** For years many oil companies outsourced crewing for their oil tankers. However, after one or two serious accidents, many of these companies decided to use their own crews, making sure that they are properly trained and fully understand their responsibilities.

- **Fear of opportunism.** As companies become increasingly interdependent, transaction costs tend to rise. Frequently the time and resources needed to manage the outsourcing relationship and to clarify contracts and expectations are too exorbitant or too daunting. Such has been the case with many IT outsourcing arrangements where aligning the objectives with the supplier has been extremely difficult.

Most of the above drivers for outsourcing and potential drawbacks are only partially related to the issue of core competence. Many activities that companies perform fall in the 'gray category' of competencies, i.e., they are neither clearly distinctive nor are they clearly unrelated to the main business. Nevertheless, companies still have to answer the fundamental question of what to outsource and what to keep in-house.

Lessons from Practice

Evidence from major manufacturing companies suggests that there is a rich variety of approaches to outsourcing. DuPont, one of the world's biggest producers of polymers, has its largest European manufacturing facilities concentrated in the Benelux region. A wide variety of industries, including consumer electronics and automobile manufacture, use DuPont's high-performance polymers to build plastic components. The manufacturing process itself consists of two major steps: (1) resin creation, a chemical process for creating the polymer from petroleum components, and (2) compounding the physical extrusion process through which the polymer is converted into small pellets sold directly to customers. DuPont has an outstanding record of product research and innovation. The company is renowned for developing proprietary manufacturing processes with the primary objective of producing high volumes at competitive prices.

There is a rich variety of approaches to outsourcing.

In 1996, outsourced activities at DuPont represented a significant proportion of sales in some divisions, yet activities considered core in one part of the business might well have been outsourced in another (Vivanco *et al.,* 1997). In DuPont's polymer business, for instance, the European operation considered that, for both competitive and economical reasons, the compounding of special compounds was a core competence. Not only was a detailed knowledge of the chemical characteristics of the product necessary for carrying out the compounding process efficiently, but DuPont Europe could compound polymers at a lower cost than other companies. However, DuPont Europe had not always had the facilities to carry out all compounding operations in-house. Prior to 1996, they had outsourced part of production. Only recently had the division decided to invest in developing the necessary facilities to be able to undertake all compounding in-house. The situation was different in the USA. There DuPont continued to outsource its compounding activities as U.S. union agreements dictated that all chemical company employees be paid according to the same guidelines. As chemical industry salaries were substantially higher than those paid in a compounding-only company, outsourcing as much as possible made economic sense.

At the same time, a set of more complex outsourcing decisions characterized DuPont's resin-creation business. With small batch sizes where the product was not a proprietary product, DuPont referred its customers directly to an outside supplier and took no responsibility for product quality. However, the company did make an exception for key customers who refused to take products DuPont had not manufactured. In such cases, the company produced small lots in-house. Similarly, DuPont had outside contractors producing its unique products with small sales volumes for key customers. However, the company ensured that the quality was the same as it would have been if the product had been made in-house.

Another example worth noting is recycling. DuPont did not consider recycling a distinctive competence. The company was aware that in the future, legislation might require chemical manufacturers to have recycling capabilities. For this reason they had invested in a recycling plant in the UK but outsourced the operation to a third party. DuPont provided the raw materials and the two companies agreed on yields and performance measures.

Outsourcing some activities allows a company to focus on developing distinctive competencies and increasing flexibility. As a case in point in addition to core competence, DuPont's outsourcing decisions took into consideration factors such as resource costs, as well as how it could best manage the potential risks in the quality of its product and in environmental issues.

Nokia Mobile Phones: Flexibility for Choosing Future Technologies

Nokia Mobile Phones is a major player in an industry characterized by phenomenal growth, rapid technology development and rapid price erosion. During the first half of 1990s, Nokia's value of purchases grew over three times faster than their sales. The price erosion of a mobile phone model could exceed 80 percent in just two years.

Nokia defined its core competence as developing and manufacturing mobile phones (Heikkliä *et al.,* 1998). Product life cycles were short and in order to utilize new technologies, technology leaders in the business had to make considerable progress with each new product generation. In Nokia's core business, technology-related competencies developed rapidly, from distinctive to widely available. The company followed a strategy of *not* being vertically integrated because this could easily lead to having 'parasitic' competencies. Essentially, differentiation meant designing and manufacturing cellular phones *and* finding and co-managing the best suppliers for each product generation. For Nokia, co-managing meant aggressively driving the price and performance characteristics of selected technologies together with their suppliers.

A good example of the user interface is the Nokia 2110 mobile phone. Introduced in 1995, the new phone needed a flexible circuit board assembly, a technology that the company did not possess at the time. In response, Nokia initially outsourced the whole model to one global supplier located in Japan. After some time, however, Nokia decided that it did not want to depend on a single supplier and decided to develop the necessary competence internally. At the same time, Nokia wanted to further increase flexibility and improve local responsiveness by having a regional European supplier. The company therefore decided to subcontract some production to Elcoteq Network, a Finnish contract manufacturer.

The history of the Nokia 2110 is basically the history of Nokia moving from having one global supplier through doing its own production to one of having several regional suppliers working in flexible roles. As the least vertically integrated company in its business, Nokia faced the contradictory challenge of avoiding vulnerability in the competencies that distinguished it from its competition, while at the same time going for the advantages of long-term partnerships with wide geographical focus. Nokia's suppliers had to be able to maintain both the immense growth and the foreseen cost reduction, while at the same time coping with the drop in model prices.

Nokia followed a supply chain strategy that was flexible enough to adjust to the changes in their business environment. Above all, in the rapidly changing business the company wanted to avoid being tied to a wrong technology partner. Partnerships were meant to last for the life of a product and Nokia did not hesitate to aggressively develop their supplier base to meet their regional responsiveness needs. Two types of competencies were involved in the company's outsourcing considerations: (1) protection from potential abuse of a sole supplier and (2) having an essential competence available regionally.

Efficiency and Risk

The fundamental issues in outsourcing decisions are the efficiency of performing the considered activity internally compared to a partner's efficiency and the risk of either keeping or outsourcing the activity. When managers start analyzing the possibility of outsourcing a particular activity, they should give serious thought to how the activity contributes to the overall success of their business. Instead of trying to oversimplify the analysis of whether to outsource or keep an activity, management should take full account of the variety of issues involved in a strategic business decision. We suggest categorizing activities that a company wants to keep in-house as belonging to one of the following three types:

- **Distinctive competencies.** Distinctive competencies are the key capabilities of an organization and invariably the ones that allow it to excel. Examples cited here include Honda's internal combustion engines, DuPont's product design and innovation and proprietary manufacturing processes, and Nokia's design and manufacture of mobile phones, combined with selecting the right technologies for future product generations.

- **Essential competencies.** Essential competencies are the activities the organization needs for sustaining its profitable operations. For DuPont, essential competencies are compounding, resin creation and recycling and, depending on the particular conditions, the company either performs them internally or outsources them. For Nokia, making technologies available globally for the entire operation is essential for their successful growth, but it alone would not distinguish Nokia from their competitors.

- **Protective competencies.** Protective competencies relate to those activities that pose a considerable risk for the success of the whole organization if they are not properly managed. For example, DuPont needs to secure product quality for their customers by keeping some of the manufacturing and Nokia Mobile Phones needs to master flexible circuit board assembly before outsourcing it regionally.

The three competencies can be depicted in a framework to reflect efficiency compared to other companies and risk. **Figure 1** describes this arrangement and thus allows a clearer examination of outsourcing choices.

Our advice for management in making decisions between retaining an activity in-house and outsourcing it, is to follow the following guidelines:

- If the efficiency of the particular operation is high, it is logical to keep the activity in-house, assuming that the company can maintain this efficiency well into the future.

- Risk can be managed by distinctive competence. Examples include firms that have special systems for handling volatile and dangerous materials, with the resulting high profitability. The competence tends to be necessary in the area of high risk,

Figure 1   Efficiency and Risk Considerations in Outsourcing

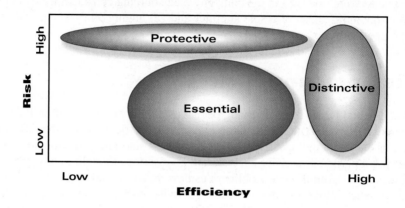

although it might be less desirable from the point of view of efficiency. Keeping a high-risk activity means protecting the firm by controlling the activity better.

- If the operating efficiency is low and the associated risks are also low, the logical action is to outsource the activity. As shown in **Figure 1** this might apply for some essential competencies.

- The main challenge comes when the activity efficiency is low and the risks are high. In this situation management either has to redesign the activity so that either the company's performance becomes more efficient or the risks are reduced. That is, for any activities in the upper left-hand quadrant of **Figure 1,** whether protective or essential, the company needs to redefine the activity to fit in a different quadrant. Thereafter, management can consider other outsourcing alternatives.

This model should be understood as dynamic and activities will move from one category to another over time. Typically, an essential activity can become a target for outsourcing if a competitive supply market develops. The model can serve as the basis for deciding what to outsource, when and how. Essential competencies and protective competencies might be outsourced if an appropriate relation can be created to ensure that the service is available continuously and the risks minimized.

Managing Outsourcing Relationships

The competence dimension of outsourcing decisions needs to be tightly coupled with the issues related to implementing the resulting outsourcing relationships. The following two cases illustrate the point.

Thomas Medical Systems: Higher-Level Purchasing

Thomas Medical Systems, or Thomas (the name of the company is disguised to maintain confidentiality), is a leading supplier of diagnostic imaging systems that used X-ray, magnetic resonance, and ultrasound technologies. The Apollo B product series was the newest addition to the Thomas cardiology product family and included many innovative new features the company had pioneered. The Apollo B was a digital cardiac imaging system that produced high-quality digital images using X-rays combined with exclusive sensor technology. It also incorporated the company's comprehensive approach to X-ray dose management, which provided the tools necessary for cardiologists to optimize the image quality while minimizing the dose applied to the patient.

To develop Apollo B, Thomas had piloted a new way of working with their suppliers. They started by purchasing assemblies rather than individual parts for assembly in-house. The company's intention was to enhance the value chain in order to provide more integrated solutions to hospitals. Making their suppliers responsible for larger assemblies was consistent with this intent and would allow the company to focus their management and financial resources on better serving their customers (Julien *et al.,* 1998).

Thomas wanted to move from purchasing individual parts towards what the company called 'higher-level purchasing.' This shift embodied management's goal of purchasing assemblies in order to reduce the quantity of parts the company had to purchase. Subcontracted assembly was expected to be cheaper than assembling the parts in-house. The fundamental objective was to turn fixed costs into variable costs.

Thomas completed the Apollo B project on time and the market received it well. Although the project came in on budget, the new way of working failed to bring the anticipated savings. In fact, while the overall cost of the system was acceptable, the two outsourced modules exceeded estimated costs by 10–15 percent. Furthermore, members of the project team were unhappy with the overall performance of the project. A lot of time and many resources had been wasted because neither Thomas nor the suppliers had understood the changes needed at the outset.

The strategic intent was directionally correct but, as often happens, the devil was in the detail. For example, the central supplier did not have compatible CAD/CAM systems and they had a different approach to engineering design and database maintenance. Also the company had seriously overestimated the supplier's competence in certain areas, including assembly. The problems were largely attributed to lack of a clear outsourcing policy and the fact that the project team had been developing in parallel both a new product and a new way of working.

As a direct result of their first outsourcing experience, Thomas Medical Systems developed an outsourcing policy that included a number of criteria for defining non-core areas that could be outsourced. The company formed eleven technology clusters that encompassed all the 'non-core' activities for which they would search for outsourcing partners. If Thomas could find no company with the necessary competencies, they would need to launch a dedicated effort to develop the competencies in the existing supplier base.

The net result of this new outsourcing policy was to ask many new questions.

- What was required from the outsourcing partners to meet Thomas's requirements?
- How long would it take to implement the policy given the constraints in the partners' skills and competencies?
- How could Thomas follow the outsourcing policy and not make outsourcing decisions that, above all, merely took care of immediate cost concerns?

Thomas's central concern became finding outsourcing partners with the right skills and competencies and in the absence of such new partners, how it could develop the right skills and competencies with the available partners.

TeStrake: Learning to Work Together in a Partnership

TeStrake, a Dutch company, recently took the initiative to find a new way to work in a consortium of suppliers for new product development (Julien *et al.,* 1997). The aim was to develop new products rapidly and cost efficiently by leveraging the best in each supplier. At the time, Stork Digital Imaging (SDI) was developing an inkjet color printer, PIP (Perfect Image Printing) for high-resolution textile printing. PIP was seen as a completely new generation of textile printers. Working on the project were SDI, which led the development; TeStrake, a second subcontractor, and DuPont, the marketing agent.

TeStrake and SDI had previously worked together developing a printer called AX4 but a host of problems had plagued the project. While TeStrake and SDI had been developing the AX4, DuPont had regularly identified and refined customers' requirements, which resulted in many changes in AX4 design. Consequently, the project ran significantly over budgeted cost and came late to market. What were the main problems with the AX4? It had taken too long, had cost too much, and communication problems had plagued the companies, which had also significantly underestimated the difficulties of system integration. Market information was inadequate and when problems surfaced, the firms resorted to time-consuming negotiations. TeStrake had not been involved early enough in the product design and no real trade-off existed between the technical specifications, the development cost and the product cost. Too much time had elapsed before the companies understood the extent of the cost increases.

With their new working methods, the companies tried to avoid making the same mistakes in the next product development project, the PIP. In the PIP, SDI involved its suppliers early, even at the stage of developing the functional specifications. SDI sought fixed-cost estimates at the beginning of the project. Development costs were not open-ended and the partner companies shared the risks and the rewards. The companies changed their approach to research and development dramatically. They resolved major uncertainties early, even if this meant increasing the overall development time. They froze design specifications early with the time to market driving the development activities.

A central concern here was who should be involved at what point in the project. Managers advocated dividing the major responsibility for different parts of the work more equally between the partners. From a relationship perspective, this desire underpinned the need to work differently in a long-term partnership from the normal working procedures in an ordinary customer–supplier relationship.

Conclusions and Recommendations

The Thomas Medical Systems and TeStrake examples illustrate the challenges companies face when they implement outsourcing partnerships according to the strategic guidelines discussed earlier. It seems clear that when the outsourced activity is crucial for the success of the companies involved, the choice of partners and the approach to co-managing the relationship become central factors in the outcome of an outsourcing arrangement. **Figure 2** captures our understanding of the essential dynamics companies need to consider when they make vital outsourcing decisions.

Companies need to consider both strategic and operational issues.

Figure 2   **The Full Scope of an Outsourcing Decision**

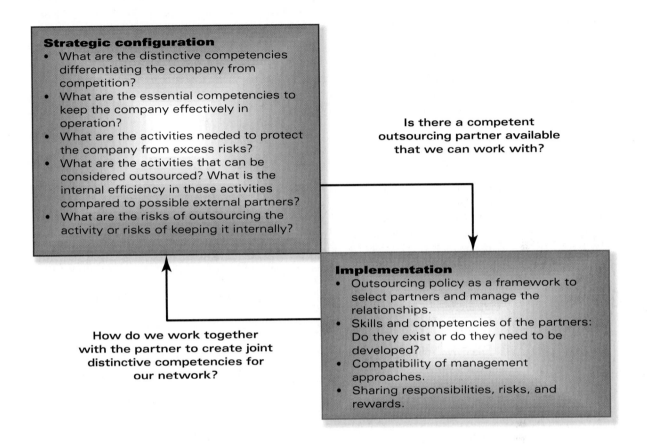

Companies need to consider both strategic and operational issues when they make outsourcing decisions. Outsourcing strongly influences the organization's ability to meet its challenges. Quick decision rules should be avoided. Managers need to evaluate from different points of view the relationship between the activity under consideration and its relationship with the rest of the organization. The following guidelines should lead to a more comprehensive outsourcing decision-making process:

1. Management should adopt a creative approach to evaluating the competencies of the company. The three types of competencies presented here, distinctive, essential and protective, serve as a useful starting point for the evaluation.

2. Managers should then engage in a wide-ranging discussion of where an activity belongs in the framework depicted in **Figure 1.** Analyzing the targeted activity in terms of its efficiency compared to other activities and risk sharpens management's understanding of the activity and its relative organizational importance.

3. Determining what actions the company might take to reposition the targeted activity in the efficiency-and-risk framework brings dynamism to the planning process. How are the competencies expected to evolve? How do we increase the value we produce to our customers? How do we develop our set of competencies in order to thwart future competition?

4. Thereafter, the next step is to evaluate the possible supply alternatives. Is there a good outsourcing option? Can another organization undertake the activity as efficiently as we can? Do we have confidence that the supplier can provide the activity *and* continually improve it? What are the risks and what are the implications of these risks?

5. Finally, each firm needs to continuously assess their ability to operate in a 'virtual organization.' The objective of real strategic outsourcing partnerships is to create joint distinctive competencies in order to change the rules of the industry and to orchestrate the whole supply chain.

References

Alexander, M. 1997. Getting to grips with the virtual organization. *Long Range Planning* 30(1): 122–124.

Dyer, J.H. 1996. Specialized supplier networks as a source of competitive advantage: evidence from the auto industry. *Strategic Management Journal* 17(4): 271–291.

Heikkilä, J., Vollmann, T.E., and Cordon, C. 1998. Nokia Mobile Phones: Supply line management. *IMD Multimedia Case Study* POM 201.

Hoffman, R.C., Gamble, J.E., and Arnold, E.W. 1996. Briggs & Stratton Corporation: Competing in the outdoor power equipment industry. In *Strategic Management: Concepts & Cases*, Thompson, A.A., Strickland A.J., Richard D. Irwin: Boston; 610–622.

Insinga, R.C., and Werle, M.J. 2000. Linking outsourcing to business strategy. *Academy of Management Executive* 14(4): 58–70.

Julien, D., Vollmann, T.E., and Cordon, C. 1997. TeStrake: Beyond early supplier involvement. *IMD Case Study* POM 202.

Julien, D., Vollmann T.E., and Cordon, C. 1998. Thomas Medical Systems' outsourcing policy (A), (B) and (C). *IMD Case Studies* POM 205–207.

Lambert, D.M., Emmelhainz, M.A., and Gardner, J.T. 1996. So you think you want a partner? *Marketing Management* 5(2): 24–29.

Porter, M.E. 1985. *Competitive Advantage: Creating and Sustaining Superior Performance.* Free Press: New York.

Prahalad, C.K., and Doz, Y.L. 1987. *The Multinational Mission—Balancing Local Demands and Global Vision.* Free Press: New York; 61–62.

Prahalad, C.K., and Hamel, G. 1990. The core competence of the corporation. *Harvard Business Review* 68(3): 79–93.

Upton, D.M., and McAfee, A. 1996. The real virtual factory. *Harvard Business Review* 74(4): 123–133.

Vivanco, L.M., Cordon, C., and Vollmann, T.E. 1996. Outsourcing and subcontracting at DuPont Europe. *IMD Case Study* POM 191.

Vollmann, T.E., Cordon, C., and Vandenbosch, M. 1997. Restructuring: how to improve your success ratio. *Financial Times.*

Why Is Knowledge Management So Difficult?

Julian Birkinshaw
London Business School

Knowledge management promises much, but often delivers very little. There are no simple solutions to this challenge. This article starts by trying to define what knowledge management is. It then identifies where the problems lie and suggests five steps to resolve those problems. The article is based on research in a dozen leading companies, including HP, Ericsson, ABB, Skandia, and Xerox.

If you keep even half an eye on the management press, chances are you have come across the concept of knowledge management. Emerging at the beginning of the 1990s, knowledge management is now a well-established school of thought with its own dedicated consulting companies, journals and management gurus.

The "big idea" with knowledge management is that in a fast-moving and increasingly competitive world, a firm's only enduring source of advantage is its knowledge—the knowledge of its individual employees, and the knowledge that gets built into its structures and systems. Consulting companies and R&D organisations have known this for years, but increasingly even "old economy" firms in oil, steel, and consumer products are recognising the importance of knowledge assets as the source of their success.

The problem with knowledge management is that most companies struggle to make it work. A Bain and Co. study found that while some companies were "extremely satisfied" with their progress in knowledge management, the majority expressed a below-average level of satisfaction. And in a survey of European and U.S. companies (Ruggles 1998), the results were even more worrying. Only 13 percent of respondents rated their ability "to transfer existing knowledge within the organisation" as good or excellent, and "measuring the value of knowledge assets and/or the impact of knowledge management" was rated good or excellent by only 4 percent of respondents.

Drawing on research in a dozen companies, this article tries to make sense of the practical implications of knowledge management. Through interviews with more than 50 executives in companies like HP, Ericsson, ABB, Skandia, and Xerox, I have looked at the approaches taken to managing knowledge and the effect on individual and company performance. While these companies have all undertaken plenty of initiatives in knowledge management, the results of their efforts typically lie somewhere

Knowledge Management at Hewlett-Packard Laboratories

HP has developed a sophisticated approach to knowledge management. Of all the companies in the study, HP has come farthest in making knowledge management work. Yet managers acknowledge that they are still experiencing some teething pains and frustrations.

A plethora of knowledge management tools and techniques has been established over a number of years.

- *IT applications for co-ordinating activities:* HP has a market research database to make research reports available to all staff, and an external standards database to help with lobbying. In addition there are databases for managing research projects and HP's patent portfolio.
- *Organisational tools for co-ordinating activities:* HP's laboratories are organised into centres that focus on specific technologies, but there is a high level of fluidity across centres, and typically strong links between centres and development groups. HP has an active rotation programme. As one person said, "There are 12 different ways to rotate here." There are also experiments underway with creating a "virtual laboratory" in which people co-ordinate their efforts remotely.
- *IT applications for problem-solving:* HP has an elaborate competence database to search for employees with specific skills. There are also communication facilitators such as intranet forums and video-conferencing.
- *Organisational tools for problem-solving:* There is a well-established best practice transfer process, including a unit that takes responsibility for best practices across the laboratories. Individuals are encouraged to seek out information from other labs and from outside HP, and to share information with others. There are also informal networks of individuals with similar technological interests. More broadly, HP has managed to develop a strong "one company culture" that prevents individuals from hoarding their knowledge.

How well do these tools and systems work? Certainly as well as in any other company that participated in the study, but not as well as HP would like. Three issues in particular stand out. First, with so many tools, people were either not aware of all of them, or were too busy to use them all. As a result, a lot of knowledge management still took place through the informal networks. Second, while knowledge flows within the labs was good, the links between labs and development groups were of very variable quality, and this constrained researchers' ability to develop technologies that would be usable on a corporate-wide basis. Third, some of the IT applications such as the patent database were developed primarily for management rather than for researchers, and were not readily accessible without explicit permission.

Note: The focus in this study was on HP's research laboratories in Palo Alto, CA, and on their links with development groups in the United States, UK, and France. For more information, see Teigland, Fey and Birkinshaw (2000).

---

between disappointing and acceptable. There were no outright failures, but no great success stories either (see the box above for a discussion of HP's experiences).

Why is knowledge management so difficult? The key problem is that knowledge management is so central to the make-up of the firm that it cannot be separated out and acted upon in the way that a single business process or management system can. In all companies, knowledge is already being "managed" through informal networks. To do it better involves not only developing new tools, but also eliminating old ways of working. As a result, changing a firm's knowledge management system is not unlike changing its culture—it involves fundamental changes to people's behaviour, and it typically takes many years to bring about.

In sum, knowledge management promises much, but often delivers very little. There are no simple solutions to this challenge, but it is possible to make some

The Related Concepts of Organisation Learning and Intellectual Capital

Knowledge management is one, but by no means the only, set of concepts concerned with how companies make the most of their knowledge assets. Two others are particularly influential—Organisation Learning and Intellectual Capital. While their key ideas overlap to a great extent with knowledge management, they also have their own particular nuances.

Organisation learning was the forerunner to knowledge management, and gained its support largely on the back of Peter Senge's (1990) *The Fifth Discipline.* The underlying premise is similar—that knowledge is a scarce and valuable resource, so for firms to succeed in a fast-changing world they have to become better at learning (i.e., sharing knowledge among individuals). The difference is that organisation learning is about managing the processes of learning while knowledge management is more con-

cerned with techniques for building up and applying stocks of knowledge.

The *Intellectual Capital* movement took shape around the same time as knowledge management. It emerged out of the world of accounting as an attempt to identify and measure intangible assets. By breaking a firm's intellectual capital down into such elements as human capital (the capabilities of employees), customer capital (existing relationships), and structural capital (patents, operating systems, practices), its advocates were able to come up with useful measures that could then be monitored and evaluated over time (Ambler 1999). The best-known example of this was the Navigator model developed by Skandia, a Swedish insurance company, in which the elements of Intellectual Capital were identified, measured, and reported on as a supplement to the Annual Report.

---

progress through a more complete understanding of what exactly knowledge management is, where the problems lie, and the steps you can take to resolve those problems. That is the purpose of this article.

What Is Knowledge Management?

At the heart of the knowledge management movement is the simple concept of the firm as a "social institution." The firm draws value from the individuals within it, and from its ability to harness their knowledge. But individuals also draw value from the firm they work for, to a far greater extent than a simple contract-based view of the world would suggest. They learn from their colleagues and are able to accomplish tasks they could not do on their own. Equally important, people are innately social animals—they like to share experiences, they like to gossip, and they like the feeling of "belonging" to a department or a firm.

This may not be an organisational philosophy that resonates with everyone, but the fact is that many firms—both small and large—do work this way, so there is potentially a great deal of value in understanding how to make it work. And to do so is essentially about creating structures and systems that enable, rather than constrain, social activity and knowledge sharing. Knowledge management, by this logic, can be seen as a set of techniques and practices that facilitate the flow of knowledge into and within the firm. Two related bodies of thinking, Organisation Learning and Intellectual Capital can also be identified (see box).

In practical terms, there are three elements to knowledge management (Figure 1). First, the firm should encourage individuals to interact—to work together on projects, or to share their ideas on an informal basis. Second, systems are needed to *codify* the knowledge of individuals so that it can be used by others. A key insight from the

Figure 1   Three Elements of Knowledge Management

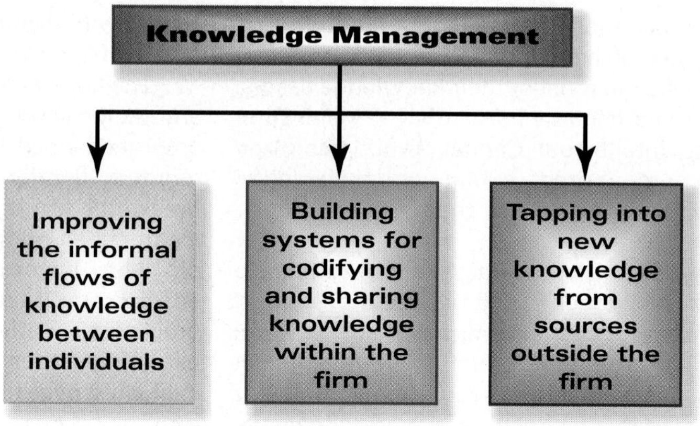

knowledge management movement is that most valuable knowledge is *tacit*—it is held so deeply by the individual that it is hard to express or write down. If ways can be found for transferring that knowledge to others in the firm, either through personal interaction or by recording it explicitly, then that knowledge becomes an asset of the firm, and a key source of advantage. Third, the firm needs to get access to new knowledge from outside its boundaries, as a means of updating and renewing its knowledge base.

Applying these concepts involves three sets of tools: information technology systems, formal and informal structures and specific KM tools.

- ■ *Information Technology systems:* In many firms, knowledge management evolved out of information management, for the obvious reason that knowledge and information are closely related concepts. McKinsey and Accenture, for example, both have highly sophisticated databases that provide libraries of information about their proprietary methodologies, clients, previous engagements and so on (see box). These are essentially repositories of *codified knowledge.* They do not capture the tacit knowledge or expertise of leading partners, but they provide a form of collective memory that consultants can tap into quickly and efficiently.

- ■ *Formal and informal structures:* A large part of knowledge management is simply about facilitating the natural interactions between people. One approach is to design the physical layout of offices so that social interaction is encouraged. Ericsson and GlaxoWellcome, for example, designed their R&D labs using lots of glass, open-plan layouts and hub-and-spoke structures to facilitate informal discussions. A second approach is to design the formal structure around the key knowledge flows. Cross-functional project teams are a case in point—a way of formalising meetings to ensure that all the individuals involved bring their relevant knowledge to bear on the project. A third approach is to facilitate informal interactions through what are usually called *communities of practice*—groups of individuals with common interests and problems who are dispersed throughout the firm. These individuals, it is argued, will naturally seek one another out to share their experiences and learn from one another, so the firm can play a subtle role in

Knowledge Databases in Accenture and McKinsey

Accenture and McKinsey have both developed very sophisticated "knowledge databases" to capture the collective knowledge of their professional staff.

Accenture (formerly Andersen Consulting) put its Knowledge Xchange system together in the early nineties. Built on Lotus Notes software, Knowledge Exchange consists of a series of information and knowledge databases to meet the needs of specific industry and competence groups. Most of these databases—and there are over 3,000 of them—are repositories of information about firm methodologies and previous consulting assignments. There are also discussion forums so that consultants can ask their peers in other parts of the firm for help with specific issues or questions.

Knowledge Xchange is very well-used but casual conversations with Accenture employees reveal that it takes considerable time to get up to speed with the system—just because of its sheer size and complexity. Because of this, the firm has worked

recently on making "Navigation" of Knowledge Xchange easier.

McKinsey developed its Practice Development Network (PDNet) in the late eighties, and like Accenture's Knowledge Xchange it provides access to proprietary methodologies, papers written by McKinsey consultants, and information about clients. For a number of years, access to PDNet was controlled by dedicated information managers, but more recently the system has been put onto Lotus Notes and can be accessed by all consultants. Nonetheless, PDNet is actively managed by a dedicated team to ensure that the information on it reflects the state-of-the-art thinking in the firm. The other key knowledge resource in McKinsey is its "Yellow Pages" which provides information on who has expertise in what competencies or industry sectors.

Source: Author interviews and cases study by Bartlett (1998) and Davenport and Hansen (1999).

---

facilitating their interaction, for example by creating discussion forums on the intranet (Wenger and Snyder 2000).

- *Specific knowledge management tools:* Finally, there are a number of specific knowledge management tools that firms use. One is the *transfer of best practice*—HP for example, has a structured process for taking a technique or practice in one laboratory and transferring it to another laboratory in a different part of the world. Another is the designation of *centres of excellence*—for example 3M Europe identified individuals or groups with specific expertise (e.g., business intelligence in the UK, key account management in Sweden), in order that their knowledge could be picked up and used in other parts of the firm (see Moore and Birkinshaw 1998).

Why Knowledge Management Often Fails

Despite the range of tools and techniques, the success rate of knowledge management is mixed, and in my own research I have seen plenty of cases of programmes and initiatives that did not deliver the results they were looking for. The following four observations summarise why this is the case:

- Firms do not sufficiently recognise that they are already doing it.
- Information technology is often regarded as a substitute for social interaction.
- Knowledge management typically focuses too much on recycling existing knowledge, rather than generating new knowledge.
- Most knowledge management techniques look like traditional techniques.

Figure 2   Typical *Actual* Rather Than Intended Flows of Best Practice

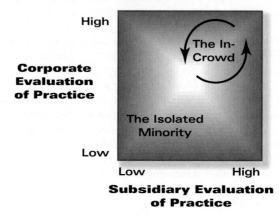

Source: Arvidsson 1999.

Knowledge Management Is Never Zero-Based: to Make It Work, You Need to Recognise That You Are Already Doing It

While the proponents of knowledge management might like to argue otherwise, the reality is that firms have been managing their knowledge since the dawn of time. For example, formal organisation structures are typically designed to ensure that knowledge exchange takes place between those who most need it. Informal social networks—the groups of people who have lunch together or go for a drink after work—are mechanisms for knowledge transfer. And industry associations are vehicles for sharing ideas and discussing common problems.

A recent study by Niklas Arvidsson (1999) looked at the sales and marketing affiliates of such Swedish firms as Alfa Laval, Ericsson, and Volvo. The study examined the flows of knowledge between these affiliates, and sure enough it found that there were plenty of knowledge transfers going on. However, when Arvidsson compared the flows of knowledge with the ratings of which affiliates were the highest performers, he discovered that most transfers did not flow from "best" to "worst"—they simply flowed along existing lines of communication. Those affiliates that were part of the "in crowd" exchanged knowledge freely, while those that were new to the group or geographically isolated were essentially shut out of the loop (Figure 2). The result was a lot of cases of "mediocre" or "worst" practice transfers. The only exception to this rule was Alfa Laval, which had gone to enormous effort to build linkages between all its affiliate companies and to hold regular management meetings at which knowledge sharing could take place.

Another example is a new media consulting company I work with. In looking at how knowledge was shared between software programmers, it became apparent that these people would often use external discussion groups with people they had never met, *rather than* the company's own intranet forum. This was a real eye-opener for the managers, because they had assumed that the intranet would be a useful tool for sharing ideas and solving problems. Armed with this insight, they were then in a position to re-think the support they gave to their software programmers, and the function of the corporate intranet.

The point, in other words, is that knowledge sharing is already taking place, but it is happening in an *ad hoc* way along the lines of people's informal networks. Knowledge management can help to make this a more systematic process, for example by monitoring and comparing the performance of different subsidiary companies or R&D units. This at least helps the firm to "know what it knows" but it still does not guarantee that the flows of knowledge will be diverted away from their traditional and well-trodden paths.

Information Technology Is Never a Substitute for Social Interaction

The internet revolution has caused some writers to make absurd claims about how the world of work will change. One popular article by Tom Malone and Robert Laubacher (1998) foresaw the emergence of the "e-lance economy" in which individuals would work as freelancers rather than as members of firms. Another line of thinking talked about the "paperless office." And many have argued that telecommuting will take over from traditional forms of commuting. These arguments are just plain wrong, for the simple reason noted earlier that individuals need social interaction—both for its own sake, and because it provides a powerful vehicle for learning. *The Social Life of Information* (Brown and Duguid 2000) provides an excellent counterpoint to the argument that technology is going to change the way we work. It explains the importance of the social interaction between people that lies at the heart of knowledge management.

This simple insight has important implications for the management of knowledge. First, it helps to explain why most knowledge databases are so poorly used. Most people would much prefer to talk to a colleague about their latest ideas rather than try to find something he or she wrote. And second, it cautions us to recognise that IT tools and "social" tools such as communities of practice are complementary. Again, this flies somewhat against the received wisdom. A recent article by Morten Hansen and colleagues (2000) suggested that firms should focus on either a "codification strategy" which involved putting the firm's knowledge onto IT databases, or on a "personalisation strategy" which involved building strong social networks. But experience suggests that the complementary nature of the two strategies is such that you need to do both.

> *IT tools and "social" tools such as communities of practice are complementary.*

Knowledge Management Typically Ends Up Focusing Too Much on the Recycling of Existing Knowledge and Not Enough on Generating New Knowledge

Most of the knowledge management literature is inherently inward-looking. It is concerned with tools such as transfer of best practice and knowledge databases. These are extremely important but ultimately focused on what I would call "operational efficiency"—making current activities work in a more streamlined way. Much more important, over the long term, is the ability to bring new knowledge into the organisation, and turn it into new products and business models. There are many ways of doing this. 3M, for example, has strategic accounts with many leading customers to pursue joint innovation projects. Ericsson and Nokia both have outposts in Silicon Valley whose job is to tap into the latest thinking there and transfer it back to head office. Cisco aggressively acquires small companies as a way of building its knowledge base. All of these approaches to knowledge generation have their own challenges, but they are critically important because they represent a way of renewing the firm's knowledge, rather than just recycling it.

Most Knowledge Management Techniques End Up Looking Just Like the Traditional Techniques You Have Been Using for Years

The deeper that firms get into these sorts of tools, the more they find that managing knowledge is integral to the working of the entire organisation. For example, Skandia, the Swedish insurance company, developed its "Navigator" model on Intellectual Capital foundations, but it ended up functioning exactly like the Balanced Scorecard. The concept of communities of practice is alluring, but essentially it is just about encouraging people to communicate with one other and share their ideas, which is an idea that is as old as the hills. Knowledge databases have an important role to play in sharing knowledge, but the challenge of aligning such tools to user needs is the same one that IT managers have always faced.

These observations are not meant to be disparaging. Good management practice always boils down to a few basic challenges, so the fact that knowledge management leads to a certain amount of déjà vu among seasoned managers is actually a reassurance that it is addressing important issues. The acid test is whether these techniques end up being better understood, and better implemented, as a result of the knowledge management "framing." In my assessment, they are certainly being better understood, but the jury is still out on whether implementation is also improving.

Making Knowledge Management Work

These arguments paint a complex and perhaps overgloomy picture of knowledge management. There are no easy quick fixes for a company that is pursuing, or considering, a knowledge management programme. But the following five basic guidelines may make it easier to think through how to structure knowledge management efforts:

- Map the knowledge flows in the organisation.
- Map the stocks of knowledge and use them to encourage sharing of best practice.
- Focus efforts on mission-critical rather than nice-to-have knowledge.
- Raise the visibility of knowledge management activities.
- Use incentives to institutionalise new knowledge-sharing activities.

Map the Knowledge Flows in the Organisation

Before starting any specific change initiatives, you need to get a handle on the current state of the knowledge flows in your company. They can best be understood through "social network" analysis, which involves mapping the web of connections between individuals in an organisation. The analysis shows very clearly which parts of the company suffer from a lack of knowledge flows, and these can then be highlighted for attention. For example, in one division of Skandia it became clear that the German subsidiary was being left out of the loop on important discussions. On closer investigation it became clear that the problem was language—the German subsidiary head did not speak good English, so he had chosen to opt out rather than embarrass himself. The problem was readily addressed by identifying one of his team with good English and bringing him into the discussions.

Map the Stocks of Knowledge and Use Them to Push the Sharing of Best Practice

A similar procedure can be used to identify the key sources of expertise in the company. One established approach is to undertake a "best practice audit" in which units or businesses are rated on a series of key metrics and then ranked in "league tables" of performance. In Ericsson, for example, R&D units are rated in this way, and the information is then used to start a discussion with each unit about how their performance can be improved, and which other units they can learn from. In Intel and GE such league tables are taken a stage further, and are used as a major input into performance evaluations. For the laggards, the incentive to learn from the units at the top of such league tables is extremely strong.

Focus Efforts on Mission-Critical Rather Than Nice-to-Have Knowledge

Good change programs always start with the "low-hanging fruit"—the stuff that can be grasped with minimal effort. In terms of knowledge management, this means groups who *need* access to new knowledge to do their job. In one pharmaceutical company, for example, this meant focusing on the project teams doing in-licensing of drugs. In a consulting company, the first knowledge initiative focused on making sure that client teams had the technological and interpersonal support they need to deliver leading-edge solutions to their clients.

Raise the Visibility of Knowledge Management Activities

Making knowledge management effective in the long term requires a fundamental shift in the behaviour of employees. The chief executive and other senior figures have an important role to play in this process, by raising the visibility of knowledge management and by demonstrating its importance. One chief executive made a point of putting best practice sharing on the table at every management meeting—by getting a subsidiary manager to present the latest thinking from his or her market. Gradually the team began to take some of these ideas home with them to share with their people. Another approach is to appoint a Chief Knowledge Officer whose role is to champion all knowledge sharing and creation activities (Earl 2000). Ultimately, however, knowledge management has to become a way of doing business, and just as with Total Quality Management this means moving it from a staff function and a couple of specific projects to an organisation-wide responsibility.

> *The problem was readily addressed by identifying one of his team with good English and bringing him into the discussions.*

Use Incentives to Institutionalise New Knowledge-Sharing Behaviours

Another useful way of instilling a shift in behaviour is by making knowledge management part of the incentive system. By this I don't mean a financial reward every time an employee shares their ideas with a colleague—this would be expensive, impossible to monitor, and would encourage exactly the wrong sort of narrow-minded behaviour. Much better—as most consulting companies have realized—is a "soft" form of incentive, typically a section of the annual performance review in which an individual's contribution to the company's knowledge is recorded and evaluated. This ensures that individuals are reminded of the importance of knowledge management on a regular basis, while avoiding the problem of specifying too narrowly what the appropriate knowledge-sharing behaviours are.

Knowledge management has been around for more than ten years, but it has got a lot of life left in it. My purpose in this article was to identify some of the core ideas, but also to show why they are so difficult to put into practice. The tone is deliberately somewhat sceptical, but I think that is appropriate if knowledge management is to move from being yet another interesting "fad" to an enduring management technique. Many of the ideas in knowledge management are, indeed, old ones with new labels. But at the same time there are some important and lasting principles that help us better understand how knowledge-based firms work.

References

Ambler, T. (1999) Valuing human assets. *Business Strategy Review,* 10.1.

Arvidsson, N. (1999) The Ignorant MNE. Doctoral Dissertation, *Institute of International Business, Stockholm School of Economics.*

Bartlett, C. A. (1998) Mckinsey & Company: Managing knowledge and learning. *Harvard Business School Case Study* 9-396-357.

Brown, J. S. and P. Duguid (2000) *The Social Life of Information.* Harvard Business School Press.

Davenport, T. and M. Hansen (1999) Knowledge management at Andersen consulting. *Harvard Business School Case Study* 9-499-032.

Earl, M. (2000) What on earth is a CKO? *Sloan Management Review.*

Hansen, M., N. Nohria and T. Tierney (2000) What's your strategy for managing knowledge? *Harvard Business Review,* Jan–Feb.

Malone, T. and R. J. Laubacher (1998) The dawn of the e-lance economy. *Harvard Business Review,* Aug–Sept.

Moore, K. and J. Birkinshaw (1998) Knowledge management in service MNCs: Centres of Excellence. *Academy of Management Executive.*

Nonaka, I. and H. Takeuchi (1995) *The Knowledge-Creating Company.* Harvard Business School Press.

Ruggles, R. (1999) Knowledge Management: The state of the notion. *California Management Review.*

Senge, P. (1990) *The Fifth Discipline.* New York: Doubleday.

Stewart, T. (1997) *Intellectual Capital.* Nicholas Brealey Publishing.

Teigland, R., C. Fey, J. Birkinshaw (2000) Knowledge dissemination in global R&D operations: An empirical study of multinationals in the high technology electronics industry. *Management International Review* 40(1): 49–77.

Wenger, E. and W. Snyder. (2000) Communities of Practice: The organisational frontier. *Harvard Business Review,* Jan–Feb: pp 139–146.

"See No Evil, Hear No Evil, Speak No Evil"—Leaders Must Respond to Employee Concerns About Wrongdoing

Bob Gandossy
Hewitt Associates

Rosabeth Moss Kanter
Harvard Business School

It wasn't the first time he discovered fraud committed by his boss—also the owner of the company. A year after he joined the firm, as the head of accounting, he came across several loans that were financed, not once, but two and three times. The owner claimed the loans were obtained "inadvertently" and, further, "it was no big deal and won't happen again." A year later, the accountant discovered it did happen again. This time his boss said, "don't worry" and promised, "I'll take care of it." Over the next few years, more signs of trouble surfaced: serious cash flow difficulties, officers' loan accounts exceeding net worth, doctored financial statements, incomplete documentation on multimillion-dollar transactions, and extravagant spending by the principals. Then, some seven years after he first came to the company, the firm pleaded guilty to check kiting and received the maximum penalty under the law.

Why would the accountant stay under these circumstances? Clearly, the company was in deep financial trouble and a principal had resorted to fraud and other forms of misconduct in the past, and, therefore, was quite capable of doing it again. Why not get out? The accountant eventually did leave, but only after he and other inside accountants had discovered hard evidence of fraud amounting to more than $40 million—and that was for only one year. On leaving, the accountant did not reveal what he knew to the authorities. Nor did the other accountants, who continued to work for the company. A year after he resigned, a massive fraud was uncovered—19 financial institutions had been swindled out of more than $220 million during a ten-year period. Could the fraud have been prevented? Why didn't the accountant and many others, who either knew or strongly suspected the fraud, take action?

Over the past several decades the business press has reported dozens of scandals, often involving leading companies that have been involved in improprieties for years before anyone took steps to bring them to an end. Why weren't illegal activities discovered

Reprinted from *Business and Society Review*, Vol. 107, No. 4, 2002, pp. 415–422. © 2002 Center for Business Ethics at Bentley College, Published by Blackwell Publishing, Inc. 350 Main Street, Malden, MA 02148, USA, and 108 Cowley Road, Oxford OX4 1JF, UK.

earlier? And, if they were, why didn't people act to bring the crimes to a halt? How can responsible managers and professionals be so blind to such massive misconduct?

As we've seen, the aftermath of scandals usually involves numerous people sifting through evidence, discovering "retrospective errors" and unheeded warnings on the part of particular players associated with the fraudulent operators. Signs of trouble are typically present, but simply missed by the persons involved. So, the question becomes, why? What factors prevent us from seeing and acting on signs of misconduct? As important, what steps can we take to reduce the likelihood of becoming a victim— or worse, blindly aiding and abetting the perpetrator? And, as leaders, what steps should we take to reassure our employees that we are what we say?

There is no single answer to these questions. Human and organizational behaviors are complex, and explanations for our actions rarely come in tidy packages. Likewise, there is no single step to protect corporations from wrongdoing, but several steps will decrease the probability that managers will become either victimized or otherwise involved in such frauds. Said differently, there are certain things we as leaders do that *can* foster criminal wrongdoing. As well, there are no simple steps to ensure leadership integrity on such matters, but we must take seriously the workforce uneasiness that ripples the corporate landscape in the wake of recent scandals.

Most of the attention in leadership today is primarily focused on the positive side of corporate life—strategies for getting results through people, the organizational value of giving people more responsibility and accountability, and the virtue of trusting in people to do the "right thing." However, alongside this "people-are-trustworthy" theme is yet another emerging set of stories about corporate crime.

In many corporate circles today, managers and leaders are writing off instances of wrongdoing as aberrations without relevance to them. *This is a mistake.* Corporate crime anchors one end of a continuum of performance problems, ranging from outright theft to more subtle instances of ripping off the company for supplies, padding expense accounts, ignoring product defects, or simply failing to perform all duties in a quality manner.

Seen in this way, the ability of leaders to detect and prevent corporate crime is related to their ability to correct ineffective performance more generally. We should look closely at corporate wrongdoing and rip-offs for lessons about how to get the *best* out of people by preventing the *worst.*

Common Warning Signs of Fraud

How do you know a fraud is being committed by a client, customer, or someone within your own organization?

- Insufficient working capital or credit
- Extremely high debt with rigid restrictions imposed by creditors
- Dependence on few products, services, or customers
- Unfavorable and declining industry or business conditions

Situational

- Profit squeeze (costs rising higher and faster than sales and revenues)
- Difficulty collecting receivables
- Significant inventories

- Long business cycles
- Urgent and intense need to report favorable earnings to support high stock price, lure customers, or obtain credit
- Unrealistic sales projections
- Extremely rapid expansion of business

Opportunity

- Management of the organization or department dominated by one or a few individuals
- Understaffed or inexperienced financial and accounting functions
- Weak internal control system
- Rapid turnover in key financial positions and/or frequent change in auditors
- Numerous unexplained and undocumented transactions
- Apparent tolerance by management of unethical and even illegal conduct

Personal

- Key personnel had rapid rise to top (responsibility and remuneration) and have considerable fear of falling from their perch
- Prior history of unethical or illegal conduct by suspects

No One Knew

"But I'd shut my eyes in the sentry box so I didn't see nothing wrong."
—Rudyard Kipling

In most cases of corporate wrongdoing, we hear that no one "knew" and no one took action. Why? How is it possible for accounting firms, other professional service providers, internal staff, and executives to remain blind to such malfeasance for so long?

In fact, in many of these cases, a number of people either knew about the infractions or strongly suspected them, but they failed to take the necessary steps to bring the crimes to an end. In some situations, individuals saw troubling signs of wrongdoing but considered them less serious than they actually were—the signals were ignored. In other situations, people tried to respond—to further investigate a sign of misconduct—but eventually gave up.

Important Lessons

Stories of corporate scandal make headlines and are interesting studies of wrongdoing, but there are important lessons that extend well beyond the prevention of illegal activity. For instance, is the ineffectiveness of managers and professionals in these cases so different from a production manager closing his eyes to substandard products about to be shipped? Or a design engineer ignoring obvious flaws in a new product design? Or the loan officer who approves credit to a customer with suspect financial records simply to get more loans on the books?

Surely there are differences, make no mistake. But our examination of many cases of corporate wrongdoing, in light of our work with dozens of ethical organizations, provides some similarities. The same pressures and opportunities that encourage otherwise responsible managers to become apathetic bystanders to fraud and other forms of misconduct also encourage blindness and paralysis to ineffective performance more generally.

First, senior and middle managers often are rewarded for short-term performance. "What have you done for me lately?" is a common phrase in corporate corridors for a reason. If salaries, bonuses, and promotions are tied to quarterly profits, it is difficult for managers to call a halt to practices that affect their bottom-line performance. Where reward systems have a performance trigger that provides multiple targets, then pressure is even greater. Corporations that don't permit admitting mistakes (without a penalty) force managers to conceal errors—they simply sweep evidence of poor performance under the rug rather than call attention to themselves.

This overriding concern for financial ends rather than means, coupled with insufficient moral and ethical guidance from senior executives, often leads managers to bend the rules or look the other way if doing otherwise prevents them from achieving their goals.

The second lesson stems from the complexity of business life today. There is virtually no significant transaction or project today that does not involve dozens of specialists, or perhaps even dozens of organizations. Specialists are used to reduce risk. But reducing risk by using multiple actors creates a structure wherein it is easy to conceal poor performance—or fraud.

Organizations that come together for a particular project, joint venture, or series of transactions generally have specific, often very narrow, concerns. And within each organization, the aspects of the deal that occupy an individual's time are further differentiated. Information is diffused and fragmented. No one pays attention to the big picture—each player has a piece of the action, but no one makes sure they are all working together on the same team. The materials managers do not seem to care about complaints from the shop floor. The marketing folks ignore the sales team, and so on.

Because many people are involved, each is quick to assume that others are responsible for certain aspects of the deal or project. When trouble appears—whether poor quality products or services or the slightest sign of misconduct—it is relatively easy to shift responsibility for acting to someone else—and claim later that no one "knew."

Inattention to Detail and Lack of Accountability

The third factor is somewhat "softer": inattention to detail and lack of accountability. Sometimes managers at many companies ignore the small things—the "minor" defect in the product, the "insignificant" liabilities of a credit applicant, or the avoidance of a "small" audit step.

These practices set a standard, a pattern others come to follow in a sort of mindless way, making it tolerable—indeed, acceptable—for managers to close their eyes to poor performance. It becomes more important to close the sale than to deliver a quality product or service. Production and service shortcuts are the norm at some companies—hustling new business is more important than delivering on the business they have.

Steps You Can Take to Reduce Your Vulnerability to Fraud

- Develop a code of ethics—disseminate widely and hold discussion meetings.
- Conduct unscheduled audits of your business practices to determine where you are vulnerable to foul play.
- Discuss with colleagues ways to shore up weak links thereby obtaining not only better solutions, but also solutions that clearly communicate your concerns.
- Discuss acceptable and unacceptable business practices with colleagues at every opportunity.
- Discuss with employees ways to resolve ethical dilemmas and the alternative courses of action if they discover wrongdoing.
- Discuss ethical issues in performance appraisals.
- Review performance and incentive programs. Minimize the overemphasis on bottom-line performance to the neglect of other factors. Set performance targets that can be met without cheating.
- Establish a reward program for exemplary ethical conduct.
- Discuss fiduciary responsibility with your accountants, lawyers, investment bankers, and other financial advisers. Find out exactly what they do to protect you. Obtain a written understanding of their responsibilities. Monitor carefully for potential conflicts of interest.
- Hold joint meetings with fiduciaries so each clearly understands the roles and responsibilities of each other.
- Ask your lawyer, accountant, and investment bankers to hold question and answer sessions with your managers and supervisors.
- Act swiftly when foul play occurs in your organization. Make the penalty fit the crime, publicize the incident, and hold discussions with employees so there is a clear understanding of what transpired.
- Hire an outsider to periodically raise ethical questions with your staff.

Organizations that live and breathe quality, that set high standards, that pay attention to detail are less vulnerable to misconduct and general ineffectiveness. Senior executives who convey a sense of moral integrity and provide opportunities to openly discuss ethical and operational dilemmas reduce confusion over proper and improper behavior.

Companies that provide multiple, and balance, rewards and forms of recognition, that tolerate reasonable mistakes, are more likely to correct problems when they occur, not after they have been ignored for so long that they have become disasters. Where teamwork and shared, overlapping responsibilities are encouraged there is less "passing the buck," and more joint resolution of problems. Individuals are able to discuss and resolve dilemmas common to the group.

To improve performance and reduce costly misbehaviors, leaders can build these factors into the organization: quality, as opposed to inattention to detail; multiple rewards and forms of recognition; rewards for individuals *and* teams; a tolerance for well-intended mistakes; and integrative cultures rather than segmented units.

Leaders who want to create a great company need to look on the dark side—at the possibility of "evil"—as well as the positive values of faith in people and trust in their integrity. They need to devote personal time and attention to making sure that performance problems do not slip by unnoticed and unpunished. Corporate philosophies saying that achievement is rewarded and good performance is valued mean nothing unless, simultaneously, bad performance is rendered impossible.

READING 13

Ethical Concerns in International Business: Are Some Issues More Important Than Others?

Turgut Guvenli
Minnesota State University

Rajib Sanyal
The College of New Jersey

Firms expanding into international business have had to contend with ethical and social dilemmas brought on by differences in economic conditions, cultural values, and competitive variables. In recent years, as economic activities have become more globally integrated, concern has been expressed over ethical practices in various countries and the role of multinational firms in making profits through conduct considered inappropriate.[1] Thanks to the activism of nongovernmental organizations (NGOs) and advancements in communication such as television, telephone, and the World Wide Web, the general public, especially in advanced industrial countries such as the United States, are now aware and conscious of economic, social, and political conditions elsewhere in the world. In this article we ascertain and rank the U.S. public's concern over a set of ethical issues in international business.

Globalization and Ethical Concern

As the world economy has become more integrated, so has the backlash against globalization. The most vivid manifestation of the backlash occurred in November 1999 in the U.S. city of Seattle when demonstrators scuttled planned negotiations by the World Trade Organization (WTO) to expand global trade.[2] Opponents of the WTO and globalization complained that unfettered trade and investment flows were responsible for a whole host of evils in the world. These included, in the developed countries, loss of high-paying jobs and stagnant or declining real incomes among low-skilled and unskilled workers; and in the developing countries, increased exploitation of workers, including children, by paying them low wages for work in sweatshop conditions; neglect of the physical environment; and denial of basic human rights.[3]

Critics maintained that the removal of trade barriers had encouraged multinational firms to locate to developing countries to take advantage of lower labor costs and nonexistent or nonenforcement of regulations. Products made in these countries, subsequently exported to developed countries, competed on an unfair basis because lower production costs could be traced to the denial of very elementary workplace standards and basic worker rights.[4]

Reprinted from *Business and Society Review*, Vol. 107, No. 2, 2002, pp. 195–206. © 2002 Center for Business Ethics at Bentley College. Published by Blackwell Publishing, Inc. 350 Main Street, Malden, MA 02148, USA, and 108 Cowley Road, Oxford OX4 1JF, UK.

453

Table 1   ETHICAL ISSUES IN INTERNATIONAL BUSINESS

Employment conditions	Low wages
	Poor working conditions
	Employment of children
	Use of prison labor
Politics and laws	Nondemocratic governments
	Lack of unionization rights
	Nonprotection of intellectual property rights (e.g., patents and trademarks)
	Corruption
Physical environment	Absence of regulations
	Weak regulatory framework
	Nonenforcement of regulations

NGOs, usually alliances of human rights activists, women's groups, labor unions, environmentalists, and church and religious leaders, have pushed for the inclusion of a social clause in bilateral and multilateral trade treaties. Such a clause would link improvements in labor standards in less developed countries to enhance access to markets in developed nations. The goal was to ensure that trade was not only free but also "fair."[5]

Literature Review

Public concern in developed countries over ethical business practices in less developed countries have focused on three main topics: (a) Employment conditions (low wages, sweatshoplike workplaces, and employment of prisoners and children); (b) Politics and laws (nondemocratic nature of governments, absence of laws protecting intellectual property rights); and (c) Environmental protection (nonexistence of regulations and lax enforcement of regulations). This is presented in Table 1. Concern extends to doing business with countries where ethical practices are questionable as well as to firms that take advantage of producing in these locations.

Note that these conditions are perceived to exist in the foreign country and are seen by firms and citizens in the home country as the basis on which products made in the foreign country have a competitive edge. Thus the competition from imported goods is seen to be "unfair" and consequently triggers a wide range of protests and opposition including the demand to stop trading with such countries or to impose other sorts of restrictions.

Employment Conditions

Data indicate that wages in many less developed countries are often a fraction of what they are in the advanced industrial countries. For instance, hourly compensation costs for production workers in Mexico were only 10 percent of what it was in the United States. Many U.S. firms had relocated to Mexico to take advantage of these lower labor costs.[6] Information available on working conditions in the factories of contractors used by Nike, a U.S. sports footwear firm, in Indonesia and Vietnam have revealed long hours of work, employment of children, poor physical conditions, use of toxic materials, absence of safety equipment and procedures, and abusive treatment by supervisors.[7] Employment of children is common in many less developed countries and has been receiving urgent attention of NGOs and the media, as well as governments.[8] Use of prisoners in China to make products for exports has been frequently reported. Prisoners or forced labor are paid a pittance if they are paid at all and work long hours in very harsh conditions.[9]

Politics and Law

While the world has seen a marked trend toward the establishment of democratic countries around the world, pockets of nondemocratic regimes exist. In addition, in many countries undergoing transition to democracy and free market, old antidemocratic practices persist as new institutions and processes take time to take hold. In nondemocratic countries recourse to justice may not be available. Workers may not have the right to form unions or go on strike; the judiciary may not be independent; one-party political systems exist; and individual rights may be circumscribed. China is often held up as an example where an unrepresentative government imposes strict restrictions on the rights and freedom of its citizens. Workers do not have the right to form independent unions and they do not enjoy rights typical of Western democracies—such as freedom of expression, right to due process, and freedom of personal choices or religion.[10]

Laws on protection of intellectual property rights may not exist or, if they do, may not be enforced. While it is true that counterfeiting, misuse of patents and trademarks, and illegal copying are widespread, they are difficult to measure. U.S. firms have long complained to their own government and to foreign governments that illegal duplication of their products—films, videos, recorded music, books, and computer software—cost them over $200 billion annually.[11] For instance, U.S. firms have complained that Mexico fails to enforce its own laws protecting intellectual property and violates the clauses on copyright protection included in NAFTA.

National laws regarding copyright, trademark, and patent protections vary with regard to their comprehensiveness and enforceability. In 1997, under the auspices of the WTO, an international agreement—Agreement on Trade-Related Aspects of Intellectual Property Rights, Including Trade in Counterfeit Goods (TRIPS)—to curb counterfeiting was signed. It requires the signatory countries to imprison and fine individuals or organizations guilty of violating copyright, trademark, and patent rights. Illegally produced goods can be seized and destroyed. However, the effect of this agreement has been mixed.[12] Violation of intellectual property rights not only leads to loss of revenues for the firm whose assets are being misused, it often leads to the devaluation of product quality and integrity. Finally, such violations create competitors who export cheap knock-off versions. Industry groups in developed countries feel that some foreign governments are unenthusiastic about stamping out illegal duplication, counterfeiting, and patents' misuse.

Corruption, primarily in the form of payment of bribes to obtain contracts in less developed countries, not only adds to the cost of doing business but also poses difficult ethical dilemmas and in many situations serious legal problems. In the United States the Foreign Corrupt Practices Act makes it illegal for American firms to bribe foreign officials with the intention of changing policies or to secure the suspension of a legal norm. In 1997 thirty-four countries signed the first Convention on Combating Bribery of Foreign Public Officials in International Business Transactions.[13] Transparency International, an NGO based in Berlin, gathers information on corruption and provides an annual ranking of countries by the amount of bribery, embezzlement, and trickery involved in doing business (www.transparency.org).

Physical Environment

A growing concern is the impact of unrestrained and unregulated economic activities in less developed countries on their physical environment—the air, water, and land. Strict regulations in developed countries impose costs and reduce the maneuvering space of manufacturing firms. In many less developed countries, laws on environmental pollution do not exist, or are weak, or are not enforced. Firms, domestic and foreign, take advantage of this lax regulatory regime to produce and export goods at lower costs with scant concern for the degradation of the physical environment.

As noted earlier, protests against globalization so far as it profits firms and nations at the expense of workers, the disadvantaged groups in society, the environment, democratic rights, and the rule of law, have led to a reassessment of the international trading regime. Among the consequences have been: (a) delay in the start of a new round of negotiations under the aegis of the WTO to further liberalize trade; (b) inclusion in the North American Free Trade Treaty side protocols on labor union rights and environmental protection; (c) continuing pressure to incorporate a social clause in trade treaties; (d) denial of fast-track negotiating authority to the U.S. president to forge new trade agreements; (e) protests and boycotts against individual firms (e.g., Nike) for manufacturing products in harsh working conditions); (f) negative media coverage of products, firms, and countries; (g) divestment of stocks in erring firms and countries by pension fund managers; (h) heightened public scrutiny of international firms and their activities in host countries; (i) enactment of laws that impose sanctions and tariffs on imports from countries believed to be insufficiently concerned about working conditions; (j) heightened lobbying by advocacy groups to bring about changes in foreign countries; (k) complaints to home and host governments by firms hurt through loss of protection of their intellectual property; and (l) creation of both corporate codes of conduct and industry codes to increase consciousness about being socially responsible.[14]

Survey and Research Methodology

A survey instrument was developed that sought responses on a five-point scale to ten most common issues of ethical concern in international business. These issues are: employment of child labor, employment of prison labor, poor working conditions, low wages, violation of human rights, absence of democracy in the country, violation of intellectual property rights, low environmental standards, lack of enforcement of environmental standards, and unfair competition based on low wages. The purpose of the questionnaire was to determine how these various ethical issues were perceived and ranked in importance by the respondents.

In the context of the notion of including a social clause in trade treaties, survey participants were asked whether they would support restrictions on the import of goods into the United States if the goods had been made in countries where employment conditions and business practices identified in the previous section prevailed. Responses could range from strongly disagree (1) to strongly agree (5). The focus was on countries, not individual firms.

Completed responses were obtained from 429 college students (55 percent men, 45 percent women) in the United States. The gender information permitted the determination of whether perception of ethical issues differed between men and women. The survey results were tabulated and analyzed.

Table 2   RANKING OF ETHICAL ISSUES

Rank	Ethical Issue	Mean	Standard Deviation
1	Use of child labor	4.27	1.11
2	Human rights violations	4.23	1.17
3	Poor working conditions	3.99	1.23
4	Violation of intellectual property rights	3.90	1.76
5	Lack of enforcement of environmental standards	3.76	1.25
6	Low environmental standards	3.61	1.21
7	Unfair competition	3.48	1.45
8	Low wages	3.21	1.52
9	Undemocratic government	2.92	1.98
10	Use of prison labor	2.88	1.90

Note. Mean responses are on a scale of 1 to 5 where 5 represents highest level of disapproval.

Table 3   GENDER DIFFERENCES ON ETHICAL ISSUES

Social Issue	Women Mean	Men Mean	t value	p value
Use of child labor	4.37	4.18	1.85	0.06*
Human rights violations	4.38	4.11	2.45	0.02*
Poor working conditions	4.16	3.84	2.63	0.01*
Violation of intellectual property rights	3.97	3.84	0.78	0.43
Lack of enforcement of environmental standards	3.81	3.71	0.85	0.39
Low environmental standards	3.70	3.54	1.41	0.16
Unfair competition	3.63	3.36	1.95	0.05*
Low wages	3.23	3.18	0.30	0.76
Undemocratic government	3.05	2.81	1.28	0.20
Use of prison labor	3.13	2.68	2.48	0.01*

*Significant at the 0.05 or 0.10 levels.

Results

Calculation of mean and standard deviation of the responses to the ten ethical issues of concern indicate a distinct ranking by the respondents. The results are presented in Table 2.

T-tests indicate that there was a distinctive division between male and female respondents on how seriously they viewed the ten issues. As Table 3 indicates, women were more disapproving of all the socially challenged business practices than men. On five of the practices, the differences between men and women were statistically significant.

Discussion

The findings point to a highly nuanced prioritization of ethical concerns in the minds of the population. All the usual ethical concerns that are reported with respect to international business activities do not arouse the same level of concern and indignation. There is a calibrated ranking of these issues. Employment of child labor, violation of human rights, and poor working conditions (sweatshops) are viewed as issues of far greater concern than the employment of prison labor or whether the foreign government is undemocratic, or even whether wage rates are low. It should be noted that in the United States, for the most part, the practice of using children in manufacturing is not only prohibited but in practice too is virtually nonexistent. Similarly, Americans enjoyed an extensive array of constitutionally protected rights including the right to form labor unions. The advanced nature of the economy, legislation with regard to workplace standards, and the enforcement of laws have generally ensured that sweatshoplike conditions are the rare exception, not the rule. In contrast, the three ethical issues that came at the bottom of the league suggest that there is less sympathy for prisoners. That they should be used to produce goods and services does not appear to cause much concern; presumably prisoners deserve this plight for crimes they have committed. The American respondents were also relatively less concerned over the political makeup of the countries where imported goods come from. Many countries with which the United States trades, though political democracies, also have poor working conditions. It may also be an acknowledgment that the U.S. notions of democracy may not be appropriate in all countries. The low wages in many foreign countries may be seen as reflective of the low level of economic development and lower productivity levels.

As noted in Table 3, men and women differed on all the ten issues. Women appear to be more concerned over social conditions of production in international business than men. The mean scores for women were consistently higher than those for men. On five of the issues—employment of child labor, violation of human rights, poor working conditions, unfair competition because of lower wages, and use of prison labor—the responses of women were significantly different from those of men. Women were more likely to oppose imports of goods produced under these conditions than men. These findings reflect the basis of one of Hofstede's four cultural dimensions, that of masculinity-femininity. He had presented this construct as a continuum where femininity characterized a greater concern for quality of life issues than masculinity.[15] An implication of the masculinity-femininity dichotomy of these findings is that as women in the United States continue to be empowered and assertive, their concerns will undoubtedly have a bearing on the formulation and implementation of U.S. trade policy.

In looking at the rankings in Table 2 and the significant differences by gender in Table 3, it appears that labor-related issues arouse more indignation and concern than issues related to politics and laws (lack of democracy, violation of intellectual property rights, and human rights) or environmental issues. There is greater empathy for the human condition and perceived human suffering than for legalistic violations, political imperfections, or the inadequacy of an environmental protection regime. Respondents appear to suggest that a nation's competitive advantage obtained through the employment of child labor, human rights violations, and harsh working conditions was clearly unethical and trade with countries where such situations prevailed should be restricted.

What do the findings mean for the different players in international business? It lends support for the thinking prevalent in many quarters that in a globally integrated system, the need for addressing labor standards in various jurisdictions cannot be brushed aside.[16] Firms engaged in international business as producers, contractors, exporters, and importers should note that the strongest opprobrium attaches to the employment of children, violation of human rights (such as right to form unions, right to due process, and right to fair treatment), and the existence of degrading working conditions. If businesses have to allocate resources to improve their social responsibility practices, priority should be given to these issues. Failure to address these issues will also draw the greatest flak. Thus, these findings can help managers focus on what issues to give immediate and higher attention than others and where to source their products or locate their manufacturing facilities. Similarly, countries concerned about the access of their products to the large and affluent U.S. market should recognize that certain activities and practices bring more negative reaction than others and thus should work to alleviate them.

Customers in the United States are willing to tolerate higher prices or nonavailability of particular products through import restrictions should imported products be made under conditions that they disapprove of strongly. In a democratic society with a highly literate population and where women are highly placed and influential in society, concerns over social issues easily influence public policy, media coverage, and lobbying activities. It also feeds into the programs of NGOs, which may be able to garner public support and exercise greater influence by focusing on those issues that are high on the ethics hierarchy of concerns.

The instrument used in this study juxtaposed concern over ethical issues in foreign countries with the imposition of restrictions of imports by the United States on those governments. This implies that respondents believe not only that they should not patronize products made under unacceptable conditions but also that import restrictions would force the exporting countries to make improvements in their social and economic policies and practices. The focus here was on countries of origin of imported products and not on the firms that make, buy, and export/import the products. Consumer wrath is often directed toward specific businesses thought to be profiting from adverse production conditions in certain countries. In response, some companies have withdrawn their operations from countries such as Myanmar, or have drawn up corporate codes of ethics (e.g., Mattel's global manufacturing principles), or have proactively sought to alleviate the worst elements of the workplace environment (e.g., working with various NGOs to eliminate child labor in the carpet making industry in Pakistan).[17]

Conclusion

The results of this pilot study point to the existence of a scale of importance with regard to ethical issues in international business among the populace and that there is a marked difference between men and women. The findings also suggest that concern over certain ethical issues in international business is strong enough to invite public opposition to doing business with countries whose practices are felt to be at fault. As the advent of globalization fuels continuing anxiety, the issue of ethical practices in international business will continue to occupy center-stage and engage the attention of policy makers, nongovernmental organizations, international firms, and the general public, all of whom have the task of reconciling competing interests, needs, and values.

This study could be expanded into a wider, multicountry comparative examination of ethical concerns. Multicountry perspectives would allow for a fuller understanding of the ranking of ethical concerns in individual societies. There is also scope for analyzing ethical perceptions along several other variables such as education, age, and income levels.

Notes

1. P. F. Buller, J. J. Kohls, and K. S. Anderson, "The Challenge of Global Ethics," *Journal of Business Ethics* 10 (1991), 767–775.
2. Nancy Dunne, "US unions take heart from Seattle talks failure," *Financial Times,* Dec. 7, 1999, p. 4.
3. Eddy Lee, "Globalization and Labour Standards: A Review of Issues," *International Labour Review* 136(2) (1997), 173–189.
4. Nigel Haworth and Stephen Hughes, "Trade and International Labor Standards: Issues and Debates over a Social Clause," *Journal of Industrial Relations* 39(2) (1997), 179–195.
5. Rajib Sanyal, "The Social Clause in Trade Treaties: Implications for International Firms," *Journal of Business Ethics* 29(4) (2001), 379–389.
6. *Statistical Abstract of the U.S., 1999,* 119th edition (Washington, DC: U.S. Census Bureau, 1999).
7. John Cushman, "Nike pledges to end child labor, apply U.S. rules abroad," *New York Times,* May 13, 1998, pp. D1, D5.
8. Janet Hilowitz, "Social Labeling to Combat Child Labour: Some Considerations," *International Labour Review* 136(20) (1997), pp. 215–232; *International Labor Office,* 1997, Protecting children in a world of work, 109. Geneva.
9. S. Kaltenheuser, "China: Doing Business under an Immoral Government," *Business Ethics* (May/June, 1995), pp. 20–23.
10. Ibid.
11. Michael Flagg, "Asian bootleggers export their CD expertise," *Wall Street Journal,* Nov. 8, 1999, p. B17A; Paul Taylor, "Internet pirates 'costing' software groups $1bn," *Financial Times,* Feb. 2, 1999, p. 6.
12. Peggy Chaudhry and Michael Walsh, "Intellectual Property Rights: Changing Levels of Protection under GATT, NAFTA, and the EU," *Columbia Journal of World Business* 30(2) (1995), pp. 80–92.
13. "Bribery: The New Global Outlaw," *Management Review* (April 1998), pp. 49–51; Catherine Yannaca-Small, "Battling International Bribery," *The OECD Observer* 172 (Feb.–March 1995), pp. 16–17.
14. Sanyal, "Social Clause in Trade Treaties"; Dinah Payne, Cecily Raibourn, and Jorn Askvik, "A Global Code of Business Ethics," *Journal of Business Ethics* 16(16) (1997), pp. 1727–1735.
15. Geert Hofstede, *Culture's Consequences: International Differences in Work-related Values* (Beverly Hills, CA: Sage, 1980).
16. Brian Langille, "Eight Ways to Think about International Labour Standards," *Journal of World Trade* 31(4) (1997), pp. 27–52.
17. Sanyal, "Social Clause in Trade Treaties"; "Some firms tout benefits of a social conscience," *Wall Street Journal,* Dec. 3, 1999, p. A6; Francis Williams, "Carpetmakers agree to end child labour," *Financial Times,* Oct. 23, 1998, p. 4.

Why Ethics and Compliance Programs Can Fail

Megan Barry
Ethics Consultant and former Ethics Officer for Nortel
Networks

Bob, a veteran, well-respected manager, calls a staff meeting to introduce his new hire, Cindy. The bad news, Bob tells the staff, is that he doesn't have any money in the capital budget—he simply can't buy Cindy the equipment she needs to do her job. But there's good news, too. Bob has plenty of money in his T&E budget and a creative solution to the problem. All his staff has to do is add $100 to each of their expense reimbursement requests (and since Bob signs off on these requests, no one will question the expenses). Then, when they get the check, they can give him the extra money, which he'll use to buy the equipment Cindy needs.

As far as Bob's subordinates are concerned, their boss—who for all practical purposes represents the leadership of the organization—has just identified a way to solve a bureaucratic problem. And Bob has also provided a valuable lesson. To thrive in the company, employees must be willing to push the envelope, to find ways to circumvent an outdated process, to get around an unrealistic policy.

So even though Bob's proposal made some of his subordinates uncomfortable, they all did as he asked. Not one questioned Bob's actions; not one raised the issue with someone in management. Only after several months had passed, and Bob still hadn't bought the equipment Cindy needed, did his staff begin to question his actions.

As it turned out, Bob had used the extra funds as a down payment on a new boat. When he invited his subordinates to join him for a day of sailing fun, the group finally realized what happened—and only then did they get angry enough to finally approach a senior manager in the company.

Most employees—like the people in Bob's group—want to do the right thing, but they can get into trouble when they think the organization expects them to behave unethically. As was the case in Bob's company, most senior managers reward people who can solve problems. But management also needs to know exactly how employees are going about solving these problems, and it needs to create a channel through which employees can raise issues and ask questions. Otherwise, employees may engage in activities and behaviors that senior management never anticipated.

Bob's company didn't have an Ethics and Compliance function. When he first explained his scheme for "paying for Cindy's equipment," his subordinates didn't know where to go or to whom they should turn for advice. Soon after this incident, the company created an Ethics Office and hired an Ethics Officer.

Reprinted from *Journal of Business Strategy,* Vol. 23, No. 6, November–December 2002, pp. 37–40. Used with permission.

Carrots and Sticks

Ethics Officers now exist in over half of all multinational companies recently surveyed by The Conference Board. The Ethics Officer Association, a U.S-based, not-for-profit membership organization for Ethics and Compliance Officers, has more than 700 members who have some kind of ethics responsibility in their organizations. When the EOA was launched in 1991, it had fewer than 10 members.

This tremendous growth was spurred by the introduction of the Federal Sentencing Guidelines in the early 1990s. When the U.S. Sentencing Commission introduced the Guidelines, it embraced a "carrot and stick" approach. The "stick" allows a judge to impose harsh penalties upon an organization whose employees or other agents commit federal crimes. The "carrot" gives organizations an opportunity to mitigate potential fines and penalties, *provided* the firms had implemented a seven-element process for compliance with the Guidelines before the transgression occurred.

The seven elements are:

1. Compliance standards and procedures

2. Oversight by high-level personnel

3. Due care in delegating substantial discretionary authority

4. Effective communication of standards and procedures to all levels of employees and other agents, e.g., through required training or clear and practical publications

5. Reasonable steps to achieve compliance with standards, including systems for monitoring, auditing, and reporting suspected wrongdoing without fear of retribution

6. Consistent enforcement of compliance standards, including disciplinary mechanisms

7. Reasonable steps to respond to and prevent further, similar offences upon detection of a violation

However, some companies use this framework and still fall short. Take Enron as an example. Much has been made about the fact that Enron had a lengthy Code of Conduct that outlined its compliance standards and procedures. Yet Enron failed to create an ethical workplace. Why? For Enron, the answer is multifaceted and complex, but one clue might be the fact that, on two separate occasions, the board of directors voted to suspend the code document in order for one board member to invest in multiple partnerships.

There are other reasons why these initiatives fail. Below are some of them.

Danger #1: Standards Are Inconsistent

"The organization must have established compliance standards and procedures to be followed by its employees and other agents that are reasonably capable of reducing the prospect of criminal conduct."

Problem: Not having clearly articulated and shared company values. When the members of the board of a small start-up discovered the company president had been submitting expenses that included charges for prostitutes, they were stunned. Asked to justify his actions, the president maintained that the charges fell under the

heading of customer entertainment. A potential customer had asked for the services, and, since sales to
this firm could bring great value to the shareholders,
the president felt his actions were justified. The
board disagreed and asked for his resignation. To
the dismissed executive, the ouster was unjust: No
one connected with the company had ever set out
specific ethical business practices.

> *The cornerstone to starting and maintaining an ethics and compliance culture is a shared set of values and standards.*

This may seem like an extreme example, but the cornerstone to starting and maintaining an ethics and compliance culture is a shared set of values and standards—and
a shared understanding that it applies to all employees, regardless of their level in the
organization.

**Problem: Senior management limits its approach to ethics by not creating a
global standard.** Just because it's legal, doesn't mean it's ethical. Take for example
the company that adhered to local laws regarding health and safety standards. The laws
differed significantly from those in the country in which the company was headquartered and, in this particular case, the standards for safeguarding employees on the job
were much more lenient. After several employees were involved in work-related accidents, the company reevaluated its position and developed a global standard that applied wherever it did business.

This problem also can arise in the application of U.S. laws regarding discrimination. Divisions operating in the U.S. might have one set of criteria, while another part
of the organization in another part of the world follows different criteria. Take for example the ad one U.S.-based multinational ran in the English-language newspaper in
an Asian country, "Wanted: Receptionist. Must be female, attractive, under 25, and
bilingual." If that company had an articulated standard that was consistent across all
geographies, it would not have run this ad.

**Problem: Lack of board of director involvement in crafting the code of con-
duct and creating an ethical environment.** A recent Conference Board study found
that today's boards of directors were more likely to take an active role in shaping an organization's principles than were their predecessors of a decade ago. However, although the 21 percent involved in 1987 grew to 78 percent in 1998, that still leaves
close to one-quarter of the boards with no involvement in the code of conduct.

Problem: Inconsistency in the messages contained in the code. One company
devoted two pages in its code to discussing its steadfast commitment to protecting the
environment, but then failed to print the code on recycled paper. When employees see
such inconsistencies, they may start to wonder about senior management's commitment to an ethics and compliance initiative.

Problem: Arcane policies and procedures that employees routinely violate.
Some companies, in an effort to monitor and control employee behavior, introduce
"zero tolerance" policies. While these are appropriate for workplace issues such as harassment and discrimination, it is possible to take this concept to the extreme.

For example, one company proclaimed, "Employees are not allowed to use their
work computer for non-work-related activities, including accessing the Internet and
sending and receiving personal e-mail." Did this approach work? No. Believing it unrealistic, employees routinely broke the rule. And by implementing such a restrictive
policy, the company created an atmosphere in which employees began to feel that they
could disregard some policies if they didn't like them.

Danger #2: Ethics Officers Lack Support

"Specific individual(s) within high-level personnel of the organization must have been assigned overall responsibility to oversee compliance with such standards and procedures."

Just because it's legal, doesn't mean it's ethical.

Problem: Ethics Officers aren't given the power they need to do their job effectively. When organizations fail to empower EOs, their effectiveness is compromised. For example, many EOs don't have a significant reporting relationship to the CEO or the board of directors. In a membership study conducted in 2000 by the Ethics Officer Association, 27 percent of the respondents stated that they reported to the CEO/president/chair, 21 percent reported to the general counsel, and 21 percent to an executive/senior vice president.

When asked about their working relationship with the board of directors, 4 percent said they meet with the board (or committees of the board) "on a regular and frequent basis" (more than four times a year). Another 30 percent meet with the board on a regular but infrequent basis (four times per year or less). Nearly a quarter (23 percent) reported that the board is "accessible when needed." The majority, 61 percent, reported that their boards are "very supportive" (down slightly from 65 percent in 1997). Also interesting to note, on the 1997 survey, 14 percent of the respondents indicated that their board was "mildly unsupportive." Significantly, this figure had dropped to 1 percent in the 2000 survey.

Danger #3: Communication Is Poor

"The organization must have taken steps to communicate effectively its standards and procedures to all employees and other agents, e.g., by requiring participation in training programs or by disseminating publications that explain in a practical manner what is required."

Problem: Training programs are one-time events, and not everyone receives the training. Although most organizations do an initial roll-out to communicate standards and procedures, the initiative often loses steam. Organizations may fail to train everyone, focusing only on mid-level managers and leaving out senior management and the board of directors.

Effective initiatives devise a communication strategy that includes training for all levels of employees, with a focus on the organization's code of conduct. Training

Effective initiatives devise a communication strategy that includes training for all levels of employees.

delivery methodologies include everything from CD-ROM training, Web-based training, video conferencing, and live trainers. The training must also be integrated into new hire training and functional training, and can include programs specifically directed at sales and marketing, supply management, and research and development.

Danger #4: Systems Are Weak

"The organization must have taken reasonable steps to achieve compliance with its standards, e.g., by utilizing monitoring and auditing systems reasonably designed to detect criminal conduct by its employees and other agents and by having in place and publicizing a reporting system whereby employees and other agents could report criminal conduct by others within the organization without fear of retribution."

Problem: Failure to give employees a safe and reliable place to report misconduct—anonymously, if necessary—without suffering retaliation. A primary role for many compliance and ethics officers is to maintain a system through which employees can raise issues and ask questions.

Consider what happened when two employees complained to Human Resources that their manager consistently harassed his subordinates. (In fact, it was a standing joke within the group that the only way to get promoted was to sleep with the boss.) HR ignored the allegations. Why? Because the VP of HR was a good friend of the offending manager. Even worse, the two employees who had come forward were fired shortly thereafter. These employees felt so strongly about the problem they tried to contact HR even after they'd left the company, but as ex-employees, they were labeled as "disgruntled," and their complaints were deemed "no longer our problem." Eventually, current employees anonymously reported the incident to the Ethics Office, triggering an investigation. The allegations were found to be true, and the manager was dismissed.

Danger #5: There's No Way to Enforce Standards

"The standards must have been consistently enforced through appropriate mechanisms, including, as appropriate, discipline of individuals responsible for the failure to detect an offense. Adequate discipline of individuals responsible for an offense is a necessary component of enforcement; however, the form of discipline that will be appropriate will be case specific."

Problem: Inconsistent application of punishments depending on the level of the offender. Remember the manager dismissed for harassing his employees? When the allegations were found to be true, and the decision was made to release him from the organization, he was allowed to retire—with full benefits and a hefty severance package. Now the standing joke in the department is "harass someone, and the company will take good care of you."

The ethics and compliance function must work closely with all corporate functions, including human resources, security, audit, and legal, making sure that discipline in the organization is consistent and appropriate.

Why It Matters

These are just a few examples of why companies fail to implement and maintain successful ethics programs. But ultimately, a successful program helps to safeguard a company's reputation. As one CEO I know said, "Reputation is that intangible asset that is so hard to gain and so easy to lose. And once you lose it, it's gone."

While in the car with me last week, my seven-year-old son helped bring this point home. As we passed an Exxon station, he said, "Mommy, don't ever buy your gas from that company because they caused a really, really big oil spill." Boy, I thought, this is a marketing person's worst nightmare. My son is making a purchase decision for a product he can't even buy yet, based on something that happened before he was born. Clearly, for many companies experiencing ethical lapses today, regaining a good reputation may take a lifetime.

Indexes

Name

Organization

Subject

Photo Credits

Chapter 1, page 2, © William Whitehurst/CORBIS
Chapter 2, page 36, © Digital Art/CORBIS
Chapter 3, page 78, © Brownie Harris Productions/CORBIS
Chapter 4, page 108, © Ron Lowery/CORBIS
Chapter 5, page160, © B.S.P.I./CORBIS
Chapter 6, page 190, © PictureNet/CORBIS
Chapter 7, page 242, © Ryan McVay/Getty Images, Inc.
Chapter 8, page 272, © Brownie Harris Productions/CORBIS
Chapter 9, page 294, © R.W. Jones/CORBIS